A forest of voices

A Forest of Voices

Reading and Writing the Environment

CHRIS ANDERSON
Oregon State University

LEX RUNCIMAN
Linfield College

Mayfield Publishing Company
Mountain View, California
London • Toronto

Copyright © 1995 by Mayfield Publishing Company

LIBRARY OF CONGRESS CATALOGING-IN-PUBLICATION DATA
Anderson, Chris
   A forest of voices : reading and writing the environment / Chris Anderson, Lex Runciman.
     p.   cm.
   ISBN 1-55934-315-X
   1. English language—Rhetoric.   2. Environmental protection—
Problems, exercises, etc.   3. Readers—Environmental
protection.   4. Nature—Problems, exercises, etc.   5. College
readers.   6. Readers—Nature.   I. Runciman, Lex.   II. Title.
PE1408.A577   1994
808'.0427—dc20   94-31080
                                                            CIP

Manufactured in the United States of America
10 9 8 7 6 5 4 3 2 1

Mayfield Publishing Company
1280 Villa Street
Mountain View, California 94041

Sponsoring editor, Thomas V. Broadbent; production editor, April Wells-Hayes; manuscript editor, Carol T. Beal; art director, Jeanne M. Schreiber; text and cover design, Linda M. Robertson; manufacturing manager, Aimee Rutter. The text was set in 11/12 Bembo by Thompson Type and printed on 45# Restorecote by the Maple Vail Book Manufacturing Group.

Cover image: Gustav Klimt (1862–1918), *Buchenwald (Beech trees)*. Oil on canvas. 1903. Oesterreichische Galerie, Vienna, Austria. © Photograph by Erich Lessing.

Acknowledgments appear on pages 769–772, which constitute an extension of the copyright page.

PREFACE: A NOTE TO STUDENTS

> Tell me the landscape in which you live, and I will tell you who you are.
>
> —Jose Ortega y Gassett

We have two related reasons for putting this book together. First, we want to help you become a better reader and a better writer about reading. Second, we want to do what we can for the environment.

The environment is a good topic for college readers because much of today's best writing is about the environment—essays, fiction, poetry, scholarly and informative articles, arguments about policy and value. Reading about the landscapes around us and the ecologies we belong to is a very good way to study what makes writing good.

We have found that reading like this leads to good class discussions and good student writing. Whoever you are and wherever you live, what's most important in your life in some way connects to questions of landscape and weather and air, to the relation of the inner and the outer worlds, imagination and fact.

But most important, the subject of the environment is a good focus for college reading and writing because it is a complex subject. The environmental question is like a forest, complicated, full of interrelationships, everything dependent upon everything else—and that is what you'll find to be true about every other topic you encounter in your college classes. There's always more than meets the eye. Things that seemed simple turn out to be complicated after all. What college is always trying to teach you, underneath everything else, is not to accept the easy answers, not to act out of prejudice and unexamined assumptions.

Moreover, environmental questions may be the most broadly cross-disciplinary questions we can ask. Their answers include chemistry and computer science, philosophy and economics, religious studies, history, biology and physics, political science and literature. Good answers to environmental questions need knowledge from all these disciplines. Put another way, environmental questions ask us to engage our whole minds.

The reading and writing assignments we suggest in this book will help you approach this kind of reading. We say: Look, this is hard, and it's supposed to be. You've got to read most pieces more than once. It's all a process. So here are some strategies—practical strategies for becoming a better reader and so a better writer—strategies, in fact, that depend on writing.

The best way to read is to write. That's what we keep emphasizing throughout this book, from the opening five chapters to the questions and activities we pose at the end of each selection. To read insightfully and with personal engagement, you need to write out your responses, not just think about them, and at every step of the way—in a word or phrase in the margins of your books, in a freewritten journal entry, in a list of questions, in an outline, in a draft of an essay, in one revision and then another revision, in a long term paper, in a bibliography. The act of writing makes the reading clearer, more interesting, more your own. And, of course, the process works the other way around, too, since reading well and reading good things always helps students become better writers themselves.

Which leads to our second main reason for doing this book. The skills of knowing how to work with complexity and read between the lines are just exactly the skills people need to solve the problems overwhelming the planet right now. One of the main stumbling blocks in the environmental debate is the simplistic, polarized language in which it is carried on. Most of the time we can't talk about the issues without squaring off into silly, naive distinctions like "spotted owls" versus "loggers," "environmentalists" versus "prodevelopers." The consequences of this superficial language are great: gridlock in government, divisions among the people, the slow death of the world.

Students who know how to read and write well can read these problems well—which means reading them more deeply. It means understanding that no important issue can be reduced to slogans. It means getting down to the reality of these questions, a reality that is rich and nuanced and layered, requiring both humility and patience. And that means maybe, finally, getting things done. If more people knew how to do the humane and reasoned thinking of our best writers—if more people really knew how to *read*—the world might not be in the mess it's in.

We've assembled this book in two major parts. The first five chapters form part I; they suggest practical ways to proceed as a reader and as a writer. We don't promise that every suggestion will work equally well; we trust that you'll be willing to experiment with what may seem difficult or unfamiliar and that in the process you'll become a better thinker—a surer reader and more practiced writer. We expect that you'll use these first five chapters often as you read in the second part.

Part II, consisting of chapters 6–12, has been arranged to encourage you to progressively enlarge your view and understanding of the environment. Chapter 6 starts with the places we know best and perhaps think about least: the places we live in every day, the places we have made and call home. Chapter 7 takes us outside, and chapter 8 shows that the landscape and the air and the water all teem with other living things—from pets to horses, to fish, to weasels, to chimpanzees—and these living things bear some complex relationship to us.

Chapter 9 focuses on our tendency to develop attachments to known landscapes, our tendency to associate our experiences with the places that saw them unfold, our continuing interest in what we can learn from and in these places. Chapter 10 turns its gaze on nature itself and tries to decide what can be seen there. Chapter 11 moves into a particular example, the forest; it's an example that holds virtually all of our current environmental tensions. Chapter 12 moves beyond the forest to a number of large and insistent issues—global warming, pesticide use, water use, and the like. Chapter 13 examines various approaches and ways of seeing, various principles that underlie whatever environmental actions we might take. And chapter 14 asks you to consider what kinds of actions might be called right actions when it comes to the environment.

We feel this arrangement makes a usable, reasonable intellectual arc, and we're equally sure that individual teachers will see their own different ways to work with these selections.

This book has been a particularly happy collaboration. We'd like to thank Tom Broadbent both for his initial interest and his thoughtful editorial suggestions. Thanks as well to his assistant, Julianna Scott Fein. Thanks to April Wells-Hayes and the Mayfield Production Department. Thanks to copy editor Carol Beal for catching our obvious gaffes (whatever gaffes remain, they are ours).

Thanks to Linfield College librarian Susan Whyte for her help with our discussion of libraries and the research process. Thanks to Debbie Runciman for her fine job as Permissions Editor. Thanks to Moira Dempsey for her useful, readable instructor's manual. Thanks to Professor Peter List of the Oregon State University philosophy department for his help identifying various reading selections. Thanks to Bill McKibben and Ted Leeson for adapting their selections for this book. Thanks to Charles Schuster, Johanna W. Atwood, Alys Chulhane, Karen Dick, Lydia Equitz, Kerry Hansen, Roberta Harvey, Matt Matcuk, and Donna Strickland for their critiques of an early version of the manuscript.

Finally, thanks to our families—Barb and Debbie, John, Maggie, Tim, Beth, and Jane—for their patience and support. Thanks to the writers in this book; their work continues to help us think about the environment and our places in it. And thanks to our students, for both their resistances and their enthusiasms.

CONTENTS

"Now a self-conscious and stricken silence overtook the neighborhood, overtook our white corner house and myself inside. 'Am I living?'"

"Behavioral sink is a term from ethology, which is the study of how animals relate to their environment. Among animals, the sink winds up with a 'population collapse' or 'massive die-off.'"

"By the end of the longest day of the year he could not stand it. . . ."

"We moved to El Cerrito. Instead of the patronizing nosiness blacks complain about in Berkeley, I found the opposite on Terrace Drive in El Cerrito."

"Community life amid tract housing is a disappointing experience. The space within the development has been equipped and staged for isolated family living and little else."

"We started with one tree nursery in the backyard of the office of the National Council of Women. Today we have over 1,500 tree nurseries, 99 percent run by women."

"When the Atomic Energy Commission described the country north of the Nevada Test Site as 'virtually uninhabited desert terrain,' my family members were some of the 'virtual uninhabitants.'"

"This was indeed a classic environmental battle, in that it seemed to exemplify just about everything that's wrong with the way we approach problems of this kind these days."

A Forest of Voices

Part I
Writing to Read

1

Keeping a Reading Journal

How do I know what I think until I see what I've said?

—E. M. FORSTER

or

How do I know what I think until I see what I've read?

By the time you get to college, you've probably already heard a lot about the writing process. You know that good writers revise and rethink, that writing is almost always hard work, and that the work of writing can lead to the satisfaction of something learned, something understood and said clearly. Getting to that satisfaction often means brainstorming, drafting, and redrafting—blank screens, crumpled hard copy.

Reading is a process, too. The kind of reading you have to do in college is usually complex and demanding, and even the best students don't understand everything the first time through. College reading asks you to think—and think again; read—and revise your readings; understand—and understand more completely.

Think about reading the Sunday comics and reading a college textbook: "Calvin and Hobbes" doesn't require much thought, you won't be asked to give a summary or an opinion, and you won't get together with your friends to discuss what you think. In fact, the reading you're asked to do in college classes is almost exactly the opposite: It offers more than quick laughs; it *does* require some thought; you often have to summarize it or analyze it or argue for or against it; and you almost always read it as a member of a class, a community of readers. Reading academically is a complicated process, but it's worth the effort. Like the process of writing, the hard work of rereading and reconsidering leads to a deeper sense of the complexities that are always there in any subject worth knowing.

ACADEMIC READING: SOME INITIAL ADVICE

1. *Read in a setting that lets you think.* Like every other act, reading depends in many ways on its environment. Some people need quiet to read. Others like a noisy, crowded room. Some people like to sit up straight at a desk or table, and others want to sprawl on a couch. Whatever environment you choose, arrange your week so that you have good reading time there.

2. *Set aside enough time.* Reading slowly isn't a problem if you set aside enough time—and even fast readers need time to reread difficult pieces. How much time is enough? Enough to work through confusions and misunderstandings. When you're planning a schedule, give yourself more time than you think you need. Then plan ahead so that you can read when you're awake, able to concentrate, and not likely to be interrupted. If your schedule is too full for large blocks of reading time, plan on several shorter ones.

3. *Don't panic, and don't give up.* By its nature, academic reading often deals with something you don't know very much about, and often this subject is complicated, with many levels of meaning. So expect some struggle and work when you read college texts. There's nothing wrong or lacking in you. No one else is having an easier time of it. Academic reading (or literary reading, for that matter) isn't meant to be disposable, something you can deal with quickly and discard. The readings in this book have been written by people who've worked hard to understand and communicate some part of the complicated truth arising from their study and their lives. These readings will repay your efforts; you'll find more in them as you read and think, listen and reread.

ACTIVITY 1.1

1. List twenty things you remember reading recently. Include everything: menus, billboards, novels, school assignments—anything you remember. Don't stop until you have at least twenty things listed.
2. From the list in item 1, identify three of your most recent and relatively long reading experiences (including at least one that involved reading for school). For each reading, indicate where you actually did this reading, what time of day you did it, and how long it took you.
3. Identify which of the three readings was easiest for you, and give two reasons why.
4. Identify the most difficult reading, and give two reasons why.

5. Identify the reading that taught you the most, and explain why these new understandings were easy or hard to gain.
6. Which of the readings (if any) forced you to reread some parts more than once? How was the second reading different from the first reading?

KEEPING A READING JOURNAL

If you read a Stephen King novel or a Sue Grafton mystery, you probably don't take notes on what you read. You just read and enjoy. On the other hand, when you read for academic reasons, you're probably aware that you should be taking notes of some kind. You know that you're supposed to be responsible for the reading in some way, that you're supposed to understand it enough to answer questions about it. Maybe you typically write in the margins of your books. Maybe you read with a highlighter in your hand.

As you read the selections in this book, we want to encourage you to keep paper and pencil handy so that you can use informal writing—writing you do quickly for yourself—as a way to make your reading process more conscious and more rewarding. Journal entries have several advantages: they're on paper (so you don't have to rely entirely on memory), they're relatively compact (you don't have to thumb through a book reading marginal notes), and they make rethinking easier (rereading a journal entry, you invariably find yourself agreeing or disagreeing with what you thought earlier).

To start a journal, buy a manila folder, loose-leaf binder, or spiral notebook—whatever feels comfortable to you or whatever your instructor assigns—and plan on keeping all your notes and reflections between those covers. Like the poet Coleridge, think of your journal as a "fly-catcher," a place to keep and preserve all the thoughts of your reading day (before they fly away).

Three examples:

March 4th. "Dogs, and the Tug of Life" is a strange essay. Odd. It's hard to follow. Keeps jumping around. I'm not clear what Hoagland's main point is—that having a dog is good or bad? That dogs are really wild after all? The idea that pets reflect their masters, maybe? (No, more than that.) I keep thinking of my dog, Max. Part border collie and part who knows what. He's just a silly, friendly dog and I love coming home to him, taking him for a walk. I don't think much about him at all. I don't *think* when I'm with him. That's the point, just to let go, to come home from college and just be with my dog, have him lick my face, be happy to see me. And so I resist Hoagland making such a big deal out of pets, reading things into what's simple and natural. (Although maybe *that's* the point, his point: all this is deeper than it seems.)

March 23rd. Today in class we talked about our first reactions to "A White Heron." It was sort of strange to read a story that seems old-fashioned—almost like a fairy tale. Ms. Blake asked us to list the sorts of technology that we take for granted now and that the story doesn't include—toasters, cars, dishwashers, radios, and so on. It made me think about how close to nature Sylvia and her grandma really were. We also talked about how the story is really set up to focus on a problem—Sylvia's decision. What I'm not quite sure about is why Sylvia climbs that big tree. I mean, she climbs it to see the view from the top, to see where the heron's nest is. But once she comes down, she decides *not* to tell the hunter where the nest is. And the story doesn't say why—that's what we're supposed to figure out, I guess. I have to say the young man in the story bugs me, too. If he's so much the scientist and bird lover, why does he kill so many birds?

May 14th. "Everything that seems empty is full of the angels of God." That really hit me. (It's St. Hilary, quoted by Norris in "The Beautiful Places.") I'd never thought of that, and I'm not sure what it means, except it makes a sort of sense. What I thought of immediately was the place on the coast where all the trees were harvested years ago. It's just fields and hills. But that's what I like about it, that it's open and clean, sort of. I normally like forests and lots of trees everywhere, but sometimes I like going to that place on the coast just because it's empty and free of other things. I feel something there I don't anywhere else. Can't put it into words—I feel empty myself, though in a good sense. I don't know about the "angel" part. That seems silly or strange. It's the word that stands out in the sentence, although of course it's a saint writing, so that's what you expect. Interesting. (I wonder: this must be what Dillard is talking about in "A Field of Silence," too. She sees an empty field and thinks something happens, though she can't put it into words. Yes.)

THE PROCESS OF READING: PREREADING

Before you actually begin reading the first word of the first sentence, preread. Prereading means scanning the assignments with the following questions in mind, jotting down your answers briefly, and then using those answers to help you plan and to give your reading a preliminary context.

What is this reading's genre? poetry? fiction? nonfiction prose? If nonfiction prose, what kind? an autobiographical account? a discussion of an issue? an argument in favor of something? part of a textbook?

Is it contemporary or older?

Is it long or short? in pieces or one whole?

Do you know anything about the author (what do the headnotes tell you, for example)?

Can you tell what audience this writer wants to talk to?

Can you tell why this writer wants to talk to these readers?

What do you already know about this subject?

Sometimes your prereading won't give you answers to all these questions, but prereading should give you a basic sense of what this reading will ask of you in terms of time and attention.

From your prereading, you should be able to answer these three basic questions.

1. What does this reading ask you to understand? plot? characters? an idea or set of ideas?
2. What general reading goals should you keep in mind as you start this reading?
3. Given what you know now, should you read the entire assignment in one sitting, or should you plan to break up the reading into parts or stages? How much time should you budget to do justice to this reading?

ACTIVITY 1.2

Preread one of the reading selections in this book and jot down your answers. From your prereading, use the preceding three questions to make reading plans.

FIRST READING

Begin reading by using your common sense and trusting your initial, intuitive responses. Some of what you'll read will be clear right from the start; other parts will seem fuzzy or only partly clear or (sometimes) entirely unclear. As you read, keep track of what you understand and what you don't.

Try this, for example. Open your journal so that you have two blank pages facing each other, or draw a line down the center of a single page. On the left side, jot down quickly what you understand or what you can relate to. Write a phrase or key word along with the page number. On the right side, jot down questions or things you don't understand or can't relate to. Do this as you actually read (read with a pencil or pen in your hand). Remember, some readings will be relatively easy; with others, almost everything you write—questions or comments about what's not clear—will end up on the right side.

Don't be surprised if this kind of reading and recording feels a little awkward or cumbersome the first few times. That's normal, especially if you're used to reading everything quickly and without much reflection. Writing as you read encourages you to make the change from a passive reader ("I'll just let this wash over me") to a reader who actively talks back to the text. And once you can establish a dialogue with your reading, once you're saying "Yes, I get this" or "Wait a minute, what does *this* mean?"— once you're speaking as a participant, an active thinker—you'll begin understanding academic reading far better than you ever have before. Questioning leads to answering.

ACTIVITY 1.3
Following the suggestions just given, take notes on your first reading from one of the selections in this book.

ACTIVITY 1.4
After your first reading of one of the selections in this book, use one of the following suggestions to write a journal entry.

1. Tell the story of your reading, in chronological order from start to finish. (For example: "When I first started, I was confused. I couldn't understand what the author was saying because I didn't understand some of the words. But then, about the second page, the passage about environmental impact statements really jumped out at me and made sense, and from then on I was right with the author. Suddenly the subtitles were very clear and logical, and I was able to read right to the end, agreeing all the way.")
2. Explain anything in the reading that surprised you, that you didn't expect.
3. What passages stood out (either in good ways or in problematic ones), and why?
4. Talk about how this reading helps you understand something in your own life.
5. Talk about how this reading complicates or confuses something you've taken for granted or not thought about much before now.

ANNOTATING

Writing *in* in your book is good, too—not just marking or highlighting passages that strike you but writing questions and comments in the margins. Think of annotating the text itself as abbreviated journal writing and of the journal as an elaboration of your reactions. Some of the same thought processes are involved.

The advantage of annotating is that you can make your comments at the moment they occur to you and right next to the passage that inspired them. It's immediate. The disadvantage, of course, is that you can't say much. There's not enough room to write more than a few fragmentary phrases or short sentences.

What good annotating encourages is what the journal encourages: active, involved reading. Sometimes students are reluctant to write in the margins because they're afraid those marks will decrease the resale value of the book. But the real way to get the value out of your books is to make them the first, immediate record of your own thinking. Mark them everywhere.

Here are some ideas on what to mark and how to comment.

Mark any passage that interests, compels, excites, confuses you—anything that seems important. Draw a line, bracket, star, or circle. In the margins, write a short phrase or question summarizing the point.

Record enthusiasms: "Yes." "I agree with this." "Of course."

Record resistances and questions: "What?" "Give me a break." "I'm not following this."

Mark statements that summarize the theme of the piece, and mark the topic sentences in important paragraphs—mark anything that summarizes main ideas.

Notice patterns and evolving themes. At the top of a page, write your reactions: "Rejection of romanticism." "Statistics used to overwhelm us." "Notice all the images of passageways."

Outline the selection. Put numbers and letters in the margins indicating the main sections.

Write subtitles for major sections.

Write questions to ask in class.

Marginal comments like these are the seeds of journal entries—the pegs for hanging longer, more considered comments.

ACTIVITY 1.5

Annotate the first two pages of any selection in this anthology. In class, exchange and discuss your annotations with one or two of your classmates. What did you mark in common? What do your annotations reveal about the way you think? about the nature of the piece?

REREADING

The next step is rereading, going back through the text and trying to understand both what it's saying and how you're responding to it. This is the stage when you start dealing with complexities and so have to be patient with yourself and the writer, avoiding panic and getting down to work. Here are some suggestions and questions to guide you.

- *Reflect.* Where did you bog down or have difficulty, and why? What in the form or content of the piece made the reading hard for you? If the reading was easy and fun, what made it easy and fun—the author's language, your prior knowledge of the subject? To put this another way, what kind of reader does the author suppose you are? What does the author assume you know? What does the author expect you to be able to do? How could you become that reader?

- *Translate.* Take any passage that isn't clear and try to put it into your own words. Make it as simple and direct and clear as you can. You can do this translation in your head, in a discussion, or in the reading journal. Imagine you're teaching the concept to a twelve-year-old or explaining it to a friend not in class. Be slangy. Find a commonsense, everyday, contemporary example of the idea or form: What would it be like if it were a soap opera, a comic book, a bumper sticker?

- *Interpret.* Do the examples support the writer's claims, or is there some slippage or disjunction? Is this a well-written, honest piece, but you just can't buy it? Does this piece overturn or call into question any of your own beliefs? Does the writing ring true in your own experience? How does it compare with other pieces you've read?

- *Organize.* You have a list of questions and comments in two columns on a sheet of paper, or you've scribbled in the margins of the book. Try to find connections among these points. Are some points subordinate to one larger point? Are there, say, three major points to which everything else is secondary? Do your comments line up as a series of oppositions, paradoxes, or contradictions? Try sketching, doodling, looping, outlining.

ACTIVITY 1.6
Reread the early two-column journal entries you made on your first reading. Underneath those reading notes, use the questions in the preceding list to reflect, translate, and interpret. Quantity counts here; messiness counts. When you've come up with at least a full page of ideas, try organizing them: Circle the main ideas, and draw lines to subordinate ideas. Use another sheet here if you need it.

ACTIVITY 1.7
Return to what you're reading and to your reading journal. Look over your earlier journal entries for this reading, identify an important question, and reread to answer that question. Then write a short entry that will help you remember what you've discovered with this rereading.

ACTIVITY 1.8
Use any of the following suggestions to make an extended journal entry (more than half a page) based on your rereading.

1. Outline a possible research project. What else would you like to know? Why would it be helpful to know these things?

2. Teach this reading to someone in the class who hasn't been able to read it. What do you say to the person that gives him or her a basic grasp of this reading?

3. Think imaginatively and metaphorically for a bit: think of this reading as medicine, for example, a cure for something. What's the disease, and why does this reading cure it? Or what kind of weather is the reading like? What would the reading look like if it were a landscape? What kind of music is the reading like, or what kind of clothes? Who would play the author or main character in the movie, and what kind of movie would it be?

FREEWRITING

The technique of freewriting can be a very useful way of responding to any of these questions and ideas. To freewrite, simply start writing and don't stop for five minutes or so, or until you've run out of steam. Write nonstop, at a comfortable pace, not letting your pen leave the page. If you don't know what to say, write "I don't know what to say" until you think of something, or repeat the last word of the last sentence until you find your way. Don't worry about making errors in grammar, punctuation, or spelling or even about saying something stupid or off the point. Just keep writing. Don't let your pen leave the page or your fingers the keyboard. Concentrate on what you're thinking, as if the words were transparent, not there at all.

Try to stay on the point, focused on the reading. But if you find yourself wandering into new territory, don't pull back too soon. You may be exploring something unusual and important.

The idea is to brainstorm *in writing,* letting the flow of words lead you to new ideas, to possibilities you hadn't known you were thinking of. In freewriting, your internal censor is silenced or postponed. There's no voice in your head saying "Be careful," "That's not true," or "That sounds silly," so your best, deepest, and truest thinking can often emerge—and in more straightforward language than you can usually manage in a finished paper.

Not every freewrite is useful. You have to give yourself permission to babble and move away from the point sometimes. Freewriting is like running or meditation or any process that takes time. You've got to get into shape, build up those muscles. If a particular freewrite doesn't yield anything worthwhile, think of it as a warm-up, a way of clearing your mind, and go on from there.

ACTIVITY 1.9

Start reading any selection in this book. At just the moment you feel yourself getting interested or confused or having something to say, stop, close the book, and freewrite for ten minutes. Record everything that's in your head at the moment, not letting your pen leave the page or your fingers the keyboard. Just write. If you don't know what to say, write "I don't know what to say." Don't think about the writing; think about the thinking. Let yourself go and really freewrite. Write for the whole ten minutes, whatever happens.

ACTIVITY 1.10
Do activity 1.9 two or three times; then reread the most productive free-write. Underline and number the major ideas. What did the freewrite yield?

FURTHER ADVICE AND PERSPECTIVES

Like the writing process, reading always involves some kind of re-vision, re-seeing. Reading once is not enough. You usually can't go straight ahead without stopping. You're always taking three steps forward and two back, at least at first; and one key to becoming a successful reader is simply accepting that process. Of course, some reading is just fun, not work at all. Reading isn't always a hard academic chore; it can be a pleasure, its content something you understand intuitively and appreciate right away. But you don't need advice for doing that kind of reading, just time and opportunity.

Here are some further ideas to keep in mind as you go through the process for the harder reading, some other perspectives for making this reading more like the kind you already enjoy.

- *Be generous and open-minded.* It's hard to understand any reading when you've made up your mind in advance. Reading involves, after all, a kind of careful listening; it requires paying attention. So try not to dismiss any author offhandedly, even when you disagree. Give the author the benefit of the doubt, the way you do when you meet someone in person; show some courtesy. Remember, too, that an editor at some point considered this work good enough and important enough to publish in a magazine or a book, and that, as the editors of this anthology, we obviously think it's good enough to include here. Some of these pieces are famous. They've been around for years, and generations of educated people have considered them important. Surely there must be something to them.

- *Keep in mind that meaning is never absolute.* A text isn't cast in concrete, its meaning fixed once and for all. Meaning is what you make for yourself as you read a text. You bring to the reading your values, beliefs, and experience, and they condition what it's possible for you to understand in that text. You shine your light on it. In other words, all readers have a right to their feelings and opinions about the reading—the instructor's reading is not the only one, the "right" one. This means, too, that it's no scandal when several different interpretations of a reading come up in a class discussion. That's the way life is.

At the same time, the language and the structure of the reading do set limits. A reading can't mean anything that readers claim; the range of reasonable interpretations is always defined by the historical context, the meaning of words, and the author's intentions.

- *Consider the rhetorical context.* A piece of writing comes from somewhere and is directed to a particular audience—that is its rhetorical context. The author wrote it for a reason. Often the context is implicit; and if you cannot figure it out, your instructor or someone else may have to explain it to you. Maybe a particular piece is a response to some other piece. Or maybe it was first a speech delivered to a particular audience. Maybe it is especially significant because the author is a woman or a person of color. Maybe the historical context is the key thing.

  In the same way, it's important to know the *aim* of a piece of expository writing. Is it intended *to inform, to argue a position,* or *to reflect and explore?* These are the three main purposes a piece of writing can serve (though a particular piece can have more than one aim or fall somewhere between the aims). Joan Didion's "On Going Home" is a reflective and exploratory piece, and so we approach it very differently from the way we approach Samuel Matthew's purely informative article, "Under the Sun," on the problems of global warming. In much the same way, we know that the facts and statistics in Ron Arnold's "Rethinking Environmentalism" can't be taken as detached and objective. Arnold is arguing a particular position in this essay, and we have to interpret his claims with that position in mind. We need to be aware that the author is writing from a particular point of view. If we're confused about aims or kinds of writing, we usually get confused about meaning. We don't know *how* to read.

  In other words, not only do the readings in this book all concern the theme of the environment, they also all *have* an environment. And that environment is as important to understand as the reading itself.

- *Look for what* isn't *said.* A literary text like a poem or short story *shows* rather than *tells.* It gives scenes, metaphors, and images that usually stand on their own without explicit commentary from the writer. Rarely does a poet or fiction writer step forward and say, "And the moral of this story is. . . ." Literature doesn't want to tell you something; it wants to make an experience for you. At its best, literature wants to make that experience so full and real that you realize any interpretation—anything you say about that experience—will only get at part of its truth. Again, the part you get—the part you can talk most readily about—will depend as much on you as on the literature itself. Reading literature means participating in the experience it wants to make and noticing every detail; reading literature means imagining you're the writer and then working to understand the writer's intentions; and reading literature means trying to make sense of your own responses.

An expository or explanatory reading is more explicit than literature. There's usually a very clear thesis statement right at the beginning, and the author tries to take us step by step through the details and information. But even in expository prose some of the most important things are not said explicitly. Often the writer will assume we know historical facts or the methods of a discipline. The writer may be continuing a discussion that's been going on for years and may assume we are aware of the background. Often there will be some key assumption that isn't stated directly, something the writer is taking for granted.

- *Think about likenesses and differences.* One key way to read is to look for how the ideas and feelings embodied in the reading are like your own, familiar, in keeping with who you already are, relevant to your situation, contemporary. Try to imaginatively close the gaps between yourself and your reading. Imagine living in the world of the author who wrote what you're reading. Only by making the imaginative leap into that author's world, however different, can you really understand the reading. Now, once you've worked hard to understand the author in these ways, step back again and think about how different that author is from you and how different that author's life and world appear to you. Understanding these human similarities and differences can make reading feel real.

- *Rely on the instructor and your classmates.* Students often worry when they can't figure out a reading all by themselves. Just as a now-outdated assumption suggested that writers worked all alone by lamplight in some lonely garret, students often seem to assume that readers are supposed to understand things on their own; and if they can't, there's something wrong with them. But reading, like writing, is a collaborative act. It depends on community and discussion. Of course teachers have insights and information you need in order to understand some of the reading you do. They're more experienced, and much college reading is hard stuff. Your responsibility is to do the best you can in advance, learn from your instructor, and then read again, bringing all you've learned into the class.

Your classmates are also part of the process. Each person in a class sees something the rest haven't; and together these insights make up a larger, fuller, richer understanding of the subject. Take advantage of any opportunities for classroom discussion. Ask that nagging question you've written in one of your journal entries. Respond to what others say. Write down what others say. Whenever your class offers opportunities for discussion, take that dialogue you've developed with the text and use it to help others and to ask for help.

ACTIVITY 1.11

As you read a selection in this book, use one of the discussion points in the preceding section as the basis for an entry in your reading journal. Use that discussion point to help you further understand the selection you're reading. Make sure that this entry runs at least half a page.

ACTIVITY 1.12

Use a lecture or a class discussion to enrich your reading of a passage, and write a journal entry organized as follows: (1) a summary of your thoughts and reactions on a first reading; (2) a summary of the main ideas from the class discussion or the teacher's comments; (3) a rereading of the passage or selection with these new ideas in mind.

WRITING AND READING

Implicit in everything we recommend in this book is the belief that writing is the best way to read. To understand a hard reading, you need to write about it, briefly and informally at first and later at length and with revision. Through writing you enter into a reading. You enter into conversation with it. You talk back to it and it talks back to you; and gradually you write your way into something that other people find is worthwhile reading for themselves.

This interaction between you and the text you're reading changes as you become more familiar with that text. You replace your first impressions with a surer understanding; and often this understanding leads you to considered judgments. Here is a list of journal questions to use as you become more familiar with a given text.

Recall your prereading of this selection, and look back over any earlier journal entries. How have those earlier understandings changed? Did what you guess at the start prove accurate? What have you understood accurately from the first? What did you misunderstand at first but now understand?

If you were going to write two questions to focus class discussion, what would they be? (Make sure that both of your questions include a specific reference to a particular section or part of the reading itself.)

What do you like in this reading? What do you find praiseworthy?

What do you dislike in this reading, and where does your dislike come from? Do you dislike it because you disagree with it? because it doesn't persuade you?

What biases, experiences, and beliefs do you bring to the reading, and how do they influence your understanding, whether or not you like the reading?

What argument (either direct or indirect) does this selection make? What does the author want readers to understand or think or do?

Think of what you've read as answering a large question that was on the writer's mind. What was this question? How would you begin to answer this question?

Write a letter to the author or to one of the characters. Tell that person what you think about what you've read. Or become one of the characters or the author and write back, or write something from that person's point of view.

Write more about the relationship between the reading and your experience. Write from both directions: How does the reading help you understand your life, and how does your life help you understand the reading? How do the reading and your life influence each other, pull against each other, warp or change each other, slide into each other—clash, merge, split?

After doing a number of entries over several weeks, review what you've written and try to summarize and analyze it. Describe your intellectual landscape. Narrate your intellectual journey. Sort and categorize the entries. What have you learned?

As you review a number of entries about different works, do you see any two or more entries that suddenly seem connected to each other? You wrote them separately, not thinking about connections. But looking back now, do you see a pattern? a series of oppositions? paradoxes? questions?

Summarize, explain, extend, illustrate, apply, react to what you think are the most important and interesting ideas from class lectures and discussions.

Write a memo to your instructor asking questions about a lecture or offering comments you didn't have a chance to make in class.

Write an open memo to the class offering comments and reactions about a class discussion.

ACTIVITY 1.13

Use any two of the preceding questions to help you further define your own response to one of your assigned readings. Make your responses journal entries; write for yourself, and don't second-guess your spelling or punctuation. Make each of your answers at least half a page long—longer if what you're writing seems sensible and useful. Overall, you should end up with a journal entry at least a page long.

Essay Topics for Chapter 1

1. Sketch a profile of yourself as a reader. Write a reading autobiography. Here are some questions to help you start brainstorming details. (Don't

feel that you have to take each one up in order. Simply start writing as soon as you've gotten enough ideas and images.)

Did you read a lot or a little growing up? Did your parents read and, if so, what did they read? Did you have books in your house? Have your tastes and interests changed? how? Do you remember one treasured book from your growing up? Do you read for pleasure now? What is your favorite book, and why? What is the last book you read, why did you read it, and what was the experience of reading it? If you don't read for pleasure, what do you do instead, and what are the benefits of doing those things? the disadvantages? What role does television play in your reading life? Have you always intended to do more reading but for some reason haven't gotten to it? Why haven't you gotten to it? What do you feel the moment you've gotten a reading assignment in one of your classes this term? dread? anticipation? What's the difference between the reading you enjoy (if you enjoy reading) and the reading you're assigned? Is there any kind of reading you enjoy, or anything else you do instead of reading? Do you know people who read a lot? What kind of people are they? Would you like to be more like these people? What do you enjoy doing most, and how does this activity compare with the act of reading? Is it at odds with reading or in keeping with it?

After you've filled in your portrait with your details, conclude by reflecting on the implications. How do you think your experiences with reading and your attitudes about reading will influence your approach to this book? to college in general? In your own life, what's the relationship between reading and writing?

2. Write an essay reflecting on how you "read" other things in your life besides books and articles—*reading* in the sense of interpreting a person, thing, or experience, decoding the details on the surface, seeing past the surface to what's underneath.

For example, a person good at auto mechanics can read an engine, figuring out the problem with the fuel filter or the wheel bearings by interpreting the external signs—the sounds, the smells, the appearance of things. A forester can read a forest, determining the best approach to logging or reforestation by the lay of the land, the health and distribution of trees, the density of wildlife, and so on. A cook can read a cake or sauce, deciding when to add ingredients or turn off the heat.

In our day-to-day experiences we're reading all the time: making inferences about people on the basis of their body language, their clothing, what they say and how they say it, and what they don't say. Reading is what we have to do whenever the answer or the reality of something isn't immediately obvious.

Write an essay describing some kind of thing you know how to read, and compare this kind of reading to the reading of books and articles. How are these acts of interpretation different and the same?

What can one tell you about the other? How did you learn to become expert in this other kind of reading? What have you gained from it?

3. Write about a time when reading really worked for you—a time when you were very moved by a book or story or poem or essay or a time when you learned something important from a reading.

What was the content of the reading? What was its style? Why did you do the reading? Was it assigned, or did you choose it yourself? Where did you read it, and how long did it take? Did you write about it or take notes on it? Describe how you felt during and after the reading—sad, elated, happy, confused. What was it that caused these feelings? If you got information from a piece, what information did you get, why did you want it, and how did the text deliver it? What did you do to make the reading successful? How were you prepared? How did you act?

Finally, compare this positive experience to a negative one—to a time when reading was hard or frustrating. What's the difference? What can you do to change things? What things can't you change, and how can you manage them?

2

Writing Essays

If my mind could gain a firm footing, I would not make essays, I would make decisions; but it is always in apprenticeship and on trial.
—ESSAYIST MICHEL EYQUEM DE MONTAIGNE *(1533–1592)*

THE ESSAY AS A REVISED JOURNAL ENTRY

Ask five different writers to tell you what an essay is and you're likely to receive five different descriptions; the same thing holds for teachers. There is no common and precise definition. For some writers and teachers an essay is a five-paragraph formula (introduction, main point, main point, main point, conclusion). And in some timed-writing or test situations this sort of formula can be useful. But we prefer Montaigne's original idea that the essay is a trial or an attempt, as in "giving something a try." We want you to think of an essay as a careful and considered piece of writing but one that's personal and informal, a record of the mind in the act of thinking.

Maybe the best way to think of the informal essay is as a revised journal entry. It's the step between the journal and the long research paper, with elements of both. If you've been keeping a journal, take one of your best and most extended entries and proofread and polish it, or blend several related entries into a finished product. The structure and movement of those entries can also be the structure and movement of the essay.

You can write the same kind of piece even if you haven't been keeping a journal or if you want to move away from your journal and on to new ideas. You can take your direction for an essay from any of the topics or questions we proposed in the previous chapter and write about it at greater length.

An essay is like journal entries in several ways:

It's informal in style, free of fancy words and unnecessary jargon.

It's personal, drawing on the writer's own experience, admitting biases and enthusiasms.

It doesn't have to come to definitive answers or demonstrate a thesis beyond any doubt; it can ask questions and try out different possibilities.

It doesn't have to follow a certain format like the traditional five-paragraph theme, but it can be organized organically, naturally.

An essay is different from a journal entry in the following ways:

It's proofread: grammar, spelling, and punctuation count.

It's precise; there are no wasted words.

It's the product of thinking, rethinking, and reconsidering. If a journal entry means "let's think about this," then an essay means "let's think about this, think about it again, raise new questions about it, look at it from another perspective, and then see if we can say what we think is true."

It's detailed and grounded in evidence. Although you don't have to come to a definite conclusion, you do need to show where your responses come from in the reading.

It's organized. It doesn't have to follow a prescribed format, but it does have to have a coherent shape and clear transitions.

A journal entry records your first thoughts. An essay records your second and third and fourth thoughts. In a journal you don't have to worry about the shape of the sentences and paragraphs. In an essay you do the same kind of thinking you do in a journal but in the clearest sentences and most organized paragraphs you can write. A journal is private, written primarily to prompt and record your thinking as it happens; an essay is public, a piece of writing for a reader who needs to have assumptions explained and detail presented.

ACTIVITY 2.1

Take an entry from your journal and experiment with revising it both to make its thinking more complete and orderly and to make its thinking clearer to readers. What would you have to delete? What would you need to add?

ACTIVITY 2.2

Do a one-page freewrite responding to a question from the reading; then experiment with revising it. What part or parts of the entry would you focus on as most promising? Circle these parts. Write two or three sentences describing what would you want to add to these parts in order to flesh out the thinking. As you look at the circled parts of your entry, what changes would you want to make in these sections? Describe them in two or three sentences.

THE NATURAL STYLE

When students move from journals to essays, they're often tempted to get wordy and abstract and indirect, giving up the gains of journal writing. Their thinking goes like this: It's all well and good to be natural and direct in the privacy of your own journal; but when you write for an audience, you've got to be stiff and formal. And you've got to be careful, too, making sure that the reader doesn't catch you in some embarrassing mistake. So talk around things; hide the real point; fancy up the language.

The students are wrong. Essays give you permission to be informal and direct, writing with the same honesty you bring to the journal. And they demand that you do. The premise of essay writing is that direct sentences are not only acceptable but also better—more precise, more insightful, more powerful stylistically. When you revise a journal entry, you often need to reword phrases for greater clarity or include clearer transitions; but the key is not to lose your natural rhythms in the process. The key is not to back off from what you really have to say.

The irony in all good writing is that readers are most persuaded by language that doesn't seem to be trying to persuade them. What's most convincing is the impression that writers are struggling to say something important for themselves, to make something clearer to themselves, and not trying to show off or gain approval.

PATTERNS

If you think of an essay as writing that grows directly out of your own thinking, then its structure can follow the natural movement of your mind as you explore and work through an important idea. You don't have to force your ideas into one required pattern.

On the other hand, it's good to have some possibilities for structure, some models to show you what's allowed and what other writers have found helpful. Formulas are good as long as there are lots of them and you realize you don't have to follow any particular one to the letter.

The sections that follow describe ten patterns that will help you understand how an essay can be structured. Feel free to combine, extend, and adapt the patterns in any way that works for you. In the end, they're simply various ways of describing what the mind naturally does as it works on material. You will recognize versions of journal questions here, applied now to structure. They all overlap. All are simplified patterns that can be varied and adapted in many ways.

1. Spot of time/mind-movie

   Spot of time: First, describe as directly and in as much detail as you can some significant moment from your recent experience, some moment that stands out from the rest, when you felt greater joy or had deeper insight into something.

   Mind-movie: In the second half of the essay, think aloud about what the experience might mean. *Read* it. Tell the story of your thinking and feeling about the experience, in chronological order, including how you feel and think about it now that it's passed. Use ideas and short quotations from your reading of other essays, stories, or articles.

This is the classic pattern of the personal essay, complicated and varied in all kinds of ways in all kinds of essays. A good example is Lewis Thomas's "The Tucson Zoo." It begins with a description of Thomas's experience watching beavers and otters at play; then it moves to a record, in stages, of his thinking about the experience, each idea succeeded by the next.

2. Passage/mind-movie

   Passage: First, take a significant passage from the reading, some passage that stands out from the rest (just as the spot of time stands out in your experiences). Describe the passage as clearly and directly as you can, putting it into your own words.

   Mind-movie: Next, tell the story of your thinking about the passage, in chronological order: what you thought first, then second, then third, along with any confusions and questions. Conclude by explaining where you are right now. Use relevant ideas and terms from lectures and class discussions, other readings in the book, and other classes.

3. Mind-movie

   Simply tell the story of your thinking about the reading or a question from the reading. You can explain what you first thought, then what you thought next, and so on, from the beginning of the process. Or you can zero in on what you're thinking at this moment—videotaping everything that's going on in your head, all the levels and layers, right now.

Another way of viewing this essay is as a "think piece," a piece sharing your current thinking about an issue. Be sure to keep your responses keyed to where they come from in the reading; quote useful passages.

4. Ideas before/ideas after

   Ideas before: Begin by describing everything you thought about a particular issue or subject before you did the reading.

   Ideas after: Next, discuss how the reading has confirmed your ideas, reinforced and strengthened them; or how it has changed your mind, overturned what you thought; or how your ideas have been complicated at least.

You can also think of this pattern as two mind-movies: one before you read, the other after. Or you can think of the pattern in this way:

Before: Describe what you thought about a reading before the class discussion and lectures.

After: Describe what you think about the reading now, in light of what you learned in class.

5. Confusion to clarity

Confusion: Start by identifying and describing why you were confused in the beginning, what the problem was.

Clarity: Then discuss what you understand now and how you came to understand it, as well as whatever problems remain.

This pattern is another variation on the mind-movie.

6. Response/sources

Response: Explain a reaction you had to one of the readings: confusion, anger, frustration, agreement, excitement.

Sources: Then try to figure out the sources of this response. What features of the style and structure of the piece caused you to feel this way? What convictions or experiences did you bring to the reading, and how have they helped to prompt your response?

7. Oppositions, paradoxes, contradictions

List and explain the ideas in the reading that seem to be at odds with each other or in some tension—on the one hand, this; on the other hand, that. An entire essay can be focused on only one such tension. Or an essay can express a confusion, the way things seem to you right now. Or you can write to express a conviction, what you're sure is at the heart of the reading, some underlying problem or paradox the reading confronts.

8. Reading/experience

Reading: Take an important passage or idea and explain it clearly in your own words.

Experience: Take an experience from your life, describe it in detail, and then explain how that experience illustrates the idea in the reading, how it is an example of it. Or show how your experience complicates, challenges, or questions the issue in the reading.

One obvious variation is to reverse the order: to begin with experience and then go on to the reading. Another possibility is to use this pattern several times with several different points.

9. Reading is like me/unlike me

Reading is like me: Begin by discussing how your experience is similar to the author's, how you can relate to it, and how you agree with it.

Reading is unlike me: Then move to contrast, to show how the author's experience is different from yours, at odds with it, its values separate and its history remote.

This pattern is a variation of pattern 8.

It makes sense to think about these patterns more than once as you work on an essay. For example, you could read over these patterns until you recognize that one of them seems to fit your earliest sense of a reading. Recognizing a promising pattern can help you push and examine and continue thinking about your response. Thus you might start with pattern 5, identifying some confusion you feel and working to understand it. In the process of thinking about that confusion, you might well find yourself forming a definite agreement or disagreement with what you've read. Seeing this stronger response might lead you to move to pattern 9.

ACTIVITY 2.3

Reread your journal. Find three entries that more or less correspond to three of the organizational patterns just discussed. Make copies of these entries. On the copies, identify the pattern, and mark the parts of the entries that reflect the pattern's logic.

ACTIVITY 2.4

Use any one of the patterns to write a short essay about the reading.

A FINAL PATTERN

Notice that most of the patterns we've suggested move in some way from the general to the particular or from the particular to the general. That's the key to any structure. A claim gets made or an idea is stated; then the writer naturally moves to defending the claim, explaining the idea, filling in the details. All writing is an ebb and flow between the general and the particular.

Often, what are missing from a journal entry are just these supporting details. You're writing quickly and without revising, so you're free to generalize. Revising the journal entry means taking that good, quick idea and showing where it came from, what details give rise to it, what particulars support it.

Sometimes it's just the opposite. Your journal entries record details and notice particulars, but you haven't realized yet what their significance is. Revising the entry for an essay involves pulling the particulars together under some unifying concept.

Here's a slightly more systematic way to understand and organize this movement. It's a structure that can be used within paragraphs and across a number of paragraphs in whole essays.

10. TRIAC

In this pattern each letter stands for a part of the essay.

T = theme, topic, thesis: State what the essay is about, the topic the essay addresses, or what you will argue or claim. This opening may run only a sentence or so; rarely will it be longer than a paragraph.

R = restatement, restriction, refinement: Rephrase the theme or thesis in sharper, slightly more particular ways. This restatement is often preceded with transitions like *that is, in other words,* or *what I mean is.* Again, this restatement may run only a sentence or a few sentences.

I = illustration, example: Support your ideas. Give examples. Illustrate. Sentences that do this are often preceded with the transitional phrases *for instance* or *for example.* These discussions form the heart of an essay or paragraph; they give the details that make the writing convincing and interesting.

A = analysis: Analysis means telling readers how to understand the examples or illustrations. It means making logical, commonsense inferences between causes and effects, intentions and actions. Words like *since, therefore, because, however,* and *nevertheless* all work to signal your logic.

C = conclusion, closure: Anytime you're ready to draw together several threads of your logic, you're making a conclusion. Such sentences or paragraphs are often preceded with *in conclusion* or *thus,* though these transitions aren't always necessary and can sound a little clunky. Conclusions can appear in the middle of an essay and more than once.

On the paragraph level TRIAC is a particularly good way of organizing a discussion of quotations or paraphrases from the reading. In essence, TRIAC gives you a recipe:

T = your claim about a passage
R = a refined statement of that claim
I = the passage itself, quoted or paraphrased
A = analysis of how the passage illustrates your claim
C = statement you now have clearly shown to be true

It's a structure that can vary, too. For example, the steps can go in different orders, such as IATC:

I = intriguing illustration or example to begin
A = analysis of this illustration, how it works, why it works this way
T = your sense of the theme of the passage, your real topic
C = your concluding discussion of what now seems true to you and should seem true to your readers

Or you could use TITITIAC—three pairs of thesis/illustrations followed by analysis of how these three add up and a concluding discussion of what now seems accurate or true. TRIAC, in other words, is a structure that can work in lots of different sequences and combinations.

_____

ACTIVITY 2.5
Use the various TRIAC headings to help you analyze and outline one of the readings in this book. As you read, see whether you can identify the logical moves the writer has made. Once you see this structure, consider the effectiveness of the author's decisions. Do you think the parts should have been rearranged?

ACTIVITY 2.6
Imitate the structure of the piece you've outlined. Put your content in its form.

ACTIVITY 2.7
Write an essay following TRIAC exactly.

ACTIVITY 2.8
Go back to your journal and use TRIAC to outline and diagram a particularly effective entry. Were you already following this scheme—or some part of it—intuitively?

_____

PARAPHRASING AND QUOTING

We've mentioned now the importance of using quotations from the reading you've done. Using quotations helps you to be specific; quotations help you (and your readers) see where an idea came from or what parts of a reading provoked your response. Let's say that you've been struck by a highly quotable passage in Wendell Berry's "Getting Along with Nature" and want to use it in an essay. You have several options.

- *You can quote the whole passage.* Quoting the whole passage tells readers that they really need to read it all in the exact words of the author. You might decide to quote a whole passage because you think it cannot be summarized accurately or because it makes such an impact that summarizing it or using only part of it wouldn't be persuasive. To quote an entire passage, use a lead-in phrase, and then indent the passage as a block.

  As Wendell Berry puts it in "Getting Along with Nature":
  > We go to wilderness places to be restored, to be instructed
  > in the natural economies of fertility and healing, to admire
  > what we cannot make. Sometimes, as we find to our surprise,
  > we go to be chastened or corrected. And we go in order to

> return with renewed knowledge by which to judge the
> health of our human economy and our dwelling places.
Wilderness, in other words, teaches us and heals us in ways that
nothing else can.

Whenever you want to quote a passage longer than three or four lines,
you need to block it like this. Notice that in a block quotation you don't
use quotation marks before and after the passage. The indentation takes
care of that.

- *You can use a shorter part of the passage.* To use just part of a passage, use a
  lead-in phrase, and then quote the lines. But this time there's no need to
  indent the passage as a block. Work the lines into the paragraph and use
  quotation marks.

  > As Wendell Berry puts it in "Getting Along with Nature," "We
  > go to wilderness places to be restored, to be instructed in the
  > natural economies of fertility and healing, to admire what we can-
  > not make." Wilderness, in other words, teaches us and heals us in
  > ways that nothing else can.

- *You can work smaller phrases into your own sentences.* Instead of quoting all
  or part of the passage in whole sentences, take some piece of the author's
  sentence and blend it into your own language.

  > Sometimes, we go to wilderness areas, as Wendell Berry says, "to
  > be chastened or corrected." This is often a surprise. We don't
  > expect to be shown the errors of our ways, but we are; and we
  > return to civilization a little sheepish, aware of our mistakes.

In general, try not to quote more than you really need to. Sometimes,
a long passage is so good that you've got to use all of it, but you should do
extensive quoting only now and then. Even in a long term paper you
shouldn't have more than one or two long quotations. Otherwise, you run
into the problem of the paper looking like nothing more than a string of
quotations hooked together with occasional pieces of your own writing.

When you're doing things the other way around, working pieces of
quotations into your own sentences, *you're* in control. *You're* doing the
work (not the other writer, and not the reader). You're showing that
you've done the reading and understood it, but you're not letting the other
writer's words overwhelm your own.

Here are further tips for all three kinds of quoting.

> Notice that commas and periods always go inside quotation marks.
> Notice that in all three examples the quotation is followed by some
>   explanation in the student's own words. It's not enough just to
>   quote the piece. You've got to explain it a little, both because
>   important quotations are usually not self-explanatory and because
>   part of your job is to show that you've actually understood what

you're quoting. You're showing that the quotation actually fits the claim you're making about it, that it belongs in the paragraph.

Lead-in and transitional phrases are always necessary: *As Berry says, According to Berry, As Berry puts it, In Berry's words, Berry says, Berry exclaims, Berry insists, Berry argues.* These phrases can go at the beginning, in the middle, or at the end of a quotation. Varying the sequence can help the sentences flow more smoothly.

As Berry insists, "whether we go to those places or not, we need to know that they exist."

Berry argues that "whether we go to those places or not, we need to know that they exist."

"Whether we go to those places or not," Berry insists, "we need to know that they exist."

- *Finally, you can paraphrase the quotation.* That is, you can put the idea into your own words, acknowledging in some way that it isn't your own. This is what the follow-up sentences—"Wilderness, in other words, teaches us and heals us in ways that nothing else can"—are doing in the earlier examples. The transition *in other words* is the obvious indication of the paraphrase.

One way to imagine the sequence when you're quoting is like this:

thesis
lead-in phrase
long or short quotation or a brief quotation worked into your own
  sentences
follow-up paraphrase

But it's also good to leave out the quotations and simply give the sense of the author's meaning yourself. You show that you've absorbed the meaning and can give it back in your own way.

Berry's point in "Getting Along with Nature" is that we all need wilderness areas. We need to get away from the unnatural "economies" that surround us everywhere in the city and encounter the "natural economies" of wilderness, because these natural economies teach us things. They teach us what we're doing wrong. They teach us by contrast—and in the process "chasten" and "correct" us.

Here is a shorter version.

Berry's point is that wilderness teaches us what we're doing wrong and shows us an alternative "economy," something different from the world of malls and tract houses, something we can "admire."

Notice that in paraphrase, too, it's good to quote a word now and then. But the student is controlling the sentence rhythms, directing the sequence, and emphasizing what he or she thinks should be emphasized.

In the next chapter we'll talk about the larger concept of summarizing, the next step beyond paraphrase.

ACTIVITY 2.9

Apply each of the strategies of quoting and paraphrasing to the following passage from "Getting Along with Nature."

> Humans, like all other creatures, must make a difference; otherwise, they cannot live. But unlike other creatures, humans must make a choice as to the kind and scale of the difference they make. If they choose to make too small a difference, they diminish their humanity. If they choose to make too great a difference, they diminish nature, and narrow their subsequent choices; ultimately, they diminish or destroy themselves.

MISCONCEPTIONS ABOUT "PERSONAL EXPERIENCE"

"Personal experience" is the other main kind of support and development we're suggesting, and here there's often a misconception: the idea that a "personal essay" is easy and self-indulgent, not demanding the hard work of a long term paper. It's as if the word *personal* were just an invitation to be fuzzy.

But the real reason to draw on your own experience is to test and complicate ideas, to think hard and with precision. Anyone can generalize. Anyone can make broad claims in the abstract. The question is whether these abstract claims are really true, whether they conform to the way life actually is; and the only way to find that out is to move to the level of concrete particulars.

When you do research, you find those particulars in the library or through interviews—statistics, historical facts, scientific information. Personal experience is another, more primary source of particulars. Writing about your own experience is a direct way of doing research, of grounding claims in the complexities of what you see and hear everyday.

The demand, then, is not for feeling but for detail. Good personal writing shows rather than tells. And in that showing the reader can see whether the writer's opinions make sense and ring true.

In the same way, students misunderstand the permission to ask questions and admit confusions in an essay. Good essays can be more rigorous than conventional term papers or articles because they're not hiding behind faked coherence or feigned authority. In the contradictions they record, the uncertainties they own up to, they're often much closer to the "truth"—which is always that things are more complicated than they look from a distance.

ACTIVITY 2.10
Write a paragraph, page, or essay following this basic pattern:

Everyone says _____.
But in my own experience I have found _____.

HOW THE ESSAY HELPS YOU WITH TERM PAPERS

Writing essays is good training for writing term papers (as well as something worthwhile to do in itself). The permissions of the essay form give you a chance to learn what's basic to all good writing.

Writing clearly and straightforwardly: Using *I* and writing in your own voice prepares you for writing the direct, precise sentences that good term papers require.

Grounding claims: Testing ideas in your own experience prepares you for grounding claims in the kinds of evidence found through research.

Getting beyond the easy generalization: Exploring meaning in your own reading experience, not settling for the easy answers, prepares you for the complexities of a longer project.

You usually don't use *I* in a term paper, of course, and you usually don't write directly about your own experience. There are further adjustments to be made, more distancing to do, as you move from the essay to the longer paper. But the essay, like the journal, is a way of learning what's fundamental to academic thinking. It's a way of learning to read past the obvious, to get to the rich particulars.

Essay Topics for Chapter 2

In addition to all the essay projects spread throughout the chapter, here are some further projects.

1. *"Screenings" or "Best Pieces."*
   This is a preliminary form, a step toward an essay. Simply go through your journal and screen out what you think are your best entries or the best parts of entries. Clean these up (proofreading and correcting any grammatical mistakes); then type them, leaving blank space between each entry. You don't need to add anything or put anything together. The pieces don't have to be arranged in any particular order.

2. *Collages.*

This is another preliminary form, a step up from a screening. Go through the same process of screening out the best pieces, proofreading, and typing; but this time, try to arrange the pieces in some kind of order. Use blank spaces as transitions; there's no need to add transitions or do any other blending. But try to see whether there's a pattern among the pieces: imagistic, associative, alternating (long/short, personal/analytical), thematic. Think of the pieces as a puzzle you've made up yourself; then try to assemble the pieces. It's helpful even to cut these pieces out (literally, with scissors) and spread them on a table so that you can see them better. Be intuitive. Be playful. Think of this task as an arts and crafts project.

As a final stage, after completing the collage, you might want to experiment with blending the pieces into a single, coherent essay. Is it possible to put some pieces together without elaborate transition—pieces that seemed unrelated at first but that now might blend? What transitions are necessary? Do you need to write a few extra pieces?

3. Write an essay reflecting on the essay. Here are some questions to get you thinking. When you hear the word *essay,* what associations immediately come to mind? what images? From past experience, come up with a list of rules and requirements for good essay writing, and then compare this list with the suggestions in this chapter. Read several of the essayists in this book, such as Joan Didion, Lewis Thomas, Wendell Berry, and Barry Lopez. Do these writers break any of the rules you learned before now? Do they surprise you? What new rules or new standards do they introduce? What values seem implicit in the way the essay was taught to you in school, and what values are implicit in the way we're talking about the essay in this chapter (assuming they are different)?

4. Write an essay reflecting on your style of thinking. Maybe you've taken a test establishing your psychological profile or read educational theorists talking about learning styles. Using any of that terminology or simply your own language, try to describe how you think you think. If you've been keeping a journal, reread it as "data" for this study. Step back and see whether you can identify patterns in the way you've written, questions you've especially liked to answer, moves you typically make as a reader and writer. Maybe you like going from the general to the particular, or maybe you find it hard to come up with particulars. Maybe you find yourself typically resisting something at first and then opening up to it, or vice versa. Maybe you're very personal as a thinker, or very abstract. Maybe you like to jump from point to point, or maybe you stick to the same idea for pages. If you haven't kept a journal, simply reflect on what happens as you do a reading for school, write a paper, or learn a new job—what you do when you think.

Try to come to some conclusions. Given the way you think, what kind of career are you best suited for? Are there things about your style that you'd just as soon change? How and why? Do the essay patterns proposed in this chapter help you in your thinking, clarify or modify it in any way? Can you come up with usable patterns that correspond to your own style of thought?

5. Write an essay reflecting on the following quotation from Thoreau's journals. Have you read any textbook or article recently that has the same problems Thoreau identifies? How does the environment of this kind of writing—the bad writing around you all the time—affect the way you write yourself? Is it possible to write differently and still succeed?

> I look over the report of the doings of a scientific association and am surprised that there is so little life to be reported; I am put off with a parcel of dry technical terms. Anything living is easily and naturally expressed in popular language. I cannot help suspecting that the life of these learned professors has been almost as inhuman and wooden as a rain-gauge or self-registering magnetic machine. They communicate no fact which rises to the temperature of blood-heat. It doesn't all amount to one rhyme.

6. Consider yourself as a writer, and report about what you learn. When given an assignment to write an essay, how do you respond; especially, what do you actually do? Do you eagerly embrace the notion of writing an essay? Does the idea fill you with dread? Which ever way you feel, can you explain why you feel this way, why you react this way? After your first reaction, then what happens? What do you actually do step by step to get to the words you actually turn in? Draw on some examples—such as your memory of earlier writing projects—to illustrate what you're saying.

Make sure that your essay also takes a close look at your habits. Have they given you good results? Do they let you make good use of your time (so that you're not rushed)? Have you modified those habits recently, and if so, how? How have the approaches in this book changed what you actually do as a writer? Are you feeling more confident as a writer, more sure of how you should proceed? Don't feel that you must answer each of these questions in turn. Instead, use them to help you think about and evaluate your own writing process.

3

Writing Summaries

Some books are to be tasted, others to be swallowed, and some few to be chewed and digested.

—FRANCIS BACON

In this chapter we move from the informal, open-ended writing of journals and short essays to the stricter, objective form of the summary. The task here is not to show *your* thinking but to report the thinking of someone else—to show that you've understood what someone else has to say. You're concentrating on the text itself, following its logic and main points. You're not thinking aloud with the reader, turning an idea over in your mind; you're beginning with the main idea and then supporting it point by point.

Like the open-ended writing of a journal, the stricter form of the summary can be a very effective way of learning through writing. Summarizing forces you to read with an attention and care that might be hard to keep up without the pressure of this assignment. Knowing that you'll be summarizing changes how you read.

If you're the reader of a summary (and it is a good, accurate one), then reading it lets you take advantage of someone else's effort. The summary tells you enough for you to understand the main points of the reading and to know whether you need to read the original piece.

READING TO WRITE A SUMMARY

Knowing that you'll be writing a summary should change how you read, focusing your attention in particular ways. You should pay special attention to figuring out the mental moves that piece of writing makes—that is, pay attention to how it's been structured. Here are some questions to be aware of as you read a piece you plan to summarize. If you're keeping a reading journal, as we suggested earlier, you can use these questions to anchor your journal entries—entries that will later become the backbone of your summary.

- What does the title and first page or so of the reading identify as this writer's main interest? If you can find a sentence that directly tells you, copy it down. If not, finish this sentence after you've read the first page: "So far, it looks like the writer in this piece aims to. . . ." Then add another sentence of your own that adds further explanation.

- Has the writer of this piece used subheadings or other divisions (for instance, asterisks or extra white space) to show shifts in content? If so, pay attention to them. Try to explain the reasons that the piece shifts where it does.

- Realizing that virtually all writing is made up of examples (stories, images, illustrations) and larger assertions, see whether you can identify which is which. Which examples or illustrations go on the longest? On what does this writer spend the most words?

- Use the TRIAC scheme to identify the major pieces in the selection as a whole: Which paragraphs or parts of paragraphs fill the T slot, which the A slot, and so on? Use TRIAC to look within paragraphs as well: Which sentences fill the T slot in a certain paragraph, which the A slot?

- Does this piece tell a story? Does it move in a chronological order (first this happened, then this, then this)? Or does it move from major topic to major topic? If it moves in chronological order to tell a story, what is the story? What is the story about? If it moves from major topic to major topic, what are these topics?

Using these questions while reading Melissa Greene's "No Rms, Jungle Vu," you might make the following notes in your journal.

> *Title, first page:* This title's a little strange. It looks like something from a classified ad, maybe an advertisement for an apartment or something. Except where would you have an apartment that has no rooms and gives a view of the jungle? Once I begin reading, things get clearer: it's a zoo—the design of a zoo—that she's talking about. And once that's clear, the title makes sense.
>
> *Subheadings, other divisions:* No subheadings, though I see that the piece does divide into sections separated by three dots. Just looking quickly, I see a first section that's sort of long, a second one that's much shorter, a third long one with a subdivision in it (white space), then a quite short ending section.
>
> *Examples, assertions:* Just looking at how the first section starts, it opens with assertions—Jon Coe telling us something he believes: how zoo design should work—it should "make the hair stand up on the back of your neck." Then the section goes on with what looks like a careful discussion of the Woodland Park gorilla exhibit

as a major example, how it's a model for other places. And this section also tells us what it's like to actually go to this exhibit, where we'd stand and what we'd see and how it's all been arranged to keep the gorillas where they're in easy view. The heated boulders is a nifty idea. This organization seems pretty straightforward: assertion, then example.

The second section looks like it's establishing the recent history of zoo design—how this kind of design started. It's telling that story.

Chronology, major topics: This piece starts by establishing its major focus: the revolution in zoo design. The second section tells the story of its immediate origin. The third section really has two topics—the changes in science and the loss of wilderness. Both have driven this new kind of design. Section three does a lot of comparing/contrasting (zoos now versus older ones) to show the changes, and it uses explanations and quotations to talk about the loss of wilderness and what that means for zoos and their goals. The last section seems to be a short example, a story really. Except for the last section, the overall organization relies on opening assertions followed by examples and explanations.

Using these questions about structure and form along with all the questions you'd normally bring to your reading should help you interrogate what you read and write useful journal entries. Remember that you cannot write an accurate, effective summary about something that still confuses you. So if what you're supposed to be summarizing still seems elusive or hard to understand, reread the piece, answering the previous list of questions again. Don't be surprised if you have to read the piece two or three times to really understand it: This isn't busywork; it's you working to make your own education. And remember that you have classmates and an instructor; involve them in your summary-writing process. Talking about the reading with others is probably the easiest way to improve your understanding.

ACTIVITY 3.1

Read Melissa Greene's "No Rms, Jungle Vu" and use your journal to take useful notes as you read. You can refer to the discussion given in this section, but make sure that your notes are just that: your notes. Try to write enough to fill at least a page and a half. (If you're not sure how to proceed, review the questions given in this section, and refer to the journal activities discussed in chapter 1.)

ACTIVITY 3.2

Read some piece designated by your instructor and use the questions given in this section (as well as any other note-taking strategies you normally use) to make useful notes as you read. Make sure that your notes fill at least a page and a half.

WRITING THE SUMMARY

Since summaries are usually short and since your role as a summary writer is really that of a reporter, the standard journalistic questions can form the framework for your summary. Usually, a summary performs three main functions: It describes *what the writing does,* it discusses *how the writing does it,* and it explains *why the author has written it.* A summary will also include any important information about the author and any crucial information about the context in which the piece was written. If the summary must be very short (say five hundred words), then these major discussion points may require only a paragraph each. And the summary might open by discussing all of them. So, for example, a summary of "No Rms, Jungle Vu" by Melissa Greene might begin in this way.

> When we go to zoos, we might not think of them as places that have actually been designed. Melissa Greene's "No Rms, Jungle Vu" shows us otherwise. Her factual essay takes us into the world of zoo design, introduces readers to some of the major designers, and explains how dramatically zoos have changed since 1970.

An opening like this gives us a good bit of information: We know who wrote the piece, we know its primary focus, we know its title, we know that it's an essay (not a poem or short story), and we know its basic aims. Later sentences and paragraphs would identify Greene's major assertions and major examples. Remember that, as a general rule, the most important points will be those that are discussed the longest. In general, then, look for the longest explanations or the longest stories: They usually focus on the most important and most complicated main points.

ACTIVITY 3.3

Draft a three-page (750-word) summary of Melissa Greene's "No Rms, Jungle Vu." You may use the sample first sentence in this section as your first sentence, if you wish. As you work to draft this summary, don't worry too much about spelling or punctuation. Focus instead on making sure that your summary accurately identifies and includes the most important parts of Greene's discussion. Be ready to explain how you've decided what's important.

ACTIVITY 3.4

Draft a three-page (750-word) summary of any piece in this book your instructor assigns. As you work to draft this summary, don't worry too much about spelling or punctuation. Focus instead on making sure that your summary accurately identifies and includes the most important parts of the reading. Be ready to explain how you've decided what's important.

USING QUOTATIONS IN SUMMARIES

Summaries are hard to write partly because they must take complicated or well-detailed information and present it briefly. The great temptation here is to generalize, to make your summary too vague, so that it doesn't really communicate a clear sense of the piece you're summarizing. Using brief quotations can remedy this problem and give your readers a clearer sense of the original.

Why use brief quotations (at most, usually no more than a sentence or so for any one purpose) rather than long ones? Remember that to be really effective and truly save readers time, a summary has to be short, concise. Thus it should use quotations to help flesh out only the most important aspects of the original piece you're summarizing. Sometimes you may decide to quote a sentence or a part of one, as in this example.

> Greene features the Woodland Park gorilla exhibit in Seattle as "an international standard for the replication of wilderness in a zoo exhibit."

Sometimes you may decide to quote parts of two sentences within a sentence of your own.

> Greene explains that in the past zoos were often designed by local architects who "did the suburban hospital," whereas today zoo architecture is a specialty aimed at creating "astoundingly realistic habitats for the animals."

ACTIVITY 3.5

Return to the rough draft of your summary and make sure that it includes at least two direct quotations from the piece you're summarizing (use more than two if you need to). Don't let any quotation run longer than two sentences from the original, and see whether you can make them briefer while still communicating clearly. Be ready to explain why you've chosen those particular quotations.

EVALUATING AND REVISING SUMMARY DRAFTS

Good summaries spend their words carefully, and they work to accurately reflect the intentions and major features of the original. Thus minor points of the original are left out of the summary or are mentioned only briefly; major points and major illustrations or explanations receive most of the attention and most of the summary's words. In addition, a good summary flows easily, its logic and progression consistently clear to readers. With these traits in mind we can make a checklist that should help you evaluate and revise your own draft. Better yet, ask others—preferably writing center staff members or other students who haven't read the original—to tell you their responses as they use this checklist.

> Read over the draft as though you have no knowledge of the original reading. On the basis of the summary draft only, list the main points (the main logic, the major explanations or illustrations) in the reading.
>
> Does your summary quote from the original, and do the quotations support the original author's most important points? Which other points (if any) should also be supported with quotations from the original? Should any quotations now in the draft be cut or shortened?
>
> What sentences or paragraphs in your summary draft seem confusingly worded or likely to be misunderstood?
>
> What parts of this draft will benefit most from revision?
>
> How do the main points in your summary draft compare with the points you first made in journal entries? Does your draft accurately reflect the original reading? Does it leave out or pay too little attention to something important? Where does it spend too much time (and too many words), and where does it spend too few?

ACTIVITY 3.6

Use the revising checklist to evaluate and revise the rough draft of your summary. In addition to answering the checklist questions yourself, ask another person to also do so, and take notes on what this person tells you. Save these notes and staple them to the final draft of your summary.

Finally, writing summaries forces you to pay attention to your reading in a more active and critical way. To summarize well, you have to be able to distinguish between what's centrally important in the reading and what's relatively less important. And to understand the main points and present them accurately, you must have a clear grasp of how the examples and illustrations (even those you don't directly include) work to explain those main points, however complicated this structure is. Writing a summary, you really learn what a piece of writing has to say.

WRITING CRITICAL SUMMARIES

A summary aims simply to give readers an accurate report, but a critical summary also wants to give readers the writer's opinion or judgment of the piece being summarized. Usually, the criteria for your opinion or your judgment gets spelled out in the assignment itself. For example, you might be asked to write a critical summary of John Muir's piece "Hetch Hetchy Valley," and the assignment might look like this:

Write a critical summary of John Muir's piece "Hetch Hetchy Valley." Make sure that your summary accurately reports Muir's argument, and end by discussing why you think this argument did not succeed. Do not let this critical summary exceed 750 words.

Your critical summary would begin as any summary does, by reporting in brief form what the reading tells you. But your critical summary would end by going a step beyond reporting: It would end by giving your brief judgment of why this essay didn't stop the damming of the Tuolumne River. Notice that a critical summary limited to 750 words cannot be a fully presented argument; the assignment doesn't give you room to do much more than state your opinions and explain them very briefly.

ACTIVITY 3.7
Write a critical summary of John Muir's piece "Hetch Hetchy Valley." Make sure that your summary accurately reports Muir's argument, and end by discussing why you think this argument did not succeed. Do not let this critical summary exceed 750 words, and make sure that it includes at least two brief quotations from the original. (For more information, see the earlier discussions in this chapter.) Staple your relevant journal entries to your final draft of this summary.

ACTIVITY 3.8
Write a critical summary of William Tucker's "Is Nature Too Good for Us?" Make sure that you report the argument accurately and clearly. End your summary by discussing briefly whether you agree with Tucker's criticism of environmentalism. Don't let your writing exceed 750 words, and make sure that you include two brief quotations.

ACTIVITY 3.9
Condense one of your 750-word summaries to a single page (250 words). With such a short summary you can only present an outline in prose form. Make sure that your shorter summary still includes at least two *brief* quotations from the original. As you work on this condensation, pay attention to what makes it hard to do. When you turn in your condensed summary, turn in a half a page or so of informal writing that talks about what made doing this assignment difficult.

Essay Topics for Chapter 3

1. In 50 words, summarize all that you did yesterday.
   In 250 words, summarize all that you did yesterday.
   In 500 words, summarize all that you did yesterday.
   Write an essay, including these three summaries as an appendix, entitled "On Summarizing a Day." What do you have to leave out in the shorter

versions, and why? What do you begin including as you write longer summaries? What good is summarizing? After doing this kind of summarizing, what are your thoughts on how we establish the importance of things, on what is important and what isn't?

2. Find a painting or poster you like, in a book or in a nearby gallery or on your walls. Summarize what you see in fifty to one hundred words. (Don't describe all the details; just summarize what's essential.) Next, find a short essay or article in this book, and write a fifty- to one-hundred-word summary. Then write an essay comparing the act of summarizing the painting and the act of summarizing the article. Begin with the two summaries—maybe include them as block quotations at the beginning—and then go on to reflect on the differences between the visual and the written language. What does this exercise tell you about the structure of a piece of writing?

   Another option is to summarize a piece of music and compare this summary to a summary of a written work.

3. Go to the library and ask for *Dissertation Abstracts.* Skim the entries until you find a dissertation in your field or some other dissertation that attracts you. Copy the abstract and study it closely. Then write an essay entitled "How to Write a Summary," using this abstract as a model. Explain how the abstract is organized, what it tells you, why it's valuable, how it's supposed to work, and why anyone would need to consult it. On the basis of this abstract, list strategies for writing good summaries. Or take the advice we give in this chapter and illustrate it with this abstract.

4. In the form of a memo, summarize a long and important conversation you've recently had—a long phone conversation about some complicated problem, a long argument, or an intense, late-night discussion. Address the memo to some interested third party, somebody who wasn't involved in the conversation or argument but would want to know about it.

5. Think about one of the other classes you have this term. Assume that you have a good friend in that class, and assume that your friend has been sick, unable to attend the last two classes. Write a summary of these two classes so that your friend won't feel entirely lost coming back to class. Don't let this summary run longer than five hundred words.

4

Writing Arguments

Writing is the act of saying I, *of imposing oneself upon other people, of saying* listen to me, see it my way, change your mind.

—JOAN DIDION

Despite what television or movies might suggest, arguing doesn't necessarily mean yelling or scoring points or being nasty. In an academic setting, when you're asked to write an argument, you're really being asked to take charge of an issue, understand it, make judgments about it, and present those judgments to readers. A good argumentative paper convinces readers of several things.

You investigated an issue thoroughly.
You understood it because you present credible evidence.
You made clear decisions about how to weigh and value that
     evidence.
You presented your findings in accessible, rational ways.
Your position is at least as well considered as their own.

When you're writing in a journal, you can be tentative and open-ended and informal; but here, as in summaries, you're moving to clearer, firmer structures. You're also writing as a person, though, someone who doesn't have all the answers. The assumption in good argument is not that your opponent is stupid and uninformed—not that you have an opponent at all, in fact.

In good argument you're speaking and writing to an audience of people just like you, people of goodwill and intelligence who may not agree with you or who may not understand your position. You're writing not to seize ground but to find common ground. And you're writing about things worth arguing about—which means complicated things, which means things that reasonable people can understand differently.

USING JOURNAL ENTRIES TO HELP YOU DECIDE YOUR POSITION

You will rarely be asked to write an argument on an issue that's simple or self-evident. Simple or obvious issues (should you stop at a red light, for instance) aren't really debatable; there is no genuine basis for argument or disagreement. Issues worth arguing about are arguable because they're complicated and because thoughtful, honest people can disagree about them.

As a thinker and writer, you can't decide your position until you've looked at a problem and understood it. Here are some useful suggestions to keep in mind as you begin this process.

- *Start by identifying the main issue.* What is the question or set of questions that forms the center of the discussion? To find them, look for (or listen for) the statements that discuss some action or outcome. Such statements will either agree with this action/outcome or disagree with it. In John Muir's piece "Hetch Hetchy Valley," for example, the immediate question can be seen in this sentence: "Sad to say, this most precious and sublime feature of the Yosemite National Park, one of the greatest of all our natural resources for the uplifting joy and peace and health of the people, is in danger of being dammed and made into a reservoir to help supply San Francisco with water and light. . . ." The possible action here is the damming of a river, and the possible outcomes are two: (1) a valley flooded and made into a reservoir and (2) additional water and electricity made available for San Francisco. And even this one sentence clearly indicates that Muir disagrees with the proposed action and possible outcomes: Thinking about it is "sad to say."

- *Think about audience and purpose.* Who cares about this issue, and why? If the situation isn't clear in your mind, try to dramatize it as concretely as you can: Someone is standing up in front of some particular group at a particular time saying these things. Visualize the group. What are they wearing? Why are they here? Visualize the speaker. What is he or she wearing? What is this person trying to accomplish? What is the occasion for the meeting—what made it necessary, brought it about?

- *State the issue in a question (or a series of questions).* Should the Tuolumne River be dammed and the Hetch Hetchy Valley be flooded? What would be gained by doing this? What would be lost by doing this? Who or what would benefit by the damming? Who or what would be sacrificed? Do the benefits outweigh the sacrifices? why or why not? Once you've identified these questions, you can begin to see the complexities, the reason that people disagree. And you can also begin to find your own answers.

- *Identify your own preliminary judgment.* If you had to pick a side or choose a position right now, what choice would you make? What reasons do you have now? Jot down anything that supports your position or that contributes to your preliminary judgment.

- *Consult those who have already taken a side.* This consultation may take the form of discussion (in class or out). Or it may take the form of reading from other sources (we'll say more about research later). As you listen or read, ask yourself whether what you're learning supports your first judgment or contradicts it. Do you feel more secure about that first judgment, or are you now thinking that you should revise that judgment?

- *Do a two-column, quick review of what you know with regard to your issue.* Put all the arguments for one side in one column, and put the rebuttals or counterarguments in the other column. Use keywords or phrases, not full sentences, and try to put all the major information you have on a single sheet of paper. In that way you can easily contrast one column with another.

- *Revise and refine your own judgment.* At some point you must make a decision about what you believe is true and why you believe it. Are you ready to do that now? If not, what nagging questions do you need to answer?

ACTIVITY 4.1

Focus on a major issue that arises from your reading. Use the suggestions in this section to do the following.

1. Write a one-sentence statement of the issue formed as a question. Phrase your question so that it identifies the major positions (for example, "Should the Tuolomne River be dammed, or should it be left free flowing?"). Put this question at the top of your page.

2. Write a brief review of the major positions taken on this controversial issue. Use a column for each position. Thus if your issue has two main sides, you'd use a column for each so that you can contrast the two sides. As you fill in these columns, use keywords or phrases instead of sentences. Make sure that your review here reflects the complexity of the issue. This review should fill your page.

3. On a separate page, informally sketch your own position now. Use this opening: "Right now I think that. . . ." Once you've stated your position, list three of your main reasons for believing as you do.

ACTIVITY 4.2

Read John Muir's "Hetch Hetchy Valley," and then read Marsden Manson's response "A Statement of San Francisco's Side of the Hetch-Hetchy Reservoir Matter." Using only these sources, write a three-part analysis as suggested in activity 4.1.

UNDERSTANDING ARGUMENT

In advertising, flashy visual images catch our eye, or an easy-to-remember jingle sticks in our minds. However, these methods of persuasion aren't appropriate for arguments in college writing. The readings in this book demonstrate a variety of approaches to more reasoned, literate persuasion. The pieces by Rachel Carson and Aldo Leopold, for instance, present straightforward discussion of issues and evidence, and they make equally direct pleas for agreement: They want readers to agree with their specific conclusions.

Other pieces in this book make their arguments through narrative, through storytelling: The story makes their argument. Stephen Crane's "The Open Boat" is a good example. And many of the essays included here use the author's direct personal experience to form the basis for powerful conclusions. These authors hope and assume that readers will become caught up in the personal experiences they read about—so caught up, in fact, that they will agree with the conclusions the writers draw.

These same two techniques—straightforward presentation of evidence leading to clear pleas for agreement, and the use of personal storytelling to make a point (or several points)—are available to you as well. The straightforward, logical presentation asks you to assemble evidence, some of it from your own experience (your own research) and some of it (maybe all of it) from your investigation of the issue and what others have found out and said about it. This latter technique is the one more likely to send you to the library or to other written and professional sources. If, on the other hand, you choose to use some of your own experience to make your point, then you're taking everything we've said about the short essay (see chapter 2) and going one more step with it by asserting that it leads to some truth wider than your own personal experience.

ACTIVITY 4.3

Take one of your earlier personal essays and assume that it makes (or begins to make) an argument. What is that argument? What does the essay assert as true? Is this truth directly stated, or is it implied? How would you revise this essay to make it more clearly and more pointedly persuasive? What parts of the essay would you revise? What would you consider adding to the essay to make it more directly persuasive? Write another page that discusses these issues.

ACTIVITY 4.4

1. Identify a piece in this book that you think makes a strong argument. Using your own words, write about a page that explains how this writer makes this persuasive argument.
2. Once you've seen how this argument has been constructed, imitate this construction in an essay of your own. Change the issue that you write

on, but try to imitate the reading's structure and the writer's decisions as you see them. If the piece you are imitating is lengthy, make your imitation a shorter (four pages or so) version.

ACTIVITY 4.5

Read any two opposing pieces in this book (for example, Lewis Thomas's "The Tucson Zoo" and Stephen Jay Gould's "Nonmoral Nature"; Gerard Manley Hopkins's "God's Grandeur" and Charles Wright's "Clear Night"; or Rodrick Nash's "A Wilderness Condition" and Barry Lopez's "Gone Back into the Earth"). From your reading of these pieces, come to some conclusion about your own stance. (To do this, follow the directions for activity 4.1.) On the basis of this analysis, do you agree with one of these writers, or would you take some new position of your own? List briefly (half a page or so) the reasons that led you to your current thinking. Keep this assignment; you may be asked to return to it later.

RETHINKING ASSUMPTIONS

One of the challenges in arguing is getting outside our own natural, instinctive assumptions. All of us feel and think certain things automatically, intuitively, because of who we are and where we come from. And while these assumptions may be right and good, they need to be taken out and examined, thought about. Sometimes, in fact, our own convictions are the result of hearing someone else's good, reasonable argument: We're moved; we're taken out of ourselves.

ACTIVITY 4.6

Here is a series of strategies and questions, borrowed from writing teacher Douglas Hunt, that can help you examine your assumptions.

1. Identify a position that seems obvious or natural to you, something you believe now without even thinking about it.
2. Write down the elements in your experience that make this idea or position seem natural to you.
3. Make a list of any reasons you can think of to question this idea. Why would others question it? Come to think of it, why should *you* question it?
4. Make a list of all the reasons you can think of to believe in this position after all. What were you thinking or feeling underneath?
5. Explain why this isn't a black-and-white issue, isn't clearly one way or the other, but is complex (and so worth arguing about).
6. Explain the consequences of persuading your readers to accept the position: What would happen if everyone agreed with you? disagreed?

THE IMPORTANCE OF EVIDENCE

Part of the point of activity 4.6 is that anyone can have opinions. Anyone can make claims. The question is whether these claims are true. What is the justification for the claim? What is the evidence?

Answering these questions is part of the writing process. The way to think through your argument is to ask yourself where your ideas come from, what gave rise to them. But just as importantly, answering these questions is your main task as a writer of argument. Your responsibility is not just to make assertions but to support them, to ground them, to make them specific.

This is argument's version of the demand for concreteness. When you write personally, your job is to show, not to tell—to give the reader concrete details of the place, time, and feeling of your experience. When you write in a journal for a grade, your job is to show the instructor and yourself that your questions and speculations are direct evidence of your active thinking and engagement. When you write an essay, the specifics of detail and description are what help readers see what you mean. Argument has this same demand for concreteness, but now it's stricter. There must be a clear, direct connection between the generalizations and the particulars.

And that means work. That means going outside yourself to find support, reading essays and articles, and doing research in the library. Things aren't true just because you say they're true.

THE POSITION PAPER: ARGUMENT AS INQUIRY

Writing an argument, then, can be a way to think more deeply about a problem, for you and for your readers.

Suppose your instructor asks you to read one of the more complicated pieces in this book, say Rachel Carson's "Elixirs of Death." Your first writing about this piece might take the form of journal entries that help you keep track of what Carson says and also help you see what you're beginning to think about as you read. Perhaps not too much later, your instructor decides that this piece is a good one for you to summarize. Working to boil down a piece like this one makes you decide what's crucially important and why.

But while a summary puts pressure on you to fully understand what you're reading, it doesn't give you any room to react or express any of your own opinions. All you can do is be as faithful as you can to what you're summarizing.

What we call a position paper is designed specifically to give you that room. A position paper asks you, "What do you think, and why do you think so?" It forces you not just to understand what others have said but also to define more coherently what *you* think, where *you* stand on this issue.

A position paper works to make your position and your reasons clear; the focus stays on your position and your reasons. In a way, you're writing to yourself. You're working to find a shape in all the information and to organize the ideas and reactions you've had into some preliminary conclusions.

At the same time, a position paper can be useful for others, particularly for what we might think of as neutral readers, people who haven't yet thought the issue through. Think of addressing people who aren't yet fully informed, who haven't taken the time and effort to ponder the issue and decide what they think. And, of course, a position paper also lets your instructor see and evaluate what you think. Here, too, your task is to present your information and evidence, tell the reader how to understand and interpret that evidence, and finally, show that reader how it all adds up.

All the questions we've asked in this chapter so far should help you work toward your own conclusions for a position paper. Once you've thoroughly understood your own position, consider these questions for other readers.

What do my readers already know (however vaguely)?

What errors do uninformed readers often make as they consider this issue? What are the common misunderstandings?

What key concepts or pieces of information will illustrate this controversy and convince readers? What are the crucial elements here?

What experience or reading or argument convinced me on this issue? How can I get neutral readers to go through this same process?

ACTIVITY 4.7

1. Identify a reading in this book that has raised questions for you. For example, after having read Rachel Carson's "Elixirs of Death," you may now be rethinking your use of pesticides if you grow vegetables, or you may now be willing to pay a few cents more for vegetables identified as organically grown.

2. Assume you will write a paper that uses as its primary source the reading you have just identified. In about a half a page, write the new truth or course of action that you're now convinced of after doing this reading. Make sure that you mention at least two main reasons for your new conviction.

DRAFTING POSITION PAPERS

Virtually all position papers begin by clearly identifying the controversial issue. Sometimes this can be accomplished in a sentence or two; more often it may take a paragraph. Once the issue or controversy has been established, readers want to know your position, and so that's what comes next. And once readers know your position, they want to understand how you've come to it and why you feel it's valid. This fundamental logic—from issue, to your stance, to your reasons—works for virtually all position papers. And you can use this organization, along with earlier journal entries and activities, to help you begin drafting.

USING TRIAC TO STRUCTURE A POSITION PAPER

In chapter 2 we discussed TRIAC as one pattern to use for an essay. We want you to look at it again here because this pattern can be particularly useful with position papers.

- *T = Topic (or Issue) and Thesis:* State the topic, the issue or controversy that you want your readers to look at. In a position paper this opening should give a wide view, mentioning the two or three major positions people have taken on the issue. The tone here is that of an objective reporter surveying the range of responses to the controversy. For example, suppose that after reading Wendell Berry's "Out of Your Car, Off Your Horse," you've decided that it is a good idea to buy locally grown food. That's your position. The overall topic is larger though. Phrased as a question, it might be, "What food should we buy?" How do most people answer this question now? by price? by convenience and what the closest store happens to carry? These are the sorts of questions a first paragraph might raise.

- *R = Restatement, Restriction, Refinement:* Return to the position that you advocate, rephrasing the overall question and restricting it in sharper, more particular ways. You don't want to just look at price or convenience; you want to also encourage readers to tie their food buying to ecological thinking. The tone here shifts, becoming less neutral and surer of its own truth. Here's where you tell readers what you think. This section establishes the foundation on which your position paper will build, and it normally includes a listing of the major reasons that the next sections of your paper will discuss at some length.

- *I = Illustrations, Examples:* By illustrations or examples we mean your reasons, your facts, data, or testimony from authorities—whatever it is that you have learned (either from your own experience or your research) that has helped you take your position. This section is your teaching section. It's the place where you introduce readers to the new information that has significantly affected your own view and presumably will (once they fully understand it) work to educate them, too.

- *A = Analysis:* Once readers feel more fully educated about the issue, they need to see how these new understandings add up. That's what your analysis section does: It tells readers how the various pieces interrelate. In a way, you are assembling a puzzle, putting together various understandings until they form a complete picture.

- *C* = *Conclusion:* Analysis inevitably leads to conclusion. In a position paper each piece of evidence, each reason you have, ought to lead to its own conclusion. Thus if you have three main reasons, you should have three conclusions, each of which asserts some truth. These three conclusions should also add up to some greater truth.

Remember, too, that TRIAC can be modified in a variety of ways. Suppose that your examples seem particularly important and convincing. It might be reasonable then to position these examples earlier, moving from the examples to the statement of your position. So TRIAC becomes TIRAC. This alternative pattern can also be a useful way to draft your position paper. Drafting your examples first can often help you more fully understand your own position.

ACTIVITY 4.8
Start drafting a position paper that will eventually be about four pages (roughly a thousand words) long. (You may base this paper on activity 4.3.) Begin by making the issue clear to readers. Follow this section with the declaration of your own belief, stance, or position. Continue by discussing your evidence and explaining your reasons. Keep working on this draft until it contains all these fundamental parts.

USING RESEARCH TO EXPLAIN AND SUPPORT YOUR POSITION

We'll devote an entire chapter to gathering and using information later, but the topic is important enough to include here, too. Most of the position papers written in college address issues that you will have to learn about; your own experience just won't be enough. Take, for example, the question of what pesticides (if any) we ingest whenever we drink a glass of orange juice. The simple act of drinking orange juice (our personal experience) doesn't tell us what we need to know; we can't taste pesticides. And assuming that we do swallow some pesticides with our juice, which ones, and at what concentrations? And (especially) should we be worried? Should we quit drinking orange juice? These are questions for research. Investigating those questions and writing what you find and telling readers how you interpret your information—these activities form the IAC in TRIAC. Don't be surprised if you begin drafting your position paper only to find that you need to do some research to more fully understand the controversy or your own position.

The readings in this book can be the first layer of research. They can provide the evidence and support you need to ground arguments, to flesh out positions.

REVISING YOUR DRAFT
POSITION PAPER

Once you have a more or less complete draft of a position paper, get responses to it from other readers. Since the draft gives them all they know of your thinking, other readers (fellow students, writing center staff) are able to see your draft's holes or inconsistencies. If you cannot involve other readers, you may still be able to pretend that you're reading for the first time. Either way, here are some directions to organize a writing group discussion or to help you see your draft as others do. As you or your respondents work through these directions, pay attention to whatever seems confusing or difficult to find; these are obvious places you'll want to return to when it comes time to revise.

> Find the part of the draft that most clearly states the overall issue. Is it as clear as it should be? Does it appear at the right place in the draft?
>
> Find the part of the draft that most clearly states the specific position the paper will work to illustrate and make clear. Is it as clear as it should be? How could it be misinterpreted? Is it placed where it should be?
>
> List the major reasons, evidence, or examples the paper gives.
>
> Evaluate each of the reasons or examples. Is each discussed clearly? What questions come up as you read this part of the discussion?
>
> Ask yourself where readers could misread or misinterpret what the paper says now. Make a list of these problem areas.
>
> Pay attention to how the paper ends. Does it close with a strongly argued set of conclusions (because W is true and X is true and Y is true, then Z is true)? Does the concluding position fit with the writing and thinking that precedes it? If not, what seems to be wrong?

You can also try filling out a chart of the argument, similar to the one that follows. In the process of filling it out, you should get a clearer view of your own draft. Use just keywords and phrases, and try to summarize each of the sections.

Opening identification of issue + range of responses

_____

_____

_____

Refocusing of issue, author's position, list of major reasons

_____

_____

_____

Discussion of reasons and evidence + preliminary conclusions

_____

_____

_____

Ending interpretations, analyses, conclusions

_____

_____

_____

Using a checklist or the chart should help you identify holes in your discussion and should help you anticipate readers' questions.

_____

ACTIVITY 4.9

Use some sort of form to obtain responses to your position paper draft. You may use the list of directions given in this section, use the chart, or construct your own list of at least four questions. You can give the form to one or more readers separately, collecting the responses yourself; or you (or your instructor) can organize several students into a writing group, using the form to guide feedback. Once you have obtained the responses, evaluate them carefully, paying particular attention to major misunderstandings and to anything that confirms a worry or concern you had about your draft. Then write four or five sentences that explain how and where you will focus your revising efforts.

_____

Don't be surprised if you find position papers more time consuming and difficult than you first anticipated. Often the deeper you look at an issue, the more you realize how genuinely complicated that issue is. Sometimes you may find it useful to repeat activity 4.1 two or three times as you work to fully grasp an issue and your own response to it.

ARGUING TO PERSUADE OTHERS

Argument is more than a form of inquiry, of course. Often the task is not to figure out what you think but to persuade someone else that what you think is valid and right, or at least worth taking seriously. You're focusing on readers now, not your own thinking. Your goal is to change minds, to move people to action. Everything we've said earlier in this chapter will help you do this. But writing to convince readers you know oppose you presents some additional challenges. To reach these readers, you also need to understand their values and their reasons, which means looking carefully at divergent viewpoints. Here are three things to look at closely.

1. *Look at how the other person frames the controversy.* Consider, for example, the question of mass transit versus individual commuters driving their own cars. Those advocating mass transit would probably frame the question in terms of air pollution (mass transit reduces it), ease (someone else drives, no parking hassles), and perhaps expense (no parking fees, less upkeep on a car, maybe even one less car). On the other hand, those who individually commute might frame the question first and foremost in terms of freedom and convenience (after all, individual cars aren't bound by transit schedules or limited to transit routes). Clearly the two sides view the question in quite different terms.

If you were to write an argumentative paper focusing on this question, you'd need to make sure that part of your paper showed your understanding of your readers' differing perspectives. Your paper certainly wouldn't need to agree with those perspectives, but you would want to show that you've considered your readers' viewpoints and so can effectively build on that understanding to offer a better, more persuasive alternative.

2. *As you look at your readers' different views, also pay attention to what they present as evidence or proof.* Try to summarize this evidence briefly in your own words as a way to test whether you really understand what you're hearing. This summary will help you as you construct your own argument, because as someone who wants to change readers' minds, you will need to counter this evidence with better evidence of your own. For example, if an argument presents a first-person story as its proof (for example, the story of how an individual commute in one's own car gives a person flexibility), then you might want to try telling a story (a different story) that illustrates your way of seeing this issue.

3. *See whether you can identify any values or truths that you and your readers share.* For example, virtually all commuters will value less tension in their lives, minimum expense, dependability of schedule, and the like. Identifying such common ground can be an important step toward understanding your opposition, and it can sometimes lead to the development of counterarguments or compromise positions.

ACTIVITY 4.10

Read Michael Pollan's "The Idea of a Garden," and then follow these directions.

1. In a sentence or two, identify the controversy that split the people in Pollan's town of Cornwall.
2. Using two columns, list the reasons that each faction advanced to support its argument.
3. Review these two columns and see whether you can identify two or three values, wishes, or beliefs that the two sides have in common.
4. In a half a page or so (no more than a page), sketch Pollan's compromise position.

5. In a half a page or so, judge Pollan's argument. Does it work? Why or why not?

ACTIVITY 4.11
Read any two opposing pieces, and then follow these directions.

1. Using two or three sentences for each piece, identify how each author frames the controversy.
2. Using phrases and keywords, identify the major evidence each offers. Contrast them in two columns.
3. As you look at the two discussions, what common ground can you identify? What would both writers agree on (even if they disagree about what it means or what action ought to be taken)? Write several sentences that make this common ground clear.

ACTIVITY 4.12
Here's another way to structure an academic argument, a simpler version of the TRIAC scheme. A four-part structure with its origins in oral debate, it works well particularly when you're arguing a strong position on something you yourself feel passionately about. Use it to frame a five-hundred-word essay agreeing or disagreeing with Michael Pollan's argument in "The Idea of the Garden."

> Part 1. A relatively brief summary of the issue and of what the opposition says on this issue.
>
> Part 2. Your counterstatement, said clearly and concisely.
>
> Part 3. The presentation of evidence—evidence that supports your position and evidence that undermines or contradicts the opposing position. This section is usually relatively lengthy because it offers the substance—the stuff, the facts or data or testimony from others—of your argument.
>
> Part 4. Your argument based on your interpretation of the evidence; your discussion of how it adds up and why it adds up as you see it. The assertions you make here are those that part 3 has supported.

THE REASONABLE VOICE

The style of your argument is important, too—the words you use or don't use, the rhythm of your sentences. The temptation is to overdo it, thundering away in grand or pushy tones about the rightness of your position and the silliness of others'. But as in all kinds of writing, less is more. Keep it down. Be yourself. In fact, in argument especially it's important to be clear, straightforward, and modest. Even if the modesty feels forced, it's persuasive—far more persuasive than pushiness and posturing. After all, nobody likes to feel pressured.

This means, too, that you need to be aware of what your opponents will think of as fighting words. Remember that in writing an argument, your first goal is to make sure that the argument is actually read by those you want to reach; an unread argument—however brilliantly constructed— always fails. So you want to be careful not to call your readers (or their views) foolish, misguided, inadequate, or uninformed. Thus instead of saying something like "these sadly incomplete views fail to fully understand X," you could work to raise more questions about X: "Let's look at X more closely. Does X really mean . . . ?" Also, try to avoid any specific words your readers will immediately object to. For example, those who prefer driving their own cars to work probably will flare up at the identification of their cars as "gas-guzzlers."

Essay Topics for Chapter 4

1. Re-create a recent argument you've had with someone. Describe the give and take, the sequence of the argument, more or less as it actually happened. You can write in the form of a dialogue (introduced with a paragraph to set the stage) or in the form of an essay. Once you've presented the give and take of the argument, talk about its outcome. When the argument was over, had either of you changed your original position? If not, why didn't any of the arguments prove to be convincing? If one of you did have a change of mind, how and why did that happen? Finally, as you look at the argument as a whole, what were the most important forces at work? Were they personal forces (your like or dislike for the other person)? Were they intellectual forces (the differing ways the issue was analyzed)? In short, why did the argument end as it did?

2. Let's say that you've recently been involved in an argument or intense discussion with a friend or acquaintance and that in the heat of the moment you weren't able to express yourself clearly or fully. Write a letter to this person, calmly setting forth your position.

3. Write an essay arguing for the view of argument presented in this chapter—that argument shouldn't be combative and antagonistic but a way of reaching mutual consent. Draw on your own experience and on your reading of the newspapers. Argue for the practical advantages of the approach we suggest. As an option, you may choose to argue against our approach.

4. Write an essay analyzing some specific environmental debate, some dispute recently covered in the newspaper or in the national magazines— water rights; the cutting of old-growth forest; commuting and pollution; restrictions on fishing, hunting, or mining; or the like. Study what's reported in the language of the opposing sides. What terms do

they use? How do they argue? What evidence do they claim? What are their attitudes toward each other? Come to some conclusions. Argue that the debate has been good and productive or bad and counterproductive, and explain your thinking.

5. Write a letter to the editor of your local or student newspaper taking a stand on some local environmental problem. Assume that you're writing to people who really haven't yet thought about the issue; assume that you're educating them. Now, write a similar letter but address those who are definitely against your position; assume that they know the issue and disagree with your stance. Once you've written both letters, explain which one seemed easier to write, and why.

6. Write an essay arguing that the best way to read well is to do the kinds of writing-to-learn assignments we've been recommending in this book. That is, argue for the journal-writing and summarizing strategies you've been trying out—assume that they're good. Assume also that you're addressing someone you know who isn't a good reader. Try to get that person to start keeping a reading journal. Use all the evidence you can, from your own experience and from what we've written here.

5

Gathering and Using Information

For excellence, the presence of others is always required.

—HANNAH ARENDT

Research isn't just something a college-writing assignment forces you into. You gather and use information from the moment you get up in the morning. Often the information comes directly from your own experience: You look out the window, see that it's raining, and decide this isn't a good day to wear shorts. Your own experience—the rain you saw—has told you what to do. Later while you're eating breakfast, you look in the paper to see what the weather forecast is for tomorrow: morning cloudiness giving way to afternoon sunshine, with temperatures in the high 60s—a good day for tennis or a bicycle ride or a walk in the park.

When you rely on what your own senses and thinking tell you, you're using experience as a form of evidence or support. When you make plans based on the weather forecast in the newspaper or on television, you're using someone else's information: You're doing research.

ACTIVITY 5.1

Consider a serious choice you've had to make lately: a purchase of $200, a move to a new town or house, a decision to take a new job or change your major. Identify your choice in a sentence or two at the top of a piece of paper.

Below this identification, draw a line down the middle of the paper so that you have two columns. In the left column, note the major personal experiences—things you did or thought about—that you drew on to make this decision. Include here both your thinking and your physical actions. Say you've recently bought a car. Your test-drive would be one of the personal experiences, as would your daydreaming about owning that car. If you talked with others as a way to help you clarify your decision, count that as a personal experience. (If those other people had suggestions or gave you input, also list this in the second column, as discussed in the next paragraph.)

In the right column, list all the information that you received from sources other than your own personal experience. If you bought the car— or decided not to—and the salesperson's pitch was part of the reason, that's something from an outside source. If you checked a consumer magazine for that particular model, that's an outside source. If you asked for input from a friend who already owned that same make and model, then that's also outside information.

Work on this two-column listing until you're convinced that it accurately presents all the major reasons for making your choice. Then review the two columns. Did you rely mostly on your personal experience? Did you rely mostly on the information given by others? Explain this review in a couple of sentences.

Finally, look only at the column showing outside sources. Which of these sources did you trust entirely, and why? Which sources did you trust less, and why?

The readings in this book depend on research not all that different from the research you do everyday. The selections fall into roughly three categories: literary readings (the poems and short stories), personal essays drawing mostly from personal experience (Joan Didion's "On Going Home," for instance), and essays that depend heavily on information from other experts and sources (Samuel W. Matthews's "Under the Sun," for example). Some involve looking out the window at the sky, in other words; others involve checking the newspaper; many involve both.

ACTIVITY 5.2

1. Think about the selections that you've read so far in this book. Identify one that relies entirely (or almost entirely) on the writer's own personal experience. Use two or three sentences to describe that personal experience. Then use another two or three sentences to describe how the writer used that personal experience. In other words, what was the aim of this writing? What was the writer trying to accomplish?

2. Do the same analysis for a reading that seems to you to draw heavily on information the writer has taken from other sources. How does the writer use this information? Is this information meant primarily to inform you, or is it used primarily to convince you to take a particular stand or course of action? Use several sentences to explain your analysis.

ACTIVITY 5.3

Look at Samuel W. Matthews's piece, "Under the Sun." Find where Matthews first quotes information from Elmer Robinson. Write a short paragraph that explains how Matthews prepares readers for Robinson's information. Later in this same article Matthews quotes another source, Stephen Leatherman. Find this part of the article, and then write another short paragraph explaining how Matthews prepares readers for Leatherman's information. Finally, compare the information in your two paragraphs; what conclusions can you draw about how Matthews uses sources?

SOME TIPS FOR COMING UP WITH TOPICS (AND KEEPING THEM SMALL)

The hard part in doing research for papers, of course, is finding a good topic you really care about—and then keeping it small and narrow enough to be doable. Most of the time library research doesn't come as naturally as, say, checking out the weather. Somehow, even the phrase *library research* is off-putting for a lot of inexperienced students, as if a library were too vast and alien to master—or to matter.

A good topic—something you care about, something you might actually want to spend time on—can give you the energy and interest you need to walk through those library doors and sit down at the CD-ROM computer screens. Here are some practical tips.

- *Think in terms of questions (large or small) that interest you.* When you buy a stereo or a car, you're interested in answering a question: Which stereo should I buy, or which car should I buy? And to answer broad questions like these, you naturally start asking smaller, more specific ones. How much do stereos cost anyway? What features do they have? Suppose something breaks—is there a warranty? Do I know anyone who already has this model (and if so, would this person buy the same stereo again)? Thinking in terms of such questions can help you see how large or small your topic really is. If your research interest is too large, you'll find yourself trying to write a book.

- *Do your thinking in writing.* Don't just let your thoughts about research swirl around in your brain, ungrounded. Get them onto the page in a reading or research journal.

The tips continue on the following pages, interwoven with activities for you to try.

ACTIVITY 5.4

Do a five-minute freewrite recording everything you can think of about a subject that intrigues you right now. Don't try to focus. Brainstorm. Come up with as many different possibilities as you can.

1. Reread the freewrite. Underline the two or three ideas that seem most interesting to you intuitively.
2. Do another freewrite. Are these three ideas connected to each other? Does one contain the others? Is one idea more practical as a research project than another? What kinds of things would you have to know to make this project doable?
3. Finally, assume that on the basis of your freewrites you need to choose a research topic right now. Write this topic in a single sentence, and phrase it as a question. Underneath this broad question, start listing the smaller ones that will need to be answered first. Once you have a list of smaller questions, look at this list. Does this research topic look too large, about right, or too narrow? Write three or four sentences that explain your analysis.

ACTIVITY 5.5

Skim chapter 1 again and find any journal topic or question that seems helpful for thinking about a possible research topic. Then choose one of the following options.

1. Tell the story of how you thought about this topic or question, in chronological order, from start to finish.
2. Explain anything about the idea that surprised you, that you didn't expect. Are there possibilities in this for research?
3. Write in your journal as if you are talking to a good friend over coffee or taking a walk somewhere. Talk in writing. Explain what you're thinking about the project and where you're not sure. Be honest.

- *Think about what's most important in your own life right now*—think about some important personal experience—and then move outward to larger issues. Let's say that in the last few months you've become bothered by the noise in the dorm or apartment where you live. The stereos are always booming. Laughter is always coming through the walls. You probably have enough energy built up on this issue to begin asking the broader questions that only research can answer.

  Is your experience representative? For example, are many people bothered by noise? Have there been other complaints locally? Have other communities struggled with noise problems?

  Is your experience part of larger trends or larger issues? What effects does noise have on the nervous system, mood, or behavior, for instance? Are they representative of the larger effects the environment has on the way we think and feel?

  Do experts agree with you, and do they have ideas that relate to your experience? For example, what do scientists think about the effects of noise? What do moralists think about the rights and responsibilities of people living in groups?

- *Think of your experience as a window into another room*—one strand on a web—one species in an ecosystem.

ACTIVITY 5.6

Reread an earlier personal essay, or write a journal entry reflecting on some important experience in your life. Then make a list of possible ways that this experience might be connected to a research project, as an example or point of departure. Imagine a term paper that begins with a shortened version of that personal essay—say a paragraph—and then leads to discussion of the larger problem. Outline it.

- *Form opinions early and often.* Play your hunches. Go into research with a possible thesis or two. No one begins research completely blank. You usually have an intuition about what you'll find or some deep bias—or something that's gotten you a little interested, at least—and it's good to use that as an organizing point, a direction finder. For instance, you might start with the conviction that "clear-cutting is bad and unnecessary, and I'm going to show why," and that's OK. It's not that you're going into the research with your mind made up completely, looking to bend information to preconceived notions. You'll change your mind several times before you're done, a new thesis replacing the old. The situation will turn out to be complicated: Good people will disagree about clear-cutting; the evidence will be conflicting; other issues will enter in, economic and social. But if you're starting the process with a clear argument or hypothesis, it gives you some perspective for handling the great amount of information you're sure to find.

ACTIVITY 5.7

Write half a page to a page of thesis statements, one after the other, as if they form the finished thesis of a research paper. Let them be different versions of the same idea, contradictory statements making opposite points, or assertions about different parts of the issue.

ACTIVITY 5.8

In the journal, do two or three outlines of a research project—before you've done any research at all, simply reflecting your thoughts as they are right now. Try to imagine different versions of the finished product. In the body of the outline, indicate the kinds of information you hope to find. Guess at the facts. Then on a separate page, make a list of all the information you'll need to fill in the blanks on your outline legitimately, to make that outline work. (Be prepared for the outlines to change.)

- *Figure out whether you're reporting or arguing.* One reason for doing research is to find statistics, scientific studies, and expert opinion to support an argument. Drawing on the ideas in chapter 4, outline your initial argument in advance and all the evidence you can think of from your experience and your own commonsense reasoning. What's missing? What will you need to find in the library?

  You can also simply report research, seeking to inform rather than persuade. Having that purpose in mind as you walk through the library doors can help guide you, too. At first, that kind of information gathering will be broader than it would be for writing argument, for example, so you'll need to narrow things down right away. You know, too, that a paper like that will involve summarizing information, so you'll be looking for sources that lend themselves to summary.

  Of course, you can start by wanting to inform and end by wanting to argue, or vice versa.

- *Be willing to let your reading suggest new questions.* After reading Rachel Carson's "Elixirs of Death," for example, you might start wondering: Why was DDT banned in the United States? Or where is DDT still used in the world? Those questions are possibly the start of a research project. Now, generate the smaller questions that will help to answer the broad one. What are the medical effects of DDT on research animals? When were these effects first discovered and first made public? What are the effects on people? What effects of DDT were actually observed in the wild? How much DDT was used in the United States in, say, 1960? Does DDT break down into other chemicals, and if so, are these chemicals dangerous? With smaller questions like these in mind, you're ready to begin searching for useful information.

  Often a reading in this book will mention some book or historical event that you'd like to know more about. Follow that up. Often an important piece of research is already dated by the time you read it. Update it. What happened to Hetch Hetchy Valley, the place John Muir wanted to preserve? What's it like today? What's the latest research on the greenhouse effect?

ACTIVITY 5.9

Read Annie Dillard's "Life on the Rocks: The Galápagos," and look for anything she mentions that you'd like to know more about. There are all kinds of possibilities: the Galápagos as they exist today, the behavior of a particular animal on those islands, and so on. Add five more possibilities to this list.

ACTIVITY 5.10

Choose a selection from this book that sparked your interest. Do a freewrite reflecting on what you'd like to know more about, what issues come up as you skim the selection again. "As I think about this piece, I start thinking about _____."

- *Think small from the beginning.* It will be obvious as soon as you start searching the data banks and indexes that a topic like "ecology" won't get you anywhere. You'll get lost in a forest of sources. And a term paper on a subject like ecology would either be a superficial and useless ten pages or a thousand-page monster. So think small from the beginning. Not hands but fingers—or fingernails, or joints. Not houses but doors—or doorknobs, or weather strips. A zoologist at Oregon State University does research on the sexual life of rough-skinned newts, for example—apparently silly, until you realize that the hormonal systems of newts can give us all kinds of information about human hormones and thus information about possible drugs for various kinds of mental disorders.

ACTIVITY 5.11

At the top of a page, write down several words or phrases that express, in the most general terms, the field or category of your possible paper: ecology, the environment. On the rest of the page, writing quickly, list as many small, tiny, even microscopic pieces of this larger issue as you can. Be playful, even silly (who knows; one of those apparently silly issues might turn out to be workable): snails, streams, alder trees, campfire smoke, environmental effects on left eardrums, the ecology of mud puddles. Go back through the list and circle two or three that might be possibilities; for those two, turn the topics into questions you could research for answers.

- *Think locally.* In any community there are always particular examples of large national events. Focus on them. If you're concerned about child abuse, begin by checking the local papers and seeing how that issue is played out in your community. Look for some community forum where issues are being debated right now—the student council, the city council, the panel discussion at the library. A research paper can focus on just the local problem, or the local problem can be a representative story leading into the larger questions.

- *Think of a real audience.* Teachers aren't the only audience for research papers. In the world outside the classroom all kinds of people want all kinds of information. Try to translate your possible research project out of the classroom (even if that's the only place the paper will go). Ask yourself, Who do I know who would need to know this? Say you have a friend that you suspect has an alcohol problem. What kind of information would this person need to begin thinking intelligently about his or her situation?

- *Be practical.* A good way to come up with a small topic is to be realistic about how long the paper is and how much time you have.

ACTIVITY 5.12

Write a memo to yourself explaining how much time you have, what mood you're in, what's going on in your mind right now, and how much energy you have to invest in a research project. Then choose a subject that will be as interesting and important as possible but still doable—something you can actually get done in a reasonable amount of time without going out of your mind. Be honest. Think in increments of an hour. Sketch out a schedule for a week, listing two or three things you can get done each day.

ACTIVITY 5.13

Bring a thesis or more general idea for research to class and share it in small groups of three to five. Consider these questions for each other:

> Is the idea narrow enough? Can it be narrower?
> What kinds of information will I have to look for?
> How much time will the project take?
> Does the project seem interesting? Are there ways of making it
>   more interesting?

MOVING FROM TOPIC TO RESEARCH: DIVING IN

So, now you've got some ideas and questions for a paper. It's time to take the plunge.

If you're starting your research project without knowing very much about your topic, ask someone for a place to start. Take advantage of your teachers' expertise. They can probably suggest a central book or article. Why thrash around trying to find it yourself when you can skip the thrashing and get right down to reading?

Also, consider starting with the obvious sources, encyclopedias in particular. The advantage of a good encyclopedia is that it gives you an overview of a topic and then breaks it up into subtopics. Use that breakdown. Think of which subtopic interests you the most as you try to narrow your topic. Use the suggestions for further reading at the end of the articles.

If you have a clear sense of purpose, you'll probably want to go directly to useful books and articles. Searching for print information today means working with computers, checking databases for sources that might give you answers to your research questions. This technology has changed quite rapidly and will no doubt continue to change; so the best advice we can give you is this: Ask for help from your research librarian. Chances are that your school library catalogue is now on-line, as are many of the indexes that you will want to consult in order to find relevant journal articles. But there is no one on-line system employed by every library; each system has its own characteristics.

We can give you a few general pointers, though, about using computer databases. To begin with, the main distinction in a library is between books and articles. Your on-line library catalogue probably lists nothing but books. The different CD-ROM (computer disk, read-only memory) indexes list primarily articles from various journals and magazines, although sometimes chapters or parts of books are also included. These two sets of databases are sometimes in different places (on different computers), and they often require slightly different procedures.

All databases are typically organized in three ways: by author, by title of a work, and by subject. If you know you want to find work by a particular author, either a book or an article, you shouldn't have much trouble, especially if you know the author's full name. But most of the time, you're looking not for a particular author but rather for answers to some particular questions. And this means searching according to subject.

All on-line library catalogues (the ones for books) can be accessed by subject. Three of the indexes for journal articles are likely to be particularly useful for subject searches (assuming that your library has these indexes). The *Humanities Index* covers subjects you'd normally associate with the word *humanities*—philosophy, art, literature, religion, and so on. The *Social Sciences Index* covers subjects you'd normally associate with social sciences, including economics, sociology, and political science. And the *General Science Index* covers subjects that fall under that category. Often your own research interest will overlap these categories; it will be worth your trouble to check the other indexes as well as the one you think logically fits your interest.

To search by subject, you need to identify the words that the particular index program will recognize in order to retrieve the information you want. Some words are so broad (and so frequently used in the titles of articles) that the search yields more information than you want. Suppose you sit down at a computer terminal in your library, access an index, and type in the word *environment*. Chances are that the screen will then present you with many more articles and citations than you know what to do with. Similarly, typing *Cherokee* and nothing else (called a single-level search) may give you a list of articles dealing with an automobile with the brand name Cherokee. Index programs typically let you type more than one search word; so after you type *ecology,* you could type *acid rain* and *New England* (a three-level search). In general, searching in this narrowed, more focused way will give you a shorter, more focused list of articles.

Remember that databases typically give you only publication information: an article's title, its author(s), publisher, volume number or month and year of publication, and page numbers. Some indexes will also give you a very brief summary. The point to remember here is that locating promising articles in a database is not the same as actually being able to read and use these articles. Does your library have these publications, or can you get a copy of this article through interlibrary loan (and get it early enough to use it)?

ACTIVITY 5.14
Visit your library's reference room and acquaint yourself with its resources.

1. Make a list of at least three indexes that might logically carry information about environmental concerns and that your library has available.
2. Obtain a copy of the front page of the *New York Times* for your date of birth.
3. Access the catalogue your library has on computer, and search for the work of a particular author included in this book. If the author isn't listed, write that down. If the author is listed, copy all the information the screen provides for one of this author's works (or print the screen if you have that option).
4. Access an index that your library has on computer, and do a two-level search. Print the screen (if your system gives you that option), or write a couple of sentences that describe the data the computer gave you as a result of your search.

ACTIVITY 5.15
In your journal, describe how you feel when you walk into the library—your thoughts, your sensations, your expectations. Describe the library—its sights, sounds, smells. Describe how you feel after an hour in a library. Recall past libraries you've used and past experiences in a library.

ACTIVITY 5.16
Double-check one citation from a reading in this book or from a textbook. That is, find a cited piece of evidence, look up that source in the library—whether book or article—find the page number, and double-check the quotation or fact against what's quoted in the reading. Record your process in your journal.

ACTIVITY 5.17
Write a short argumentative essay using exactly one piece of library research as support.

ACTIVITY 5.18
Find an obscure, even silly fact or piece of information in the library, and then write a short essay presenting the fact and explaining how you found it. Be playful. Argue for the pleasure and value of finding this obscure fact. Celebrate the obscure. Celebrate finding useless information as something good to do, if only for fun. (Or argue that the information isn't all that silly after all.) Here are some examples.

How fast can a black-capped chickadee fly?
How many gallons of gas are consumed by lawn mowers each year?
Who invented granola?
Who invented the paper clip?

HANDLING WHAT YOU FIND

It's not hard to find information. More often, the problem is the opposite: You've got more information than you know what to do with, and it all looks equally important at first, deserving of your attention. How can you make sense of it? How can you find your way through the forest—or see the forest for the trees?

Research is like the writing process and the reading process—a process, too, just as messy and time consuming sometimes—and it helps just to know that. Don't panic. Everyone else has the same problems of focusing and organizing at first. Don't give up. Plan on setting aside enough time, because as always that's the key. And, as always, be suspicious of any claim that one way of doing research is the only way or the right way. You have your own habits of mind and ways of looking at things, and in the end you have to develop your own style of research and your own system.

Here's some initial advice for handling the panic everyone feels as the sources start piling up.

- *Go back to your original reasons for doing this research.* What are you looking for anyhow? What are you trying to find out? Remembering why you're researching should help you see what's important and what's not.

- *Read your material just closely enough to get an overview.* "Freeread" and plan on rereading later. Get a feel for what seems important, and set those sources aside. Reject sources that don't seem useful. Get a sense of the lay of the land, the topography. Look for repetitions in different sources, the ideas and questions that keep coming up. Look for contradictions.

- *Find a central book or article in the subject and move out from there.* Often a particular source will seem the most authoritative. It's the one everyone else refers to, or it's the one that you understood and liked the best, trusted the most. Usually it's a book-length study, and usually (though not always) it's fairly recent. Use that book to organize your other reading. Read it carefully. Use its endnotes and bibliography to find further research.

- *Keep a research log.* A research log is a very practical tool, partly because it records everything you actually *did* on any given day: not just the title of the book or article you found but also where in your particular library you found it; whether the book was missing from the shelves and how long it will take to get it; and so on. Buy a separate little notebook and write down everything, especially call numbers, authors, and titles. (It's probably best to keep this notebook separate from your reading journal, at least for long projects.) Looking back through it at various points will remind you of what you've done and what you still need to. And later on, when you've lost your other notes and can't remember who said what, you can find out where to find something again.

  Thursday, March 10th. Today I discovered that there are computer terminals on each floor of the library where I can search the on-line catalogue for our library. I can just go to the seventh floor now, which is where all the books I need are anyway. Found the Gifford Pinchot book on conservation but had to put a call out on John Muir. Should come in a week. (Note: Gerry, at the reference desk, was very helpful.)

- *Read only as carefully as you need to.* There are three kinds of sources, three piles to put things in: (1) the central source or sources, the ones you read line by line; (2) the useless sources, the ones you can put aside; (3) the sources that might be good or have some useful information but don't demand close reading. Skim the third group; read them quickly. Jump through the subtitles until you get to what you want. Read quickly until something in the piece catches your eye.

- *Remember how little material you can actually use.* In chapter 2 we suggested that it's good to avoid using block quotations more than once or twice, even in a long paper. In fact, the hardest part about writing a research paper is leaving things out: It was so hard to find the material in the first place, it's a shame not to include it. But you've got to be ruthless. Look for three or four long quotations at the most. Make a list of a half-dozen to a dozen phrases and short passages you want to include, too. Leave everything else aside (although in reserve, in case you need it later). The rest of the research hasn't been wasted: It forms the background for the paper. You're generally informed now. You know enough not to talk about everything; you can focus.

    Knowing how few quotations you'll need can free you to read more deeply as you start working through your material. You don't need to stop and slavishly quote everything you find. You're just looking for those two or three outstanding quotations, those two or three absolutely essential statements.

- *Summarize and paraphrase as much as you can.* These are skills we've talked about before, and they're essential now. The majority of the information you've found won't appear in the form of direct quotations. It will appear in your own words (with sources cited). Your job is to show that you've mastered the material, that you understand it well enough to explain it yourself. Anyone can string together quotations. If that were the task, why not just turn in your note cards?

    As you summarize each source in a notebook or on an index card, you're writing what may be drafts of actual parts of your final paper. Much of a research paper is the weaving together of summaries.

- *Find the quotatable quotations.* Look for the passage or sentence that stood out most to you as you read—the one that best explained or summarized the piece, that was the most beautiful or interesting. Find the passage that summarizes the idea of the selection. This passage often appears at the beginning or at the end, though it can appear elsewhere. Keep TRIAC in mind; often the most quotable statements are the T and R and C statements.

You usually will not make quotations of illustrations, examples, or statistics. Long stories and anecdotes are too long to quote. Statistics aren't quotable because they're just statistics. What you're always looking for is an unusual phrasing or wording of a statement, evidence of the author's own voice and opinion, or something unique and personal.

ACTIVITY 5.19

Read Al Gore's "Ships in the Desert" and annotate it, marking one block quotation you might use in a paper and three to five shorter quotations you could work into your own sentences.

- *Work from the books and articles themselves.* On short projects that don't need too many sources, it's useful sometimes simply to pile up the books and journals on your desk, with slips of paper to mark the passages you want to use. And having all the books and journals at your fingertips means you won't have any trouble when it comes to documenting your sources.

- *Make copies.* Copying makes elaborate note taking unnecessary most of the time, particularly for short to medium-length projects. Simply copy the half-dozen major sources or parts of sources; then annotate the copy, marking the passages you want to quote. It's useful sometimes to put numbers in the margins to keep track of things, though you may be able to keep all this organization in your head if there aren't too many sources. *Copy whatever other pages you'll need in order to document the source: its title, author, magazine or journal name, volume and/or issue, and page numbers.*

- *Keep a project notebook.* This is distinct from the research log, though it makes sense to use the same spiral notebook, simply drawing a line after the last entry on research and beginning notes for the paper itself. Write (or paste in) the major quotations that seem important to you, indicating their source. Summarize and paraphrase other major ideas, indicating their source. There's no need to write these ideas in any particular order. When it's time to do the paper, reread the project journal, mark the quotations and summaries you actually want to use (you'll have written more than you can fit into a paper), and then number them. The margins of the notebook might have this sequence: 3, 2, 5, 1, 4, 6 (the quotations are in the order they appear in in the notebook, but you want to use them in a different order). Again, this method works best when you don't have an overwhelming amount of material.

  You can follow this same process if you type up your quotations and summaries on the computer and print out a hard copy. You can then use those sheets as they are. Or you can take the next step and cut them up into separate pieces, tape them onto index cards, title the cards, and establish categories.

- *Try using index cards.* The advantage of index cards is that they allow you to establish categories, and for long, complex projects that's sometimes the only way to make sense of all the information. Typically you use one index card for each source.

    Remember to record all the publication information you'll need later: author, title, library call number or location (in case you need to find this source again), publisher, publication date, volume number (for magazines or journals), and page numbers. In the heat of your search this record keeping may seem tedious or unnecessary, but doing it accurately (rather than sloppily or not at all) will save your sanity later.

    Next, indicate in your own words how or why you might use this source. Using index cards pushes you to summarize, and they make it easier for you to find order in your information (by ordering and reordering the cards themselves).

- *Stop now and then to write.* There will come moments when you feel overwhelmed, tired, or frustrated. So stop and write for a few minutes. Freewrite. Make a list. There will also be moments when you feel that things are coming together, that you've found your theme. There will be moments (believe it or not) when you feel elated. Again, stop and write. Periodically in the process, write out progress reports, interim stories of your thinking.

    A particularly good journal topic at this point is the notion of surprise. You started with a thesis but maybe it's changed now. How? What material wasn't there that you expected to find? How has your research challenged, complicated, undermined your assumptions?

    There's probably a new thesis here, a good focus for a paper. Write it down: "Like everyone else, I used to think _____. But research shows, in fact, that _____." Let this statement be your guide for the remainder of your work in the library.

ACTIVITY 5.20

Stop now and take stock of what you've done, what information you've found, and particularly what information you've not found or haven't yet received. As you look over the situation, do you reasonably feel that you'll be able to finish this research project on time and as you originally expected to? If so, what schedule will you need to follow? If not, how can you revise your research goals and your research topic in order to take advantage of the information that you now have (or that you're sure you will have very soon)? Write a paragraph that explains all this briefly. If you can see that the project is in trouble, seek advice. Talk with your instructor about it. Talk with your research librarian, who may be able to suggest other, quicker ways to get the information you need.

ACTIVITY 5.21

Bring your research log to class and share your experiences in groups. Commiserate. Swap stories. Exchange practical tips.

ACTIVITY 5.22

Establish a research group or team with two to five other students. Meet to decide strategy and to divide up responsibility. Duplicate and share all that you've found, and then have each student write his or her own paper from that material. Option: Write a paper collaboratively, producing one project with multiple authors.

AN IDEA FOR PULLING MATERIAL TOGETHER

As we've suggested, outline early and often. Stop and outline your project at various points in the process, both to reflect where you are at that moment and to predict where you might be going. Sometimes a project journal may be made up of nothing but outlines, a dozen or so, each giving way to the next as you shape and reshape your material.

Another way to develop a shape is to work from the opposite end. That is, take your six or seven best index cards (or best sources) and spread them out on a table. Or cut out your six or seven best quotations from a notebook—several long block quotations and several shorter sentences and phrases. Or line up your best quotations on one or two sheets of paper. Now, working intuitively, arrange the pieces in order. Move the cards around. Number the quotations on the sheet.

Think of the quotations as pieces of a collage you're now pulling together—puzzle pieces you're now assembling. Think of patterns and rhythms: long and short quotations alternating, facts and anecdotes alternating, or a series of facts followed by a summary quotation, and so on. Think of the structure of the paper as emerging from the best material you actually have.

ACTIVITY 5.23

Read Marc Reisner's "A Semidesert with a Desert Heart." Now think about how Reisner actually put this piece together. What do you think he used as its original pieces? Say he used twelve index cards or twelve major pieces of information before he started writing, in whatever order. Indicate what you think these pieces or cards were.

DOCUMENTING SOURCES IN THE PAPER AND IN A SOURCES LIST AT THE END

When you look at the reading selections in this book, you'll see that they vary quite a bit in terms of how much (or in what ways) they document their sources. In general, if the article is written for an academic or expert audience, then it's likely to use academic documentation.

When it comes to using sources in your own papers, you should assume that your readers (your teacher and your peers) expect full documentation of your sources. Full documentation typically means using quotation marks for direct quotations (or indenting long block quotations) and giving a citation in the text, as well as including a separate page at the end of your paper that shows all the sources you quoted.

The specific ways that writers cite their sources in the paper itself vary among academic disciplines. In the humanities (literature, music, art, and so on) most writers follow the guidelines of the Modern Language Association (MLA). The social sciences and many natural sciences follow the guidelines of the American Psychological Association (APA). And there are many other such guidelines. We can't tell you which set of guidelines is right for you, especially since much of the material in this book could easily be classified as literature and as natural science. We can tell you, though, that the old system of numbered footnotes has been almost entirely replaced by a system that uses parentheses to indicate source information; both the current MLA and APA systems use parenthetical citations in the text itself. And both systems rely on a page at the end of the paper that lists all the sources cited.

ACTIVITY 5.24

Consult a handbook or stylebook specified by your teacher, and write two separate paragraphs, each with a quotation from a different source in this book. In your first paragraph, name the author of your quoted material only in the citation itself. In your second paragraph, name the author as part of your discussion. Note that this difference should make your citations different in format, too.

Once you have written the two paragraphs with the two citations, assume that these two paragraphs are part of the same paper, and write a list of these two sources for the bibliography that would appear at the end of the paper. Make sure that this list accurately presents both sources.

CONDUCTING INTERVIEWS

When assigned a research project, many students overlook the possibility of interviewing an expert. But if you have the option to do an interview (or more than one, if time permits), you may find your project coming alive in a new way.

To decide which questions you should ask, you need to think about what you want to find out.

ACTIVITY 5.25

Look at Chris Anderson's piece, "Forest of Voices." As you read it, pay attention to who Anderson talks to, and pay special attention to why Anderson talks to them. Identify the two people who seem to provide him with the most important information. What kind of information do these sources offer? For each of these two sources, make a list of the questions Anderson asked (or must have asked) in order to get the information he needed.

ACTIVITY 5.26

Identify an issue that arose from your reading of a selection in this book, and write it in the form of a question. (If an issue doesn't immediately come to mind, try some freewriting; if you've been keeping a journal, review your entries for possible questions.) For example, after reading Dixy Lee Ray's piece on greenhouse warming, you might wonder whether there's been any more current research on the levels of carbon dioxide in the atmosphere. So you might ask, "What does the most current research say about carbon dioxide levels and the greenhouse effect?"

Once you've written your question, ask yourself if there's a local expert who might be able to help you answer it. For example, does your campus have an atmospheric sciences department? If so, someone in that department might be able to tell you about the current research on the greenhouse effect. See whether you can come up with two people or two groups of people (like the atmospheric sciences department) who you could actually speak with face to face.

_____

COMING UP WITH QUESTIONS

Your first few questions in the interview should be about the person you're interviewing. Why is this person considered an expert?

What formal training, degrees, or work experiences have led to your interest in _____ ?
How long have you been interested in _____ ?
Have you received any professional recognition (awards, prizes, grants, or the like) for your work in _____ ?

The rest of your questions will focus on the issue or problem itself. They often begin broadly and get progressively more specific. Let's stay with the greenhouse effect example. The early, broadly worded interview questions might ask the interviewee to begin by summarizing the overall issue: "Thinking back to 1990 [when the Dixy Lee Ray piece was published], what did scientists know then about the greenhouse effect, and what did they suspect was true?" A question like this one will usually prompt a fairly long answer, and you should anticipate that you'll have to ask other questions in order to make sure you understand that answer.

Your next question would take you directly to your reason for the interview itself: "What research has been done since 1990? What have we learned since then?" Again, such questions often prompt long and complicated answers. And often you'll need to ask follow-up questions in order to make sure you understand what you're hearing. Finally, you'd probably also want to ask what conclusions your interviewee draws from this new research. Again, this broad question would probably lead to a long and complicated answer—one that would lead you to ask follow-up questions.

Don't forget to ask a last open-ended question that lets your interviewee tell you anything else that she or he feels is important for you to know: "What have I forgotten to ask you?" Or "What else should I know in order to fully understand _____ ?"

ACTIVITY 5.27

Using your writing from activity 5.26, draw up a list of at least five (and no more than ten) basic questions that you could use in an interview. Make sure that two of these questions work to establish your interviewee's credentials, and make sure that at least three pose the major questions that form the reason for the interview itself. Finally, as you look at this list of questions, decide which ones will probably yield long answers and hence require that you ask new questions to help you understand those answers. Identify these questions by number.

KEEPING TRACK OF THE INTERVIEW

We recommend that you both record the interview *and* take notes as you listen. The tape recording will give you a word-for-word record; your notes will help you remember what parts of the interview you'll want to pay particular attention to.

If you've gotten permission to tape the interview (and you should ask for permission), experiment a bit with the tape recorder you plan to use so that you know how sensitive the microphone is and how close to it your interviewee needs to be. Prepare the paper that you'll use to take notes. Write your first question, and then leave space to make notes about what the interviewee says; write your second question and leave space for your notes; and so on. If your question is complicated and thus is likely to prompt follow-up questions, leave room for them, too. Leave more room than you think you'll need. Make sure that you write down this question for yourself: what's a good time for follow-up questions?

ACTIVITY 5.28

Prepare for and schedule an interview. Turn in to your instructor the following information.

1. the overall question you hope your interview will answer (in other words, your reason for doing this interview)
2. a copy of your question list
3. the name of your interviewee and how you found out about this person

4. the scheduled day and time of your interview
5. a sentence or two indicating how you plan to remember what your interviewee said (tape recording? notes? both?)
6. a sentence or two indicating how confident or worried you feel about conducting an interview

During the interview itself, don't be surprised or flustered if you need to ask your interviewee to repeat part of an answer, especially if you're trying to make sure that you quote accurately. Don't be surprised if you need to ask your interviewee to slow down so that you can take notes.

Let the conversation take its natural course. Ask the questions that come to you in the course of things, whether you planned them or not. Improvise. Interviewing is like writing itself: Outlines are useful mostly because they give you something to deviate from.

Once you've finished the question-answer session, plan on spending the next hour or so working on your notes. Doing this right after the interview itself lets you add to your notes and make sense of them while the interview is still quite fresh. Keep a list of the new questions that occur to you; some may be answered as you continue to mull over the interview, but others might prompt you to ask your interviewee for clarification.

ACTIVITY 5.29

On the basis of earlier activities you've done in this chapter, conduct your interview. Once you've conducted it, turn in the following information to your instructor.

who you interviewed, where the interview was held, and when
how you recorded what your interviewee said
two or three sentences describing whether you feel the interview
went well and why you feel that way
a sentence indicating whether you now anticipate having to ask any
follow-up questions

WRITING UP THE INTERVIEW

If you've been keeping a journal, use it to record your informal reaction to your interview; tell yourself how it went and what surprised you.

How does this new information change your original thinking?
Does it deepen and confirm something you already half understood
or half believed?
Does it challenge something you thought was true?

Does it introduce new variables that you hadn't even considered before?

Don't be surprised if this new information prompts new questions and even additional research.

Sometimes, however, rather than using the interview to help you make some larger point, you want to present the interview itself to readers. If your assignment or aim is to report what you've learned, you can write up this interview in either of two ways: as a report organized according to major topics or major sections, or as an interview presented in question-and-answer format.

The report format uses the same sort of organization that you've probably used with other papers: It opens with an introduction that presents your broad overall question (the reason for your interview) and identifies who you interviewed. Later sections tell readers what you learned. The paper uses paragraphs and moves logically and reasonably. Usually this means taking the raw material of your interview and thinking hard about what readers need to know first, what they need to know second, and so on. Sometimes your resulting paragraphs will follow the order of the questions you asked in the interview. But often you will need to reorder those answers, putting them in the sequence that readers will find easiest to understand.

There's another format that printed interviews often take: the question-answer format. If you use this option, your written interview typically begins with the same sort of introductory paragraph identifying your major question and the interviewee. But once the reason for the interview is clear and the interviewee's credentials are established, then the rest of the paper is composed of questions followed by answers. Often the questions are indented or italicized so that readers can easily distinguish between your words (as interviewee) and your expert's responses.

Here is an example using the question-answer format.

Interview Title

In question-answer format the opening of your interview looks like any other introduction. It explains to readers the interview's purpose, making clear what broad questions prompted it. And it also tells readers enough about the interviewee that they understand this person's credentials; readers can see that this person is an expert.

Q: *Following the introductory paragraph, the first question is presented. Often questions are italicized or underlined.*

A: The answer to that question follows immediately. Practices differ about putting answers inside quotation marks. Some instructors will say that since all the answers are quoted material, and since the question-answer format makes identifying answers quite easy, the quotation marks aren't necessary. Others disagree and require the quotation marks. So ask your instructor what you should do. In general, answers are typically longer than questions.

Q: *By wording your questions carefully, you can give the written interview a sense of flow. For example, a question like "Now that we've discussed X, let's turn to Y; what can you tell us about Y?" tells readers that the interview is moving to a new topic.*

If you're using the question-answer format, you're particularly obligated to be faithful to what your interviewee actually said. Thus a tape recorder is essential. Also, you'll need to deal with the wandering and digressing that always take place in an interview. Your obligation is to present the interviewee's information as clearly and concisely as you can, not simply to reproduce the interview as it happened, warts and all. You may need to take parts of several answers and combine them. You'll need to cut parts of some answers (the parts that wandered off the subject). Almost always you'll need to present the questions and answers in an order that readers will find clear and lucid—not necessarily the order in which you actually asked the questions and heard the answers.

ACTIVITY 5.30

Take all your interview notes and tape recordings and start working this material into something readers can understand. Begin by identifying the major points you want to make sure that your write-up includes. List them briefly on a single sheet of paper, and work with this list until you have your main points arranged in a logical order that you're reasonably sure readers can follow. Once you have this list, explain it to someone else in the class; that is, talk it through from introduction to conclusion. Don't hesitate to rearrange your order to make it clearer. Turn in a copy of this new list (it should still be stated briefly enough that you can show all your major sections or major points on a single sheet of paper); keep the original so that you can work from it.

ACTIVITY 5.31

Decide on a format that will let you best present your interview information. Write a paragraph that explains why you're using that format.

ACTIVITY 5.32

Write a rough draft of your interview, following the order of main points that you identified in activity 5.30. Make any changes in this order that seem reasonable, but be ready to explain why you've reordered. Continue to polish and revise this draft as you would for any other writing assignment.

Essay Topics for Chapter 5

1. Research a researcher. Take a well-known writer of carefully researched information—John McPhee, Barbara Tuchman, Tom Wolfe—and research that person's life and work. Write a profile.

2. Interview a researcher in your field. Find out what this person researches and how this research is conducted. Ask any questions that seem useful and interesting to you, but make sure that one of your questions asks about how research in this field has changed in recent years. Assume that your readers are other majors who want to know more about research in their field.

3. Do research on guides to research. Survey a dozen composition textbooks that discuss techniques for library research, and then synthesize, categorize, and interpret what you find.

4. Write a research paper predicting the future of library research. On the basis of developing technology, project yourself ten years ahead: How will a student in this or a similar class go about a research project?

5. Write a history and profile of your particular university or community library. Who started it? Why? How was the money raised and the building built? How has the library changed? Who have been the important people in the history of the library? Include interviews with one or more members of the library staff, past and present, and possibly with several students who often use the library.

6. Spend an afternoon observing people on the main floor of the library. Record impressions, snatches of conversation, clothing, gestures, patterns of movement. Write an essay entitled "On Spending an Afternoon Watching People in a Library." A variation is to do this observation in some other similarly public place—an airport, train station, mall, or the like.

7. Write a personal essay about a time when research of some sort changed your life or a time when the absence of information changed your life.

8. Interview a book (yes, a book!), and write the interview up using the question-answer format. That is, go through exactly the same process as you would for interviewing a person, but apply it now to the book—as if it could talk back to you. Choose an important book, one that deserves close attention. In the place of the person's spoken answers, use relevant passages from the book. At the beginning of the interview, in the place of a quick profile of the person, write a short profile of the book.

Part II
Reading to Write

6

Created Worlds

When we first think of the environment or of environmental issues, we naturally start thinking about rocks and trees and birds and things. But *environment* really means something larger: It means all the places we inhabit, all the things that surround and affect us. And for most of us that means created worlds—environments that we've made ourselves. It means the dorm rooms and apartments and houses we live in now. It means cities, towns, shopping malls, roads, fences, yards; it means the places where we study or work. When we stop to think about it, stop to look around at where we really are right now, we find ourselves surrounded by structures—rooms, walls, buildings, streets, cars. Clearly, then, the environments we most associate with our daily lives have been constructed, arranged.

To begin understanding the importance of environment, we need to reflect on the influence of these structures and designs on our thoughts and feelings, on our patterns of work and play. The pieces in this opening section all concern the urban and suburban worlds—created worlds—that most of us grew up in and live in now. They work to help us see such places, to look closely; they are celebrations of that world or critiques of it.

"THE SILENT NEIGHBORHOOD"

Annie Dillard

> *At age twenty-nine Annie Dillard won the Pulitzer Prize for her first book,* Pilgrim at Tinker's Creek *(1974). Since then she has been our most influential writer of creative nonfiction. Her subsequent books include* Teaching a Stone to Talk, *a collection of essays, and* The Writing Life, *a meditation on the writing process. The following evocation of early childhood is from the opening section of her autobiography,* An American Childhood.

The story starts back in 1950, when I was five.

Oh, the great humming silence of the empty neighborhoods in those days, the neighborhoods abandoned everywhere across continental America—the city residential areas, the new "suburbs," the towns and villages on the peopled highways, the cities, towns, and villages on the rivers, the shores, in the Rocky and Appalachian mountains, the piedmont, the dells, the bayous, the hills, the Great Basin, the Great Valley, the Great Plains— oh, the silence!

For every morning the neighborhoods emptied, and all vital activity, it seemed, set forth for parts unknown.

The men left in a rush: they flung on coats, they slid kisses at everybody's cheeks, they slammed house doors, they slammed car doors; they ground their cars' starters till the motors caught with a jump.

And the Catholic schoolchildren left in a rush; I saw them from our dining-room windows. They burst into the street buttoning their jackets; they threw dry catalpa pods at the stop sign and at each other. They hugged their brown-and-tan workbooks to them, clumped and parted, and proceeded toward St. Bede's church school almost by accident.

The men in their oval, empty cars drove slowly among the schoolchildren. The boys banged the cars' fenders with their hands, with their jackets' elbows, or their books. The men in cars inched among the children; they edged around corners and vanished from sight. The waving knots of children zigzagged and hollered up the street and vanished from sight. And inside all the forgotten houses in all the abandoned neighborhoods, the day of silence and waiting had begun.

The war was over. People wanted to settle down, apparently, and calmly blow their way out of years of rationing. They wanted to bake sugary cakes, burn gas, go to church together, get rich, and make babies.

I had been born at the end of April 1945, on the day Hitler died; Roosevelt had died eighteen days before. My father had been 4-F in the war, because of a collapsing lung—despite his repeated and chagrined efforts to enlist. Now—five years after V-J Day—he still went out one night a week as a volunteer to the Civil Air Patrol; he searched the Pittsburgh skies for new enemy bombers. By day he worked downtown for American Standard.

Every woman stayed alone in her house in those days, like a coin in a safe. Amy and I lived alone with our mother most of the day. Amy was three years younger than I. Mother and Amy and I went our separate ways in peace.

The men had driven away and the schoolchildren had paraded out   10 of sight. Now a self-conscious and stricken silence overtook the neighborhood, overtook our white corner house and myself inside. "Am I living?" In the kitchen I watched the unselfconscious trees through the screen door, until the trees' autumn branches like fins waved away the silence. I forgot myself, and sank into dim and watery oblivion.

A car passed. Its rush and whine jolted me from my blankness. The sound faded again and I faded again down into my hushed brain until the icebox motor kicked on and prodded me awake. "You are living," the icebox motor said. "It is morning, morning, here in the kitchen, and you are in it," the icebox motor said, or the dripping faucet said, or any of the hundred other noisy things that only children can't stop hearing. Cars started, leaves rubbed, trucks' brakes whistled, sparrows peeped. Whenever it rained, the rain spattered, dripped, and ran, for the entire length of the shower, for the entire length of days-long rains, until we children were almost insane from hearing it rain because we couldn't stop hearing it rain. "Rinso white!" cried the man on the radio. "Rinso blue." The silence, like all silences, was made poignant and distinct by its sounds.

What a marvel it was that the day so often introduced itself with a firm footfall nearby. What a marvel it was that so many times a day the world, like a church bell, reminded me to recall and contemplate the durable fact that I was here, and had awakened once more to find myself set down in a going world.

In the living room the mail slot clicked open and envelopes clattered down. In the back room, where our maid, Margaret Butler, was ironing, the steam iron thumped the muffled ironing board and hissed. The walls squeaked, the pipes knocked, the screen door trembled, the furnace banged, and the radiators clanged. This was the fall the loud trucks went by. I sat mindless and eternal on the kitchen floor, stony of head and solemn, playing with my fingers. Time streamed in full flood beside me on the kitchen floor; time roared raging beside me down its swollen banks; and when I woke I was so startled I fell in.

Who could ever tire of this heart-stopping transition, of this breakthrough shift between seeing and knowing you see, between being and knowing you be? It drives you to a life of concentration, it does, a life in which effort draws you down so very deep that when you surface you twist up exhilarated with a yelp and a gasp.

Who could ever tire of this radiant transition, this surfacing to aware-   *15*
ness and this deliberate plunging to oblivion—the theater curtain rising
and falling? Who could tire of it when the sum of those moments at the
edge—the conscious life we so dread losing—is all we have, the gift at the
moment of opening it?

Six xylophone notes chimed evenly from the radio in the back room
where Margaret was ironing, and then seven xylophone notes chimed.
With carefully controlled emotion, a radio woman sang:

What will the weather be?
Tell us, Mister Weather Man.

Mother picked up Amy, who was afraid of the trucks. She called the
painters on the phone; it was time to paint the outside trim again. She
ordered groceries on the phone. Larry, from Lloyd's Market, delivered. He
joked with us in the kitchen while Mother unpacked the groceries' cardboard box.

I wandered outside. It was afternoon. No cars passed on the empty
streets; no people passed on the empty sidewalks. The brick houses, the
frame and stucco houses, white and red behind their high hedges, were
still. A small woman appeared at the far, high end of the street, in silhouette
against the sky; she pushed a black baby carriage tall and chromed as a
hearse. The leaves in the Lombardy poplars were turning brown.

"Lie on your back," my mother said. She was kind, imaginative. She
had joined me in one of the side yards. "Look at the clouds and figure out
what they look like. A hat? I see a camel."

Must I? Could this be anybody's idea of something worth doing?   *20*

I was hoping the war would break out again, here. I was hoping the
streets would fill and I could shoot my cap gun at people instead of at
mere sparrows. My project was to ride my swing all around, over the top.
I bounced a ball against the house; I fired gravel bits from an illegal sling-
shot Mother gave me. Sometimes I looked at the back of my hand and
tried to memorize it. Sometimes I dreamed of a coal furnace, a blue lake,
a redheaded woodpecker who turned into a screeching hag. Sometimes I
sang uselessly in the yard, "Blithar, blithar, blithar, blithar."

It rained and it cleared and I sent Popsicle sticks and twigs down the
gritty rivulet below the curb. Soon the separated neighborhood trees lost
their leaves, one by one. On Saturday afternoons I watched the men rake
leaves into low heaps at the curb. They tried to ignite the heaps with
matches. At length my father went into the house and returned with a
yellow can of lighter fluid. The daylight ended early, before all the men
had burned all their leaves.

It snowed and it cleared and I kicked and pounded the snow. I
roamed the darkening snowy neighborhood, oblivious. I bit and crumbled
on my tongue the sweet, metallic worms of ice that had formed in rows
on my mittens. I took a mitten off to fetch some wool strands from my

mouth. Deeper the blue shadows grew on the sidewalk snow, and longer; the blue shadows joined and spread upward from the streets like rising water. I walked wordless and unseeing, dumb and sunk in my skull, until— what was that?

The streetlights had come on—yellow, bing—and the new light woke me like noise. I surfaced once again and saw: it was winter now, winter again. The air had grown blue dark; the skies were shrinking; the streetlights had come on; and I was here outside in the dimming day's snow, alive.

Reading and Responding

1. Imagine that you're five years old and at home, wherever home was. It's morning. Do a one-page freewrite—not letting your pen leave the page, not worrying about grammar and punctuation, just recording your thoughts and feelings as they come to you—describing what you see and feel.
2. Freewrite about some early memory that you connect with home. Write quickly and don't worry about errors; just write what you remember and speculate about what you don't remember.

Working Together

1. Make a list of all the many details Annie Dillard uses in this essay, all the concrete sensations she describes, all the sights, sounds, and smells. List the nouns, verbs, adjectives. Combine your list with those of classmates. As a group, come to a conclusion about how all those details add up: What's their effect on you as a reader?
2. Dillard describes a time when she was glad to be alive, full of energy and awareness and attention. Try to remember how you felt when you were five. Did you feel the same as Dillard? Compare that five-year-old feeling with the feeling you had just this morning, on the way to class. As a group, come up with a list of five phrases that describe how you felt when you were young and another list of five phrases describing how you felt this morning. As you look at these two lists, how do you account for the differences?

Rethinking and Rewriting

1. Return to your earlier freewrite, and make a list of new details—new sights and sounds and smells—that you can add to it.
2. Revise and extend your earlier freewrite into a short essay remembering what home was for you when you were five years old. Add the list of details and as many more as you can think of. Your task in this essay is to re-create the experience of being where you were all those years ago.

Like Dillard, re-create a single day in that life. As you polish this essay, try to make your sentences as direct and straightforward, as strong and clear, as Dillard's.

3. Option: Make this the first part of a two-part essay comparing home when you were five and home for you now, the way you felt then and the way you feel right now.

"O ROTTEN GOTHAM"

Tom Wolfe

As a journalist writing features for Esquire *and other publications in the sixties, Tom Wolfe developed the approach to nonfiction he later called the "New Journalism," a style of writing that applies the techniques of fiction to the telling of "true" stories. His new journalistic treatment of the sixties counterculture,* The Electric Kool-Aid Acid Test *(1968), and his later portrayal of the first astronauts,* The Right Stuff *(1979), established him as one of our most important writers of literary journalism. In this study of the effects of overcrowding in New York City, Wolfe demonstrates the rule-breaking intensity of style that made him famous.*

I just spent two days with Edward T. Hall, an anthropologist, watching thousands of my fellow New Yorkers short-circuiting themselves into hot little twitching death balls with jolts of their own adrenalin. Dr. Hall says it is overcrowding that does it. Overcrowding gets the adrenalin going, and the adrenalin gets them hyped up. And here they are, hyped up, turning bilious, nephritic, queer, autistic, sadistic, barren, batty, sloppy, hot-in-the-pants, chancred-on-the-flankers, leering, puling, numb—the usual in New York, in other words, and God knows what else. Dr. Hall has the theory that overcrowding has already thrown New York into a state of behavioral sink. Behavioral sink is a term from ethology, which is the study of how animals relate to their environment. Among animals, the sink winds up with a "population collapse" or "massive die-off." O rotten Gotham.

It got to be easy to look at New Yorkers as animals, especially looking down from some place like a balcony at Grand Central at the rush hour Friday afternoon. The floor was filled with the poor white humans, running around, dodging, blinking their eyes, making a sound like a pen full of starlings or rats or something.

"Listen to them skid," says Dr. Hall.

He was right. The poor old etiolate animals were out there skidding on their rubber soles. You could hear it once he pointed it out. They stop short to keep from hitting somebody or because they are disoriented and they suddenly stop and look around, and they skid on their rubber-sole shoes, and a screech goes up. They pour out onto the floor down the escalators from the Pan-Am Building, from 42nd Street, from Lexington Avenue, up out of subways, down into subways, railroad trains, up into helicopters—

"You can also hear the helicopters all the way down here," says Dr. Hall. The sound of the helicopters using the roof of the Pan-Am Building nearly fifty stories up beats right through. "If it weren't for this ceiling"—he is referring to the very high ceiling in Grand Central—"this place

5

would be unbearable with this kind of crowding. And yet they'll probably never 'waste' space like this again."

They screech! And the adrenal glands in all those poor white animals enlarge, micrometer by micrometer, to the size of cantaloupes. Dr. Hall pulls a Minox camera out of a holster he has on his belt and starts shooting away at the human scurry. The Sink!

Dr. Hall has the Minox up to his eye—he is a slender man, calm, 52 years old, young-looking, an anthropologist who has worked with Navajos, Hopis, Spanish-Americans, Negroes, Trukese. He was the most important anthropologist in the government during the crucial years of the foreign aid program, the 1950's. He directed both the Point Four training program and the Human Relations Area Files. He wrote *The Silent Language* and *The Hidden Dimension,* two books that are picking up the kind of "underground" following his friend Marshall McLuhan started picking up about five years ago. He teaches at the Illinois Institute of Technology, lives with his wife, Mildred, in a high-ceilinged town house on one of the last great residential streets in downtown Chicago, Astor Street; has a grown son and daughter, loves good food, good wine, the relaxed, civilized life—but comes to New York with a Minox at his eye to record—perfect!—The Sink.

We really got down in there by walking down into the Lexington Avenue line subway stop under Grand Central. We inhaled those nice big fluffy fumes of human sweat, urine, effluvia, and sebaceous secretions. One old female human was already stroked out on the upper level, on a stretcher, with two policemen standing by. The other humans barely looked at her. They rushed into line. They bellied each other, haunch to paunch, down the stairs. Human heads shone through the gratings. The species North European tried to create bubbles of space around themselves, about a foot and a half in diameter

"See, he's reacting against the line," says Dr. Hall.

—but the species Mediterranean presses on in. The hell with bubbles   *10*
of space. The species North European resents that, this male human behind him presses forward toward the booth . . . *breathing* on him, he's disgusted, he pulls out of the line entirely, the species Mediterranean resents him for resenting it, and neither of them realizes what the hell they are getting irritable about exactly. And in all of them the old adrenals grow another micrometer.

Dr. Hall whips out the Minox. Too perfect! The bottom of The Sink.

It is the sheer overcrowding, such as occurs in the business sections of Manhattan five days a week and in Harlem, Bedford-Stuyvesant, southeast Bronx every day—sheer overcrowding is converting New Yorkers into animals in a sink pen. Dr. Hall's argument runs as follows: all animals, including birds, seem to have a built-in, inherited requirement to have a certain amount of territory, space, to lead their lives in. Even if they have all the food they need, and there are no predatory animals threatening them, they cannot tolerate crowding beyond a certain point. No more than two hundred wild Norway rats can survive on a quarter acre of ground, for example, even when they are given all the food they can eat. They just die off.

But why? To find out, ethologists have run experiments on all sorts of animals, from stickleback crabs to Sika deer. In one major experiment, an ethologist named John Calhoun put some domesticated white Norway rats in a pen with four sections to it, connected by ramps. Calhoun knew from previous experiments that the rats tend to split up into groups of ten to twelve and that the pen, therefore, would hold forty to forty-eight rats comfortably, assuming they formed four equal groups. He allowed them to reproduce until there were eighty rats, balanced between male and female, but did not let it get any more crowded. He kept them supplied with plenty of food, water, and nesting materials. In other words, all their more obvious needs were taken care of. A less obvious need—space—was not. To the human eye, the pen did not even look especially crowded. But to the rats, it was crowded beyond endurance.

The entire colony was soon plunged into a profound behavioral sink. "The sink," said Calhoun, "is the outcome of any behavioral process that collects animals together in unusually great numbers. The unhealthy connotations of the term are not accidental: a behavioral sink does act to aggravate all forms of pathology that can be found within a group."

For a start, long before the rat population reached eighty, a status 15 hierarchy had developed in the pen. Two dominant male rats took over the two end sections, acquired harems of eight to ten females each, and forced the rest of the rats into the two middle pens. All the overcrowding took place in the middle pens. That was where the "sink" hit. The aristocrat rats at the ends grew bigger, sleeker, healthier, and more secure the whole time.

In The Sink, meanwhile, nest building, courting, sex behavior, reproduction, social organization, health—all of it went to pieces. Normally, Norway rats have a mating ritual in which the male chases the female, the female ducks down into a burrow and sticks her head up to watch the male. He performs a little dance outside the burrow, then she comes out, and he mounts her, usually for a few seconds. When The Sink set in, however, no more than three males—the dominant males in the middle sections—kept up the old customs. The rest tried everything from satyrism to homosexuality or else gave up on sex altogether. Some of the subordinate males spent all their time chasing females. Three or four might chase one female at the same time, and instead of stopping at the burrow entrance for the ritual, they would charge right in. Once mounted, they would hold on for minutes instead of the usual seconds.

Homosexuality rose sharply. So did bisexuality. Some males would mount anything—males, females, babies, senescent rats, anything. Still other males dropped sexual activity altogether, wouldn't fight and, in fact, would hardly move except when the other rats slept. Occasionally a female from the aristocrat rats' harems would come over the ramps and into the middle sections to sample life in The Sink. When she had had enough, she would run back up the ramp. Sink males would give chase up to the top of the ramp, which is to say, to the very edge of the aristocratic preserve. But one glance from one of the king rats would stop them cold and they would return to The Sink.

The slumming females from the harems had their adventures and then returned to a placid, healthy life. Females in The Sink, however were ravaged, physically and psychologically. Pregnant rats had trouble continuing pregnancy. The rate of miscarriages increased significantly, and females started dying from tumors and other disorders of the mammary glands, sex organs, uterus, ovaries, and Fallopian tubes. Typically, their kidneys, livers, and adrenals were also enlarged or diseased or showed other signs associated with stress.

Child-rearing became totally disorganized. The females lost the interest or the stamina to build nests and did not keep them up if they did build them. In the general filth and confusion, they would not put themselves out to save offspring they were momentarily separated from. Frantic, even sadistic competition among the males was going on all around them and rendering their lives chaotic. The males began unprovoked and senseless assaults upon one another, often in the form of tail-biting. Ordinarily, rats will suppress this kind of behavior when it crops up. In The Sink, male rats gave up all policing and just looked out for themselves. The "pecking order" among males in The Sink was never stable. Normally, male rats set up a three-class structure. Under the pressure of overcrowding, however, they broke up into all sorts of unstable subclasses, cliques, packs—and constantly pushed, probed, explored, tested one another's power. Anyone was fair game, except for the aristocrats in the end pens.

Calhoun kept the population down to eighty, so that the next stage, "population collapse" or "massive die-off," did not occur. But the autopsies showed that the pattern—as in the diseases among the female rats—was already there.

20

The classic study of die-off was John J. Christian's study of Sika deer on James Island in the Chesapeake Bay, west of Cambridge, Maryland. Four or five of the deer had been released on the island, which was 280 acres and uninhabited, in 1916. By 1955 they had bred freely into a herd of 280 to 300. The population density was only about one deer per acre at this point, but Christian knew that this was already too high for the Sikas' inborn space requirements, and something would give before long. For two years the number of deer remained 280 to 300. But suddenly, in 1958, over half the deer died; 161 carcasses were recovered. In 1959 more deer died and the population steadied at about 80.

In two years, two-thirds of the herd had died. Why? It was not starvation. In fact, all the deer collected were in excellent condition, with well-developed muscles, shining coats, and fat deposits between the muscles. In practically all the deer, however, the adrenal glands had enlarged by 50 percent. Christian concluded that the die-off was due to "shock following severe metabolic disturbance, probably as a result of prolonged adrenocortical hyperactivity. . . . There was no evidence of infection, starvation, or other obvious cause to explain the mass mortality." In other words, the constant stress of overpopulation, plus the normal stress of the cold of the winter, had kept the adrenalin flowing so constantly in the deer that their systems were depleted of blood sugar and they died of shock.

Well, the white humans are still skidding and darting across the floor of Grand Central. Dr. Hall listens a moment longer to the skidding and the darting noises, and then says, "You know, I've been on commuter trains here after everyone has been through one of these rushes and I'll tell you, there is enough acid flowing in the stomachs in every car to dissolve the rails underneath."

Just a little invisible acid bath for the linings to round off the day. The ulcers the acids cause, of course, are the one disease people have already been taught to associate with the stress of city life. But overcrowding, as Dr. Hall sees it, raises a lot more hell with the body than just ulcers. In everyday life in New York—just the usual, getting to work, working in massively congested areas like 42nd Street between Fifth Avenue and Lexington, especially now that the Pan-Am Building is set in there, working in cubicles such as those in the editorial offices at Time-Life, Inc., which Dr. Hall cites as typical of New York's poor handling of space, working in cubicles with low ceilings and, often, no access to a window, while construction crews all over Manhattan drive everybody up the Masonite wall with air-pressure generators with noises up to the boil-a-brain decibel levels, then rushing to get home, piling into subways and trains, fighting for time and for space, the usual day in New York—the whole now-normal thing keeps shooting jolts of adrenalin into the body, breaking down the body's defenses and winding up with the work-a-daddy human animal stroked out at the breakfast table with his head apoplexed like a cauliflower out of his $6.95 semispread Pima-cotton shirt, and nosed over into a plate of No-Kloresto egg substitute, signing off with the black thrombosis, cancer, kidney, liver, or stomach failure, and the adrenals ooze to a halt, the size of eggplants in July.

One of the people whose work Dr. Hall is interested in on this score   25
is Rene Dubos at the Rockefeller Institute. Dubos's work indicates that specific organisms, such as the tuberculosis bacillus or a pneumonia virus, can seldom be considered "the cause" of a disease. The germ or virus, apparently, has to work in combination with other things that have already broken the body down in some way—such as the old adrenal hyperactivity. Dr. Hall would like to see some autopsy studies made to record the size of adrenal glands in New York, especially of people crowded into slums and people who go through the full rush-hour-work-rush-hour cycle every day. He is afraid that until there is some clinical, statistical data on how overcrowding actually ravages the human body, no one will be willing to do anything about it. Even in so obvious a thing as air pollution, the

pattern is familiar. Until people can actually see the smoke or smell the sulphur or feel the sting in their eyes, politicians will not get excited about it, even though it is well known that many of the lethal substances polluting the air are invisible and odorless. For one thing, most politicians are like the aristocrat rats. They are insulated from The Sink by practically sultanic buffers—limousines, chauffeurs, secretaries, aides-de-camp, doormen, shuttered houses, high-floor apartments. They almost never ride subways, fight rush hours, much less live in the slums or work in the Pan-Am Building.

We took a cab from Grand Central to go up to Harlem, and by 48th Street we were already socked into one of those great, total traffic jams on First Avenue on Friday afternoon. Dr. Hall motions for me to survey the scene, and there they all are, humans, male and female, behind the glass of their automobile windows, soundlessly going through the torture of their own adrenalin jolts. This male over here contracts his jaw muscles so hard that they bunch up into a great cheese Danish pattern. He twists his lips, he bleeds from the eyeballs, he shouts . . . soundlessly behind glass . . . the fat corrugates on the back of his neck, his whole body shakes as he pounds the heel of his hand into the steering wheel. The female human in the car ahead of him whips her head around, she bares her teeth, she screams . . . soundlessly behind glass . . . she throws her hands up in the air, Whaddya expect me—Yah, yuh stupid—and they all sit there, trapped in their own congestion, bleeding hate all over each other, shorting out the ganglia and—goddam it—

Dr. Hall sits back and watches it all. This is it! The Sink! And where is everybody's wandering boy?

Dr. Hall says, "We need a study in which drivers who go through these rush hours every day would wear GSR bands."

GSR?

"Galvanic skin response. It measures the electric potential of the skin, which is a function of sweating. If a person gets highly nervous, his palms begin to sweat. It is an index of tension. There are some other fairly simple devices that would record respiration and pulse. I think everybody who goes through this kind of experience all the time should take his own pulse—not literally—but just be aware of what's happening to him. You can usually tell when stress is beginning to get you physically." *30*

In testing people crowded into New York's slums, Dr. Hall would like to take it one step further—gather information on the plasma hydrocortisone level in the blood or the corticosteroids in the urine. Both have been demonstrated to be reliable indicators of stress, and testing procedures are simple.

The slums—we finally made it up to East Harlem. We drove into 101st Street, and there was a new, avant-garde little church building, the Church of the Epiphany, which Dr. Hall liked—and, next to it, a pile of rubble where a row of buildings had been torn down, and from the back windows of the tenements beyond several people were busy "airmailing," throwing garbage out the window, into the rubble, beer cans, red shreds, the No-Money-Down Eames roller stand for a TV set, all flying through the air onto the scaggy sump. We drove around some more in Harlem, and a sequence was repeated, trash, buildings falling down, buildings torn down, rubble, scaggy sumps or, suddenly, a cluster of high-rise apartment projects, with fences around the grass.

"You know what this city looks like?" Dr. Hall said. "It looks bombed out. I used to live at Broadway and 124th Street back in 1946 when I was studying at Columbia. I can't tell you how much Harlem has changed in twenty years. It looks bombed out. It's broken down. People who live in New York get used to it and don't realize how filthy the city has become. The whole thing is typical of a behavioral sink. So is something like the Kitty Genovese case—a girl raped and murdered in the courtyard of an apartment complex and forty or fifty people look on from their apartments and nobody even calls the police. That kind of apathy and anomie is typical of the general psychological deterioration of The Sink."

He looked at the high-rise housing projects and found them mainly testimony to how little planners know about humans' basic animal requirements for space.

"Even on the simplest terms," he said, "it is pointless to build one of these blocks much over five stories high. Suppose a family lives on the fifteenth floor. The mother will be completely cut off from her children if they are playing down below, because the elevators are constantly broken in these projects, and it often takes half an hour, literally half an hour, to get the elevator if it is running. That's very common. A mother in that situation is just as much a victim of overcrowding as if she were back in the tenement block. Some Negro leaders have a bitter joke about how the white man is solving the slum problem by stacking Negroes up vertically, and there is a lot to that."

For one thing, says Dr. Hall, planners have no idea of the different space requirements of people from different cultures, such as Negroes and Puerto Ricans. They are all treated as if they were minute, compact middle-class whites. As with the Sika deer, who are overcrowded at one per acre, overcrowding is a relative thing for the human animal, as well. Each species has its own feeling for space. The feeling may be "subjective," but it is quite real.

Dr. Hall's theories on space and territory are based on the same information, gathered by biologists, ethologists, and anthropologists, chiefly, as Robert Ardrey's. Ardrey has written two well-publicized books, *African Genesis* and *The Territorial Imperative*. *Life* magazine ran big excerpts from *The Territorial Imperative*, all about how the drive to acquire territory and property and add to it and achieve status is built into all animals, including man, over thousands of centuries of genetic history, etc., and is a more powerful drive than sex. *Life*'s big display prompted Marshall McLuhan to crack, "They see this as a great historic justification for free enterprise and Republicanism. If the birds do it and the stickle-back crabs do it, then it's right for man." To people like Hall and McLuhan, and Ardrey, for that matter, the right or wrong of it is irrelevant. The only thing they find inexcusable is the kind of thinking, by influential people, that isn't even aware of all this. Such as the thinking of most city planners.

"The planners always show you a bird's-eye view of what they are doing," he said. "You've seen those scale models. Everyone stands around the table and looks down and says that's great. It never occurs to anyone that they are taking a bird's-eye view. In the end, these projects do turn out fine, when viewed from an airplane."

As an anthropologist, Dr. Hall has to shake his head every time he hears planners talking about fully integrated housing projects for the year 1980 or 1990, as if by then all cultural groups will have the same feeling for space and will live placidly side by side, happy as the happy burghers who plan all the good clean bird's-eye views. According to his findings, the very fact that every cultural group does have its own peculiar, unspoken feeling for space is what is responsible for much of the uneasiness one group feels around the other.

It is like the North European and the Mediterranean in the subway line. The North European, without ever realizing it, tries to keep a bubble of space around himself, and the moment a stranger invades that sphere, he feels threatened. Mediterranean peoples tend to come from cultures where everyone is much more involved physically, publicly, with one another on a day-to-day basis and feels no uneasiness about mixing it up in public, but may have very different ideas about space inside the home. Even Negroes brought up in America have a different vocabulary of space and gesture from the North European Americans who, historically, have been their models, according to Dr. Hall. The failure of Negroes and whites to communicate well often boils down to things like this: some white will be interviewing a Negro for a job; the Negro's culture has taught him to show somebody you are interested by looking right at him and listening intently to what he has to say. But the species North European requires something more. He expects his listener to nod from time to time, as if to say, "Yes, keep going." If he doesn't get this nodding, he feels anxious, for fear the listener doesn't agree with him or has switched off. The Negro may learn that the white expects this sort of thing, but he isn't used to the precise kind of nodding that is customary, and so he may start overresponding, nodding like mad, and at this point the North European is liable to think he has some kind of stupid Uncle Tom on his hands, and the guy still doesn't get the job.

The whole handling of space in New York is so chaotic, says Dr. Hall, that even middle-class housing now seems to be based on the bird's-eye models for slum projects. He took a look at the big Park West Village development, set up originally to provide housing in Manhattan for families in the middle-income range, and found its handling of space very much like a slum project with slightly larger balconies. He felt the time has come to start subsidizing the middle class in New York on its own

40

terms—namely, the kind of truly "human" spaces that still remain in brownstones.

"I think New York City should seriously consider a program of encouraging the middle-class development of an area like Chelsea, which is already starting to come up. People are beginning to renovate houses there on their own, and I think if the city would subsidize that sort of thing with tax reliefs and so forth, you would be amazed at what would result. What New York needs is a string of minor successes in the housing field, just to show everyone that it can be done, and I think the middle class can still do that for you. The alternative is to keep on doing what you're doing now, trying to lift a very large lower class up by main force almost and finding it a very slow and discouraging process.

"But before deciding how to redesign space in New York," he said, "people must first simply realize how severe the problem already is. And the handwriting is already on the wall."

"A study published in 1962," he said, "surveyed a representative sample of people living in New York slums and found only 18 percent of them free from emotional symptoms. Thirty-eight percent were in need of psychiatric help, and 23 percent were seriously disturbed or incapacitated. Now, this study was published in 1962, which means the work probably went on from 1955 to 1960. There is no telling how bad it is now. In a behavioral sink, crises can develop rapidly."

Dr. Hall would like to see a large-scale study similar to that undertaken by two sociopsychologists, Chombart de Lauwe and his wife, in a French working-class town. They found a direct relationship between crowding and general breakdown. In families where people were crowded into the apartment so that there was less than 86 to 108 square feet per person, social and physical disorders doubled. That would mean that for four people the smallest floor space they could tolerate would be an apartment, say, 12 by 30 feet.

What would one find in Harlem? "It is fairly obvious," Dr. Hall wrote in *The Hidden Dimension,* "that the American Negroes and people of Spanish culture who are flocking to our cities are being very seriously stressed. Not only are they in a setting that does not fit them, but they have passed the limits of their own tolerance of stress. The United States is faced with the fact that two of its creative and sensitive peoples are in the process of being destroyed and like Samson could bring down the structure that houses us all."

Dr. Hall goes out to the airport, to go back to Chicago, and I am coming back in a cab, along the East River Drive. It is four in the afternoon, but already the damned drive is clogging up. There is a 1959 Oldsmobile just to the right of me. There are about eight people in there, a lot of popeyed silhouettes against a leopard-skin dashboard, leopard-skin seats—and the driver is classic. He has a mustache, sideburns down to his jaw socket, and a tattoo on his forearm with a Rossetti painting of Jane Burden Morris with her hair long. All right; it is even touching, like a

45

postcard photo of the main drag in San Pedro, California. But suddenly Sideburns guns it and cuts in front of my cab so that my driver has to hit the brakes, and then hardly 100 feet ahead Sideburns hits a wall of traffic himself and has to hit his brakes, and then it happens. A stuffed white Angora animal, a dog, no, it's a Pekingese cat, is mounted in his rear window—as soon as he hits the brakes its *eyes* light up, Nighttown pink. To keep from ramming him, my driver has to hit the brakes again, too, and so here I am, out in an insane, jammed-up expressway at four in the afternoon, shuddering to a stop while a stuffed Pekingese grows bigger and bigger and brighter in the eyeballs directly in front of me. Jolt! Nighttown pink! Hey— that's me the adrenalin is hitting, *I* am this white human sitting in a projectile heading amid a mass of clotted humans toward white Angora stuffed goddam leopard-dash Pekingese freaking cat—kill that damned Angora—Jolt!— got me—another micrometer on the old adrenals—

Reading and Responding

1. Explain anything in the language or ideas of this essay that surprised you.
2. Mark a passage you especially liked or a passage that confused you, and explain why you had the reaction you did.
3. Freewrite about a city you know. Does the term *behavioral sink* apply? Talk about why it does and/or why it doesn't.

Working Together

1. Make a list of all the *do*'s and *don't*'s you've been taught for writing term papers or research papers, particularly for the style and form of those papers. Make a list of all the ways Tom Wolfe fulfills those requirements and all the ways he violates those rules.
2. Discuss why you think Wolfe would want to stretch and intensify the conventional forms of writing the way he does. How do you think he wants readers to respond? How did you respond?
3. Discuss whether you want to live in a big city. Make a list of advantages and disadvantages as seen by the members of your group.

Rethinking and Rewriting

1. Both Dillard in "The Silent Neighborhood" and Wolfe in "O Rotten Gotham" talk about the ways that environment affects behavior. Explain, first, how the empty suburb affects how Dillard felt as a girl and, second, how overcrowding in New York influences behavior according to Wolfe.
2. Go to the library and look up the works of Edward T. Hall. Write a paper comparing his language and form with Wolfe's and arguing for the style or approach you like best.

3. Take any textbook or academic article you're reading for another course, and write about those ideas in a Wolfe-like, completely non- or even anti-academic way. Juice up the term paper. Write a hyper–term paper.

"SUMMER SOLSTICE, NEW YORK CITY"

Sharon Olds

A winner of the Lamont Poetry Award in 1983 (for her book The Dead and the Living*), Sharon Olds has published four collections of startlingly direct and humane poems. Her work has earned her fellowships from the National Endowment for the Arts and from the Guggenheim Foundation. She teaches a variety of poetry workshops with writers in the New York area, including those at Goldwater Hospital. This poem comes from her third book,* The Gold Cell, *published in 1987.*

Before You Read

Before you even read this poem, write for five minutes (quickly and without stopping) about your experience with poems. Then read the poem straight through (don't reread). Now, write for another five minutes about this poem: Is it like the other poems you've read?

By the end of the longest day of the year he could not stand it,
he went up the iron stairs through the roof of the building
and over the soft, tarry surface
to the edge, put one leg over the complex green tin cornice
and said if they came a step closer that was it.   *5*
Then the huge machinery of the earth began to work for his life,
the cops came in their suits blue-grey as the sky on a cloudy evening,
and one put on a bullet-proof vest, a
black shell around his own life,
life of his children's father, in case   *10*
the man was armed, and one, slung with a
rope like the sign of his bounden duty,
came up out of a hole in the top of the neighboring building
like the gold hole they say is in the top of the head,
and began to lurk toward the man who wanted to die.   *15*
The tallest cop approached him directly,
softly, slowly, talking to him, talking, talking,
while the man's leg hung over the lip of the next world
and the crowd gathered in the street, silent, and the
hairy net with its implacable grid was   *20*
unfolded near the curb and spread out and
stretched as the sheet is prepared to receive at a birth.
Then they all came a little closer
where he squatted next to his death, his shirt
glowing its milky glow like something   *25*
growing in a dish at night in the dark in a lab and then

everything stopped
as his body jerked and he
stepped down from the parapet and went toward them
and they closed on him, I thought they were going to   *30*
beat him up, as a mother whose child has been
lost will scream at the child when it's found, they
took him by the arms and held him up and
leaned him against the wall of the chimney and the
tall cop lit a cigarette   *35*
in his own mouth, and gave it to him, and
then they all lit cigarettes, and the
red, glowing ends burned like the
tiny campfires we lit at night
back at the beginning of the world.   *40*

Reading and Responding

Have you ever been part of a crowd watching some accident or other
terrible event (a fire, a shooting, a fight)? If so, write about that for half a
page or so. What were the circumstances, and what did it feel like to
watch?

Working Together

1. Summarize the action of this poem in a few sentences. If you have
   questions about what actually happens, make a list of those questions.
2. Take a look at the length of the sentences that Sharon Olds uses in this
   poem. As a group, decide what effects these long sentences make on
   readers.
3. Talk together about how this poem ends. If you've also read Tom Wolfe's
   piece earlier, talk about whether this poem agrees with Wolfe or disagrees. Write a group paragraph that explains your conclusions here.

Rethinking and Rewriting

1. Copy this poem word for word and line for line in your own handwriting. Then write a short essay that discusses what you've learned by
   doing this careful copying. Don't worry about being an expert on anything; just explain what difference it makes to have actually copied
   down the poem yourself. (Write the essay itself on a computer if you
   wish.)
2. After reading this one poem, would you be inclined to read other
   poems by Sharon Olds? Whatever your answer is here, make sure that
   it includes at least two quotations from the poem in order to illustrate
   your points.

"MY NEIGHBORHOOD"

Ishmael Reed

> *Afro-American novelist, playwright, and essayist Ishmael Reed teaches at the University of California, Berkeley. His work includes the novels* Mumbo Jumbo *(1978) and* Reckless Eyeballing *(1986) and the essay collections* Shrovetide in Old New Orleans *(1979) and* Writing Is Fightin' *(1988). In this essay, first published in* California *magazine, Reed praises the Oakland, California, neighborhood where he lives.*

My stepfather is an evolutionist. He worked for many years at the Chevrolet division of General Motors in Buffalo, a working-class auto and steel town in upstate New York, and was able to rise from relative poverty to the middle class. He believes that each succeeding generation of Afro-Americans will have it better than its predecessor. In 1979 I moved into the kind of neighborhood that he and my mother spent about a third of their lives trying to escape. According to the evolutionist integrationist ethic, this was surely a step backward, since "success" was seen as being able to live in a neighborhood in which you were the only black and joined your neighbors in trying to keep out "them."

My neighborhood, bordered by Genoa, Market Street, and 48th and 55th streets in North Oakland, is what the media refer to as a "predominantly black neighborhood." It's the kind of neighborhood I grew up in before leaving for New York City in 1962. My last New York residence was an apartment in a brownstone, next door to the building in which poet W. H. Auden lived. There were trees in the backyard, and I thought it was a swell neighborhood until I read in Robert Craft's biography of [the composer] Stravinsky that "when Stravinsky sent his chauffeur to pick up his friend Auden, the chauffeur would ask, 'Are you sure Mr. Auden lives in this neighborhood?'" By 1968 my wife and I were able to live six months of the year in New York and the other six in California. This came to an end when one of the people I sublet the apartment to abandoned it. He had fled to England to pursue a romance. He didn't pay the rent, and so we were evicted long distance.

My first residence in California was an apartment on Santa Ynez Street, near Echo Park Lake in Los Angeles, where I lived for about six months in 1967. I was working on my second novel, and Carla Blank, my wife, a dancer, was teaching physical education at one of Eddie Rickenbacker's camps, located on an old movie set in the San Bernardino Mountains. Carla's employers were always offering me a cabin where they promised I could write without interruption. I never took them up on the offer, but for years I've wondered about what kind of reception I would have received had they discovered that I am black.

During my breaks from writing I would walk through the shopping areas near Santa Ynez, strolling by vending machines holding newspapers whose headlines screamed about riots in Detroit. On some weekends we'd visit novelist Robert Gover (*The One Hundred Dollar Misunderstanding*) and his friends in Malibu. I remember one of Gover's friends, a scriptwriter for the *Donna Reed Show,* looking me in the eye and telling me that if he were black he'd be "on a Detroit rooftop, sniping at cops," as he reclined, glass of scotch in hand, in a comfortable chair whose position gave him a good view of the rolling Pacific.

My Santa Ynez neighbors were whites from Alabama and Mississippi, and we got along fine. Most of them were elderly, left behind by white flight to the suburbs, and on weekends the street would be lined with cars belonging to relatives who were visiting. While living here I observed a uniquely Californian phenomenon. Retired men would leave their houses in the morning, enter their cars, and remain there for a good part of the day, snoozing, reading newspapers, or listening to the radio.

I didn't experience a single racial incident during my stay in this Los Angeles neighborhood of ex-southerners. Once, however, I had a strange encounter with the police. I was walking through a black working-class neighborhood on my way to the downtown Los Angeles library. Some cops drove up and rushed me. A crowd gathered. The cops snatched my briefcase and removed its contents books and notebooks having to do with my research of voodoo. The crowd laughed when the cops said they thought I was carrying a purse.

In 1968 my wife and I moved to Berkeley, where we lived in one Bauhaus box after another until about 1971, when I received a three-book contract from Doubleday. Then we moved into the Berkeley Hills, where we lived in the downstairs apartment of a very grand-looking house on Bret Harte Way. There was a Zen garden with streams, waterfalls, and bridges outside, along with many varieties of flowers and plants. I didn't drive, and Carla was away at Mills College each day, earning a master's degree in dance. I stayed holed up in that apartment for two years, during which time I completed my third novel, *Mumbo Jumbo.*

During this period I became exposed to some of the racism I hadn't detected on Santa Ynez or in the Berkeley flats. As a black male working at home, I was regarded with suspicion. Neighbors would come over and warn me about a heroin salesman they said was burglarizing the neighborhood, all the while looking over my shoulder in an attempt to pry into what I was up to. Once, while I was eating breakfast, a policeman entered through the garden door, gun drawn. "What on earth is the problem, officer?" I asked. He said they got word that a homicide had been committed in my apartment, which I recognized as an old police tactic used to gain entry into somebody's house. Walking through the Berkeley Hills on Sundays, I was greeted by unfriendly stares and growling, snarling dogs. I remember one pest who always poked her head out of her window whenever I'd walk down Bret Harte Way. She was always hassling me about parking my car in front of her house. She resembled Miss Piggy. I came to think of this section of Berkeley as "Whitetown."

Around 1974 the landlord raised the rent on the house in the hills, and we found ourselves again in the Berkeley flats. We spent a couple of peaceful years on Edith Street, and then moved to Jayne Street, where we encountered another next-door family of nosy, middle-class progressives. I understand that much time at North Berkeley white neighborhood association meetings is taken up with discussion of and fascination with blacks who move through the neighborhoods, with special concern given those who tarry, or who wear dreadlocks. Since before the Civil War, vagrancy laws have been used as political weapons against blacks. Appropriately, there has been talk of making Havana—where I understand a woman can get turned in by her neighbors for having too many boyfriends over—Berkeley's sister city.

In 1976 our landlady announced that she was going to reoccupy the Jayne Street house. I facetiously told a friend that I wanted to move to the most right-wing neighborhood he could think of. He mentioned El Cerrito. There, he said, your next-door neighbor might even be a cop. We moved to El Cerrito. Instead of the patronizing nosiness blacks complain about in Berkeley, I found the opposite on Terrace Drive in El Cerrito. The people were cold, impersonal, remote. But the neighborhood was quiet, serene even—the view was Olympian, and our rented house was secluded by eucalyptus trees. The annoyances were minor. Occasionally a car would careen down Terrace Drive full of white teenagers, and one or two would shout, "Hey, nigger!" Sometimes as I walked down The Arlington toward Kensington Market, the curious would stare at me from their cars, and women I encountered would give me nervous, frightened looks. Once, as I was walking to the market to buy magazines, a white child was sitting directly in my path. We were the only two people on the street. Two or three cars actually stopped, and their drivers observed the scene through their rearview mirrors until they were assured I wasn't going to abduct the child.

At night the Kensington Market area was lit with a yellow light, especially eerie during a fog. I always thought that this section of Kensington would be a swell place to make a horror movie—the residents would make great extras—but whatever discomfort I felt about traveling through this area at 2 a.m. was mixed with the relief that I had just navigated safely through Albany, where the police seemed always to be lurking in the shadows, prepared to ensnare blacks, hippies, and others they didn't deem suitable for such a neighborhood.

In 1979 our landlord, a decent enough fellow in comparison to some of the others we had had (who made you understand why the communists shoot the landlords first when they take over a country), announced he was going to sell the house on Terrace Drive. This was the third rented house to be sold out from under us. The asking price was way beyond our means, and so we started to search for another home, only to find that the ones within our price range were located in North Oakland, in a "predominantly black neighborhood." We finally found a huge Queen Anne

Victorian, which seemed to be about a month away from the wrecker's ball if the termites and the precarious foundation didn't do it in first, but I decided that I had to have it. The oldest house on the block, it was built in 1906, the year the big earthquake hit Northern California, but left Oakland unscathed because, according to Bret Harte, "there are some things even the earth can't swallow." If I was apprehensive about moving into this neighborhood—on television all black neighborhoods resemble the commotion of the station house on *Hill Street Blues*—I was later to learn that our neighbors were just as apprehensive about us. Were we hippies? Did I have a job? Were we going to pay as much attention to maintaining our property as they did to theirs? Neglected, the dilapidated monstrosity I'd got myself into would blight the entire block.

While I was going to college I worked as an orderly in a psychiatric hospital, and I remember a case in which a man was signed into the institution, after complaints from his neighbors that he mowed the lawn at four in the morning. My neighbors aren't that finicky, but they keep very busy pruning, gardening, and mowing their laws. Novelist Toni Cade Bambara wrote of the spirit women in Atlanta who plant by moonlight and use conjure to reap gorgeous vegetables and flowers. A woman on this block grows roses the size of cantaloupes.

On New Year's Eve, famed landscape architect John Roberts accompanied me on my nightly walk, which takes me from 53rd Street to Aileen, Shattuck, and back to 53rd Street. He was able to identify plants and trees that had been imported from Asia, Africa, the Middle East, and Australia. On Aileen Street he discovered a banana tree! And Arthur Monroe, a painter and art historian, traces the "Tabby" garden design—in which seashells and plates are mixed with lime, sand, and water to form decorative borders, found in this Oakland neighborhood, and others—to the influence of Islamic slaves brought to the Gulf Coast.

I won over my neighbors, I think, after I triumphed over a dozen *15* generations of pigeons that had been roosting in the crevices of this house for many years. It was a long and angry war, and my five year old constantly complained to her mother about Daddy's bad words about the birds. I used everything I could get my hands on, including chicken wire and mothballs, and I would have tried the clay owls if the only manufacturer hadn't gone out of business. I also learned never to underestimate the intelligence of pigeons; just when you think you've got them whipped, you'll notice that they've regrouped on some strategic rooftop to prepare for another invasion. When the house was free of pigeons and their droppings, which had spread to the adjoining properties, the lady next door said, "Thank you."

Every New Year's Day since then our neighbors have invited us to join them and their fellow Louisianans for the traditional Afro-American good luck meal called Hoppin' John. This year the menu included blackeyed peas, ham, corn bread, potato salad, chitterlings, greens, fried chicken, yams, head cheese, macaroni, rolls, sweet potato pie, and fruitcake. I got up that morning weighing 214 pounds and came home from the party weighing 220.

We've lived on 53rd Street for three years now. Carla's dance and theater school, which she operates with her partner, Jody Roberts—Roberts and Blank Dance/Drama—is already five years old. I am working on my seventh novel and a television production of my play *Mother Hubbard*. The house has yet to be restored to its 1906 glory, but we're working on it.

I've grown accustomed to the common sights here—teenagers moving through the neighborhood carrying radios blasting music by Grandmaster Flash and Prince, men hovering over cars with tools and rags in hand, decked-out female church delegations visiting the sick. Unemployment up, one sees more men drinking from sacks as they walk through Market Street or gather in Helen McGregor Plaza, on Shattuck and 52nd Street, near a bench where mothers sit with their children, waiting for buses. It may be because the bus stop is across the street from Children's Hospital (exhibiting a brand-new antihuman, postmodern wing), but there seem to be a lot of sick black children these days. The criminal courts and emergency rooms of Oakland hospitals, both medical and psychiatric, are also filled with blacks.

White men go from door to door trying to unload spoiled meat. Incredibly sleazy white contractors and hustlers try to entangle people into shady deals that sometimes lead to the loss of a home. Everybody knows of someone, usually a widow, who has been gypped into paying thousands of dollars more than the standard cost for, say, adding a room to a house. It sure ain't El Cerrito. In El Cerrito the representatives from the utilities were very courteous. If they realize they're speaking to someone in a black neighborhood, however, they become curt and sarcastic. I was trying to arrange for the gas company to come out to fix a stove when the woman from Pacific Gas and Electric gave me some snide lip. I told her, "Lady, if you think what you're going through is an inconvenience, you can imagine my inconvenience paying the bills every month." Even she had to laugh.

The clerks in the stores are also curt, regarding blacks the way the media regard them, as criminal suspects. Over in El Cerrito the cops were professional, respectful—in Oakland they swagger about like candidates for a rodeo. In El Cerrito and the Berkeley Hills you could take your time paying some bills, but in this black neighborhood if you miss paying a bill by one day, "reminders" printed in glaring and violent typefaces are sent to you, or you're threatened with discontinuance of this or that service. Los Angeles police victim Eulia Love, who was shot in the aftermath of an argument over an overdue gas bill, would still be alive if she had lived in El Cerrito or the Berkeley Hills.

I went to a bank a few weeks ago that advertised easy loans on television, only to be told that I would have to wait six months after opening an account to be eligible for a loan. I went home and called the same bank, this time putting on my Clark Kent voice, and was informed

²⁰

that I could come in and get the loan the same day. Other credit unions and banks, too, have different lending practices for black and white neighborhoods, but when I try to tell white intellectuals that blacks are prevented from developing industries because the banks find it easier to lend money to communist countries than to American citizens, they call me paranoid. Sometimes when I know I am going to be inconvenienced by merchants or creditors because of my 53rd Street address, I give the address of my Berkeley studio instead. Others are not so fortunate.

Despite the inconveniences and antagonism from the outside world one has to endure for having a 53rd Street address, life in this neighborhood is more pleasant than grim. Casually dressed, well-groomed elderly men gather at the intersections to look after the small children as they walk to and from school, or just to keep an eye on the neighborhood. My next-door neighbor keeps me in stitches with his informed commentary on any number of political comedies emanating from Washington and Sacramento. Once we were discussing pesticides and the man who was repairing his porch told us that he had a great garden and didn't have to pay all that much attention to it. As for pesticides, he said, the bugs have to eat, too.

There are people on this block who still know the subsistence skills many Americans have forgotten. They can hunt and fish (and if you don't fish, there is a man who covers the neighborhood selling fresh fish and yelling, "Fishman," recalling a period of ancient American commerce when you didn't have to pay the middleman). They are also loyal Americans—they vote, they pay taxes—but you don't find the extreme patriots here that you find in white neighborhoods. Although Christmas, Thanksgiving, New Year's, and Easter are celebrated with all get-out, I've never seen a flag flying on Memorial Day, or on any holiday that calls for the showing of the flag. Blacks express their loyalty in concrete ways. For example, you rarely see a foreign car in this neighborhood. And this 53rd Street neighborhood, as well as black neighborhoods like it from coast to coast, will supply the male children who will bear the brunt of future jungle wars, just as they did in Vietnam.

We do our shopping on a strip called Temescal, which stretches from 46th to 51st streets. Temescal, according to Oakland librarian William Sturm, is an Aztec word for "hothouse," or "bathhouse." The word was borrowed from the Mexicans by the Spanish to describe similar hothouses, early saunas, built by the California Indians in what is now North Oakland. Some say the hothouses were used to sweat out demons; others claim the Indians used them for medicinal purposes. Most agree that after a period of time in the steam, the Indians would rush en masse into the streams that flowed through the area. One still runs underneath my backyard—I have to mow the grass there almost every other day.

Within these five blocks are the famous Italian restaurant Bertola's, *25* "Since 1932"; Siam restaurant; La Belle Creole, a French-Caribbean restaurant; Asmara, an Ethiopian restaurant; and Ben's Hof Brau, where white and black senior citizens, dressed in the elegance of a former time, congregate to talk or to have an inexpensive though quality breakfast provided by Ben's hardworking and courteous staff.

The Hof Brau shares its space with Vern's market, where you can shop to the music of DeBarge. To the front of Vern's is the Temescal Delicatessen, where a young Korean man makes the best po'boy sandwiches north of Louisiana, and near the side entrance is Ed Fraga's Automotive. The owner is always advising his customers to avoid stress, and he says goodbye with a "God bless you." The rest of the strip is taken up by the Temescal Pharmacy, which has a resident health advisor and a small library of health literature; the Aikido Institute; an African bookstore; and the internationally known Genova deli, to which people from the surrounding cities travel to shop. The strip also includes the Clausen House thrift shop, which sells used clothes and furniture. Here you can buy novels by J. D. Salinger and John O'Hara for ten cents each.

Space that was recently occupied by the Buon Gusto Bakery is now for rent. Before the bakery left, an Italian lady who worked there introduced me to a crunchy, cookie-like treat called "bones," which she said went well with Italian wine. The Buon Gusto had been a landmark since the 1940s, when, according to a guest at the New Year's Day Hoppin' John supper, North Oakland was populated by Italians and Portuguese. In those days a five-room house could be rented for $45 a month, she said.

The neighborhood is still in transition. The East Bay Negro Historical Society, which was located around the corner on Grove Street, included in its collection letters written by nineteenth-century macho man Jack London to his black nurse. They were signed, "Your little white pickaninny." It's been replaced by the New Israelite Delight restaurant, part of the Israelite Church, which also operates a day care center. The restaurant offers homemade Louisiana gumbo and a breakfast that includes grits.

Unlike the other California neighborhoods I've lived in, I know most of the people on this block by name. They are friendly and cooperative, always offering to watch your house while you're away. The day after one of the few whites who lives on the block—a brilliant muckraking journalist and former student of mine—was robbed, neighbors gathered in front of his house to offer assistance.

In El Cerrito my neighbor was indeed a cop. He used pomade on   *30*
his curly hair, sported a mustache, and there was a grayish tint in his brown eyes. He was a handsome man, with a smile like a movie star's. His was the only house on the block I entered during my three-year stay in that neighborhood, and that was one afternoon when we shared some brandy. I wanted to get to know him better. I didn't know he was dead until I saw people in black gathered on his doorstep.

I can't imagine that happening on 53rd Street. In a time when dour thinkers view alienation and insensitivity toward the plight of others as characteristics of the modern condition, I think I'm lucky to live in a neighborhood where people look out for one another.

A human neighborhood.

Reading and Responding

1. Have you ever moved to a new home? If so, freewrite about that experience. What was it like to move?
2. As you read about the reactions that various neighbors and others have to Ishmael Reed's presence, what's your reaction? Talk about the parts of this essay that provoke the strongest reaction from you.

Working Together

1. Talk about the various groups that you belong to and about the ways that other people judge you simply because you're a member of that group. Identify three examples that you can present to the class.
2. Pretend that you are Ishmael Reed. What do you say to your father about the neighborhood you live in now (at the end of the essay)? Does living where you live now mean "success"?

Rethinking and Rewriting

1. Write an essay that begins by discussing the very best place you've ever lived and then goes on to describe your ideal neighborhood. What are its features, and who are your neighbors? What would you take from that very best place, and what would you add to it to make this ideal neighborhood?
2. Write an essay that discusses an occasion when you've been uncomfortable in some part of a city. Make sure the essay explains where you were, how you got there, and why you were uncomfortable. Then talk about some occasion when you had a great time in a city (again, make this clear). End by looking at these two experiences. What made for the comfort; what made for the discomfort?

"THE PROBLEM OF PLACE IN AMERICA"

Ray Oldenburg

Ray Oldenburg, a sociologist, teaches at the University of West Florida in Pensacola. After publishing a scholarly article on the subject of place in America, he "wrestled," he says, for over six years to complete a book-length treatment of the topic for a general audience. What follows is the opening chapter of that book, published in 1989: The Great Good Place: Cafés, Coffee Shops, Community Centers, Beauty Parlors, General Stores, Bars, Hangouts and How They Get You Through the Day.

> A number of recent American writings indicate that the nostalgia for the small town need not be construed as directed toward the town itself: it is rather a "quest for community" (as Robert Nisbet puts it)—a nostalgia for a compassable and integral living unit. The critical question is not whether the small town can be rehabilitated in the image of its earlier strength and growth—for clearly it cannot—but whether American life will be able to evolve any other integral community to replace it. This is what I call the problem of place in America, and unless it is somehow resolved, American life will become more jangled and fragmented than it is, and American personality will continue to be unquiet and unfulfilled.
>
> MAX LERNER, *America as a Civilization*, 1957

The ensuing years have confirmed Lerner's diagnosis. The problem of place in America has not been resolved and life *has* become more jangled and fragmented. No new form of integral community has been found; the small town has yet to greet its replacement. And Americans are not a contented people.

What may have seemed like the new form of community—the automobile suburb—multiplied rapidly after World War II. Thirteen million plus returning veterans qualified for single-family dwellings requiring no down payments in the new developments. In building and equipping these millions of new private domains, American industry found a major alternative to military production and companionate marriages appeared to have found ideal nesting places. But we did not live happily ever after.

Life in the subdivision may have satisfied the combat veteran's longing for a safe, orderly, and quiet haven, but it rarely offered the sense of place and belonging that had rooted his parents and grandparents. Houses alone do not a community make, and the typical subdivision proved hostile to the emergence of any structure or space utilization beyond the uniform houses and streets that characterized it.

Like all-residential city blocks, observed one student of the American condition, the suburb is "merely a base from which the individual reaches out to the scattered components of social existence."[1] Though proclaimed as offering the best of both rural and urban life, the automobile suburb had the effect of fragmenting the individual's world. As one observer wrote: "A man works in one place, sleeps in another, shops somewhere else, finds pleasure or companionship where he can, and cares about none of these places."

The typical suburban home is easy to leave behind as its occupants   *5* move to another. What people cherish most in them can be taken along in the move. There are no sad farewells at the local taverns or the corner store because there are no local taverns or corner stores. Indeed, there is often more encouragement to leave a given subdivision than to stay in it, for neither the homes nor the neighborhoods are equipped to see families or individuals through the cycle of life. Each is designed for families of particular sizes, incomes, and ages. There is little sense of place and even less opportunity to put down roots.

Transplanted Europeans are acutely aware of the lack of a community life in our residential areas. We recently talked with an outgoing lady who had lived in many countries and was used to adapting to local ways. The problem of place in America had become her problem as well:

> After four years here, I still feel more of a foreigner than in any other place in the world I have been. People here are proud to live in a "good" area, but to us these so-called desirable areas are like prisons. There is no contact between the various households, we rarely see the neighbors and certainly do not know any of them. In Luxembourg, however, we would frequently stroll down to one of the local cafés in the evening, and there pass a very congenial few hours in the company of the local fireman, dentist, bank employee or whoever happened to be there at the time. There is no pleasure to be had in driving to a sleazy, dark bar where one keeps strictly to one's self and becomes fearful if approached by some drunk.

Sounding the same note, Kenneth Harris has commented on one of the things British people miss most in the United States. It is some reasonable approximation of the village inn or local pub; our neighborhoods do not have it. Harris comments: "The American does not walk around to the local two or three times a week with his wife or with his son, to have his pint, chat with the neighbors, and then walk home. He does not take out the dog last thing every night, and break his journey with a quick one at the Crown."[2]

The contrast in cultures is keenly felt by those who enjoy a dual residence in Europe and America. Victor Gruen and his wife have a large place in Los Angeles and a small one in Vienna. He finds that: "In Los Angeles we are hesitant to leave our sheltered home in order to visit friends or to participate in cultural or entertainment events because every such outing involves a major investment of time and nervous strain in driving long distances."[3] But, he says, the European experience is much different: "In Vienna, we are persuaded to go out often because we are within easy walking distance of two concert halls, the opera, a number of theatres, and a variety of restaurants, cafés, and shops. Seeing old friends does not have to be a prearranged affair as in Los Angeles, and more often than not, one bumps into them on the street or in a café." The Gruens have a hundred times more residential space in America but give the impression that they don't enjoy it half as much as their little corner of Vienna.

But one needn't call upon foreign visitors to point up the shortcomings of the suburban experiment. As a setting for marriage and family life, it has given those institutions a bad name. By the 1960s, a picture had emerged of the suburban housewife as "bored, isolated, and preoccupied with material things."[4] The suburban wife without a car to escape in epitomized the experience of being alone in America.[5] Those who could afford it compensated for the loneliness, isolation, and lack of community with the "frantic scheduling syndrome" as described by a counselor in the northeastern region of the United States:

> The loneliness I'm most familiar with in my job is that of wives and mothers of small children who are dumped in the suburbs and whose husbands are commuters . . . I see a lot of generalized loneliness, but I think that in well-to-do communities they cover it up with a wealth of frantic activity. That's the reason tennis has gotten so big. They all go out and play tennis.[6]

A majority of the former stay-at-home wives are now in the labor force. As both father and mother gain some semblance of a community life via their daily escapes from the subdivision, children are even more cut off from ties with adults. Home offers less and the neighborhood offers nothing for the typical suburban adolescent. The situation in the early seventies as described by Richard Sennett is worsening:

> In the past ten years, many middle-class children have tried to break out of the communities, the schools and the homes that their parents have spent so much of their own lives creating. If any one feeling can be said to run through the diverse groups and lifestyles of the youth movements, it is a feeling that these middle-class communities of the parents were like pens, like cages keeping the youth from being free and alive. The source of the feeling lies in the perception that while these middle-class environments are secure and orderly regimes, people suffocate there for lack of the new, the unexpected, the diverse in their lives.[7]

The adolescent houseguest, I would suggest, is probably the best and quickest test of the vitality of a neighborhood; the visiting teenager in the subdivision soon acts like an animal in a cage. He or she paces, looks unhappy and uncomfortable, and by the second day is putting heavy pressure on the parents to leave. There is no place to which they can escape and join their own kind. There is nothing for them to do on their own. There is nothing in the surroundings but the houses of strangers and nobody on the streets. Adults make a more successful adjustment, largely because they demand less. But few at any age find vitality in the housing developments. David Riesman, an esteemed elder statesman among social scientists, once attempted to describe the import of suburbia upon most of those who live there. "There would seem," he wrote, "to be an aimlessness, a pervasive low-keyed unpleasure."[8] The word he seemed averse to using is *boring.* A teenager would not have had to struggle for the right phrasing.

Their failure to solve the problem of place in America and to provide a community life for their inhabitants has not effectively discouraged the growth of the postwar suburbs. To the contrary, there have emerged new generations of suburban development in which there is even less life outside the houses than before. Why does failure succeed? Dolores Hayden supplies part of the answer when she observes that Americans have substituted the vision of the ideal home for that of the ideal city.[9] The purchase of the even larger home on the even larger lot in the even more lifeless neighborhood is not so much a matter of joining community as retreating from it. Encouraged by a continuing decline in the civilities and amenities of the public or shared environment, people invest more hopes in their private acreage. They proceed as though a house can substitute for a community if only it is spacious enough, entertaining enough, comfortable enough, splendid enough—and suitably isolated from that common horde that politicians still refer to as our "fellow Americans."

Observers disagree about the reasons for the growing estrangement between the family and the city in American society.[10] Richard Sennett, whose research spans several generations, argues that as soon as an American family became middle class and could afford to do something about its fear of the outside world and its confusions, it drew in upon itself, and "in America, unlike France or Germany, the urban middle-class shunned public forms of social life like cafés and banquet halls."[11] Philippe Ariès, who also knows his history, counters with the argument that modern urban development has killed the essential relationships that once made a city and, as a consequence, "the role of the family overexpanded like a hypertrophied cell" trying to take up the slack.[12]

In some countries, television broadcasting is suspended one night a week so that people will not abandon the habit of getting out of their homes and maintaining contact with one another. This tactic would probably not work in America. Sennett would argue that the middle-class family, given its assessment of the public domain, would stay at home anyway. Ariès would argue that most would stay home for want of places to get together with their friends and neighbors. As Richard Goodwin declared, "there is virtually no place where neighbors can anticipate unplanned meetings—no pub or corner store or park."[13] The bright spot in this dispute is that the same set of remedies would cure both the family and the city of major ills.

Meantime, new generations are encouraged to shun a community life
in favor of a highly privatized one and to set personal aggrandizement
above public good. The attitudes may be learned from parents but they are
also learned in each generation's experiences. The modest housing developments, those *un*exclusive suburbs from which middle-class people graduate as they grow older and more affluent, teach their residents that future
hopes for a good life are pretty much confined to one's house and yard.
Community life amid tract housing is a disappointing experience. The
space within the development has been equipped and staged for isolated
family living and little else. The processes by which potential friends might
find one another and by which friendships not suited to the home might
be nurtured outside it are severely thwarted by the limited features and
facilities of the modern suburb.

The housing development's lack of informal social centers or informal public gathering places puts people too much at the mercy of their
closest neighbors. The small town taught us that people's best friends and
favorite companions rarely lived right next door to one another. Why
should it be any different in the automobile suburbs? What are the odds,
given that a hundred households are within easy walking distance, that one
is most likely to hit it off with the people next door? Small! Yet, the closest
neighbors are the ones with whom friendships are most likely to be attempted, for how does one even find out enough about someone a block
and a half away to justify an introduction?

What opportunity is there for two men who both enjoy shooting,
fishing, or flying to get together and gab if their families are not compati-
ble? Where do people entertain and enjoy one another if, for whatever
reason, they are not comfortable in one another's homes? Where do people
have a chance to get to know one another casually and without commitment before deciding whether to involve other family members in their
relationship? Tract housing offers no such places.

Getting together with neighbors in the development entails considerable hosting efforts, and it depends upon continuing good relationships
between households and their members. In the usual course of things,
these relationships are easily strained or ruptured. Having been lately
formed and built on little, they are not easy to mend. Worse, some of the
few good friends will move and are not easily replaced. In time, the over-
tures toward friendship, neighborliness, and a semblance of community
hardly seem worth the effort.

In the Absence of an Informal Public Life

We have noted Sennett's observation that middle-class Americans are
not like their French or German counterparts. Americans do not make
daily visits to sidewalk cafés or banquet halls. We do not have that third
realm of satisfaction and social cohesion beyond the portals of home and
work that for others is an essential element of the good life. Our comings

and goings are more restricted to the home and work settings, and those two spheres have become preemptive. Multitudes shuttle back and forth between the "womb" and the "rat race" in a constricted pattern of daily life that easily generates the familiar desire to "get away from it all."

A two-stop model of daily routine is becoming fixed in our habits as the urban environment affords less opportunity for public relaxation. Our most familiar gathering centers are disappearing rapidly. The proportion of beer and spirits consumed in public places has declined from about 90 percent of the total in the late 1940s to about 30 percent today.[14] There's been a similar decline in the number of neighborhood taverns in which those beverages are sold. For those who avoid alcoholic refreshments and prefer the drugstore soda fountain across the street, the situation has gotten even worse. By the 1960s, it was clear that the soda fountain and the lunch counter no longer had a place in "the balanced drug store."[15] "In this day of heavy unionization and rising minimum wages for unskilled help, the traditional soda fountain should be thrown out," advised an expert on drugstore management. And so it has been. The new kinds of places emphasize fast service, not slow and easy relaxation.

In the absence of an informal public life, people's expectations toward work and family life have escalated beyond the capacity of those institutions to meet them. Domestic and work relationships are pressed to supply all that is wanting and much that is missing in the constricted life-styles of those without community. The resulting strain on work and family institutions is glaringly evident. In the measure of its disorganization and deterioration, the middle-class family of today resembles the low-income family of the 1960s.[16] The United States now leads the world in the rate of divorce among its population. Fatherless children comprise the fastest-growing segment of the infant population. The strains that have eroded the traditional family configuration have given rise to alternate life-styles, and though their appearance suggests the luxury of choice, none are as satisfactory as was the traditional family when embedded in a supporting community.

It is estimated that American industry loses from $50 billion to $75 billion annually due to absenteeism, company-paid medical expenses, and lost productivity.[17] Stress in the lives of the workers is a major cause of these industrial losses. Two-thirds of the visits to family physicians in the United States are prompted by stress-related problems.[18] "Our mode of life," says one medical practitioner, "is emerging as today's principal cause of illness."[19] Writes Claudia Wallis, "It is a sorry sign of the times that the three best-selling drugs in the country are an ulcer medication (Tagamet), a hypertension drug (Inderal), and a tranquilizer (Valium)."[20]

In the absence of an informal public life, Americans are denied those means of relieving stress that serve other cultures so effectively. We seem not to realize that the means of relieving stress can just as easily be built into an urban environment as those features which produce stress. To our considerable misfortune, the pleasures of the city have been largely reduced

20

to consumerism. We don't much enjoy our cities because they're not very enjoyable. The mode of urban life that has become our principal cause of illness resembles a pressure cooker without its essential safety valve. Our urban environment is like an engine that runs hot because it was designed without a cooling system.

Unfortunately, opinion leans toward the view that the causes of stress are social but the cures are individual. It is widely assumed that high levels of stress are an unavoidable condition of modern life, that these are built into the social system, and that one must get outside the system in order to gain relief. Even our efforts at entertaining and being entertained tend toward the competitive and stressful. We come dangerously close to the notion that one "gets sick" in the world beyond one's domicile and one "gets well" by retreating from it. Thus, while Germans relax amid the rousing company of the *bier garten* or the French recuperate in their animated little bistros, Americans turn to massaging, meditating, jogging, hot-tubbing, or escape fiction. While others take full advantage of their freedom to associate, we glorify our freedom *not* to associate.

In the absence of an informal public life, living becomes more expensive. Where the means and facilities for relaxation and leisure are not publicly shared, they become the objects of private ownership and consumption. In the United States, about two-thirds of the GNP is based on personal consumption expenditures. That category, observes Goodwin, contains "the alienated substance of mankind."[21] Some four *trillion* dollars spent for individual aggrandizement represents a powerful divisive force indeed. In our society, insists one expert on the subject, leisure has been perverted into consumption.[22] An aggressive, driving force behind this perversion is advertising, which conditions "our drive to consume and to own whatever industry produces."[23]

Paragons of self-righteousness, advertisers promulgate the notion that society would languish in a state of inertia but for their efforts. "Nothing happens until somebody sells something," they love to say. That may be true enough within a strictly commercial world (and for them, what else is there?) but the development of an informal public life depends upon people finding and enjoying one another outside the cash nexus. Advertising, in its ideology and effects, is the enemy of an informal public life. It breeds alienation. It convinces people that the good life can be individually purchased. In the place of the shared camaraderie of people who see themselves as equals, the ideology of advertising substitutes competitive acquisition. It is the difference between loving people for what they are and envying them for what they own. It is no coincidence that cultures with a highly developed informal public life have a disdain for advertising.[24]

The tremendous advantage enjoyed by societies with a well-developed informal public life is that, within them, poverty carries few burdens other than that of having to live a rather Spartan existence. But there is no stigma and little deprivation of experience. There is an engaging and sustaining public life to supplement and complement home and work routines. For

25

those on tight budgets who live in some degree of austerity, it compensates for the lack of things owned privately. For the affluent, it offers much that money can't buy.

The American middle-class life-style is an exceedingly expensive one—especially when measured against the satisfaction it yields. The paucity of collective rituals and unplanned social gatherings puts a formidable burden upon the individual to overcome the social isolation that threatens. Where there are homes without a connection to community, where houses are located in areas devoid of congenial meeting places, the enemy called boredom is ever at the gate. Much money must be spent to compensate for the sterility of the surrounding environment. Home decoration and redecoration becomes a never-ending process as people depend upon new wallpaper or furniture arrangements to add zest to their lives. Like the bored and idle rich, they look to new clothing fashions for the same purpose and buy new wardrobes well before the old ones are past service. A lively round of after-dinner conversation isn't as simple as a walk to the corner pub—one has to host the dinner.

The home entertainment industry thrives in the dearth of the informal public life among the American middle class. Demand for all manner of electronic gadgetry to substitute vicarious watching and listening for more direct involvement is high. Little expense is spared in the installation of sound and video systems, VCRs, cable connections, or that current version of heaven on earth for the socially exiled—the satellite dish. So great is the demand for electronic entertainment that it cannot be met with quality programming. Those who create for this insatiable demand must rely on formula and imitation.

Everyone old enough to drive finds it necessary to make frequent   *30* escapes from the private compound located amid hundreds of other private compounds. To do so, each needs a car, and that car is a means of conveyance as privatized and antisocial as the neighborhoods themselves. Fords and "Chevys" now cost from ten to fifteen thousand dollars, and the additional expenses of maintaining, insuring, and fueling them constitute major expenditures for most families. Worse, each drives his or her own car. About the only need that suburbanites can satisfy by means of an easy walk is that which impels them toward their bathroom.

In the absence of an informal public life, industry must also compensate for the missing opportunity for social relaxation. When the settings for casual socializing are not provided in the neighborhoods, people compensate in the workplace. Coffee breaks are more than mere rest periods; they are depended upon more for sociable human contact than physical relaxation. These and other "time-outs" are extended. Lunch hours often afford a sufficient amount of reveling to render the remainder of the working day ineffectual. The distinction between work-related communications and "shooting the breeze" becomes blurred. Once-clear parameters separating work from play become confused. The individual finds that neither work nor play are as satisfying as they should be.

The problem of place in America manifests itself in a sorely deficient informal public life. The structure of shared experience beyond that offered by family, job, and passive consumerism is small and dwindling. The essential group experience is being replaced by the exaggerated self-consciousness of individuals. American life-styles, for all the material acquisition and the seeking after comforts and pleasures, are plagued by boredom, loneliness, alienation, and a high price tag. America can point to many areas where she has made progress, but in the area of informal public life she has lost ground and continues to lose it.

Unlike many frontiers, that of the informal public life does not remain benign as it awaits development. It does not become easier to tame as technology evolves, as governmental bureaus and agencies multiply, or as population grows. It does not yield to the mere passage of time and a policy of letting the chips fall where they may as development proceeds in other realms of urban life. To the contrary, neglect of the informal public life can make a jungle of what had been a garden while, at the same time, diminishing the ability of people to cultivate it.

In the sustained absence of a healthy and vigorous informal public life, the citizenry may quite literally forget how to create one. A facilitating public etiquette consisting of rituals necessary to the meeting, greeting, and enjoyment of strangers is not much in evidence in the United States. It is replaced by a set of strategies designed to avoid contact with people in public, by devices intended to preserve the individual's circle of privacy against any stranger who might violate it. Urban sophistication is deteriorating into such matters as knowing who is safe on whose "turf," learning to minimize expression and bodily contact when in public, and other survival skills required in a world devoid of the amenities. Lyn Lofland notes that the 1962 edition of Amy Vanderbilt's *New Complete Book of Etiquette* "contains not a single reference to proper behavior in the world of strangers."[25] The cosmopolitan promise of our cities is diminished. Its ecumenic spirit fades with our ever-increasing retreat into privacy.

Toward a Solution: The Third Place

Though none can prescribe the total solution to the problem of place in America, it is possible to describe some important elements that any solution will have to include. Certain basic requirements of an informal public life do not change, nor does a healthy society advance beyond them. To the extent that a thriving informal public life belongs to a society's past, so do the best of its days, and prospects for the future should be cause for considerable concern.

Towns and cities that afford their populations an engaging public life are easy to identify. What urban sociologists refer to as their interstitial spaces are filled with people. The streets and sidewalks, parks and squares, parkways and boulevards are being used by people sitting, standing, and walking. Prominent public space is not reserved for that well-dressed, middle-class crowd that is welcomed at today's shopping malls. The elderly and poor, the ragged and infirm, are interspersed among those looking and doing well. The full spectrum of local humanity is represented. Most of the streets are as much the domain of the pedestrian as of the motorist. The typical street can still accommodate a full-sized perambulator and still encourages a new mother's outing with her baby. Places to sit are abundant. Children play in the streets. The general scene is much as the set director for a movie would arrange it to show life in a wholesome and thriving town or city neighborhood.

Beyond the impression that a human scale has been preserved in the architecture, however, or that the cars haven't defeated the pedestrians in the battle for the streets, or that the pace of life suggests gentler and less complicated times, the picture doesn't reveal the *dynamics* needed to produce an engaging informal public life. The secret of a society at peace with itself is not revealed in the panoramic view but in examination of the average citizen's situation.

The examples set by societies that have solved the problem of place and those set by the small towns and vital neighborhoods of our past suggest that daily life, in order to be relaxed and fulfilling, must find its balance in three realms of experience. One is domestic, a second is gainful or productive, and the third is inclusively sociable, offering both the basis of community and the celebration of it. Each of these realms of human experience is built on associations and relationships appropriate to it; each has its own physically separate and distinct places; each must have its measure of autonomy from the others.

What the panoramic view of the vital city fails to reveal is that the third realm of experience is as distinct a place as home or office. The informal public life only seems amorphous and scattered; in reality, it is highly focused. It emerges and is sustained in *core settings*. Where the problem of place has been solved, a generous proliferation of core settings of informal public life is sufficient to the needs of the people.

Pierre Salinger was asked how he liked living in France and how he would compare it with life in the United States. His response was that he likes France where, he said, everyone is more relaxed. In America, there's a lot of pressure. The French, of course, have solved the problem of place. The Frenchman's daily life sits firmly on a tripod consisting of home, place of work, and another setting where friends are engaged during the midday and evening *aperitif* hours, if not earlier and later. In the United States, the middle classes particularly are attempting a balancing act on a bipod consisting of home and work. That alienation, boredom, and stress are endemic among us is not surprising. For most of us, a third of life is either deficient or absent altogether, and the other two-thirds cannot be successfully integrated into a whole.

Before the core settings of an informal public life can be restored to the urban landscape and reestablished in daily life, it will be necessary to articulate their nature and benefit. It will not suffice to describe them in a mystical or romanticized way such as might warm the hearts of those already convinced. Rather, the core settings of the informal public life must be analyzed and discussed in terms comprehensible to these rational and individualistic outlooks dominant in American thought. We must dissect, talk in terms of specific payoffs, and reduce special experiences to common labels. We must, urgently, begin to defend these Great Good Places against the unbelieving and the antagonistic and do so in terms clear to all.

The object of our focus—the core settings of the informal public life—begs for a simpler label. Common parlance offers few possibilities and none that combine brevity with objectivity and an appeal to common sense. There is the term *hangout,* but its connotation is negative and the word conjures up images of the joint or dive. Though we refer to the meeting places of the lowly as hangouts, we rarely apply the term to yacht clubs or oak-paneled bars, the "hangouts" of the "better people." We have nothing as respectable as the French *rendez-vous* to refer to a public meeting place or a setting in which friends get together away from the confines of home and work. The American language reflects the American reality—in vocabulary as in fact the core settings of an informal public life are underdeveloped.

For want of a suitable existing term, we introduce our own: the third place will hereafter be used to signify what we have called "the core settings of informal public life." The third place is a generic designation for a great variety of public places that host the regular, voluntary, informal, and happily anticipated gatherings of individuals beyond the realms of home and work. The term will serve well. It is neutral, brief, and facile. It underscores the significance of the tripod and the relative importance of its three legs. Thus, the first place is the home—the most important place of all. It is the first regular and predictable environment of the growing child and the one that will have greater effect upon his or her development. It will harbor individuals long before the workplace is interested in them and well after the world of work casts them aside. The second place is the work setting, which reduces the individual to a single, productive role. It fosters competition and motivates people to rise above their fellow creatures. But it also provides the means to a living, improves the material quality of life, and structures endless hours of time for a majority who could not structure it on their own.

Before industrialization, the first and second places were one. Industrialization separated the place of work from the place of residence, removing productive work from the home and making it remote in distance, morality, and spirit from family life. What we now call the third place existed long before this separation, and so our term is a concession to the sweeping effects of the Industrial Revolution and its division of life into private and public spheres.

The ranking of the three places corresponds with individual dependence upon them. We need a home even though we may not work, and most of us need to work more than we need to gather with our friends and neighbors. The ranking holds, also, with respect to the demands upon the individual's time. Typically, the individual spends more time at home than at work and more at work than in a third place. In importance, in claims on time and loyalty, in space allocated, and in social recognition, the ranking is appropriate.

In some countries, the third place is more closely ranked with the others. In Ireland, France, or Greece, the core settings of informal public life rank a *strong* third in the lives of the people. In the United States, third places rank a weak third with perhaps the majority lacking a third place and denying that it has any real importance.

The prominence of third places varies with cultural setting and historical era. In preliterate societies, the third place was actually foremost, being the grandest structure in the village and commanding the central location. They were the men's houses, the earliest ancestors of those grand, elegant, and pretentious clubs eventually to appear along London's Pall Mall. In both Greek and Roman society, prevailing values dictated that the *agora* and the *forum* should be great, central institutions; that homes should be simple and unpretentious; that the architecture of cities should assert the worth of the public and civic individual over the private and domestic one. Few means to lure and invite citizens into public gatherings were overlooked. The forums, colosseums, theaters, and ampitheaters were grand structures, and admission to them was free.

Third places have never since been as prominent. Attempts at elegance and grand scale continued to be made but with far less impact. Many cultures evolved public baths on a grand scale. Victorian gin palaces were elegant (especially when contrasted to the squalor that surrounded them). The winter gardens and palm gardens built in some of our northern cities in the previous century included many large and imposing structures. In modern times, however, third places survive without much prominence or elegance.

Where third places remain vital in the lives of people today, it is far more because they are prolific than prominent. The geographic expansion of the cities and their growing diversity of quarters, or distinct neighborhoods, necessitated the shift. The proliferation of smaller establishments kept them at the human scale and available to all in the face of increasing urbanization.

In the newer American communities, however, third places are nei-   50
ther prominent nor prolific. They are largely prohibited. Upon an urban landscape increasingly hostile to and devoid of informal gathering places, one may encounter people rather pathetically trying to find some spot in which to relax and enjoy each other's company.

Sometimes three or four pickups are parked under the shade near a convenience store as their owners drink beers that may be purchased but not consumed inside. If the habit ever really catches on, laws will be passed to stop it. Along the strips, youths sometimes gather in or near their cars in the parking lots of hamburger franchises. It's the best they can manage, for they aren't allowed to loiter inside. One may encounter a group of women in a laundromat, socializing while doing the laundry chores. One encounters parents who have assumed the expense of adding a room to the house or converting the garage to a recreation room so that, within neighborhoods that offer them nothing, their children might have a decent place to spend time with their friends. Sometimes too, youth will develop a special attachment to a patch of woods not yet bulldozed away in the relentless spread of the suburbs. In such a place they enjoy relief from the confining overfamiliarity of their tract houses and the monotonous streets.

American planners and developers have shown a great disdain for those earlier arrangements in which there was life beyond home and work. They have condemned the neighborhood tavern and disallowed a suburban version. They have failed to provide modern counterparts of once-familiar gathering places. The gristmill or grain elevator, soda fountains, malt shops, candy stores, and cigar stores—places that did not reduce a human being to a mere customer, have not been replaced. Meantime, the planners and developers continue to add to the rows of regimented loneliness in neighborhoods so sterile as to cry out for something as modest as a central mail drop or a little coffee counter at which those in the area might discover one another.

Americans are now confronted with that condition about which the crusty old arch-conservative Edmund Burke warned us when he said that the bonds of community are broken at great peril for they are not easily replaced. Indeed, we face the enormous task of making "the mess that is urban America" suitably hospitable to the requirements of gregarious, social animals.[26] Before motivation or wisdom is adequate to the task, however, we shall need to understand exactly what it is that an informal public life can contribute to both national and individual life. Therein lies the purpose of this book.

Successful exposition demands that some statement of a problem precede a discussion of its solution. Hence, I've begun on sour and unpleasant notes and will find it necessary to sound them again. I would have preferred it otherwise. It is the solution that intrigues and delights. It is my hope that the discussion of life in the third place will have a similar effect upon the reader, just as I hope that the reader will allow the bias that now and then prompts me to substitute Great Good Place for third place. I am confident that those readers who have a third place will not object.

Notes

1. Richard N. Goodwin, "The American Condition," *The New Yorker* (28 January 1974), 38.
2. Kenneth Harris, *Travelling Tongues* (London: John Murray, 1949), 80.
3. Victor Gruen, *Centers for Urban Environment* (New York: Van Nostrand Reinhold Co., 1973), 217.

4. Philip E. Slater, "Must Marriage Cheat Today's Young Women?" *Redbook Magazine* (February 1971).

5. Suzanne Gordon, *Lonely in America* (New York: Simon & Schuster, 1976).

6. *Ibid.,* 105.

7. Richard Sennett, "The Brutality of Modern Families," in *Marriages and Families,* ed. Helena Z. Lopata. (New York: D. Van Nostrand Company, 1973), 81.

8. David Riesman, "The Suburban Dislocation," *The Annals of the American Academy of Political and Social Science* (November 1957), 142.

9. Dolores Hayden, *Redesigning the American Dream* (New York: W. W. Norton & Company, 1984), Chapter 2.

10. See Sennett (*op. cit.*) and Aries, Philippe. "The Family and the City." *Daedalus,* Spring, 1977. Pp. 227–237 for succinct statements of the two views.

11. Sennett, *op. cit.,* 84.

12. Philippe Aries, "The Family and the City," *Daedalus* (Spring 1977), 227.

13. Goodwin, *op. cit.,* 38.

14. P. F. Kluge, "Closing Time," *Wall Street Journal* (27 May 1982).

15. Frank L. Ferguson, *Efficient Drug Store Management* (New York: Fairchild Publications, 1969), 202.

16. Urie Bronfenbrenner, "The American Family: An Ecological Perspective," in *The American Family: Current Perspectives* (Cambridge, Mass.: Harvard University Press, Audiovisual Division, 1979), (audio cassette).

17. Claudia Wallis, "Stress: Can We Cope?" *Time* (6 June 1983).

18. *Ibid.*

19. *Ibid.*

20. *Ibid.*

21. Richard Goodwin, "The American Condition," *New Yorker* (4 February 1970) 75.

22. Thomas M. Kando, *Leisure and Popular Culture in Transition,* 2d ed. (St. Louis: The C. V. Mosby Company, 1980).

23. *Ibid.,* 101.

24. Generally, the Mediterranean cultures.

25. Lyn H. Lofland, *A World of Strangers* (Prospect Heights, Ill.: Waveland Press, Inc., 1973), 117.

26. Sometimes the phrase employed is "the mess that is man-made America." Planners appear to use it as much as anyone else.

Reading and Responding

1. This is a carefully organized and sequenced piece. Outline it, paying attention to Oldenburg's use of subheadings and topic sentences at the beginning of paragraphs.

2. Is Ray Oldenburg easy or hard to read? He's the most textbookish writer in this section (not necessarily in a negative sense): Is that a problem or a strength for you? Compare him to Wolfe: Did you have an easier or harder time understanding Oldenburg's main points?

3. Do a short page of freewriting explaining anything in the reading that complicated or confused something you've taken for granted. That is, have you ever thought about anything Oldenburg discusses before? Does it make sense now? Does Oldenburg help you see something you didn't see before? Does he make you uneasy?

Working Together

1. Write a quick page (1) summarizing what Oldenburg means by a "third place" and (2) giving an example from your own experience, some "third place" you often go to, on campus or back home.

   • Sitting in a group of three to five, pass the pages around, round-robin style: pass to the right, read that piece, pass to the right again, read another piece—continue until you get your own piece back.

   • With all these ideas in mind, discuss the following questions as a group. What is Oldenburg saying? Are there third places in your lives?

2. Find the section where Oldenburg contrasts American and European experience; once you've found this section, list three or four features of what Oldenburg identifies as European. Once you have that list, think about your own college campus; how does your campus fit (or not fit) those European features?

Rethinking and Rewriting

1. Write an essay explaining Oldenburg's idea of the third place and describing that kind of place in your own experience. Assume that your readers haven't read "The Problem of Place in America," and make sure that your essay tells them what they need to know.

2. Go to a third place, take notes on everything you see and hear for an hour, and write a portrait of that place, a profile. At some point, include Oldenburg's definition.

3. At the heart of Oldenburg's critique is an analysis of how the car has completely changed the structure of our cities and towns and the rhythms of our lives. Keep a log for a week recording how often you drive your car, where you drive your car, how far, and so on. Take notes, too, on where you live, the size of your garage, how close you are to other houses, whether you drive to malls, how many of the places you drive to are designed expressly for cars, and so on. (If you're living on campus now, you might compare the arrangement and design of the

buildings and the use of cars there with the design of your city or neighborhood back home.) Write an essay. Try imagining living for a week without your car: What wouldn't you be able to do? How would you go about your daily routines? Finally, try to imagine your hometown or neighborhood without cars. What would it look like? What redesigning would be necessary?

4. Using CD-ROM and other sources in the library, gather and synthesize information from the past five years on the environmental impact of automobiles. Gather figures on pollution, automobile accidents, mass transit or the lack of it, and so on. (You might want to look in particular at the effect of the 1994 Los Angeles earthquake on traffic patterns there and the lives of the people.) (See also John McPhee's "Duty of Care.") Write an informative paper outlining some of the major problems and issues.

5. Write a paper arguing that people should stop driving to your campus or that additional bus service should be implemented. Use your library research to support your argument. (See Wendell Berry's "Out of Your Car, Off Your Horse.")

"ENCLOSED. ENCYCLOPEDIC. ENDURED. ONE WEEK AT THE MALL OF AMERICA"

David Guterson

The author of an earlier book on education, Family Matters: Why Home Schooling Makes Sense, *David Guterson is a frequent contributor to* Harper's Magazine, *where this essay first appeared. In this piece Guterson's writing combines factual research with his own intellectual and emotional responses in an effort to come to some clear understanding of both Minneapolis's Mall of America and the country and society that has spent $625 million to build such a place.*

Last April, on a visit to the new Mall of America near Minneapolis, I carried with me the public-relations press kit provided for the benefit of reporters. It included an assortment of "fun facts" about the mall: 140,000 hot dogs sold each week, 10,000 permanent jobs, 44 escalators and 17 elevators, 12,750 parking places, 13,300 short tons of steel, $1 million in cash disbursed weekly from 8 automatic-teller machines. Opened in the summer of 1992, the mall was built on the 78-acre site of the former Metropolitan Stadium, a five-minute drive from the Minneapolis–St. Paul International Airport. With 4.2 million square feet of floor space—including twenty-two times the retail footage of the average American shopping center—the Mall of America was "the largest fully enclosed combination retail and family entertainment complex in the United States."

Eleven thousand articles, the press kit warned me, had already been written on the mall. Four hundred trees had been planted in its gardens, $625 million had been spent to build it, 350 stores had been leased. Three thousand bus tours were anticipated each year along with a half-million Canadian visitors and 200,000 Japanese tourists. Sales were projected at $650 million for 1993 and at $1 billion for 1996. Donny and Marie Osmond had visited the mall, as had Janet Jackson and Sally Jesse Raphael, Arnold Schwarzenegger, and the 1994 Winter Olympic Committee. The mall was five times larger than Red Square and twenty times larger than St. Peter's Basilica; it incorporated 2.3 miles of hallways and almost twice as much steel as the Eiffel Tower. It was also home to the nation's largest indoor theme park, a place called Knott's Camp Snoopy.

On the night I arrived, a Saturday, the mall was spotlit dramatically in the manner of a Las Vegas casino. It resembled, from the outside, a castle or fort, the Emerald City or Never-Never Land, impossibly large and vaguely unreal, an unbroken, windowless multi-storied edifice the size of an airport terminal. Surrounded by parking lots and new freeway ramps, monolithic and imposing in the manner of a walled city, it loomed brightly against the Minnesota night sky with the disturbing magnetism of a mirage.

I knew already that the Mall of America had been imagined by its creators not merely as a marketplace but as a national tourist attraction, an immense zone of entertainments. Such a conceit raised provocative questions, for our architecture testifies to our view of ourselves and to the condition of our souls. Large buildings stand as markers in the lives of nations and in the stream of a people's history. Thus I could only ask myself: Here was a new structure that had cost more than half a billion dollars to erect—what might it tell us about ourselves? If the Mall of America was part of America, what was that going to mean?

I passed through one of the mall's enormous entranceways and took   5
myself inside. Although from a distance the Mall of America had appeared menacing—exuding the ambience of a monstrous hallucination—within it turned out to be simply a shopping mall, certainly more vast than other malls but in tone and aspect, design and feel, not readily distinguishable from them. Its nuances were instantly familiar as the generic features of the American shopping mall at the tail end of the twentieth century: polished stone, polished tile, shiny chrome and brass, terrazzo floors, gazebos. From third-floor vistas, across vaulted spaces, the Mall of America felt endlessly textured—glass-enclosed elevators, neon-tube lighting, bridges, balconies, gas lamps, vaulted skylights—and densely crowded with hordes of people circumambulating in an endless promenade. Yet despite the mall's expansiveness, it elicited claustrophobia, sensory deprivation, and an unnerving disorientation. Everywhere I went I spied other pilgrims who had found, like me, that the straight way was lost and that the YOU ARE HERE landmarks on the map kiosks referred to nothing in particular.

Getting lost, feeling lost, being lost—these states of mind are intentional features of the mall's psychological terrain. There are, one notices, no clocks or windows, nothing to distract the shopper's psyche from the alternate reality the mall conjures. Here we are free to wander endlessly and to furtively watch our fellow wanderers, thousands upon thousands of milling strangers who have come with the intent of losing themselves in the mall's grand, stimulating design. For a few hours we share some common ground—a fantasy of infinite commodities and comforts—and then we drift apart forever. The mall exploits our acquisitive instincts without honoring our communal requirements, our eternal desire for discourse and intimacy, needs that until the twentieth century were traditionally met in our marketplaces but that are not met at all in giant shopping malls.

On this evening a few thousand young people had descended on the mall in pursuit of alcohol and entertainment. They had come to Gators, Hooters, and Knuckleheads, Puzzles, Fat Tuesday, and Ltl Ditty's. At Players, a sports bar, the woman beside me introduced herself as "the pregnant wife of an Iowa pig farmer" and explained that she had driven five hours with friends to "do the mall party scene together." She left and was replaced by Kathleen from Minnetonka, who claimed to have "a real shopping thing—I can't go a week without buying new clothes. I'm not fulfilled until I buy something."

Later a woman named Laura arrived, with whom Kathleen was acquainted. "I *am* the mall," she announced ecstatically upon discovering I was a reporter. "I'd move in here if I could bring my dog," she added. "This place is heaven, it's a *mecca.*"

"We egg each other on," explained Kathleen, calmly puffing on a cigarette. "It's like, sort of, an addiction."

"You want the truth?" Laura asked. "I'm constantly suffering from   10
megamall withdrawal. I come here all the time."

Kathleen: "It's a sickness. It's like cocaine or something; it's a drug."

Laura: "Kathleen's got this thing about buying, but I just need to *be* here. If I buy something it's an added bonus."

Kathleen: "She buys stuff all the time; don't listen."

Laura: "Seriously, I feel sorry for other malls. They're so small and *boring.*"

Kathleen seemed to think about this: "Richdale Mall," she blurted   15
finally. She rolled her eyes and gestured with her cigarette. "Oh, my God, Laura. Why did we even *go* there?"

There is, of course, nothing naturally abhorrent in the human impulse to dwell in marketplaces or the urge to buy, sell, and trade. Rural Americans traditionally looked forward to the excitement and sensuality of market day; Native Americans traveled long distances to barter and trade at sprawling, festive encampments. In Persian bazaars and in the ancient Greek agoras the very soul of the community was preserved and could be seen, felt, heard, and smelled as it might be nowhere else. All over the planet the humblest of people have always gone to market with hope in their hearts and in expectation of something beyond mere goods—seeking a place where humanity is temporarily in ascendance, a palette for the senses, one another.

But the illicit possibilities of the marketplace also have long been acknowledged. The Persian bazaar was closed at sundown; the Greek agora was off-limits to those who had been charged with certain crimes. One myth of the Old West we still carry with us is that market day presupposes danger; the faithful were advised to make purchases quickly and repair without delay to the farm, lest their attraction to the pleasures of the marketplace erode their purity of spirit.

In our collective discourse the shopping mall appears with the tract house, the freeway, and the backyard barbecue as a product of the American postwar years, a testament to contemporary necessities and desires and an invention not only peculiarly American but peculiarly of our own era too. Yet the mall's varied and far-flung predecessors—the covered bazaars of the Middle East, the stately arcades of Victorian England, Italy's vaulted and skylit galleries, Asia's monsoon-protected urban markets—all suggest that the rituals of indoor shopping, although in their nuances not often like our own, are nevertheless broadly known. The late twentieth-century American contribution has been to transform the enclosed bazaar into an economic institution that is vastly profitable yet socially enervated, one that redefines in fundamental ways the human relationship to the marketplace. At the Mall of America—an extreme example—we discover ourselves thoroughly lost among strangers in a marketplace intentionally designed to serve no community needs.

In the strict sense the Mall of America is not a marketplace at all—the soul of a community expressed as a *place*—but rather a tourist attraction. Its promoters have peddled it to the world at large as something more profound than a local marketplace and as a destination with deep implications. "I believe we can make Mall of America stand for all of America," asserted the mall's general manager, John Wheeler, in a promotional video entitled *There's a Place for Fun in Your Life.* "I believe there's a shopper in all of us," added the director of marketing, Maureen Hooley. The mall has memorialized its opening-day proceedings by producing a celebratory videotape: Ray Charles singing "America the Beautiful," a laser show followed by fireworks, "The Star-Spangled Banner" and "The Stars and Stripes Forever," the Gatlin Brothers, and Peter Graves. "Mall of America . . . ," its narrator intoned. "The name alone conjures up images of greatness, of a retail complex so magnificent it could only happen in America."

Indeed, on the day the mall opened, Miss America visited. The mall's   20
logo—a red, white, and blue star bisected by a red, white, and blue ribbon—decorated everything from the mall itself to coffee mugs and the flanks of buses. The idea, director of tourism Colleen Hayes told me, was to position America's largest mall as an institution on the scale of Disneyland or the Grand Canyon, a place simultaneously iconic and totemic, a revered symbol of the United States and a mecca to which the faithful would flock in pursuit of all things purchasable.

On Sunday I wandered the hallways of the pleasure dome with the sensation that I had entered an M. C. Escher drawing—there was no such thing as up or down, and the escalators all ran backward. A 1993 Ford Probe GT was displayed as if popping out of a giant packing box; a full-size home, complete with artificial lawn, had been built in the mall's rotunda. At the Michael Ricker Pewter Gallery I came across a miniature tableau of a pewter dog peeing on a pewter man's leg; at Hologram Land I pondered 3-D hallucinations of the Medusa and Marilyn Monroe. I passed a kiosk called The Sportsman's Wife; I stood beside a life-size statue of the Hamm's Bear, carved out of pine and available for $1,395 at a store called Minnesot-ah! At Pueblo Spirit I examined a "dream catcher"—a small hoop made from deer sinew and willow twigs and designed to be hung over its owner's bed as a tactic for filtering bad dreams. For a while I sat in front of Glamour Shots and watched while women were groomed and brushed for photo sessions yielding high-fashion self-portraits at $34.95

each. There was no stopping, no slowing down. I passed Mug Me, Queen for a Day, and Barnyard Buddies, and stood in the Brookstone store examining a catalogue: a gopher "eliminator" for $40 (it's a vibrating, anodized-aluminum stake), a "no-stoop" shoehorn for $10, a nose-hair trimmer for $18. At the arcade inside Knott's Camp Snoopy I watched while teenagers played Guardians of the 'Hood, Total Carnage, Final Fight, and Varth Operation Thunderstorm; a small crowd of them had gathered around a lean, cool character who stood calmly shooting video cowpokes in a game called Mad Dog McCree. Left thumb on his silver belt buckle, biceps pulsing, he banged away without remorse while dozens of his enemies crumpled and died in alleyways and dusty streets.

At Amazing Pictures a teenage boy had his photograph taken as a bodybuilder—his face smoothly grafted onto a rippling body—then proceeded to purchase this pleasing image on a poster, a sweatshirt, and a coffee mug. At Painted Tipi there was wild rice for sale, hand-harvested from Leech Lake, Minnesota. At Animalia I came across a polyresin figurine of a turtle retailing for $3,200. At Bloomingdale's I pondered a denim shirt with its sleeves ripped away, the sort of thing available at used-clothing stores (the "grunge look," a Bloomingdale's employee explained), on sale for $125. Finally, at a gift shop in Knott's Camp Snoopy, I came across a game called Electronic Mall Madness, put out by Milton Bradley. On the box, three twelve-year-old girls with good features happily vied to beat one another to the game-board mall's best sales.

At last I achieved an enforced self-arrest, anchoring myself against a bench while the mall tilted on its axis. Two pubescent girls in retainers and braces sat beside me sipping coffees topped with whipped cream and chocolate sprinkles, their shopping bags gathered tightly around their legs, their eyes fixed on the passing crowds. They came, they said, from Shakopee— "It's nowhere," one of them explained. The megamall, she added, was "a buzz at first, but now it seems pretty normal. 'Cept my parents are like Twenty Questions every time I want to come here. 'Specially since the shooting."

On a Sunday night, she elaborated, three people had been wounded when shots were fired in a dispute over a San Jose Sharks jacket. "In the *mall,*" her friend reminded me. "Right here at megamall. A shooting."

"It's like nowhere's safe," the first added.   *25*

They sipped their coffees and explicated for me the plot of a film they saw as relevant, a horror movie called *Dawn of the Dead,* which they had each viewed a half-dozen times. In the film, they explained, apocalypse had come, and the survivors had repaired to a shopping mall as the most likely place to make their last stand in a poisoned, impossible world. And this would have been perfectly all right, they insisted, except that the place had also attracted hordes of the infamous living dead—sentient corpses who had not relinquished their attraction to indoor shopping.

I moved on and contemplated a computerized cash register in the infant's section of the Nordstrom store: "The Answer Is Yes!!!" its monitor reminded clerks. "Customer Service Is Our Number One Priority!" Then back at Bloomingdale's I contemplated a bank of televisions playing incessantly an advertisement for Egoïste, a men's cologne from Chanel. In the ad a woman on a wrought-iron balcony tossed her black hair about and screamed long and passionately; then there were many women screaming passionately, too, and throwing balcony shutters open and closed, and this was all followed by a bottle of the cologne displayed where I could get a good look at it. The brief, strange drama repeated itself until I could no longer stand it.

America's first fully enclosed shopping center—Southdale Center, in Edina, Minnesota—is a ten-minute drive from the Mall of America and thirty-six years its senior. (It is no coincidence that the Twin Cities area is such a prominent player in mall history: Minnesota is subject to the sort of severe weather that makes climate-controlled shopping seductive.) Opened in 1956, Southdale spawned an era of fervid mall construction and generated a vast new industry. Shopping centers proliferated so rapidly that by the end of 1992, says the National Research Bureau, there were nearly 39,000 of them operating everywhere across the country. But while malls recorded a much-ballyhooed success in the America of the 1970s and early 1980s, they gradually became less profitable to run as the exhausted and overwhelmed American worker inevitably lost interest in leisure shopping. Pressed for time and short on money, shoppers turned to factory outlet centers, catalogue purchasing, and "category killers" (specialty stores such as Home Depot and Price Club) at the expense of shopping malls. The industry, unnerved, re-invented itself, relying on smaller and more convenient local centers—especially the familiar neighborhood strip mall—and building far fewer large regional malls in an effort to stay afloat through troubled times. With the advent of cable television's Home Shopping Network and the proliferation of specialty catalogue retailers (whose access to computerized market research has made them, in the Nineties, powerful competitors), the mall industry reeled yet further. According to the International Council of Shopping Centers, new mall construction in 1992 was a third of what it had been in 1989, and the value of mall-construction contracts dropped 60 percent in the same three-year period.

Anticipating a future in which millions of Americans will prefer to shop in the security of their living rooms—conveniently accessing online retail companies as a form of quiet evening entertainment—the mall industry, after less than forty years, experienced a full-blown mid-life crisis. It was necessary for the industry to re-invent itself once more, this time with greater attentiveness to the qualities that would allow it to endure relentless change. Anxiety-ridden and sapped of vitality, mall builders fell back on an ancient truth, one capable of sustaining them through troubled seasons: they discovered what humanity had always understood, that shopping and frivolity go hand in hand and are inherently symbiotic. *If you build it fun, they will come.*

The new bread-and-circuses approach to mall building was first ven-   *30*
tured in 1985 by the four Ghermezian brothers—Raphael, Nader, Bah-
man, and Eskandar—builders of Canada's $750 million West Edmonton
Mall, which included a water slide, an artificial lake, a miniature-golf
course, a hockey rink, and forty-seven rides in an amusement park known
as Fantasyland. The complex quickly generated sales revenues at twice the
rate per square foot of retail space that could be squeezed from a conventional outlet mall, mostly by developing its own shopping synergy: people
came for a variety of reasons and to do a variety of things. West Edmonton's carnival atmosphere, it gradually emerged, lubricated pocketbooks
and inspired the sort of impulse buying on which malls everywhere thrive.
To put the matter another way, it was time for a shopping-and-pleasure
palace to be attempted in the United States.

After selling the Mall of America concept to Minnesotans in 1985,
the Ghermezians joined forces with their American counterparts—Mel
and Herb Simon of Indianapolis, owners of the NBA's Indiana Pacers and
the nation's second-largest developers of shopping malls. The idea, in the
beginning, was to outdo West Edmonton by building a mall far larger and
more expensive—something visionary, a wonder of the world—and to
include such attractions as fashionable hotels, an elaborate tour de force
aquarium, and a monorail to the Minneapolis–St. Paul airport. Eventually
the project was downscaled substantially: a million square feet of floor space
was eliminated, the construction budget was cut, and the aquarium and
hotels were never built (reserved, said marketing director Maureen Hooley,
for "phase two" of the mall's development). Japan's Mitsubishi Bank, Mitsui
Trust, and Chuo Trust together put up a reported $400 million to finance
the cost of construction, and Teachers Insurance and Annuity Association
(the majority owner of the Mall of America) came through with another
$225 million. At a total bill of $625 million, the mall was ultimately a less
ambitious project than its forebear up north on the Canadian plains, and
neither as large nor as gaudy. Reflecting the economy's downturn, the
parent companies of three of the mall's anchor tenants—Sears, Macy's, and
Bloomingdale's—were battling serious financial trouble and needed substantial transfusions from mall developers to have their stores ready by
opening day.

The mall expects to spend millions on marketing itself during its
initial year of operation and has lined up the usual corporate sponsors—
Ford, Pepsi, US West—in an effort to build powerful alliances. Its public-
relations representatives travel to towns such as Rapid City, South Dakota,
and Sioux City, Iowa, in order to drum up interest within the Farm Belt.
Northwest Airlines, another corporate sponsor, offers package deals from
London and Tokyo and fare adjustments for those willing to come from
Bismarck, North Dakota; Cedar Rapids, Iowa; and Kalamazoo or Grand
Rapids, Michigan. Calling itself a "premier tourism destination," the mall
draws from a primary tourist market that incorporates the eleven Midwest
states (and two Canadian provinces) lying within a day's drive of its parking
lots. It also estimates that in its first six months of operation, 5.3 million

out of 16 million visitors came from beyond the Twin Cities metropolitan area.

The mall has forecast a much-doubted figure of 46 million annual visits by 1996—four times the number of annual visits to Disneyland, for example, and twelve times the visits to the Grand Canyon. The number, Maureen Hooley explained, seems far less absurd when one takes into account that mall pilgrims make far more repeat visits—as many as eighty in a single year—than visitors to theme parks such as Disneyland. Relentless advertising and shrewd promotion, abetted by the work of journalists like myself, assure the mall that visitors will come in droves—at least for the time being. The national media have comported themselves as if the new mall were a place of light and promise, full of hope and possibility. Meanwhile the Twin Cities' media have been shameless: on opening night Minneapolis's WCCO-TV aired a one-hour mall special, hosted by local news anchors Don Shelby and Colleen Needles, and the *St. Paul Pioneer Press* (which was named an "official" sponsor of the opening) dedicated both a phone line and a weekly column to answering esoteric mall questions. Not to be outdone, the *Minneapolis Star Tribune* developed a special graphic to draw readers to mall stories and printed a vast Sunday supplement before opening day under the heading A WHOLE NEW MALLGAME. By the following Wednesday all perspective was in eclipse: the local press reported that at 9:05 a.m., the mall's Victoria's Secret outlet had recorded its first sale, a pair of blue/green silk men's boxer shorts; that mall developers Mel and Herb Simon ate black-bean soup for lunch at 12:30 p.m.; that Kimberly Levis, four years old, constructed a rectangular column nineteen bricks high at the mall's Lego Imagination Center; and that mall officials had retained a plumber on standby in case difficulties arose with the mall's toilets.

From all of this coverage—and from the words you now read—the mall gains status as a phenomenon worthy of our time and consideration: place as celebrity. The media encourage us to visit our megamall in the obligatory fashion we flock to *Jurassic Park*—because it is there, all glitter and glow, a piece of the terrain, a season's diversion, an assumption on the cultural landscape. All of us will want to be in on the conversation and, despite ourselves, we will go.

Lost in the fun house I shopped till I dropped, but the scale of the mall eventually overwhelmed me and I was unable to make a purchase. Finally I met Chuck Brand on a bench in Knott's Camp Snoopy; he was seventy-two and, in his personal assessment of it, had lost at least 25 percent of his mind. "It's fun being a doozy," he confessed to me. "The security cops got me figured and keep their distance. I don't get hassled for hanging out, not shopping. Because the deal is, when you're seventy-two, man, you're just about all done shopping."

After forty-seven years of selling houses in Minneapolis, Chuck comes to the mall every day. He carries a business card with his picture on it, his company name and phone number deleted and replaced by his pager

35

code. His wife drops him at the mall at 10:00 a.m. each morning and picks him up again at six; in between he sits and watches. "I can't sit home and do nothing," he insisted. When I stood to go he assured me he understood: I was young and had things I had to do. "Listen," he added, "thanks for talking to me, man. I've been sitting in this mall for four months now and nobody ever said nothing."

The next day I descended into the mall's enormous basement, where its business offices are located. "I'm sorry to have to bring this up," my prearranged mall guide, Michelle Biesiada, greeted me. "But you were seen talking to one of our housekeepers—one of the people who empty the garbage?—and really, you aren't supposed to do that."

Later we sat in the mall's security center, a subterranean computerized command post where two uniformed officers manned a bank of television screens. The Mall of America, it emerged, employed 109 surveillance cameras to monitor the various activities of its guests, and had plans to add yet more. There were cameras in the food courts and parking lots, in the hallways and in Knott's Camp Snoopy. From where we sat, it was possible to monitor thirty-six locations simultaneously; it was also possible, with the use of a zoom feature, to narrow in on an object as small as a hand, a license plate, or a wallet.

While we sat in the darkness of the security room, enjoying the voyeuristic pleasures it allowed (I, for one, felt a giddy sense of power), a security guard noted something of interest occurring in one of the parking lots. The guard engaged a camera's zoom feature, and soon we were given to understand that a couple of bored shoppers were enjoying themselves by fornicating in the front seat of a parked car. An officer was dispatched to knock on their door and discreetly suggest that they move themselves along; the Mall of America was no place for this. "If they want to have sex they'll have to go elsewhere," a security officer told me. "We don't have anything against sex, per se, but we don't want it happening in our parking lots."

I left soon afterward for a tour of the mall's basement, a place of perpetual concrete corridors and home to a much-touted recyclery. Declaring itself "the most environmentally conscious shopping center in the industry," the Mall of America claims to recycle up to 80 percent of its considerable refuse and points to its "state-of-the-art" recycling system as a symbol of its dedication to Mother Earth. Yet Rick Doering of Browning-Ferris Industries—the company contracted to manage the mall's 700 tons of monthly garbage—described the on-site facility as primarily a public-relations gambit that actually recycles only a third of the mall's tenant waste and little of what is discarded by its thousands of visitors; furthermore, he admitted, the venture is unprofitable to Browning-Ferris, which would find it far cheaper to recycle the mall's refuse somewhere other than in its basement.

A third-floor "RecycleNOW Center," located next to Macy's and featuring educational exhibits, is designed to enhance the mall's self-styled

40

image as a national recycling leader. Yet while the mall's developers gave Macy's $35 million to cover most of its "build-out" expenses (the cost of transforming the mall's basic structure into finished, customer-ready floor space), Browning-Ferris got nothing in build-out costs and operates the center at a total loss, paying rent equivalent to that paid by the mall's retailers. As a result, the company has had to look for ways to keep its costs to a minimum, and the mall's garbage is now sorted by developmentally disabled adults working a conveyor belt in the basement. Doering and I stood watching them as they picked at a stream of paper and plastic bottles; when I asked about their pay, he flinched and grimaced, then deflected me toward another supervisor, who said that wages were based on daily productivity. Did this mean that they made less than minimum wage? I inquired. The answer was yes.

Upstairs once again, I hoped for relief from the basement's oppressive, concrete gloom, but the mall felt densely crowded and with panicked urgency I made an effort to leave. I ended up instead at Knott's Camp Snoopy—the seven-acre theme park at the center of the complex—a place intended to alleviate claustrophobia by "bringing the outdoors indoors." Its interior landscape, the press kit claims, "was inspired by Minnesota's natural habitat—forests, meadows, river banks, and marshes . . ." And "everything you see, feel, smell and hear adds to the illusion that it's summertime, seventy degrees and you're outside enjoying the awesome splendor of the Minnesota woods."

Creators of this illusion had much to contend with, including sixteen carnival-style midway rides, such as the Pepsi Ripsaw, the Screaming Yellow Eagle, Paul Bunyan's Log Chute by Brawny, Tumbler, Truckin', and Huff 'n' Puff; fifteen places for visitors to eat, such as Funnel Cakes, Stick Dogs and Campfire Burgers, Taters, Pizza Oven, and Wilderness Barbecue; seven shops with names like Snoopy's Boutique, Joe Cool's Hot Shop, and Camp Snoopy Toys; and such assorted attractions as Pan for Gold, Hunter's Paradise Shooting Gallery, the Snoopy Fountain, and the video arcade that includes the game Mad Dog McCree.

As if all this were not enough to cast a serious pall over the Minnesota woods illusion, the theme park's designers had to contend with the fact that they could use few plants native to Minnesota. At a constant temperature of seventy degrees, the mall lends itself almost exclusively to tropical varieties— orange jasmine, black olive, oleander, hibiscus—and not at all to the conifers of Minnesota, which require a cold dormancy period. Deferring ineluctably to this troubling reality, Knott's Camp Snoopy brought in 526 tons of plants—tropical rhododendrons, willow figs, buddhist pines, azaleas—from such places as Florida, Georgia, and Mississippi.

Anne Pryor, a Camp Snoopy marketing representative, explained to me that these plants were cared for via something called "integrated pest management," which meant the use of predators such as ladybugs instead of pesticides. Yet every member of the landscape staff I spoke to described a campaign of late-night pesticide spraying as a means of controlling the theme park's enemies—mealybugs, aphids, and spider mites. Two said they had argued for integrated pest management as a more environmentally sound method of controlling insects but that to date it had not been tried.

Even granting that Camp Snoopy is what it claims to be—an authentic version of Minnesota's north woods tended by environmentally correct means—the question remains whether it makes sense to place a forest in the middle of the country's largest shopping complex. Isn't it true that if people want woods, they are better off not going to a mall?

On Valentine's Day last February—cashing in on the promotional scheme of a local radio station—ninety-two couples were married en masse in a ceremony at the Mall of America. They rode the roller coaster and the Screaming Yellow Eagle and were photographed beside a frolicking Snoopy, who wore an immaculate tuxedo. "As we stand here together at the Mall of America," presiding district judge Richard Spicer declared, "we are reminded that there is a place for fun in your life and you have found it in each other." Six months earlier, the Reverend Leith Anderson of the Wooddale Church in Eden Prairie conducted services in the mall's rotunda. Six thousand people had congregated by 10:00 a.m., and Reverend Anderson delivered a sermon entitled "The Unknown God of the Mall." Characterizing the mall as a "direct descendant" of the ancient Greek agoras, the reverend pointed out that, like the Greeks before us, we Americans have many gods. Afterward, of course, the flock went shopping, much to the chagrin of Reverend Delton Krueger, president of the Mall Area Religious Council, who told the *Minneapolis Star Tribune* that as a site for church services, the mall may trivialize religion. "A good many people in the churches," said Krueger, "feel a lot of the trouble in the world is because of materialism."

But a good many people in the mall business today apparently think the trouble lies elsewhere. They are moving forward aggressively on the premise that the dawning era of electronic shopping does not preclude the building of shopping-and-pleasure palaces all around the globe. Japanese developers, in a joint venture with the Ghermezians known as International Malls Incorporated, are planning a $400 million Mall of Japan, with an ice rink, a water park, a fantasy-theme hotel, three breweries, waterfalls, and a sports center. We might shortly predict, too, a Mall of Europe, a Mall of New England, a Mall of California, and perhaps even a Mall of the World. The concept of shopping in a frivolous atmosphere, concocted to loosen consumers' wallets, is poised to proliferate globally. We will soon see monster malls everywhere, rooted in the soil of every nation and offering a preposterous, impossible variety of commodities and entertainments.

The new malls will be planets unto themselves, closed off from this world in the manner of space stations or of science fiction's underground cities. Like the Mall of America and West Edmonton Mall—prototypes for a new generation of shopping centers—they will project a separate and distinct reality in which an "outdoor café" is not outdoors, a "bubbling brook" is a concrete watercourse, and a "serpentine street" is a hallway. Safe, surreal, and outside of time and space, they will offer the mind a potent dreamscape from which there is no present waking. This carefully controlled fantasy—now operable in Minnesota—is so powerful as to inspire psychological addiction or to elicit in visitors a catatonic obsession with the mall's various hallucinations. The new malls will be theatrical, high-tech illusions capable of attracting enormous crowds from distant points and foreign ports. Their psychology has not yet been tried pervasively on the scale of the Mall of America, nor has it been perfected. But in time our marketplaces, all over the world, will be in essential ways interchangeable, so thoroughly divorced from the communities in which they sit that they will appear to rest like permanently docked spaceships against the landscape, windowless and turned in upon their own affairs. The affluent will travel as tourists to each, visiting the holy sites and taking photographs in the catacombs of far-flung temples.

Just as Victorian England is acutely revealed beneath the grandiose   *50* domes of its overwrought train stations, so is contemporary America well understood from the upper vistas of its shopping malls, places without either windows or clocks where the temperature is forever seventy degrees. It is facile to believe, from this vantage point, that the endless circumambulations of tens of thousands of strangers—all loaded down with the detritus of commerce—resemble anything akin to community. The shopping mall is not, as the architecture critic Witold Rybczynski has concluded, "poised to become a real urban place" with "a variety of commercial and noncommercial functions." On the contrary, it is poised to multiply around the world as an institution offering only a desolate substitute for the rich, communal lifeblood of the traditional marketplace, which will not survive its onslaught.

Standing on the Mall of America's roof, where I had ventured to inspect its massive ventilation units, I finally achieved a full sense of its vastness, of how it overwhelmed the surrounding terrain—the last sheep farm in sight, the Mississippi River incidental in the distance. Then I peered through the skylights down into Camp Snoopy, where throngs of my fellow citizens caroused happily in the vast entrails of the beast.

Reading and Responding

1. David Guterson starts this piece by giving you quite a number of facts. What's your response to these facts? In a paragraph or so, talk about the effects they have on you.
2. Once Guterson gets inside the mall, he both observes (tells you what he sees, hears, and so on) and judges (tells you what he thinks of what he sees, hears, and so on). As you read, make a list of these observations; and next to it, make a list of his judgments.

Working Together

1. Look closely at how Guterson ends this piece. Paying special attention to this ending, see whether you can summarize his main points in a paragraph.

2. As a group, talk about how reading Guterson's piece has made you think about malls in new ways. Phrased another way, how has reading Guterson changed the way you look at malls? What aspects of his view are new to you?

Rethinking and Rewriting

1. Go to a mall and take your notebook with you. As you walk in and walk around, assume that the mall is a town. What's in this town? What's not in this town? Who lives in this town? Who do you not see in this town? Is it pleasant to be in this town? Is it not pleasant to be in this town? What can you do here, and what can you not do here? Finally, draw on your notes and experience and write an essay that presents your answers to these questions and ends by discussing the advantages and the disadvantages of this town.

2. As you look at David Guterson's piece, does his writing seem objective and neutral, or does it seem as though Guterson wants to convince you of something? In an essay, describe at least one section where the writing seems objective, and describe another where you feel the writing wants to convince readers of something. End your essay by arguing either that Guterson is, in fact, a neutral observer or that he writes to persuade.

"NO RMS, JUNGLE VU"

Melissa Greene

> *In her first book of nonfiction,* Praying for Sheetrock *(1991), freelance writer Melissa Greene describes the struggle for civil rights in McIntosh Country, Georgia. In this earlier essay from the December 1987* Atlantic Monthly, *printed here in a slightly shorter form, she explores the very different topic of zoo design. Zoos, like malls, are quite carefully and consciously constructed worlds. The piece comes last in this chapter because it looks forward both to chapter 7, "Excursions" (going to a zoo is usually an excursion), and to chapter 8, "Observing the Other" (since we go to zoos to observe other animals).*

As You Read

As you read, pay particular attention to the description of the Woodland Park gorilla exhibit. Ask yourself why Melissa Greene allows so many words for this part of her essay. Sometimes writers feel that if they give too much detail, readers will be bored. Does Greene give too much detail here? Are you bored? Write a half page or so that talks about this idea.

"The Egyptians have been civilized for four thousand years . . . my own ancestors probably a lot less," Jon Charles Coe says. "We evolved over millions of years in the wild, where survival depended on our awareness of the landscape, the weather, and the animals. We haven't been domesticated long enough to have lost those senses. In my opinion, it is the business of the zoo to slice right through that sophisticated veneer, to recall us to our origins. I judge the effectiveness of a zoo exhibit in the pulse rate of the zoo-goer. We can design a zoo that will make the hair stand up on the back of your neck."

A revolution is under way in zoo design, which was estimated to be a $20 million business last year. Jon Coe and Grant Jones are the vanguard. Coe, forty-six, is a stocky man with a long, curly beard. He is an associate professor of landscape architecture at the University of Pennsylvania and a senior partner in the zoo-design firm of Coe Lee Robinson Roesch, in Philadelphia. Grant Jones, a senior partner in the architectural firm Jones & Jones, in Seattle, is at forty-eight a trendsetter in the design of riverfront areas, botanical gardens, and historical parks, as well as zoos. Coe and Jones were classmates at the Harvard School of Design, and Coe worked for Jones & Jones until 1981.

Ten years ago in Seattle they created the Woodland Park gorilla exhibit in collaboration with Dennis Paulson, a biologist, and with David

Hancocks, an architect and the director of the Woodland Park Zoo. The exhibit is still praised by experts as the best ever done. It has become an international standard for the replication of wilderness in a zoo exhibit and for the art of including and engaging the zoo-goer. Dian Fossey, the field scientist who lived for fifteen years near the wild mountain gorillas of Rwanda before her murder there, in December of 1985, flew to Seattle as a consultant to the designers of Woodland Park. When the exhibit was completed, Johnpaul Jones, Grant Jones's partner (the two are not related), sent photographs to her. She wrote back that she had shown the photos to her colleagues at the field station and they had believed them to be photos of wild gorillas in Rwanda. "Your firm, under the guidance of [Mr.] Hancocks, has made a tremendously important advancement toward the captivity conditions of gorillas," Fossey wrote. "Had such existed in the past, there would undoubtedly be more gorillas living in captivity."

"Woodland Park has remained a model for the zoo world," says Terry Maple, the new director of Zoo Atlanta, a professor of comparative psychology (a field that examines the common origins of animal and human behavior) at the Georgia Institute of Technology, and the author of numerous texts and articles on primate behavior. "Woodland Park changed the way we looked at the zoo environment. Before Woodland Park, if the gorillas weren't in cages, they were on beautiful mown lawns, surrounded by moats. In good zoos they had playground equipment. In Woodland Park the staff had to teach the public not to complain that the gorilla exhibit looked unkempt."

"As far as gorilla habitats go," Maple says, "Cincinnati's is pretty good;   5
San Diego's is pretty good; Columbus's has a huge cage, so aesthetically it loses a great deal, but socially it's terrific; San Francisco's is a more technical solution, naturalistic but surrounded by walls. Woodland Park's is the best in the world."

In Woodland Park the zoo-goer must step off the broad paved central boulevard onto a narrow path engulfed by vegetation to get to the gorillas. Coe planted a big-leaf magnolia horizontally, into the bank of a man-made hill, so that it would grow over the path. ("People forget that a landscape architect not only can do this," he said on a recent tour of the exhibit, indicating a pretty circle of peonies, "but can also do *this*"—he pointed to a shaggy, weed-covered little hill. "I *designed* that hill.")

The path leads to a wooden lean-to with a glass wall on one side that looks into a rich, weedy, humid clearing. Half a dozen heavy-set, agile gorillas part the tall grasses, stroll leaning on their knuckles, and sit nonchalantly among clumps of comfrey, gnawing celery stalks. The blue-black sheen of their faces and fur on a field of green is electrifying. The social organization of the gorillas is expressed by their interaction around a couple of boulders in the foreground of the exhibit. All the gorillas enjoy climbing on the boulders, but the young ones yield to their elders and the adult females yield to the adult males, two silverback gorillas. The silverbacks drum their chests with their fists rapidly and perfunctorily while briefly rising on two feet—not at all like Tarzan. The fists make a rapid thudding noise, which seems to mean, "Here I come." Each silverback climbs to his rostrum, folds his arms, and glares at the other. As in nature, their relationship is by turns civil but not friendly, and contentious but not bullying.

The zoo-goers in the lean-to, observing all this, feel fortunate that the troop of gorillas chooses to stay in view, when it apparently has acres and acres in which to romp. Moss-covered boulders overlap other boulders in the distance, a stream fringed with ferns wanders among them, birds roost in the forty-foot-high treetops, and caves and nests beyond the bend in the stream are available to the gorillas as a place of retreat. "Flight distance" is the zoological term for the distance an animal needs to retreat from an approaching creature in order to feel safe—the size of the cushion of empty space it wishes to maintain around itself. (Several years ago Jon Coe accepted an assignment to design a nursing home, a conventional job that was unusual for him. He designed the home with flight distance. Sitting rooms and visiting areas were spacious near the front door but grew smaller as one progressed down the hall toward the residents' rooms. A resident overwhelmed by too much bustle in the outer areas could retreat down the hall to quieter and quieter environments.)

In fact the gorillas in Woodland Park do not have so much space to explore. The exhibit is 13,570 square feet (about a third of an acre), which is generous but not limitless. The arrangement of overlapping boulders and trees in the distance is meant to trick the eye. There are no fences or walls against which to calculate depth, and the visitor's peripheral vision is deliberately limited by the dimensions of the lean-to. Wider vision might allow a visitor to calculate his position within Woodland Park, or might give him an inappropriate glimpse—as happens in almost every other zoo in the world—of a snowshoe rabbit or an Amazon porcupine or a North American zoo-goer, over the heads of the West African gorillas. Coe measured and calculated the sight lines to ensure that the view was an uncorrupted one into the heart of the rain forest.

The boulders themselves contain a trick. Coe designed them to con- *10* tain heating coils, so that in the miserable, misty Seattle winter they give off a warm aura, like an electric blanket. The boulders serve two purposes: they help the tropical gorillas put up with the Seattle winter, and they attract the gorillas to within several feet of the lean-to and the zoo-goers. It is no coincidence that much of the drama of the gorillas' everyday life is enacted three feet away from the lean-to. The patch of land in front of the lean-to is shady and cool in summer. The gorillas freely choose where to spend their day, but the odds have been weighted heavily in favor of their spending it in front of the lean-to.

"Their old exhibit was a six-hundred-square-foot tile bathroom," says Grant Jones, a tall, handsome, blue-eyed man. "The gorillas displayed a lot of very neurotic behavior. They were aggressive, sad, angry, lethargic. They had no flight distance. The people were behind the glass day and night, the people pounded on the glass, the gorillas were stressed out, totally, all the time. Their only way to deal with it was to sleep or to show intense anger. They'd pick up their own feces and smear it across the glass. They were not interacting with one another.

"My assumption was that when they left their cage to enter their new outdoor park, that behavior would persist. On the first day, although they were frightened when they came into the new park, they were tranquil. They'd never felt the wind; they'd never seen a bird fly over; they'd never seen water flowing except for the drain in the bottom of their cubicle. Instantly they became quiet and curious. The male was afraid to enter into the environment and stood at the door for hours. His mate came and took him by the hand and led him. They only went about halfway. They stopped at a small stream. They sat and picked up some leaves and dipped them in the water and took a bite of the leaves. They leaned back and saw clouds moving over. It was spellbinding. I assumed they would never recover from the trauma of how they'd been kept. It turned out to be a matter of two or three days."

"Picture the typical zoo exhibit," Jon Coe says. "You stroll along a sidewalk under evenly spaced spreading maples, beside colorful bedding plants. On your right is a polar-bear exhibit. There is a well-pruned hedge of boxwood with a graphic panel in it. The panel describes interesting features of the species, including the fact that polar bears often are seen swimming far out to sea. In the exhibit a bear is splashing in a bathtub. Very little is required of the viewers and very little is gained by them. The visitor is bored for two reasons: first because the setting is too obvious, and second because of a feeling of security despite the close presence of a wild animal.

"When planning this exhibit, we learned that in the wild, gorillas like to forage at the edge of a forest, in clearings created by tribal people who fell the trees, burn off the undergrowth, farm for a couple of years, then move on. After they move on, the forest moves back in and the gorillas forage there. We set about to re-create that scene. We got lots of charred stumps, and we took a huge dead tree from a power-line clearing a few miles from here. The story is plant succession, and how the gorillas exploit the early plants growing back over the abandoned farmland."

Coe relies on stagecraft and drama to break down the zoo-goer's   *15*
sense of security. When walking through a client zoo for the first time, long before he has prepared a master plan, he offers a few suggestions: Get rid of the tire swings in the chimp exhibit. Get rid of the signs saying NIMBA THE ELEPHANT and JOJO THE CHEETAH. Stop the publicized feeding of the animals, the baby elephant's birthday party, and any other element contributing to either an anthropomorphized view ("Do the elephants call each *other* Nimba and Bomba?") or a view of wild beasts as tame pets.

"How can we improve our ability to get and hold the attention of the zoo-goer?" he asks. "We must create a situation that transcends the range of stimulation people are used to and enhances the visitor's perception of the animal. A zoo animal that *appears* to be unrestrained and dangerous should receive our full attention, possibly accompanied by an adrenal rush, until its potential for doing us harm is determined."

For ten years Coe and others have been experimenting with the relative positions of zoo-goers and zoo animals. Coe now designs exhibits in which the animal terrain surrounds and is actually higher than the zoo paths, so that zoo-goers must look up to see the animals. The barriers between animals and people are camouflaged so effectively that zoo-goers may be uncertain whether an animal has access to them or not. In JungleWorld, the Bronx Zoo's recently opened $9.5 million indoor tropical forest nearly an acre in size, conceived by William Conway, the director of the zoo, a python lives inside a tree trunk that apparently has fallen across the zoo-goers' walkway. "We made the interior of the log brighter and tilted the glass away from the outside light to avoid all reflections," says Charles Beier, an associate curator. "It's an old jeweler's trick. When people glance overhead, there appears to be no barrier between them and the snake." The screams of horror provoked by the python are quite a different matter from the casual conversations that people engage in while strolling past rows of terrariums with snakes inside.

"We are trying to get people to be prepared to look for animals in the forest, not have everything brightly lighted and on a platform in front of them," says John Gwynne, the deputy director for design of the New York Zoological Society, which operates the Bronx Zoo. "We have lots of dead trees and dead grass in here. It's actually very hard to train a gardener not to cut off the dead branches. We're trying to create a wilderness, not a garden—something that can catch people by surprise."

The profession of zoo design is a relatively new one. In the past, when a zoo director said that a new lion house was required, the city council solicited bids and hired a popular local architect—the one who did the suburban hospital and the new high school—and paid him to fly around the country and get acquainted with lion houses. He visited four or five and learned design tips from each: how wide to space the bars, for example, and how thick to pour the cement. Then he flew home and drew a lion house.

"As recently as fifteen years ago there was no Jones & Jones or Jon   20
Coe," says William Conway, of the Bronx Zoo. "There were very few architects around then who had any concept of what animals were all about or who would go—as Jon Coe has gone—to Africa to see and sketch and try to understand, so that he knew what the biologist was talking about. The problem of the zoologist in the zoo was that, in the past, he was very often dealing with an architect who wanted to make a monument."

"The downfall of most zoos has been that they've hired architects," says Ace Torre, a designer in New Orleans, who holds degrees in architecture and landscape architecture. "Some of the more unfortunate zoos hired six different architects. Each one made his own statement. As a result, the zoo is a patchwork of architectural tributes."

In 1975 the City of Seattle asked Grant Jones, whose firm had restored the splendid Victorian copper-roofed pergolas and the elegant walkways and the granite statuary of the city's Pioneer Square Historic District, to design the Woodland Park Zoo gorilla house. The City of Seattle—specifically, David Hancocks, the zoo director—had made a novel choice. Jones was an anomaly in the world of architecture in that he prided himself on having never designed anything taller than three stories. Most of his buildings were made of wood, and they tended to be situated in national parks. Instead of making a grand tour of gorilla houses, Jones consulted field scientists and gorilla experts who had seen how gorillas lived in the wild.

"When they asked me to design a gorilla exhibit," Jones says, "I naturally rephrased the problem in my own mind as designing a landscape with gorillas in it. In what sort of landscape would I want to behold gorillas? I would want to include mystery and discovery. I'd like to see the gorillas from a distance first, and then up close. I'd like to be able to intrude on them and see what's going on without their knowing I'm there. I'd want to give them flight distance, a place to back off and feel secure. And I would want an experience that would take me back to a primordial depth myself. How did I spend my day some millions of years ago, living in proximity to this animal?"

"We asked Dian Fossey to visit Seattle," David Hancocks says, "and she became the most crucial member of the design team. We had so many people telling us we were being very foolish. A zoo director on the East Coast called to say he'd put a potted palm in a cage where a gorilla had lived for fifteen years. The gorilla pulled it out by the roots, ate it, and got sick."

"Driving in from the airport, we asked Fossey what the rain forest looked like," Jon Coe says. "She kept turning this way and that way in her seat, saying, 'It looks like that! It looks just like that!' Of course, Seattle is in a belt of temperate rain forest. Fossey was in an alpine tropical rain forest. The plants are not identical, but they are very similar. We realized that we could stand back and let the native plants take over the exhibit and the overall effect would be very much the same.

"And there were trees, forty-foot-tall trees, in the area slated for the gorillas. What to do about the trees? No zoo in the world had let gorillas have unlimited access to trees. We thought of the gorilla as a terrestrial animal. The wisdom at the time said that the trees had to come down. We brought George Schaller, probably the world's preeminent field scientist, to Seattle, and asked him about the trees. His response was, 'I don't know if they're going to fall out of them or not, but somebody has to do this.'"

"They didn't fall out of the trees," Jones says, "but Kiki [one of the silverbacks] escaped. We'd brought in some rock-climbers to try to get out of the exhibit when it was finished, and we'd made a few modifications based on their suggestions. Jon figured out an elaborate jumping matrix: if a gorilla can jump this far on the horizontal, how far can he go on a downward slope, et cetera. The problem is, you can't program in motivation. At some point the motivation may be so great that you'll find yourself saying, 'Whoops, the tiger can jump thirteen feet, not twelve. Guess we should have made it wider.'

"We had planted some hawthorn trees about four to five inches in diameter, ten feet high, and had hoped they were large enough that the gorillas would accept them. They accepted everything else, but these trees were standing too much alone, too conspicuous. Kiki pulled all the branches off of one, then ripped it out of the ground. It stood by itself; the roots were like a tripod. He played with that thing for a number of days.

"The keepers were aware of how we must never let them have a big long stick because they might put it across the moat, walk across it, and get out. They saw that tree but it was clearly not long enough to bridge the moat. We all discussed it, and decided it wasn't a problem. During that same period Kiki began disappearing for three hours at a time, and we didn't know where he was. It's a large environment, and he could have been off behind some shrubbery. One of the keepers told us later that he'd seen Kiki sitting on the edge of the big dry moat at the back of the habitat. One day Kiki climbed down into the moat.

"I imagine he took his tree with him to the far corner, leaned it up   *30* against the wall, and considered it. At some point he must have made a firm decision. He got a toehold on the roots, pressed his body to the wall, lifted himself up in one lunge, and hung from the top of the moat. Then he pulled himself up and landed in the rhododendrons. He was out, he was in the park."

"He was sitting in the bushes and some visitors saw him," Coe says. "They raced to the director's office and reported it to Hancocks." His response was calm, according to Coe. Anxious visitors often reported that there were gorillas loose in the trees. "The gorilla's not out," said Hancocks. "The exhibit, you see, is called landscape immersion. It's intended to give you the *impression* that the gorillas are free."

The visitors thanked Hancocks and left. He overheard one remark to the other, "Still, it just doesn't seem right having him sit there on the sidewalk like that."

"Sidewalk?" Hancocks said.

"We called the police," says Hancocks, "not to control the gorilla but to stop people from coming into the zoo. Jim Foster, the vet, fed fruit to Kiki and calmed him down while we tried to figure out what to do. We put a ladder across the moat and Jim climbed on it to show Kiki how to cross. Kiki actually tried it, but the ladder wobbled and fell, and he retreated. It was getting dark. We finally had to tranquilize him and carry him back."

"It's been seven years since," Jones says, "and Kiki never has tried   *35* again, although he clearly knows how to do it. He doesn't want to leave.

In fact I am frequently called in by zoos that are having problems with escape. They always want to know, Should we make the moats wider? The bars closer together? Should we chain the animal? Yet escape is almost never a design problem. It is a question of motivation. It is a social problem."

"One of the roles a silverback has in life," Coe says, "is to patrol his territory. Kiki wasn't escaping *from* something. He was exploring outward from the center of his territory to define its edges."

"If Kiki had escaped from a conventional ape house, the city would have panicked," Hancocks says. "But in the year or two the exhibit had been open, Seattle had lost the hairy-monster-of-the-ape-house image, and saw gorillas as quiet and gentle."

Shortly after, one of the local papers carried a cartoon of Kiki roller-skating arm-in-arm with two buxom beauties through the adjacent Green-lake Park, and another had a cartoon of him pole-vaulting over the moat.

The current revolution in zoo design—the landscape revolution—is driven by three kinds of change that have occurred during this century. First are great leaps in animal ecology, veterinary medicine, landscape design, and exhibit technology, making possible unprecedented realism in zoo exhibits. Second, and perhaps most important, is the progressive disappearance of wilderness—the very subject of zoos—from the earth. Third is knowledge derived from market research and from environmental psychology, making possible a sophisticated focus on the zoo-goer.

Zoo-related sciences like animal ecology and veterinary medicine for exotic animals barely existed fifty years ago and tremendous advances have been made in the last fifteen years. Zoo veterinarians now inoculate animals against diseases they once died of. Until recently, keeping the animals alive required most of a zoo's resources. A cage modeled after a scientific laboratory or an operating room—tile-lined and antiseptic, with a drain in the floor—was the best guarantee of continued physical health. In the late 1960s and early 1970s zoo veterinarians and comparative psychologists began to realize that stress was as great a danger as disease to the captive wild animals. Directors thus sought less stressful forms of confinement than the frequently-hosed-down sterile cell.

Field scientists also published findings about the complex social relations among wild animals. Zoos began to understand that captive animals who refused to mate often were reacting to the improper social configurations in which they were confined. Gorillas, for example, live in large groups in the wild. Zoos had put them in pairs, and then only at breeding time—"believing them monogamous, as we'd like to think we are," Coe says. Interaction between the male and the female gorilla was stilted, hostile, abnormal. Successful breeding among captive gorillas didn't begin until they were housed in large family groups. Golden lion tamarins, in contrast, refused to mate when they were caged in groups. Only very recently did researchers affiliated with the National Zoo discover that these beautiful little monkeys *are* monogamous.

Science first affected the design of zoos in 1735, when Linnaeus published his *Systema Naturae* and people fell in love with classification. The resultant primate house, carnivore house, and reptile house allowed the public to grasp the contemporary scientific understanding of the animal world. "At the turn of the century a zoo was a place where you went to learn what kinds of animals there were," Conway says. "The fact that they were in little cages didn't matter. You could see this was an Arabian oryx, a scimitar-horned oryx, a beisa oryx, and so on. It wasn't at that time so important to have an idea of what they do, or the way they live, or how they evolved." The taxonomic approach informed the design of science museums, aquariums, botanical gardens, and arboretums.

Today zoo directors and designers can draw on whole libraries of information about animal behavior and habitat. Exhibit designers can create entire forests of epoxy and fiber-glass trees, reinforced concrete boulders, waterfalls, and artificial vines, with mist provided by cloud machines. A zoo director can oversee the creation of astoundingly realistic habitats for the animals.

But zoo directors and designers cannot simply create magnificent animal habitats and call them a zoo. That would be something else—a wildlife preserve, a national park. A zoo director has to think about bathrooms: zoos are for people, not animals. A zoo director has to think about bond issues and the fact that the city council, which also finances garbage collection, trims a little more from his budget each year. He has to be aware that the zoo is competing with a vast entertainment industry for the leisure hours and dollars of the public.

"If you're not smiling at Disney World, you're fired the next day," says Robert Yokel, the director of the Miami Metrozoo. He is a laid-back, blue-jeaned, suntanned man with wild, scant hair. "Happy, happy, happy, that's the whole concept. They are the premier operators. They taught the rest of the industry how a park should be run: keep it clean, make it convenient, make the ability to spend dollars very easy. They do everything top drawer. They drew over thirteen million people last year. It's an escape. It's a fantasy." Obviously, the director of the Miami zoo, more than most, has to worry about Disney World. He is surrounded, as well, by Monkey Jungle, the Miami Seaquarium, Busch Gardens, Parrot Jungle, Orchid Jungle, Flamingo Gardens, Lion Country Safari, and the beach. If Florida legalizes gambling, he may never see anyone again. But Yokel is not alone in the zoo world in appreciating what commercial entertainment parks offer the public.

The public today has more leisure time and disposable income than ever before, more children than at any time since the 1950s, and more sophistication about animals—thanks to television, movies, and libraries—than at any time in history. Although a Greek in the age of Homer might not have been able to identify an anteater or a koala, many two-year-olds today can. However, there are other claims on people's time. Although, according to statistics, zoo-going is an entrenched habit with Americans, it is no longer likely that a station wagon packed with kids and heading down the highway on Sunday afternoon will turn in at the zoo. The family has been to Disney World, to Six Flags; they've been to theme parks where the hot-dog vendors wear period costumes and the concession stands look like log cabins; they've visited amusement parks where the whole environment, from the colorful banners to the trash cans, all sparkling clean and brightly painted, shrieks of fun. The local zoo, with its broad tree-lined avenues, pacing leopards, and sleeping bears, seems oddly antiquated and sobering by comparison. So zoo directors must ask, Are our visitors having a good time? Will they come back soon? Would they rather be at Disney World? What will really excite them?

Zoos used to be simpler. Once upon a time—in pharaonic Egypt, in Imperial Rome, in the Austro-Hungarian Empire, in the traveling menageries and bear shows of Western Europe and Russia in the 1800s, even in the United States at the turn of the century—it was sufficient for the zoo to pluck an animal from the teeming wild populations in Asia and Africa and display it, as an exotic specimen, to an amazed populace. (And if the animal sickened in captivity, there was nothing to do but wait for it to die and send for another one. Not only had veterinary medicine not evolved adequately but there was no pressure by concerned wildlife groups for zoos to maintain and reproduce their own stock. The animals were out there.)

Already occupied with the welfare of their animals and the amusement of their zoo-goers, zoo directors today must be responsible to the larger reality that the wilderness is disappearing and the animals with it. Today the cement-block enclosure or quarter-acre plot allotted by a zoo may be the last protected ground on earth for an animal whose habitat is disappearing under farmland, villages, or cities. The word *ark* is used with increasing frequency by zoo professionals. In this country, zoos house members of half a dozen species already extinct in the wild, and of hundreds more on the verge of extinction. Zoo-goers are confronted by skull logos denoting vanishing animals. The new designers like Coe and Jones, and directors like Conway, Maple, Graham, Dolan, George Rabb, at Chicago Brookfield, and Michael Robinson, at the National Zoo, belong as no designers or directors ever before belonged to the international community of zoologists and conservationists who have as their goal the preservation of the wild.

"This is a desperate time," William Conway says. The New York Zoological Society, under his leadership, also operates one of the largest and oldest wildlife-conservation organizations in the world, Wildlife Conservation International, which sponsors sixty-two programs in thirty-two countries. Conway is a slender, distinguished, avuncular gentleman with a pencil-line moustache. For him it seems quite a personal matter, a subject of intense private distress, that the earth is losing its wildlife and he doesn't know how many species are going, or what they are, or where they are, or how to save them.

"We are certainly at the rate of losing a species a day now, probably   *50* more," he says. "Who knows how many species there are on earth? Suppose, for the sake of argument, there are ten million species of animals out there. If we have one million in the year 2087 we will be doing very well. The human population is increasing at the rate of a hundred and fifty a minute. The tropical moist forest is decreasing at the rate of fifty acres a minute. And there is not a hope in the world of slowing this destruction and this population increase for quite some time. Most of the animals we hold dear, the big, charismatic megavertebrates, almost all of them will be endangered within the next twenty years. The people who are going to do that have already been born.

"And the destruction is being effected by some poor guy and his wife and their five children who are hacking out a few acres of ground to try to eat. That's where most of the fifty acres a minute are going: forty-eight that way and two to the bulldozers. In Rwanda there is a mountain-gorilla preserve that supports two hundred and forty gorillas. It recently was calculated that the park could sustain two thousand human families, people with no other place to live, no land. Now, how can you justify saving the land for two hundred and forty gorillas when you could have two thousand human families? That's one side of the story. Here's the other: if you were to do that, to put those two thousand families in there, the mountain gorilla would disappear completely, and that would take care of Rwanda's population-expansion needs for slightly less than three months. It's a very discouraging picture."

Michael Robinson, the director of the National Zoo, is a rotund and rosy-cheeked Englishman. "I have spent twenty years in the tropics, and it is difficult to talk about them in a detached, scientific manner," he says. "They are the richest ecosystem on earth. They have been here for millions of years. Perhaps eighty percent of all the animals in the world live there and have evolved relationships of breathtaking complexity. The northern hardwood forests have perhaps forty species of trees per hectare. The rain forest has closer to a hundred and fifty to two hundred species per hectare. Once the rain forest is cut down, it takes about a hundred years for the trees to grow back. We estimate that it would take at least six hundred years before the forest has returned to its original state, with all the plants and animals there."

"The American Association of Zoological Parks and Aquariums Species Survival Plan has only thirty-seven endangered species," Conway says. "We should have at least a thousand. How are we going to do it? My God, there are only one thousand seven hundred and eighty-five spaces for big cats in the United States. One thousand seven hundred and eighty-five. How many races of tigers are out there? Five or six. Several races of lions. Several races of leopards, to say nothing of snow leopards, jaguars, fishing cats, cheetahs, and so on. And you have to maintain a minimum population of two to three hundred animals each to have a population that is genetically and demographically sound. What in bloody hell are we going to do?"

Zoos in America are doing two things to try to save the wild animals. The front-line strategy is conservation biology and captive propagation, employing all the recent discoveries in human fertility, such as *in vitro* fertilization, embryo transplantation, and surrogate motherhood. Zoos around the world have hooked into a computerized database called ISIS, so that if a rare Indian rhino goes into heat in Los Angeles—or, for that matter, in the wilds of India—a healthy male rhino to donate sperm can be located.

The second-line strategy is to attempt to save the wilderness itself *55* through educating the public. Zoo directors and designers point out that there are 115 million American zoo-goers each year, and that if even 10 percent of them were to join conservation organizations, to boycott goods produced from the bones, horns, organs, and hides of endangered species, to vote to assist poor nations that are attempting to preserve their forests (perhaps by allowing debt payments to be eased in proportion to the numbers of wild acres preserved), their strength would be felt. The point of the landscape-immersion exhibits is to give the public a taste of what is out there, what is being lost.

It is dawning on zoo professionals that they are, in part, responsible for the American public's unfamiliarity with ecology and lack of awareness that half a dozen species a week are being driven into extinction, and that the precious tropical rain forest may vanish within our lifetime. "By itself, the sight of caged animals does not engender respect for animals," the environmental psychologist Robert Sommer wrote in 1972 in a pioneering essay titled "What Did We Learn at the Zoo?" "Despite excellent intentions, even the best zoos may be creating animal stereotypes that are not only incorrect but that actually work against the interests of wildlife preservation." Terry Maple says, "Zoos used to teach that animals are weird and they live alone."

In the past the only zoo people who paid much attention to zoo-goers were the volunteers assigned to drum up new members. The question they usually asked about zoo-goers was, Can we attract ten thousand of them in August? rather than, How have we influenced their attitudes about wildlife? With the decline of the wild and the dedication of zoos to educating the public, zoo professionals have grown curious about zoo-goers. What do they think? What are they saying as they nudge each other and point? Why do they shoot gum balls at the hippos? What exactly *are* they learning at the zoo? In search of answers to such questions, behavioral scientists are strolling through zoos around the country. They clock the number of seconds zoo-goers look at an exhibit. They count how many zoo-goers read the educational placards. They record the casual utterances of passers-by. And they note the age and gender of the zoo-goers who carve their initials on the railings. (They excite the envy of their co-equals in the science-museum world. "Researchers [at zoos] can linger for inordinate amounts of time at exhibits under the guise of waiting for an animal to do something," Beverly Serrell wrote in *Museum News* in 1980. "Standing next to a skeleton doesn't afford such a convenient cover.")

A fairly sharply focused portrait of the average North American zoo-goer has emerged. For example, data collected by the Smithsonian Institution at the National Zoo in 1979 revealed that zoo-goers arrive at the gates in any one of eighty-four "visitor constellations." One of the most common constellations is one parent accompanied by one or more children. On weekdays mothers predominate. On weekends fathers are sighted. In another study Professor Edward G. Ludwig, of State University College at Fredonia, New York, observed that the adult unaccompanied by children seemed to have "an aura of embarrassment." A survey published in 1976 found that zoo-goers tend to have more education and larger annual incomes than the population at large, and a 1979 survey found that zoo-goers are ignorant of basic ecological principles much more than are back-packers, birdwatchers, and members of wildlife organizations.

In a group of four zoo-goers, it's likely that only one or two will read an informational sign. Nearly all conversation will be confined to the friends and family members with whom the zoo-goer arrives. The most common form of conversation at the zoo is a declarative sentence following "Watch!" or "Look!" The second most common form is a question. Robert Yokel, in Miami, believes that the two questions asked most frequently by zoo-goers are "Where is the bathroom?" and "Where is the snack bar?" Zoo-goers typically look at exhibits for about ninety seconds. Some never stop walking. Ludwig found that most people will stop for animals that beg, animals that are feeding, baby animals, animals that make sounds, or animals that are mimicking human behavior. People express irritation or annoyance with animals that sleep, eliminate, or regurgitate.

Zoo visitors do not like to lose their way within a zoo, and they get *60* disgruntled when they find themselves backtracking. "We do not enjoy walking in circles and we invariably do," said one of the 300 respondents to the Smithsonian study. "Then we get irritated with ourselves."

Jim Peterson, a senior partner in the natural-history exhibit design firm of Bios, in Seattle, has identified the "first-fish syndrome." Within twenty feet of the entrance to an aquarium, visitors need to see a fish or they become unhappy. They will rush past the finest backlighted high-tech hands-on exhibitry to find that first fish. Similarly, Peterson has noted that visitors in zoos can tolerate only fifty feet between animals. Any greater distance inspires them to plow through foliage and create their own viewing blind.

Most "noncompliant behavior" such as unauthorized feeding of animals or attempting to climb over barriers, comes from juveniles and teens in mixed-gender groupings and children accompanied by both parents. A 1984 study by Valerie D. Thompson suggested that two parents tend to be involved with each other, freeing the children to perform antisocial acts; and that among teenagers there is "a close tie between noncompliant behavior and attempting to impress a member of the opposite sex."

Ted Finlay, a graduate student working with Terry Maple at Zoo Atlanta, wrote a master's thesis titled "The Influence of Zoo Environments on Perceptions of Animals," one of the first studies to focus on zoo design. Finlay majored in psychology and animal behavior with a minor in architecture, with the intention of becoming a zoo psychologist. For the research for his dissertation he prepared a slide show of animals in three environments: free, caged, and in various types of naturalistic zoo exhibits. Two hundred and sixty-seven volunteers viewed the slides and rated their feelings about the animals. The free animals were characterized as "free," "wild," and "active." Caged animals were seen as "restricted," "tame," and "passive." Animals in naturalistic settings were rated like the free animals if no barrier was visible. If the barrier *was* visible, they were rated like caged animals—that is to say, less favorably.

The zoo-goer who emerges from the research literature—benighted and happy-go-lucky, chomping his hot dog, holding his nose in the elephant house and scratching under his arms in the monkey house to make his children laugh—is a walking anachronism. He is the creation of an outmoded institution—the conventional zoo—in which the primate house, carnivore house, and reptile house, all lined with tile, glow with an unreal greenish light as if the halls were subterranean, and in which giraffes, zebras, and llamas stand politely, and as if on tiptoe, on the neatly mown lawns of the moated exhibits.

Once it was education enough for the public to file past the captive   65
gorilla in its cage and simply absorb the details of its peculiar or frightening countenance. "One ape in a cage, shaking its steel bars," Terry Maple says, "was a freak show, a horror show, King Kong! You'd go there to be scared, to scream, to squeeze your girlfriend." Despite gilded, or dingy, surroundings, a tusked creature in eighteenth-century Versailles, or downtown Pittsburgh, had the aura of a savage, strange, flowered wilderness.

"Pee-you!" is the primal, universal response of schoolchildren herded into an elephant house. Adults more discreetly crinkle their noses, turn their heads, and laugh. The unspoken impressions are that elephants are filthy, tread in their own feces, attract flies, require hosing down, eat mush, and no wonder they are housed in cinder-block garages. These are not the sort of impressions that might inspire a zoo-goer to resist—much less protest—the marketing of souvenirs made of ivory.

Moated exhibits display animals in garden-like settings, with bedding plants along cement walkways. A koala seated alone in the branch of a single artificial tree above a bright-green lawn looks as if he'd be at home in a Southern California back yard, next to the patio. The visitors looking at such exhibits appreciate the animals in them more and pronounce them "beautiful" or "interesting," but the subliminal message here is that animals are like gentle pets and thrive nicely in captivity. The visitors are hard pressed to explain what the big deal is about the rain forest or why zoologists talk about it, their voices cracking, the way twelfth-century Crusaders must have discussed the Holy Land.

One evening, just at dusk, Coe hurried alone through the Woodland Park Zoo. He'd worked late on some sketches, and the zoo had closed. He would have to let himself out. The lions in the Serengeti Plains exhibit galloped back and forth through their yellow grass, whipping their tails. They ran and ran and pulled up short at the brink of their hidden moat, panting, their nostrils flaring. Coe just happened to be passing by. One of the dun-colored male lions approached and crouched at the very edge of the moat, and growled. Jon Coe froze.

Now, Coe had designed the exhibit. He knew that he was looking up at the lion because he'd elevated its territory to instill fear and respect in the zoo-goer. He knew that he seemed to be walking beside the wild, dark African plains because he'd considered issues like sight lines and cross-viewing. He knew that a concealed moat lay between him and the lion, and that the width of the moat was the standard width used by zoos all over the world. But he also knew that you can't program in motivation. The lion looked at him and crouched; he could hear it snorting. Then it growled again—king of the darkness on the grassy plain. The hair stood up on the back of Coe's neck.

Reading and Responding

1. It might be surprising to see a piece in this chapter discussing zoo design. What do zoos have in common with malls or cities, anyhow? Run with this; do a ten-minute freewrite that addresses this question.
2. Visit your closest zoo and take your notebook with you. Make notes about what you see, and try to make sure that each note about what you see (or hear, or smell) also includes some mention of how this makes you feel.

Working Together

1. Assuming that you've all visited your local zoo and made notes (as suggested in "Reading and Responding"), pool your observations. Make a list of ten of those observations, and then write a few sentences that draw some conclusions on the basis of those observations. As you think about these conclusions, ask yourself this question: is your zoo a good zoo?
2. Assume that, as a group, you are speaking for zoo architect Jon Coe. Write a paragraph that expresses your central philosophy regarding zoo design. Use your own words, not Coe's.

3. As a group, walk around your campus. Take note of the kinds of decisions that you can see reflected in the landscape around you. For example, are the walkways straight, or do they meander? Are the buildings designed so that you walk right into them, or do you climb stairs to get to the "first" floor? Where are the plants, and what kinds do you see? Do you find any sculpture or other public art? If so, where is it, and why is it there rather than somewhere else? Where are the benches or other places that encourage people to gather, and how have these places been designed to encourage that gathering? Think of it this way: Your campus has been designed by people, and these people made decisions on the basis of various values and assumptions. See whether you can observe these decisions. For now, just make a list of the things you observe.

Rethinking and Rewriting

1. Greene ends this piece by making connections between zoos and environmental awareness. Explain what she's talking about to someone who hasn't read this piece and doesn't see any immediate relationship between seeing an elephant in a zoo and deciding whether to purchase something made of ivory. What does zoo design and zoo-goers experience have to do with the environment anyhow?
2. Discuss your own experience as a designer of living space. If you've ever decided how to arrange the furniture in a room (or decided what furniture ought to go in it in the first place), if you've ever decided what ought to go on blank walls and what shouldn't, or if you've ever made gardening decisions about what ought to be planted where, then you've been a designer.
3. From the notes your group collected on the design of your campus, focus on one part of the campus that seems to clearly reflect design decisions. Write an essay that presents this part of the campus (like Greene does with her description of the Woodland Park gorilla exhibit), and make sure that readers understand both the design decisions that must have been made here and the results of these decisions on people who actually use this part of the campus.

Essay Topics for Chapter 6

1. Apply Oldenburg's analysis of the problem of place in America to three or four other essays in this chapter. How do "The Silent Neighborhood," "O Rotten Gotham," or "My Neighborhood," for example, illustrate and confirm Oldenburg's main ideas? Or what would Oldenburg say about these three essays? How would he analyze them as evidence of his conclusions?

2. Trace the role of the car in three or more of these essays. Look carefully at how the car figures into Dillard's, Wolfe's, and Guterson's essays of place, for example. How is the role of the car everywhere implicit in the shopping mall? In what way does the car make possible the places described? In what way is the car necessary for these places—or the source of problems? This writing can be an expansion of the essay idea suggested following the Oldenburg selection—the reflection on the role of cars in your own life. Use your own experience in the beginning, middle, or end of the essay as a further kind of development.

3. One of the major themes running through this chapter is the influence of environment on behavior, mood, and spirit. Trace this theme, using three or more of the essays. Your thesis is that environment does have an influence. Your evidence and illustrations should include examples from these essays.

4. Address the theme of the influence of surroundings from the perspective of your own experience. Tell one or more stories of how place makes a difference to how you feel and act. Use quotations from the readings here and there—use the readings as a jumping off point or a way of summarizing what you're trying to say.

5. Analyze the shopping mall as a way of re-creating American small-town life, of creating healthy, wholesome environments—or what we imagine and hope are healthy and wholesome environments. That is, connect Guterson to Dillard, Wolfe, and all the others—see the malls as efforts to keep what is good about these human communities and solve what is bad. From your experience and your reading, are shopping malls successful places, good for the mind and heart, genuine? Imagine what Dillard or Wolfe would say about malls.

6. Write an essay celebrating a created world—the suburb, small town, or large city you grew up in; the campus of your university; a highway; a car. Do your celebrating through concrete description. Work in several brief quotations from at least two of the readings in this section. Or write an essay condemning a created world, taking the same descriptive approach.

7. On the basis of your experience with the readings in this chapter, write an essay describing the challenges and demands of college reading. Does your experience confirm some of the ideas about reading we introduced in chapter 1? Which suggestions for reading and writing in chapter 1 helped you the most? the least? What attitude can you bring to the rest of the readings in this book? What strategies, both practical and intellectual, are you planning to apply to these further readings?

7

Excursions

An excursion carries with it three related notions: the idea of leaving something behind, the sense of moving forward toward something else, and the curiosity and anticipation of not knowing what we will find. And whether we're talking about a stroll in the local park or an expedition to the Andes, excursions take us out of our normal routines.

The excursions in this chapter embody this movement; they all consciously take readers outside the created worlds of chapter 6. And they all seek something—some change or connection or renewed awareness. They urge fresh understanding of our places in landscapes and systems (like weather, for instance) not originally created by people. In simplest terms these readings urge us to get up from our desks, go outside, look, pay attention, feel, and think. These readings claim that we can't know ourselves or our created worlds without exploring and experiencing and learning from our context: the physical world—the planet—that supports all the life we know.

"TO MY SISTER"

William Wordsworth

Early-nineteenth-century English poet William Wordsworth is one of the major figures in the literary and philosophical movement known as romanticism, a movement that celebrates imagination, spontaneity, and the direct, individual experience of the natural world. This brief lyric from the revolutionary volume of poetry he coauthored with Samuel Taylor Coleridge, The Lyrical Ballads *(1798), is a good example both of Wordsworth's love of nature and his deceptively simple poetic style.*

[Composed 1798.—Published 1798.]

It is the first mild day of March:
Each minute sweeter than before,
The redbreast sings from the tall larch
That stands beside our door.

There is a blessing in the air,   5
Which seems a sense of joy to yield
To the bare trees, and mountains bare,
And grass in the green field.

My sister! ('tis a wish of mine)
Now that our morning meal is done,   10
Make haste, your morning task resign;
Come forth and feel the sun.

Edward will come with you;—and, pray,
Put on with speed your woodland dress;
And bring no book: for this one day   15
We'll give to idleness.

No joyless forms shall regulate
Our living calendar:
We from to-day, my Friend, will date
The opening of the year.   20

Love, now a universal birth,
From heart to heart is stealing,
From earth to man, from man to earth:
—It is the hour of feeling.

One moment now may give us more   25
Than years of toiling reason:
Our minds shall drink at every pore
The spirit of the season.

Some silent laws our hearts will make,
Which they shall long obey: *30*
We for the year to come may take
Our temper from to-day.

And from the blessed power that rolls
About, below, above,
We'll frame the measure of our souls: *35*
They shall be tuned to love.

Then come, my Sister! come, I pray,
With speed put on your woodland dress;
And bring no book: for this one day
We'll give to idleness.   *40*

Reading and Responding

Put this poem into your own words, as directly and straightforwardly as you can. Be awkward even, or slangy, but try to work in all the major reasons the poem offers. Make this a brief paragraph.

Working Together

1. Share your paraphrases, and then list all the things left out—all the things that Wordsworth's language does that the paraphrase doesn't, all the things that don't directly or obviously express the main meaning. (Rhyme, for example, or line breaks, or particular words and images.)
2. Talk about the effects of the paraphrase on the reader: what kinds of demands the paraphrase puts on a reader, what a reader has to do. Compare these demands to the demands a poem puts on a reader: what a reader has to do when confronted with a poem.

Rethinking and Rewriting

1. Write a letter or a short note to your sister—or your brother, friend, girlfriend, or boyfriend—urging this person to stop what he or she is doing and come outside with you on a walk or a drive somewhere out of town. Imitate Wordsworth, but in your own contemporary terms.
2. Write an essay about spring fever. Try to re-create how you feel in the spring when you're tired of school and ready to get out of town, back home, to the mountains, to the lake, or to the beach.

"DAYBREAK"

Bill McKibben

Author of several hundred pieces for the New Yorker *magazine, Bill McKibben is best known for* The End of Nature *(1989), a lament about the physical and spiritual effects of global warming. In this excerpt from his recent book* The Age of Missing Information *adapted by the author for this anthology, McKibben explores how television has changed the way we perceive the world around us.*

A little mist hangs above the pond, which is still save for a single mallard paddling slowly back and forth. From time to time it dives—sticks its rump in the air. From time to time it climbs out on a rock and airs its wings in the breeze, which is visible now and again on the surface of the pond. I watched for about an hour, and mostly the duck just swam back and forth, back and forth, back and forth.

Ducks are not necessarily placid. At certain times of the year male mallards flick water at females, or engage in what the bird books call a "grunt-whistle," while females perform "nod-swimming." At other seasons they may pull feathers from their bodies to insulate their eggs. And ducks are peculiarly susceptible to "imprinting." If, between thirteen and sixteen hours after they hatch, they are exposed to a moving object—a man or a dog or an Infiniti Q-45—they will thereafter follow it.

But on this particular morning this particular duck was doing nothing much, just swimming slowly back and forth.

We believe that we live in the "age of information," that there has been an information "explosion," an information "revolution." While in a certain narrow sense this is the case, in many important ways just the opposite is true. We also live at a moment of deep ignorance, when vital knowledge that humans have always possessed about who we are and where we live seems beyond our reach. An Unenlightenment. An age of missing information.

This account of that age takes the form of an experiment—a contrast 5 between two days. One day, May 3, 1990, lasted well more than a thousand hours—I collected on videotape nearly every minute of television that came across the enormous Fairfax cable system from one morning to the next, and then I watched it all. The other day, later that summer, lasted the conventional twenty-four hours. A mile from my house, camped on a mountaintop by a small pond, I awoke, took a day hike up a neighboring peak, returned to the pond for a swim, made supper, and watched the stars till I fell asleep. This book is about the results of that experiment—about the information that each day imparted.

These are, of course, straw days. No one spends twenty-four hours a day watching television (though an impressive percentage of the population gives it their best shot). And almost no one spends much time alone outdoors—the hermit tradition, never strong in America, has all but died away. (Thoreau came up twice on television during May 3. Once, he was an answer on *Tic Tac Dough* in the category "Bearded Men," and later that evening, in the back of a limousine, a man toasted his fiancée with champagne and said, "You know how we've always talked about finding our Walden Pond, our own little utopia? Well, here it is. This is Falconcrest.") I'm not interested in deciding which of these ways of spending time is "better." Both are caricatures, and neither strikes me as a model for a full and happy life. But caricatures have their uses—they draw attention to what is important about the familiar. Our society is moving steadily from natural sources of information toward electronic ones, from the mountain and the field toward the television; this great transition is very nearly complete. And so we need to understand the two extremes. One is the target of our drift. The other an anchor that might tug us gently back, a source of information that once spoke clearly to us and now hardly even whispers.

About the mountain first. Crow Mountain is no Himalaya, no Alp. Even in the company of its fellow Adirondacks it keeps a low profile. It is not one of the fifty highest peaks in New York State, nor is it particularly difficult to climb—I was at the top with a two-hour hike from my back door. A day on Crow, then, offers little in the way of drama or danger or overcoming odds. Still, this mountain has its charms, including half a mile of bare ridge, with marvelous views in all directions, and an uncommonly large pond, perhaps ten acres in size, nestled just below the peak. It is an uncrowded summit—the day described here came at the end of a week I spent alone on Crow, a week in which I encountered no other human beings. And yet it is not isolated. From the ridge I could see down to the valley where my wife and I live—could see the volunteer firehouse and the few homes and grown-in pastures that form our community. Though my house was hidden behind a ridge of hemlock, I could see where Mill Creek twists through the yard. So Crow is wilderness softened by familiarity.

If climbing the mountain was easy, assembling a video record of May 3, 1990, was not. No machine exists that can tape nearly a hundred channels simultaneously; instead, you need a hundred people with video-cassette recorders who will simultaneously do you a favor. With their help I compiled what I think is a unique snapshot of American culture—a sort of video Domesday that for twenty-four hours captures the images and voices that normally vanish like birdcalls on the breeze. For even in the age of the VCR, the invisible-ink effect of television is amazing. One day last year, for instance, a reporter for *The New York Times* needed to find out how the local ABC affiliate had covered a story the previous night. He failed, reporting only that a spokesman "could not release what was said on Sunday night's newscast without the permission of William Applegate, the news director, and Mr. Applegate did not respond to repeated requests left with his secretary for a transcript." In other words, the most powerful newspaper in the world could not get its hands on a newscast watched by millions only hours before. So I was pleased with my archive of tape, even if there were hours blanked out here and there, and MTV was nothing but snow so I had to retape it and a few others a couple of days later, and several hours of CBS were in black and white.

I chose Fairfax solely because of the astounding size of the system, which in 1990 was roughly 40 percent larger than its nearest competitor. There were five Christian channels, four shopping channels, two country music video channels, even a channel that broadcasts all the arrival and departure information off the Dulles and National airport screens. Its *Cable Guide* lists nearly a thousand movies each month; in May 1990 they ranged from *About Last Night* ("1986, Romantic Comedy, A young man and woman find themselves confused, frustrated, enthralled") to *Zombie* ("1964, Horror, Friends vacationing on a remote island find it inhabited by disfigured ghouls"), with everything in between from *Slumber Party Massacre II* to *The Son of Hercules Versus Medusa* to *It Happened One Night* to *Bonzo Goes to College* to *Sagebrush Law* to *Shaft* (and *Shaft in Africa*) to *Watchers* ("1988, Science Fiction, A dog, the subject of experiments in fostering superintelligence, escapes from a CIA compound"). For those who want *more*, a six-channel pay-per-view setup offers first-run films—on May 3: *Lethal Weapon 2; Honey, I Shrunk the Kids; Welcome Home; Field of Dreams; Alienator* ("She's programmed to kill anything in her path"); and *Enraptured*. Two comedy channels, nine public-access and government channels, a national sports channel and a local one, two weather channels, even a unique "four-in-one" channel that splits your screen into quarters and lets you watch the three networks and PBS simultaneously. Before the nineties are out, technology could permit six hundred channels per set, but even with a hundred stations you can watch virtually every national TV program aired in America on Fairfax Cable. On a single day you can hear about virtually every topic on earth.

Fairfax turned out to be ideal in another way, too—it is hard to imagine a place more devoid of quirky regional tradition. The county has grown quickly in recent years, till large stretches of it have the relentlessly standardized look of neutral America, the placeless Edge City of interchange plazas and malls with crowded chain restaurants and housing developments (Foxfield, Brookfield, Century Oak) named for the things they replaced. Only in its wealth is it extreme. The town of Falls Church ranks first in the nation in per capita income; nearly 80 percent of the county's households earn more than $35,000 and 75 percent of their children, who score seventy points above the national average on the SAT, will go on to college. On the other hand, a lot of the local programming comes from the District of Columbia, which is like a photographic negative of Fairfax.

Once my friends in Fairfax had mailed me the cardboard boxes full of tape, I began spending eight or ten hours a day in front of the VCR—I watched it all, more or less. A few programs repeat endlessly, with half-hour "infomercials" for DiDi 7 spot remover and Liquid Lustre car wax leading the list at more than a dozen appearances apiece. Having decided that once or twice was enough to mine their meanings, I would fast-forward through them, though I always slowed down to enjoy the part where the car-wax guy sets fire to the hood of his car. Otherwise, however, I dutifully spent many months of forty-hour weeks staring at, say, *Outdoors Wisconsin,* the kind of show that appears on minor cable channels across the nation because there's nowhere near enough programming produced to fill all the available time. On *Outdoors Wisconsin* ("summer to fall, winter to spring, Green Bay to where the St. Croix sings") they were "sucker-grabbing" in a creek near Fond du Lac. Sucker-grabbing involves wading up behind suckers, which are a variety of fish, and grabbing them. "They're really good if you grind 'em and mix 'em with a little egg and soda cracker," the host contended.

Which leads pretty directly into the question "Why bother?" *Outdoors Wisconsin* clearly has little direct effect on anyone but the suckers. But TV is cumulative, and over a lifetime ten minutes here and there of watching fishing or car racing or *Divorce Court* has added up to a lot of hours and had a certain effect on all of us. When people write about television, especially the critics who have to do it regularly, they usually have no choice but to concentrate on the new and the interesting as if they were reviewing plays or films. But TV is different—the new is relatively unimportant. The most popular program in 1990, *Cheers,* was in its ninth season; several weeks it was topped in the ratings by twenty-two-year-old *60 Minutes,* or challenged by *Murder, She Wrote,* which turned a hardy seven. Programs that first aired twenty or thirty years ago are still on the air, shown more often than ever in ceaseless rerun. You could argue that *The Brady Bunch,* not *Twin Peaks,* is the really important show to understand—simply by dint of repetition and familiarity it has won its way into the culture. (In March of 1991, the Associated Press reported that a Florida police officer had pleaded guilty to battery charges. He had lined up fourteen juveniles he had caught skateboarding, and then gone down the line whacking them with a nightstick as he sang the theme from *The Brady Bunch*. "He was singing that *Brady Bunch* tune, and each time he'd say like two words, he would hit one person in the butt," one of the boys told investigators.) People don't watch TV the way critics have to watch it. They don't watch it the way I watched it either—I have no way of re-creating the discussions the next day at work, say, or the easy familiarity with a show that you've seen every Thursday for a decade. But I did watch everything. The commercials, the filler, the reruns, the videos—all of it counts. *My Three Sons* still alters people's orbits, at least a little, just as Cosby will still be a force in 2010.

I grew up in the sixties and seventies, watching a great deal of television. Not the "quality TV" of television's Golden Era in the 1950s—not *Playhouse 90* or *The Honeymooners.* I was watching TV TV. Friday night meant ABC—*The Brady Bunch, The Partridge Family,* and *Room 222* in that order. TV was like a third parent—a source of ideas and information and impressions. And not such a bad parent—always with time to spare, always eager to please, often funny. TV filled dull hours and it made me a cosmopolite at an early age. I have great affection for it—I can remember waiting anxiously for *Room 222* to come on, remember that the high school it showed (Bernie with the red Afro! Karen Valentine!) seemed impossibly, enticingly sophisticated. People who didn't grow up with television tend not to understand its real power—they already had a real world to compare with the pictures on the screen. People my age didn't—we were steeped in television, flavored for life. A few years ago my wife and I moved to a mountain-rimmed valley—there's no cable, and even with a big antenna you get mostly snow. Since necessity is the mother of acquiescence, TV proved a fairly easy habit to kick. But of course I hadn't escaped it entirely—it lingered in my temperament, attitudes, outlook. And only with some distance, some time away, was I starting to get a sense of just how much. As I embarked on this project, then, I was not some Martian suddenly confronted with television; I was a traveler returning to a cozy home, able to see that home with new eyes. Going back to television was like spending the holidays with your parents once you've grown up—in three days you comprehend more on a conscious level about your mother than you did in twenty years of living with her.

Television is the chief way that most of us partake of the larger world, of the information age, and so, though none of us owe our personalities and habits entirely to the tube and the world it shows, none of us completely escape its influence either. Why do we do the things we do? Because of the events of our childhood, and because of class and race and gender, and because of our political and economic system and because of "human nature"—but also because of what we've been told about the world, because of the information we've received.

Television researchers tend to ignore the content, taking their cue   *15* from Marshall McLuhan, who argued that the "content of a medium is like the juicy piece of meat carried by the burglar to distract the watchdog of the mind." One study after another, not to mention the experience of most of us, indicates that McLuhan was largely right—that we do in fact often watch television because of our mood or out of habit, instead of tuning in to see something in particular. Even so, we're not staring at test patterns. We also often eat because we're bored or depressed, but the effects are different if we scarf carrot sticks or Doritos.

Two thirds of Americans tell researchers they get "most of their information" about the world from television, and the other statistics are so familiar we hardly notice them—more American homes have TVs than plumbing and they're on an average of seven hours a day; children spend more time watching TV than doing anything else save sleeping; on weekday evenings in the winter half the American population is sitting in front of television; as many as 12 percent of adults (that is, one in eight) feel they are physically addicted to the set, watching an average of fifty-six hours a week; and so on. The industry works hard to make this absorption seem glamorous: the Fairfax system runs an around-the-clock Cable Welcome Channel for instance, which tells viewers how to operate their systems ("If you can't get a picture on your TV, make sure it is plugged in"), but mainly congratulates them endlessly on "being part of a complete communications system that puts the whole world at your fingertips, from the far reaches of outer space to the heart of Fairfax." Outer space! Satellites! Fiber optics! Data! The final installment of an A&E series called *The Romantic Spirit* gushes, "Computers and satellites and silicon chips signal that we are in sight of a post–Romantic Age, of a fresh start." Communications are now "almost instantaneous," a documentary on the computer age explains. "Communications are the currency we trade in, the currency of the information age."

But what is this vaunted information currency? If you're a commodity broker or a bond trader, it's a blizzard of constantly changing green numbers on a flashing screen. If you're a vice president for marketing, it's a cataract of data about how much people earn in a certain zip code and what kind of car they drive. For most of us, though, this romantic, mind-boggling Niagara of communications washes up in our living rooms in the form of, say, Cory Everson's hunky husband, Jeff. Cory has an exercise program on ESPN called *Body Shaping,* and she lets Jeff handle the show's Nutrition Corner. If you're in the supermarket, Jeff advises, and you open up a carton and see that one of the eggs is broken, "don't buy that carton."

To be fair, there's a lot of other information you didn't already know, some of which is vaguely fascinating. On the Discovery Channel, for instance, Dr. Frank Field explains that in Switzerland white bread is taxed and the money is given to whole-wheat bakers so their loaves can be competitively priced. According to Casey Kasem on *Oprah,* Neil Sedaka went to the same high school as Neil Diamond and Barbra Streisand, and while he was there he wrote a song about a girl called Carole Klein who went on to become Carole King and of course have several number-one records, not only for herself but for the Shirelles. Sea otters wrap themselves in kelp before going to sleep, and three thousand matings are required to produce one lion cub that will live past its second year, and hyenas usually bear twins. And according to Showtime, the Voyager space probe carries a recording offering our planet's greetings to the entire universe in the voice of—Kurt Waldheim.

Some of the information on TV could win you fabulous prizes. "In American literature, what Mark Twain character had a girlfriend named Becky Thatcher?" As English teachers across the nation held their collective breath, a team on *Super Sloppy Double Dare* who had earlier recalled the name of the Flintstones' pet dinosaur failed to remember Tom Sawyer, and so had to turn themselves into "human tacos" by pouring vats of guacamole on their heads.

On other occasions, the information is more speculative: John Os- 20
borne, in a special edition of *Prophecy Countdown* called "Angels—God's Special Space Shuttles," calculated that angels travel eleven million miles a minute versus 283 for a NASA rocket.

And once in a while the information is just a shade less than honest, as when the Travel Channel claimed that "three things make Nuremberg famous—its Christmas market, the Nuremberg gingerbread, and the Nuremberg sausage."

Most of the time, though, the information that TV has to offer is not spelled out in such tidy little factlets. It is at least a little hidden in the fabric of movies and newscasts and commercials and reruns. Not so hidden that you need to hire a team of deconstruction contractors to analyze it all—just hidden enough that the messages are passed over, absorbed through the eyes without triggering the entire brain. People used to claim you could see "sex" written on Ritz crackers in their advertisements. Despite careful examination I never could, and that's not what I'm talking about. What I'm talking about is what happens when you see an ad, over and over, for small Ritz crackers pre-smeared and pre-stuck together with peanut butter and sold under the slogan "No assembly required." What habits of mind and body does this, in concert with a hundred other similar messages, help produce? And how do those habits differ from the habits, the attitudes people got from the natural world?

Occasionally, in between old World War II documentaries on A&E, a promotion for the network showed a man named Jack Perkins who said proudly that his channel showed "the entire scope of television, which is of course the entire scope of life." This is more or less the claim of all those who herald the new age now upon us—that our flow of data replaces nearly all that came before, including nature. Mark Fowler, the Reagan-era director of the Federal Communications Commission, appeared on C-SPAN to make this point explicitly. He talked about the range of environmental problems we face, including the depletion of the ozone, the destruction of the rain forests, and the spread of acid rain. "Pretty dreary stuff," he said, "except that as the ecological system has deteriorated, I think the man-made information ecology—the ebb and flow of words, voice, data—has vastly improved, so that we now live in a world more tightly bound, more in touch one part with another, than at any moment in its history."

Set aside the question of whether it's a worthwhile trade-off to be able to fax your aunt in Australia so that you can tell her it's bloody hot out and all the fish are dying—simply realize that an awful lot of people have come to see this "information ecology" as a sort of substitute for the other, older, natural ecology. "Ours is an economy increasingly dependent not on our natural resources or geographic location," President Bush told the members of the class of 1991 as they left the California Institute of Technology. "Ours is an age of microchips and MTV." And most of us vaguely agree with the president, I think—the world seems to be evolving into an "information economy" where the occupants of every country will busy themselves selling each other computer chips and watching the whole process on Esperanto CNN.

Against such a tide of opinion it sounds a little romantic to say: If you sat by a pond beside a hemlock tree under the sun and stars for a day, you might acquire some information that would serve you well. I don't fret about TV because it's decadent or shortens your attention span or leads to murder. It worries me because it alters perception. TV, and the culture it anchors, masks and drowns out the subtle and vital information contact with the real world once provided. There are lessons—small lessons, enormous lessons, lessons that may be crucial to the planet's persistence as a green and diverse place and also to the happiness of its inhabitants—that nature teaches and TV can't. Subversive ideas about how much you need, or what comfort is, or beauty, or time, that you can learn from the one great logoless channel and not the hundred noisy ones or even the pay-per-view.

For instance, as the sun comes up I'm sitting by the edge of the pond on Crow, drinking tea and wondering idly if the weather will hold all day so I can hike to the cliffs on nearby Blackberry Mountain. Ransacking my brain for weather lore, I recall that red skies at night are a sailor's delight, a ring around the moon heralds snow, and woolly caterpillars are woolliest before a hard winter, none of which is much help. I find myself wishing that I could gauge the wind direction and its speed, add the feel of the air and the type of clouds overhead, and make a reasonable guess, as most Americans once could, of what the day would bring. Of course this is no longer an essential skill—on the Fairfax cable system alone you can watch not only the twenty-four-hour national Weather Channel but also a local radar weather channel that shows storms moving inexorably, pixel by pixel, in your direction. You'd be crazy to devote any time to learning to forecast from the clouds and the wind—you wouldn't be as accurate as the giggly guy in the loud sports coat, and who would teach you anyhow? Jeffersonian farmers would doubtless have welcomed accurate predictions. Still, let this stand as one small example of information people once had and no longer possess.

Or another small example: an oft-repeated ad on May 3 was for a product called Jimmy Dean Microwave Mini Burgers, prefabricated hamburgers in a microwavable container. Silly as it sounds, think of the information you would have needed a century ago if you lived in a place like the Adirondacks and wanted to make yourself a hamburger. You'd have needed to be able to raise cattle, which implies knowing how to clear land, how to rotate pastures, how to build a barn—probably you'd have needed to know how to get your neighbors to *help* you raise a barn. You'd have

25

needed to know how to kill an animal, and what to do with it once it was hanging there dead. You might have bought your grain at the store or you might have used cornmeal, but certainly you needed to know how to bake bread. Baking and cooking would have required wood, which meant you had to know which trees to cut down, and when, and how to build an even fire. And so on.

If we're ever to recapture these fundamental kinds of information, it's necessary to start by remembering just how divorced from the physical world many of us have become. In a refreshingly honest piece of reporting, food writer Dena Kleiman recently told readers of *The New York Times* about a trip she'd taken to the lake district of southern Chile. "I had always fantasized about eating my own catch—staring down at a plate of fresh fish and knowing it would never have got there without me. The whole idea was appealing: braving the elements, testing my skill, indulging in one of the oldest battles of time—man versus nature." So she jumped at the chance to go fishing in Chile, although not before consulting with a passel of experts. George J. Armelagos, an anthropologist at the University of Florida, told her that "it was not until about ten thousand years ago that humans first turned from hunting and fishing to farming and herding in what was the start of the Neolithic Age." After that "nothing was ever the same," explained Mr. Armelagos, who is also the author of *Consuming Passions: An Anthology of Eating.* Ultimately, added California anthropology professor Eugene Anderson, "it is capitalism that has distanced us from all stages and phases of the food preparation process." Having heard this, Kleiman was ready. The management of the hotel sent her off in a boat with a guide, and the chef promised he would sauté her catch with a touch of garlic. "Time passes slowly in a fishing boat," she reported. "The routine, in fact, is tedious. Cast out. Reel in." To fill the time, "I tried to envision what kind of weapon I would devise, what kind of skill might be required, what kind of mind-set I would need to develop if I were lost in the wilderness and confronted with starvation." While mulling over this problem, she caught a fish, the guide motored her in, and she handed it to the chef and dressed for dinner. But presented with her catch, she reports, "I was stunned to find myself suddenly feeling nauseated," unable to eat for the memory of the vibrant living creature of some hours before. Despite the assurances of one Robert Cialdini, a social psychologist at the University of Arizona, that "it is natural for us to generate food for ourselves," she went without her supper.

Her squeamishness is not the point—that may be her only natural reaction, and in any event it's not deep enough to stop her eating the flesh of animals she didn't catch herself. It's how profoundly disconnected an obviously intelligent and educated person can be from the natural world. She is perhaps a slight caricature in this regard—only a true Manhattanite would actually consult a professor for the news that it is okay for us to "generate" our own food—but she offers a pretty accurate drawing of our society as a whole. Even most of us who do hike and fish do so sporadically, and out of such a single-minded desire for recreation that we don't absorb a lot of meaning from the experience. What you do every day, after all, is what forms your mind, and precious few of us can or would spend most days outdoors. "Despite all the lip service we give to craving nature and wanting to spend more time away from cities, I suppose that in the end we are grateful to live in a society where foraging requires only a walk to the local market," Kleiman writes. And that is fine—we don't need a nation of hunter-gatherers. But it does, as she demonstrates, come at a real cost in your comprehension of the world—it robs her of the ability, in this instance, to squarely address her own participation in the drama of life and death.

Even for the few modern farmers who do appear on television, the industrial scale of the business has changed it so dramatically that much of this information is diluted, drowned out in the roar of the tractor piloting its noisy course across a vast sea of crops. The Lifetime network ran a short feature on a farm family in northern California. They ran such a large dairy operation (950 head) that the mother said she spent most of her day on the computer doing records while Dad was out minding the help. The kids took care of the house pets, and helped in other small ways, but they weren't really a part of farm life any more than a banker's children make loans. The message she tried to teach them, Mom said, was that "hard work pays off in nice things—toys, cars." Which is probably better than our culture's usual message—Buy a lottery ticket so you won't have to work hard—but it doesn't yield much in the way of wisdom about death or limits or the cycles of the seasons. Even home gardeners, presumably planting for love of working the soil, are hectored around the clock to purchase products like Miracle-Gro—hectored by "world championship gardeners," which is to say not the people who grow the tastiest vegetables or produce them most thriftily, or with the most care for their soils. No, these are the people who through constant application of chemicals have managed to produce the *largest* vegetables, great pulpy squashes and melons.

The narrow valley at the foot of Crow Mountain was once a farm— we know how grand it looked because a poet, Jeanne Robert Foster, lived in the mountain's shadow as a girl. But the farmer who had built it watched as his children left for other, shinier pursuits. An old man, he looked on in despair as his fields began the slow return to forest:

> I must find a man who still loves the soil
> Walk by his side unseen, pour in his mind
> What I loved when I lived until he builds
> Sows, reaps, and covers these hill pastures here
> With sheep and cattle, mows the meadowland
> Grafts the old orchard again, makes it bear again
> Knowing that we are lost if the land does not yield.

As I stand on the ridge this morning, looking at the sumac and the birch covering the pasture, it is clear he never found his man. And clear that

30

most of us will need some way other than a life of growing crops to get at this fundamental information.

There are other paths to this kind of deeper understanding of the world, but they too are overgrown and hard to find; a day of watching television makes it obvious that farming is not the only skill we've lost. Often, in fact, the television culture celebrates incompetence. One American Express ad depicts a couple who have chartered a sailboat in the tropics but are having a difficult time operating it. Suddenly they see a cruise schooner round the point, and to the triumphant Big Chill strains of "Rescue Me" they ditch their scow and jump aboard the luxury yacht, where there's a crew to attend to stuff like *sails* and *wind* and *lines* and *rocks* so they can concentrate on drinking. Money supplants skill; its possession allows us to become happily stupid. Presumably the crew members on the yacht make enough money pursuing *their* specialty that they don't need to know about anything else themselves either. Certainly most TV characters don't possess many skills; except for tending bar and solving murders, virtually no one in a drama or comedy actually works.

Occasionally, though, television offers a few glimpses of people who have developed very deep mastery, become real craftsmen. There are baseball games (on this evening the Braves were losing to the Pirates) where you get to watch men employ an enormous accretion of specialized knowledge—"There's a good hitter's pitch coming here," "He's shading him to right." On public TV, a man demonstrated the art of Chinese calligraphy. And off in the back alleys of cable there are a great many cooking shows run by chefs who can chop, whisk, separate, fold, knead, and roll, all in a blur.

These kinds of skills come from long, repetitive, and disciplined apprenticeships. Societies have always, at least since the beginning of agriculture, needed and valued certain specialized abilities; while the great majority of people were learning from their parents to produce food and otherwise care for themselves, a few were spending years with a master of some craft or art. Where the one education was broad, the other was deep—deeper, say, than law school. *So* deep that it may have produced some of the same kinds of fundamental knowledge that farming produces, because the master taught not just cooking or painting but universal things. As the poet and longtime Buddhist novice Gary Snyder wrote recently, "The youngsters left home to go and sleep in the back of the potting shed and would be given the single task of mixing clay for three years. . . . It was understood that the teacher would test one's patience and fortitude endlessly. One could not think of turning back, but just take it, go deep, and have no other interests." In the TV era, we're more comfortable with, say, Robert Warren, who has a cable art show and today is teaching all of America how to paint "Majestic Mountain Meadow." No three seasons of watching Robert mix paints! Or perhaps the amazing piano course sold by former Detroit Lion Alex Karras and endorsed by Davy Jones—"Now the Monkees can play their own instruments." Or maybe you'd like the Paint by Numbers Last Supper Painting Kit from the QVC shopping channel. "Duplicate Leonardo da Vinci's beautiful painting—you get 42 shades, so many that you're going to get very close to da Vinci. . . . You'll be able to learn just what goes into making an intricate painting like this. Give yourself the pride of accomplishment."

Still, there are echoes. The notion of apprenticeship as an almost   35
religious vocation survives best, oddly, in martial arts movies like *Bloodsport* on Showtime. Representative of its type, it featured a young Caucasian who had studied for many years under a Japanese master. His command of body and soul was complete—he had reached the point where he fought not for external reward (for the teacher gave none, not even a smile) or for his liking for blood (he hated it—his master left Japan after his family was killed at Hiroshima). Instead he fought for an essentially spiritual satisfaction—because it made him feel close to some universal force. We thrill to this in part because it's a ridiculous excuse to let people kick each other's teeth in. But there's also something deeply attractive about that depth of training, that self-abnegation. We secretly believe that people who have gone through it *may* understand more about who they are. *Bloodsport* was followed on Showtime by Championship Boxing (Michael "The Silk" Olaajide losing a decision to Thomas "Hitman" Hearns). In an even more degraded way, boxing is about the same kind of issues. The great dramas in the sport only occasionally take place in the ring—usually they're outside it, where we watch to see if young men "stick to their training" or at the first flush of victory begin buying Italian cars and fancy women and letting their hangers-on coax them into staying up late at night. That is, will they trade their secrets and their discipline for the glitter of the world? Almost invariably flash wins out, in part because by old master-apprentice standards the training is not very rigorous (and because most other sorts of apprentices don't make $20 million a year). Still, we always find ourselves hoping.

Handcrafting pottery and samurai fighting and growing corn may be outmoded skills, but perhaps all the discipline and wisdom they offer can be acquired through more modern devotions, in which case my day on the mountain would be unnecessary. That is one of the arguments Robert Pirsig makes in *Zen and the Art of Motorcycle Maintenance* when he says "the Buddha, the Godhead, resides quite as comfortably in the circuits of a digital computer or the gears of a cycle transmission as he does at the top of a mountain or in the petals of a flower." ("I am master of my fate, captain of my soul," intones an ad for BMW motorcycles.) The Buddha, for all I know, *is* as comfortable in the gearbox, but he's increasingly inaccessible. Albert Borgmann, in a book called *Technology and the Character of Contemporary Life,* argues convincingly that Pirsig's approach becomes less and less helpful as technology progresses. When Pirsig wrote his book, a motorcycle was essentially a mechanical device; with each passing year it becomes more and more a microelectronic one, and you can't sit by the road and find God by looking at a bunch of incomprehensibly microscopic silicon chips. (You also can't repair your motorcycle anymore.) TV itself began as a toy for hobbyists, a gee-whiz gadget to build in the basement. Now it is too complex even for individual corporations—great manufacturing combines are getting together to develop High Definition TV. The great push is always *away* from individual skill and engagement—a horse took all sorts of information and insight to handle, and a Model T a little, and a Honda Accord virtually none.

It's a comfortable notion that as we progress we simply add to our store of understanding about the world—that we know more about the world by kindergarten than our grandparents knew when they died, and that our grandchildren will in turn be infinitely wiser than we are. In truth, though, we usually learn a new way of doing things at the expense of the old way. In this case we've traded away most of our physical sense of the world, and with it a whole category of information, of understanding. We have a new understanding, reflected most ubiquitously by television, which in many ways is sophisticated and powerful. And democratic—TV's obvious virtues, that it is cheap and always accessible—should not be overlooked. But there's much that it leaves out, that it can't include.

For only a few people anymore will this other information come from farming, and I don't anticipate a sudden, statistically significant boom in pot-throwing apprenticeships. So I'll concentrate on contrasting television's message with the ideas about the world and our place in it that come from a day in the natural world. In a way, I suppose, I'm hunting for a shortcut, which is the curse of the age. But it's a useful shortcut, since though few of us will farm, most people can still manage regular excursions into the natural world. It's not elitist—it's subversively easy.

To pull in this broadest of broadcasts you do not need pristine wilderness—there's very little, perhaps nothing, left that's entirely "natural." A city park or a suburban woodlot or a rural hedgerow or a backyard garden will do—anyplace that will let you take a conscious step away from the entirely man-made world. In all these places you can read what John Muir called "the inexhaustible pages of nature . . . written over and over uncountable times, written in characters of every size and color, sentences composed of sentences, every part of a character a sentence."

That this broadcast has gone on since the start of time—that some of   *40* its messages still live in our genes and instincts—does not mean, however, that it will go on forever. Parts of Muir's grammar are wiped off the slate each day—species lost, ecosystems altered. You have to listen harder to the natural world so you can separate out the primal song from the songs of our civilization and from our static. A team of Canadian scientists recently finished a study of several lakes in a remote part of northern Ontario, an area where the temperature had increased 3.5 degrees in the last two decades—the kind of warming that other scientists tell us the whole planet can expect in the next two generations. The Canadian researchers reported all sorts of highly complex alterations of the environment. Warmer air had meant more evaporation, for instance. Hence, stream flows dropped and the lakes became clearer and therefore warmer. As a result, many cold-water species, including trout, faced extinction. But beyond their practical impact, the changes were simply one more sign that Muir's alphabet was turning into indecipherable hieroglyphics—one more sign that the great simplification had begun.

Much of this simplification may be irreversible. If so, we had best listen closely, since we will not get another chance. And what chance we *do* have of preserving this natural world also depends on listening—on absorbing the information of the mountain and garden and park as thoroughly as we soak up the information on the screen. And on letting it play as large a role in shaping the way we live. It depends, that is, on turning the present moment into a true age of information.

Reading and Responding

1. Freewrite about a camping trip, hike, or other outdoor activity you've done. Talk specifically about what you did, what you saw, how you felt—just try to remember it on paper.
2. Brainstorm about the sources of the information you tap on any normal day. Make a list of as many of these sources as you can (10 minimum). Then divide them as Bill McKibben does—either "natural" or "electronic." If something doesn't fit either category, call it "other."
3. Fold a paper in half from left to right so that you have a crease running down the middle. To the left of the crease, write words or phrases that describe reading; to the right of the crease, write words or phrases describing watching television. Once you have at least half a dozen items on each side of the crease, look at what you've written, and write two or three sentences about what you see.
4. Freewrite about the role that television plays in your life right now. What do you tend to watch, when is it on, and why do you watch it?

Working Together

1. Bring your comparison of TV watching and reading to class and share as a class or in groups. Brainstorm on the board or on paper together about all the ways the two acts differ.
2. In light of item 1, work together to make a list of practical tips for anyone outside the class who sits down to read this piece by McKibben. Address someone who hasn't read very much, if at all, who's grown up only with television and not with books. What, exactly, should this person do when he or she starts this assignment? (For example, should she turn off the TV first?) Then what?
3. Talk as a group about the outdoor activities that you do, and make a list of them. As you think about these outdoor activities, also think about what they teach you about the natural world. For example, if you

go hiking in the mountains, you may learn how to pay attention to the shifting weather (and so avoid getting drenched); or walking the dog in the afternoon, you may learn that your neighbor's cherry trees have bloomed and the camas grass has sprouted in the field. Make a list of these "lessons," too. Finally, how important are these "lessons" to your everyday life? As a group, write a couple of sentences that answer that question.

4. Talk as a group about the things that you make for yourself (or used to make for yourself) rather than buy. Make a list of these things. Then make a list of all the reasons you can think of to make things for yourself. Finally, as a group, write a few sentences either agreeing or disagreeing with this statement: assuming we had the money, we'd rather buy everything we need or want, even if we knew how to make it ourselves.

Rethinking and Rewriting

1. Watch television for an hour. Record everything you see; and try to record *how* you're seeing it: what your body is doing, what your eyes are doing in particular, what's going on in your mind as you watch, whether you get up to get a snack, and so on. Then go outside—to your backyard, to a park, out of town to a mountain or a stream, or to some place on campus where you can sit and simply watch things for an hour. Record everything you see. Write both these lists into an essay, imitating the structure of McKibben's "Daybreak." At some point, include a summary of McKibben's main point in your own words. Does your own small version of McKibben's experiment support his ideas or help you understand them better?

2. Identify three of your favorite things to eat. In an essay, look at each of them in turn, paying attention to how this food is made and where it comes from. Do some research if necessary. End your essay by asking yourself how natural your favorite foods (or dishes) are. Could you trace how they're made, could you identify their ingredients, and could you find out where those ingredients were grown or raised? Finally, on the basis of these three examples, would you say that you look at food as something that comes from nature or something that comes from a box, can, or freezer case?

3. Find Neil Postman's book about television, *Amusing Ourselves to Death: Public Discourse in the Age of Television*. Summarize his main argument in the first few chapters and then compare it with McKibben's. McKibben and Postman agree about how television changes the way we process information, the way we see the world. Explain. What does Postman add to McKibben's charge?

4. Write an essay that describes the experience of making something and then using it. Talk about the process and about the frustrations and pleasures that are part of that process.

5. Using your library's computer bibliography and CD-ROM, gather information in books and articles from the past five years about the effects of television on viewers. Write this information into a position paper, explaining and supporting your own initial conclusions about the "problem of television."

"ROLLING NAKED IN
THE MORNING DEW"

Pattiann Rogers

In her five books of poems Pattiann Rogers consistently wonders about and examines the relationships between the natural world and ourselves. Winner of grants from both the National Endowment for the Arts and the Guggenheim Foundation, Rogers has taught widely and lives now in Colorado. Reviewers have called her "an insider in nature, finding and defining her own metaphysic." The poem reprinted here comes from her fourth volume, Splitting and Binding.

Out among the wet grasses and wild barley-covered
Meadows, backside, frontside, through the white clover
And feather peabush, over spongy tussocks
And shaggy-mane mushrooms, the abandoned nests
Of larks and bobolinks, face to face   5
With vole trails, snail niches, jelly
Slug eggs; or in a stone-walled garden, level
With the stemmed bulbs of orange and scarlet tulips,
Cricket carcasses, the bent blossoms of sweet william,
Shoulder over shoulder, leg over leg, clear   10
To the ferny edge of the goldfish pond—some people
Believe in the rejuvenating powers of this act—naked
As a toad in the forest, belly and hips, thighs
And ankles drenched in the dew-filled gulches
Of oak leaves, in the soft fall beneath yellow birches,   15
All of the skin exposed directly to the *killy* cry
Of the kingbird, the buzzing of grasshopper sparrows,
Those calls merging with the dawn-red mists
Of crimson steeplebush, entering the bare body then
Not merely through the ears but through the skin   20
Of every naked person willing every event and potentiality
Of a damp transforming dawn to enter.

Lillie Langtry practiced it, when weather permitted,
Lying down naked every morning in the dew,
With all of her beauty believing the single petal   25
Of her white skin could absorb and assume
That radiating purity of liquid and light.
And I admit to believing myself, without question,
In the magical powers of dew on the cheeks
And breasts of Lillie Langtry believing devotedly   30
In the magical powers of early morning dew on the skin

Of her body lolling in purple beds of bird's-foot violets,
Pink prairie mimosa. And I believe, without doubt,
In the mystery of the healing energy coming
From that wholehearted belief in the beneficent results   *35*
Of the good delights of the naked body rolling
And rolling through all the silked and sun-filled,
Dusky-winged, sheathed and sparkled, looped
And dizzied effluences of each dawn
Of the rolling earth.   *40*

Just consider how the mere idea of it alone
Has already caused me to sing and sing
This whole morning long.

Reading and Responding

1. This poem starts out with a long list of things before it gets to anything like a normal sentence ("—some people/ Believe in the rejuvenating powers of this act—"). Pretend you're Pattiann Rogers: Why did you start the poem this way? What are you trying to do? Freewrite on these questions for half a page or so.
2. Do you know of any people who do similarly crazy or excessive things to experience nature more fully (like go swimming in an otherwise ice-covered lake on January 1)? Or have you yourself done anything that's similarly crazy (such as taking a walk *because* it's raining, or going camping in January so you can sleep in an ice cave), either intentionally or not? If you have, what's it feel like to be outside in this crazy kind of way? Write about that for ten minutes or so.

Working Together

1. Read through the poem carefully in order to answer this question: Does Pattiann Rogers say that she rolls naked in the morning dew, or doesn't she? Be ready to point to two places in the poem that support your answer.
2. This poem frequently includes various forms of the word *believe*. Take a look at those places in the poem, and as a group, decide what this poem says we ought to believe in. Write a group paragraph that discusses this idea.

Rethinking and Rewriting

1. Write your own version of "Rolling Naked," except write a paragraph. Title the paragraph by using an *ing* word to anchor it (for example, "Playing Mudball at Midnight"). In your paragraph, try to capture the spirit—the fun and craziness—of whatever you're discussing. Write as

much as you want to for a rough draft; but for your final draft, do not write more than 200 words.

2. Write a short essay in which you imagine doing something like rolling naked in the morning dew—something a little wild or daring that you probably wouldn't actually try yourself. Write as though you've actually done this (whatever it is), and try to use sensory details that convince readers.

"NEW YEAR'S DAY"

Barbara Kingsolver

> *Her three novels set in the American Southwest—*The Bean Trees
> *(1988),* Animal Dreams *(1990), and* Pigs in Heaven *(1993)—have
> established Barbara Kingsolver as an accomplished, literate, and popular con-
> temporary novelist. In this excerpt from* The Bean Trees *Taylor Greer's
> employer, Mattie, decides to close up shop for the afternoon and take Taylor
> and a number of friends on a short expedition out of town. Once they've
> made some child care arrangements, that's exactly what they do. The "I" in
> this excerpt is Taylor Greer, a Kentuckian still new to Arizona.*

At three o'clock in the afternoon all the cicadas stopped buzzing at
once. They left such an emptiness in the air it hurt your ears. Around four
o'clock we heard thunder. Mattie turned over the "Closed" sign in the
window and said, "Come on. I want you to smell this."

She wanted Esperanza to come too, and surprisingly she agreed. I
went upstairs to phone Edna and Mrs. Parsons, though I practically could
have yelled to them across the park, to say I'd be home later than usual.
Edna said that was fine, just fine, the kids were no trouble, and we prepared
to leave. At the last minute it turned out that Estevan could come too; he
had the night off. The restaurant was closed for some unexpected family
celebration. We all piled into the cab of Mattie's truck with Esperanza on
Estevan's lap and me straddling the stick shift. The three of us had no idea
where we were headed, or why, but the air had sparks in it. I felt as though
I had a blind date with destiny, and someone had heard a rumor that
destiny looked like Christopher Reeve.

Mattie said that for the Indians who lived in this desert, who had
lived here long before Tucson ever came along, today was New Year's Day.

"What, July the twelfth?" I asked, because that's what day it was, but
Mattie said not necessarily. They celebrated it on whatever day the summer's first rain fell. That began the new year. Everything started over then,
she said: they planted their crops, the kids ran naked through the puddles
while their mothers washed their clothes and blankets and everything else
they owned, and they all drank cactus-fruit wine until they fell over from
happiness. Even the animals and plants came alive again when the drought
finally broke.

"You'll see," Mattie said. "You'll feel the same way."   5

Mattie turned onto a gravel road. We bounced through several stream
beds with dry, pebbled bottoms scorched white, and eventually pulled over
on high ground about a mile or so out of town. We picked our way on
foot through the brush to a spot near a grove of black-trunked mesquite
trees on the very top of the hill.

The whole Tucson Valley lay in front of us, resting in its cradle of
mountains. The sloped desert plain that lay between us and the city was

like a palm stretched out for a fortuneteller to read, with its mounds and hillocks, its life lines and heart lines of dry stream beds.

A storm was coming up from the south, moving slowly. It looked something like a huge blue-gray shower curtain being drawn along by the hand of God. You could just barely see through it, enough to make out the silhouette of the mountains on the other side. From time to time nervous white ribbons of lightning jumped between the mountaintops and the clouds. A cool breeze came up behind us, sending shivers along the spines of the mesquite trees.

The birds were excited, flitting along the ground and perching on thin, wildly waving weed stalks.

What still amazed me about the desert was all the life it had in it.   10 Hillbilly that I was, I had come to Arizona expecting an endless sea of sand dunes. I'd learned of deserts from old Westerns and Quickdraw McGraw cartoons. But this desert was nothing like that. There were bushes and trees and weeds here, exactly the same as anywhere else, except that the colors were different, and everything alive had thorns.

Mattie told us the names of things, but the foreign words rolled right back out of my ears. I only remembered a few. The saguaros were the great big spiny ones, as tall as normal trees but so skinny and personlike that you always had the feeling they were looking over your shoulder. Around their heads, at this time of year, they wore crowns of bright red fruits split open like mouths. And the ocotillos were the dead-looking thorny sticks that stuck up out of the ground in clusters, each one with a flaming orange spike of flower buds at its top. These looked to me like candles from hell.

Mattie said all the things that looked dead were just dormant. As soon as the rains came they would sprout leaves and grow. It happened so fast, she said, you could practically watch it.

As the storm moved closer it broke into hundreds of pieces so that the rain fell here and there from the high clouds in long, curving gray plumes. It looked like maybe fifty or sixty fires scattered over the city, except that the tall, smoky columns were flowing in reverse. And if you looked closely you could see that in some places the rain didn't make it all the way to the ground. Three-quarters of the way down from the sky it just vanished into the dry air.

Rays of sunlight streamed from between the clouds, like the Holy Ghost on the cover of one of Mattie's dead husband's magazines. Lightning hit somewhere nearby and the thunder made Esperanza and me jump. It wasn't all that close, really, about two miles according to Mattie. She counted the seconds between the lightning strike and the thunder. Five seconds equaled one mile, she told us.

One of the plumes of rain was moving toward us. We could see big   15 drops spattering on the ground, and when it came closer we could hear them, as loud as pebbles on a window. Coming fast. One minute we were dry, then we were being pelted with cold raindrops, then our wet shirts were clinging to our shoulders and the rain was already on the other side of us. All four of us were jumping and gasping because of the way the sudden cold took our breath away. Mattie was counting out loud between the lightning and thunderclaps: six, seven, boom! . . . four, five, six, boom! Estevan danced with Esperanza, then with me, holding his handkerchief under his arm and then twirling it high in the air—it was a flirtatious, marvelous dance with thunder for music. I remembered how he and I had once jumped almost naked into an icy stream together, how long ago that seemed, and how innocent, and now I was madly in love with him, among other people. I couldn't stop laughing. I had never felt so happy.

That was when we smelled the rain. It was so strong it seemed like more than just a smell. When we stretched out our hands we could practically feel it rising up from the ground. I don't know how a person could ever describe that scent. It certainly wasn't sour, but it wasn't sweet either, not like a flower. "Pungent" is the word Estevan used. I would have said "clean." To my mind it was like nothing so much as a wonderfully clean, scrubbed pine floor.

Mattie explained that it was caused by the greasewood bushes, which she said produced a certain chemical when it rained. I asked her if anybody had ever thought to bottle it, it was so wonderful. She said no, but that if you paid attention you could even smell it in town. That you could always tell if it was raining in any part of the city.

I wondered if the smell was really so great, or if it just seemed that way to us. Because of what it meant.

It was after sunset when we made our way back to the truck. The clouds had turned pink, then blood red, and then suddenly it was dark. Fortunately Mattie, who was troubled by night-blindness, had thought to bring a flashlight. The night was full of sounds—bird calls, a high, quivery owl hoot, and something that sounded like sheep's baahs, only a hundred times louder. These would ring out from the distance and then startle us by answering right from under our feet. Mattie said they were spadefoot toads. All that noise came from something no bigger than a quarter. I would never have believed it, except that I had seen cicadas.

"So how does a toad get into the middle of the desert?" I wanted to know. "Does it rain toad frogs in Arizona?"

"They're here all along, smarty. Burrowed in the ground. They wait out the dry months kind of deadlike, just like everything else, and when the rain comes they wake up and crawl out of the ground and start to holler."

I was amazed. There seemed to be no end to the things that could be hiding, waiting it out, right where you thought you could see it all.

"Jeez," I said, as one of them let out a squall next to my sneaker.

"Only two things are worth making so much noise about: death and sex," Estevan said. He had the devil in him tonight. I remembered a dream about him from a few nights before, one that I had not until that minute known I'd had. A very detailed dream. I felt a flush crawling up my neck and was glad for the dusk. We were following Mattie's voice to keep to the trail, concentrating on avoiding the embrace of spiny arms in the darkness.

"It's all one to a toad," Mattie said. "If it's not the one, it's the other. *25* They don't have long to make hay in weather like this. We might not get another good rain for weeks. By morning there'll be eggs in every one of these puddles. In two days' time, even less, you can see tadpoles. Before the puddles dry up they've sprouted legs and hit the high road."

We were following behind Mattie in single file now, holding to one another's damp sleeves and arms in the darkness. All at once Esperanza's fingers closed hard around my wrist. The flashlight beam had found a snake, just at eye level, its muscular coils looped around a smooth tree trunk.

"Better step back easy, that's a rattler," Mattie said in a calm voice. With the flashlight she followed the coils to the end and pointed out the bulbs on the tail, as clear and fragile-looking as glass beads. The rattle was poised upright but did not shake.

"I didn't know they could get up in trees," I said.

"Sure, they'll climb. After birds' eggs."

A little noise came from my throat. I wasn't really afraid, but there is *30* something about seeing a snake that makes your stomach tighten, no matter how you make up your mind to feel about it.

"Fair's fair," Mattie pointed out, as we skirted a wide path around the tree. "Everybody's got her own mouths to feed."

Reading and Responding

1. Though you may not feel fully acquainted with the characters in this excerpt, they've clearly decided to drop their usual daily routine. Why have they done this? And what do they find when they get out of town? Freewrite about these two questions for half a page or more.
2. In this piece Mattie acts as the tour guide; she's the one who's familiar with the local area. Can you recall a time when you acted as a tour guide and showed visitors some landscape you feel attached to? Write a journal entry that talks about what was it like to act in this role.
3. As readers, we see through the eyes of someone (the "I" in the story) who's from Kentucky and who is therefore seeing this part of Arizona for the first time. Can you remember a time when you saw some impressive place for the first time? Write a journal entry about one of those experiences.

Working Together

1. Make a list of all the reactions that Mattie's friends have as she leads them into this new landscape (aim for a list of ten reactions).
2. As a group, discuss how the tone in this piece changes after the sun goes down. Make a list of words that describe the overall feeling of this

piece in daylight, and then make a new list for its overall feeling after sundown. Finally, summarize these lists and their differences in a short, group-written paragraph.

3. As a group, make a list of all the times that each person can remember seeing a landscape or special place for the first time. Then on the basis of these experiences, make a list of all the reactions that seeing such a landscape can trigger—all of them.

Rethinking and Rewriting

1. Describe a time when you've acted as a tour guide (as Mattie does). Then discuss the ways that you and Mattie felt alike and the ways that your experience and responses differed from Mattie's. End by discussing what it means to know a place and act as a guide to it. What obligations (if any) go with such knowledge? What's complicated—and what's easy—about knowing a place well and showing it to people who don't yet know it?

2. Describe a time when you've visited a place for the first time with a guide. Discuss what you remember and what you've forgotten. Would you consider the visit successful or not, and why? Would you go back to this place? What was it about this place—or your response to it—that would call you back?

"THE FARTHEST DISTANCE BETWEEN TWO POINTS"

Ted Leeson

Ted Leeson teaches English at Oregon State University and is a contributing editor to Fly and Reel *magazine. His essays on fly fishing have appeared in* Field and Stream, Gray's Sporting Journal, *and* Fly Fisherman. *The following piece, adapted by the author for this anthology, is from his recent book of essays,* The Habits of Rivers: Reflections on Trout Streams and Fly Fishing *(1994).*

A good traveler has no fixed plans
and is not intent upon arriving.

—LAO-TZU, *Tao Te Ching*

We know by experience it selfe, that it is a
maruelous paine, to finde oute but a short waie,
by long wandering.

—ROGER ASCHAM, *The Scholemaster*

As You Read
Ted Leeson says that he set out on an "unprescribed, directionless" trip, a trip without a map or plan in advance. As you read, keep track of the transitions between major sections describing this trip. Circle the transitional words and phrases, or write a note in the margins suggesting how you think Leeson moves from one piece to the other. Give a subtitle to the major sections. Once you've seen this organization, write a few sentences about it. Talk about whether the piece seems carefully organized or directionless and apparently random.

April may indeed be the cruellest month. In the tight tongue-and-groove of the angling year, it seems somehow to have slipped between the cracks. The season seems out of sync with itself. Under warm rains and mild air, the land greens up with promise and propels you forward. But the water holds you back, a brown and roily disappointment, the lagtime of altitude. Some time zones are vertical, and the rivers answer to their origins on mountain peaks still packed in snow, melting with glacial slowness. Remote winters drain into the valley in icy, turbid water, running between grassy banks.

April is a jagged seam, a fault line of the year where the massive plate of winter grinds against the immensity of summer, and the force of occlusion erupts in freak winds, warm deluges, and berserk barometers. The months appear to me as places, fitted like flagstones in a year. Except for April. April is not a place—it is a behavior, the irascible shucking of an itchy skin.

Last month's clocklike hatches of March Browns on the big valley rivers have wound down and with them the first foretaste of a summer's dry-fly fishing. Now you might fish all afternoon for a small flurry of mayflies that comes and goes in fifteen minutes and a rise of trout that lasts half as long. Just as often, there's nothing at all. Still six weeks away, the Deschutes stonefly hatch is just beyond the range of fruitful anticipation. The winter steelhead have spawned and gone and the first swell of summer fish is just now gathering off the coast. A few shad have arrived, but not yet in numbers worth troubling about. You can cobble together only odds and ends: a few hours nymphing whitefish; casting at midnight off jetties on the coast for black rockfish; taking a beating in the afternoon surf, fishing perch; half a morning indulging the eternal vanity of taking a spring chinook on a fly. But it's hard to find a mainstay in these acrobatics. They don't even feel much like fishing, just something to do with your hands.

Driven indoors this April, I tied flies by the pound, tore down reels and oiled them, built leaders, cleaned out my vest, patched waders, and organized my rods (first by length, then line size, and finally by degrees of affection). I spent a couple weeks in this methadone fishing, a substitute less important for what it does than for what it prevents from happening. Outside my window, a white camellia bloomed feebly, and from a rusted gutter left unrepaired during sea-run cutthroat season, rain leaked down to a concrete block and tapped impatiently. Having only so much tackle to fuss with, I eventually tinkered myself into a corner—all dressed up and no place to go.

But at certain times, in certain moods, it simply feels better to be moving than standing still. And rather than go no place, I decided to go no place in particular, on the kind of trip defined only by its impelling energy. You don't go somewhere, you just go. Instead of seeking a place that conforms to the shape of your desire, you allow desire to shape itself around whatever places happen to present themselves.

After a winter of good fishing, focused tightly on a few stretches of a few rivers, April came as an abrupt dislocation, and primed me for just such a trip. In a season when everything rejuvenates by taking root, there can be a kind of renewal in rootlessness too. The novelist Don DeLillo once observed, "Plots carry their own logic. There is a tendency of plots to move toward death." Plans and plots are inertial, with an order and direction governed by the inexorable gravity of an endpoint. They imply patterns of inevitability which, from forceps to headstone, are the shortest distance between two points. The kind of trip I had in mind, on the other hand—unprescribed, directionless, and entropic—is the farthest.

If just about anywhere is possible, just about anything may be necessary. I packed up trout rods from 3- to 6-weight and a vest with everything from big streamers to midges. The prospect of lake fishing occurred to me, and I tossed in another rod, a long 7-weight; a few reels with assorted sinking lines; a float tube and fins; a pump to blow it up. There was a separate vest, a rod, and two reels for steelhead, along with a wading staff and cleats. Rain gear, a fly-tying kit, extra flies, hatch books, neoprene waders and lightweight ones, and boots. On impulse, I added a huge eleven-and-a-half-foot surf rod and a big spinning reel to the growing pile, and then took them out. No point in overdoing it.

I headed north for the simple reason that the nearest gas station lay in that direction. Along the highway, I began seeing unusual numbers of hawks and counted eleven of them in less than ten miles, perched on fence-posts, utility poles, and billboards, hunched against the drizzle. Sometimes it's hard not to look for omens and signs. My knowledge of birds is only middling, but I knew at once these were rough-legged hawks. I'd seen them featured in countless miles of raptor footage that aired on public television in the last decade, when legions of sleekly groomed Reagan-youth fueled a national fascination with handsome predators. I weighed the various interpretations of the omen, inconclusively.

When I began to hit the Portland traffic, I veered east toward the mountains, and eventually stopped some time later at a sagging little diner near the Clackamas River for coffee and information. Behind the counter, tiny red lights flashed silently in sequence on a police scanner, and an amber power lamp glowed on the front of a CB base unit. The only sound, however, issued from the tinny speaker of a transistor radio hung on a nail, a drone I recognized at once as the National Weather Service broadcast. Parked on a counter stool, an aged waitress in a peach uniform and white Adidas poured coffee without getting up. The fishing was slow, she said, "maybe some winter fish below the dam." She put on a pair of half-moon reading glasses and leaned over to a handwritten chart taped to the cash register.

"Six-point-three feet. That's last night. Radio man," she nodded *10* vaguely behind her, "says more weather's moving in. River's blowed out as it is. Get caught in that and you won't stop floatin' till the Japs fish you out." She looked meaningfully over the tops of her glasses, "A Jap'll eat fish eyes, you know."

I drove to see the river anyway. It was empty except for two bait plunkers huddled like a pair of hams by a damp, smoky fire. I watched for a time, waiting for something in the scene to lure me past the effort of unpacking my gear, and in the end moved higher up the river, away from any fishing. The season closed here three weeks ago, but there were fish in the river. Getting out to stretch my legs, I walked along a little tributary and found a pair of spawning steelhead, finning over the gravel, looking bushed. Disjunctions in scale have a way of magnifying things that is rare in the natural world, and the sight of big fish in small water is a magnetic spectacle. You couldn't help but wonder how, through the gauntlet of seals, gill nets, dams, and fishermen, they ever made it up here, if they were somehow better than other fish or just got the breaks. . . .

The radio man, as it turned out, didn't lie. Late in the day, a squall-like storm moved in, dropping sheets of rain that turned to clots of heavy, wet snow near Blue Box Pass, and finally thinned to a drizzle east of the Cascades when I pulled into Maupin at nightfall.

Flanking the Deschutes River, Maupin is the last major boat landing before the near-certain fatality of Sherars Falls. In six weeks, the first packs of summer rafters would arrive and the town would come alive, renting equipment, selling beer and groceries, frying burgers, running shuttles, and generally laying on some fat against the long, unprosperous winter. But now, in April, the place just waited, lean, vacant, and cheerless. Some time during the night, the rain stopped. I fished an hour in the raw, wintry morning, and left.

You don't take a trip like this. It takes you. It is indeterminate, open-ended, almost a succession of tangents except that there is no main line of navigation and so nothing is really tangential. A small body in space, I understand—an asteroid, a meteor, a particle of dust—may travel in just this way. Drawn by some distant star or planet, it bends around the gravitational field, and momentum carries it in a new direction, toward some other star or planet that diverts it yet again. A chunk of matter zigzags through space in a trajectory largely defined by things other than itself. There is, at certain times, the same inertness to being, when what you sense most clearly are the currents outside yourself, shifting forces of uncertain direction. And in such moments, what's needed most is to throw up a sail, pull in the keelboard, and just see where the drift takes you.

Still, traveling like this with no destination and no steam of your own   *15* takes some getting used to. It is difficult not to look ahead, not to see yourself on the way to somewhere. The whole thrust bucks a lifetime of habit by inverting the accustomed relation of destination and desire. Even temporary dislocations are unsettling—which is exactly why they're good for you—and for the first few days, I reluctantly picked at the trip like a plate of existential vegetables. I missed my wife, worried about the weather, about work left undone, about where to go next.

My notes record only fragments. Half a sentence for a river, a highway in an aside, a parenthetical stopping place. Spot-fishing the John Day River for hungry eight-inch smallmouth. Up the gulches and dry washes near Dayville, hunting for thunder-egg geodes. On the Crooked River, a handful of aquatic weeds squirming with hundreds of shrimplike scuds, a tantalizing fact I was unable to translate into trout. And driving, long, long, textureless miles of greening desert. All of these felt somehow preliminary. I waited, bored by my own company, and considered turning back. There seemed to be no point, which was true, and was also precisely the point.

But unpatterned time and routineless days tug at you with a sly, seductive insistence; bit by bit, they persuade you to themselves and begin to win you over. The ordinary formulae of daily life give way to pleasantly odd private jags, eating when the mood strikes, sleeping when it suits you, fishing or not, abruptly deciding to move on or content to linger, keeping irregular hours. I stopped taking notes. As always, change began with the rivers. Strangely (or not so strangely as I discovered later), I ran into no other fishermen over the course of nearly a week. I could work the best water without hurry, move when I wished, humor any whim of technique or method, and generally indulge the luxury of a man who has a trout stream entirely to himself. Inevitably, the tone and timbre of the fishing rippled back into the trip and subsumed it. According to Jung, crossing a river represents a fundamental change of attitude. Pity he didn't fish; he would have recognized that rivers are far more powerful as agents of transformation than symbols for it.

The turning point came one day along the Deschutes. I'm still not quite sure what led me back there—habit, accident, the simple consequence of unchecked momentum. I just found myself there one overcast afternoon standing on Lower Bridge, seventy-five miles above Maupin, scanning the water for rises. Against the cattails and willow thickets, a few trout dimpled sporadically. In late winter, big browns feed on the surface, first to a hatch of small black stoneflies and, later, March Browns. The odds of hitting a fish four pounds or better on a dry fly suddenly fall into betting range. But in a place like this, I care less for the stakes than for the game, for sight-fishing to individual risers on glassy, unforgiving currents. So I whittled an afternoon down to evening, sitting on the banks, marking rises, and fishing among flooded tule and current-swept brush to shy, jittery trout, one at a time.

This is a tough, technical kind of fishing, careful, deliberate, and intensely absorbing; that I'm not very good at it doesn't diminish its particular satisfactions. In fishing (among other things) style and technique are important only insofar as they define the shape of one's appreciation. Alter the style, and you change as well the nature of your pleasure. In blind fishing, for instance, say in searching a riffle with a floating fly or nymphing pocket water, you prospect for the unknown, wondering always where the trout might lie, what fly might tempt it, what cast it might come on. You fish, in essence, for surprise out of nowhere, for an instant in which you suddenly become aware that you're attached to a heartbeat. Fishing a heavy hatch—in most other respects the antithesis of blind-casting—nonetheless holds much the same appeal. I think it's fair to say that most anglers are apt to flock shoot a good rise of fish, picking out a density of rings, dropping a fly in the middle of them, and trusting to the numbers. Here, too, we fish for that moment of uncertainty, that tiny interval of unresolvedness in which we strain to assess just what it is we have hold of, how big it might be, and what will happen next. As in blind fishing, much of the thrill lies in seeing what you come up with.

But the deliberate, studied fishing to a single rising trout reverses the   20
circumstances and kindles an altogether different type of engagement.
Here, the fish is the given. You know its precise location, the form and
pattern of rises, often the size, and quite possibly the insect it's feeding on.
With the endpoint defined, getting there becomes the question. From the
particularities there emerges a kind of abstract problem, almost geometric
in design—a calculation of drift lines, curve casts, and angles of presentation, superimposed on the tempo of the rise, and predicated on the cagi-
ness of your own surmise. Alternatives must be weighed; small adaptations
undertaken; adjustments made one at a time; a solution converged upon;
and, sometimes, the final luxury of knowing exactly when you got it right.
You want to catch the fish, but you want more to figure it out, and the
particular satisfactions stem less from the eventuality than the process by
which the whole thing unfolds.

I doubt that I cast to more than ten or twelve fish that day and
hooked only a few of them. But I did, at last, catch the rhythm of the trip.

From the road map, Bend, Oregon, rose up as an enormous hot
shower. Finding one proved little trouble. Once an unassuming little town
at the edge of the desert, Bend suffered the irreparable misfortune, some
years back, of being "discovered." Now it sprawls in random ugliness, a
casualty of too much money too fast. The old center of town is ringed
with low-slung motels, fast-food huts, strange extraterrestrial boutiques,
minimalls, and inflatable subdivisions, and overall, looks like something
you might find if Dante had been a real estate developer. I had plenty of
opportunity to see it all, touring the place two or three times when I got
lost looking for a fly shop. It turned out to be three blocks from the motel.

I needed only some tippet material, which I asked for in a strange
glottal croak, far too loud and edged with the faint inflection of hysteria.
For the past six days, it suddenly occurred to me, I hadn't spoken to a soul.
The fly-shop clerk . . . said that the fishing had been "only fair," a revelation that surprised me. A fly shop is the only place I know of where the
fishing is always "excellent," since there's no reason to provide a customer
with less than best. As a result, any fly-shop report must be adjusted for
inflation, which in this case meant fishing was lousy. We talked a bit, he
suggesting a few places I might try, when our conversation drew the attention of a customer who seemed to browse the shop solely for this opportunity. He leaned an elbow on the glass counter, beamed an indulgent
smile, and introduced himself: "Can I tell you a little something about fly
fishing?" Statistically, my chances of running into someone who can "tell
me a little something about fly fishing" are pretty good, so I had to wonder
how this person so soundly whipped the odds. The type is regrettably
familiar—polar fleece and a haircut stretched over a hideous bubble of gas.
They never brag. It is too merciful. Instead, they insist upon "explaining"
things to you, benevolently strolling among the worldlings and torturing

them with little lectures. This one was particularly insufferable, droning at length about the previous weekend spent on a two-hundred-dollar-a-day fee-lake, hitting fish after fish on midges, modestly subordinating his own Olympian achievements to more general proclamations on the proper way to fish *Chironomids* on still water and play large trout on light tippets. It was amply clear that his actual knowledge of midge fishing was dwarfed even by my own pale understanding of the subject. Worst of all, he repeatedly referred to the insects as "Geronimos," and each authoritative mispronunciation seemed like a tiny pellet expelled solely for my irritation.

I left Bend in a pounding rainstorm, looping southeast toward drier skies (which I eventually caught up with) and a rumored pond (which I never found). Another day and a half of continuous prospecting turned up nothing, and I was well into the second of the truck's two twenty-three-gallon fuel tanks. In the eerie moonscape of the Warner Valley, I spread a map on the dust and pinned the corners with rocks. Unchecked, the prevailing momentum would bring me south to Pyramid Lake in Nevada by the next day. The road to the nearest gas station ran north. I debated, then took it.

There's little to say about long drives that hasn't already been said. 25 They dislocate your sense of reality, and the outside world becomes less a place than a medium through which you vaguely move. Whatever is real is contained within the jarring shell of a pickup cab, and the landscape rolls by like a long, plotless movie projected from all sides. After a while, you can't remember a time when you weren't driving, and what you might have seen or done seem like things told to you by someone else.

More than anything, though, is the weird introspection that it induces. On a small tape recorder, I started taking notes again. I dictated replies to long-neglected correspondence, made lists of various kinds, pondered out loud the big questions. I composed a letter of resignation from my job, a churlish and huffy little speech (never delivered) that trailed off into a rambling indictment of the American university, which gleefully split the atom while solemnly guarding the integrity of the infinitive. For a time, I just let the tape run—recording the road vibration and wind noise, the gargle of a perforated exhaust, John Hiatt singing about a band of Indians—to remind me of the traveling (I am listening to it now). Seized by some morbidity, I made out my will.

The gas station at Brothers came just in time, right at the point when it occurred to me that I wasn't really taking notes. I was talking to myself. In a dingy little restroom, I stripped to the waist, washed up in the sink and shaved, and got my bearings again. Half an hour away lay a small reservoir I'd heard about. An astonishing number of these impoundments are scattered about this arid, unremittingly exposed landscape. People call them "lakes," though this is an insult to real lakes everywhere. Most are manmade, little more than shallow depressions with a bulldozed earthen dam just high enough to trap a thin film of turbid, ugly water. Some are seasonal, some more or less permanent, and of those, a few manage one deeply redeeming quality—they grow trout at a phenomenal rate. The one I made camp on had this reputation.

In the morning, for the first time since setting out, the sun rose in a cloudless sky. It woke me early. A few fishermen were already on the water; offshore, a guy in a float tube netted a trout. I raised my rod and pointed with exaggerated gestures at the fly on my hook keeper. He cupped a hand to his mouth and shouted, "Nimps!" I walked on, led much of the way by a horned lark hopping through sagebrush in a highly convincing crippled-wing performance. On a small arm of the lake where I could get the morning sun to my back and the glare from my eyes, I tried nimp after nimp. Big dragonfly nymphs on sink-tips, olive marabou damsels on intermediate lines, and finally, by luck, a floating line and a #14 Prince. That one rang the bell.

In a rare inversion of the normal order, the catching was comparatively brisk, although the fishing itself was slow. I made maybe twenty casts an hour. There was the long delivery, an even longer pause to let the fly sink, followed by an agonizingly deliberate, inching retrieve almost to the rod tip. Then, just the smallest resistance. Not a tug, only the faint feeling of a little extra weight. I missed the first few fish, assuming that the take would be more decisive and palpable, but eventually got the hang of it. None of the trout jumped; in the cold water, they dogged the bottom amid the flooded sagebrush; by noon, I'd taken seven thick rainbows, and lost as many more.

The weather continued to moderate—cool, sunny days, cold and clear nights—and time passed in the kind of pleasant rhythm that comes easily when you are alone. Yet at the same time I became aware again of a vague feeling I'd had off and on since the beginning. It was more inkling than idea, a vague perception that something was hovering on the perimeter of this trip. I sensed it only as an indistinct significance, possibly a place or a direction, something to find or be found by, or perhaps only a reason for coming. It didn't drive the trip, but seemed to accumulate along with it, and though I now understand what it was, at the time it remained at the edge of intuition and would not be thought or coaxed into the open, or snuck up on and surprised. Nor would it quite go away.

The trip through Hines was a strange hallucination. A gas station attendant discovered a grotesque swelling on the sidewall of a rear tire. I was sent to a specialist who diagnosed the bulge as terminal, indicating as well that the other tire, to all appearances in good health, was in fact rapidly failing. Skeptical but helpless, I surrendered the keys and walked a few blocks to a diner. For reasons that became abundantly clear, it announced itself with a handlettered sign—no name, just a message: "The Worst Food in Oregon." This, I discovered, was no joke. The coffee might just have been the worst in the world. I ordered up the breakfast special (recorded in my notes as "Toast-and-Eggs Regret"), and under the circumstances, found it difficult to complain about the result, the cook having lived up so fully to his end of the agreement. The place itself was scarcely larger than a Fotomat, with a few picnic tables inside, and walls covered in graffiti of a spooky and unvarying "Go Jesus!" type. The management apparently encouraged the practice, which seemed appropriate to an establishment where mere matters of the flesh, like food, commanded so little regard.

Outside the tire dealer, my pickup awaited as promised. I paid the bill, and the clerk handed over a receipt along with a package wrapped neatly in white paper and hard as a brick, a promotional bonus, I was told, for the new radials. I asked what was in it. "Seven pounds of ground beef," he said, walking off. One might have expected a stainless-steel tire gauge or a Naugahyde litter bag. Instead, burger—the national solvent. Only in America.

An hour south, the Steens first appeared, an isolated mountain range in remote country riven with geological fault lines. Ten million years ago, the area was a broad basalt plateau; over time, stresses along the faults fractured the sheet of rock into immense blocks. Some of the blocks sank, like the ones to the east in the Alvord Valley. Others pushed upward in abrupt, sheared escarpments, forming the Steens that rise a mile above the valley floor and 10,000 feet above sea level. The western approach to the Steens rim, near Frenchglen, is a gradual rise, cut intermittently by deep glacial valleys. At the foot of the mountains runs the Blitzen River. Moving water again.

The Blitzen, I've been told repeatedly, holds some large rainbows, though I've never hooked one or seen one or been in the presence of anyone who has. Rumors take on a life of their own whenever big fish are involved. But it is a hard, jagged, beautiful place, and in past years I've hiked upstream for the small native redbands, a subspecies of rainbow trout that long ago adapted to the desert. Mostly, they inhabit the steep canyon of the upper river, and I wouldn't go there on this trip. The jeep trail is tenuous enough in the best weather; at this time of year, it would be five miles of thigh-deep mudholes.

I worked the lower river, where it levels out onto a marshy plain *35* that, in a month or so, would breed a quantity of mosquitoes impossible to believe in this dry landscape. Again, only the small fish were willing, though plenty of those.

Nothing gnaws like a detail, and comfortably encamped with fishing enough to satisfy, I became strangely consumed with the burger question. A windfall, even a small one, is not to be taken lightly. Thawing in the cooler, the package had bled on the beer and stained the water a thin, milky pink. I weighed the options against its obviously accelerating half-life, and the next night mashed the whole lump into a big cast-iron skillet over a white-gas stove, and for the better part of an hour tended the largest hamburger with which I've ever personally come into contact. Out of duty, I ate as much as I could, wrapped a few cold wedges in a plastic bag, and laid the remainder on a stump near camp. In the morning it was gone, a second windfall for some other creature and an occasion for musing: a bad tire was transformed into a hunk of ground beef, which in turn became a skunk or porcupine, which might eventually meet its own fate beneath a careless tire. "Burger to burger, dust to dust." Clearly, it was time to move on.

Down the Catlow Valley, the flatland was already greening and the hillside sprouted shoots of monkey flower that would soon line the seeps and springs with their absurdly pure yellow flowers. On the long grade between the Steens and Pueblos, I coasted into Fields and another one of the oddest little eateries on the planet, a low-ceilinged white-enamel cubicle, like the inside of a refrigerator, heavy with the smell of grilling hamburgers. I ordered the fish.

By early evening I was headed back north on the Fields-Denio Road, a fifty-mile stretch of washboard gravel that follows the eastern base of the Steens. Twenty minutes out of Fields, I stopped at a hot springs that bubbled through fissures in the hillside. Someone, some time ago, had cozied it up with a cement basin and a corrugated steel windbreak, and it's become a regular stopping point for the few travelers on this road. Sitting and soaking, I watched the water steam in the cool air and trickle down to the Alvord Desert spread out before me, sixty square miles of dust, sand, and baked dirt, flat as a griddle and almost completely devoid of vegetation. Over the desert floor, columns of soil swirled in dust devils, coalescing suddenly, traveling a random spin over the flats, and settling back into powder when the wind quieted.

With the mountains to your back and Tule Springs Rim on the far side of the valley, you get the distinct and accurate impression that you're sitting at the bottom of a lake. By the time of the last ice age, the Alvord Basin was filled with water, forming a lake nearly a hundred miles long, though still dwarfed by the huge inland seas of Lake Bonneville and Lake Lahontan to the south. Long cut off from any connection with other waters, the cutthroat in the Alvord Basin evolved into a distinct subspecies that, like the redband, adapted to tolerate the increasingly harsh conditions of the region—burning cold winters; frigid runoff; the splintering heat of high summer; streams that almost disappear in rainless spells; and warm slackwater creeks so saturated with dissolved minerals that the water leaves a white film on waders when it evaporates.

About 8,000 years ago, the lake dried up completely and the trout retreated to the small mountain streams, their numbers dwindling until, in this century, they were thought to have become extinct. In spite of their evolutionary handstands, the cutthroats couldn't compete with cattle herds and irrigators for habitat and were too willing to interbreed with introduced trout to maintain an undiluted wild gene pool. But in recent years, a handful of fish believed to be the Alvord strain were discovered toughing it out in a remote creek, a remarkable fact that holds only the grimmest reassurances. *40*

But this ancient lakebed validates the overwhelming sense of this desert as a world of its own. Even now, the streams that head in the mountains are part of no larger river system. Willow Creek, Whitehorse Creek, Trout Creek, Indian, Pike, and Alvord Creeks are their own watersheds. They simply flow out of the mountains to a dish in the dust, as if nothing had changed in 10,000 years, though now the waters simply sink into nothingness or evaporate in alkaline sumps. Few sights can affect a fisherman more profoundly than to walk downstream along one of these creeks and watch it, in just a few yards, disappear into the desert floor. You know you are in a different place, self-enclosed, with its own rules.

As always, some people just don't get it. One morning, a few years back, the handful of residents here awoke to find an enormous geometric design carved into the hard desert flat. It immediately occasioned the usual titillating speculation about extra-terrestrial beings that, in the twentieth century, have become technology's way of accommodating the persistent human need for a metaphysic. I strongly suspect that should such a visitation ever occur, it would run a disappointing second to the expectation, like meeting the Buddha and discovering he had hemorrhoids and a short temper. On the other hand, no spacemen have so far appeared, which at least argues for superior intelligence.

As it turned out, a certain "artist" stepped forward to take credit for the design, explaining that when no one was looking (which could be almost any time out here), he and a few accomplices laid out the pattern with stakes and string and harrowed it into the dirt with a hand plow. The figure, he patiently elaborated, reproduced an ancient, mystical pattern, meditating upon which would heal the aura, grow hair on a bald soul, cure existential dyspepsia, and administer karmic medicaments of various sorts, of which a misty, Miss America-like version of peace on earth was the very least to be expected.

In an unrelated incident, Bill Witherspoon, a name terminally associated with frauds of this type, erected a similar monument to himself—several hundred three-story logs stuck upright over sixty acres of desert to form a "cosmic transducer." (It is my great hope that a real visionary will come along and plant a giant, stuffed coyote by each pole, a hind leg lifted in salute to Witherspoon's achievement.) The cosmic transducer was erected, he said, to make contact with nature, because "to make contact with nature is to make contact with the most intimate part of oneself." Personally, I prefer that he just went somewhere in private and made contact with the most intimate part of himself in an essentially similar, but less obtrusive, fashion. The arrogance and obtuseness of spirit are staggering, as though the place somehow needed these portraits of the artist to invest it with significance.

It was after dark when I pulled off on the rutted two-track leading   *45* to Mann Lake. I made camp in the light of a half-moon. Despite the clear sky, the surest sign of a cold night in the desert, the air was inexplicably mild.

At certain moments, this can be a deeply serene place, one of those landscapes in which you feel a kind of reparative and healing power, even when you don't believe yourself to be in need of these things. In part, I think, it is a consequence of perspective. To the west, two miles off but feeling much closer, the white peaks of the Steens rise a mile high. In saddles between angular summits, snow and ice linger into summer. Below them, the mountains fall away in a steep, smooth arc, sloping more gradually at the foot, and finally leveling down to the shore of the lake, forming one of the most beautiful curves of landscape I've ever seen. The scale is impossible to hold out against; the land coaxes you into a kind of equilibrium with itself.

At other times, however, it simply beats you into submission, and five or six days out here can leave you feeling pretty worked over. The high-summer sun will simmer your brain in its own juice, and there is no shade anywhere; in winter, eyes ache from the cold and the hair in your nose crackles like icicles. The distance from one extreme to the other is sometimes a matter of minutes. With mountains so close on the west, you can never see the change coming. The weather is on top of you in an instant. I've fished the far shore of the lake in shirtsleeves, bolted for camp when I felt the first waves of cold air rolling down the mountain, and jogged the last hundred yards in snow.

Mostly, it's the wind, the most difficult element to convey because people think they understand it already. They know windy days and believe they can imagine one after another after another. Yet they still have no idea of a place where the wind doesn't die down, not at evening, not in early morning. It rocks a tent all night long. There is nothing to block or blunt the incessant tunnel of moving air and all that goes with it— alkalai dust, cinders, bits of dry grass and sage bark; the lip-cracking dryness; and perhaps in the end, most inescapable of all, the noise rushing ceaselessly past your ears like traffic, so unremitting that it finally seems to be coming from inside your head.

On a windy afternoon, every angler on the lake will be lined up on the lee shore, hunched against the weather, with forty feet of fly line held stiffly horizontal over the water. You must dip the rod tip in the lake to set down a fly. And most of the fish are on the other side of the lake anyway, feeding on the drift and churn of the windward shore.

Still, it can be worth the trouble. The Lahontan cutthroats here—   50
another ice-age subspecies genetically groomed for desert life—are remarkably handsome fish and grow to a size that seems impossible in this thin pan of water. They can sometimes be caught on big woolly buggers or leeches, sometimes on damsel or *Callibaetis* nymphs, sometimes on nothing at all. Day-in and day-out, though, the staple is *Chironomid* pupae, midges, Geronimos. They flourish here in unimaginable abundance, and on a warm summer evening, enormous numbers of adults collect along the shore, swarming about, clinging to grasses or to one another, vibrating in the wind. From some distance away, you can hear their collective sound,

a continuous low-level whine, everywhere in general but nowhere in particular, nearly subsonic, like the hum of a power plant.

When I finished making camp, I walked down to the lake and there, for the first time, noticed something strange. There was no wind. It was absolutely still.

There is, I'm convinced, an innate human predisposition toward pattern-making. From three random dots on a blank page, the mind's eye constructs a triangle. We find familiar outlines in the night sky and transform clouds into recognizable shapes. We discern as well geometries of experience and order them in narrative. History, to us, has a structure and we read it like a long, untidy novel. Our own life stretches behind us as a story told, and ahead like a plot unfolding around a hero named after ourselves.

At home in the Willamette Valley, looking back on the trip and tracing on a map where I'd been, I saw just such a pattern unexpectedly emerge from a route that seemed at the time shapeless and undesigned. Though I had deliberately taken a trip with no particular direction, it now seemed to have a particular indirection, which can be just as certain, and sometimes truer. I'd driven wide, looping curves, wandering back and forth, zigzagging across a hypothetical line that marked the shortest distance from my doorstep to the shore of Mann Lake. And whether drawn or impelled, I still can't say.

That first morning I awoke, about as far away from home as I could get and still find trout, in a landscape as capricious and as little to be counted on as any I know, and discovered what couldn't be seen the night before. A vast expanse of purple lupine on the desert floor tinted the landscape with a deep amethyst, cupped between broken ridges. The air, still calm, was spiced with the odor of rabbitbrush blooming in a million tiny yellow blossoms. Bees worked the morning nectar flow, and the calls of meadowlarks chimed off the rimrock. And I remember standing there and thinking that back home in the valley, it must be spring now, too.

Reading and Responding

In the margins of the book, mark the passage you think expresses the main idea of the essay, its central point. Where does this passage occur, and how does this positioning influence the way you read the essay?

Working Together

1. Leeson says that all along, without knowing it, he was headed for Mann Lake. Why? Given what you learn about him in the essay, why would he be drawn to this particular place?

2. The concluding scene at Mann Lake is composed mostly of details, with only a little direct commentary from the author. Leeson shows rather than tells. Make a list of all the details that seem important in this description, then discuss what they seem to imply. Why is this an appropriate ending for both the journey and the essay?

3. One theme of this essay is "the innate human predisposition toward pattern-making." Working in groups, compare and combine your individual maps of the organization of this essay in order to make one group map. Think about the pattern of Leeson's trip and the pattern of his thinking; and suggest a geometric shape to describe this pattern: a circle, a spiral, or something else.

Rethinking and Rewriting

1. Take an "unprescribed, directionless" walk, drive, or ride. Just take off for an hour, not planning your route or destination; go where your whims take you. Immediately when you come back—or better yet, during the trip itself—write down everything of importance that you see, hear, and feel; and record, as clearly as you can, the route you took. Using these notes and your memory, write an essay of your travels; conclude as Leeson does, with some sense of how these apparently random movements assume some sort of pattern after all.

2. Reread your reading journal for this term, an old personal journal or diary, or a series of old letters. Copy the passages that seem the most interesting or fruitful, and spread them out on a table. With these pieces in front of you, assume they are pieces of a puzzle; assume there's an order to be found here, even though you weren't aware of it when you originally wrote. Find this order. Once you have it, type these pieces, thus making them into a collage essay. Use spaces to indicate shifts, and write some transitions if you feel the material needs it. For more on collage essays, see chapter 2.

3. Think about how you tend to make patterns in your own life, in small or large ways (how you order your socks, how you shelve your tapes, how you plan your school work, and so on). Write an essay that explains the kind of order you seem to need (or at least seem to live with).

4. Using the textbooks you're reading and working from this term, write an essay that discusses the ways your textbooks organize and present information. Using only these textbooks, discuss how the different disciplines organize their knowledge. What do these organizational patterns have in common, and how are they different? Finally, which organizational patterns seem easy (or relatively easy) for you to read and understand? Which patterns give you trouble?

"GONE BACK INTO THE EARTH"— hook

Barry Lopez

> *Essayist and nature writer Barry Lopez lives and writes near Finn Rock,*
> *along the McKenzie River, in Oregon. His* Of Wolves and Men *(1978)*
> *won the John Burroughs Medal;* Arctic Dreams *(1986) won the National*
> *Book Award. This piece from his essay collection* Crossing Open Ground
> *(1988) illustrates the intense environmentalism and stylistic power that have*
> *made him one of the most important environmental writers in America.*

Before and As You Read

Freewrite about the pressures and stresses in your life right now. Go on for
at least half a page. Then read the opening few pages of this essay. What (if
anything) happens to those pressures and stresses as you read? Write a few
sentences that simply record what happens as you read; then continue
reading.

Sensy
/touch

I am up to my waist in a basin of cool, acid-clear water, at the head
of a box canyon some 600 feet above the Colorado River. I place my
outstretched hands flat against a terminal wall of dark limestone which
rises more than a hundred feet above me, and down which a sheet of water
falls—the thin creek in whose pooled waters I now stand. The water splits
at my fingertips into wild threads; higher up, a warm canyon wind lifts
water off the limestone in a fine spray; these droplets intercept and shatter
sunlight. Down, down another four waterfalls and fern-shrouded pools
below, the water spills into an eddy of the Colorado River, in the shadow
of a huge boulder. Our boat is tied there.

This lush crease in the surface of the earth is a cleft in the precipitous
desert walls of Arizona's Grand Canyon. Its smooth outcrops of purple-
tinged travertine stone, its heavy air rolled in the languid perfume of columbine, struck by the sharp notes of a water ouzel, the trill of a disturbed
black phoebe—all this has a name: Elves Chasm.

A few feet to my right, a preacher from Maryland is staring straight
up at a blue sky, straining to see what flowers those are that nod at the top
of the falls. To my left a freelance automobile mechanic from Colorado sits
with an impish smile by helleborine orchids. Behind, another man, a
builder and sometime record producer from New York, who comes as
often as he can to camp and hike in the Southwest, stands immobile at the
pool's edge.

Sprawled shirtless on a rock is our boatman. He has led twelve or
fifteen of us on the climb up from the river. The Colorado entrances him.
He has a well-honed sense of the ridiculous, brought on, one believes, by
so much time in the extreme remove of this canyon.

In our descent we meet others in our group who stopped climbing   *5*
at one of the lower pools. At the second to the last waterfall, a young
woman with short hair and dazzling blue eyes walks with me back into
the canyon's narrowing V. We wade into a still pool, swim a few strokes to
its head, climb over a boulder, swim across a second pool and then stand
together, giddy, in the press of limestone, beneath the deafening cascade—
filled with euphoria.

One at a time we bolt and glide, fishlike, back across the pool,
grounding in fine white gravel. We wade the second pool and continue
our descent, stopping to marvel at the strategy of a barrel cactus and at the
pale shading of color in the ledges to which we cling. We share few words.
We know hardly anything of each other. We share the country.

The group of us who have made this morning climb are in the
middle of a ten-day trip down the Colorado River. Each day we are
upended, if not by some element of the landscape itself then by what the
landscape does, visibly, to each of us. It has snapped us like fresh-laundered
sheets.

After lunch, we reboard three large rubber rafts and enter the Colorado's quick, high flow. The river has not been this high or fast since Glen
Canyon Dam—135 miles above Elves Chasm, 17 miles above our starting
point at Lee's Ferry—was closed in 1963. Jumping out ahead of us, with
its single oarsman and three passengers, is our fourth craft, a twelve-foot
rubber boat, like a water strider with a steel frame. In Sockdolager Rapid
the day before, one of its welds burst and the steel pieces were bent apart.
(Sockdolager: a nineteenth-century colloquialism for knockout punch.)

Such groups as ours, the members all but unknown to each other on
the first day, almost always grow close, solicitous of each other, during
their time together. They develop a humor that informs similar journeys
everywhere, a humor founded in tomfoolery, in punning, in a continuous
parody of the life-in-civilization all have so recently (and gleefully) left.
Such humor depends on context, on an accretion of small, shared events;
it seems silly to those who are not there. It is not, of course. Any more
than that moment of fumbling awe one feels on seeing the Brahma schist
at the dead bottom of the canyon's Inner Gorge. Your fingertips graze the
1.9-billion-year-old stone as the boat drifts slowly past.

With the loss of self-consciousness, the landscape opens.   *10*

There are forty-one of us, counting a crew of six. An actor from
Florida, now living in Los Angeles. A medical student and his wife. A
supervisor from Virginia's Department of Motor Vehicles. A health-store
owner from Chicago. An editor from New York and his young son.

That kind of diversity seems normal in groups that seek such vacations—to trek in the Himalaya, to dive in the Sea of Cortez, to go birding
in the Arctic. We are together for two reasons: to run the Colorado River,
and to participate with jazz musician Paul Winter, who initiated the trip,
in a music workshop.

Winter is an innovator and a listener. He had thought for years about coming to the Grand Canyon, about creating music here in response to this particular landscape—collared lizards and prickly pear cactus, Anasazi Indian ruins and stifling heat. But most especially he wanted music evoked by the river and the walls that flew up from its banks—Coconino sandstone on top of Hermit shale on top of the Supai formations, stone exposed to sunlight, a bloom of photons that lifted colors—saffron and ochre, apricot, madder orange, pearl and gray green, copper reds, umber and terra-cotta browns—and left them floating in the air.

Winter was searching for a reintegration of music, landscape and people. For resonance. Three or four times during the trip he would find it for sustained periods: drifting on a quiet stretch of water below Bass Rapids with oboist Nancy Rumbel and cellist David Darling; in a natural amphitheater high in the Muav limestone of Matkatameba Canyon; on the night of a full June moon with euphonium player Larry Roark in Blacktail Canyon.

Winter's energy and passion, and the strains of solo and ensemble music, were sewn into the trip like prevailing winds, like the canyon wren's clear, whistled, descending notes, his glissando—seemingly present, close by or at a distance, whenever someone stopped to listen. *15*

But we came and went, too, like the swallows and swifts that flicked over the water ahead of the boats, intent on private thoughts.

On the second day of the trip we stopped at Redwall Cavern, an undercut recess that spans a beach of fine sand, perhaps 500 feet wide by 150 feet deep. Winter intends to record here, but the sand absorbs too much sound. Unfazed, the others toss a Frisbee, practice Tai-chi, jog, meditate, play recorders, and read novels.

No other animal but the human would bring to bear so many activities, from so many different cultures and levels of society, with so much energy, so suddenly in a new place. And no other animal, the individuals so entirely unknown to each other, would chance together something so unknown as this river journey. In this frenetic activity and difference seems a suggestion of human evolution and genuine adventure. We are not the first down this river, but in the slooshing of human hands at the water's edge, the swanlike notes of an oboe, the occasional hugs among those most afraid of the rapids, there *is* exploration.

Each day we see or hear something that astounds us. The thousand-year-old remains of an Anasazi footbridge, hanging in twilight shadow high in the canyon wall above Harding Rapid. Deer Creek Falls, where we stand knee-deep in turquoise water encircled by a rainbow. Havasu Canyon, wild with grapevines, cottonwoods and velvet ash, speckled dace and mule deer, wild grasses and crimson monkey flowers. Each evening we enjoy a vespers: cicadas and crickets, mourning doves, vermilion flycatchers. And the wind, for which chimes are hung in a salt cedar. These notes leap above the splash and rattle, the grinding of water and the roar of rapids.

The narrow, damp, hidden worlds of the side canyons, with their   *20*
scattered shards of Indian pottery and ghost imprints of 400-million-year-
old nautiloids, open onto the larger world of the Colorado River itself;
but nothing conveys to us how far into the earth's surface we have come.
Occasionally we glimpse the South Rim, four or five thousand feet above.
From the rims the canyon seems oceanic; at the surface of the river the
feeling is intimate. To someone up there with binoculars we seem utterly
remote down here. It is this known dimension of distance and time and
the perplexing question posed by the canyon itself—What is consequen-
tial? (in one's life, in the life of human beings, in the life of a planet)—that
reverberate constantly, and make the human inclination to judge (another
person, another kind of thought) seem so eerie.

Two kinds of time pass here: sitting at the edge of a sun-warmed pool
watching blue dragonflies and black tadpoles. And the rapids: down the
glassy-smooth tongue into a yawing trench, climb a ten-foot wall of standing
water and fall into boiling, ferocious hydraulics, sucking whirlpools,
drowned voices, stopped hearts. Rapids can fold and shatter boats and take
lives if the boatman enters at the wrong point or at the wrong angle.

Some rapids, like one called Hermit, seem more dangerous than they
are and give us great roller-coaster rides. Others—Hance, Crystal, Upset—
seem less spectacular, but are technically difficult. At Crystal, our boat
screeches and twists against its frame. Its nose crumples like cardboard in
the trough; our boatman makes the critical move to the right with split-
second timing and we are over a standing wave and into the haystacks of
white water, safely into the tail waves. The boatman's eyes cease to blaze.

The first few rapids—Badger Creek and Soap Creek—do not overwhelm us. When we hit the Inner Gorge—Granite Falls, Unkar Rapid,
Horn Creek Rapid—some grip the boat, rigid and silent. (On the ninth
day, when we are about to run perhaps the most formidable rapid, Lava
Falls, the one among us who has had the greatest fear is calm, almost
serene. In the last days, it is hard to overestimate what the river and the
music and the unvoiced concern for each other have washed out.)

There are threats to this separate world of the Inner Gorge. Down
inside it one struggles to maintain a sense of what they are, how they
impinge.

In 1963, Glen Canyon Dam cut off the canyon's natural flow of   *25*
water. Spring runoffs of more than two hundred thousand cubic feet per
second ceased to roar through the gorge, clearing the main channel of rock
and stones washed down from the side canyons. Fed now from the bottom
of Lake Powell backed up behind the dam, the river is no longer a warm,
silt-laden habitat for Colorado squawfish, razorback sucker and several kinds
of chub, but a cold, clear habitat for trout. With no annual scouring and a
subsequent deposition of fresh sand, the beaches show the evidence of continuous human use: they are eroding. The postflood eddies where squawfish
bred have disappeared. Tamarisk (salt cedar) and camel thorn, both exotic

plants formerly washed out with the spring floods, have gained an apparently permanent foothold. At the old high-water mark, catclaw acacia, mesquite and Apache plume are no longer watered and are dying out.

On the rim, far removed above, such evidence of human tampering seems, and perhaps is, pernicious. From the river, another change is more wrenching. It floods the system with a kind of panic that in other animals induces nausea and the sudden evacuation of the bowels: it is the descent of helicopters. Their sudden arrival in the canyon evokes not jeers but staring. The violence is brutal, an intrusion as criminal and as random as rape. When the helicopter departs, its rotor-wind walloping against the stone walls, I want to wash the sound off my skin.

The canyon finally absorbs the intrusion. I focus quietly each day on the stone, the breathing of time locked up here, back to the Proterozoic, before there were seashells. Look up to wisps of high cirrus overhead, the hint of a mare's tail sky. Close my eyes: tappet of water against the boat, sound of an Anasazi's six-hole flute. And I watch the bank for beaver tracks, for any movement.

The canyon seems like a grandfather.

One evening, Winter and perhaps half the group carry instruments and recording gear back into Blacktail Canyon to a spot sound engineer Mickey Houlihan says is good for recording.

Winter likes to quote from Thoreau: "The woods would be very *30* silent if no birds sang except those that sing best." The remark seems not only to underscore the ephemeral nature of human evolution but the necessity in evaluating any phenomenon—a canyon, a life, a song—of providing for change.

After several improvisations dominated by a cappella voice and percussion, Winter asks Larry Roark to try something on the euphonium; he and Rumbel and Darling will then come up around him. Roark is silent. Moonlight glows on the canyon's lips. There is the sound of gurgling water. After a word of encouragement, feeling shrouded in anonymous darkness like the rest of us, Larry puts his mouth to the horn.

For a while he is alone. God knows what visions of waterfalls or wrens, of boats in the rapids, of Bach or Mozart, are in his head, in his fingers, to send forth notes. The whine of the soprano sax finds him. And the flutter of the oboe. And the rumbling of the choral cello. The exchange lasts perhaps twenty minutes. Furious and sweet, anxious, rolling, delicate and raw. The last six or eight hanging notes are Larry's. Then there is a long silence. Winter finally says, "My God."

I feel, sitting in the wet dark in bathing suit and sneakers and T-shirt, that my fingers have brushed one of life's deep, coursing threads. Like so much else in the canyon, it is left alone. Speak, even notice it, and it would disappear.

I had come to the canyon with expectations. I had wanted to see snowy egrets flying against the black schist at dusk; I saw blue-winged teal against the deep green waters at dawn. I had wanted to hear thunder rolling in the thousand-foot depths; I heard Winter's soprano sax resonating in Matkatameba Canyon, with the guttural caws of four ravens which circled above him. I had wanted to watch rattlesnakes; I saw in an abandoned copper mine, in the beam of my flashlight, a wall of copper sulphate that looked like a wall of turquoise. I rose each morning at dawn and washed in the cold river. I went to sleep each night listening to the cicadas, the pencil-ticking sound of some other insect, the soughing of river waves in tamarisk roots, and watching bats plunge and turn, looking like leaves blown around against the sky. What any of us had come to see or do fell away. We found ourselves at each turn with what we had not imagined.

The last evening it rained. We had left the canyon and been carried   35
far out onto Lake Mead by the river's current. But we stood staring backward, at the point where the canyon had so obviously and abruptly ended.

A thought that stayed with me was that I had entered a private place in the earth. I had seen exposed nearly its oldest part. I had lost my sense of urgency, rekindled a sense of what people were, clambering to gain access to high waterfalls where we washed our hair together; and a sense of our endless struggle as a species to understand time and to estimate the consequences of our acts.

It rained the last evening. But before it did, Nancy Rumbel moved to the highest point on Scorpion Island in Lake Mead and played her oboe before a storm we could see hanging over Nevada. Sterling Smyth, who would return to programming computers in twenty-four hours, created a twelve-string imitation of the canyon wren, a long guitar solo. David Darling, revealed suddenly stark, again and then again, against a white-lightning sky, bowed furious homage to the now overhanging cumulonimbus.

In the morning we touched the far shore of Lake Mead, boarded a bus and headed for the Las Vegas airport. We were still wrapped in the journey, as though it were a Navajo blanket. We departed on various planes and arrived home in various cities and towns and at some point the world entered again and the hardest thing, the translation of what we had touched, began.

I sat in the airport in San Francisco, waiting for a connecting flight to Oregon, dwelling on one image. At the mouth of Nankoweap Canyon, the river makes a broad turn, and it is possible to see high in the orange rock what seem to be four small windows. They are entrances to granaries, built by the Anasazi who dwelled in the canyon a thousand years ago. This was provision against famine, to ensure the people would survive.

I do not know, really, how we will survive without places like the   40
Inner Gorge of the Grand Canyon to visit. Once in a lifetime, even, is enough. To feel the stripping down, an ebb of the press of conventional time, a radical change of proportion, an unspoken respect for others that elicits keen emotional pleasure, a quick, intimate pounding of the heart.

Some parts of the trip will emerge one day on an album. Others will be found in a gesture of friendship to some stranger in an airport, in a letter of outrage to a planner of dams, in a note of gratitude to nameless faces in the Park Service, in wondering at the relatives of the ubiquitous wren, in the belief, passed on in whatever fashion—a photograph, a chord, a sketch—that nature can heal.

The living of life, any life, involves great and private pain, much of which we share with no one. In such places as the Inner Gorge the pain trails away from us. It is not so quiet there or so removed that you can hear yourself think, that you would even wish to; that comes later. You can hear your heart beat. That comes first.

Reading and Responding

1. Does it surprise you to find that part of the reason for this trip is to play music? Are you surprised to find that jazz musician Paul Winter has organized this trip? What do you think of that? Would you normally associate jazz with a rafting trip? Write about these questions for half a page or so.
2. Write something you would share with no one. Then decide whether to keep it somewhere or shred it or burn it or throw it away.

Working Together

1. Assume that "Gone Back into the Earth" is an example of strong, effective narrative and descriptive writing. Read over the opening paragraphs (up to "After lunch, we reboard . . ."), and as a group, decide on three reasons why this writing is in fact strong and effective narrative, descriptive writing. List your reasons and a part of Lopez's essay that illustrates each of your reasons. (*Hint:* Look for the writing that grabs you.)
2. As a group, talk about whether or not you think jazz has any place on a rafting trip. Come to a consensus if you can, and write a short paragraph that explains your group's conclusion. If you can't agree, write a paragraph about why you can't agree.

Rethinking and Rewriting

1. Write about a time when you've "gone back" to some wild or natural place. Put yourself and your readers right back into that landscape and that time. In your opening paragraph, consciously try to imitate Lopez's opening paragraph. And try to end as Lopez does, too, by reflecting on the trip and what it might mean—or does mean—to you.
2. On the basis of only this one Barry Lopez piece, write about why you would or would not be interested in reading more by this author. What is it that appeals to you in this writing? What is it that doesn't appeal to

you? How do these likes and dislikes, interests and disinterests, add up? Make sure that you make your thoughts and opinions clear, and make sure that you actually quote the essay at least twice to illustrate and explain what you're saying. One of these quotations should be short—less than a sentence. Another one should be long (more than three lines of text). For explanations of how to use quotations, see chapter 2.

"THE GREAT AMERICAN DESERT"

Edward Abbey

The late Edward Abbey was famous for his passionate love of the South-
west desert and his cranky impatience with those who failed to love and respect
it, too. After writing several novels early in his career, he first became well-
known for Desert Solitaire *(1968), a "personal history" of his experience*
as a park ranger in the canyon country of Utah and Arizona. His subsequent
work includes several collections of essays and a best-selling novel about eco-
sabotage, The Monkey Wrench Gang *(1975). The essay that follows is*
from Desert Solitaire.

Before You Read

Read just the first four paragraphs of this essay (stop after the business
about the kissing bug); then write briefly about your response. What's
Edward Abbey's logic, his reason for starting his essay in this way? What
response does he want to get from you as a reader? Does it work?

In my case it was love at first sight. This desert, all deserts, any desert.
No matter where my head and feet may go, my heart and my entrails stay
behind, here on the clean, true, comfortable rock, under the black sun of
God's forsaken country. When I take on my next incarnation, my bones
will remain bleaching nicely in a stone gulch under the rim of some
faraway plateau, way out there in the back of beyond. An unrequited and
excessive love, inhuman no doubt but painful anyhow, especially when I
see my desert under attack. "The one death I cannot bear," said the
Sonoran-Arizonan poet Richard Shelton. The kind of love that makes a
man selfish, possessive, irritable. If you're thinking of a visit, my natural
reaction is like a rattlesnake's—to warn you off. What I want to say goes
something like this.

Survival Hint #1: Stay out of there. Don't go. Stay home and read a
good book, this one for example. The Great American Desert is an awful
place. People get hurt, get sick, get lost out there. Even if you survive,
which is not certain, you will have a miserable time. The desert is for
movies and God-intoxicated mystics, not for family recreation.

Let me enumerate the hazards. First the Walapai tiger, also known as
conenose kissing bug. *Triatoma protracta* is a true bug, black as sin, and it
flies through the night quiet as an assassin. It does not attack directly like a
mosquito or deerfly, but alights at a discreet distance, undetected, and
creeps upon you, its hairy little feet making not the slightest noise. The
kissing bug is fond of warmth and like Dracula requires mammalian blood
for sustenance. When it reaches you the bug crawls onto your skin so
gently, so softly that unless your senses are hyperacute you feel nothing.

Selecting a tender point, the bug slips its conical proboscis into your flesh, injecting a poisonous anesthetic. If you are asleep you will feel nothing. If you happen to be awake you may notice the faintest of pinpricks, hardly more than a brief ticklish sensation, which you will probably disregard. But the bug is already at work. Having numbed the nerves near the point of entry the bug proceeds (with a sigh of satisfaction, no doubt) to withdraw blood. When its belly is filled, it pulls out, backs off, and waddles away, so drunk and gorged it cannot fly.

At about this time the victim awakes, scratching at a furious itch. If you recognize the symptoms at once, you can sometimes find the bug in your vicinity and destroy it. But revenge will be your only satisfaction. Your night is ruined. If you are of average sensitivity to a kissing bug's poison, your entire body breaks out in hives, skin aflame from head to toe. Some people become seriously ill, in many cases requiring hospitalization. Others recover fully after five or six hours except for a hard and itchy swelling, which may endure for a week.

After the kissing bug, you should beware of rattlesnakes; we have half   5 a dozen species, all offensive and dangerous, plus centipedes, millipedes, tarantulas, black widows, brown recluses, Gila monsters, the deadly poisonous coral snakes, and giant hairy desert scorpions. Plus an immense variety and near-infinite number of ants, midges, gnats, bloodsucking flies, and blood-guzzling mosquitoes. (You might think the desert would be spared at least mosquitoes? Not so. Peer in any water hole by day: swarming with mosquito larvae. Venture out on a summer's eve: The air vibrates with their mournful keening.) Finally, where the desert meets the sea, as on the coasts of Sonora and Baja California, we have the usual assortment of obnoxious marine life: sandflies, ghost crabs, stingrays, electric jellyfish, spiny sea urchins, man-eating sharks, and other creatures so distasteful one prefers not even to name them.

It has been said, and truly, that everything in the desert either stings, stabs, stinks, or sticks. You will find the flora here as venomous, hooked, barbed, thorny, prickly, needled, saw-toothed, hairy, stickered, mean, bitter, sharp, wiry, and fierce as the animals. Something about the desert inclines all living things to harshness and acerbity. The soft evolve out. Except for sleek and oily growths like the poison ivy—oh yes, indeed—that flourish in sinister profusion on the dank walls above the quicksand down in those corridors of gloom and labyrinthine monotony that men call canyons.

We come now to the third major hazard, which is sunshine. Too much of a good thing can be fatal. Sunstroke, heatstroke, and dehydration are common misfortunes in the bright American Southwest. If you can avoid the insects, reptiles, and arachnids, the cactus and the ivy, the smog of the southwestern cities, and the lung fungus of the desert valleys (carried by dust in the air), you cannot escape the desert sun. Too much exposure to it eventually causes, quite literally, not merely sunburn but skin cancer.

Much sun, little rain also means an arid climate. Compared with the high humidity of more hospitable regions, the dry heat of the desert seems at first not terribly uncomfortable—sometimes even pleasant. But that sensation of comfort is false, a deception, and therefore all the more dangerous, for it induces overexertion and an insufficient consumption of water, even when water is available. This leads to various internal complications, some immediate—sunstroke, for example—and some not apparent until much later. Mild but prolonged dehydration, continued over a span of months or years, leads to the crystallization of mineral solutions in the urinary tract, that is, to what urologists call urinary calculi or kidney stones. A disability common in all the world's arid regions. Kidney stones, in case you haven't met one, come in many shapes and sizes, from pellets smooth as BB shot to highly irregular calcifications resembling asteroids, Vietcong shrapnel, and crown-of-thorns starfish. Some of these objects may be "passed" naturally; others can be removed only by means of the Davis stone basket or by surgery. Me—I was lucky; I passed mine with only a groan, my forehead pressed against the wall of a pissoir in the rear of a Tucson bar that I cannot recommend.

You may be getting the impression by now that the desert is not the most suitable of environments for human habitation. Correct. Of all the Earth's climatic zones, excepting only the Antarctic, the deserts are the least inhabited, the least "developed," for reasons that should now be clear.

You may wish to ask, Yes, okay, but among North American deserts   10 which is the *worst?* A good question—and I am happy to attempt to answer.

Geographers generally divide the North American desert—what was once termed "the Great American Desert"—into four distinct regions or subdeserts. These are the Sonoran Desert, which comprises southern Arizona, Baja California, and the state of Sonora in Mexico; the Chihuahuan Desert, which includes west Texas, southern New Mexico, and the states of Chihuahua and Coahuila in Mexico; the Mojave Desert, which includes southeastern California and small portions of Nevada, Utah, and Arizona; and the Great Basin Desert, which includes most of Utah and Nevada, northern Arizona, northwestern New Mexico, and much of Idaho and eastern Oregon.

Privately, I prefer my own categories. Up north in Utah somewhere is the canyon country—places like Zeke's Hole, Death Hollow, Pucker Pass, Buckskin Gulch, Nausea Crick, Wolf Hole, Mollie's Nipple, Dirty Devil River, Horse Canyon, Horseshoe Canyon, Lost Horse Canyon, Horsethief Canyon, and Horseshit Canyon, to name only the more classic places. Down in Arizona and Sonora there's the cactus country; if you have nothing better to do, you might take a look at High Tanks, Salome Creek, Tortilla Flat, Esperero ("Hoper") Canyon, Holy Joe Peak, Depression Canyon, Painted Cave, Hell Hole Canyon, Hell's Half Acre, Iceberg Canyon, Tiburon (Shark) Island, Pinacate Peak, Infernal Valley, Sykes Crater,

Montezuma's Head, Gu Oidak, Kuakatch, Pisinimo, and Baboquivari Mountain, for example.

Then there's The Canyon. *The* Canyon. The Grand. That's one world. And North Rim—that's another. And Death Valley, still another, where I lived one winter near Furnace Creek and climbed the Funeral Mountains, tasted Badwater, looked into the Devil's Hole, hollered up Echo Canyon, searched for and never did find Seldom Seen Slim. Looked for *satori* near Vana, Nevada, and found a ghost town named Bonnie Claire. Never made it to Winnemucca. Drove through the Smoke Creek Desert and down through Big Pine and Lone Pine and home across the Panamints to Death Valley again—home sweet home that winter.

And which of these deserts is the worst? I find it hard to judge. They're all bad—not half bad but all bad. In the Sonoran Desert, Phoenix will get you if the sun, snakes, bugs, and arthropods don't. In the Mojave Desert, it's Las Vegas, more sickening by far than the Glauber's salt in the Death Valley sinkholes. Go to Chihuahua and you're liable to get busted in El Paso and sandbagged in Ciudad Juárez—where all old whores go to die. Up north in the Great Basin Desert, on the Plateau Province, in the canyon country, your heart will break, seeing the strip mines open up and the power plants rise where only cowboys and Indians and J. Wesley Powell ever roamed before.

Nevertheless, all is not lost; much remains, and I welcome the pros-   15
pect of an army of lug-soled hiker's boots on the desert trails. To save what wilderness is left in the American Southwest—and in the American Southwest only the wilderness is worth saving—we are going to need all the recruits we can get. All the hands, heads, bodies, time, money, effort we can find. Presumably—and the Sierra Club, the Wilderness Society, the Friends of the Earth, the Audubon Society, the Defenders of Wildlife operate on this theory—those who learn to love what is spare, rough, wild, undeveloped, and unbroken will be willing to fight for it, will help resist the strip miners, highway builders, land developers, weapons testers, power producers, tree chainers, clear cutters, oil drillers, dam beavers, subdividers—the list goes on and on—before that zinc-hearted, termite-brained, squint-eyed, nearsighted, greedy crew succeeds in completely californicating what still survives of the Great American Desert.

So much for the Good Cause. Now what about desert hiking itself, you may ask. I'm glad you asked that question. I firmly believe that one should never—I repeated *never*—go out into that formidable wasteland of cactus, heat, serpents, rock, scrub, and thorn without careful planning, thorough and cautious preparation, and complete—never mind the expense!—*complete* equipment. My motto is: Be Prepared.

That is my belief and that is my motto. My practice, however, is a little different. I tend to go off in a more or less random direction myself, half-baked, half-assed, half-cocked, and half-ripped. Why? Well, because I have an indolent and melancholy nature and don't care to be bothered getting all those *things* together—all that bloody *gear*—maps, compass, binoculars, poncho, pup tent, shoes, first-aid kit, rope, flashlight, inspirational poetry, water, food—and because anyhow I approach nature with a certain surly ill-will, daring Her to make trouble. Later when I'm deep into Natural Bridges Natural Moneymint or Zion National Parkinglot or say General Shithead National Forest Land of Many Abuses why then, of course, when it's a bit late, then I may wish I had packed that something extra: matches perhaps, to mention one useful item, or maybe a spoon to eat my gruel with.

If I hike with another person it's usually the same; most of my friends have indolent and melancholy natures too. A cursed lot, all of them. I think of my comrade John De Puy, for example, sloping along for mile after mile like a goddamned camel—indefatigable—with those J. C. Penney hightops on his feet and that plastic pack on his back he got with five books of Green Stamps and nothing inside it but a sketchbook, some homemade jerky and a few cans of green chiles. Or Douglas Peacock, ex–Green Beret, just the opposite. Built like a buffalo, he loads a ninety-pound canvas pannier on his back at trailhead, loaded with guns, ammunition, bayonet, pitons and carabiners, cameras, field books, a 150-foot rope, geologist's sledge, rock samples, assay kit, field glasses, two gallons of water in steel canteens, jungle boots, a case of C-rations, rope hammock, pharmaceuticals in a pig-iron box, raincoat, overcoat, two-man mountain tent, Dutch oven, hibachi, shovel, ax, inflatable boat, and near the top of the load and distributed through side and back pockets, easily accessible, a case of beer. Not because he enjoys or needs all that weight—he may never get to the bottom of that cargo on a ten-day outing—but simply because Douglas uses his packbag for general storage both at home and on the trail and prefers not to have to rearrange everything from time to time merely for the purposes of a hike. Thus my friends De Puy and Peacock; you may wish to avoid such extremes.

A few tips on desert etiquette:

1. Carry a cooking stove, if you must cook. Do not burn desert wood, which is rare and beautiful and required ages for its creation (an ironwood tree lives for over 1,000 years and juniper almost as long).
2. If you must, out of need, build a fire, then for God's sake allow it to burn itself out before you leave—do not bury it, as Boy Scouts and Campfire Girls do, under a heap of mud or sand. Scatter the ashes; replace any rocks you may have used in constructing a fireplace; do all you can to obliterate the evidence that you camped here. (The Search & Rescue Team may be looking for you.)
3. Do not bury garbage—the wildlife will only dig it up again. Burn what will burn and pack out the rest. The same goes for toilet paper: Don't bury it, *burn it.*

4. Do not bathe in desert pools, natural tanks, *tinajas,* potholes. Drink what water you need, take what you need, and leave the rest for the next hiker and more important for the bees, birds, and animals—bighorn sheep, coyotes, lions, foxes, badgers, deer, wild pigs, wild horses—whose *lives* depend on that water.

5. Always remove and destroy survey stakes, flagging, advertising signboards, mining claim markers, animal traps, poisoned bait, seismic exploration geophones, and other such artifacts of industrialism. The men who put those things there are up to no good and it is our duty to confound them. Keep America Beautiful. Grow a Beard. Take a Bath. Burn a Billboard.

Anyway—why go into the desert? Really, why do it? That sun, roaring at you all day long. The fetid, tepid, vapid little water holes slowly evaporating under a scum of grease, full of cannibal beetles, spotted toads, horsehair worms, liver flukes, and down at the bottom, inevitably, the pale cadaver of a ten-inch centipede. Those pink rattlesnakes down in The Canyon, those diamondback monsters thick as a truck driver's wrist that lurk in shady places along the trail, those unpleasant solpugids and unnecessary Jerusalem crickets that scurry on dirty claws across your face at night. Why? The rain that comes down like lead shot and wrecks the trail, those sudden rockfalls of obscure origin that crash like thunder ten feet behind you in the heart of a dead-still afternoon. The ubiquitous buzzard, so patient—but only so patient. The sullen and hostile Indians, all on welfare. The ragweed, the tumbleweed, the Jimson weed, the snakeweed. The scorpion in your shoe at dawn. The dreary wind that blows all spring, the psychedelic Joshua trees waving their arms at you on moonlight nights. Sand in the soup du jour. Halazone tablets in your canteen. The barren hills that always go up, which is bad, or down, which is worse. Those canyons like catacombs with quicksand lapping at your crotch. Hollow, mummified horses with forelegs casually crossed, dead for ten years, leaning against the corner of a barbed-wire fence. Packhorses at night, iron-shod, clattering over the slickrock through your camp. The last tin of tuna, two flat tires, not enough water and a forty-mile trek to Tule Well. An osprey on a cardón cactus, snatching the head off a living fish—always the best part first. The hawk sailing by at 200 feet, a squirming snake in its talons. Salt in the drinking water. Salt, selenium, arsenic, radon and radium in the water, in the gravel, in your bones. Water so hard it bends light, drills holes in rock and chokes up your radiator. Why go there? Those places with the hardcase names: Starvation Creek, Poverty Knoll, Hungry Valley, Bitter Springs, Last Chance Canyon, Dungeon Canyon, Whipsaw Flat, Dead Horse Point, Scorpion Flat, Dead Man Draw, Stinking Spring, Camino del Diablo, Jornado del Muerto . . . Death Valley.

Well then, why indeed go walking into the desert, that grim ground, that bleak and lonesome land where, as Genghis Khan said of India, "the heat is bad and the water makes men sick"?

20

Why the desert, when you could be strolling along the golden beaches of California? Camping by a stream of pure Rocky Mountain spring water in colorful Colorado? Loafing through a laurel slick in the misty hills of North Carolina? Or getting your head mashed in the greasy alley behind the Elysium Bar and Grill in Hoboken, New Jersey? Why the desert, given a world of such splendor and variety?

A friend and I took a walk around the base of a mountain up beyond Coconino County, Arizona. This was a mountain we'd been planning to circumambulate for years. Finally we put on our walking shoes and did it. About halfway around this mountain, on the third or fourth day, we paused for a while—two days—by the side of a stream, which the Navajos call Nasja because of the amber color of the water. (Caused perhaps by juniper roots—the water seems safe enough to drink.) On our second day there I walked down the stream, alone, to look at the canyon beyond. I entered the canyon and followed it for half the afternoon, for three or four miles, maybe, until it became a gorge so deep, narrow and dark, full of water and the inevitable quagmires of quicksand, that I turned around and looked for a way out. A route other than the way I'd come, which was crooked and uncomfortable and buried—I wanted to see what was up on top of this world. I found a sort of chimney flue on the east wall, which looked plausible, and sweated and cursed my way up through that until I reached a point where I could walk upright, like a human being. Another 300 feet of scrambling brought me to the rim of the canyon. No one, I felt certain, had ever before departed Nasja Canyon by that route.

But someone had. Near the summit I found an arrow sign, three feet long, formed of stones and pointing off into the north toward those same old purple vistas, so grand, immense, and mysterious, of more canyons, more mesas and plateaus, more mountains, more cloud-dappled sun-spangled leagues of desert sand and desert rock, under the same old wide and aching sky.

The arrow pointed into the north. But what was it pointing *at?* I   25
looked at the sign closely and saw that those dark, desert-varnished stones had been in place for a long, long, time; they rested in compacted dust. They must have been there for a century at least. I followed the direction indicated and came promptly to the rim of another canyon and a drop-off straight down of a good 500 feet. Not that way, surely. Across this canyon was nothing of any unusual interest that I could see—only the familiar sun-blasted sandstone, a few scrubby clumps of blackbrush and prickly pear, a few acres of nothing where only a lizard could graze, surrounded by a few square miles of more nothingness interesting chiefly to horned toads. I returned to the arrow and checked again, this time with field glasses, looking away for as far as my aided eyes could see toward the north, for ten, twenty, forty miles into the distance. I studied the scene with care, looking for an ancient Indian ruin, a significant cairn, perhaps an abandoned mine, a hidden treasure of some inconceivable wealth, the mother of all mother lodes. . . .

But there was nothing out there. Nothing at all. Nothing but the desert. Nothing but the silent world.

That's why.

Reading and Responding

Pay attention to the various sideways glimpses you get of Abbey, the narrator of this piece. How would you describe him? (Find two places where you think Abbey shows through clearly.)

Working Together

1. Discuss the ending of this essay. Abbey doesn't so much explain his reasons as make his essay itself an arrow that points at something (or several somethings). Guess at what the arrow (this essay, that is) points at. As a group, come up with three possibilities. (*Hint:* Looking at his tips on desert etiquette might help here.)
2. Each of you identify some animal mentioned in this essay. Do a little bit of research about this animal. For your next class, be ready to read a short paragraph that summarizes what you've learned about this animal. End your paragraph by talking about whether Abbey's information was accurate. Finally, as a group, decide whether Abbey's essay is a reliable source of information on what one can find in the desert.
3. As a group, decide what Abbey values and doesn't value. Make a list of each category.

Rethinking and Rewriting

1. On the basis of only your reading of "The Great American Desert," write an essay that identifies what Abbey values and doesn't value. Structure your essay so that it starts by discussing what he doesn't value and ends by focusing on what you think he values most.
2. On the basis of only this essay, write a one-page introduction to Edward Abbey for those who haven't ever read anything he's written.
3. Regardless of your own beliefs, assume that you're going to write an essay that argues with Abbey. What would you argue with him about? How would you make such an argument? Who would be likely to agree with your arguments?

"LIFE ON THE ROCKS: THE GALÁPAGOS"

Annie Dillard

> *This essay is from Annie Dillard's* Teaching a Stone to Talk *(1982), a collection subtitled "Expeditions and Encounters." In contrast to much of her work, which seeks the mystery in the everyday world around us, it's a piece about an expedition to an exotic, faraway place, a place very remote from Tinker's Creek in Virginia or the Pittsburgh suburb of her childhood. (See, too, Dillard's "The Silent Neighborhood" in chapter 6.)*

Before and As You Read

1. As you read, assume that you are Annie Dillard and you are the one on this trip. What's fun about it? Why are you making this trip? Freewrite about these questions for at least half a page. As you continue reading, mark places where you can see what makes this trip an interesting or rewarding one.

2. Look only at the first two paragraphs of this essay. Why are they there? What's Dillard suggesting about the Galápagos? Write a sentence that explains this question.

3. As you read this piece, what sections stand out as particularly remarkable? Once you're done reading, go back and pick out two such sections. Write three or four sentences that explain why you've chosen them.

I

First there was nothing, and although you know with your reason that nothing is nothing, it is easier to visualize it as a limitless slosh of sea— say, the Pacific. Then energy contracted into matter, and although you know that even an invisible gas is matter, it is easier to visualize it as a massive squeeze of volcanic lava spattered inchoate from the secret pit of the ocean and hardening mute and intractable on nothing's lapping shore— like a series of islands, an archipelago. Like: the Galápagos. Then a softer strain of matter began to twitch. It was a kind of shaped water; it flowed, hardening here and there at its tips. There were blue-green algae; there were tortoises.

The ice rolled up, the ice rolled back, and I knelt on a plain of lava boulders in the islands called Galápagos, stroking a giant tortoise's neck. The tortoise closed its eyes and stretched its neck to its greatest height and vulnerability. I rubbed that neck, and when I pulled away my hand, my palm was green with a slick of single-celled algae. I stared at the algae, and at the tortoise, the way you stare at any life on a lava flow, and thought: Well—here we all are.

Being here is being here on the rocks. These Galapagonian rocks, one of them seventy-five miles long, have dried under the equatorial sun between five and six hundred miles west of the South American continent; they lie at the latitude of the Republic of Ecuador, to which they belong.

There is a way a small island rises from the ocean affronting all reason. It is a chunk of chaos pounded into visibility *ex nihilo:* here rough, here smooth, shaped just so by a matrix of physical necessities too weird to contemplate, here instead of there, here instead of not at all. It is a fantastic utterance, as though I were to open my mouth and emit a French horn, or a vase, or a knob of tellurium. It smacks of folly, of first causes.

I think of the island called Daphnecita, little Daphne, on which I   5 never set foot. It's in half of my few photographs, though, because it obsessed me: a dome of gray lava like a pitted loaf, the size of the Plaza Hotel, glazed with guano and crawling with red-orange crabs. Sometimes I attributed to this island's cliff face a surly, infantile consciousness, as though it were sulking in the silent moment after it had just shouted, to the sea and the sky, "I didn't ask to be born." Or sometimes it aged to a raging adolescent, a kid who's just learned that the game is fixed, demanding, "What did you have me for, if you're just going to push me around?" Daphnecita: again, a wise old island, mute, leading the life of pure creaturehood open to any antelope or saint. After you've blown the ocean sky-high, what's there to say? What if we the people had the sense or grace to live as cooled islands in an archipelago live, with dignity, passion, and no comment?

It is worth flying to Guayaquil, Ecuador, and then to Baltra in the Galápagos just to see the rocks. But these rocks are animal gardens. They are home to a Hieronymus Bosch assortment of windblown, stowaway, castaway, flotsam, and shipwrecked creatures. Most exist nowhere else on earth. These reptiles and insects, small mammals and birds, evolved unmolested on the various islands on which they were cast into unique species adapted to the boulder-wrecked shores, the cactus deserts of the lowlands, or the elevated jungles of the large islands' interiors. You come for the animals. You come to see the curious shapes soft proteins can take, to impress yourself with their reality, and to greet them.

You walk among clattering four-foot marine iguanas heaped on the shore lava, and on each other, like slag. You swim with penguins; you watch flightless cormorants dance beside you, ignoring you, waving the black nubs of their useless wings. Here are nesting blue-footed boobies, real birds with real feathers, whose legs and feet are nevertheless patently fake, manufactured by Mattel. The tortoises are big as stoves. The enormous land iguanas at your feet change color in the sunlight, from gold to blotchy red as you watch.

There is always some creature going about its beautiful business. I missed the boat back to my ship, and was left behind momentarily on uninhabited South Plaza island, because I was watching the Audubon's shearwaters. These dark pelagic birds flick along pleated seas in stitching flocks, flailing their wings rapidly—because if they don't, they'll stall. A shearwater must fly fast, or not at all. Consequently it has evolved two nice behaviors which serve to bring it into its nest alive. The nest is a shearwater-sized hole in the lava cliff. The shearwater circles over the water, ranging out from the nest a quarter of a mile, and veers gradually toward the cliff, making passes at its nest. If the flight angle is precisely right, the bird will fold its wings at the hole's entrance and stall directly onto its floor. The angle is perhaps seldom right, however; one shearwater I watched made a dozen suicidal-looking passes before it vanished into a chink. The other behavior is spectacular. It involves choosing the nest hole in a site below a prominent rock with a downward-angled face. The shearwater comes careering in at full tilt, claps its wings, stalls itself into the rock, and the rock, acting as a backboard, banks it home.

The animals are tame. They have not been persecuted, and show no fear of man. You pass among them as though you were wind, spindrift, sunlight, leaves. The songbirds are tame. On Hood Island I sat beside a nesting waved albatross while a mockingbird scratched in my hair, another mockingbird jabbed at my fingernail, and a third mockingbird made an exquisite progression of pokes at my bare feet up the long series of eyelets in my basketball shoes. The marine iguanas are tame. One settler, Carl Angermeyer, built his house on the site of a marine iguana colony. The gray iguanas, instead of moving out, moved up on the roof, which is corrugated steel. Twice daily on the patio, Angermeyer feeds them a mixture of boiled rice and tuna fish from a plastic basin. Their names are all, unaccountably, Annie. Angermeyer beats on the basin with a long-handled spoon, calling, "Here AnnieAnnieAnnieAnnie"—and the spiny reptiles, fifty or sixty strong, click along the steel roof, finger their way down the lava boulder and mortar walls, and swarm round his bare legs to elbow into the basin and be elbowed out again smeared with a mash of boiled rice on their bellies and on their protuberant, black, plated lips.

The wild hawk is tame. The Galápagos hawk is related to North   10
America's Swainson's hawk; I have read that if you take pains, you can walk up and pat it. I never tried. We people don't walk up and pat each other; enough is enough. The animals' critical distance and mine tended to coincide, so we could enjoy an easy sociability without threat of violence or unwonted intimacy. The hawk, which is not notably sociable, nevertheless endures even a blundering approach, and is apparently as content to perch on a scrub tree at your shoulder as anyplace else.
    In the Galápagos, even the flies are tame. Although most of the land is Ecuadorian national park, and as such rigidly protected, I confess I gave

the evolutionary ball an offsides shove by dispatching every fly that bit me, marveling the while at its pristine ignorance, its blithe failure to register a flight trigger at the sweep of my descending hand—an insouciance that was almost, but not quite, disarming. After you kill a fly, you pick it up and feed it to a lava lizard, a bright-throated four-inch lizard that scavenges everywhere in the arid lowlands. And you walk on, passing among the innocent mobs on every rock hillside; or you sit, and they come to you.

We are strangers and sojourners, soft dots on the rocks. You have walked along the strand and seen where birds have landed, walked, and flown; their tracks begin in sand, and go, and suddenly end. Our tracks do that: but we go down. And stay down. While we're here, during the seasons our tents are pitched in the light, we pass among each other crying "greetings" in a thousand tongues, and "welcome," and "good-bye." In-habitants of uncrowded colonies tend to offer the stranger famously warm hospitality—and such are the Galápagos sea lions. Theirs is the greeting the first creatures must have given Adam—a hero's welcome, a universal and undeserved huzzah. Go, and be greeted by sea lions.

I was sitting with ship's naturalist Soames Summerhays on a sand beach under cliffs on uninhabited Hood Island. The white beach was a havoc of lava boulders black as clinkers, sleek with spray, and lambent as brass in the sinking sun. To our left a dozen sea lions were body-surfing in the long green combers that rose, translucent, half a mile offshore. When the combers broke, the shoreline boulders rolled. I could feel the roar in the rough rock on which I sat; I could hear the grate inside each long backsweeping sea, the rumble of a rolled million rocks muffled in splashes and the seethe before the next wave's heave.

To our right, a sea lion slipped from the ocean. It was a young bull; in another few years he would be dangerous, bellowing at intruders and biting off great dirty chunks of the ones he caught. Now this young bull, which weighed maybe 120 pounds, sprawled silhouetted in the late light, slick as a drop of quicksilver, his glistening whiskers radii of gold like any crown. He hauled his packed bulk toward us up the long beach; he flung himself with an enormous surge of fur-clad muscle onto the boulder where I sat. "Soames," I said—very quietly, "he's here because *we're* here, isn't he?" The naturalist nodded. I felt water drip on my elbow behind me, then the fragile scrape of whiskers, and finally the wet warmth and weight of a muzzle, as the creature settled to sleep on my arm. I was catching on to sea lions.

Walk into the water. Instantly sea lions surround you, even if none has been in sight. To say that they come to play with you is not especially anthropomorphic. Animals play. The bull sea lions are off patrolling their territorial shores; these are the cows and young, which range freely. A five-foot sea lion peers intently into your face, then urges her muzzle gently against your underwater mask and searches your eyes without blinking.

Next she rolls upside down and slides along the length of your floating body, rolls again, and casts a long glance back at your eyes. You are, I believe, supposed to follow, and think up something clever in return. You can play games with sea lions in the water using shells or bits of leaf, if you are willing. You can spin on your vertical axis and a sea lion will swim circles around you, keeping her face always six inches from yours, as though she were tethered. You can make a game of touching their back flippers, say, and the sea lions will understand at once; somersaulting conveniently before your clumsy hands, they will give you an excellent field of back flippers.

And when you leave the water, they follow. They don't want you to go. They porpoise to the shore, popping their heads up when they lose you and casting about, then speeding to your side and emitting a choked series of vocal notes. If you won't relent, they disappear, barking; but if you sit on the beach with so much as a foot in the water, two or three will station with you, floating on their backs and saying, Urr.

Few people come to the Galápagos. Buccaneers used to anchor in the bays to avoid pursuit, to rest, and to lighter on fresh water. The world's whaling ships stopped here as well, to glut their holds with fresh meat in the form of giant tortoises. The whalers used to let the tortoises bang around on deck for a few days to empty their guts; then they stacked them below on their backs to live—if you call that living—without food or water for a year. When they wanted fresh meat, they killed one.

Early inhabitants of the islands were a desiccated assortment of grouches, cranks, and ships' deserters. These hardies shot, poisoned, and enslaved each other off, leaving behind a fecund gang of feral goats, cats, dogs, and pigs whose descendants skulk in the sloping jungles and take their tortoise hatchlings neat. Now scientists at the Charles Darwin Research Station, on the island of Santa Cruz, rear the tortoise hatchlings for several years until their shells are tough enough to resist the crunch; then they release them in the wilds of their respective islands. Today, some few thousand people live on three of the islands; settlers from Ecuador, Norway, Germany, and France make a livestock or pineapple living from the rich volcanic soils. The settlers themselves seem to embody a high degree of courteous and conscious humanity, perhaps because of their relative isolation.

On the island of Santa Cruz, eleven fellow passengers and I climb in an open truck up the Galápagos' longest road; we shift to horses, burros, and mules, and visit the lonely farm of Alf Kastdalen. He came to the islands as a child with his immigrant parents from Norway. Now a broad, blond man in his late forties with children of his own, he lives in an isolated house of finished timbers imported from the mainland, on four hundred acres he claimed from the jungle by hand. He raises cattle. He walks us round part of his farm, smiling expansively and meeting our chatter with a willing, open gaze and kind words. The pasture looks like any pasture—but the rocks under the grass are round lava ankle-breakers, the copses are a tangle of thorny bamboo and bromeliads, and the bordering trees dripping in epiphytes are breadfruit, papaya, avocado, and orange.

Kastdalen's isolated house is heaped with books in three languages. He knows animal husbandry; he also knows botany and zoology. He feeds us soup, chicken worth chewing for, green *naranjilla* juice, noodles, pork in big chunks, marinated mixed vegetables, rice, and bowl after bowl of bright mixed fruits.

And his isolated Norwegian mother sees us off; our beasts are ready. We will ride down the mud forest track to the truck at the Ecuadorian settlement, down the long road to the boat, and across the bay to the ship. I lean down to catch her words. She is gazing at me with enormous warmth. "Your hair," she says softly. I am blond. *Adiós.*

II

Charles Darwin came to the Galápagos in 1835, on the *Beagle;* he was twenty-six. He threw the marine iguanas as far as he could into the water; he rode the tortoises and sampled their meat. He noticed that the tortoises' carapaces varied wildly from island to island; so also did the forms of various mockingbirds. He made collections. Nine years later he wrote in a letter, "I am almost convinced (quite contrary to the opinion I started with) that species are not (it is like confessing a murder) immutable." In 1859 he published *On the Origin of Species,* and in 1871 *The Descent of Man.* It is fashionable now to disparage Darwin's originality; not even the surliest of his detractors, however, faults his painstaking methods or denies his impact.

Darwinism today is more properly called neo-Darwinism. It is organic evolutionary theory informed by the spate of new data from modern genetics, molecular biology, paleobiology—from the new wave of the biologic revolution which spread after Darwin's announcement like a tsunami. The data are not all in. Crucial first appearances of major invertebrate groups are missing from the fossil record—but these early forms, sometimes modified larvae, tended to be fragile either by virtue of their actual malleability or by virtue of their scarcity and rapid variation into "hardened," successful forms. Lack of proof in this direction doesn't worry scientists. What neo-Darwinism seriously lacks, however, is a description of the actual mechanism of mutation in the chromosomal nucleotides.

In the larger sense, neo-Darwinism also lacks, for many, sheer plausibility. The triplet splendors of random mutation, natural selection, and Mendelian inheritance are neither energies nor gods; the words merely describe a gibbering tumult of materials. Many things are unexplained, many discrepancies unaccounted for. Appending a very modified neo-Lamarckism to Darwinism would solve many problems—and create new ones. Neo-Lamarckism holds, without any proof, that certain useful ac-

20

quired characteristics may be inherited. Read C. H. Waddington, *The Strategy of the Genes,* and Arthur Koestler, *The Ghost in the Machine.* The Lamarckism/Darwinism issue is not only complex, hinging perhaps on whether DNA can be copied from RNA, but also politically hot. The upshot of it all is that while a form of Lamarckism holds sway in Russia, neo-Darwinism is supreme in the West, and its basic assumptions, though variously modified, are not overthrown.

So much for scientists. The rest of us didn't hear Darwin as a signal   25
to dive down into the wet nucleus of a cell and surface with handfuls of strange new objects. We were still worried about the book with the unfortunate word in the title: *The Descent of Man.* It was dismaying to imagine great-grandma and great-grandpa effecting a literal, nimble descent from some liana-covered tree to terra firma, scratching themselves, and demanding bananas.

Fundamentalist Christians, of course, still reject Darwinism because it conflicts with the creation account in Genesis. Fundamentalist Christians have a very bad press. Ill feeling surfaces when, from time to time in small towns, they object again to the public schools' teaching evolutionary theory. Tragically, these people feel they have to make a choice between the Bible and modern science. They live and work in the same world as we, and know the derision they face from people whose areas of ignorance are perhaps different, who dismantled their mangers when they moved to town and threw out the baby with the straw.

Even less appealing in their response to the new evolutionary picture were, and are, the social Darwinists. Social Darwinists seized Herbert Spencer's phrase, "the survival of the fittest," applied it to capitalism, and used it to sanction ruthless and corrupt business practices. A social Darwinist is unlikely to identify himself with the term; social Darwinism is, as the saying goes, not a religion but a way of life. A modern social Darwinist wrote the slogan "If you're so smart, why ain't you rich?" The notion still obtains, I believe, wherever people seek power: that the race is to the swift, that everybody is *in* the race, with varying and merited degrees of success or failure, and that reward is its own virtue.

Philosophy reacted to Darwin with unaccustomed good cheer. William Paley's fixed and harmonious universe was gone, and with it its meticulous watchmaker god. Nobody mourned. Instead philosophy shrugged and turned its attention from first and final causes to analysis of certain values here in time. "Faith in progress," the man-in-the-street philosophy, collapsed in two world wars. Philosophers were more guarded; pragmatically, they held a very refined "faith in process"—which, it would seem, could hardly lose. Christian thinkers, too, outside of Fundamentalism, examined with fresh eyes the world's burgeoning change. Some Protestants, taking their cue from Whitehead, posited a dynamic god who lives alongside the universe, himself charged and changed by the process of becoming.

Catholic Pierre Teilhard de Chardin, a paleontologist, examined the evolution of species itself, and discovered in that flow a surge toward complexity and consciousness, a free ascent capped with man and propelled from within and attracted from without by god, the holy freedom and awareness that is creation's beginning and end. And so forth. Like flatworms, like languages, ideas evolve. And they evolve, as Arthur Koestler suggests, not from hardened final forms, but from the softest plasmic germs in a cell's heart, in the nub of a word's root, in the supple flux of an open mind.

Darwin gave us time. Before Darwin (and Huxley, Wallace, et al.) there was in the nineteenth century what must have been a fairly nauseating period: people knew about fossils of extinct species, but did not yet know about organic evolution. They thought the fossils were litter from a series of past creations. At any rate, for many, this creation, the world as we know it, had begun in 4004 B.C., a date set by Irish Archbishop James Ussher in the seventeenth century. We were all crouched in a small room against the comforting back wall, awaiting the millennium which had been gathering impetus since Adam and Eve. Up there was a universe, and down here would be a small strip of man come and gone, created, taught, redeemed, and gathered up in a bright twinkling, like a sprinkling of confetti torn from colored papers, tossed from windows, and swept from the streets by morning.

The Darwinian revolution knocked out the back wall, revealing eerie lighted landscapes as far back as we can see. Almost at once, Albert Einstein and astronomers with reflector telescopes and radio telescopes knocked out the other walls and the ceiling, leaving us sunlit, exposed, and drifting— leaving us puckers, albeit evolving puckers, on the inbound curve of spacetime. *30*

III

It all began in the Galápagos, with these finches. The finches in the Galápagos are called Darwin's finches; they are everywhere in the islands, sparrowlike, and almost identical but for their differing beaks. At first Darwin scarcely noticed their importance. But by 1839, when he revised his *Journal* of the *Beagle* voyage, he added a key sentence about the finches' beaks: "Seeing this gradation and diversity of structure in one small, intimately related group of birds, one might really fancy that from an original paucity of birds in this archipelago, one species had been taken and modified for different ends." And so it was.

The finches come when called. I don't know why it works, but it does. Scientists in the Galápagos have passed down the call: you say psssssh psssssh psssssh psssssh psssssh until you run out of breath; then you say it again until the island runs out of birds. You stand on a flat of sand by a shallow lagoon rimmed in mangrove thickets and call the birds right out of the sky. It works anywhere, from island to island.

Once, on the island of James, I was standing propped against a leafless *palo santo* tree on a semiarid inland slope, when the naturalist called the birds.

From other leafless *palo santo* trees flew the yellow warblers, speckling the air with bright bounced sun. Gray mockingbirds came running. And from the green prickly pear cactus, from the thorny acacias, sere grasses, bracken and manzanilla, from the loose black lava, the bare dust, the fern-hung mouths of caverns or the tops of sunlit logs—came the finches. They fell in from every direction like colored bits in a turning kaleidoscope. They circled and homed to a vortex, like a whirlwind of chips, like draining water. The tree on which I leaned was the vortex. A dry series of puffs hit my cheeks. Then a rough pulse from the tree's thin trunk met my palm and rang up my arm—and another, and another. The tree trunk agitated against my hand like a captured cricket: I looked up. The lighting birds were rocking the tree. It was an appearing act: before there were barren branches; now there were birds like leaves.

Darwin's finches are not brightly colored; they are black, gray, brown,   *35*
or faintly olive. Their names are even duller: the large ground finch, the medium ground finch, the small ground finch; the large insectivorous tree finch; the vegetarian tree finch; the cactus ground finch, and so forth. But the beaks are interesting, and the beaks' origins even more so.

Some finches wield chunky parrot beaks modified for cracking seeds. Some have slender warbler beaks, short for nabbing insects, long for probing plants. One sports the long chisel beak of a woodpecker; it bores wood for insect grubs and often uses a twig or cactus spine as a pickle fork when the grub won't dislodge. They have all evolved, fanwise, from one bird.

The finches evolved in isolation. So did everything else on earth. With the finches, you can see how it happened. The Galápagos islands are near enough to the mainland that some strays could hazard there; they are far enough away that those strays could evolve in isolation from parent species. And the separate islands are near enough to each other for further dispersal, further isolation, and the eventual reassembling of distinct species. (In other words, finches blew to the Galápagos, blew to various islands, evolved into differing species, and blew back together again.) The tree finches and the ground finches, the woodpecker finch and the warbler finch, veered into being on isolated rocks. The witless green sea shaped those beaks as surely as it shaped the beaches. Now on the finches in the *palo santo* tree you see adaptive radiation's results, a fluorescent splay of horn. It is as though an archipelago were an arpeggio, a rapid series of distinct but related notes. If the Galápagos had been one unified island, there would be one dull note, one super-dull finch.

IV

Now let me carry matters to an imaginary, and impossible, extreme. If the earth were one unified island, a smooth ball, we would all be one species, a tremulous muck. The fact is that when you get down to this business of species formation, you eventually hit some form of reproductive isolation. Cells tend to fuse. Cells tend to engulf each other; primitive creatures tend to move in on each other and on us, to colonize, aggregate, blur. (Within species, individuals have evolved immune reactions, which help preserve individual integrity; you might reject my liver—or someday my brain.) As much of the world's energy seems to be devoted to keeping us apart as was directed to bringing us here in the first place. All sorts of different creatures can mate and produce fertile offspring: two species of snapdragon, for instance, or mallard and pintail ducks. But they don't. They live apart, so they don't mate. When you scratch the varying behaviors and conditions behind reproductive isolation, you find, ultimately, geographical isolation. Once the isolation has occurred, of course, forms harden out, enforcing reproductive isolation, so that snapdragons will never mate with pintail ducks.

Geography is the key, the crucial accident of birth. A piece of protein could be a snail, a sea lion, or a systems analyst, but it had to start somewhere. This is not science; it is merely metaphor. And the landscape in which the protein "starts" shapes its end as surely as bowls shape water.

We have all, as it were, blown back together like the finches, and it's hard to imagine the isolation from parent species in which we evolved. The frail beginnings of great phyla are lost in the crushed histories of cells. Now we see the embellishments of random chromosomal mutations selected by natural selection and preserved in geographically isolate gene pools as *faits accomplis,* as the differentiated fringe of brittle knobs that is life as we know it. The process is still going on, but there is no turning back; it happened, in the cells. Geographical determination is not the cow-caught-in-a-crevice business I make it seem. I'm dealing in imagery, working toward a picture. 40

Geography is life's limiting factor. Speciation—life itself—is ultimately a matter of warm and cool currents, rich and bare soils, deserts and forests, fresh and salt waters, deltas and jungles and plains. Species arise in isolation. A plaster cast is as intricate as its mold; life is a gloss on geography. And if you dig your fists into the earth and crumble geography, you strike geology. Climate is the wind of the mineral earth's rondure, tilt, and orbit modified by local geological conditions. The Pacific Ocean, the Negev Desert, and the rain forest in Brazil are local geological conditions. So are the slow carp pools and splashing trout riffles of any backyard creek. It is all, God help us, a matter of rocks.

The rocks shape life like hands around swelling dough. In Virginia, the salamanders vary from mountain ridge to mountain ridge; so do the fiddle tunes the old men play. All this is because it is hard to move from mountain to mountain. These are not merely anomalous details. This is what life is all about: salamanders, fiddle tunes, you and me and things, the split and burr of it all, the fizz into particulars. No mountains and one salamander, one fiddle tune, would be a lesser world. No continents, no fiddlers. No possum, no sop, no taters. The earth, without form, is void.

The mountains are time's machines; in effect, they roll out protoplasm like printers' rollers pressing out news. But life is already part of the landscape, a limiting factor in space; life too shapes life. Geology's rocks and climate have already become Brazil's rain forest, yielding shocking bright birds. To say that all life is an interconnected membrane, a weft of linkages like chain mail, is truism. But in this case, too, the Galápagos islands afford a clear picture.

On Santa Cruz island, for instance, the saddleback carapaces of tortoises enable them to stretch high and reach the succulent pads of prickly pear cactus. But the prickly pear cactus on that island, and on other tortoise islands, has evolved a treelike habit; those lower pads get harder to come by. Without limiting factors, the two populations could stretch right into the stratosphere.

Ça va. It goes on everywhere, tit for tat, action and reaction, triggers   45
and inhibitors ascending in a spiral like spatting butterflies. Within life, we are pushing each other around. How many animal forms have evolved just so because there are, for instance, trees? We pass the nitrogen around, and vital gases; we feed and nest, plucking this and that and planting seeds. The protoplasm responds, nudged and nudging, bearing the news.

And the rocks themselves shall be moved. The rocks themselves are not pure necessity, given, like vast, complex molds around which the rest of us swirl. They heave to their own necessities, to stirrings and prickings from within and without.

The mountains are no more fixed than the stars. Granite, for example, contains much oxygen and is relatively light. It "floats." When granite forms under the earth's crust, great chunks of it bob up, I read somewhere, like dumplings. The continents themselves are beautiful pea-green boats. The Galápagos archipelago as a whole is surfing toward Ecuador; South America is sliding toward the Galápagos; North America, too, is sailing westward. We're on floating islands, shaky ground.

So the rocks shape life, and then life shapes life, and the rocks are moving. The completed picture needs one more element: life shapes the rocks.

Life is more than a live green scum on a dead pool, a shimmering scurf like slime mold on rock. Look at the planet. Everywhere freedom twines its way around necessity, inventing new strings of occasions, lassoing time and putting it through its varied and spirited paces. Everywhere live things lash at the rocks. Softness is vulnerable, but it has a will; tube worms bore and coral atolls rise. Lichens in delicate lobes are chewing the granite mountains; forests in serried ranks trammel the hills. Man has more freedom than other live things; anti-entropically, he batters a bigger dent in the given, damming the rivers, planting the plains, drawing in his mind's eye dotted lines between the stars.

The old ark's a moverin'. Each live thing wags its home waters,   *50*
rumples the turf, rearranges the air. The rocks press out protoplasm; the
protoplasm pummels the rocks. It could be that this is the one world, and
that world a bright snarl.

Like boys on dolphins, the continents ride their crustal plates. New
lands shoulder up from the waves, and old lands buckle under. The very
landscapes heave; change burgeons into change. Gray granite bobs up, red
clay compresses; yellow sandstone tilts, surging in forests, incised by
streams. The mountains tremble, the ice rasps back and forth, and the
protoplasm furls in shock waves, up the rock valleys and down, ramifying
possibilities, riddling the mountains. Life and the rocks, like spirit and
matter, are a fringed matrix, lapped and lapping, clasping and held. It is
like hand washing hand. It is like hand washing hand and the whole tumult
hurled. The planet spins, rapt inside its intricate mists. The galaxy is a
flung thing, loose in the night, and our solar system is one of many dotted
campfires ringed with tossed rocks. What shall we sing?

What shall we sing, while the fire burns down? We can sing only
specifics, time's rambling tune, the places we have seen, the faces we have
known. I will sing you the Galápagos islands, the sea lions soft on the
rocks. It's all still happening there, in real light, the cool currents upwelling,
the finches falling on the wind, the shearwaters looping the waves. I could
go back, or I could go on; or I could sit down, like Kubla Khan:

> Weave a circle round him thrice,
>   And close your eyes with holy dread,
> For he on honey-dew hath fed,
>   And drunk the milk of Paradise.

Working Together

1. As a group, look at the first section of this essay (marked I) and then at
   the second (marked II). What kind of writing—and what sorts of topics—do you find in section I and not in section II? What do you find
   in section II that you don't find in section I? Make two separate lists of
   words and phrases that describe these sections; make these descriptions
   as clear as you can, and link each one with a specific place where it's
   illustrated in the essay. Finally, discuss why Dillard divided this essay in
   this way, and write a brief paragraph that explains the division.
2. Continue looking at the sections of this essay (specifically now sections
   III and IV). Describe and explain them in the same ways that you did
   for sections I and II.

Rethinking and Rewriting

1. Write an essay that presents the structure of Dillard's essay from section
   I through section IV. Use at least two quotations to help explain what

you say. End by arguing that the structure is either loose and mostly without plan: Changing the order here wouldn't matter. Or argue that this structure is carefully sequenced so that the parts can't be shifted; they have to be in the order they're given in now so that Dillard can end the essay as she does.

2. Do some research about the geology and geological history of where you live now. What was the countryside like five hundred years ago; what was it like five thousand years ago; and what was it like fifty thousand years ago? (Feel free to change these ages to accommodate whatever information your research gives you.) Write an essay for residents of your area telling them about the how the ground they walk on and drive on has changed over the years. At the end of your essay, skip some space and write a short paragraph that tells readers where the information in your essay comes from.

Essay Topics for Chapter 7

1. Write an essay that starts with Wordsworth's basic suggestion and goes on to discuss what can happen once we do leave the routine places and the routine schedules of our lives for travel or "idleness." Talk about what happens when we travel, when we see places entirely new to us. Use one of the essays in this chapter as an example of what can happen—what we might start to think about—once we get away from the social whirl and the concentration of our daily work.

2. Compare some travel or similar experience to the experience presented by Leeson, Lopez, or Dillard (choose one). Start your essay by giving readers your experience; then move on to how your experience is similar to or different from the experience described in the essay in this chapter. End your essay by explaining what you've learned.

3. Write an essay about the ways that you are affected (or unaffected) by the landscape around you. Structure your essay in three numbered sections. In section I, present your own experience of some urban landscape; in section II, present your experience of some nonurban, wild (or nearly wild) landscape; and in section III, talk about these two experiences. Come to conclusions that make sense given the experiences you present in sections I and II.

4. Consider the place that excursions played in your family as you grew up. Where did your family typically go, what would you do, and how do you feel about these trips now?

5. Think about work time and workplaces versus free time and nonworkplaces. Where do we typically work? Would you call the typical work environment a created world? Use a work example that you're familiar with and describe that work environment; explain how its design reflects the work that people do there. Then contrast this environment with an environment you'd choose to visit on an excursion. How are these environments different, and what (if anything) do these environments have in common? To what extent does the work environment

you know leave out what you think of as "nature" or "natural environments?" Using your example, discuss the ways that "natural environments" and "workplaces" overlap or exclude each other.

6. What's the difference between seeing animals in a zoo and seeing animals where they normally live? Draw on your own experience of zoos (on the one hand) and your experience of seeing animals in their natural habitats (on the other). What do these experiences have in common, and how do they significantly differ?

7. Consider some experience that you know about because you've participated in it and that television also presents in some form or another. What's the difference between the television experience and actually doing whatever's being televised? For example, if you fish, you could write about how televised fishing programs are like (or are not like) the fishing you've done. If you play a sport that's also televised sometimes, that could work here. Use this comparison to argue that television tells the truth or to argue that television distorts the truth.

8

Observing the Other

Once we leave our desks and televisions and walk out the door, we start to notice other animals besides human beings. Parks support populations of both resident and migratory birds, not to mention squirrels or fish in ponds. In cities with skyscrapers peregrine falcons have taken to nesting in the crannies of what they see as cliffs. And though we don't live with animals in the ways that people did before gasoline engines, we often keep pets.

The first observation we make about animals is that they're not us: They're different. They fly or walk on all fours or swim; they move in different ways than we do, see in different ways, smell in different ways, act and react in different ways. Their lives are theirs, not ours. And yet, sometimes, they surprise us with behavior that seems out of character for them—hardly animal-like, more like us. So we like to watch them. Observing animals offers us unpredictability; it offers the rich data of comparison and contrast. It becomes a way of telling us about ourselves—or holds the tantalizing promise that it will.

The readings in this chapter all present accounts of people in contact with animals. It's a subject frequently written about, perhaps because animals themselves seem (much of the time) beyond or outside language as we know it and use it. Maybe since we can't converse with animals, since we can't directly ask them questions and understand their answers, we write about them, making observations, posing our questions, and working to answer them ourselves. In any case, observing animals gives our imaginations more than they know how to use, suggesting the many ways that life is larger and more various than we are.

"DOGS, AND THE TUG OF LIFE"

Edward Hoagland

> *After writing several novels early in his career, Edward Hoagland shifted to the form of the personal essay. Since then, in a number of essay collections and travel books, including* The Courage of Turtles *(1971) and* Walking the Dead Diamond River *(1973), he has used the essay form to explore a wide range of topics, from tugboats to black bears to human psychology. This essay suggests Hoagland's abiding interest in the natural world, particularly the behavior of animals.*

Before and As You Read

1. Before you start reading, write a short paragraph describing how you feel about dogs right now. What experiences have you had with dogs? Talk about whether or not these experiences have been good ones.
2. As you read, mark two or three passages in the margins that surprise you—things you've never thought about, ideas that disturb you or make you uneasy. Once you've finished reading, return to one of these passages and freewrite about it, exploring whatever makes you uneasy.

It used to be that you could tell just about how poor a family was by how many dogs they had. If they had one, they were probably doing all right. It was only American to keep a dog to represent the family's interests in the intrigues of the back alley; not to have a dog at all would be like not acknowledging one's poor relations. Two dogs meant that the couple were dog lovers, with growing children, but still might be members of the middle class. But if a citizen kept three, you could begin to suspect he didn't own much else. Four or five irrefutably marked the household as poor folk, whose yard was also full of broken cars cannibalized for parts. The father worked not much, fancied himself a hunter; the mother's teeth were black. And an old bachelor living in a shack might possibly have even more, but you knew that if one of them, chasing a moth, didn't upset his oil lamp some night and burn him up, he'd fetch up in the poorhouse soon, with the dogs shot. Nobody got poor feeding a bunch of dogs, needless to say, because the more dogs a man had, the less he fed them. Foraging as a pack, they led an existence of their own, but served as evidence that life was awfully lonesome for him and getting out of hand. If a dog really becomes a man's best friend his situation is desperate.

That dogs, low-comedy confederates of small children and ragged bachelors, should have turned into an emblem of having made it to the middle class—like the hibachi, like golf clubs and a second car—seems at the very least incongruous. Puppies which in the country you would have to carry in a box to the church fair to give away are bringing seventy-five dollars apiece in some of the pet stores, although in fact dogs are in such oversupply that one hundred and fifty thousand are running wild in New York City alone.

There is another line of tradition about dogs, however. Show dogs, toy dogs, foxhounds for formal hunts, Doberman guard dogs, bulldogs as ugly as a queen's dwarf. An aristocratic Spanish lady once informed me that when she visits her Andalusian estate each fall the mastiffs rush out and fawn about her but would tear to pieces any of the servants who have accompanied her from Madrid. In Mississippi it was illegal for a slave owner to permit his slaves to have a dog, just as it was to teach them how to read. A "negro dog" was a hound trained by a bounty hunter to ignore the possums, raccoons, hogs and deer in the woods that other dogs were supposed to chase, and trail and tree a runaway. The planters themselves, for whom hunting was a principal recreation, whooped it up when a man unexpectedly became their quarry. They caught each other's slaves and would often sit back and let the dogs do the punishing. Bennet H. Barrow of West Feliciana Parish in Louisiana, a rather moderate and representative plantation owner, recounted in his diary of the 1840s, among several similar incidents, this for November 11, 1845: In "5 minutes had him up & a going, And never in my life did I ever see as excited beings as R & myself, ran ½ miles & caught him dogs soon tore him naked, took him Home Before the other negro(es) at dark & made the dogs give him another over hauling." Only recently in Louisiana I heard what happened to two Negroes who happened to be fishing in a bayou off the Blind River, where four white men with a shotgun felt like fishing alone. One was forced to pretend to be a scampering coon and shinny up a telephone pole and hang there till he fell, while the other impersonated a baying, bounding hound.

Such memories are not easy to shed, particularly since childhood, the time when people can best acquire a comradeship with animals, is also when they are likely to pick up their parents' fears. A friend of mine hunts quail by jeep in Texas with a millionaire who brings along forty bird dogs, which he deploys in eight platoons that spell each other off. Another friend, though, will grow apprehensive at a dinner party if the host lets a dog loose in the room. The toothy, mysterious creature lies dreaming on the carpet, its paws pulsing, its eyelids open, the nictitating membranes twitching; how can he be certain it won't suddenly jump up and attack his legs under the table? Among Eastern European Jews, possession of a dog was associated with the hard-drinking goyishe° peasantry, traditional antagonists, or else with the gentry, and many carried this dislike to the New World. An immigrant fleeing a potato famine or the hunger of Calabria°

---

goyishe: Non-Jewish.
Calabria: Region in southern Italy.

might be no more equipped with the familiar British-German partiality to dogs—a failing which a few rugged decades in a great city's slums would not necessarily mend. The city had urbanized plenty of native farmers' sons as well, and so it came about that what to rural America had been the humblest, most natural amenity—friendship with a dog—has been transmogrified into a piece of the jigsaw of moving to the suburbs: there to cook outdoors, another bit of absurdity to the old countryman, whose toilet was outdoors but who was pleased to be able to cook and eat his meals inside the house.

There are an estimated forty million dogs in the United States (nearly two for every cat). Thirty-seven thousand of them are being destroyed in humane institutions every day, a figure which indicates that many more are in trouble. Dogs are hierarchal beasts, with several million years of submission to the structure of a wolf pack in their breeding. This explains why the Spanish lady's mastiffs can distinguish immediately between the mistress and her retainers, and why it is about as likely that one of the other guests at the dinner party will attack my friend's legs under the table as that the host's dog will, once it has accepted his presence in the room as proper. Dogs need leadership, however; they seek it, and when it's not forthcoming quickly fall into difficulties in a world where they can no longer provide their own.

"Dog" is "God" spelled backwards—one might say, way backwards. There's "a dog's life," "dog days," "dog-sick," "dog-tired," "dog-cheap," "dog-eared," "doghouse," and "dogs" meaning villains or feet. Whereas a wolf's stamina was measured in part by how long he could go without water, a dog's is becoming a matter of how long he can *hold* his water. He retrieves a rubber ball instead of coursing deer, chases a broom instead of hunting marmots. His is the lowest form of citizenship: that tug of life at the end of the leash is like the tug at the end of a fishing pole, and then one doesn't have to kill it. On stubby, amputated-looking feet he leads his life, which if we glance at it attentively is a kind of cutout of our own, all the more so for being riskier and shorter. Bam! A member of the family is dead on the highway, as we expected he would be, and we just cart him to the dump and look for a new pup.

Simply the notion that he lives on four legs instead of two has come to seem astonishing—like a goat or cow wearing horns on its head. And of course to keep a dog is a way of attempting to bring nature back. The primitive hunter's intimacy, telepathy, with the animals he sought, surprising them at their meals and in their beds, then stripping them of their warm coats to expose a frame so like our own, is all but lost. Sport hunters, especially the older ones, retain a little of it still; and naturalists who have made up their minds not to kill wild animals nevertheless appear to empathize primarily with the predators at first, as a look at the tigers, bears, wolves, mountain lions on the project list of an organization such as the World Wildlife Fund will show. This is as it should be, these creatures having suffered from our brotherly envy before. But in order to really enjoy a dog, one doesn't merely try to train him to be semihuman. The point of it is to open oneself to the possibility of becoming partly a dog (after all, there are plenty of sub- or semihuman beings around whom we don't wish to adopt). One wants to rediscover the commonality of animal and man—to see an animal eat and sleep that hasn't forgotten how to enjoy doing such things—and the directness of its loyalty.

The trouble with the current emphasis on preserving "endangered species" is that, however beneficial to wildlife the campaign works out to be, it makes all animals seem like museum pieces, worth saving for sentimental considerations and as figures of speech (to "shoot a sitting duck"), but as a practical matter already dead and gone. On the contrary, some animals are flourishing. In 1910 half a million deer lived in the United States, in 1960 seven million, in 1970 sixteen million. What has happened is that now that we don't eat them we have lost that close interest.

Wolf behavior prepared dogs remarkably for life with human beings. So complete and complicated was the potential that it was only a logical next step for them to quit their packs in favor of the heady, hopeless task of trying to keep pace with our own community development. The contortions of fawning and obeisance which render group adjustment possible among such otherwise forceful fighters—sometimes humping the inferior members into the shape of hyenas—are what squeezes them past our tantrums, too. Though battling within the pack is mostly accomplished with body checks that do no damage, a subordinate wolf bitch is likely to remain so in awe of the leader that she will cringe and sit on her tail in response to his amorous advances, until his female co-equal has had a chance to notice and dash over and redirect his attention. Altogether, he is kept so busy asserting his dominance that this top-ranked female may not be bred by him, finally, but by the male which occupies the second rung. Being breadwinners, dominant wolves feed first and best, just as we do, so that to eat our scraps and leavings strikes a dog as normal procedure. Nevertheless, a wolf puppy up to eight months old is favored at a kill, and when smaller can extract a meal from any pack member—uncles and aunts as well as parents—by nosing the lips of the adult until it regurgitates a share of what it's had. The care of the litter is so much a communal endeavor that the benign sort of role we expect dogs to play within our own families toward children not biologically theirs comes naturally to them.

For dogs and wolves the tail serves as a semaphore of mood and social *10* code, but dogs carry their tails higher than wolves do, as a rule, which is appropriate, since the excess spirits that used to go into lengthy hunts now have no other outlet than backyard negotiating. In addition to an epistolary anal gland, whose message-carrying function has not yet been defined, the anus itself, or stool when sniffed, conveys how well the animal has been eating—in effect, its income bracket—although most dog foods are sorrily monotonous compared to the hundreds of tastes a wolf encounters, perhaps dozens within the carcass of a single moose. We can speculate on a dog's powers of taste because its olfactory area is proportionately fourteen times larger than a man's, its sense of smell at least a hundred times as keen.

The way in which a dog presents his anus and genitals for inspection indicates the hierarchal position that he aspires to, and other dogs who sniff his genitals are apprised of his sexual condition. From his urine they can undoubtedly distinguish age, build, state of sexual activity and general health, even hours after he's passed by. Male dogs dislike running out of urine, as though an element of potency were involved, and try to save a little; they prefer not to use a scent post again until another dog has urinated there, the first delight and duty of the ritual being to stake out a territory, so that when they are walked hurriedly in the city it is a disappointment to them. The search is also sexual, because bitches in heat post notices about. In the woods a dog will mark his drinking places, and watermark a rabbit's trail after chasing it, as if to notify the next predator that happens by exactly who it was that put such a whiff of fear into the rabbit's scent. Similarly, he squirts the tracks of bobcats and of skunks with an aloof air unlike his brisk and cheery manner of branding another dog's or fox's trail, and if he is in a position to do so, will defecate excitedly on a bear run, leaving behind his best effort, which no doubt he hopes will strike the bear as a bombshell.

The chief complaint people lodge against dogs is their extraordinary stress upon lifting the leg and moving the bowels. Scatology did take up some of the slack for them when they left behind the entertainments of the forest. The forms of territoriality replaced the substance. But apart from that, a special zest for life is characteristic of dogs and wolves—in hunting, eating, relieving themselves, in punctiliously maintaining a home territory, a pecking order and a love life, and educating the resulting pups. They grin and grimace and scrawl graffiti with their piss. A lot of inherent strategy goes into these activities: the way wolves spell each other off, both when hunting and in their governess duties around the den, and often "consult" as a pack with noses together and tails wagging before flying in to make a kill. (Tigers, leopards, house cats base their social relations instead upon what ethologists call "mutual avoidance.") The nose is a dog's main instrument of discovery, corresponding to our eyes, and so it is that he is seldom offended by organic smells, such as putrefaction, and sniffs intently for the details of illness, gum bleeding and diet in his master and his fellows, and for the story told by scats, not closing off the avenue for any reason—just as we rarely shut our eyes against new information, even the tragic or unpleasant kind.

Though dogs don't see as sharply as they smell, trainers usually rely on hand signals to instruct them, and most firsthand communication in a wolf pack also seems to be visual—by the expressions of the face, by body english and the cant of the tail. A dominant wolf squares his mouth, stares at and "rides up" on an inferior, standing with his front legs on its back, or will pretend to stalk it, creeping along, taking its muzzle in his mouth, and performing nearly all of the other discriminatory pranks and practices familiar to anybody who has a dog. In fact, what's funny is to watch a homely mutt as tiny as a shoebox spin through the rigmarole which a whole series of observers in the wilderness have gone to great pains to document for wolves.

Dogs proffer their rear ends to each other in an intimidating fashion, but when they examine the region of the head it is a friendlier gesture, a snuffling between pals. One of them may come across a telltale bone fragment caught in the other's fur, together with a bit of mud to give away the location of bigger bones. On the same impulse, wolves and free-running dogs will sniff a wanderer's toes to find out where he has been roaming. They fondle and propitiate with their mouths also, and lovers groom each other's fur with tongues and teeth adept as hands. A bitch wolf's period in heat includes a week of preliminary behavior and maybe two weeks of receptivity—among animals, exceptionally long. Each actual copulative tie lasts twenty minutes or a half an hour, which again may help to instill affection. Wolves sometimes begin choosing a mate as early as the age of one, almost a year before they are ready to breed. Dogs mature sexually a good deal earlier, and arrive in heat twice a year instead of once—at any season instead of only in midwinter, like a wolf, whose pups' arrival must be scheduled unfailingly for spring. Dogs have not retained much responsibility for raising their young, and the summertime is just as perilous as winter for them because, apart from the whimsy of their owners, who put so many of them to sleep, their nemesis is the automobile. Like scatology, sex helps fill the gulf of what is gone.

The scientist David Mech has pointed out how like the posture of a 15 wolf with a nosehold on a moose (as other wolves attack its hams) are the antics of a puppy playing tug-of-war at the end of a towel. Anybody watching a dog's exuberance as it samples bites of long grass beside a brook, or pounds into a meadow bristling with the odors of woodchucks, snowshoe rabbits, grouse, a doe and buck, field mice up on the seedheads of the weeds, kangaroo mice jumping, chipmunks whistling, weasels and shrews on the hunt, a plunging fox, a porcupine couched in a tree, perhaps can begin to imagine the variety of excitements under the sky that his ancestors relinquished in order to move indoors with us. He'll lie down with a lamb to please us, but as he sniffs its haunches, surely he must remember atavistically that this is where he'd start to munch.

There is poignancy in the predicament of a great many animals: as in the simple observation which students of the California condor have made that this huge, most endangered bird prefers the carrion meat of its old standby, the deer, to all the dead cows, sheep, horses and other substitutes it sees from above, sprawled about. Animals are stylized characters in a kind of old saga—stylized because even the most acute of them have little leeway as they play out their parts. (*Rabbits,* for example, I find terribly affecting, imprisoned in their hop.) And as we drift away from any cognizance of them, we sacrifice some of the intricacy and grandeur of life. Having already lost so much, we are hardly aware of what remains, but to a primitive snatched forward from an earlier existence it might seem as if we had surrendered a richness comparable to all the tapestries of childhood. Since this is a matter of the imagination as well as of animal demographics, no Noah projects, no bionomic discoveries on the few sanctuaries that have been established are going to reverse the swing. The very specialists in the forefront of finding out how animals behave, when one meets them, appear to be no more intrigued than any ordinary Indian was.

But we continue to need—as aborigines did, as children do—a parade of morality tales which are more concise than those that politics, for instance, later provides. So we've had Aesop's and medieval and modern fables about the grasshopper and the ant, the tiger and Little Black Sambo, the wolf and the three pigs, Br'er Rabbit and Br'er Bear, Goldilocks and her three bears, Pooh Bear, Babar and the rhinos, Walt Disney's animals, and assorted humbler scary bats, fat hippos, funny frogs, and eager beavers. Children have a passion for clean, universal definitions, and so it is that animals have gone with children's literature as Latin has with religion. Through them they first encountered death, birth, their own maternal feelings, the gap between beauty and cleverness, or speed and good intentions. The animal kingdom boasted the powerful lion, the mothering goose, the watchful owl, the tardy tortoise, Chicken Little, real-life dogs that treasure bones, and mink that grow posh pelts from eating crawfish and mussels.

In the cartoons of two or three decades ago, Mouse doesn't get along with Cat because Cat must catch Mouse or miss his supper. Dog, on the other hand, detests Cat for no such rational reason, only the capricious fact that dogs don't dote on cats. Animal stories are bounded, yet enhanced, by each creature's familiar lineaments, just as a parable about a prince and peasant, a duchess and a milkmaid, a blacksmith and a fisherman, would be. Typecasting, like the roll of a metered ode, adds resonance and dignity, summoning up all of the walruses and hedgehogs that went before: the shrewd image of Br'er Rabbit to assist his suburban relative Bugs Bunny behind the scenes. But now, in order to present a tale about the contest between two thieving crows and a scarecrow, the storyteller would need to start by explaining that once upon a time crows used to eat a farmer's corn if he didn't defend it with a mock man pinned together from old clothes. Crows are having a hard go of it and may soon receive game-bird protection.

One way childhood is changing, therefore, is that the nonhuman figures—"Wild Things" or puppet monsters—constructed by the best of the new artificers, like Maurice Sendak or the *Sesame Street* writers, are distinctly humanoid, ballooned out of faces, torsos met on the subway. The televised character Big Bird does not resemble a bird the way Bugs Bunny remained a rabbit—though already he was less so than Br'er or Peter Rabbit. Big Bird's personality, her confusion, haven't the faintest connection to an ostrich's. Lest she be confused with an ostrich, her voice has been slotted unmistakably toward the prosaic. Dr. Seuss did transitional composites of worldwide fauna, but these new shapes—a beanbag like the

Sesame Street Grouch or Cookie Monster or Herry Monster, and the floral creations in books—have been conceived practically from scratch by the artist ("in the night kitchen," to use a Sendak phrase), and not transferred from the existing caricatures of nature. In their conversational conflicts they offer him a fresh start, which may be a valuable commodity, whereas if he were dealing with an alligator, it would, while giving him an old-fashioned boost in the traditional manner, at the same time box him in. A chap called Alligator, with that fat snout and tail, cannot squirm free of the solidity of actual alligators. Either it must stay a heavyweight or else play on the sternness of reality by swinging over to impersonate a cream puff and a Ferdinand.

Though animal programs on television are popular, what with the [20] wave of nostalgia and "ecology" in the country, we can generally say about the animal kingdom, "The King is dead, long live the King." Certainly the talent has moved elsewhere. Those bulbous Wild Things and slant-mouthed beanbag puppets derived from the denizens of Broadway—an argumentative night news vendor, a lady on a traffic island—have grasped their own destinies, as characters on the make are likely to. It was inevitable they would. There may be a shakedown to remove the elements that would be too bookish for children's literature in other hands, and another shakedown because these first innovators have been more city-oriented than suburban. New authors will shift the character sources away from Broadway and the subway and the ghetto, but the basic switch has already been accomplished—from the ancient juxtaposition of people, animals, and dreams blending the two, to people and monsters that grow solely out of people by way of dreams.

Which leaves us in the suburbs, with dogs as a last link. Cats are too independent to care, but dogs are in an unenviable position, they hang so much upon our good opinion. We are coming to *have* no opinion; we don't pay enough attention to form an opinion. Though they admire us, are thrilled by us, heroize us, we regard them as a hobby or a status symbol, like a tennis racquet, and substitute leash laws for leadership—expect them not simply to learn English but to grow hands, because their beastly paws seem stranger to us every year. If they try to fondle us with their handy-jack mouths, we read it as a bite; and like used cars, they are disposed of when the family relocates, changes its "bag," or in the scurry of divorce. The first reason people kept a dog was to acquire an ally on the hunt, a friend at night. Then it was to maintain an avenue to animality, as our own nearness began to recede. But as we lose our awareness of all animals, dogs are becoming a bridge to nowhere. We can only pity their fate.

Reading and Responding

If you've owned a dog, quickly list three different stories you could tell about that dog. Then pick one of these stories and flesh it out so that you have about a page worth of notes or freewriting.

Working Together

1. Make a list of three or four strange, odd, or different ideas from the Edward Hoagland essay and discuss each one. Do you agree or disagree?
2. How are the ideas you noted in item 1 related? Are they subpoints of a larger point? How would you draw their relationship—spokes of a wheel, islands in a stream, scattered pieces of something?
3. What is Hoagland's central idea in this piece? What reasons, observations, or arguments pushed him to write? As a group, compose a paragraph that expresses you answer(s).
4. Imagine going out to lunch with Edward Hoagland. Describe what he looks like, what he's wearing. What kind of restaurant would you go to? What would he order? What would you talk about?

Rethinking and Rewriting

1. Describe the behavior of your own dog. Tell a story of a dog you've loved. Variation: Tell a story about a cat you've loved.
2. Write an essay about the reasons you've kept a pet. Describe the pet, but focus mostly on whatever role the pet actually played (or still plays) in your life. Finally, does your experience lead you to agree with Hoagland that we've almost entirely lost our links to the animal world?
3. Describe the life and behavior of several people you know by describing their dogs (or other pets): How does a person's pet reveal his or her own character and values?
4. Write a paper reporting the latest research on the behavior of dogs. To help you focus, assume that you're writing an article for would-be dog owners who aren't sure how the various breeds differ.

"AM I BLUE?"

"Ain't these tears in these eyes tellin' you?" [1]

Alice Walker

> *Afro-American novelist, poet, and essayist Alice Walker is probably best known for* The Color Purple *(1983), her novel about the southern black experience that won the National Book Award and the Pulitzer Prize before being made into a successful movie. Her essays have been collected into several books, including* Living by the Word *(1988), from which "Am I Blue?" is taken.*

For about three years my companion and I rented a small house in the country that stood on the edge of a large meadow that appeared to run from the end of our deck straight into the mountains. The mountains, however, were quite far away, and between us and them there was, in fact, a town. It was one of the many pleasant aspects of the house that you never really were aware of this.

It was a house of many windows, low, wide, nearly floor to ceiling in the living room, which faced the meadow, and it was from one of these that I first saw our closest neighbor, a large white horse, cropping grass, flipping its mane, and ambling about—not over the entire meadow, which stretched well out of sight of the house, but over the five or so fenced-in acres that were next to the twenty-odd that we had rented. I soon learned that the horse, whose name was Blue, belonged to a man who lived in another town, but was boarded by our neighbors next door. Occasionally, one of the children, usually a stocky teen-ager, but sometimes a much younger girl or boy, could be seen riding Blue. They would appear in the meadow, climb up on his back, ride furiously for ten or fifteen minutes, then get off, slap Blue on the flanks, and not be seen again for a month or more.

There were many apple trees in our yard, and one by the fence that Blue could almost reach. We were soon in the habit of feeding him apples, which he relished, especially because by the middle of summer the meadow grasses—so green and succulent since January—had dried out from lack of rain, and Blue stumbled about munching the dried stalks half-heartedly. Sometimes he would stand very still just by the apple tree, and when one of us came out he would whinny, snort loudly, or stamp the ground. This meant, of course: I want an apple.

---

1. © 1929 Warner Bros., Inc. (renewed). By Grant Clarke and Harry Akst. All rights reserved. Used by permission.

It was quite wonderful to pick a few apples, or collect those that had fallen to the ground overnight, and patiently hold them, one by one, up to his large, toothy mouth. I remained as thrilled as a child by his flexible dark lips, huge, cubelike teeth that crunched the apples, core and all, with such finality, and his high, broad-breasted *enormity;* beside which, I felt small indeed. When I was a child, I used to ride horses, and was especially friendly with one named Nan until the day I was riding and my brother deliberately spooked her and I was thrown, head first, against the trunk of a tree. When I came to, I was in bed and my mother was bending worriedly over me; we silently agreed that perhaps horseback riding was not the safest sport for me. Since then I have walked, and prefer walking to horseback riding—but I had forgotten the depth of feeling one could see in horses' eyes.

I was therefore unprepared for the expression in Blue's. Blue was   5 lonely. Blue was horribly lonely and bored. I was not shocked that this should be the case; five acres to tramp by yourself, endlessly, even in the most beautiful of meadows—and his was—cannot provide many interesting events, and once rainy season turned to dry that was about it. No, I was shocked that I had forgotten that human animals and nonhuman animals can communicate quite well; if we are brought up around animals as children we take this for granted. By the time we are adults we no longer remember. However, the animals have not changed. They are in fact *completed* creations (at least they seem to be, so much more than we) who are not likely *to* change; it is their nature to express themselves. What else are they going to express? And they do. And, generally speaking, they are ignored.

After giving Blue the apples, I would wander back to the house, aware that he was observing me. Were more apples not forthcoming then? Was that to be his sole entertainment for the day? My partner's small son had decided he wanted to learn how to piece a quilt; we worked in silence on our respective squares as I thought . . .

Well, about slavery: about white children, who were raised by black people, who knew their first all-accepting love from black women, and then, when they were twelve or so, were told they must "forget" the deep levels of communication between themselves and "mammy" that they knew. Later they would be able to relate quite calmly, "My old mammy was sold to another good family." "My old mammy was _____." Fill in the blank. Many more years later a white woman would say: "I can't understand these Negroes, these blacks. What do they want? They're so different from us."

And about the Indians, considered to be "like animals" by the "settlers" (a very benign euphemism for what they actually were), who did not understand their description as a compliment.

And about the thousands of American men who marry Japanese, Korean, Filipina, and other non-English-speaking women and of how happy they report they are, "*blissfully,*" until their brides learn to speak

English, at which point the marriages tend to fall apart. What then did the men see, when they looked into the eyes of the women they married, before they could speak English? Apparently only their own reflections.

I thought of society's impatience with the young. "Why are they playing the music so loud?" Perhaps the children have listened to much of the music of oppressed people their parents danced to before they were born, with its passionate but soft cries for acceptance and love, and they have wondered why their parents failed to hear. 10

I do not know how long Blue had inhabited his five beautiful, boring acres before we moved into our house; a year after we had arrived—and had also traveled to other valleys, other cities, other worlds—he was still there.

But then, in our second year at the house, something happened in Blue's life. One morning, looking out the window at the fog that lay like a ribbon over the meadow, I saw another horse, a brown one, at the other end of Blue's field. Blue appeared to be afraid of it, and for several days made no attempt to go near. We went away for a week. When we returned, Blue had decided to make friends and the two horses ambled or galloped along together, and Blue did not come nearly as often to the fence underneath the apple tree.

When he did, bringing his new friend with him, there was a different look in his eyes. A look of independence, of self-possession, of inalienable *horse*ness. His friend eventually became pregnant. For months and months there was, it seemed to me, a mutual feeling between me and the horses of justice, of peace. I fed apples to them both. The look in Blue's eyes was one of unabashed "this is *it*ness."

It did not, however, last forever. One day, after a visit to the city, I went out to give Blue some apples. He stood waiting, or so I thought, though not beneath the tree. When I shook the tree and jumped back from the shower of apples, he made no move. I carried some over to him. He managed to half-crunch one. The rest he let fall to the ground. I dreaded looking into his eyes—because I had of course noticed that Brown, his partner, had gone—but I did look. If I had been born into slavery, and my partner had been sold or killed, my eyes would have looked like that. The children next door explained that Blue's partner had been "put with him' (the same expression that old people used, I had noticed, when speaking of an ancestor during slavery who had been impregnated by her owner) so that they could mate and she conceive. Since that was accomplished, she had been taken back by her owner, who lived somewhere else.

Will she be back? I asked. 15

They didn't know.

Blue was like a crazed person. Blue *was,* to me, a crazed person. He galloped furiously, as if he were being ridden, around and around his five beautiful acres. He whinnied until he couldn't. He tore at the ground with his hooves. He butted himself against his single shade tree. He looked always and always toward the road down which his partner had gone. And then, occasionally, when he came up for apples, or I took apples to him, he looked at me. It was a look so piercing, so full of grief, a look so *human,* I almost laughed (I felt too sad to cry) to think there are people who do not know that animals suffer. People like me who have forgotten, and daily forget, all that animals try to tell us. "Everything you do to us will happen to you; we are your teachers, as you are ours. We are one lesson" is essentially it, I think. There are those who never once have even considered animals' rights: those who have been taught that animals actually want to be used and abused by us, as small children "love" to be frightened, or women "love" to be mutilated and raped. . . . They are the great-grand-children of those who honestly thought, because someone taught them this: "Women can't think," and "niggers can't faint." But most disturbing of all, in Blue's large brown eyes was a new look, more painful than the look of despair: the look of disgust with human beings, with life; the look of hatred. And it was odd what the look of hatred did. It gave him, for the first time, the look of a beast. And what that meant was that he had put up a barrier within to protect himself from further violence; all the apples in the world wouldn't change that fact.

And so Blue remained, a beautiful part of our landscape, very peaceful to look at from the window, white against the grass. Once a friend came to visit and said, looking out on the soothing view: "And it *would* have to be a *white* horse; the very image of freedom." And I thought, yes, the animals are forced to become for us merely "images" of what they once so beautifully expressed. And we are used to drinking milk from containers showing "contented" cows, whose real lives we want to hear nothing about, eating eggs and drumsticks from "happy" hens, and munching hamburgers advertised by bulls of integrity who seem to command their fate.

As we talked of freedom and justice one day for all, we sat down to steaks. I am eating misery, I thought, as I took the first bite. And spit it out.

1986

Reading and Responding

1. Mark the place in this essay where you think you know what it's about, what the main theme is. Briefly paraphrase this passage.
2. Write quickly and freely about a horse or other animal that you know or have known well enough to describe its personality.

Working Together

1. Do a short freewrite explaining what you think Blue represents for Alice Walker. Then as a group, discuss your responses. Trace each interpretation back to a particular place in the text. Finally, identify two

points you feel sure that Walker wants readers to understand. Write two or three sentences to explain each of them.

2. Imagine that you're Walker and that you're getting ready to write this essay. Explain what's going through your mind: what moved you to begin writing? What main point are you planning to make? What are you thinking about strategy?

Rethinking and Rewriting

1. Write an essay centering on a particular animal but using that animal as a way of reflecting on larger issues as well. Use the animal as a point of departure, a representative example, a symbol.

2. Write an essay arguing for vegetarianism. Use Walker's essay as a source, do other research to support your arguments, or, like Walker, draw on personal experience.

"MY HORSE AND I"

N. Scott Momaday

> *Part Kiowa and part Cherokee Indian, N. Scott Momaday has written*
> *two novels, including* House Made of Dawn *(1968), winner of the Pulit-*
> *zer Prize; several collections of poetry; and a number of nonfiction books and*
> *essays, including his best-known and most influential book,* The Way to
> Rainy Mountain *(1969), a collage of Kiowa legends and autobiographical*
> *stories. He teaches now at the University of Arizona. In the following essay*
> *Momaday writes about his boyhood relationship to his horse.*

As You Read

1. Stop somewhere in your reading and write half a page or so in response
   to this question: How are you like N. Scott Momaday, and how do you
   differ from him?
2. As you're reading, look for sentences that really grab you, either because
   of what they say or because of how they're made. Note them in the
   margin and keep reading. Once you're done reading, go back and copy
   out three of them.

I sometimes think of what it means that in their heyday—in 1830,
say—the Kiowas owned more horses *per capita* than any other tribe on the
Great Plains, that the Plains Indian culture, the last culture to evolve in
North America, is also known as "the horse culture" and "the centaur
culture," that the Kiowas tell the story of a horse that died of shame after
its owner committed an act of cowardice, that I am a Kiowa, that therefore
there is in me, as there is in the Tartars, an old, sacred notion of the horse.
I believe that at some point in my racial life, this notion must needs be
expressed in order that I may be true to my nature.

It happened so: I was thirteen years old, and my parents gave me a
horse. It was a small nine-year-old gelding of that rare, soft color that is
called strawberry roan. This my horse and I came to be, in the course of
our life together, in good understanding, of one mind, a true story and
history of that large landscape in which we made the one entity of whole
motion, one and the same center of an intricate, pastoral composition,
evanescent, ever changing. And to this my horse I gave the name Pecos.

On the back of my horse I had a different view of the world. I could
see more of it, how it reached away beyond all the horizons I had ever
seen; and yet it was more concentrated in its appearance, too, and more
accessible to my mind, my imagination. My mind loomed upon the farthest edges of the earth, where I could feel the full force of the planet

whirling into space. There was nothing of the air and light that was not pure exhilaration, and nothing of time and eternity. Oh, Pecos, *un poquito mas!* Oh, my hunting horse! Bear me away, bear me away!

It was appropriate that I should make a long journey. Accordingly I set out one early morning, traveling light. Such a journey must begin in the nick of time, on the spur of the moment, and one must say to himself at the outset: Let there be wonderful things along the way; let me hold to the way and be thoughtful in my going; let this journey be made in beauty and belief.

I sang in the sunshine and heard the birds call out on either side. Bits   *5* of down from the cottonwoods drifted across the air, and butterflies fluttered in the sage. I could feel my horse under me, rocking at my legs, the bobbing of the reins in my hand; I could feel the sun on my face and the stirring of a little wind at my hair. And through the hard hooves, the slender limbs, the supple shoulders, the fluent back of my horse I felt the earth under me. Everything was under me, buoying me up; I rode across the top of the world. My mind soared; time and again I saw the fleeting shadow of my mind moving about me as it went winding upon the sun.

When the song, which was a song of riding, was finished, I had Pecos pick up the pace. Far down on the road to San Ysidro I overtook my friend Pasqual Fragua. He was riding a rangy, stiff-legged black and white stallion, half wild, which horse he was breaking for the rancher Cass Goodner. The horse skittered and blew as I drew up beside him. Pecos began to prance, as he did always in the company of another horse. "Where are you going?" I asked in the Jemez language. And he replied, "I am going down the road." The stallion was hard to manage, and Pasqual had to keep his mind upon it; I saw that I had taken him by surprise. "You know," he said after a moment, "when you rode up just now I did not know who you were." We rode on for a time in silence, and our horses got used to each other, but still they wanted their heads. The longer I looked at the stallion the more I admired it, and I suppose that Pasqual knew this, for he began to say good things about it: that it was a thing of good blood, that it was very strong and fast, that it felt very good to ride it. The thing was this: that the stallion was half wild, and I came to wonder about the wild half of it; I wanted to know what its wildness was worth in the riding. "Let us trade horses for a while," I said, and, well, all right, he agreed. At first it was exciting to ride the stallion, for every once in a while it pitched and bucked and wanted to run. But it was heavy and raw-boned and full of resistance, and every step was a jolt that I could feel deep down in my bones. I saw soon enough that I had made a bad bargain, and I wanted my horse back, but I was ashamed to admit it. There came a time in the late afternoon, in the vast plain far south of San Ysidro, after thirty miles, perhaps, when I no longer knew whether it was I who was riding the stallion or the stallion who was riding me. "Well, let us go back now," said Pasqual at last. "No, I am going on; and I will have my horse back, please," I said, and he was surprised and sorry to hear it, and we said goodbye. "If you are going south or east," he said, "look out for the sun, and keep your face in the shadow of your hat. *Vaya con Dios*." And I went on my way alone then, wiser and better mounted, and thereafter I held on to my horse. I saw no one for a long time, but I saw four falling stars and any number of jackrabbits, roadrunners, and coyotes, and once, across a distance, I saw a bear, small and black, lumbering in a ravine. The mountains drew close and withdrew and drew close again, and after several days I swung east.

Now and then I came upon settlements. For the most part they were dry, burnt places with Spanish names: Arroyo Seco, Las Piedras, Tres Casas. In one of these I found myself in a narrow street between high adobe walls. Just ahead, on my left, was a door in the wall. As I approached the door was flung open, and a small boy came running out, rolling a hoop. This happened so suddenly that Pecos shied very sharply, and I fell to the ground, jamming the thumb of my left hand. The little boy looked very worried and said that he was sorry to have caused such an accident. I waved the matter off, as if it were nothing; but as a matter of fact my hand hurt so much that tears welled up in my eyes. And the pain lasted for many days. I have fallen many times from a horse, both before and after that, and a few times I fell from a running horse on dangerous ground, but that was the most painful of them all.

In another settlement there were some boys who were interested in racing. They had good horses, some of them, but their horses were not so good as mine, and I won easily. After that, I began to think of ways in which I might even the odds a little, might give some advantage to my competitors. Once or twice I gave them a head start, a reasonable head start of, say, five or ten yards to the hundred, but that was too simple, and I won anyway. Then it came to me that I might try this: we should all line up in the usual way, side by side, but my competitors should be mounted and I should not. When the signal was given I should then have to get up on my horse while the others were breaking away; I should have to mount my horse during the race. This idea appealed to me greatly, for it was both imaginative and difficult, not to mention dangerous; Pecos and I should have to work very closely together. The first few times we tried this I had little success, and over a course of a hundred yards I lost four races out of five. The principal problem was that Pecos simply could not hold still among the other horses. Even before they broke away he was hard to manage, and when they were set running nothing could hold him back, even for an instant. I could not get my foot in the stirrup, but I had to throw myself up across the saddle on my stomach, hold on as best I could, and twist myself into position, and all this while racing at full speed. I could ride well enough to accomplish this feat, but it was a very awkward and inefficient business. I had to find some way to use the whole energy of my horse, to get it all into the race. Thus far I had managed only to break his motion, to divert him from his purpose and mine. To correct this I took Pecos away and worked with him through the better part of a long afternoon on a broad reach of level ground beside an irrigation ditch. And it was hot, hard work. I began by teaching him to run straight away while I ran beside him a few steps, holding on to the saddle horn, with no pressure on the reins. Then, when we had mastered this trick, we proceeded to the next one, which was this: I placed my weight on my arms, hanging from the saddle horn, threw my feet out in front of me, struck them to the ground, and sprang up against the saddle. This I did again and again, until Pecos came to expect it and did not flinch or lose his stride. I sprang a little higher each time. It was in all a slow process of trial and error, and after two or three hours both Pecos and I were covered with bruises and soaked through with perspiration. But we had much to show for our efforts, and at last the moment came when we must put the whole performance together. I had not yet leaped into the saddle, but I was quite confident that I could now do so; only I must be sure to get high enough. We began this dress rehearsal then from a standing position. At my signal Pecos lurched and was running at once, straight away and smoothly. And at the same time I sprinted forward two steps and gathered myself up, placing my weight precisely at my wrists, throwing my feet out and together, perfectly. I brought my feet down sharply to the ground and sprang up hard, as hard as I could, bringing my legs astraddle of my horse—and everything was just right, except that I sprang too high. I vaulted all the way over my horse, clearing the saddle by a considerable margin, and came down into the irrigation ditch. It was a good trick, but it was not the one I had in mind, and I wonder what Pecos thought of it after all. Anyway, after a while I could mount my horse in this way and so well that there was no challenge in it, and I went on winning race after race.

I went on, farther and farther into the wide world. Many things happened. And in all this I knew one thing: I knew where the journey was begun, that it was itself a learning of the beginning, that the beginning was infinitely worth the learning. The journey was well undertaken, and somewhere in it I sold my horse to an old Spanish man of Vallecitos. I do not know how long Pecos lived. I had used him hard and well, and it may be that in his last days an image of me like thought shimmered in his brain.

Reading and Responding

1. Is this a hard or easy piece to read? why? What exactly in the words and sentences makes it one way or the other?

Working Together

1. Compare Walker's and Momaday's experiences of horses, their attitudes and values. Speculate: How much of these differences are attributable to race and gender—to Walker being a black woman and Momaday a Native American man?

2. Just on the basis of these two essays—assuming for the sake of argument that both are representative—discuss the words, phrases, images, and attitudes that are typically black and feminine and those that are typically Native American and "masculine." Or do you think this is a silly thing to do? Are there any significant differences in these two pieces? If there are, do they necessarily relate to race and gender?

3. Make a list of the simple facts of the journey that Momaday describes taking with his horse Pecos. Then discuss the aspects of the journey that don't show up in a list of the simple facts. As you think about this, pay some attention to the essay's opening and final paragraphs.

Rethinking and Rewriting

1. Take the class discussion and your own rereading and make them the basis of an essay with this thesis: Walker's and Momaday's essays illustrate how race and gender influence the way people look at the world. Be specific. Quote the texts. Use ideas and phrases from the class discussion.

2. Add your own view to this essay idea—your view as a white male from California, or a Jewish woman from Brooklyn, or whoever you are. How do you look at horses? What experiences have you had with horses, if any? Compare and contrast them with those of Walker and Momaday, emphasizing the ways that race and gender influence not just how we see things but also what we've experienced in the first place.

3. Write an essay about some significant journey you've taken, one that you can now see gave you important experience—experience that changed your outlook, your understanding, or your character. Give readers both the journey itself (the basic facts) and your reflections on it.

"ALAMO CANYON CREEK"

Kathleen Dean Moore

Kathleen Dean Moore chairs the Philosophy Department at Oregon State University. She has written extensively on justice and the judicial process in Pardons: Justice, Mercy, and the Public Interest *(Oxford, 1989), and she has also authored two textbooks on writing, thinking, and argument. Married to a zoologist (he appears in this essay), Moore is no sheltered academic. As this essay makes clear, her intelligence and interests range widely indeed. "Alamo Canyon Creek" is one of a series of essays exploring the connections among people, landscape, animals, and water.*

As You Read

1. This essay starts with people looking for rattlesnakes. Why would any-one do this? As you read, see whether you can find places in the essay that begin to suggest good reasons. Make a note of these places in the margins so that you can return to them later.

2. As you read, look for places where Kathleen Moore simply describes action or scenery, and mark them with a wiggly line in the margin. Also as you read, look for places where Moore talks about what she finds, places where she explains or analyzes or speculates; mark these places with a straight line in the margin.

We found the first rattlesnake no more than a hundred yards from the foot of Alamo Canyon. At this point, the Ajo Mountains form two rough ridgelines parallel to each other, trending north and south. The Alamo Canyon breaches the first ridge and gives access in both directions to the valley between them, a valley clogged with saguaro, palo verde, yellow mounds of coreopsis, mesquite with thorns two inches long, and huge blocks of volcanic rock, black rock heaped against a bleached sky. It was quiet in the canyon, and hot, the kind of heat that makes a person's face glow and his eyes narrow. Frank and I had picked our way down one side of an arroyo, across the wash at the bottom, and then up over broken basalt on the other side, on a trail barely wide enough for a pair of hiking boots. It cut between rock ledges and brushed past thickets, detoured around slab-sided prickly pears and dropped over boulders, forcing us to walk altogether too close to vegetation that often hides snakes.

Sure enough, the first rattlesnake was resting in leaf litter under a mesquite that brushed across the trail. It was coiled as perfectly as a Zuni pot, with its neck poking out the middle like a lily and its broad head resting on the top coil. The snake lay in easy striking range of the trail and could have picked off hikers one after another if it had chosen to, but apparently it had not. Instead, it sat quiet and cool, gloriously beautiful, while we inspected it from every angle, and from a fair distance away.

After the first snake, we hiked on full alert, peeking under the bushes, then scanning the trail, then inspecting the margins, flinching whenever a cicada rasped in branches overhanging the track or a lizard dodged from rock to rock like a gunfighter. Even so, we didn't see the second snake until I stepped one small step off the trail to get a better look at a cowboy's line cabin, if that's what it was—I never did get a closer look. A rattlesnake set off an alarm buzz and I whooped, leaped away, and froze in place, all before the thought of a snake had time to cross my mind.

I used to worry really quite a lot about whether I would recognize the sound of a rattlesnake in time to take evasive measures. Would I stand there wondering *Is that a cicada, or is that a rattlesnake?* until the rattlesnake decided I wasn't going to get the message and nailed me? *Is the sound more like a rattle?* I would ask people, *or more like a door-buzzer?* Useless questions, all of them. The sound of that snake had not entered my consciousness before I was gone; my spinal column recognized the rattlesnake, and that was all it took.

From a safe distance, I watched the snake raise its head and sway like   5
a cobra, darting its head around branches to get a clear shot at me I thought, but maybe, as Frank said, to taste the air on its tongue. The snake was as thick as a man's arm, but what I had never figured out about that cliché is that anything as thick as a man's arm could also be as strong as a man's arm, and this snake broadcast strength. Rearing back to strike, drawing up to full height as if it wanted to arm wrestle me, the snake was five long feet of power and menace and fury, but mostly power. I could see his rattle sticking up in the air like a finger, vibrating so fast it blurred, making a terrible racket. He was hot, he was mad, and I was afraid—for the first time in my life afraid of a snake, afraid in my muscles and bones. I backed away down the trail.

Finding rattlesnakes is one of those things you want to do until you succeed, and then it doesn't necessarily seem like such a brilliantly conceived project. Still, it has its advantages as a hobby. Unlike birds, up at the crack of dawn, snakes are comfortable in temperatures that feel comfortable to humans, and so they tend to sleep in until the sun has warmed the rocks, and they nap in bushes during the heat of the day. When you find a snake, it doesn't fly off and leave you wondering what it was; usually it sits still while you dig in your pack for a field guide and watches you warily while you try to count the scales between its eyes.

For many years, our mentor in the snake-searching business was Albert Zimbelman, a herpetologist from the university down the road. Dr. Zimbelman liked to take university students out on field trips into the high desert canyons each spring, and our family would tag along for the fun of it. His practice was to sit in a lawnchair by an oversized campfire and tell horrible snake stories long into the night. As a result, nobody ever saw Dr. Zimbelman at a decent hour in the morning. We were always impatient, we converted birdwatchers, pacing around camp and checking our watches, sure that the snakes would get tired of waiting and go take a nap. But along about ten o'clock, he would crawl out of his tent, bolt down a cup of coffee and suggest, as if he were the first one to think of it, "let's go find snakes." Thirty undergraduate students fanned out across the hillsides, turning stones, peering into bushes, calling Dr. Zimbelman to come identify what they had discovered. He knew everything. Side-blotched lizards in the sagebrush. Prairie rattlers in the desert holly. Gopher snakes everywhere. Western whiptail lizards under the junipers. Scorpions under a log. A coachwhip by the road. Who would ever think all those animals would be hiding on one hillside?—a hillside as full of surprises as an advent calendar, with something scaled and occasionally lethal behind every little rock.

From Dr. Zimbelman, we learned that rattlesnakes can strike a distance no greater than two-thirds their body length. That the rattles form from the dry skin a snake sheds as it grows. That rattlesnakes have heat sensors in their faces and hunt mice after dark by the heat the little mouse bodies give off. That ninety percent of the people bitten by rattlesnakes in Arizona each year are drunken males. That one percent of those die. That rattlesnakes—even roadkill rattlesnakes—taste like chicken and iguanas. That a snake will continue to strike after its head is cut off. That in the spring, if you see one snake you'll probably see several, because they are just then leaving the caverns where they winter underground, wound together in shifting, sifting, rasping skeins.

Forewarned, we moved even more carefully up the Alamo Canyon after we had seen the second snake, and we made a wide detour around the old ranch buildings. Just at the point where the canyon intersects the valley between the ridges and two sandstone rocks lean toward each other across the trail, we thought we heard water. Great loping strides toward the sound, and we looked down on a thousand rivulets trickling under gravel into a rockbound basin. Has anyone ever heard water in the desert and not turned toward it, glad, shouting aloud and bounding over rocks to the source of the sound? We stood at the basin's edge and listened: an insistent, fluttering sound, soft as seeds sifting in a sack, a sound that might have been leaves falling through dry branches or wind in cottonwoods.

Like the snake's warning, the sound of the water lodged somewhere   10
near the muscles in my back—a lovely wash of comfort and safety, unmediated by any thoughts, the simple assurance of something good. How to explain an emotion in the muscles? As far as I know, the only person who comes close is Thomas Hobbes, an English philosopher dead now for four hundred years, a materialist who thought that the body is a collection of particles. The way Hobbes described it, desire is the movement of all those particles toward an object of desire, particles simultaneously surging toward what is good. Aversion is movement away, a million cells recoiling. I used to think the whole idea was silly, imagining some kind of microscopic chorus line of cells. But I don't think it's so silly any more. In the desert, I

felt all the parts of my body leap away from that snake, every cell, every nerve fiber in full retreat from the slam of intracellular fear. And the joyous movement toward water was prickly, every cell responding. I dropped my pack on the beach and knelt over the water.

Where Alamo Canyon Creek pools up under a boulder, the water carried clouds of algae, brilliant bilious green algae, dotted with—of all things in the desert—polliwogs, the young of the spadefoot toad. You wouldn't think an amphibian could survive a desert summer when all surface water evaporates and temperatures reach 125 degrees. You'd think that all you'd find in the way of desert amphibians would be little dried up toadskins, tough and dark under the desert sun. But the spadefoot toads show up in wet years, digging themselves out of the earth.

Thunder brings them out. The rolling vibrations of sand pounded by thunder, the echoing pap pap pap of hard rain, the low-frequency waves of the heaviest storms, startle them to life after such a long time of torpor, and they start to dig. Toad after toad, they pop out of the sand and hop to water for their first drink of the year, or two years, or three. They lower their hindquarters into cool, ozone-soaked water and suck up moisture through their skin.

Frank is the one who has taught me about toads, spinning long, biological tales of sex and violence. The toads mate piggyback and lay eggs in the desert pools, the eggs hatch into polliwogs, and then the race is on to mature into toads before the sun dries up the pool. In this race, there are no scruples, only winners and desiccated polliwog corpses, little dried-up commas stuck in the crust at the edge of the rock basin. To win, the polliwogs turn to cannibalism. Those who eat the most protein from brine shrimp grow a hard, beakish tooth on their upper lip. They turn the tooth against their egg-mates, eating each other's tails, tearing off bites of flesh, growing at phenomenal rates off the rich flesh of their kin, hopping out of the basin as the last water steams out of the algae.

I took off my boots and my socks and arranged them in the sun. Then I dropped down onto the rock and stretched my feet into the water, leaning back into the shade of the sandstone slab, scattering polliwogs that soon regrouped in the shadow of my right foot. I was feeling most satisfied by the progress of this hike. We had set out to encounter the desert, to find the animals that bring the landscape alive, or maybe to find the animals that enliven us to the landscape by raising our heartbeats and focussing our attention. We had set out to connect with the animals we encountered, at least in a scientific way, which in my experience is a matter of close attention to detail.

Encounters with animals are a gold mine of interest because the more you learn about an animal, the more improbable it seems, and you realize suddenly that there is more than one way to skin a cat, that the categories that *limit* your life—five senses, daylight vision, a certain moral compunction about eating relatives, a daily schedule, and nowhere near enough time to wait for a good storm—these categories that restrict the way hu-

15

mans live, do not impose any such limits on an animal's life. Snakes can see pictures drawn by heat. Toads can go underground without any more fuss than going to the grocery store, living a life that would be, for a human, the most exquisite, brutalizing torture, buried for years, deprived of every sense but touch.

Observing animals, you also learn that the categories that *enrich* your life—long-distance vision, self-righteousness, reflective thought, empathy, planning to a purpose—are utterly absent from the experiences of the animals, or at least that's what I am assuming from what I know about the structure of their brains. Snakes and toads have a primitive brain, hardwired for fear and the detection of prey, for sex, hunger, and thirst. We primates have that brain too, and on top of that, the layered accretions of the cerebral cortex. So I come the closest to thinking like a snake, to seeing the world through the brain of a toad, when my body reacts to a stimulus—terror, elation—and leaves my conscious mind out of the process.

I study the issue: What was I thinking about when I was thinking with my reptilian precursor of a brain, when I was frightened by the snake and yowled, and leaped back, and froze? In the effort to remember, I reconstruct the sequence of events in my mind, and at the point where the snake buzzed, I find . . . nothing. Nothing. No visual images. I don't even find a memory of the sound. No memory of jumping. A step off the trail toward the adobe bricks, a blank space (maybe a dark space), and then I'm ten feet behind where I was before, my shout echoing in my ears, my mind ablaze with interest in a snake that is still ripping off a buzz to terrify the world. My reptile's brain did its job and then passed responsibility back to my cerebral cortex.

So maybe I know what it is like to think like a snake, because I know what it is like to think not at all—to act with no memory, with no decision, with no awareness, to do the right thing at the right time and nothing more. In this vacuum, this unawareness extended through time, a snake or a toad lives out its life, eats its sisters, absorbs its tail, lays its eggs, hops out of the pond, and in increasing heat, swims backwards into the sand, one foot down, two feet, and waits for the storms. It is possible that the coolness of mud behind his knees gives a groggy toad the most glorious excitement and pleasure. But if so, he never knows it.

Sometimes I wonder what happens to all the emotion that is never experienced by the snakes and the toads in the desert. Where is the terror of an animal being eaten by its brother? What happens to the pleasure that washes over a toad when he eases his rump into a desert pool? If a snake doesn't experience the anger that is so evident in the curve of its spine, where does the anger go?

In a desert landscape, a landscape without consciousness, emptier of 20 intellect than any other landscape I have ever seen, I find emotion lying like heat on the surface of the sand and seeping into cracks between boulders. There is joy in the wind in the spines of the saguaro and fear in bare rocks. Anger flies with the ravens and sits waiting under stones. Excitement pools in the low places, the dry river courses, the cracked arroyos, and is sucked by low-pressure ridges up into storm clouds that blow east toward the Alamo Canyon.

Reading and Responding

Freewrite about a time you went on some sort of expedition (or hike or outing) expressly to look for some particular animal (or animals). What were you looking for, where did you go, and were you successful?

Working Together

1. As a group, write a paragraph that explains Moore's motivations for looking for rattlesnakes. Make sure that you identify at least two persuasive reasons.
2. Discuss what rattlesnakes and water have in common in this essay. Write four or five sentences that explain the links you see.
3. Draw up two lists, one composed of the ways that people live and a contrasting list composed of the ways that animals live. Draw from Moore's essay to get your lists started, but make sure that your group adds at least one item of its own to each list.

Rethinking and Rewriting

1. Think about your typical day or your typical week: How much of what you do seems thoughtless and automatic? Talk about the sorts of things you do that fall into this category. Then think about the things you do that result specifically from careful planning and decision making. As you look at these two categories, which one yields the most satisfaction, the most pleasure in being alive?
2. Write about an enounter with an animal, a vivid encounter—one that taught you something you might not have otherwise learned. Make the encounter real to your readers, and make sure that they understand how you were affected and what you learned.

"SLEEPING WITH ANIMALS"

Maxine Kumin

*An accomplished novelist and poet, Maxine Kumin is perhaps most fa-
mous for her book* Up Country, *which draws many of its themes and locales
from rural New England and which won the 1973 Pulitzer Prize for poetry.
Reprinted from* Nurture *(1989), "Sleeping with Animals" turns what could
easily be considered an obligation—spending a night in the barn while waiting
for a mare to foal—into both meditation and celebration.*

As You Read

1. As you read, make two lists, one list detailing whatever you know about
   the person speaking in this poem and the other list relating to whatever
   you know about the horse. Read slowly and add to your lists as you go.
2. The person talking to us in this poem says "I choose" to keep this horse
   company. As you read, keep an eye out for some of the reasons for this
   choice.

Nightly I choose to keep this covenant
with a wheezing broodmare who, ten days past due,
grunts in her sleep in the vocables
of the vastly pregnant. She lies down
on sawdust of white pine, its turp smell blending   5
with the rich scent of ammonia and manure.
I in my mummy bag just outside her stall
observe the silence, louder than the catch
in her breathing, observe gradations of
the ancient noneditorial dark; against   10
the open doorway looking south, observe
the paddock posts become a chain gang, each
one shackled leg and wrist; the pasture wall
a graveyard of bones that ground fog lifts and swirls.

Sleeping with animals,   15
loving my animals too much,
letting them run like a perfectly detached
statement by Mozart through all the other lines
of my life, a handsome family of serene
horses glistening in their thoughtlessness,   20
fear ghosts me still for my two skeletons:
one stillborn foal eight years ago.
One, hours old, dead of a broken spine.

Five others swam like divers into air,
dropped on clean straw, were whinnied to, tongued dry,   25
and staggered, stagey drunkards, to their feet,
nipped and nudged by their mothers to the teat.

Restless, dozy, between occasional coughs
the mare takes note of me and nickers. Heaves
herself up, explores the corners of   30
her feed tub. Sleeps a little, leg joints locked.
I shine my light across the bar to watch
the immense contours of her flanks rise and fall.
Each double-inhale is threaded to the life
that still holds back in its safe sac.   35
What we say to each other in the cold black
of April, conveyed in a wordless yet perfect
language of touch and tremor, connects
us most surely to the wet cave we all
once burst from gasping, naked or furred,   40
into our separate species.

Everywhere on this planet, birth.
Everywhere, curled in the amnion,
an unborn wonder.
Together we wait for this still-clenched burden.   45

Working Together

1. Clearly, Maxine Kumin has divided this poem into four sections. As a group, look at each of these sections, and summarize each one in a sentence or two. Then from your brief summaries, make a list of questions that each section works to answer. For example, here's one of the questions that the first section works to answer: What's the horse's condition?

2. As a group, discuss the reasons why the person in this poem is spending the night in the barn. What connects the person and the pregnant mare? Decide on the three most important links or connections, and write a sentence for each.

Rethinking and Rewriting

1. Tell the story of a birth that you watched or participated in and try to do justice to how it affected you.

2. Assume that someone has made a quick reading of "Sleeping with Animals" and just doesn't seem to understand it. Lead this reader pa-

tiently through the poem, explaining both what's going on and what the speaker thinks about.

3. Using this poem as your starting point, discuss why you'd be inclined (or not) to read other work by Kumin. Be honest, and make your explanation a careful and thoughtful one.

"THE FISH"

Elizabeth Bishop

> *Winner of both the Pulitzer Prize (for her second book,* Poems, *in 1956) and the National Book Award (for* The Complete Poems *in 1969), Elizabeth Bishop has steadily gained a wider audience since her death in 1979. "The Fish" is reprinted from her first book,* North and South. *Now often anthologized, this poem reveals the kind of attention so characteristic of Bishop's work.*

Before and As You Read

1. Before you even begin reading this poem, make a list of the kind of things you'd expect to hear about in an everyday, run-of-the-mill fish story. Or think about it this way: If you told a fishing story, what would you include?
2. Stop reading after the fourth sentence (after "battered and venerable/ and homely," line 9) and summarize what's happened before the poem started as well as what you've actually read about. When you're not sure, guess from the available evidence.

I caught a tremendous fish
and held him beside the boat
half out of water, with my hook
fast in a corner of his mouth.
He didn't fight.   5
He hadn't fought at all.
He hung a grunting weight,
battered and venerable
and homely. Here and there
his brown skin hung in strips   10
like ancient wallpaper,
and its pattern of darker brown
was like wallpaper:
shapes like full-blown roses
stained and lost through age.   15
He was speckled with barnacles,
fine rosettes of lime,
and infested
with tiny white sea-lice,
and underneath two or three   20
rags of green weed hung down.
While his gills were breathing in
the terrible oxygen

—the frightening gills,
fresh and crisp with blood,   *25*
that can cut so badly—
I thought of the coarse white flesh
packed in like feathers,
the big bones and the little bones,
the dramatic reds and blacks   *30*
of his shiny entrails,
and the pink swim-bladder
like a big peony.
I looked into his eyes
which were far larger than mine   *35*
but shallower, and yellowed,
the irises backed and packed
with tarnished tinfoil
seen through the lenses
of old scratched isinglass.   *40*
They shifted a little, but not
to return my stare.
—It was more like the tipping
of an object toward the light.
I admired his sullen face,   *45*
the mechanism of his jaw,
and then I saw
that from his lower lip
—if you could call it a lip—
grim, wet, and weaponlike,   *50*
hung five old pieces of fish-line,
or four and a wire leader
with the swivel still attached,
with all their five big hooks
grown firmly in his mouth.   *55*
A green line, frayed at the end
where he broke it, two heavier lines,
and a fine black thread
still crimped from the strain and snap
when it broke and he got away.   *60*
Like medals with their ribbons
frayed and wavering,
a five-haired beard of wisdom
trailing from his aching jaw.
I stared and stared   *65*
and victory filled up
the little rented boat,
from the pool of bilge
where oil had spread a rainbow

around the rusted engine   70
to the bailer rusted orange,
the sun-cracked thwarts,
the oarlocks on their strings,
the gunnels—until everything
was rainbow, rainbow, rainbow!   75
And I let the fish go.

Reading and Responding

What's the effect of having this poem presented to you in such short lines? Do they speed up your reading or slow it down? Write a short paragraph about what it's like for you to read this poem.

Working Together

1. As a group, make sure that you understand what the speaker in this poem actually does. Think of the poem as a short film; what's the film actually show? Write a quick description of what we'd see if we saw the movie of this poem.
2. Focus on the word *victory* in lines 66 and 67: "and victory filled up/ the little rented boat." As a group, discuss this victory. Whose victory is it? Where does it come from? And how does this victory (whatever it is) explain that the person who caught this fish lets it go at the end of the poem? Be ready to report your answers.
3. As a group, assume that you are actually the fish in this poem. Why don't you fight? How do you win? And what does winning mean in this poem?

Rethinking and Rewriting

1. Write an essay that either agrees with or disagrees with this statement: Although most of the lines in this poem seem to describe the fish someone caught, this poem really tells you more about the person doing the fishing than about the fish itself.
2. Write an essay explaining why this poem has to be as long as it is now. Argue that none of this poem could be cut because cutting it would confuse the reader or lessen its impact. Explain why the poem couldn't be any longer, too.
3. Write a story about a successful fishing trip you've taken. Make sure readers understand both the trip itself and the reasons you view it as successful.

"THE BIRD AND THE MACHINE"

Loren Eiseley

> *A distinguished physical anthropologist, Loren Eiseley also wrote evocative, lyrical personal essays about his own experience of the natural world. In his first book of these essays,* The Immense Journey *(1957), he meditates on the evolution of life from Precambrian times to the formation of the human mind. His other prose meditations include* The Firmament of Time *(1960),* The Unexpected Universe *(1969), and* Night Country *(1971), as well as a haunting autobiography,* All the Strange Hours *(1975). In "The Bird and the Machine," as in all his essays, Eiseley celebrates the mystery and wonder of living things.*

As You Read

Reading slowly and patiently, annotate this essay, marking passages you don't understand, asking questions in the margins, recording your reactions.

I suppose their little bones have years ago been lost among the stones and winds of those high glacial pastures. I suppose their feathers blew eventually into the piles of tumbleweed beneath the straggling cattle fences and rotted there in the mountain snows, along with dead steers and all the other things that drift to an end in the corners of the wire. I do not quite know why I should be thinking of birds over the *New York Times* at breakfast, particularly the birds of my youth half a continent away. It is a funny thing what the brain will do with memories and how it will treasure them and finally bring them into odd juxtapositions with other things, as though it wanted to make a design, or get some meaning out of them, whether you want it or not, or even see it.

It used to seem marvelous to me, but I read now that there are machines that can do these things in a small way, machines that can crawl about like animals, and that it may not be long now until they do more things—maybe even make themselves—I saw that piece in the *Times* just now. And then they will, maybe—well, who knows—but you read about it more and more with no one making any protest, and already they can add better than we and reach up and hear things through the dark and finger the guns over the night sky.

This is the new world that I read about at breakfast. This is the world that confronts me in my biological books and journals, until there are times when I sit quietly in my chair and try to hear the little purr of the cogs in my head and the tubes flaring and dying as the messages go through them and the circuits snap shut or open. This is the great age, make no mistake about it; the robot has been born somewhat appropriately along with the atom bomb, and the brain they say now is just another type of more complicated feedback system. The engineers have its basic principles worked out; it's mechanical, you know; nothing to get superstitious about; and man can always improve on nature once he gets the idea. Well, he's got it all right and that's why, I guess, that I sit here in my chair, with the article crunched in my hand, remembering those two birds and that blue mountain sunlight. There is another magazine article on my desk that reads "Machines Are Getting Smarter Every Day." I don't deny it, but I'll still stick with the birds. It's life I believe in, not machines.

Maybe you don't believe there is any difference. A skeleton is all joints and pulleys, I'll admit. And when man was in his simpler stages of machine building in the eighteenth century, he quickly saw the resemblances. "What," wrote Hobbes, "is the heart but a spring, and the nerves but so many strings, and the joints but so many wheels, giving motion to the whole body?" Tinkering about in their shops it was inevitable in the end that men would see the world as a huge machine "subdivided into an infinite number of lesser machines."

The idea took on with a vengeance. Little automatons toured the country—dolls controlled by clockwork. Clocks described as little worlds were taken on tours by their designers. They were made up of moving figures, shifting scenes, and other remarkable devices. The life of the cell was unknown. Man, whether he was conceived as possessing a soul or not, moved and jerked about like these tiny puppets. A human being thought of himself in terms of his own tools and implements. He had been fashioned like the puppets he produced and was only a more clever model made by a greater designer.

Then in the nineteenth century, the cell was discovered, and the single machine in its turn was found to be the product of millions of infinitesimal machines—the cells. Now, finally, the cell itself dissolved away into an abstract chemical machine, and that into some intangible, inexpressible flow of energy. The secret seems to lurk all about, the wheels get smaller and smaller, and they turn more rapidly, but when you try to seize it the life is gone—and so, by popular definition, some would say that life was never there in the first place. The wheels and the cogs are the secret and we can make them better in time—machines that will run faster and more accurately than real mice to real cheese.

I have no doubt it can be done, though a mouse harvesting seeds on an autumn thistle is to me a fine sight and more complicated, I think, in his multiform activity than a machine "mouse" running a maze. Also, I like to think of the possible shape of the future brooding in mice, just as it brooded once in a rather mousy insectivore who became a man. It leaves a nice fine indeterminate sense of wonder that even an electronic brain hasn't got, because you know perfectly well that if the electronic brain changes, it will be because of something man has done to it. But what man will do to himself he doesn't really know. A certain scale of time and a ghostly intangible thing called change are ticking in him. Powers and potentialities like the oak in the seed, or a red and awful ruin. Either way, it's impressive; and the mouse has it, too. Or those birds, I'll never forget those birds—yet before I measured their significance, I learned the lesson of time first of all. I was young then and left alone in a great desert—part of an expedition that had scattered its men over several hundred miles in order to carry on research more effectively. I learned there that time is a series of planes existing superficially in the same universe. The tempo is a human illusion, a subjective clock ticking in our own kind of protoplasm.

As the long months passed, I began to live on the slower planes and to observe more readily what passed for life there. I sauntered, I passed more and more slowly up and down the canyons in the dry baking heat of midsummer. I slumbered for long hours in the shade of huge brown boulders that had gathered in tilted companies out on the flats. I had forgotten the world of men and the world had forgotten me. Now and then I found a skull in the canyons, and these justified my remaining there. I took a serene cold interest in these discoveries. I had come, like many a naturalist before me, to view life with a wary and subdued attention. I had grown to take pleasure in the divested bone.

I sat once on a high ridge that fell away before me into a waste of sand dunes. I sat through hours of a long afternoon. Finally, as I glanced beside my boot an indistinct configuration caught my eye. It was a coiled rattlesnake, a big one. How long he had sat with me I do not know. I had not frightened him. We were both clocked in the sleepwalking tempo of the earlier world, baking in the same high air and sunshine. Perhaps he had been there when I came. He slept on as I left, his coils, so ill-discerned by me, dissolving once more among the stones and gravel from which I had barely made him out.

Another time I got on a higher ridge, among some tough little wind-warped pines half covered over with sand in a basinlike depression that caught everything carried by the air up to those heights. There were a few thin bones of birds, some cracked shells of indeterminable age, and the knotty fingers of pine roots bulged out of shape from their long and agonizing grasp upon the crevices of the rock. I lay under the pines in the sparse shade and went to sleep once more. 10

It grew cold finally, for autumn was in the air by then, and the few things that lived thereabouts were sinking down into an even chillier scale of time. In the moments between sleeping and waking I saw the roots about me and slowly, slowly, a foot in what seemed many centuries, I moved my sleep-stiffened hands over the scaling bark and lifted my numbed face after the vanishing sun. I was a great awkward thing of knots and aching limbs, trapped up there in some long, patient endurance that involved the necessity of putting living fingers into rocks and by slow, aching expansion bursting those rocks asunder. I suppose, so thin and slow was the time of my pulse by then, that I might have stayed on to drift still deeper into the lower cadences of the frost, or the crystalline life that glistens pebbles, or shines in a snowflake, or dreams in the meteoric iron between the worlds.

It was a dim descent, but time was present in it. Somewhere far down in that scale the notion struck me that one might come the other way. Not many months thereafter I joined some colleagues heading higher into a remote windy tableland where huge bones were reputed to protrude like boulders from the turf. I had drowsed with reptiles and moved with the century-long pulse of trees; now, lethargically, I was climbing back up some invisible ladder of quickening hours. There had been talk of birds in connection with my duties. Birds are intense, fast-living creatures—reptiles, I suppose one might say, that have escaped out of the heavy sleep of time, transformed fairy creatures dancing over sunlit meadows. It is a youthful fancy, no doubt, but because of something that happened up there among the escarpments of that range, it remains with me a lifelong impression. I can never bear to see a bird imprisoned.

We came into that valley through the trailing mists of a spring night. It was a place that looked as though it might never have known the foot of man, but our scouts had been ahead of us and we knew all about the abandoned cabin of stone that lay far up on one hillside. It had been built in the land rush of the last century and then lost to the cattlemen again as the marginal soils failed to take to the plow.

There were spots like this all over that country. Lost graves marked by unlettered stones and old corroding rim-fire cartridge cases lying where somebody had made a stand among the boulders that rimmed the valley. They are all that remain of the range wars; the men are under the stones now. I could see our cavalcade winding in and out through the mist below us: torches, the reflection of the truck lights on our collecting tins, and the far-off bumping of a loose dinosaur thigh bone in the bottom of a trailer. I stood on a rock a moment looking down and thinking what it cost in money and equipment to capture the past.

We had, in addition, instructions to lay hands on the present. The *15* word had come through to get them alive—birds, reptiles, anything. A zoo somewhere abroad needed restocking. It was one of those reciprocal matters in which science involves itself. Maybe our museum needed a stray ostrich egg and this was the payoff. Anyhow, my job was to help capture some birds and that was why I was there before the trucks.

The cabin had not been occupied for years. We intended to clean it out and live in it, but there were holes in the roof and the birds had come in and were roosting in the rafters. You could depend on it in a place like this where everything blew away, and even a bird needed some place out of the weather and away from coyotes. A cabin going back to nature in a wild place draws them till they come in, listening at the eaves, I imagine, pecking softly among the shingles till they find a hole, and then suddenly the place is theirs and man is forgotten.

Sometimes of late years I find myself thinking the most beautiful sight in the world might be the birds taking over New York after the last man has run away to the hills. I will never live to see it, of course, but I know just how it will sound because I've lived up high and I know the sort of watch birds keep on us. I've listened to sparrows tapping tentatively on the outside of air conditioners when they thought no one was listening, and I know how other birds test the vibrations that come up to them through the television aerials.

"Is he gone?" they ask, and the vibrations come up from below, "Not yet, not yet."

Well, to come back, I got the door open softly and I had the spotlight all ready to turn on and blind whatever birds there were so they couldn't see to get out through the roof. I had a short piece of ladder to put against the far wall where there was a shelf on which I expected to make the biggest haul. I had all the information I needed, just like any skilled assassin. I pushed the door open, the hinges squeaking only a little. A bird or two stirred—I could hear them—but nothing flew and there was a faint starlight through the holes in the roof.

I padded across the floor, got the ladder up and the light ready, and 20 slithered up the ladder till my head and arms were over the shelf. Everything was dark as pitch except for the starlight at the little place back of the shelf near the eaves. With the light to blind them, they'd never make it. I had them. I reached my arm carefully over in order to be ready to seize whatever was there and I put the flash on the edge of the shelf where it would stand by itself when I turned it on. That way I'd be able to use both hands.

Everything worked perfectly except for one detail—I didn't know what kind of birds were there. I never thought about it at all, and it wouldn't have mattered if I had. My orders were to get something interesting. I snapped on the flash and sure enough there was a great beating and feathers flying, but instead of my having them, they, or rather he, had me. He had my hand, that is, and for a small hawk not much bigger than my fist he was doing all right. I heard him give one short metallic cry when the light went on and my hand descended on the bird beside him; after that he was busy with his claws and his beak was sunk in my thumb. In the struggle I knocked the lamp over on the shelf, and his mate got her sight back and whisked neatly through the hole in the roof and off among the stars outside. It all happened in fifteen seconds and you might think I would have fallen down the ladder, but no, I had a professional assassin's reputation to keep up, and the bird, of course, made the mistake of thinking the hand was the enemy and not the eyes behind it. He chewed my thumb up pretty effectively and lacerated my hand with his claws, but in the end I got him, having two hands to work with.

He was a sparrow hawk and a fine young male in the prime of life. I was sorry not to catch the pair of them, but as I dripped blood and folded his wings carefully, holding him by the back so that he couldn't strike again, I had to admit the two of them might have been more than I could have handled under the circumstances. The little fellow had saved his mate by diverting me, and that was that. He was born to it and made no outcry now, resting in my hand hopelessly but peering toward me in the shadows behind the lamp with a fierce, almost indifferent glance. He neither gave nor expected mercy and something out of the high air passed from him to me, stirring a faint embarrassment.

I quit looking into that eye and managed to get my huge carcass with its fist full of prey back down the ladder. I put the bird in a box too small to allow him to injure himself by struggle and walked out to welcome the arriving trucks. It had been a long day, and camp still to make in the darkness. In the morning that bird would be just another episode. He would go back with the bones in the truck to a small cage in a city where he would spend the rest of his life. And a good thing, too. I sucked my aching thumb and spat out some blood. An assassin has to get used to these things. I had a professional reputation to keep up.

In the morning, with the change that comes on suddenly in that high country, the mist that had hovered below us in the valley was gone. The sky was a deep blue, and one could see for miles over the high outcroppings of stone. I was up early and brought the box in which the little hawk was imprisoned out onto the grass where I was building a cage. A wind as cool as a mountain spring ran over the grass and stirred my hair. It was a fine day to be alive. I looked up and all around and at the hole in the cabin roof out of which the other little hawk had fled. There was no sign of her anywhere that I could see.

"Probably in the next county by now," I thought cynically, but before *25* beginning work I decided I'd have a look at my last night's capture.

Secretively, I looked again all around the camp and up and down and opened the box. I got him right out in my hand with his wings folded properly and I was careful not to startle him. He lay limp in my grasp and I could feel his heart pound under the feathers but he only looked beyond me and up.

I saw him look that last look away beyond me into a sky so full of light that I could not follow his gaze. The little breeze flowed over me again, and nearby a mountain aspen shook all its tiny leaves. I suppose I must have had an idea then of what I was going to do, but I never let it come up into consciousness. I just reached over and laid the hawk on the grass.

He lay there a long minute without hope, unmoving, his eyes still fixed on that blue vault above him. It must have been that he was already so far away in heart that he never felt the release from my hand. He never even stood. He just lay with his breast against the grass.

In the next second after that long minute he was gone. Like a flicker of light, he had vanished with my eyes full on him but without actually seeing even a premonitory wing beat. He was gone straight into that towering emptiness of light and crystal that my eyes could scarcely bear to penetrate. For another long moment there was silence. I could not see him. The light was too intense. Then from far up somewhere a cry came ringing down.

I was young then and had seen little of the world, but when I heard   30
that cry my heart turned over. It was not the cry of the hawk I had captured; for, by shifting my position against the sun, I was now seeing farther up. Straight out of the sun's eye, where she must have been soaring restlessly above us for untold hours, hurtled his mate. And from far up, ringing from peak to peak of the summits over us, came a cry of such unutterable and ecstatic joy that it sounds down across the years and tingles among the cups of my quiet breakfast table.

I saw them both now. He was rising fast to meet her. They met in a great soaring gyre that turned to a whirling circle and a dance of wings. Once more, just once, their two voices, joined in a harsh wild medley of question and response, struck and echoed against the pinnacles of the valley. Then they were gone forever somewhere into those upper regions beyond the eyes of men.

I am older now, and sleep less, and have seen most of what there is to see and am not very much impressed any more, I suppose, by anything. "What Next in the Attributes of Machines?" my morning headline runs. "It Might Be the Power to Reproduce Themselves."

I lay the paper down and across my mind a phrase floats insinuatingly: "It does not seem that there is anything in the construction, constituents, or behavior of the human being which it is essentially impossible for science to duplicate and synthesize. On the other hand . . ."

All over the city the cogs in the hard, bright mechanisms have begun to turn. Figures move through computers, names are spelled out, a thoughtful machine selects the fingerprints of a wanted criminal from an array of thousands. In the laboratory an electronic mouse runs swiftly through a maze toward the cheese it can neither taste nor enjoy. On the second run it does better than a living mouse.

"On the other hand . . ." Ah, my mind takes up, on the other hand   35
the machine does not bleed, ache, hang for hours in the empty sky in a torment of hope to learn the fate of another machine, nor does it cry out with joy nor dance in the air with the fierce passion of a bird. Far off, over a distance greater than space, that remote cry from the heart of heaven makes a faint buzzing among my breakfast dishes and passes on and away.

Working Together

1. In groups of four or five, read each other's annotations: read, pass to the right; read, pass to the right—until you get your own book back.
2. Discuss: What passages did you and your group members mark? What challenges and demands does Eiseley present for the reader? What are the best strategies for meeting these challenges?

3. This essay falls into several pieces, each separated with blank space. Number each piece, label or give it a subheading, put the structure on the board, and insert transitional phrases or sentences between the pieces: "and this makes me think of . . . ," or "here's an example of what I was talking about," or "and that brings me back to what I was thinking of earlier."

Rethinking and Rewriting

1. Write an essay comparing any animal you know well to any machine you know well: a gerbil and a word processor, a cat and a mountain bike, a dog and a pickup truck. Think of all the comparisons you can, however odd or apparently trivial. Somewhere in your essay, quote Eiseley's main point, and agree or disagree.
2. Write an essay on any subject, imitating Eiseley's structure: the same number of pieces, each piece doing the same kind of thing Eiseley does here, each piece separated with blank space.

"LIVING LIKE WEASELS"
Annie Dillard

This essay marks Annie Dillard's third appearance in this book. Here, Dillard writes about her encounter with a weasel. As always, Dillard's perceptions offer readers ways of seeing and ways of thinking.

A weasel is wild. Who knows what he thinks? He sleeps in his underground den, his tail draped over his nose. Sometimes he lives in his den for two days without leaving. Outside, he stalks rabbits, mice, muskrats, and birds, killing more bodies than he can eat warm, and often dragging the carcasses home. Obedient to instinct, he bites his prey at the neck, either splitting the jugular vein at the throat or crunching the brain at the base of the skull, and he does not let go. One naturalist refused to kill a weasel who was socketed into his hand deeply as a rattlesnake. The man could in no way pry the tiny weasel off, and he had to walk half a mile to water, the weasel dangling from his palm, and soak him off like a stubborn label.

And once, says Ernest Thompson Seton—once, a man shot an eagle out of the sky. He examined the eagle and found the dry skull of a weasel fixed by the jaws to his throat. The supposition is that the eagle had pounced on the weasel and the weasel swiveled and bit as instinct taught him, tooth to neck, and nearly won. I would like to have seen that eagle from the air a few weeks or months before he was shot: was the whole weasel still attached to his feathered throat, a fur pendant? Or did the eagle eat what he could reach, gutting the living weasel with his talons before his breast, bending his beak, cleaning the beautiful airborne bones?

I have been reading about weasels because I saw one last week. I startled a weasel who startled me, and we exchanged a long glance.

Twenty minutes from my house, through the woods by the quarry and across the highway, is Hollins Pond, a remarkable piece of shallowness, where I like to go at sunset and sit on a tree trunk. Hollins Pond is also called Murray's Pond; it covers two acres of bottomland near Tinker Creek with six inches of water and six thousand lily pads. In winter, brown-and-white steers stand in the middle of it, merely dampening their hooves; from the distant shore they look like miracle itself, complete with miracle's nonchalance. Now, in summer, the steers are gone. The water lilies have blossomed and spread to a green horizontal plane that is terra firma to plodding blackbirds, and tremulous ceiling to black leeches, crayfish, and carp.

This is, mind you, suburbia. It is a five-minute walk in three directions to rows of houses, though none is visible here. There's a 55 mph highway at one end of the pond, and a nesting pair of wood ducks at the 5 other. Under every bush is a muskrat hole or a beer can. The far end is an alternating series of fields and woods, fields and woods, threaded everywhere with motorcycle tracks—in whose bare clay wild turtles lay eggs.

So. I had crossed the highway, stepped over two low barbed-wire fences, and traced the motorcycle path in all gratitude through the wild rose and poison ivy of the pond's shoreline up into high grassy fields. Then I cut down through the woods to the mossy fallen tree where I sit. This tree is excellent. It makes a dry, upholstered bench at the upper, marshy end of the pond, a plush jetty raised from the thorny shore between a shallow blue body of water and a deep blue body of sky.

The sun had just set. I was relaxed on the tree trunk, ensconced in the lap of lichen, watching the lily pads at my feet tremble and part dreamily over the thrusting path of a carp. A yellow bird appeared to my right and flew behind me. It caught my eye; I swiveled around—and the next instant, inexplicably, I was looking down at a weasel, who was looking up at me.

Weasel! I'd never seen one wild before. He was ten inches long, thin as a curve, a muscled ribbon, brown as fruitwood, soft-furred, alert. His face was fierce, small and pointed as a lizard's; he would have made a good arrowhead. There was just a dot of chin, maybe two brown hairs' worth, and then the pure white fur began that spread down his underside. He had two black eyes I didn't see, any more than you see a window.

The weasel was stunned into stillness as he was emerging from beneath an enormous shaggy wild rose bush four feet away. I was stunned into stillness twisted backward on the tree trunk. Our eyes locked, and someone threw away the key.

Our look was as if two lovers, or deadly enemies, met unexpectedly   *10* on an overgrown path when each had been thinking of something else: a clearing blow to the gut. It was also a bright blow to the brain, or a sudden beating of brains, with all the charge and intimate grate of rubbed balloons. It emptied our lungs. It felled the forest, moved the fields, and drained the pond; the world dismantled and tumbled into that black hole of eyes. If you and I looked at each other that way, our skulls would split and drop to our shoulders. But we don't. We keep our skulls. So.

He disappeared. This was only last week, and already I don't remember what shattered the enchantment. I think I blinked, I think I retrieved my brain from the weasel's brain, and tried to memorize what I was seeing, and the weasel felt the yank of separation, the careening splashdown into real life and the urgent current of instinct. He vanished under the wild rose. I waited motionless, my mind suddenly full of data and my spirit with pleadings, but he didn't return.

Please do not tell me about "approach-avoidance conflicts." I tell you I've been in that weasel's brain for sixty seconds, and he was in mine. Brains are private places, muttering through unique and secret tapes—but the weasel and I both plugged into another tape simultaneously, for a sweet and shocking time. Can I help it if it was a blank?

What goes on in his brain the rest of the time? What does a weasel think about? He won't say. His journal is tracks in clay, a spray of feathers, mouse blood and bone: uncollected, unconnected, loose-leaf, and blown.

I would like to learn, or remember, how to live. I come to Hollins Pond not so much to learn how to live as, frankly, to forget about it. That is, I don't think I can learn from a wild animal how to live in particular—shall I suck warm blood, hold my tail high, walk with my footprints precisely over the prints of my hands?—but I might learn something of mindlessness, something of the purity of living in the physical senses and the dignity of living without bias or motive. The weasel lives in necessity and we live in choice, hating necessity and dying at the last ignobly in its talons. I would like to live as I should, as the weasel lives as he should. And I suspect that for me the way is like the weasel's: open to time and death painlessly, noticing everything, remembering nothing, choosing the given with a fierce and pointed will.

I missed my chance. I should have gone for the throat. I should have   *15* lunged for that streak of white under the weasel's chin and held on, held on through mud and into the wild rose, held on for a dearer life. We could live under the wild rose wild as weasels, mute and uncomprehending. I could very calmly go wild. I could live two days in the den, curled, leaning on mouse fur, sniffing bird bones, blinking, licking, breathing musk, my hair tangled in the roots of grasses. Down is a good place to go, where the mind is single. Down is out, out of your ever-loving mind and back to your careless senses. I remember muteness as a prolonged and giddy fast, where every moment is a feast of utterance received. Time and events are merely poured, unremarked, and ingested directly, like blood pulsed into my gut through a jugular vein. Could two live that way? Could two live under the wild rose, and explore by the pond, so that the smooth mind of each is as everywhere present to the other, and as received and as unchallenged, as falling snow?

We could, you know. We can live any way we want. People take vows of poverty, chastity, and obedience—even of silence—by choice. The thing is to stalk your calling in a certain skilled and supple way, to locate the most tender and live spot and plug into that pulse. This is yielding, not fighting. A weasel doesn't "attack" anything; a weasel lives as he's meant to, yielding at every moment to the perfect freedom of single necessity.

I think it would be well, and proper, and obedient, and pure, to grasp your one necessity and not let it go, to dangle from it limp wherever it takes you. Then even death, where you're going no matter how you live, cannot you part. Seize it and let it seize you up aloft even, till your eyes burn out and drop; let your musky flesh fall off in shreds, and let your very bones unhinge and scatter, loosened over fields, over fields and woods, lightly, thoughtless, from any height at all, from as high as eagles.

Reading and Responding

1. This is the third Annie Dillard piece in this book (the other two are "The Silent Neighborhood" and "Life on the Rocks: The Galápagos"). If you've read the two previous pieces, what expectations do you now have for Dillard? What do you know about her themes and style? How do you have to read her work?
2. Dillard comes on very strong here. Her language is intense and direct, and it makes powerful claims about her experience, asks us to believe a lot. Look for an example of this language, and then record your reaction: How do you respond to this high-powered language?

Working Together

1. In two or three sentences, explain what the weasel represents for Dillard—why she admires it, the qualities in the weasel she'd like to have for herself. Share these sentences as a class or in groups. Find two or three specific sentences that best summarize her idea.
2. Is there anything "weasely" about Dillard's language here? Does she perform her argument, practice what she preaches? Any "bright blows to the brain"? Do we react to the essay the way Dillard reacted to the weasel?
3. What would "living like weasels" mean in your own life? What would it mean to study, read, go to school, write, and rewrite like a weasel?

Rethinking and Rewriting

1. Take the class discussion about "living like weasels" in your own life as a student and turn it into a complete essay: "Going to School Like a Weasel," "Writing Like Weasels," or "Reading Like Weasels."
2. Write an essay with this title, filling in the blank with some animal of your own choosing: "Living Like _____." In the essay, describe as clearly and concretely as you can the physical attributes of this animal; and then, only at the end, briefly, discuss why these qualities appeal to you. Choose an unlikely animal (like the weasel)—not some admirable, popular animal but something odd and at first glance even silly; not a lion, eagle, or dog but a squirrel, slug, stellar jay, or black-capped chickadee.
3. Do research on the animal you chose in item 2, the way Dillard researches the weasel. Write the essay in item 2, and then include this research, moving back and forth from fact to experience in a kind of collage structure, using blank space as transitions.

"THE RAINS"

Jane Goodall

Published in 1971, Jane Goodall's landmark book In the Shadow of
Man *has changed our view of chimpanzees and ourselves. Goodall first ventured to Tanzania and the area around Gombe Stream (now Gombe National Park) near Lake Tanganyika in 1960. She worked with Dr. Louis
Leakey on excavations at Olduvai Gorge, where Leakey and his team discovered remains of some of the earliest of our human ancestors. And it was
Leakey who suggested she might undertake a study of chimpanzees. Now in
its fourth decade, Jane Goodall's research continues. Reprinted here is an
excerpt from the opening pages of chapter 5, "The Rains," from* In the
Shadow of Man.

As You Read

As you read this piece, pretend you're Jane Goodall. Are you having fun?
Why are you doing this? What are you getting from it? What times stand
out as frustrating to you, and what times stand out as moments of success?

At about noon the first heavy drops of rain began to fall. The chimpanzees climbed out of the tree and one after the other plodded up the
steep grassy slope toward the open ridge at the top. There were seven adult
males in the group, including Goliath and David Graybeard, several females, and a few youngsters. As they reached the ridge the chimpanzees
paused. At that moment the storm broke. The rain was torrential, and the
sudden clap of thunder, right overhead, made me jump. As if this were a
signal, one of the big males stood upright and as he swayed and swaggered
rhythmically from foot to foot I could just hear the rising crescendo of his
pant-hoots above the beating of the rain. Then he charged off, flat-out
down the slope toward the trees he had just left. He ran some thirty yards,
and then, swinging round the trunk of a small tree to break his headlong
rush, leaped into the low branches and sat motionless.

Almost at once two other males charged after him. One broke off a
low branch from a tree as he ran and brandished it in the air before hurling
it ahead of him. The other, as he reached the end of his run, stood upright
and rhythmically swayed the branches of a tree back and forth before
seizing a huge branch and dragging it farther down the slope. A fourth
male, as he too charged, leaped into a tree and, almost without breaking
his speed, tore off a large branch, leaped with it to the ground, and continued down the slope. As the last two males called and charged down, so the
one who had started the whole performance climbed from his tree and
began plodding up the slope again. The others, who had also climbed into
trees near the bottom of the slope, followed suit. When they reached the

ridge, they started charging down all over again, one after the other, with equal vigor.

The females and youngsters had climbed into trees near the top of the rise as soon as the displays had begun, and there they remained watching throughout the whole performance. As the males charged down and plodded back up, so the rain fell harder, jagged forks or brilliant flares of lightning lit the leaden sky, and the crashing of the thunder seemed to shake the very mountains.

My enthusiasm was not merely scientific as I watched, enthralled, from my grandstand seat on the opposite side of the narrow ravine, sheltering under a plastic sheet. In fact it was raining and blowing far too hard for me to get at my notebook or use my binoculars. I could only watch, and marvel at the magnificence of those splendid creatures. With a display of strength and vigor such as this, primitive man himself might have challenged the elements.

Twenty minutes from the start of the performance the last of the males plodded back up the slope for the last time. The females and youngsters climbed down from their trees and the whole group moved over the crest of the ridge. One male paused, and with his hand on a tree trunk, looked back—the actor taking his final curtain. Then he too vanished over the ridge.

I continued to sit there, staring almost in disbelief at the white scars on the tree trunks and the discarded branches on the grass—all that remained, in that rain-lashed landscape, to prove that the wild "rain dance" had taken place at all. I should have been even more amazed had I known then that I would only see such a display twice more in the next ten years. Often, it is true, male chimpanzees react to the start of heavy rain by performing a rain dance, but this is usually an individual affair.

As the rainy season progressed the grass shot up until it was over twelve feet in some places, and even on the exposed ridges it often reached heights of at least six feet. When I left the tracks that I knew—if indeed I could find them at all—I could not tell where I was going and had to stop every so often and climb a tree to get my bearings. Also, I was no longer able to sit down wherever I happened to be or wherever was convenient when I came across a group of chimpanzees, for usually my view would then be totally obscured by grasses. I have never been able to work with binoculars for long periods of time when standing, so I had either to bend down hundreds of grass stems or else climb a tree. As the rainy season progressed I became increasingly arboreal in my habits, but despite my love for trees it was not very satisfactory, because I lost time both in looking for a suitable tree and in breaking away branches that obstructed my view of the chimps. And when there was a wind, which was often, I couldn't keep the binoculars steady anyway.

I found it difficult, also, to shield my binoculars from the rain. I made a sort of tube from a sheet of plastic which kept out much of the wet, and I pulled a large piece of plastic material forward over my head, like a peaked cap, when I was watching chimps. Even so, there were many days when I couldn't use my binoculars because the lenses were clouded over inside with droplets of condensed moisture.

Also, when it was not actually raining the long grass remained drenched nearly all day either with rain or the heavy nightly dew, and there were periods when I seemed to be wet through for days on end. I think I spent some of the coldest hours of my life in those mountains, sitting in clammy clothes in an icy wind watching chimpanzees. There was even a time when I dreaded the early morning climb to the Peak: I left my warm bed in the darkness, had my slice of bread and cup of coffee by the cozy glow of a hurricane lamp, and then had to steel myself for the plunge into that icy, water-drenched grass. After a while, though, I took to bundling my clothes into a plastic bag and carrying them. There was no one to see my ascent, and it was dark anyway. Then, when I knew there were dry clothes to put on at my destination, the shock of the cold grass against my naked skin was a sensual pleasure. For the first few days my body was crisscrossed by scratches from the tooth-edged grass, but after that my skin hardened.

One morning, in the first light of dawn, I plodded up the last steep slope to the Peak. As I reached the top my foot seemed to freeze in midair, for no less than four yards from me, a lone buffalo lay, half hidden in the long grass. He must have been asleep, or surely he would have heard me; and luckily the breeze was blowing his rich cowlike scent my way. Had it been the other way around . . . As it was, I was able to creep quietly away, and he was not disturbed.   *10*

It was at this time, too, that a leopard actually passed within a few yards of me as I sat in some long grass. I never knew he was there until I saw the white tip of his tail just ahead of me, and there was no time to retreat. So I just held my breath. I doubt if he ever knew how close to a human being he had been.

On the whole I loved that rainy season at the Gombe. It was cool most of the time and there was no heat to distort long-distance observations. The crunching of my feet on the crackling leaf carpet of the forest floor in the dry season had always bothered me, but when the leaves became soft and damp during the rains I could move through the trees silently, and catch more than fleeting glimpses of some of the shyer creatures. Best of all, of course, I was continuously learning more and more about chimpanzees and their behavior.

In the dry season the chimpanzees, I knew, usually rested on the ground at midday; I had often glimpsed them lying stretched out in the shade. In the rainy season, though, the ground is frequently sodden and I found that the chimpanzees made quite elaborate day nests on which to rest. To my surprise they often made these while it was still actually raining and then sat hunched up, with their arms around their knees and their heads bowed, until the rain stopped. In the mornings they got up later and at times, after feeding or just sitting about, made new nests and lay down again only two or three hours later. I suppose this was because they some-times had such miserably wet and cold nights that they couldn't sleep, and so were tired in the morning. They usually went to bed earlier, too. Often when I left the chimps in their nests, soaking wet from a late afternoon storm, I felt not only sorry for them but guilty because I was returning to a warm meal, dry clothes, and a tent. And I felt even worse when I woke in the middle of the night to hear the rain lashing down on the canvas and thought of all the poor huddled chimps shivering on their leafy platforms while I snuggled cozily into my warm bed.

Sometimes at the beginning of a storm a chimpanzee would shelter under an overhanging trunk or tangle of vegetation, but then, when the rain began to drip through, he usually emerged and just sat in the open, hunched and looking miserable. Small infants appeared to fare the best in a heavy storm. Quite often I saw old Flo, who of all the females was least afraid of me at that time, sitting hunched over two-year-old Fifi. At the end of a deluge Fifi would crawl from her mother's embrace looking completely dry. Flo's son Figan, about four years older than Fifi, often swung wildly through the tree on such occasions, dangling from one hand and kicking his legs, leaping from branch to branch, jumping up and down above Flo, until she was showered with debris and she hunched even lower to avoid the twigs that lashed her face. It was a good way of keeping his blood warm—rather like the wild rain display with which older males frequently greeted the start of heavy rain.

As the weeks went by I found that I could usually get closer to a group of chimpanzees when it was cold and wet than when the weather was dry. It was as though they were too fed up with the conditions to bother about me. One day I was moving silently through the dripping forest. Overhead the rain pattered onto the leaves and all around it dripped from leaf to leaf to the ground. The smell of rotten wood and wet vege-tation was pungent; under my hands the tree trunks were cold and slippery and alive. I could feel the water trickling through my hair and running warmly into my neck. I was looking for a group of chimps I had heard before the rain began.

Unexpectedly, only a few yards ahead of me, I saw a black shape hunched up on the ground with its back to me. I hunched down onto the ground myself: the chimp hadn't seen me. For a few minutes there was silence save for the pattering of the rain, and then I heard a slight rustle and a soft *hoo* to my right. Slowly I turned my head, but saw nothing in the thick undergrowth. When I looked back, the black shape that had been in front of me had vanished. Then came a sound from above. I looked up and there saw a large male directly overhead: it was Goliath. He stared down at me with his lips tensed and very slightly shook a branch. I looked away, for a prolonged stare can be interpreted as a threat. I heard another rustle to my left, and when I looked I could just make out the black shape of a chimp behind a tangle of vines. Ahead I saw two eyes staring toward me and a large black hand gripping a hanging liana. Another soft *hoo,* this time from behind. I was surrounded.

All at once Goliath uttered a long drawn-out *wraaaa,* and I was showered with rain and twigs as he threatened me, shaking the branches. The call was taken up by the other dimly seen chimps. It is one of the most savage sounds of the African forests, second only to the trumpeting scream of an enraged elephant. All my instincts bade me flee, but I forced myself to stay, trying to appear uninterested and busy eating some roots from the ground. The end of the branch above me hit my head. With a stamping and slapping of the ground a black shape charged through the undergrowth ahead, veering away from me at the last minute and running at a tangent into the forest. I think I expected to be torn to pieces. I do not know how long I crouched there before I realized that everything was still and silent again, save for the *drip-drip* of the raindrops. Cautiously I looked around. The black hand and the glaring eyes were no longer there; the branch where Goliath had been was deserted; all the chimpanzees had gone. Admittedly, my knees shook when I got up, but there was the sense of exhilaration that comes when danger has threatened and left one unharmed—and the chimpanzees were surely less afraid of me.

It lasted for about five months, this period of aggression and hostility toward me following the initial fear and hasty retreat that had taken place whenever the chimps saw me. There is one other incident that stands out in my memory: it took place about three weeks after the one I have just described. I was waiting on one side of a narrow ravine, hoping that chimpanzees would arrive in a fruit-laden tree on the opposite slope. When I heard the deliberate footsteps of approaching chimpanzees behind me I lay down flat and kept still—for often, if the apes saw me on their way to feed, they changed their minds and fed elsewhere. Once they had started to feed, however, once they were surrounded by the delicious taste and sight and smell of the fruit, their hunger usually proved stronger than their distrust of me. On this occasion the footsteps came on and abruptly stopped, quite close. There was a soft *hoo,* the call of a worried, slightly fearful individual. I had been seen. I kept still, and presently the footsteps came even closer. Then I heard one chimpanzee run for a few yards; this was followed by a loud scream.

Suddenly I saw a large male chimpanzee climbing a tree only a couple of yards away. He moved over into the branches above my head and began screaming at me, short, loud, high-pitched sounds, with his mouth open. I stared up into his dark face and brown eyes. He began climbing down toward me until he was no more than ten feet above me and I could see his yellow teeth and, right inside his mouth, the pinkness of his tongue. He shook a branch, showering me with twigs. Then he hit the trunk and shook more branches, and continued to scream and scream and work himself into a frenzy of rage. All at once he climbed down and went out of sight behind me.

It was then that I saw a female with a tiny baby and an older child   20
sitting in another tree and staring at me with wide eyes. They were quite
silent and quite still. I could hear the old male moving about behind me
and then this footsteps stopped. He was so close I could hear his breathing.

Without warning there was a loud bark, a stamping in the leaves, and
my head was hit, hard. At this I had to move, had to sit up. The male was
standing looking at me, and for a moment I believed he would charge; but
he turned and moved off, stopping often to turn and stare at me. The
female with her baby and the youngster climbed down silently and moved
after him. A few moments later I was alone again. There was a sense of
triumph: I had made real contact with a wild chimpanzee—or perhaps it
should be the other way round.

When I looked back some years later at my description of that male,
I was certain it was the bad-tempered, irascible, paunchy J. B. The behavior fits in perfectly with the irritable, fearless character that I later came to
know so well. I suppose he was puzzled by my immobility and the plastic
sheet that was protecting me from the light rain. He simply had to find
out exactly what I was and make me move—he must have known, from
my eyes, that I was alive.

Reading and Responding

What do you (or any of us, for that matter) typically do when it rains?
Contrast this normal human response to bad weather with the response
made by the chimpanzees. From just the differences you can see here, talk
about how our way of living in the world differs from the ways chimpanzees live in the world. Run with this for half a page at least.

Working Together

Look back over this piece together, and work to make two lists, one that
describes Jane Goodall herself and another that describes the chimpanzees
she observes. From your lists and your collective understanding of this
piece, what motivations lead the chimpanzees to act as they do? What
motivations lead Goodall to act as she does?

Rethinking and Rewriting

1. Write a three-page profile of Jane Goodall. Describe who she is and
   what she's done. In addition to whatever research you find necessary,
   use at least one quotation from this piece to help make her clear to
   readers.
2. This chapter of readings is titled "Observing the Other." Using just Jane
   Goodall's piece as your source, discuss the ways that "observing the
   other" also means learning about ourselves. (*Hint:* Think about what

Jane Goodall learns about herself as well as what she learns about the chimpanzees.)

Essay Topics for Chapter 8

1. Contrast a time when you've felt scared or threatened by an animal with a time when you've felt some kinship or quickened interest or awe for an animal. From these two different experiences, what can you say about your own particular personal relationship with other animals?

2. All the readings in chapter 6 discuss created, human-made worlds—the worlds we live in. Contrast one of the readings in chapter 6 with a reading from this chapter. Focus on the differences (and/or similarities) between our lives in created worlds and the lives animals live. (For another suggestion that also involves reading from chapter 6, see topic 6 in this list.)

3. Consider some local ecological conflict that pits the rights of an animal species against the rights of people. Don't take the usual slant here—don't talk about politics or economics. Instead, use this local conflict as a way to focus on how the animal (the other) views its world (on the one hand) and how we view it (on the other). Don't try to resolve the conflict; don't even take a side. Just use this conflict as an example that illustrates how we view the world and how that differs from the way animals do.

4. Both Kathleen Dean Moore's essay and Jane Goodall's include fear as one response to animals. Yet the other pieces in this chapter celebrate animals. Use Moore or Goodall and contrast the reading of your choice with one of the other readings in this chapter. That is, contrast a fearful response to animals with a response that's more celebratory. End by discussing how you think we should view animals.

5. Imagine your life without *any* experiences with animals—none. What would you have missed? What would you not understand (or understand less well)? Explain at some length and in detail.

6. Read Melissa Greene's piece in chapter 6 and then read Jane Goodall's in this chapter. Assuming both options were equally available to you, would you rather be an observer at the Woodland Park Gorilla Exhibit or an observer at Gombe Stream? How would your relationship to the gorillas at Woodland Park be similar to your relationship to the chimpanzees at Gombe; how would these relationships differ? Discuss the advantages and disadvantages of each observation post.

9

Spirit of Place

We all have places we feel most at home in, places we keep coming back to or only leave when we have to. Within those walls or among those trees, we feel most like ourselves. Somehow in that landscape, with all that particular weather, things have their proper proportion, and so we are in balance, too. We are in right relation to the world around us and that changes how we feel inside.

All the pieces that follow explore this relationship between the inner and the outer worlds in the places we call home. They are about places where we stay put long enough to know every detail. They are about beloved, remembered places we can't get out of our minds. They are about our longing for that kind of landscape, that kind of home, even if we can never find it.

The world isn't just something we travel through and explore. Sometimes we stop and begin to belong to it. The world isn't just something we observe from a distance. Being in it changes who we are. In some hard-to-measure way, where we are is who we are. The spirit, the unique character, of each individual and separate place has much to do with forming our own spirit and character.

"FIVE A.M. IN THE PINEWOODS"

Mary Oliver

Mary Oliver's poems consistently explore the relationship between human beings and natural landscapes. Her book American Primitive *won the Pulitzer Prize for poetry in 1984, and her* New and Selected Poems *was awarded the National Book Award in 1992. The poem here tells a small story that gathers large implications by the time it ends. "Five a.m. in the Pinewoods" originally appeared in* House of Light.

Before You Read

Read just the first 18 lines of this poem (up through "nibbled some damp/ tassels of weeds"), stop there, and summarize the main action in a sentence or two, using your own words. Make sure your summary includes all the action to that point. Once you've finished your summary, underline a part of it that surprises you—something you couldn't have guessed or wouldn't have expected.

I'd seen
their hoofprints in the deep
needles and knew
they ended the long night

under the pines, walking   5
like two mute
and beautiful women toward
the deeper woods, so I

got up in the dark and
went there. They came   10
slowly down the hill
and looked at me sitting under

the blue trees, shyly
they stepped
closer and stared   15
from under their thick lashes and even

nibbled some damp
tassels of weeds. This
is not a poem about a dream,
though it could be.   20

This is a poem about the world
that is ours, or could be.

Finally
one of them—I swear it!—

would have come to my arms.   *25*
But the other
stamped sharp hoof in the
pine needles like

the tap of sanity,
and they went off together through   *30*
the trees. When I woke
I was alone,

I was thinking:
so this is how you swim inward,
so this is how you flow outward,   *35*
so this is how you pray.

Reading and Responding

1. Read the whole poem. Write down three things you're clear about;
   write down one thing that puzzles you or you don't quite get. (You
   should end up with four sentences.)
2. Write about a time when you've gotten close to a deer or other similarly impressive wild animal; tell the story in a page or so, and focus
   mostly on that time when you were closest to the animal.

Working Together

1. As a group, figure out why the poem goes from roughly eighteen lines
   of storytelling to roughly five lines of commentary. Why not just tell
   the story? What place does the commentary have? (*Hint:* Is the story
   about the deer, about the speaker, or both?)
2. This speaker gets up early to go see some deer. Why get up early to do
   this? What do the lines "This is a poem about the world/ that is ours,
   or could be" mean? Do they help explain why the speaker goes to the
   pinewoods at 5 a.m.? Discuss this question as a group, and come up
   with some answers that make sense and do the poem justice.
3. Toward the end of this poem one deer stamps a hoof. Why does this
   deer stamp a hoof? Explain.

Rethinking and Rewriting

1. Write an essay that contrasts the first hour of a normal morning for you
   with the experience given in this poem. In the middle of your essay,
   discuss a time that you've been outside, somewhere in the country

perhaps, just as it's getting light. End by discussing what you understand makes the experience in this poem so valuable to the speaker.

2. Assume you were going to send a copy of this poem to someone. Who would you send it to? Write that person a one-page letter that you would send with the poem.

3. Write your instructor a letter explaining why you like—or don't like—poetry. Use this poem as an example. Don't be mean or nasty or wildly enthusiastic. Just try to explain your feelings carefully and honestly.

"WHERE I LIVED AND WHAT I LIVED FOR"

Henry David Thoreau

> *Henry David Thoreau's* Walden, or Life in the Woods *(1854) is the most influential book of nature writing ever published. Its account of one man's attempt to live a simpler, sparer life in the woods outside Concord, Massachusetts, haunts most of the other pieces in this collection. The following essay from that book contains many of its most famous pronouncements.*

At a certain season of our life we are accustomed to consider every spot as the possible site of a house. I have thus surveyed the country on every side within a dozen miles of where I live. In imagination I have bought all the farms in succession, for all were to be bought, and I knew their price. I walked over each farmer's premises, tasted his wild apples, discoursed on husbandry with him, took his farm at his price, at any price, mortgaging it to him in my mind; even put a higher price on it,—took every thing but a deed of it,—took his word for his deed, for I dearly love to talk,—cultivated it, and him too to some extent, I trust, and withdrew when I had enjoyed it long enough, leaving him to carry it on. This experience entitled me to be regarded as a sort of real-estate broker by my friends. Wherever I sat, there I might live, and the landscape radiated from me accordingly. What is a house but a *sedes,* a seat?—better if a country seat. I discovered many a site for a house not likely to be soon improved, which some might have thought too far from the village, but to my eyes the village was too far from it. Well, there I might live, I said; and there I did live, for an hour, a summer and a winter life; saw how I could let the years run off, buffet the winter through, and see the spring come in. The future inhabitants of this region, wherever they may place their houses, may be sure that they have been anticipated. An afternoon sufficed to lay out the land into orchard, woodlot, and pasture, and to decide what fine oaks or pines should be left to stand before the door, and whence each blasted tree could be seen to the best advantage; and then I let it lie, fallow perchance, for a man is rich in proportion to the number of things which he can afford to let alone.

My imagination carried me so far that I even had the refusal of several farms,—the refusal was all I wanted,—but I never got my fingers burned by actual possession. The nearest that I came to actual possession was when I bought the Hollowell place,° and had begun to sort my seeds, and collected materials with which to make a wheelbarrow to carry it on or off with; but before the owner gave me a deed of it, his wife—every

---

Hollowell place: A farm near Walden Pond.

man has such a wife—changed her mind and wished to keep it, and he offered me ten dollars to release him. Now, to speak the truth, I had but ten cents in the world, and it surpassed my arithmetic to tell, if I was that man who had ten cents, or who had a farm, or ten dollars, or all together. However, I let him keep the ten dollars and the farm too, for I had carried it far enough; or rather, to be generous, I sold him the farm for just what I gave for it, and, as he was not a rich man, made him a present of ten dollars, and still had my ten cents, and seeds, and materials for a wheelbarrow left. I found thus that I had been a rich man without any damage to my poverty. But I retained the landscape, and I have since annually carried off what it yielded without a wheelbarrow. With respect to landscapes,—°

"I am monarch of all I *survey*,
My right there is none to dispute."

I have frequently seen a poet withdraw, having enjoyed the most valuable part of a farm, while the crusty farmer supposed that he had got a few wild apples only. Why, the owner does not know it for many years when a poet has put his farm in rhyme, the most admirable kind of invisible fence, has fairly impounded it, milked it, skimmed it, and got all the cream, and left the farmer only the skimmed milk.

The real attractions of the Hollowell farm, to me, were; its complete retirement, being about two miles from the village, half a mile from the nearest neighbor, and separated from the highway by a broad field; its bounding on the river, which the owner said protected it by its fogs from frosts in the spring, though that was nothing to me; the gray color and ruinous state of the house and barn, and the dilapidated fences, which put such an interval between me and the last occupant; the hollow and lichen-covered apple trees, gnawed by rabbits, showing what kind of neighbors I should have; but above all, the recollection I had of it from my earliest voyages up the river, when the house was concealed behind a dense grove of red maples, through which I heard the house-dog bark. I was in haste to buy it, before the proprietor finished getting out some rocks, cutting down the hollow apple trees, and grubbing up some young birches which had sprung up in the pasture, or, in short, had made any more of his improvements. To enjoy these advantages I was ready to carry it on; like Atlas,° to take the world on my shoulders,—I never heard what compensation he received for that,—and do all those things which had no other motive or excuse but that I might pay for it and be unmolested in my possession of it; for I knew all the while that it would yield the most abundant crop of the kind I wanted if I could only afford to let it alone. But it turned out as I have said.

With respect to landscapes,—: The lines are by William Cowper (1731–1800), English poet.
Atlas: The Greek god who supported the world on his shoulders.

All that I could say, then, with respect to farming on a large scale, (I 5
have always cultivated a garden,) was, that I had had my seeds ready. Many
think that seeds improve with age. I have no doubt that time discriminates
between the good and the bad; and when at last I shall plant, I shall be less
likely to be disappointed. But I would say to my fellows, once for all, As
long as possible live free and uncommitted. It makes but little difference
whether you are committed to a farm or the county jail.

Old Cato,° whose "De Re Rusticâ" is my "Cultivator," says, and the
only translation I have seen makes sheer nonsense of the passage, "When
you think of getting a farm, turn it thus in your mind, not to buy greedily;
nor spare your pains to look at it, and do not think it enough to go round
it once. The oftener you go there the more it will please you, if it is good."
I think I shall not buy greedily, but go round and round it as long as I live,
and be buried in it first, that it may please me the more at last.

The present was my next experiment of this kind, which I purpose
to describe more at length; for convenience, putting the experience of two
years into one. As I have said, I do not propose to write an ode to dejection, but to brag as lustily as chanticleer in the morning, standing on his
roost, if only to wake my neighbors up.

When first I took up my abode in the woods, that is, began to spend
my nights as well as days there, which, by accident, was on Independence
day, or the fourth of July, 1845, my house was not finished for winter, but
was merely a defence against the rain, without plastering or chimney, the
walls being of rough weather-stained boards, with wide chinks, which
made it cool at night. The upright white hewn studs and freshly planed
door and window casings gave it a clean and airy look, especially in the
morning, when its timbers were saturated with dew, so that I fancied that
by noon some sweet gum would exude from them. To my imagination it
retained throughout the day more or less of this auroral character, reminding me of a certain house on a mountain which I had visited the year
before. This was an airy and unplastered cabin, fit to entertain a travelling
god, and where a goddess might trail her garments. The winds which
passed over my dwelling were such as sweep over the ridges of mountains,
bearing the broken strains, or celestial parts only, of terrestrial music. The
morning wind forever blows, the poem of creation is uninterrupted; but
few are the ears that hear it. Olympus° is but the outside of the earth every
where.

The only house I had been the owner of before, if I except a boat,
was a tent, which I used occasionally when making excursions in the
summer, and this is still rolled up in my garret; but the boat, after passing

---

Marcus Porcius Cato: A Roman statesman (234–149 B.C.) who also wrote books about
farming.
Olympus: The home of the ancient Greek gods.

from hand to hand, has gone down the stream of time. With this more substantial shelter about me, I had made some progress toward settling in the world. This frame, so slightly clad, was a sort of crystallization around me, and reacted on the builder. It was suggestive somewhat as a picture in outlines. I did not need to go out doors to take the air, for the atmosphere within had lost none of its freshness. It was not so much within doors as behind a door where I sat, even in the rainiest weather. The Harivansa° says, "An abode without birds is like a meat without seasoning." Such was not my abode, for I found myself suddenly neighbor to the birds; not by having imprisoned one, but having caged myself near them. I was not only nearer to some of those which commonly frequent the garden and the orchard, but to those wilder and more thrilling songsters of the forest which never, or rarely, serenade a villager,—the wood-thrush, the veery, the scarlet tanager, the field-sparrow, the whippoorwill, and many others.

I was seated by the shore of a small pond, about a mile and a half   10
south of the village of Concord and somewhat higher than it, in the midst of an extensive wood between that town and Lincoln, and about two miles south of that our only field known to fame, Concord Battle Ground;° but I was so low in the woods that the opposite shore, half a mile off, like the rest, covered with wood, was my most distant horizon. For the first week, whenever I looked out on the pond it impressed me like a tarn high up on the side of a mountain, its bottom far above the surface of other lakes, and, as the sun arose, I saw it throwing off its nightly clothing of mist, and here and there, by degrees, its soft ripples or its smooth reflecting surface was revealed, while the mists, like ghosts, were stealthily withdrawing in every direction into the woods, as at the breaking up of some nocturnal conventicle. The very dew seemed to hang upon the trees later into the day than usual, as on the sides of mountains.

This small lake was of most value as a neighbor in the intervals of a gentle rain storm in August, when, both air and water being perfectly still, but the sky overcast, mid-afternoon had all the serenity of evening, and the wood-thrush sang around, and was heard from shore to shore. A lake like this is never smoother than at such a time; and the clear portion of the air above it being shallow and darkened by clouds, the water, full of light and reflections, becomes a lower heaven itself so much the more important. From a hill top near by, where the wood had been recently cut off, there was a pleasing vista southward across the pond, through a wide indentation in the hills which form the shore there, where their opposite sides sloping toward each other suggested a stream flowing out in that direction through a wooded valley, but stream there was none. That way I looked between and over the near green hills to some distant and higher ones in the horizon, tinged with blue. Indeed, by standing on tiptoe I

Harivansa: An epic Hindu poem of the fifth century A.D.
Concord Battle Ground: The first battle of the American Revolution took place here, April 19, 1775.

could catch a glimpse of some of the peaks of the still bluer and more distant mountain ranges in the north-west, those true-blue coins from heaven's own mint, and also of some portion of the village. But in other directions, even from this point, I could not see over or beyond the woods which surrounded me. It is well to have some water in your neighborhood, to give buoyancy to and float the earth. One value even of the smallest well is, that when you look into it you see that earth is not continent but insular. This is as important as that it keeps butter cool. When I looked across the pond from this peak toward the Sudbury meadows, which in time of flood I distinguished elevated perhaps by a mirage in their seething valley, like a coin in a basin, all the earth beyond the pond appeared like a thin crust insulated and floated even by this small sheet of intervening water, and I was reminded that this on which I dwelt was but *dry land*.

Though the view from my door was still more contracted, I did not feel crowded or confined in the least. There was pasture enough for my imagination. The low shrub-oak plateau to which the opposite shore arose, stretched away toward the prairies of the West and the steppes of Tartary, affording ample room for all the roving families of men. "There are none happy in the world but beings who enjoy freely a vast horizon,"—said Damodara,° when his herds required new and larger pastures.

Both place and time were changed, and I dwelt nearer to those parts of the universe and to those eras in history which had most attracted me. Where I lived was as far off as many a region viewed nightly by astronomers. We are wont to imagine rare and delectable places in some remote and more celestial corner of the system, behind the constellation of Cassiopeia's Chair, far from noise and disturbance. I discovered that my house actually had its site in such a withdrawn, but forever new and unprofaned, part of the universe. If it were worth the while to settle in those parts near to the Pleiades or the Hyades, to Aldebaran or Altair,° then I was really there, or at an equal remoteness from the life which I had left behind, dwindled and twinkling with as fine a ray to my nearest neighbor, and to be seen only in moonless nights by him. Such was that part of creation where I had squatted;—

> "There was a shepherd that did live,
>   And held his thoughts as high
> As were the mounts whereon his flocks
>   Did hourly feed him by."°

What should we think of the shepherd's life if his flocks always wandered to higher pastures than his thoughts?

Damodara: Another name for the Hindu god Krishna.
Cassiopeia . . . Altair: Cassiopeia's Chair, Pleiades, and Aldebaran are constellations of stars.
"Did hourly . . . by": An anonymous seventeenth-century poem.

Every morning was a cheerful invitation to make my life of equal simplicity, and I may say innocence, with Nature herself. I have been as sincere a worshipper of Aurora as the Greeks. I got up early and bathed in the pond; that was a religious exercise, and one of the best things which I did. They say that characters were engraven on the bathing tub of king Tching-thang° to this effect: "Renew thyself completely each day; do it again, and again, and forever again." I can understand that. Morning brings back the heroic ages. I was as much affected by the faint hum of a mosquito making its invisible and unimaginable tour through my apartment at earliest dawn, when I was sitting with door and windows open, as I could be by any trumpet that ever sang of fame. It was Homer's requiem; itself an Iliad and Odyssey in the air, singing its own wrath and wanderings. There was something cosmical about it; a standing advertisement, till forbidden, of the everlasting vigor and fertility of the world. The morning, which is the most memorable season of the day, is the awakening hour. Then there is least somnolence in us; and for an hour, at least, some part of us awakes which slumbers all the rest of the day and night. Little is to be expected of that day, if it can be called a day, to which we are not awakened by our Genius, but by the mechanical nudgings of some servitor, are not awakened by our own newly-acquired force and aspirations from within, accompanied by the undulations of celestial music, instead of factory bells, and a fragrance filling the air—to a higher life than we fell asleep from; and thus the darkness bear its fruit, and prove itself to be good, no less than the light. That man who does not believe that each day contains an earlier, more sacred, and auroral hour than he has yet profaned, has despaired of life, and is pursuing a descending and darkening way. After a partial cessation of his sensuous life, the soul of man, or its organs rather, are reinvigorated each day, and his Genius tries again what noble life it can make. All memorable events, I should say, transpire in morning time and in a morning atmosphere. The Vedas° say, "All intelligences awake with the morning." Poetry and art, and the fairest and most memorable of the actions of men, date from such an hour. All poets and heroes, like Memnon, are the children of Aurora, and emit their music at sunrise. To him whose elastic and vigorous thought keeps pace with the sun, the day is a perpetual morning. It matters not what the clocks say or the attitudes and labors of men. Morning is when I am awake and there is a dawn in me. Moral reform is the effort to throw off sleep. Why is it that men give so poor an account of their day if they have not been slumbering? They are not such poor calculators. If they had not been overcome with drowsiness they would have performed something. The millions are awake enough for physical labor; but only one in a million is awake enough for effective

---

Tching-thang: Confucius.
Vedas: The Hindu scriptures.

intellectual exertion, only one in a hundred millions to a poetic or divine life. To be awake is to be alive. I have never yet met a man who was quite awake. How could I have looked him in the face?

We must learn to reawaken and keep ourselves awake, not by me- *15* chanical aids, but by an infinite expectation of the dawn, which does not forsake us in our soundest sleep. I know of no more encouraging fact than the unquestionable ability of man to elevate his life by a conscious endeavor. It is something to be able to paint a particular picture, or to carve a statue, and so to make a few objects beautiful; but it is far more glorious to carve and paint the very atmosphere and medium through which we look, which morally we can do. To affect the quality of the day, that is the highest of arts. Every man is tasked to make his life, even in its details, worthy of the contemplation of his most elevated and critical hour. If we refused, or rather used up, such paltry information as we get, the oracles would distinctly inform us how this might be done.

I went to the woods because I wished to live deliberately, to front only the essential facts of life, and see if I could not learn what it had to teach, and not, when I came to die, discover that I had not lived. I did not wish to live what was not life, living is so dear; nor did I wish to practise resignation, unless it was quite necessary. I wanted to live deep and suck out all the marrow of life, to live so sturdily and Spartan-like° as to put to rout all that was not life, to cut a broad swath and shave close, to drive life into a corner, and reduce it to its lowest terms, and, if it proved to be mean, why then to get the whole and genuine meanness of it, and publish its meanness to the world; or if it were sublime, to know it by experience, and be able to give a true account of it in my next excursion. For most men, it appears to me, are in a strange uncertainty about it, whether it is of the devil or of God, and have *somewhat hastily* concluded that it is the chief end of man here to "glorify God and enjoy him forever."

Still we live meanly, like ants; though the fable tells us that we were long ago changed into men; like pygmies we fight with cranes; it is error upon error, and clout upon clout, and our best virtue has for its occasion a superfluous and evitable wretchedness. Our life is frittered away by detail. An honest man has hardly need to count more than his ten fingers, or in extreme cases he may add his ten toes, and lump the rest. Simplicity, simplicity, simplicity! I say, let your affairs be as two or three, and not a hundred or a thousand; instead of a million count half a dozen, and keep your accounts on your thumb nail. In the midst of this chopping sea of civilized life, such are the clouds and storms and quicksands and thousand-and-one items to be allowed for, that a man has to live, if he would not founder and go to the bottom and not make his port at all, by dead reckoning, and he must be a great calculator indeed who succeeds. Simplify, simplify. Instead of three meals a day, if it be necessary eat but one;

Spartan-like: A reference to the rigorous lives of the ancient Greek Spartans.

instead of a hundred dishes, five; and reduce other things in proportion. Our life is like a German Confederacy,° made up of petty states, with its boundary forever fluctuating, so that even a German cannot tell you how it is bounded at any moment. The nation itself, with all its so called internal improvements, which, by the way, are all external and superficial, is just such an unwieldy and overgrown establishment, cluttered with furniture and tripped up by its own traps, ruined by luxury and heedless expense, by want of calculation and a worthy aim, as the million households in the land; and the only cure for it as for them is in a rigid economy, a stern and more than Spartan simplicity of life and elevation of purpose. It lives too fast. Men think that it is essential that the *Nation* have commerce, and export ice, and talk through a telegraph, and ride thirty miles an hour, without a doubt, whether *they* do or not; but whether we should live like baboons or like men, is a little uncertain. If we do not get out sleepers, and forge rails, and devote days and nights to the work, but go to tinkering upon our *lives* to improve *them,* who will build railroads? And if railroads are not built, how shall we get to heaven in season? But if we stay at home and mind our business, who will want railroads? We do not ride on the railroad; it rides upon us. Did you ever think what those sleepers are that underlie the railroad? Each one is a man, an Irishman, or a Yankee man. The rails are laid on them, and they are covered with sand, and the cars run smoothly over them. They are sound sleepers, I assure you. And every few years a new lot is laid down and run over; so that, if some have the pleasure of riding on a rail, others have the misfortune to be ridden upon. And when they run over a man that is walking in his sleep, a supernumerary sleeper in the wrong position, and wake him up, they suddenly stop the cars, and make a hue and cry about it, as if this were an exception. I am glad to know that it takes a gang of men for every five miles to keep the sleepers down and level in their beds as it is, for this is a sign that they may sometime get up again.

Why should we live with such hurry and waste of life? We are determined to be starved before we are hungry. Men say that a stitch in time saves nine, and so they take a thousand stitches today to save nine tomorrow. As for *work,* we haven't any of any consequence. We have the Saint Vitus' dance,° and cannot possibly keep our heads still. If I should only give a few pulls at the parish bell-rope, as for a fire, that is, without setting the bell, there is hardly a man on his farm in the outskirts of Concord, notwithstanding that press of engagements which was his excuse so many times this morning, nor a boy, nor a woman, I might almost say, but would forsake all and follow that sound, not mainly to save property from the flames, but, if we will confess the truth, much more to see it burn, since burn it must, and we, be it known, did not set it on fire,—or

---

German Confederacy: A confederation of German states that existed from 1815 to 1866.
Saint Vitus' dance: A reference to a nervous disease known as chorea.

to see it put out, and have a hand in it, if that is done as handsomely; yes, even if it were the parish church itself. Hardly a man takes a half hour's nap after dinner, but when he wakes he holds up his head and asks, "What's the news?" as if the rest of mankind had stood his sentinels. Some give directions to be waked every half hour, doubtless for no other purpose; and then, to pay for it, they tell what they have dreamed. After a night's sleep the news is as indispensable as the breakfast. "Pray tell me any thing new that has happened to a man any where on this globe,"—and he reads it over his coffee and rolls, that a man has had his eyes gouged out this morning on the Wachito River;° never dreaming the while that he lives in the dark unfathomed mammoth cave of this world, and has but the rudiment of an eye himself.

For my part, I could easily do without the post-office. I think that there are very few important communications made through it. To speak critically, I never received more than one or two letters in my life—I wrote this some years ago—that were worth the postage. The penny-post is, commonly, an institution through which you seriously offer a man that penny for his thoughts which is so often safely offered in jest. And I am sure that I never read any memorable news in a newspaper. If we read of one man robbed, or murdered, or killed by accident, or one house burned, or one vessel wrecked, or one steamboat blown up, or one cow run over on the Western Railroad, or one mad dog killed, or one lot of grasshoppers in the winter,—we never need read of another. One is enough. If you are acquainted with the principle, what do you care for a myriad instances and applications? To a philosopher all *news*, as it is called, is gossip, and they who edit and read it are old women over their tea. Yet not a few are greedy after this gossip. There was such a rush, as I hear, the other day at one of the offices to learn the foreign news by the last arrival, that several large squares of plate glass belonging to the establishment were broken by the pressure,—news which I seriously think a ready wit might write a twelvemonth or twelve years beforehand with sufficient accuracy. As for Spain, for instance, if you know how to throw in Don Carlos and the Infanta, and Don Pedro° and Seville and Granada, from time to time in the right proportions,—they may have changed the names a little since I saw the papers,—and serve up a bull-fight when other entertainments fail, it will be true to the letter, and give us as good an idea of the exact state or ruin of things in Spain as the most succinct and lucid reports under this head in the newspapers: and as for England, almost the last significant scrap of news from that quarter was the revolution of 1649; and if you have learned the history of her crops for an average year, you never need attend

---

Wachito River: An Arkansas river now called the Ouachita.
Don Carlos . . . Don Pedro: Men active in Portuguese and Spanish politics in the 1830s and 1840s.

to that thing again, unless your speculations are of a merely pecuniary character. If one may judge who rarely looks into the newspapers, nothing new does ever happen in foreign parts, a French revolution not excepted.

What news! how much more important to know what that is which   20
was never old! "Kieou-he-yu° (great dignitary of the state of Wei) sent a man to Khoung-tseu to know his news. Khoung-tseu caused the messenger to be seated near him, and questioned him in these terms: What is your master doing? The messenger answered with respect: My master desires to diminish the number of his faults, but he cannot accomplish it. The messenger being gone, the philosopher remarked: What a worthy messenger! What a worthy messenger!" The preacher, instead of vexing the ears of drowsy farmers on their day of rest at the end of the week,—for Sunday is the fit conclusion of an ill-spent week, and not the fresh and brave beginning of a new one,—with this one other draggletail of a sermon, should shout with thundering voice,—"Pause! Avast! Why so seeming fast, but deadly slow?"

Shams and delusions are esteemed for soundest truths, while reality is fabulous. If men would steadily observe realities only, and not allow themselves to be deluded, life, to compare it with such things as we know, would be like a fairy tale and the Arabian Nights' Entertainments.° If we respected only what is inevitable and has a right to be, music and poetry would resound along the streets. When we are unhurried and wise, we perceive that only great and worthy things have any permanent and absolute existence,—that petty fears and petty pleasures are but the shadow of the reality. This is always exhilarating and sublime. By closing the eyes and slumbering, and consenting to be deceived by shows, men establish and confirm their daily life of routine and habit every where, which still is built on purely illusory foundations. Children, who play life, discern its true law and relations more clearly than men, who fail to live it worthily, but who think that they are wiser by experience, that is, by failure. I have read in a Hindoo book, that "there was a king's son, who, being expelled in infancy from his native city, was brought up by a forester, and, growing up to maturity in that state, imagined himself to belong to the barbarous race with which he lived. One of his father's ministers having discovered him, revealed to him what he was, and the misconception of his character was removed, and he knew himself to be a prince. So soul," continues the Hindoo philosopher, "from the circumstances in which it is placed, mistakes its own character, until the truth is revealed to it by some holy teacher, and then it knows itself to be *Brahme.*" I perceive that we inhabitants of New England live this mean life that we do because our vision does not penetrate the surface of things. We think that that *is* which *appears*

Kieou-he-yu: A character in a book by Confucius.
Arabian Nights' Entertainments: A tenth-century collection of Middle East stories.

to be. If a man should walk through this town and see only the reality, where, think you, would the "Mill-dam"° go to? If he should give us an account of the realities he beheld there, we should not recognize the place in his description. Look at a meeting-house, or a court-house, or a jail, or a shop, or a dwelling-house, and say what that thing really is before a true gaze, and they would all go to pieces in your account of them. Men esteem truth remote, in the outskirts of the system, behind the farthest star, before Adam and after the last man. In eternity there is indeed something true and sublime. But all these times and places and occasions are now and here. God himself culminates in the present moment, and will never be more divine in the lapse of all the ages. And we are enabled to apprehend at all what is sublime and noble only by the perpetual instilling and drenching of the reality that surrounds us. The universe constantly and obediently answers to our conceptions; whether we travel fast or slow, the track is laid for us. Let us spend our lives in conceiving then. The poet or the artist never yet had so fair and noble a design but some of his posterity at least could accomplish it.

Let us spend one day as deliberately as Nature, and not be thrown off the track by every nutshell and mosquito's wing that falls on the rails. Let us rise early and fast, or break fast, gently and without perturbation; let company come and let company go, let the bells ring and the children cry,—determined to make a day of it. Why should we knock under and go with the stream? Let us not be upset and overwhelmed in that terrible rapid and whirlpool called a dinner, situated in the meridian shallows. Weather this danger and you are safe, for the rest of the way is down hill. With unrelaxed nerves, with morning vigor, sail by it, looking another way, tied to the mast like Ulysses.° If the engine whistles, let it whistle till it is hoarse for its pains. If the bell rings, why should we run? We will consider what kind of music they are like. Let us settle ourselves, and work and wedge our feet downward through the mud and slush of opinion, and prejudice, and tradition, and delusion, and appearance, that alluvion which covers the globe, through Paris and London, through New York and Boston and Concord, through church and state, through poetry and philosophy and religion, till we come to a hard bottom and rocks in place, which we can call *reality,* and say, This is, and no mistake; and then begin, having a *point d'appui,*° below freshet and frost and fire, a place where you might found a wall or a state, or set a lamppost safely, or perhaps a gauge, not a Nilometer,° but a Realometer, that future ages might know how deep a freshet of shams and appearances had gathered from time to time. If you

---

Mill-dam: A meeting place for the townspeople in Concord.
Ulysses: The name of Odysseus in Roman mythology.
point d'appui: A foundation; a point of support.
Nilometer: An ancient instrument used in ancient Egypt to measure the rise and fall of the Nile River.

stand right fronting and face to face to a fact, you will see the sun glimmer on both its surfaces, as if it were a cimeter, and feel its sweet edge dividing you through the heart and marrow, and so you will happily conclude your mortal career. Be it life or death, we crave only reality. If we are really dying, let us hear the rattle in our throats and feel cold in the extremities; if we are alive, let us go about our business.

Time is but the stream I go a-fishing in. I drink at it; but while I drink I see the sandy bottom and detect how shallow it is. Its thin current slides away, but eternity remains. I would drink deeper; fish in the sky, whose bottom is pebbly with stars. I cannot count one. I know not the first letter of the alphabet. I have always been regretting that I was not as wise as the day I was born. The intellect is a cleaver; it discerns and rifts its way into the secret of things. I do not wish to be any more busy with my hands than is necessary. My head is hands and feet. I feel all my best faculties concentrated in it. My instinct tells me that my head is an organ for burrowing, as some creatures use their snout and fore-paws, and with it I would mine and burrow my way through these hills. I think that the richest vein is somewhere hereabouts; so by the divining rod° and thin rising vapors I judge; and here I will begin to mine.

Reading and Responding

1. Mark any passage you have trouble understanding, and do a short free-write explaining what you think is causing the trouble.
2. More famous, quotable passages can be found in this chapter from *Walden* than in any other chapter of that book—and for that matter in any other selection in this anthology. Mark all the famous passages you find. If you've never heard of Thoreau or don't know enough about him to know which passages are famous, mark the passages you think are famous—the ones that seem the most quotable.
3. Write a two-page letter to a fellow classmate and explain your overall first response to reading this chapter of Thoreau's. Don't revise; just explain what you understand or don't understand, what your reading here makes you think about. Save the letter for group work later.

Working Together

1. Share the passages you found difficult to understand and make a list of all the features in Thoreau's language that make reading difficult.
2. Given the difficulties you outlined in item 1, make a list giving practical advice for first-time readers of Thoreau: what to expect, what to do in case of emergency, how to take notes, how much time to take.

---

divining rod: A wishbone-shaped branch used to detect the presence of underground water.

3. Given the difficulties you outlined in item 1, make a list of things you can do and learn in order to prepare for a second reading of Thoreau's chapter. What does the essay demand, and how can you meet those demands a second time?

4. Read the letter written by one of your classmates describing that person's response to Thoreau's chapter. Once you've read the letter, write a response that points out one area where you agree with the letter and one area where you disagree with the letter or just hadn't thought of that point.

Rethinking and Rewriting

1. Do a "rereading" essay: First, describe your first reading of the essay; then summarize what seem to you to be the most important ideas from your teacher's lecture or from the class discussion; then apply those ideas in a second reading of the essay. Conclude by explaining what you now understand that you didn't understand before and noting what questions remain.

2. Take one of the famous, quotable quotes from the essay, paraphrase it as plainly and straightforwardly as you can, and then write an essay describing a personal experience that you think illustrates the idea. That is, apply the idea to your own life. See how Thoreau and you speak to each other.

3. Write an essay of your own with the same title: "Where I Live and What I Live For."

"ONCE MORE TO THE LAKE"

E. B. White

In the decades that he wrote for The New Yorker *and* Harpers *maga-zine, E. B. White redefined the form of the personal essay and became its most beloved practioner. His many essays on themes ranging from pigs and racoons to nuclear disarmament and world government were collected in several books over the years, including* One Man's Meat *(1944) and* The Points of My Compass *(1962). His selected essays were published in 1977. White is also well-known for his children's books,* Stuart Little *(1945) and* Charlotte's Web *(1952). In "Once More to the Lake," first published in 1941, White evokes the sights and sounds of a summer lake as a way of reflecting on time, change, and loss.*

One summer, along about 1904, my father rented a camp on a lake in Maine and took us all there for the month of August. We all got ringworm from some kittens and had to rub Pond's Extract on our arms and legs at night and morning, and my father rolled over in a canoe with all his clothes on; but outside of that the vacation was a success and from then on none of us ever thought there was any place in the world like that lake in Maine. We returned summer after summer—always on August 1 for one month. I have since become a salt-water man, but sometimes in summer there are days when the restlessness of the tides and the fearful cold of the sea water and the incessant wind that blows across the afternoon and into the evening make me wish for the placidity of a lake in the woods. A few weeks ago this feeling got so strong I bought myself a couple of bass hooks and a spinner and returned to the lake where we used to go, for a week's fishing and to revisit old haunts.

I took along my son, who had never had any fresh water up his nose and who had seen lily pads only from train windows. On the journey over to the lake I began to wonder what it would be like. I wondered how time would have marred this unique, this holy spot—the coves and streams, the hills that the sun set behind, the camps and the paths behind the camps. I was sure that the tarred road would have found it out, and I wondered in what other ways it would be desolated. It is strange how much you can remember about places like that once you allow your mind to return into the grooves that lead back. You remember one thing, and that suddenly reminds you of another thing. I guess I remembered clearest of all the early mornings, when the lake was cool and motionless, remembered how the bedroom smelled of the lumber it was made of and of the wet woods whose scent entered through the screen. The partitions in the camp were thin and did not extend clear to the top of the rooms, and as I was always the first up I would dress softly so as not to wake the others, and sneak out into the sweet outdoors and start out in the canoe, keeping close along the shore in the long shadows of the pines. I remembered being very careful never to rub my paddle against the gunwale for fear of disturbing the stillness of the cathedral.

The lake had never been what you would call a wild lake. There were cottages sprinkled around the shores, and it was in farming country although the shores of the lake were quite heavily wooded. Some of the cottages were owned by nearby farmers, and you would live at the shore and eat your meals at the farmhouse. That's what our family did. But although it wasn't wild, it was a fairly large and undisturbed lake and there were places in it that, to a child at least, seemed infinitely remote and primeval.

I was right about the tar: it led to within half a mile of the shore. But when I got back there, with my boy, and we settled into a camp near a farmhouse and into the kind of summertime I had known, I could tell that it was going to be pretty much the same as it had been before—I knew it, lying in bed the first morning, smelling the bedroom and hearing the boy sneak quietly out and go off along the shore in a boat. I began to sustain the illusion that he was I, and therefore, by simple transposition, that I was my father. This sensation persisted, kept cropping up all the time we were there. It was not an entirely new feeling, but in this setting it grew much stronger. I seemed to be living a dual existence. I would be in the middle of some simple act, I would be picking up a bait box or laying down a table fork, or I would be saying something, and suddenly it would be not I but my father who was saying the words or making the gesture. It gave me a creepy sensation.

We went fishing the first morning. I felt the same damp moss cover-   *5* ing the worms in the bait can, and saw the dragonfly alight on the tip of my rod as it hovered a few inches from the surface of the water. It was the arrival of this fly that convinced me beyond any doubt that everything was as it always had been, that the years were a mirage and that there had been no years. The small waves were the same, chucking the rowboat under the chin as we fished at anchor, and the boat was the same boat, the same color green and the ribs broken in the same places, and under the floor-boards the same fresh-water leavings and débris—the dead helgramite, the wisps of moss, the rusty discarded fishhook, the dried blood from yester-day's catch. We stared silently at the tips of our rods, at the dragonflies that came and went. I lowered the tip of mine into the water, tentatively, pensively dislodging the fly, which darted two feet away, poised, darted two feet back, and came to rest again a little farther up the rod. There had been no years between the ducking of this dragonfly and the other one—the one that was part of memory. I looked at the boy, who was silently watching his fly, and it was my hands that held his rod, my eyes watching. I felt dizzy and didn't know which rod I was at the end of.

We caught two bass, hauling them in briskly as though they were mackerel, pulling them over the side of the boat in a businesslike manner without any landing net, and stunning them with a blow on the back of the head. When we got back for a swim before lunch, the lake was exactly where we had left it, the same number of inches from the dock, and there was only the merest suggestion of a breeze. This seemed an utterly enchanted sea, this lake you could leave to its own devices for a few hours and come back to, and find that it had not stirred, this constant and trustworthy body of water. In the shallows, the dark, water-soaked sticks and twigs, smooth and old, were undulating in clusters on the bottom against the clean ribbed sand, and the track of the mussel was plain. A school of minnows swam by, each minnow with its small individual shadow, doubling the attendance, so clear and sharp in the sunlight. Some of the other campers were in swimming, along the shore, one of them with a cake of soap, and the water felt thin and clear and unsubstantial. Over the years there had been this person with the cake of soap, this cultist, and here he was. There had been no years.

Up to the farmhouse to dinner through the teeming, dusty field, the road under our sneakers was only a two-track road. The middle track was missing, the one with the marks of the hooves and the splotches of dried, flaky manure, There had been three tracks to choose from in choosing which track to walk in; now the choice was narrowed down to two. For a moment I missed terribly the middle alternative. But the way led past the tennis court, and something about the way it lay there in the sun reassured me; the tape had loosened along the backline, the alleys were green with plantains and other weeds, and the net (installed in June and removed in September) sagged in the dry noon, and the whole place steamed with midday heat and hunger and emptiness. There was a choice of pie for dessert, and one was blueberry and one was apple, and the waitresses were the same country girls, there having been no passage of time, only the illusion of it as in a dropped curtain—the waitresses were still fifteen; their hair had been washed, that was the only difference—they had been to the movies and seen the pretty girls with clean hair.

Summertime, oh, summertime, pattern of life indelible, the fade-proof lake, the woods unshatterable, the pasture with the sweetfern and the juniper forever and ever, summer without end; this was the background, and the life along the shore was the design, the cottagers with their innocent and tranquil design, their tiny docks with the flagpole and the American flag floating against the white clouds in the blue sky, the little paths over the roots of the trees leading from camp to camp and the paths leading back to the outhouses and the can of lime for sprinkling, and at the souvenir counters at the store the miniature birch-bark canoes and the postcards that showed things looking a little better than they looked. This was the American family at play, escaping the city heat, wondering whether the newcomers in the camp at the head of the cove were "common" or "nice," wondering whether it was true that the people who drove up for Sunday dinner at the farmhouse were turned away because there wasn't enough chicken.

It seemed to me, as I kept remembering all this, that those times and those summers had been infinitely precious and worth saving. There had been jollity and peace and goodness. The arriving (at the beginning of

August) had been so big a business in itself, at the railway station the farm wagon drawn up, the first smell of the pine-laden air, the first glimpse of the smiling farmer, and the great importance of the trunks and your father's enormous authority in such matters, and the feel of the wagon under you for the long ten-mile haul, and at the top of the last long hill catching the first view of the lake after eleven months of not seeing this cherished body of water. The shouts and cries of the other campers when they saw you, and the trunks to be unpacked, to give up their rich burden. (Arriving was less exciting nowadays, when you sneaked up in your car and parked it under a tree near the camp and took out the bags and in five minutes it was all over, no fuss, no loud wonderful fuss about trunks.)

Peace and goodness and jollity. The only thing that was wrong now, really, was the sound of the place, an unfamiliar nervous sound of the outboard motors. This was the note that jarred, the one thing that would sometimes break the illusion and set the years moving. In those other summertimes all motors were inboard; and when they were at a little distance, the noise they made was a sedative, an ingredient of summer sleep. They were one-cylinder and two-cylinder engines, and some were make-and-break and some were jump-spark, but they all made a sleepy sound across the lake. The one-lungers throbbed and fluttered, and the twin-cylinder ones purred and purred, and that was a quiet sound, too. But now the campers all had outboards. In the daytime, in the hot mornings, these motors made a petulant, irritable sound; at night, in the still evening when the afterglow lit the water, they whined about one's ears like mosquitoes. My boy loved our rented outboard, and his great desire was to achieve single-handed mastery over it, and authority, and he soon learned the trick of choking it a little (but not too much), and the adjustment of the needle valve. Watching him I would remember the things you could do with the old one-cylinder engine with the heavy flywheel, how you could have it eating out of your hand if you got really close to it spiritually. Motorboats in those days didn't have clutches, and you would make a landing by shutting off the motor at the proper time and coasting in with a dead rudder. But there was a way of reversing them, if you learned the trick, by cutting the switch and putting it on again exactly on the final dying revolution of the flywheel, so that it would kick back against compression and begin reversing. Approaching a dock in a strong following breeze, it was difficult to slow up sufficiently by the ordinary coasting method, and if a boy felt he had complete mastery over his motor, he was tempted to keep it running beyond its time and then reverse it a few feet from the dock. It took a cool nerve, because if you threw the switch a twentieth of a second too soon you would catch the flywheel when it still had speed enough to go up past center, and the boat would leap ahead, charging bull-fashion at the dock.

We had a good week at the camp. The bass were biting well and the sun shone endlessly, day after day. We would be tired at night and lie down in the accumulated heat of the little bedrooms after the long hot day and

10

the breeze would stir almost imperceptibly outside and the smell of the swamp drift in through the rusty screens. Sleep would come easily and in the morning the red squirrel would be on the roof, tapping out his gay routine. I kept remembering everything, lying in bed in the mornings— the small steamboat that had a long rounded stern like the lip of a Ubangi, and how quietly she ran on the moonlight sails, when the older boys played their mandolins and the girls sang and we ate doughnuts dipped in sugar, and how sweet the music was on the water in the shining night, and what it had felt like to think about girls then. After breakfast we would go up to the store and the things were in the same place—the minnows in a bottle, the plugs and spinners disarranged and pawed over by the youngsters from the boys' camp, the Fig Newtons and the Beeman's gum. Outside, the road was tarred and cars stood in front of the store. Inside, all was just as it had always been, except there was more Coca-Cola and not so much Moxie and root beer and birch beer and sarsaparilla. We would walk out with the bottle of pop apiece and sometimes the pop would backfire up our noses and hurt. We explored the streams, quietly, where the turtles slid off the sunny logs and dug their way into the soft bottom; and we lay on the town wharf and fed worms to the tame bass. Everywhere we went I had trouble making out which was I, the one walking at my side, the one walking in my pants.

One afternoon while we were there at that lake a thunderstorm came up. It was like the revival of an old melodrama that I had seen long ago with childish awe. The second-act climax of the drama of the electrical disturbance over a lake in America had not changed in any important respect. This was the big scene, still the big scene. The whole thing was so familiar, the first feeling of oppression and heat and a general air around camp of not wanting to go very far away. In mid-afternoon (it was all the same) a curious darkening of the sky, and a lull in everything that had made life tick; and then the way the boats suddenly swung the other way at their moorings with the coming of a breeze out of the new quarter, and the premonitory rumble. Then the kettle drum, then the snare, then the bass drum and cymbals, then crackling light against the dark, and the gods grinning and licking their chops in the hills. Afterward the calm, the rain steadily rustling in the calm lake, the return of light and hope and spirits, and the campers running out in joy and relief to go swimming in the rain, their bright cries perpetuating the deathless joke about how they were getting simply drenched, and the children screaming with delight at the new sensation of bathing in the rain, and the joke about getting drenched linking the generations in a strong indestructible chain. And the comedian who waded in carrying an umbrella.

When the others went swimming, my son said he was going in, too. He pulled his dripping trunks from the line where they had hung all through the shower and wrung them out. Languidly, and with no thought of going in, I watched him, his hard little body, skinny and bare, saw him wince slightly as he pulled up around his vitals the small, soggy, icy garment. As he buckled the swollen belt, suddenly my groin felt the chill of death.

August 1941

Reading and Responding

1. Mark several sentences or passages that you especially like, that seem especially evocative.
2. After reading the rest of the essay, free-associate in a ten-minute free-write, jumping off from one of these sentences or passages. Don't let your pen leave the page. Let some word or phrase or detail in the essay set off a chain of memories or images in your mind, and simply record them as they come.

Working Together

1. Share the passage you used as a jumping-off point; read it aloud. Did other students mark the same or similar passages? What do these passages have in common?
2. Share or talk through your free association. What do your free associations—your memories or images—have in common with those recorded by others in your group? Finally, write a group paragraph that describes what your group tended to think about as a result of the free associations.
3. Does the class seem to identify with E. B. White? Is your experience like his? Or is your experience generally different from his? What accounts for those differences or similarities (or both)—what factors of age, culture, historical period, or gender?

Rethinking and Rewriting

1. Assume that E. B. White is your father and that you're the son, the one pulling up his swimming trunks, the "boy." Rewrite the essay from his perspective. Once you've done this, add a one-paragraph postscript that talks about what it was like for you to assume this role.
2. Rewrite this essay for the 1990s—"Once More (Again) to the Lake." How much more has changed?
3. Write an essay with this title, filling in the blank with some special place from your own life, some place you love returning to but that may have changed: "Once More to the _____." Try to write as clearly, directly, and in as much detail as White, avoiding adjectives and adverbs as much as you can and doing the work with nouns and verbs.

"THE SOLACE OF OPEN SPACES"

Gretel Ehrlich

> *Gretel Ehrlich's book of essays about the landscape and people of Wyo-*
> *ming,* The Solace of Open Spaces *(1985), won an award from the Amer-*
> *ican Academy of Arts and Letters and wide acclaim in literary circles. She is*
> *also the author of poems, stories, and novels, as well as a subsequent book of*
> *essays,* Islands, the Universe, Home *(1991). In this, the title piece of her*
> *first book, Ehrlich describes the relationship between the Wyoming landscape*
> *and the character of the people who live in it.*

As You Read

1. Gretel Ehrlich's thesis in this essay is that landscape affects character, that there is a connection between where you live and who you are. As you read the first time, look for one or two central passages that explain how she thinks the western landscape affects the character of the people who live there.
2. As you read, underline any words you can't understand. Once you're finished reading, go back, pick two words that seem especially puzzling to you, and look them up in a dictionary. Write a one- or two-line definition for each. Then pretend you're Ehrlich and write a sentence explaining why you used exactly that word in that sentence.

It's May and I've just awakened from a nap, curled against sagebrush the way my dog taught me to sleep—sheltered from wind. A front is pulling the huge sky over me, and from the dark a hailstone has hit me on the head. I'm trailing a band of two thousand sheep across a stretch of Wyoming badlands, a fifty-mile trip that takes five days because sheep shade up in hot sun and won't budge until it's cool. Bunched together now, and excited into a run by the storm, they drift across dry land, tumbling into draws like water and surge out again onto the rugged, choppy plateaus that are the building blocks of this state.

The name Wyoming comes from an Indian word meaning "at the great plains," but the plains are really valleys, great arid valleys, sixteen hundred square miles, with the horizon bending up on all sides into mountain ranges. This gives the vastness a sheltering look.

Winter lasts six months here. Prevailing winds spill snowdrifts to the east, and new storms from the northwest replenish them. This white bulk is sometimes dizzying, even nauseating, to look at. At twenty, thirty, and forty degrees below zero, not only does your car not work, but neither do your mind and body. The landscape hardens into a dungeon of space. During the winter, while I was riding to find a new calf, my jeans froze to the saddle, and in the silence that such cold creates I felt like the first person on earth, or the last.

Today the sun is out—only a few clouds billowing. In the east, where the sheep have started off without me, the benchland tilts up in a series of eroded red-earthed mesas, planed flat on top by a million years of water; behind them, a bold line of muscular scarps rears up ten thousand feet to become the Big Horn Mountains. A tidal pattern is engraved into the ground, as if left by the sea that once covered this state. Canyons curve down like galaxies to meet the oncoming rush of flat land.

To live and work in this kind of open country, with its hundred-mile   *5* views, is to lose the distinction between background and foreground. When I asked an older ranch hand to describe Wyoming's openness, he said, "It's all a bunch of nothing—wind and rattlesnakes—and so much of it you can't tell where you're going or where you've been and it don't make much difference." John, a sheepman I know, is tall and handsome and has an explosive temperament. He has a perfect intuition about people and sheep. They call him "Highpockets," because he's so long-legged; his graceful stride matches the distances he has to cover. He says, "Open space hasn't affected me at all. It's all the people moving in on it." The huge ranch he was born on takes up much of one county and spreads into another state; to put 100,000 miles on his pickup in three years and never leave home is not unusual. A friend of mine has an aunt who ranched on Powder River and didn't go off her place for eleven years. When her husband died, she quickly moved to town, bought a car, and drove around the States to see what she'd been missing.

Most people tell me they've simply driven through Wyoming, as if there were nothing to stop for. Or else they've skied in Jackson Hole, a place Wyomingites acknowledge uncomfortably because its green beauty and chic affluence are mismatched with the rest of the state. Most of Wyoming has a "lean-to" look. Instead of big, roomy barns and Victorian houses, there are dugouts, low sheds, log cabins, sheep camps, and fence lines that look like driftwood blown haphazardly into place. People here still feel pride because they live in such a harsh place, part of the glamorous cowboy past, and they are determined not to be the victims of a mining-dominated future.

Most characteristic of the state's landscape is what a developer euphemistically describes as "indigenous growth right up to your front door"— a reference to waterless stands of salt sage, snakes, jack rabbits, deerflies, red dust, a brief respite of wildflowers, dry washes, and no trees. In the Great Plains the vistas look like music, like Kyries of grass, but Wyoming seems to be the doing of a mad architect—tumbled and twisted, ribboned with faded, deathbed colors, thrust up and pulled down as if the place had been startled out of a deep sleep and thrown into a pure light.

I came here four years ago. I had not planned to stay, but I couldn't make myself leave. John, the sheepman, put me to work immediately. It was spring, and shearing time. For fourteen days of fourteen hours each, we moved thousands of sheep through sorting corrals to be sheared, branded, and deloused. I suspect that my original motive for coming here was to "lose myself" in new and unpopulated territory. Instead of producing the numbness I thought I wanted, life on the sheep ranch woke me up. The vitality of the people I was working with flushed out what had become a hallucinatory rawness inside me. I threw away my clothes and bought new ones; I cut my hair. The arid country was a clean slate. Its absolute indifference steadied me.

Sagebrush covers 58,000 square miles of Wyoming. The biggest city has a population of fifty thousand, and there are only five settlements that could be called cities in the whole state. The rest are towns, scattered across the expanse with as much as sixty miles between them, their populations two thousand, fifty, or ten. They are fugitive-looking, perched on a barren, windblown bench, or tagged onto a river or a railroad, or laid out straight in a farming valley with implement stores and a block-long Mormon church. In the eastern part of the state, which slides down into the Great Plains, the new mining settlements are boomtowns, trailer cities, metal knots on flat land.

Despite the desolate look, there's a coziness to living in this state. There are so few people (only 470,000) that ranchers who buy and sell cattle know one another statewide; the kids who choose to go to college usually go to the state's one university, in Laramie; hired hands work their way around Wyoming in a lifetime of hirings and firings. And despite the physical separation, people stay in touch, often driving two or three hours to another ranch for dinner. 10

Seventy-five years ago, when travel was by buckboard or horseback, cowboys who were temporarily out of work rode the grub line—drifting from ranch to ranch, mending fences or milking cows, and receiving in exchange a bed and meals. Gossip and messages traveled this slow circuit with them, creating an intimacy between ranchers who were three and four weeks' ride apart. One old-time couple I know, whose turn-of-the-century homestead was used by an outlaw gang as a relay station for stolen horses, recall that if you were traveling, desperado or not, any lighted ranch house was a welcome sign. Even now, for someone who lives in a remote spot, arriving at a ranch or coming to town for supplies is cause for celebration. To emerge from isolation can be disorienting. Everything looks bright, new, vivid. After I had been herding sheep for only three days, the sound of the camp tender's pickup flustered me. Longing for human company, I felt a foolish grin take over my face; yet I had to resist an urgent temptation to run and hide.

Things happen suddenly in Wyoming, the change of seasons and weather; for people, the violent swings in and out of isolation. But good-naturedness is concomitant with severity. Friendliness is a tradition. Strangers passing on the road wave hello. A common sight is two pickups stopped side by side far out on a range, on a dirt track winding through the sage.

The drivers will share a cigarette, uncap their thermos bottles, and pass a battered cup, steaming with coffee, between windows. These meetings summon up the details of several generations, because, in Wyoming, private histories are largely public knowledge.

Because ranch work is a physical and, these days, economic strain, being "at home on the range" is a matter of vigor, self-reliance, and common sense. A person's life is not a series of dramatic events for which he or she is applauded or exiled but a slow accumulation of days, seasons, years, fleshed out by the generational weight of one's family and anchored by a land-bound sense of place.

* * *

In most parts of Wyoming, the human population is visibly outnumbered by the animal. Not far from my town of fifty, I rode into a narrow valley and startled a herd of two hundred elk. Eagles look like small people as they eat car-killed deer by the road. Antelope, moving in small, graceful bands, travel at sixty miles an hour, their mouths open as if drinking in the space.

The solitude in which westerners live makes them quiet. They tele- 15 graph thoughts and feelings by the way they tilt their heads and listen; pulling their Stetsons into a steep dive over their eyes, or pigeon-toeing one boot over the other, they lean against a fence with a fat wedge of Copenhagen beneath their lower lips and take in the whole scene. These detached looks of quiet amusement are sometimes cynical, but they can also come from a dry-eyed humility as lucid as the air is clear.

Conversation goes on in what sounds like a private code; a few phrases imply a complex of meanings. Asking directions, you get a curious list of details. While trailing sheep I was told to "ride up to that kinda upturned rock, follow the pink wash, turn left at the dump, and then you'll see the water hole." One friend told his wife on roundup to "turn at the salt lick and the dead cow," which turned out to be a scattering of bones and no salt lick at all.

Sentence structure is shortened to the skin and bones of a thought. Descriptive words are dropped, even verbs; a cowboy looking over a corral full of horses will say to a wrangler, "Which one needs rode?" People hold back their thoughts in what seems to be a dumbfounded silence, then erupt with an excoriating perceptive remark. Language, so compressed, becomes metaphorical. A rancher ended a relationship with one remark: "You're a bad check," meaning bouncing in and out was intolerable, and even coming back would be no good.

What's behind this laconic style is shyness. There is no vocabulary for the subject of feelings. It's not a hangdog shyness, or anything coy—always there's a robust spirit in evidence behind the restraint, as if the earth-dredging wind that pulls across Wyoming had carried its people's voices away but everything else in them had shouldered confidently into the breeze.

I've spent hours riding to sheep camp at dawn in a pickup when nothing was said; eaten meals in the cookhouse when the only words spoken were a mumbled "Thank you, ma'am" at the end of dinner. The silence is profound. Instead of talking, we seem to share one eye. Keenly observed, the world is transformed. The landscape is engorged with detail, every movement on it chillingly sharp. The air between people is charged. Days unfold, bathed in their own music. Nights become hallucinatory; dreams, prescient.

Spring weather is capricious and mean. It snows, then blisters with   20
heat. There have been tornadoes. They lay their elephant trunks out in the sage until they find houses, then slurp everything up and leave. I've noticed that melting snowbanks hiss and rot, viperous, then drip into calm pools where ducklings hatch and livestock, being trailed to summer range, drink. With the ice cover gone, rivers churn a milkshake brown, taking culverts and small bridges with them. Water in such an arid place (the average annual rainfall where I live is less than eight inches) is like blood. It festoons drab land with green veins; a line of cottonwoods following a stream; a strip of alfalfa; and, on ditch banks, wild asparagus growing.

I've moved to a small cattle ranch owned by friends. It's at the foot of the Big Horn Mountains. A few weeks ago, I helped them deliver a calf who was stuck halfway out of his mother's body. By the time he was freed, we could see a heartbeat, but he was straining against a swollen tongue for air. Mary and I held him upside down by his back feet, while Stan, on his hands and knees in the blood, gave the calf mouth-to-mouth resuscitation. I have a vague memory of being pneumonia-choked as a child, my mother giving me her air, which may account for my romance with this wind-swept state.

If anything is endemic to Wyoming, it is wind. This big room of space is swept out daily, leaving a bone yard of fossils, agates, and carcasses in every stage of decay. Though it was water that initially shaped the state, wind is the meticulous gardener, raising dust and pruning the sage.

I try to imagine a world in which I could ride my horse across uncharted land. There is no wilderness left; wildness, yes, but true wilderness has been gone on this continent since the time of Lewis and Clark's overland journey.

Two hundred years ago, the Crow, Shoshone, Arapaho, Cheyenne, and Sioux roamed the intermountain West, orchestrating their movements according to hunger, season, and warfare. Once they acquired horses, they traversed the spines of all the big Wyoming ranges—the Absarokas, the Wind Rivers, the Tetons, the Big Horns—and wintered on the unprotected plains that fan out from them. Space was life. The world was their home.

What was life-giving to Native Americans was often nightmarish to   25
sodbusters who had arrived encumbered with families and ethnic pasts to

be transplanted in nearly uninhabitable land. The great distances, the shortage of water and trees, and the loneliness created unexpected hardships for them. In her book *O Pioneers!,* Willa Cather gives a settler's version of the bleak landscape:

> The little town behind them had vanished as if it had never been, had fallen behind the swell of the prairie, and the stern frozen country received them into its bosom. The homesteads were few and far apart; here and there a windmill gaunt against the sky, a sod house crouching in a hollow.

The emptiness of the West was for others a geography of possibility. Men and women who amassed great chunks of land and struggled to preserve unfenced empires were, despite their self-serving motives, unwitting geographers. They understood the lay of the land. But by the 1850s the Oregon and Mormon trails sported bumper-to-bumper traffic. Wealthy landowners, many of them aristocratic absentee landlords, known as remittance men because they were paid to come West and get out of their families' hair, overstocked the range with more than a million head of cattle. By 1885 the feed and water were desperately short, and the winter of 1886 laid out the gaunt bodies of dead animals so closely together that when the thaw came, one rancher from Kaycee claimed to have walked on cowhide all the way to Crazy Woman Creek, twenty miles away.

Territorial Wyoming was a boy's world. The land was generous with everything but water. At first there was room enough, food enough, for everyone. And, as with all beginnings, an expansive mood set in. The young cowboys, drifters, shopkeepers, schoolteachers, were heroic, lawless, generous, rowdy, and tenacious. The individualism and optimism generated during those times have endured.

John Tisdale rode north with the trail herds from Texas. He was a college-educated man with enough money to buy a small outfit near the Powder River. While driving home from the town of Buffalo with a buckboard full of Christmas toys for his family and a winter's supply of food, he was shot in the back by an agent of the cattle barons who resented the encroachment of small-time stockmen like him. The wealthy cattlemen tried to control all the public grazing land by restricting membership in the Wyoming Stock Growers Association, as if it were a country club. They ostracized from roundups and brandings cowboys and ranchers who were not members, then denounced them as rustlers. Tisdale's death, the second such cold-blooded murder, kicked off the Johnson County cattle war, which was no simple good-guy-bad-guy shoot-out but a complicated class struggle between landed gentry and less affluent settlers—a shocking reminder that the West was not an egalitarian sanctuary after all.

Fencing ultimately enforced boundaries, but barbed wire abrogated space. It was stretched across the beautiful valleys, into the mountains, over desert badlands, through buffalo grass. The "anything is possible" fever—

the lure of any new place—was constricted. The integrity of the land as a geographical body, and the freedom to ride anywhere on it, were lost.

I punched cows with a young man named Martin, who is the great-grandson of John Tisdale. His inheritance is not the open land that Tisdale knew and prematurely lost but a rage against restraint.   30

Wyoming tips down as you head northeast; the highest ground—the Laramie Plains—is on the Colorado border. Up where I live, the Big Horn River leaks into difficult, arid terrain. In the basin where it's dammed, sandhill cranes gather and, with delicate legwork, slice through the stilled water. I was driving by with a rancher one morning when he commented that cranes are "old-fashioned." When I asked why, he said, "Because they mate for life." Then he looked at me with a twinkle in his eyes, as if to say he really did believe in such things but also understood why we break our own rules.

In all this open space, values crystalize quickly. People are strong on scruples but tenderhearted about quirky behavior. A friend and I found one ranch hand, who's "not quite right in the head," sitting in front of the badly decayed carcass of a cow, shaking his finger and saying, "Now, I don't want you to do this ever again!" When I asked what was wrong with him, I was told, "He's goofier than hell, just like the rest of us." Perhaps because the West is historically new, conventional morality is still felt to be less important than rock-bottom truths. Though there's always a lot of teasing and sparring, people are blunt with one another, sometimes even cruel, believing honesty is stronger medicine than sympathy, which may console but often conceals.

The formality that goes hand in hand with the rowdiness is known as the Western Code. It's a list of practical do's and don'ts, faithfully observed. A friend, Cliff, who runs a trapline in the winter, cut off half his foot while chopping a hole in the ice. Alone, he dragged himself to his pickup and headed for town, stopping to open the ranch gate as he left, and getting out to close it again, thus losing, in his observance of rules, precious time and blood. Later, he commented, "How would it look, them having to come to the hospital to tell me their cows had gotten out?"

Accustomed to emergencies, my friends doctor each other from the vet's bag with relish. When one old-timer suffered a heart attack in hunting camp, his partner quickly stirred up a brew of red horse liniment and hot water and made the half-conscious victim drink it, then tied him onto a horse and led him twenty miles to town. He regained consciousness and lived.

The roominess of the state has affected political attitudes as well.   35 Ranchers keep up with world politics and the convulsions of the economy but are basically isolationists. Being used to running their own small empires of land and livestock, they're suspicious of big government. It's a "don't fence me in" holdover from a century ago. They still want the elbow room their grandfathers had, so they're strongly conservative, but with a populist twist.

Summer is the season when we get our "cowboy tans"—on the lower parts of our faces and on three fourths of our arms. Excessive heat, in the nineties and higher, sends us outside with the mosquitoes. In winter we're tucked inside our houses, and the white wasteland outside appears to be expanding, but in summer all the greenery abridges space. Summer is a go-ahead season. Every living thing is off the block and in the race: battalions of bugs in flight and biting; bats swinging around my log cabin as if the bases were loaded and someone had hit a home run. Some of summer's high-speed growth is ominous: larkspur, death camas, and green greasewood can kill sheep—an ironic idea, dying in this desert from eating what is too verdant. With sixteen hours of daylight, farmers and ranchers irrigate feverishly. There are first, second, and third cuttings of hay, some crews averaging only four hours of sleep a night for weeks. And, like the cowboys who in summer ride the night rodeo circuit, nighthawks make daredevil dives at dusk with an eerie whirring sound like a plane going down on the shimmering horizon.

In the town where I live, they've had to board up the dance-hall windows because there have been so many fights. There's so little to do except work that people wind up in a state of idle agitation that becomes fatalistic, as if there were nothing to be done about all this untapped energy. So the dark side to the grandeur of these spaces is the small-mindedness that seals people in. Men become hermits; women go mad. Cabin fever explodes into suicides, or into grudges and lifelong family feuds. Two sisters in my area inherited a ranch but found they couldn't get along. They fenced the place in half. When one's cows got out and mixed with the other's, the women went at each other with shovels. They ended up in the same hospital room but never spoke a word to each other for the rest of their lives.

After the brief lushness of summer, the sun moves south. The range grass is brown. Livestock is trailed back down from the mountains. Water holes begin to frost over at night. Last fall Martin asked me to accompany him on a pack trip. With five horses, we followed a river into the mountains behind the tiny Wyoming town of Meeteetse. Groves of aspen, red and orange, gave off a light that made us look toasted. Our hunting camp was so high that clouds skidded across our foreheads, then slowed to sail out across the warm valleys. Except for a bull moose who wandered into our camp and mistook our black gelding for a rival, we shot at nothing.

One of our evening entertainments was to watch the night sky. My dog, a dingo bred to herd sheep, also came on the trip. He is so used to the silence and empty skies that when an airplane flies over he always looks up and eyes the distant intruder quizzically. The sky, lately, seems to be much more crowded than it used to be. Satellites make their silent passes in the dark with great regularity. We counted eighteen in one hour's viewing. How odd to think that while they circumnavigated the planet, Martin and I had moved only six miles into our local wilderness and had seen no other human for the two weeks we stayed there.

At night, by moonlight, the land is whittled to slivers—a ridge, a   40
river, a strip of grassland stretching to the mountains, then the huge sky. One morning a full moon was setting in the west just as the sun was rising. I felt precariously balanced between the two as I loped across a meadow. For a moment, I could believe that the stars, which were still visible, work like cooper's bands, holding together everything above Wyoming.

Space has a spiritual equivalent and can heal what is divided and burdensome in us. My grandchildren will probably use space shuttles for a honeymoon trip or to recover from heart attacks, but closer to home we might also learn how to carry space inside ourselves in the effortless way we carry our skins. Space represents sanity, not a life purified, dull, or "spaced out" but one that might accommodate intelligently any idea or situation.

From the clayey soil of northern Wyoming is mined bentonite, which is used as a filler in candy, gum, and lipstick. We Americans are great on fillers, as if what we have, what we are, is not enough. We have a cultural tendency toward denial, but, being affluent, we strangle ourselves with what we can buy. We have only to look at the houses we build to see how we build *against* space, the way we drink against pain and loneliness. We fill up space as if it were a pie shell, with things whose opacity further obstructs our ability to see what is already there.

Working Together

1. In the center of the board, or in the center of a sheet of paper if you're working in pairs or groups, write one or two phrases that explain Ehrlich's central idea. That is, in one or two brief phrases, explain how she thinks the West influences character. Circle those phrases.
2. On the rest of the board or sheet of paper (see item 1), moving out from that center, write down all the illustrating details you can think of that support this idea, all the concrete images and characters and examples Ehrlich uses to flesh out her idea.

Rethinking and Rewriting

1. Brainstorm for a paper on your own. In the center of a sheet of paper, write down several short phrases that express what you think is the relationship between your own landscape and the people who live in it. How does the campus, the town, the country, the neighborhood, the

forest, or the ocean influence the attitudes and moods of the people you know or your own attitudes and moods?

2. On the rest of the sheet (see item 1), brainstorm as many details as you can.

3. Write the essay.

"SACRED AND ANCESTRAL GROUND"

N. Scott Momaday

In this brief essay N. Scott Momaday describes his return to an important place in the history of his ancestors, the Kiowa Indians. (See also "My Horse and I" in chapter 8.)

As You Read

As you read this essay, underline or highlight every use of the word *sacred* (start with the title).

There is great good in returning to a landscape that has had extraordinary meaning in one's life. It happens that we return to such places in our minds irresistibly. There are certain villages and towns, mountains and plains that, having seen them, walked in them, lived in them, even for a day, we keep forever in the mind's eye. They become indispensable to our well-being; they define us, and we say: I am who I am because I have been there, or there. There is good, too, in actual, physical return.

Some years ago I made a pilgrimage into the heart of North America. I began the journey proper in western Montana. From there I traveled across the high plains of Wyoming into the Black Hills, then southward to the southern plains, to a cemetery at Rainy Mountain, in Oklahoma. It was a journey made by my Kiowa ancestors long before. In the course of their migration they became a people of the Great Plains, and theirs was the last culture to evolve in North America. They had been for untold generations a mountain tribe of hunters. Their ancient nomadism, which had determined their way of life even before they set foot on this continent, perhaps 30,000 years ago, was raised to its highest level of expression when they entered upon the Great Plains and acquired horses. Their migration brought them to a Golden Age. At the beginning of their journey they were a people of hard circumstances, often hungry and cold, fighting always for sheer survival. At its end, and for a hundred years, they were the lords of the land, a daring race of centaurs and buffalo hunters whose love of freedom and space was profound.

Recently I returned to the old migration route of the Kiowas. I had in me a need to behold again some of the principal landmarks of that long, prehistoric quest, to descend again from the mountain to the plain.

With my close friend Charles, a professor of American literature at a South Dakota university, I headed north to the Montana-Wyoming border. I wanted to intersect the Kiowa migration route at the Bighorn Medicine Wheel, high in the Bighorn Mountains. We ascended to 8,000 feet gradually, on a well-maintained but winding highway. Then we climbed sharply, bearing upon the timberline. Although the plain below had been comfortable, even warm at midday, the mountain air was cold, and much of the ground was covered with snow. We turned off the pavement, on a dirt road that led three miles to the Medicine Wheel. The road was forbidding, it was narrow and winding, and the grades were steep and slippery; here and there the shoulders fell away into deep ravines. But at the same time something wonderful happened: we crossed the line between civilization and wilderness. Suddenly the earth persisted in its original being. Directly in front of us a huge white-tailed buck crossed our path, ambling without haste into a thicket of pines. As we drove over his tracks we saw four does above on the opposite bank, looking down at us, their great black eyes bright and benign, curious. There seemed no wariness, nothing of fear or alienation. Their presence was a good omen, we thought; somehow in their attitude they bade us welcome to their sphere of wilderness.

There was a fork in the road, and we took the wrong branch. At a   5
steep, hairpin curve we got out of the car and climbed to the top of a peak. An icy wind whipped at us; we were among the bald summits of the Bighorns. Great flumes of sunlit snow erupted on the ridges and dissolved in spangles on the sky. Across a deep saddle we caught sight of the Medicine Wheel. It was perhaps two miles away.

When we returned to the car we saw another vehicle approaching. It was a very old Volkswagen bus, in much need of repair, cosmetic repair, at least. Out stepped a thin, bearded young man in thick glasses. He wore a wool cap, a down parka, jeans and well-worn hiking boots. "I am looking for Medicine Wheel," he said, having nodded to us. He spoke softly, with a pronounced accent. His name was Jürg, and he was from Switzerland; he had been traveling for some months in Canada and the United States. Chuck and I shook his hand and told him to follow us, and we drove down into the saddle. From there we climbed on foot to the Medicine Wheel.

The Medicine Wheel is a ring of stones, some 80 feet in diameter. Stone spokes radiate from the center to the circumference. Cairns are placed at certain points on the circumference, one in the center and one just outside the ring to the southwest. We do not know as a matter of fact who made this wheel or to what purpose. It has been proposed that it was an astronomical observatory, a solar calendar and the ground design of a Kiowa sun dance lodge. What we know without doubt is that it is a sacred expression, an equation of man's relation to the cosmos.

There was a great calm upon that place. The hard, snowbearing wind that had burned our eyes and skin only minutes before had died away altogether. The sun was warm and bright, and there was a profound silence. On the wire fence that had been erected to enclose and protect the wheel were fixed offerings, small prayer bundles. Chuck and Jürg and I walked about slowly, standing for long moments here and there, looking into the wheel or out across the great distances. We did not say much; there was little to be said. But we were deeply moved by the spirit of that place. The silence was such that it must be observed. To the north we could see down to the timberline, to the snowfields and draws that marked the black planes of forest among the peaks of the Bighorns. To the south and west the mountains fell abruptly to the plains. We could see thousands of feet down and a hundred miles across the dim expanse.

When we were about to leave, I took from my pocket an eagle-bone whistle that my father had given me, and I blew it in the four directions. The sound was very high and shrill, and it did not break the essential silence. As we were walking down we saw far below, crossing our path, a coyote sauntering across the snow into a wall of trees. It was just there, a wild being to catch sight of, and then it was gone. The wilderness which had admitted us with benediction, with benediction let us go.

When we came within a stone's throw of the highway, Chuck and I   10
said goodbye to Jürg, but not before Jürg had got out his camp stove and boiled water for tea. There in the dusk we enjoyed a small ceremonial feast of tea and crackers. The three of us had become friends. Only later did I begin to understand the extraordinary character of that friendship. It was the friendship of those who come together in recognition of the sacred. If we never meet again, I thought, we shall not forget this day.

On the plains the fences and roads and windmills and houses seemed almost negligible, all but overwhelmed by the earth and sky. It is a landscape of great clarity; its vastness is that of the ocean. It is the near revelation of infinity. Antelope were everywhere in the grassy folds, grazing side by side with horses and cattle. Hawks sailed above, and crows scattered before us. The place names were American—Tensleep, Buffalo, Dull Knife, Crazy Woman, Spotted Horse.

The Black Hills are an isolated and ancient group of mountains in South Dakota and Wyoming. They lie very close to both the geographic center of the United States (including Alaska and Hawaii) and the geographic center of the North American continent. They form an island, an elliptical area of nearly 6,000 square miles, in the vast sea of grasses that is the northern Great Plains. The Black Hills form a calendar of geologic time that is truly remarkable. The foundation rocks of these mountains are older than much of the sedimentary layer of which the Americas are primarily composed. An analysis of this foundation, made in 1975, indicates an age of between two billion and three billion years.

A documented record of exploration in this region is found in the Lewis and Clark journals, 1804–6. The first white party known definitely to have entered the Black Hills proper was led by Jedediah Smith in 1823. The diary of this expedition, kept by one James Clyman, is notable. Clyman reports a confrontation between Jedediah Smith and a grizzly bear, in which Smith lost one of his ears. There is also reported the discovery of a petrified ("putrified," as Clyman has it) forest, where petrified birds sing petrified songs.

Toward the end of the century, after rumors of gold had made the Black Hills a name known throughout the country, Gen. (then Lieut. Col.)

George Armstrong Custer led an expedition from Fort Abraham Lincoln into the Black Hills in July and August, 1874. The Custer expedition traveled 600 miles in 60 days. Custer reported proof of gold, but he had an eye to other things as well:

> Every step of our march that day was amid flowers of the most exquisite colors and perfume. So luxuriant in growth were they that men plucked them without dismounting from the saddle. . . . It was a strange sight to glance back at the advancing columns of cavalry and behold the men with beautiful bouquets in their hands, while the headgear of the horses was decorated with wreaths of flowers fit to crown a queen of May. Deeming it a most fitting appellation, I named this Floral Valley.

In the evening of that same day, sitting at mess in a meadow, the officers competed to see how many different flowers could be picked by each man, without leaving his seat. Seven varieties were gathered so. Some 50 different flowers were blooming then in Floral Valley. 15

The Lakota, or Teton Sioux, called these mountains Paha Sapa, "Hills That Are Black." Other tribes, besides the Kiowa and the Sioux, thought of the Black Hills as sacred ground, a place crucial in their past. The Arapaho lived here. So did the Cheyenne. Bear Butte, near Sturgis, S.D., on the northeast edge of the Black Hills, is the Cheyenne's sacred mountain. It remains, like the Medicine Wheel, a place of the greatest spiritual intensity. So great was thought to be the power inherent in the Black Hills that the Indians did not camp there. It was a place of rendezvous, a hunting ground, but above all inviolate, a place of thunder and lightning, a dwelling place of the gods.

On the edge of the Black Hills nearest the Bighorn Mountains is Devils Tower, the first of our National Monuments. The Lakotas called it Mateo Tepee, "Grizzly Bear Lodge." The Kiowas called it Tsoai, "Rock Tree." Devils Tower is a great monolith that rises high above the timber of the Black Hills. In conformation it closely resembles the stump of a tree. It is a cluster of rock columns (phonolite porphyry) 1,000 feet across at the base and 275 feet across the top. It rises 865 feet above the high ground on which it stands and 1,280 feet above the Belle Fourche River, in the valley below.

It has to be seen to be believed. "There are things in nature that engender an awful quiet in the heart of man; Devils Tower is one of them." I wrote these words almost 20 years ago. They remain true to my experience. Each time I behold this Tsoai, I am more than ever in awe of it.

Two hundred years ago, more or less, the Kiowas came upon this place. They were moved to tell a story about it:

Eight children were there at play, seven sisters and their brother. Suddenly the boy was struck dumb; he trembled and began to run upon his hands and feet. His fingers became claws and his body was covered 20 with fur. Directly there was a bear where the boy had been. The sisters were terrified; they ran, and the bear ran after them. They came to the stump of a great tree, and the tree spoke to them. It bade them climb upon it, and as they did so it began to rise into the air. The bear came to kill them, but they were just beyond its reach. It reared against the tree and scored the bark all around with its claws. The seven sisters were borne into the sky, and they became the stars of the Big Dipper.

This story, which I have known from the time I could first understand language, exemplifies the sacred for me. The storyteller, that anonymous, illiterate man who told the story for the first time, succeeded in raising the human condition to the level of universal significance. Not only did he account for the existence of the rock tree, but in the process he related his human race to the stars.

When Chuck and I had journeyed over this ground together, when we were about to go our separate ways, I reminded him of our friend Jürg, knowing well enough that I needn't have: Jürg was on our minds. He had touched us deeply with his trust, not unlike that of the wild animals we had seen. I can't account for it. Jürg had touched us deeply with his generosity of spirit, his concern to see beneath the surface of things, his attitude of free, direct, disinterested kindness.

"Did he tell us what he does?" I asked. "Does he have a profession?"

"I don't think he said," Chuck replied. "I think he's a pilgrim."

"Yes."   25

"Yes."

Reading and Responding

1. Copy out the first paragraph of this essay in your own writing. Then draw a line under what you've copied and write a paragraph of your own that responds to it, discussing what it makes you think about.
2. Copy out any paragraph in this essay—except the first—in your own handwriting. Draw a line under this paragraph and write a paragraph of your own, talking about why you chose to copy the paragraph you did.

Working Together

1. Read to each other your responses to the first paragraph of N. Scott Momaday's essay. On the basis of your individual responses, write a group paragraph explaining your group's response.
2. As a group, review the various places where Momaday uses the word *sacred*. As you look at these places, make a list of characteristics that go with *sacred*.
3. Reread the Kiowa story accounting for the Big Dipper. Assume that some students in class don't understand why the story is important (it simply sounds childish to them). As a group, figure out how you'd

explain to these classmates what makes the story work and why it's powerful. (*Hint:* Pay attention to the paragraph following the story.)

Rethinking and Rewriting

1. Write a three- to five-page letter that you would send to Momaday. In your letter, explain where you might go or the journey you might take to imitate the return that Momaday speaks of. If you have no such journey or place to talk about, then explain your situation as simply and clearly as you can. Once you finish the letter, add a postscript to your instructor. In the postscript, briefly tell your instructor what it was like to write this letter.

2. Research a native people who once lived where your campus is now (or lived nearby, or lived near your hometown). What is known about these people, and what happened to them? If you can find a story from their culture, include it in your paper. (Remember to consider not just print sources but also living ones.)

3. Tell a story from your own familial or cultural background. Introduce the story with only a few sentences, tell the story itself, and then add whatever commentary or explanation is needed to make the story and its importance clear to readers outside your family or your culture.

"THE SOW IN THE RIVER"

Mary Clearman Blew

Author of two collections of stories as well as a book-length memoir, Mary Clearman Blew was born and raised in Fergus County in central Montana and teaches now at Lewis-Clark State College in Lewiston, Idaho. In this, the opening piece from All But the Waltz: A Memoir of Five Generations in the Life of a Montana Family, *Blew returns to a landscape rich with her childhood memories, comparing those memories to the actual ground as she finds it now.*

Before and As You Read

1. Preread this piece and make some notes on what you find. (If you're not familiar with prereading, refer to chapter 1.)
2. Read Blew's essay with a piece of paper in front of you. As you come to a detail that seems especially surprising, clear, or important, copy down a phrase that captures this detail. Make sure that you copy down at least six phrases (reread the piece if you need to). Once you've finished reading the entire essay and made your list, look at the phrases you've copied. What do they have in common? Write three or four sentences that comment on these details, these phrasings.

In the sagebrush to the north of the mountains in central Montana, where the Judith River deepens its channel and threads a slow, treacherous current between the cutbanks, a cottonwood log house still stands. It is in sight of the highway, about a mile downriver on a gravel road. From where I have turned off and stopped my car on the sunlit shoulder of the highway, I can see the house, a distant and solitary dark interruption of the sagebrush. I can even see the lone box elder tree, a dusty green shade over what used to be the yard.

I know from experience that if I were to keep driving over the cattle guard and follow the gravel road through the sage and alkali to the log house, I would find the windows gone and the door sagging and the floor rotting away. But from here the house looks hardly changed from the summer of my earliest memories, the summer before I was three, when I lived in that log house on the lower Judith with my mother and father and grandmother and my grandmother's boyfriend, Bill.

My memories seem to me as treacherous as the river. Is it possible, sitting here on this dry shoulder of a secondary highway in the middle of Montana where the brittle weeds of August scratch at the sides of the car, watching the narrow blue Judith take its time to thread and wind through the bluffs on its way to a distant northern blur, to believe in anything but today? The past eases away with the current. I cannot watch a single drop of water out of sight. How can I trust memory, which slips and wobbles and grinds its erratic furrows like a bald-tired truck fighting for traction on a wet gumbo road?

Light flickers. A kerosene lamp in the middle of the table has driven the shadows back into the corners of the kitchen. Faces and hands emerge in a circle. Bill has brought apples from the box in the dark closet. The coil of peel follows his pocketknife. I bite into the piece of quartered apple he hands me. I hear its snap, taste the juice. The shadows hold threats: mice and the shape of nameless things. But in the circle around the lamp, in the certainty of apples, I am safe.

The last of the kerosene tilts and glitters around the wick. I cower *5* behind Grammy on the stairs, but she boldly walks into the shadows, which reel and retreat from her and her lamp. In her bedroom the window reflects large pale her and timorous me. She undresses herself, undresses me; she piles my pants and stockings on the chair with her dress and corset. After she uses it, her pot is warm for me. Her bed is cold, then warm. I burrow against her back and smell the smoke from the wick she has pinched out. Bill blows his nose from his bedroom on the other side of the landing. Beyond the eaves the shapeless creatures of sound, owls and coyotes, have taken the night. But I am here, safe in the center.

I am in the center again on the day we look for Bill's pigs. I am sitting between him and Grammy in the cab of the old Ford truck while the rain sheets on the windshield. Bill found the pigpen gate open when he went to feed the pigs this morning, their pen empty, and now they are nowhere to be found. He has driven and driven through the sagebrush and around the gulches, peering out through the endless gray rain as the truck spins and growls on the gumbo in low gear. But no pigs. He and Grammy do not speak. The cab is cold, but I am bundled well between them with my feet on the clammy assortment of tools and nails and chains on the floorboards and my nose just dashboard level, and I am at home with the smell of wet wool and metal and the feel of a broken spring in the seat.

But now Bill tramps on the brakes, and he and Grammy and I gaze through the streaming windshield at the river. The Judith has risen up its cutbanks, and its angry gray current races the rain. I have never seen such a Judith, such a tumult of water. But what transfixes me and Grammy and Bill behind our teeming glass is not the ruthless condition of the river— no, for on a bare ait at midcurrent, completely surrounded and only inches above that muddy roiling water, huddle the pigs.

The flat top of the ait is so small that the old sow takes up most of it by herself. The river divides and rushes around her, rising, practically at her hooves. Surrounding her, trying to crawl under her, snorting in apprehension at the water, are her little pigs. Watching spellbound from the cab of the truck, I can feel their small terrified rumps burrowing against her sides, drawing warmth from her center even as more dirt crumbles under their hooves. My surge of understanding arcs across the current, and my flesh shrivels in the icy sheets of rain. Like the pigs I cringe at the roar of the river, although behind the insulated walls of the cab I can hear and feel nothing. I am in my center and they are in theirs. The current separates us irrevocably, and suddenly I understand that my center is as precarious as theirs, that the chill metal cab of the old truck is almost as fragile as their ring of crumbling sod.

And then the scene darkens and I see no more.

For years I would watch for the ait. When I was five my family   10
moved, but I learned to snatch a glimpse whenever we drove past our old turnoff on the road from Lewistown to Denton. The ait was in plain view, just a hundred yards downriver from the highway, as it is today. *Ait* was a fancy word I learned afterward. It was a fifteen-foot-high steep-sided, flat-topped pinnacle of dirt left standing in the bed of the river after years of wind and water erosion. And I never caught sight of it without the same small thrill of memory: that's where the pigs were.

One day I said it out loud. I was grown by then. "That's where the pigs were."

My father was driving. We would have crossed the Judith River bridge, and I would have turned my head to keep sight of the ait and the lazy blue threads of water around the sandbars.

My father said, "What pigs?"

"The old sow and her pigs," I said, surprised. "The time the river flooded. I remember how the water rose right up to their feet."

My father said, "The Judith never got that high, and there never was   15
any pigs up there."

"Yes there were! I remember!" I could see the little pigs as clearly as I could see my father, and I could remember exactly how my own skin had shriveled as they cringed back from the water and butted the sow for cold comfort.

My father shook his head. "How did you think pigs would get up there?" he asked.

Of course they couldn't.

His logic settled on me like an awakening in ordinary daylight. Of course a sow could not lead nine or ten suckling pigs up those sheer fifteen-foot crumbling dirt sides, even for fear of their lives. And why, after all, would pigs even try to scramble to the top of such a precarious perch when they could escape a cloudburst by following any one of the cattle trails or deer trails that webbed the cutbanks on both sides of the river?

Had there been a cloudburst at all? Had there been pigs?   20

No, my father repeated. The Judith had never flooded anywhere near that high in our time. Bill Hafer had always raised a few pigs when we lived down there on the river, but he kept them penned up. No.

Today I lean on the open window of my car and yawn and listen to the sounds of late summer. The snapping of grasshoppers. Another car approaching on the highway, roaring past my shoulder of the road, then fading away until I can hear the faint scratches of some small hidden creature in the weeds. I am bone-deep in landscape. In this dome of sky and river and undeflected sunlight, in this illusion of timelessness, I can almost feel my body, blood, and breath in the broken line of the bluffs and the pervasive scent of ripening sweet clover and dust, almost feel the sagging fence line of ancient cedar posts stapled across my vitals.

The only shade in sight is across the river where box elders lean over a low white frame house with a big modern house trailer parked behind it. Downstream, far away, a man works along a ditch. I think he might be the husband of a second cousin of mine who still lives on her old family place. My cousins wouldn't know me if they stopped and asked me what I was doing here.

Across the highway, a trace of a road leads through a barbed-wire gate and sharply up the bluff. It is the old cutoff to Danvers, a town that has dried up and blown away. I have heard that the cutoff has washed out, further up the river, but down here it still holds a little bleached gravel. Almost as though my father might turn off in his battered truck at fifteen miles an hour, careful of his bald wartime tires, while I lie on the seat with my head on his thigh and take my nap. Almost as though at the end of that road will be the two grain elevators pointing sharply out of the hazy olives and ochers of the grass into the rolling cumulus, and two or three graveled streets with traffic moving past the pool hall and post office and dug-out store where, when I wake from my nap and scramble down from the high seat of the truck, Old Man Longin will be waiting behind his single glass display case with my precious wartime candy bar.

Yes, that little girl was me, I guess. A three-year-old standing on the unswept board floor, looking up at rows of canned goods on shelves that were nailed against the logs in the 1880s, when Montana was still a territory. The dust smelled the same to her as it does to me now.

25

Across the river, that low white frame house where my cousin still lives is the old Sample place. Ninety years ago a man named Sample fell in love with a woman named Carrie. Further up the bottom—you can't see it from here because of the cottonwoods—stands Carrie's deserted house in what used to be a fenced yard. Forty years ago Carrie's house was full of three generations of her family, and the yard was full of cousins at play. Sixty years ago the young man who would be my father rode on horseback down that long hill to Carrie's house, and Sample said to Carrie, *Did your brother Albert ever have a son? From the way the kid sits his horse, he must be your brother's son.*

Or so the story goes. Sample was murdered. Carrie died in her sleep. My father died of exposure.

The Judith winds toward its mouth. Its current seems hardly to move. Seeing it in August, so blue and unhurried, it is difficult to believe how many drownings or near drownings the Judith has counted over the years. To a stranger it surely must look insignificant, hardly worth calling a river.

In 1805 the explorers Lewis and Clark, pausing in their quest for the Pacific, saw the mountains and the prairies of central Montana and the wild game beyond reckoning. They also noted this river, which they named after a girl. Lewis and Clark were the first white recorders of this place. In recording it, they altered it. However indifferent to the historical record, those who see this river and hear its name, *Judith,* see it in a slightly different way because Lewis and Clark saw it and wrote about it.

In naming the river, Lewis and Clark claimed it for a system of governance that required a wrenching of the fundamental connections between landscape and its inhabitants. This particular drab sagebrush pocket of the West was never, perhaps, holy ground. None of the landmarks here is invested with the significance of the sacred buttes to the north. For the Indian tribes that hunted here, central Montana must have been commonplace, a familiar stretch of their lives, a place to ride and breathe and be alive.

But even this drab pocket is now a part of the history of the West, which, through a hundred and fifty years of white settlement and economic development, of rapid depletion of water and coal and timber and topsoil, of dependence upon military escalation and federal subsidies, has been a history of the transformation of landscape from a place to be alive in into a place to own. This is a transformation that breaks connections, that holds little in common. My deepest associations with this sunlit river are private. Without a connection between outer and inner landscape, I cannot tell my father what I saw. "There never was a sow in the river," he said, embarrassed at my notion. And yet I know there was a sow in the river.

All who come and go bring along their own context, leave their mark, however faint. If the driver glanced out the window of that car that just roared past, what did he see? Tidy irrigated alfalfa fields, a small green respite from the dryland miles? That foreshortened man who works along the ditch, does he straighten his back from his labors and see his debts spread out in irrigation pipes and electric pumps?

It occurs to me that I dreamed the sow in the river at a time when I was too young to sort out dreams from daylight reality or to question why they should be sorted out and dismissed. As I think about it, the episode does contain some of the characteristics of a dream. That futile, endless, convoluted search in the rain, for example. The absence of sound in the cab of the truck, and the paralysis of the onlookers on the brink of that churning current. For now that I know she never existed outside my imagination, I think I do recognize that sow on her slippery pinnacle.

Memory lights upon a dream as readily as an external event, upon a set of rusty irrigation pipes and a historian's carefully detailed context through which she recalls the collective memory of the past. As memory saves, discards, retrieves, fails to retrieve, its logic may well be analogous to the river's inexorable search for the lowest ground. The trivial and the profound roll like leaves to the surface. Every ripple is suspect.

Today the Judith River spreads out in the full sunlight of August, oblivious of me and my precious associations, indifferent to the emotional context I have framed it with. My memory seems less a record of landscape and event than a superimposition upon what otherwise would continue to flow, leaf out, or crumble according to its lot. What I remember is far less trustworthy than the story I tell about it. The possibility for connection lies in story.   *35*

Whether or not I dreamed her, the sow in the river is my story. She is what I have saved, up there on her pinnacle where the river roils.

Reading and Responding

In this essay Mary Clearman Blew is driving to a place that holds significance for her; and as the essay opens, she pulls off the road so that she can think. If you were driving to some place that holds significance for you, where would you be going? Where would you pull off the road to think? What would you think about? Write freely about these questions for a page or so.

Working Together

1. Summarize the story of the sow in the river with her offspring (the second section of this essay). Who's watching this little drama, and what do you know about her? What does she see, and how is she affected by what she sees? Don't worry about any of the essay but this second section.
2. Look only at the third section of this essay and assume that you're Mary Clearman Blew. What's just happened in this third section? What did you just learn from your father? As a group, write two or three sentences that explain what just happened.
3. In the last section of this essay Blew explains the contradiction at its center, and she says "The possibility for connection lies in story." What's she mean? If you think you know what she means, write a group paragraph that explains it. If, as a group, you're too puzzled to do that, then write a list of questions that puzzle you.

Rethinking and Rewriting

1. At the end of this essay Blew keeps her story about the sow in the river; that is, she doesn't shrug it off as a mistake she made—something childish and foolish. Write an essay that explains why she keeps the story even though she knows from her father that it never really happened.

2. Write your own personal version of "The Sow in the River," and begin it as Blew does. Divide your essay into at least three sections. As a variation, write your own personal version of "The Sow in the River," but write it using the third person. That is, instead of saying *I,* talk about yourself as *she* or *he.* Begin your essay with your main character en route to some important place (as Blew begins her essay).

3. Using your own experience and using Blew's essay, argue that our personal histories are inevitably caught up with the landscapes that we know best, the landscapes that saw our most important life experiences.

"ON GOING HOME"

Joan Didion

> *Though the author of several important novels—including* Play It as It
> Lays *(1970) and* A Book of Common Prayer *(1977)—Joan Didion is*
> *most respected for her incisive, brilliantly imagistic essays about her own ex-*
> *perience and the crises of American culture. They have been collected in several*
> *books, including* Slouching Towards Bethlehem *(1968) and* The White
> Album *(1979). "On Going Home," first published in 1967, explores the*
> *breakdown of family life and the passing away of tradition.*

Before You Read

Before you begin Joan Didion's essay, write about a time that you've lived
away from your family and then returned to see them again. Explain
briefly where you lived and what you did, but focus mostly on what it was
like to return to your family or your home place. Talk about what it felt
like to go back. Talk about what felt familiar and what felt different. Write
a quick page or so.

I am home for my daughter's first birthday. By "home" I do not
mean the house in Los Angeles where my husband and I and the baby live,
but the place where my family is, in the Central Valley of California. It is
a vital although troublesome distinction. My husband likes my family but
is uneasy in their house, because once there I fall into their ways, which
are difficult, oblique, deliberately inarticulate, not my husband's ways. We
live in dusty houses ("D-U-S-T," he once wrote with his finger on surfaces
all over the house, but no one noticed it) filled with mementos quite
without value to him (what could the Canton dessert plates mean to him?
how could he have known about the assay scales, why should he care if he
did know?), and we appear to talk exclusively about people we know who
have been committed to mental hospitals, about people we know who
have been booked on drunk-driving charges, and about property, particularly about property, land, price per acre and C-2 zoning and assessments
and freeway access. My brother does not understand my husband's inability
to perceive the advantage in the rather common real-estate transaction
known as "sale-leaseback," and my husband in turn does not understand
why so many of the people he hears about in my father's house have
recently been committed to mental hospitals or booked on drunk-driving
charges. Nor does he understand that when we talk about sale-leasebacks
and right-of-way condemnations we are talking in code about the things
we like best, the yellow fields and the cottonwoods and the rivers rising
and falling and the mountain roads closing when the heavy snow comes
in. We miss each other's points, have another drink and regard the fire. My

brother refers to my husband, in his presence, as "Joan's husband." Marriage is the classic betrayal.

Or perhaps it is not any more. Sometimes I think that those of us who are now in our thirties were born into the last generation to carry the burden of "home," to find in family life the source of all tension and drama. I had by all objective accounts a "normal" and a "happy" family situation, and yet I was almost thirty years old before I could talk to my family on the telephone without crying after I had hung up. We did not fight. Nothing was wrong. And yet some nameless anxiety colored the emotional charges between me and the place that I came from. The question of whether or not you could go home again was a very real part of the sentimental and largely literary baggage with which we left home in the fifties; I suspect that it is irrelevant to the children born of the fragmentation after World War II. A few weeks ago in a San Francisco bar I saw a pretty young girl on crystal take off her clothes and dance for the cash prize in an "amateur-topless" contest. There was no particular sense of moment about this, none of the effect of romantic degradation, of "dark journey," for which my generation strived so assiduously. What sense could that girl possibly make of, say, *Long Day's Journey into Night?* Who is beside the point?

That I am trapped in this particular irrelevancy is never more apparent to me than when I am home. Paralyzed by the neurotic lassitude engendered by meeting one's past at every turn, around every corner, inside every cupboard, I go aimlessly from room to room. I decide to meet it head-on and clean out a drawer, and I spread the contents on the bed. A bathing suit I wore the summer I was seventeen. A letter of rejection from *The Nation,* an aerial photograph of the site for a shopping center my father did not build in 1954. Three teacups hand-painted with cabbage roses and signed "E.M.," my grandmother's initials. There is no final solution for letters of rejection from *The Nation* and teacups hand-painted in 1900. Nor is there any answer to snapshots of one's grandfather as a young man on skis, surveying around Donner Pass in the year 1910. I smooth out the snapshot and look into his face, and do and do not see my own. I close the drawer, and have another cup of coffee with my mother. We get along very well, veterans of a guerrilla war we never understood.

Days pass. I see no one. I come to dread my husband's evening call, not only because he is full of news of what by now seems to me our remote life in Los Angeles, people he has seen, letters which require attention, but because he asks what I have been doing, suggests uneasily that I get out, drive to San Francisco or Berkeley. Instead I drive across the river to a family graveyard. It has been vandalized since my last visit and the monuments are broken, overturned in the dry grass. Because I once saw a rattlesnake in the grass I stay in the car and listen to a country-and-Western station. Later I drive with my father to a ranch he has in the foothills. The man who runs his cattle on it asks us to the roundup, a week from Sunday, and although I know that I will be in Los Angeles I say, in the oblique way my family talks, that I will come. Once home I mention the broken monuments in the graveyard. My mother shrugs.

I go to visit my great-aunts. A few of them think now that I am my cousin, or their daughter who died young. We recall an anecdote about a relative last seen in 1948, and they ask if I still like living in New York City. I have lived in Los Angeles for three years, but I say that I do. The baby is offered a horehound drop, and I am slipped a dollar bill "to buy a treat." Questions trail off, answers are abandoned, the baby plays with the dust motes in a shaft of afternoon sun.

It is time for the baby's birthday party: a white cake, strawberry-marshmallow ice cream, a bottle of champagne saved from another party. In the evening, after she has gone to sleep, I kneel beside the crib and touch her face, where it is pressed against the slats, with mine. She is an open and trusting child, unprepared for and unaccustomed to the ambushes of family life, and perhaps it is just as well that I can offer her little of that life. I would like to give her more. I would like to promise her that she will grow up with a sense of her cousins and of rivers and of her great-grandmother's teacups, would like to pledge her a picnic on a river with fried chicken and her hair uncombed, would like to give her *home* for her birthday, but we live differently now and I can promise her nothing like that. I give her a xylophone and a sundress from Madeira, and promise to tell her a funny story.

[1967]

Reading and Responding

1. When someone asks you where you're from, how do you answer? Do you feel like you're really from some particular place, or is your routine answer just a way to make conversation? Explain.
2. Use metaphors to describe the voice or tone of the essay: What clothes is the writing wearing? What is the weather in this essay? What kind of music is this writing most like?
3. Use metaphors to describe, in particular, the rhythm of Didion's sentences: fast or slow, hard or soft, like a clarinet or like a drum, and so on.
4. Find a sentence in this essay that seems to match something in your experience or your thinking; then find a sentence that seems quite different from your experience or your thinking. Copy down each sentence, and explain your choices in a paragraph.

Working Together

1. Outline this piece by using the TRIAC scheme. What do you notice? What slot does Didion fill most often? What slot does she fill least? What does this tell you about the experience of reading her? What's demanded?

5

2. Take a piece of paper and draw a line down the middle from top to bottom. On the left side, write "Los Angeles—husband and I and baby." On the right side, write "Central Valley—where my family is." Now as a group, start listing the characteristics of these two places as you see them described.

3. Within your group, discuss whether you have a sense of home. If you don't have a sense of home, can you figure out why you don't? If you do have a sense of home, how do you account for that? Write a group paragraph that describes the responses in your group.

Rethinking and Rewriting

1. Write an essay of your own called "On Going Home."
2. Write an essay that talks about how your experience differs from Didion's. Show how you're not similar. Or write an essay that shows how your experience actually echoes Didion's; show how your experience and Didion's agree in substantial ways. Whatever direction you take, make sure that your essay talks about your experience in clear, detailed ways, and make sure that your essay discusses your experience in comparison to Didion's.
3. At the end of her essay Didion wishes she could give her daughter a sense of home, but she cannot. So the essay ends by expressing sadness and regret. Write an essay of your own that aims to cheer up Joan Didion. Tell her why feeling less attachment to home might actually be a good thing.
4. Re-create a day (or part of a day) at home. Or re-create a time when you actually felt at home. Pack your essay with descriptions of that place and time.

"SETTLING DOWN"

Scott Russell Sanders

> *After writing several novels early in his career, Scott Sanders won the Associated Writing Programs Award in Creative Nonfiction for his collection of personal essays* The Paradise of Bombs *(1987). He has since published two more essay collections,* Secrets of the Universe *(1992) and* Staying Put *(1993), from which this essay is taken.*

Two friends arrived at our house for supper one May evening along with the first rumblings of thunder. As Ruth and I sat talking with them on our front porch, we had to keep raising our voices a notch to make ourselves heard above the gathering storm. The birds, more discreet, had already hushed. The huge elm beside our door began to sway, limbs creaking, leaves hissing. Black sponges of clouds blotted up the light, fooling the street lamps into coming on early. Above the trees and rooftops, the murky southern sky crackled with lightning. Now and again we heard the pop of a transformer as a bolt struck the power lines in our neighborhood. The pulses of thunder came faster and faster, until they merged into a continuous roar.

We gave up on talking. The four of us, all Midwesterners teethed on thunderstorms, sat down there on the porch to our meal of lentil soup, cheddar cheese, bread warm from the oven, sliced apples and strawberries. We were lifting the first spoonfuls to our mouths when a stroke of lightning burst so nearby that it seemed to suck away the air, and the lights flickered out, plunging the whole street into darkness.

After we had caught our breath, we laughed—respectfully, as one might laugh at the joke of a giant. The sharp smell of ozone and the musty smell of damp earth mingled with the aroma of bread. A chill of pleasure ran up my spine. I lit a pair of candles on the table, and the flames rocked in the gusts of wind.

In the time it took for butter to melt on a slice of bread, the wind fell away, the elm stopped thrashing, the lightning let up, and the thunder ceased. The sudden stillness was more exciting than the earlier racket. A smoldering yellow light came into the sky, as though the humid air had caught fire. We gazed at one another over the steady candle flames and knew without exchanging a word what this eerie lull could mean.

"Maybe we should go into the basement," Ruth suggested.⁵

"And leave this good meal?" one of our friends replied.

The wail of a siren broke the stillness—not the lesser cry of ambulance or fire engine or squad car, but the banshee howl of the civil defense siren at the park a few blocks away.

"They must have sighted one," I said.

"We could take the food down with us on a tray," Ruth told our guests.

"It's up to you," I told them. "We can go to the basement like   _10_
sensible people, or we can sit here like fools and risk our necks."

"What do you want to do?" one of them asked me.

"You're the guests."

"You're the hosts."

"I'd like to stay here and see what comes," I told them.

Ruth frowned at me, but there we stayed, savoring our food and the   _15_
sulphurous light. Eventually the siren quit. When my ears stopped ringing,
I could hear the rushing of a great wind, like the whoosh of a waterfall.
An utter calm stole over me. The hair on my neck bristled. My nostrils
flared. Heat rose in my face as though the tip of a wing had raked over it.

Although I found myself, minutes later, still in the chair, the faces of
my wife and friends gleaming in the candlelight, for a spell I rode the
wind, dissolved into it, and there was only the great wind, rushing.

The tornado missed us by half a mile. It did not kill anyone in our
vicinity, but it ripped off chimneys, toyed with cars, and plucked up a fat
old maple by the roots.

Prudent folks would have gone to the basement. I do not recommend our decision; I merely report it. Why the others tarried on the porch
I cannot say, but what kept me there was a mixture of curiosity and awe. I
had never seen the whirling black funnel except in cautionary films, where
it left a wake of havoc and tears. And now here was that tremendous
power, paying us a visit. When a god comes calling, no matter how bad
its reputation, would you go hide? If the siren had announced the sighting
of a dragon, I would have sat there just the same, hoping to catch a glimpse
of the spiked tail or fiery breath.

As a boy in Ohio I knew a farm family, the Millers, who not only
saw but suffered from three tornadoes. The father, mother, and two sons
were pulling into their driveway after church when the first tornado
hoisted up their mobile home, spun it around, and carried it off. With the
insurance money, they built a small frame house on the same spot. Several
years later, a second tornado peeled off the roof, splintered the garage, and
rustled two cows. The younger of the sons, who was in my class at school,
told me that he had watched from the barn as the twister passed through,
"And it never even mussed up my hair." The Millers rebuilt again, raising
a new garage on the old foundation and adding another story to the house.
That upper floor was reduced to kindling by a third tornado, which also
pulled out half the apple trees and slurped water from the stock pond.
Soon after that I left Ohio, snatched away by college as forcefully as by any
cyclone. Last thing I heard, the family was preparing to rebuild yet again.

Why did the Millers refuse to budge? I knew them well enough to   _20_
say they were neither stupid nor crazy. After the garage disappeared, the
father hung a sign from the mailbox that read: TORNADO ALLEY. He
figured the local terrain would coax future whirlwinds in their direction.
Then why not move? Plain stubbornness was a factor. These were people

who, once settled, might have remained at the foot of a volcano or on the bank of a flood-prone river or beside an earthquake fault. They had relatives nearby, helpful neighbors, jobs and stores and school within a short drive, and those were all good reasons to stay. But the main reason, I believe, was because the Millers had invested so much of their lives in the land, planting orchards and gardens, spreading manure on the fields, digging ponds, building sheds, seeding pastures. Out back of the house were groves of walnuts, hickories, and oaks, all started by hand from acorns and nuts. Honeybees zipped out from a row of white hives to nuzzle clover in the pasture. April through October, perennial flowers in the yard pumped out a fountain of blossoms. This farm was not just so many acres of dirt, easily exchanged for an equal amount elsewhere; it was a particular place, intimately known, worked on, dreamed over, cherished.

Psychologists tell us that we answer trouble with one of two impulses, either fight or flight. I believe that the Millers' response to tornadoes and my own keen expectancy on the porch arose from a third instinct, that of staying put. When the pain of leaving behind what we know outweighs the pain of embracing it, or when the power we face is overwhelming and neither fight nor flight will save us, there may be salvation in sitting still. And if salvation is impossible, then at least before perishing we may gain a clearer vision of where we are. By sitting still I do not mean the paralysis of dread, like that of a rabbit frozen beneath the dive of a hawk. I mean something like reverence, a respectful waiting, a deep attentiveness to forces much greater than our own. If indulged only for a moment, as in my case on the porch, this reverent impulse may amount to little; but if sustained for months and years, as by the Millers on their farm, it may yield marvels. The Millers knew better than to fight a tornado, and they chose not to flee. Instead they devoted themselves, season after season, to patient labor. Instead of withdrawing, they gave themselves more fully. Their commitment to the place may have been foolhardy, but it was also grand. I suspect that most human achievements worth admiring are the result of such devotion.

These tornado memories dramatize a choice we are faced with constantly: whether to go or stay, whether to move to a situation that is safer, richer, easier, more attractive, or to stick where we are and make what we can of it. If the shine goes off our marriage, our house, our car, do we trade it for a new one? If the fertility leaches out of our soil, the creativity out of our job, the money out of our pocket, do we start over somewhere else? There are voices enough, both inner and outer, urging us to deal with difficulties by pulling up stakes and heading for new territory. I know them well, for they have been calling to me all my days. I wish to raise here a contrary voice, to say a few words on behalf of standing your ground, confronting the powers, going deeper.

In a poem written not long before he leapt from a bridge over the Mississippi River, John Berryman ridiculed those who asked about his "roots" ("as if I were a *plant*"), and he articulated something like a credo for the dogma of rootlessness:

> Exile is in our time like blood. Depend on
> interior journeys taken anywhere.
>
> I'd rather live in Venice or Kyoto,
> except for the languages, but
> O really I don't care where I live or have lived.
> Wherever I am, young Sir, my wits about me,
>
> memory blazing, I'll cope & make do.

It is a bold claim, but also a hazardous one. For all his wits, Berryman in the end failed to cope well enough to stave off suicide. The truth is, none of us can live by wits alone. For even the barest existence, we depend on the labors of other people, the fruits of the earth, the inherited goods of our given place. If our interior journeys are cut loose entirely from that place, then both we and the neighborhood will suffer.

Exile usually suggests banishment, a forced departure from one's homeland. Famines and tyrants and wars do indeed force entire populations to flee; but most people who move, especially within the industrialized world, do so by choice. Salman Rushdie chose to leave his native India for England, where he has written a series of brilliant books from the perspective of a cultural immigrant. Like many writers, he has taken his own condition to represent not merely a possibility but a norm. In the essays of *Imaginary Homelands* he celebrates "the migrant sensibility," whose development he regards as "one of the central themes of this century of displaced persons." Rushdie has also taken this condition to represent something novel in history:

> The effect of mass migrations has been the creation of radically new types of human being: people who root themselves in ideas rather than places, in memories as much as in material things; people who have been obliged to define themselves—because they are so defined by others—by their otherness; people in whose deepest selves strange fusions occur, unprecedented unions between what they were and where they find themselves.

In the history of America, that description applies just as well to the Pilgrims in Plymouth, say, or to Swiss homesteading in Indiana, to Chinese trading in California, to former slaves crowding into cities on the Great Lakes, or to Seminoles driven onto reservations a thousand miles from their traditional land. Displaced persons are abundant in our century, but hardly a novelty.

Claims for the virtues of shifting ground are familiar and seductive to   *25* Americans, this nation of restless movers. From the beginning, our heroes have been sailors, explorers, cowboys, prospectors, speculators, backwoods ramblers, rainbow-chasers, vagabonds of every stripe. Our Promised Land has always been over the next ridge or at the end of the trail, never under our feet. One hundred years after the official closing of the frontier, we have still not shaken off the romance of unlimited space. If we fish out a stream or wear out a field, or if the smoke from a neighbor's chimney begins to crowd the sky, why, off we go to a new stream, a fresh field, a clean sky. In our national mythology, the worst fate is to be trapped on a farm, in a village, in the sticks, in some dead-end job or unglamorous marriage or played-out game. Stand still, we are warned, and you die. Americans have dug the most canals, laid the most rails, built the most roads and airports of any nation. In the newspaper I read that, even though our sprawling system of interstate highways is crumbling, the president has decided that we should triple it in size, and all without raising our taxes a nickel. Only a populace drunk on driving, a populace infatuated with the myth of the open road, could hear such a proposal without hooting.

So Americans are likely to share Rushdie's enthusiasm for migration, for the "hybridity, impurity, intermingling, the transformation that comes of new and unexpected combinations of human beings, cultures, ideas, politics, movies, songs." Everything about us is mongrel, from race to language, and we are stronger for it. Yet we might respond more skeptically when Rushdie says that "to be a migrant is, perhaps, to be the only species of human being free of the shackles of nationalism (to say nothing of its ugly sister, patriotism)." Lord knows we could do with less nationalism (to say nothing of its ugly siblings, racism, religious sectarianism, or class snobbery). But who would pretend that a history of migration has immunized the United States against bigotry? And even if, by uprooting ourselves, we shed our chauvinism, is that all we lose?

In this hemisphere, many of the worst abuses—of land, forests, animals, and communities—have been carried out by "people who root themselves in ideas rather than places." Rushdie claims that "migrants must, of necessity, make a new imaginative relationship with the world, because of the loss of familiar habitats." But migrants often pack up their visions and values with the rest of their baggage and carry them along. The Spaniards devastated Central and South America by imposing on this New World the religion, economics, and politics of the Old. Colonists brought slavery with them to North America, along with smallpox and Norway rats. The Dust Bowl of the 1930s was caused not by drought but by the transfer onto the Great Plains of farming methods that were suitable to wetter regions. The habit of our industry and commerce has been to force identical schemes onto differing locales, as though the mind were a cookie-cutter and the land were dough.

I quarrel with Rushdie because he articulates as eloquently as anyone the orthodoxy that I wish to counter: the belief that movement is inherently good, staying put is bad; that uprooting brings tolerance, while rootedness breeds intolerance; that imaginary homelands are preferable to geographical ones; that to be modern, enlightened, fully of our time is to be displaced. Wholesale dis-placement may be inevitable; but we should not suppose that it occurs without disastrous consequences for the earth and for ourselves. People who root themselves in places are likelier to know and care for those places than are people who root themselves in ideas. When we cease to be migrants and become inhabitants, we might begin to pay enough heed and respect to where we are. By settling in, we have a chance of making a durable home for ourselves, our fellow creatures, and our descendants. . . .

Half a century ago, in *A Sand County Almanac,* Aldo Leopold gave us an ecological standard for judging our actions: "A thing is right when it tends to preserve the integrity, stability, and beauty of the biotic community. It is wrong when it tends otherwise." We can only apply that standard if, in every biotic community, there are residents who keep watch over what is preserved and what is lost, who see the beauty that escapes the frame of the tourist's windshield or the investor's spreadsheet. "The problem," Leopold observed, "is how to bring about a striving for harmony with land among a people many of whom have forgotten there is any such thing as land, among whom education and culture have become almost synonymous with landlessness."

The question is not whether land belongs to us, through titles registered in a courthouse, but whether we belong to the land, through our loyalty and awareness. In the preface to his *The Natural History and Antiquities of Selborne,* the eighteenth-century English vicar, Gilbert White, notes that a comprehensive survey of England might be compiled if only "stationary men would pay some attention to the districts on which they reside." Every township, every field and creek, every mountain and forest on Earth would benefit from the attention of stationary men and women. No one has understood this need better than Gary Snyder: 30

> One of the key problems in American society now, it seems to me, is people's lack of commitment to any given place—which, again, is totally unnatural and outside of history. Neighborhoods are allowed to deteriorate, landscapes are allowed to be stripmined, because there is nobody who will live there and take responsibility; they'll just move on. The reconstruction of a people and of a life in the United States depends in part on people, neighborhood by neighborhood, county by county, deciding to stick it out and make it work where they are, rather than flee.

We may not have forty years, let alone forty thousand, to reconcile our mythology with our ecology. If we are to reshape our way of thinking to fit the way of things . . . many more of us need to *know* our local ground, walk over it, care for it, fight for it, bear it steadily in mind.

But if you stick in one place, won't you become a stick-in-the-mud? If you stay put, won't you be narrow, backward, dull? You might. I have met ignorant people who never moved; and I have also met ignorant people who never stood still. Committing yourself to a place does not guarantee that you will become wise, but neither does it guarantee that you will become parochial. Who knows better the limitations of a province or a culture than the person who has bumped into them time and again? The history of settlement in my own district and the continuing abuse of land hereabouts provoke me to rage and grief. I know the human legacy here too well to glamorize it.

To become intimate with your home region, to know the territory as well as you can, to understand your life as woven into the local life does not prevent you from recognizing and honoring the diversity of other places, cultures, ways. On the contrary, how can you value other places if you do not have one of your own? If you are not yourself *placed,* then you wander the world like a sightseer, a collector of sensations, with no gauge for measuring what you see. Local knowledge is the grounding for global knowledge. Those who care about nothing beyond the confines of their parish are in truth parochial, and are at least mildly dangerous to their parish; on the other hand, those who *have* no parish, those who navigate ceaselessly among postal zones and area codes, those for whom the world is only a smear of highways and bank accounts and stores, are a danger not just to their parish but to the planet.

Since birth, my children have been surrounded by images of the earth as viewed from space, images that I first encountered when I was in my twenties. Those photographs show vividly what in our sanest moments we have always known—that the earth is a closed circle, lovely and rare. On the wall beside me as I write there is a poster of the big blue marble encased in its white swirl of clouds. That is one pole of my awareness; but the other pole is what I see through my window. I try to keep both in sight at once.

For all my convictions, I still have to wrestle with the fear—in myself, in my children, and in some of my neighbors—that our place is too remote from the action. This fear drives many people to pack their bags and move to some resort or burg they have seen on television, leaving behind what they learn to think of as the boondocks. I deal with my own unease by asking just what action I am remote *from*—a stock market? a debating chamber? a drive-in mortuary? The action that matters, the work of nature and community, goes on everywhere.

Since Copernicus we have known better than to see the earth as the center of the universe. Since Einstein, we have learned that there is no center; or alternatively, that any point is as good as any other for observing the world. I take this to be roughly what medieval theologians meant when they defined God as a circle whose circumference is nowhere and whose center is everywhere. I find a kindred lesson in the words of the Zen master, Thich Nhat Hanh: "This spot where you sit is your own spot. It is on this very spot and in this very moment that you can become enlightened. You don't have to sit beneath a special tree in a distant land." There are no privileged locations. If you stay put, your place may become a holy center, not because it gives you special access to the divine, but because in your stillness you hear what might be heard anywhere. All there is to see can be seen from anywhere in the universe, if you know how to look; and the influence of the entire universe converges on every spot.

Except for the rare patches of wilderness, every place on earth has been transformed by human presence. "Ecology becomes a more complex but far more interesting science," René Dubos observes in *The Wooing of Earth,* "when human aspirations are regarded as an integral part of the landscape." Through "long periods of intimate association between human beings and nature," Dubos argues, landscape may take on a "quality of blessedness." The intimacy is crucial: the understanding of how to dwell in a place arises out of a sustained conversation between people and land. When there is no conversation, when we act without listening, when we impose our desires without regard for the qualities or needs of our place, then landscape may be cursed rather than blessed by our presence.

If our fidelity to place is to help renew and preserve our neighborhoods, it will have to be informed by what Wendell Berry calls "an ecological intelligence: a sense of the impossibility of acting or living alone or solely in one's own behalf, and this rests in turn upon a sense of the order upon which any life depends and of the proprieties of place within that order." Proprieties of place: actions, words, and values that are *proper* to your home ground. I think of my home ground as a series of nested rings, with house and marriage and family at the center, surrounded by the wider and wider hoops of neighborhood and community, the bioregion within walking distance of my door, the wooded hills and karst landscape of southern Indiana, the watershed of the Ohio River, and so on outward—and inward—to the ultimate source.

The longing to become an inhabitant rather than a drifter sets me against the current of my culture, which nudges everyone into motion. Newton taught us that a body at rest tends to stay at rest, unless acted on by an outside force. We are acted on ceaselessly by outside forces—advertising, movies, magazines, speeches—and also by the inner force of biology. I am not immune to their pressure. Before settling in my present home, I lived in seven states and two countries, tugged from place to place in childhood by my father's work and in early adulthood by my own. This itinerant life is so common among the people I know that I have been slow to conceive of an alternative. Only by knocking against the golden calf of mobility, which looms so large and shines so brightly, have I come to realize that it is hollow. Like all idols, it distracts us from the true divinity.

The ecological argument for staying put may be easier for us to see than the spiritual one, worried as we are about saving our skins. Few of us worry about saving our souls, and fewer still imagine that the condition of our souls has anything to do with the condition of our neighborhoods. Talk about enlightenment makes us jittery because it implies that we pass our ordinary days in darkness. You recall the scene in *King Lear* when blind and wretched old Gloucester, wishing to commit suicide, begs a young man to lead him to the brink of a cliff. The young man is Gloucester's son, Edgar, who fools the old man into thinking they have come to a high bluff at the edge of the sea. Gloucester kneels, then tumbles forward onto the level ground; on landing, he is amazed to find himself alive. He is transformed by the fall. Blind, at last he is able to see his life clearly; despairing, he discovers hope. To be enlightened, he did not have to leap to someplace else; he only had to come hard against the ground where he already stood.

My friend Richard, who wears a white collar to his job, recently   40
bought forty acres of land that had been worn out by the standard local regimen of chemicals and corn. Evenings and weekends, he has set about restoring the soil by spreading manure, planting clover and rye, and filling the eroded gullies with brush. His pond has gathered geese, his young orchard has tempted deer, and his nesting boxes have attracted swallows and bluebirds. Now he is preparing a field for the wildflowers and prairie grasses that once flourished here. Having contemplated this work since he was a boy, Richard will not be chased away by fashions or dollars or tornadoes. On a recent airplane trip he was distracted from the book he was reading by thoughts of renewing the land. So he sketched on the flyleaf a plan of labor for the next ten years. Most of us do not have forty acres to care for, but that should not keep us from sowing and tending local crops.

I think about Richard's ten-year vision when I read a report chronicling the habits of computer users who, apparently, grow impatient if they have to wait more than a second for their machine to respond. I use a computer, but I am wary of the haste it encourages. Few answers that matter will come to us in a second; some of the most vital answers will not come in a decade, or a century.

When the chiefs of the Iroquois nation sit in council, they are sworn to consider how their decisions will affect their descendants seven generations into the future. Seven generations! Imagine our politicians thinking beyond the next opinion poll, beyond the next election, beyond their own lifetimes, two centuries ahead. Imagine our bankers, our corporate executives, our advertising moguls weighing their judgments on that scale. Looking seven generations into the future, could a developer pave another farm? Could a farmer spray another pound of poison? Could the captain of an oil tanker flush his tanks at sea? Could you or I write checks and throw switches without a much greater concern for what is bought and sold, what is burned?

As I write this, I hear the snarl of earthmovers and chain saws a mile away destroying a farm to make way for another shopping strip. I would rather hear a tornado, whose damage can be undone. The elderly woman who owned the farm had it listed in the National Register, then willed it to her daughters on condition they preserve it. After her death, the daughters, who live out of state, had the will broken, so the land could be turned over to the chain saws and earthmovers. The machines work around the clock. Their noise wakes me at midnight, at three in the morning, at dawn. The roaring abrades my dreams. The sound is a reminder that we are living in the midst of a holocaust. I do not use the word lightly. The earth is being pillaged, and every one of us, willingly or grudgingly, is taking part. We ask how sensible, educated, supposedly moral people could have tolerated slavery or the slaughter of Jews. Similar questions will be asked about us by our descendants, to whom we bequeath an impoverished planet. They will demand to know how we could have been party to such waste and ruin. They will have good reason to curse our memory.

What does it mean to be alive in an era when the earth is being devoured, and in a country which has set the pattern for that devouring? What are we called to do? I think we are called to the work of healing, both inner and outer: healing of the mind through a change in consciousness, healing of the earth through a change in our lives. We can begin that work by learning how to abide in a place. I am talking about an active commitment, not a passive lingering. If you stay with a husband or wife out of laziness rather than love, that is inertia, not marriage. If you stay put through cowardice rather than conviction, you will have no strength to act. Strength comes, healing comes, from aligning yourself with the grain of your place and answering to its needs.

"The man who is often thinking that it is better to be somewhere else   45
than where he is excommunicates himself," we are cautioned by Thoreau, that notorious stay-at-home. The metaphor is religious: to withhold yourself from where you are is to be cut off from communion with the source. It has taken me half a lifetime of searching to realize that the likeliest path to the ultimate ground leads through my local ground. I mean the land itself, with its creeks and rivers, its weather, seasons, stone outcroppings, and all the plants and animals that share it. I cannot have a spiritual center without having a geographical one; I cannot live a grounded life without being grounded in a *place*.

In belonging to a landscape, one feels a rightness, at-homeness, a knitting of self and world. This condition of clarity and focus, this being fully present, is akin to what the Buddhists call mindfulness, what Christian contemplatives refer to as recollection, what Quakers call centering down. I am suspicious of any philosophy that would separate this-worldly from other-worldly commitment. There is only one world, and we participate in it here and now, in our flesh and our place.

Reading and Responding

1. Describe Sanders's voice. Does he remind you of anyone you know, for example? How old does the voice sound? What clothes do you imagine Sanders wearing? Is he angry, sad, self-satisfied, passionate? What other

kinds of writing or language does this remind you of? How does Sanders's voice differ from Didion's voice, or Lopez's, or Blew's?

2. What kind of reader does Sanders assume or require you to be? What
do you have to be willing to do? What he does he assume you know
or want to know?

Working Together

1. The thesis of this essay is simple: It's good to "stay put." List the different arguments, images, quotations, and stories Sanders uses to support
this claim. Then assume that you were going to argue with him. What
argument would you have to make to disagree with him?
2. Agree or disagree: Do you think it's good to stay put? Have you stayed
put in your life, or have you moved around a lot?

Rethinking and Rewriting

1. On the basis of the class discussion and a rereading of the essay, write
an essay of your own agreeing or disagreeing with Sanders. Draw on
both your experience and your reading.
2. Compare Sanders's essay with Kathleen Norris's essay "The Beautiful
Places." What is their common claim? How do they differ in their
approach to this claim?
3. Write an essay developing the following idea, using other essays in this
anthology: Staying put is a fundamentally ecological idea; all truly
ecological thinking depends in some way or another on staying put,
remaining connected to a single, beloved place.

Essay Topics for Chapter 9

1. Introduce readers to a literal place that you know well and that you
return to (either literally or in memory) in order to recharge your
batteries and find some genuine rest. Talk about your previous experience in this place, and make readers understand how the place works
to calm people and awaken a new sense of attention. Tell people what
they'd see and hear and smell, as well as how they'd feel. Be as clear as
you can be about your descriptions and their effects (but if you want to
be a little fuzzy about the actual directions for getting to this place—if
you want to keep the place secret—that's OK).
2. Describe your ideal place to live. Describe the physical layout of the
area, describe your residence, describe what you'd see out the windows
and hear when the door's open. Tell how close your neighbors are, tell
whether a city is nearby, tell how close you are to your work, and so on.
3. Take any essay in this chapter (you decide which essay) and assume that
it has not been read by one of the other writers in this chapter (you
decide which other writer). For example, you could take Mary Clear-

man Blew's essay "The Sow in the River" and assume that Joan Didion hasn't read it. Your task would be to talk to Didion, telling her about this essay she has not read and explaining to her whether you think she'd find the essay interesting or similar to her own. And you'd end by explaining why you think Didion should read more of Blew, or why Didion probably wouldn't like Blew's work.

4. Think about what it means to be connected to a place (as in "Once More to the Lake" or "Sacred and Ancestral Ground") and what it means to be connected to a community (clearest in "Settling Down"). Write an essay that discusses the places and the communities you feel connected to. Are they entirely separate allegiances, or do they overlap in any ways? Use any two of the essays in this chapter to help you explain what you mean.

5. Compare "Once More to the Lake" to either "The Sow in the River" or "On Going Home." On the basis of the two essays you compare, explain what makes places valuable to people. Or if you wish, choose any two other essays in this chapter for your comparison.

6. Find a book of Mary Oliver's poems. Compare two of the poems in the book you find to "Five a.m. in the Pinewoods," and use these three poems to explain the kind of experience that draws Mary Oliver's attention. Make copies of the two other poems you use and staple them to your essay.

7. Write a dialogue between any two of the writers in this chapter, assuming that each has just finished reading the writing of the other. As a suggestion only, think about what Henry Thoreau would say to Mary Oliver after reading her poem, then imagine what she'd say in reply, and so on. Use the dialogue to suggest what you think the two writers have in common and/or what you think might cause them to argue.

10

The Nature of Nature

The origin of a word can often tell us something useful about its meaning. Looking at the word *nature* gives us *native, nation, national, natural*—all of them carrying that *nat-* opening, which comes from the Latin word for "birth." In fact, this notion of birth is probably the deepest, oldest meaning attached to the word *nature*. Nature is what gives birth to us; nature is that wholeness of matter and space and time that holds and sustains us.

This understanding of nature encourages us to see everything—rocks, soil, water, sky, animals, insects, people—as seamless and connected, part of a larger whole (something so large we have trouble imagining it). Yet our human birthright also gives us consciousness, the conviction that we are each of us separate from everything and everyone else. We certainly feel like unique individuals, and most of our actions and judgments assume that we are free, separate, independent people. So we're able to see ourselves as part of nature—part of the wealth of offspring—and we're able to see ourselves as separate from nature, individually and collectively capable of manipulating nature, examining it, probing it, and (presumably, eventually) understanding it. But it is duality, doubleness, that forms the center of our relationship with and inside nature.

The readings in this chapter all acknowledge (in one way or another) this fundamental duality, this tension between inclusion and separation. Many of them try to solve it. That is, many of these writers offer resolutions of the tension at its center: nature as the source of all consciousness, nature as the source of religious experience and (potentially) religious understanding; or nature as mute, indifferent, radically nonintelligent—nature only as what we say it is, the result only of biological, astronomical, and geological processes, all of which are themselves essentially mechanical.

Some of the writers in this chapter say we go to nature and find God (however one defines God); others say we go to nature and find only what we can make of it. The resolutions change from writer to writer. But all of these writers are bound by language. All of them try to understand nature in human terms, which are, after all, the only terms we have ready to hand. And all of these writers recognize that how we understand nature strongly influences how we act toward nature.

"EXPOSTULATION AND REPLY" AND "THE TABLES TURNED"

William Wordsworth

> *In these two brief poems from* The Lyrical Ballads, *the English romantic poet William Wordsworth dramatizes a playful debate between his younger, restless self and his schoolmaster, Matthew. Wordsworth gives himself the best lines—several famous phrases defending his idleness and praising the natural world. (See also "To My Sister" in chapter 7.)*

To allow the reader to compare these two poems more easily, we have placed them side by side on pages 342–343. In this instance only, therefore, the questions and suggestions for discussion and writing appear *before* the reading, on page 341.

Reading and Responding

1. In a few sentences, summarize Matthew's (the teacher's) arguments for the value of books and education.
2. In a few sentences, summarize Wordsworth's arguments for leaving books behind and going out into the natural world.
3. Which person gets the better of the argument? Use two sentences to explain why you think so.

Working Together

1. Divide the class into half. One half: Do a five-minute freewrite arguing that everyone in the class should work harder at school: writing more drafts of papers, doing more and better reading, partying not at all.
2. The other half: Do a five-minute freewrite arguing that everyone should forget about school entirely and head out for the hills, hiking, skiing, mountain-biking, or bird-watching.
3. Then switch positions. In another short freewrite, argue the other side.
4. In a discussion, share your arguments and update the debate Wordsworth gives readers in these two poems.

Rethinking and Rewriting

1. Write a paper with this as an epigraph: "One impulse from a vernal wood / May teach you more of man, / Of moral evil and of good, / Than all the sages can." Be concrete. Draw on personal experience.
2. Write a paper seriously defending Matthew's position. Argue as strongly and effectively as you can that, though nature has much to teach, books are necessary and important, too (including the books of Wordsworth's own poetry). Include in your discussion at least one book (one you read or that was read to you) that you feel you couldn't do without.

"EXPOSTULATION AND REPLY"

[Composed 1798.—Published 1798.]

'Why, William, on that old grey stone,
Thus for the length of half a day,
Why, William, sit you thus alone,
And dream your time away?

'Where are your books?—that light bequeathed   5
To Beings else forlorn and blind!
Up! up! and drink the spirit breathed
From dead men to their kind.

'You look round on your Mother Earth,
As if she for no purpose bore you;   10
As if you were her first-born birth,
And none had lived before you!'

One morning thus, by Esthwaite lake,
When life was sweet, I knew not why,
To me my good friend Matthew spake,   15
And thus I made reply:

'The eye—it cannot choose but see;
We cannot bid the ear be still;
Our bodies feel, where'er they be,
Against or with our will.   20

'Nor less I deem that there are Powers
Which of themselves our minds impress;
That we can feed this mind of ours
In a wise passiveness.

'Think you, 'mid all this mighty sum   25
Of things for ever speaking,
That nothing of itself will come,
But we must still be seeking?

'—Then ask not wherefore, here, alone,
Conversing as I may,   30
I sit upon this old grey stone,
And dream my time away.'

"THE TABLES TURNED
An Evening Scene on the Same Subject"

[Composed 1798.—Published 1798.]

Up! up! my Friend, and quit your books;
Or surely you'll grow double:
Up! up! my Friend, and clear your looks;
Why all this toil and trouble?

The sun, above the mountain's head,   5
A freshening lustre mellow
Through all the long green fields has spread,
His first sweet evening yellow.

Books! 'tis a dull and endless strife:
Come, hear the woodland linnet,   10
How sweet his music! on my life,
There's more of wisdom in it.

And hark! how blithe the throstle sings!
He, too, is no mean preacher:
Come forth into the light of things,   15
Let Nature be your Teacher.

She has a world of ready wealth,
Our minds and hearts to bless—
Spontaneous wisdom breathed by health,
Truth breathed by cheerfulness.   20

One impulse from a vernal wood
May teach you more of man,
Of moral evil and of good,
Than all the sages can.

Sweet is the lore which Nature brings;   25
Our meddling intellect
Mis-shapes the beauteous forms of things:—
We murder to dissect.

Enough of Science and of Art;
Close up those barren leaves;   30
Come forth, and bring with you a heart
That watches and receives.

"WALKING"

Henry David Thoreau

> Walking *was written shortly before Henry David Thoreau's death from tuberculosis in 1862 and was published a month later in the* Atlantic Monthly. *It also appeared as part of a larger collection of essays,* Excursions, *published in 1863. This excerpt contains Thoreau's famous statement that "in Wildness is the preservation of the World." (See also "Where I Lived and What I Lived For" in chapter 9.)*

Before You Read
When you're feeling frustrated or perplexed, what do you typically do to take your mind off your troubles? Are you a walker? Write a quick half page answering this question *before* you read this piece. Then once you've read the piece, come back to your half page and write another half page talking about how you'd recover what Thoreau calls "hope and the future." If you'd not take a walk, what would you do?

The West of which I speak is but another name for the Wild; and what I have been preparing to say is, that in Wildness is the preservation of the World. Every tree sends its fibres forth in search of the Wild. The cities import it at any price. Men plough and sail for it. From the forest and wilderness come the tonics and barks which brace mankind. Our ancestors were savages. The story of Romulus and Remus being suckled by a wolf is not a meaningless fable. The founders of every State which has risen to eminence have drawn their nourishment and vigor from a similar wild source. It was because the children of the Empire were not suckled by the wolf that they were conquered and displaced by the children of the Northern forests who were.

I believe in the forest, and in the meadow, and in the night in which the corn grows. We require an infusion of hemlock-spruce or arborvitæ in our tea. There is a difference between eating and drinking for strength and from mere gluttony. The Hottentots eagerly devour the marrow of the koodoo and other antelopes raw, as a matter of course. Some of our Northern Indians eat raw the marrow of the Arctic reindeer, as well as various other parts, including the summits of the antlers, as long as they are soft. And herein, perchance, they have stolen a march on the cooks of Paris. They get what usually goes to feed the fire. This is probably better than stall-fed beef and slaughter-house pork to make a man of. Give me a wildness whose glance no civilization can endure,—as if we lived on the marrow of koodoos devoured raw.

There are some intervals which border the strain of the wood-thrush, to which I would migrate,—wild lands where no settler has squatted; to which, methinks, I am already acclimated.

The African hunter Cummings tells us that the skin of the eland, as well as that of most other antelopes just killed, emits the most delicious perfume of trees and grass. I would have every man so much like a wild antelope, so much a part and parcel of Nature, that his very person should thus sweetly advertise our senses of his presence, and remind us of those parts of Nature which he most haunts. I feel no disposition to be satirical, when the trapper's coat emits the odor of musquash even; it is a sweeter scent to me than that which commonly exhales from the merchant's or the scholar's garments. When I go into their wardrobes and handle their vestments, I am reminded of no grassy plains and flowery meads which they have frequented, but of dusty merchants' exchanges and libraries rather.

A tanned skin is something more than respectable, and perhaps olive   5 is a fitter color than white for a man,—a denizen of the woods. "The pale white man!" I do not wonder that the African pitied him. Darwin the naturalist says, "A white man bathing by the side of a Tahitian was like a plant bleached by the gardener's art, compared with a fine, dark green one, growing vigorously in the open fields."

Ben Jonson exclaims,—

"How near to good is what is fair!"

So I would say,—

How near to good is what is *wild!*

Life consists with wildness. The most alive is the wildest. Not yet subdued to man, its presence refreshes him. One who pressed forward incessantly and never rested from his labors, who grew fast and made infinite demands on life, would always find himself in a new country or wilderness, and surrounded by the raw material of life. He would be climbing over the prostrate stems of primitive forest-trees.

Hope and the future for me are not in lawns and cultivated fields, not in towns and cities, but in the impervious and quaking swamps. When, formerly, I have analyzed my partiality for some farm which I had contemplated purchasing, I have frequently found that I was attracted solely by a few square rods of impermeable and unfathomable bog,—a natural sink in one corner of it. That was the jewel which dazzled me. I derive more of my subsistence from the swamps which surround my native town than from the cultivated gardens in the village. There are no richer parterres to my eyes than the dense beds of dwarf andromeda (*Cassandra calyculata*) which cover these tender places on the earth's surface. Botany cannot go farther than tell me the names of the shrubs which grow there,—the high-blueberry, panicled andromeda, lamb-kill, azalea, and rhodora,—all standing in the quaking sphagnum. I often think that I should like to have my house front on this mass of dull red bushes, omitting other flower plots and borders, transplanted spruce and trim box, even gravelled walks,—to have this fertile spot under my windows, not a few imported barrow-fulls of soil only to cover the sand which was thrown out in digging the cellar.

Why not put my house, my parlor, behind this plot, instead of behind that meagre assemblage of curiosities, that poor apology for a Nature and Art, which I call my front-yard? It is an effort to clear up and make a decent appearance when the carpenter and mason have departed, though done as much for the passer-by as the dweller within. The most tasteful front-yard fence was never an agreeable object of study to me; the most elaborate ornaments, acorn-tops, or what not, soon wearied and disgusted me. Bring your sills up to the very edge of the swamp, then, (though it may not be the best place for a dry cellar,) so that there be no access on that side to citizens. Front-yards are not made to walk in, but, at most, through, and you could go in the back way.

Yes, though you may think me perverse, if it were proposed to me to dwell in the neighborhood of the most beautiful garden that ever human art contrived, or else of a Dismal swamp, I should certainly decide for the swamp. How vain, then, have been all your labors, citizens, for me!

My spirits infallibly rise in proportion to the outward dreariness. Give me the ocean, the desert or the wilderness! In the desert, pure air and solitude compensate for want of moisture and fertility. The traveller Burton says of it,—"Your *morale* improves; you become frank and cordial, hospitable and single-minded. . . . In the desert, spirituous liquors excite only disgust. There is a keen enjoyment in a mere animal existence." They who have been travelling long on the steppes of Tartary say,—"On reëntering cultivated lands, the agitation, perplexity, and turmoil of civilization oppressed and suffocated us; the air seemed to fail us, and we felt every moment as if about to die of asphyxia." When I would recreate myself, I seek the darkest wood, the thickest and most interminable, and, to the citizen, most dismal swamp. I enter a swamp as a sacred place,—a *sanctum sanctorum*. There is the strength, the marrow of Nature. The wild-wood covers the virgin mould,—and the same soil is good for men and for trees. A man's health requires as many acres of meadow to his prospect as his farm does loads of muck. There are the strong meats on which he feeds. A town is saved, not more by the righteous men in it than by the woods and swamps that surround it. A township where one primitive forest waves above, while another primitive forest rots below,—such a town is fitted to raise not only corn and potatoes, but poets and philosophers for the coming ages. In such a soil grew Homer and Confucius and the rest, and out of such a wilderness comes the Reformer eating locusts and wild honey.

To preserve wild animals implies generally the creation of a forest for them to dwell in or resort to. So it is with man. A hundred years ago they sold bark in our streets peeled from our own woods. In the very aspect of those primitive and rugged trees, there was, methinks, a tanning principle which hardened and consolidated the fibres of men's thoughts. Ah! already I shudder for these comparatively degenerate days of my native village, when you cannot collect a load of bark of good thickness,—and we no longer produce tar and turpentine.

10

Reading and Responding

1. Underline the key sentences and passages.
2. Write the passages you underlined in item 1 on a sheet of paper, in order.
3. Consider these questions: How are the passages you noted in items 1 and 2 connected? What is their sequence? What pattern do they fit into? What transitions connect them?

Working Together

1. Design a poster illustrating the idea that "in wildness is the preservation of the world."
2. Design a thirty-second commercial illustrating the idea noted in item 1.

Rethinking and Rewriting

1. Write an essay in which you imagine what the world would be like if everybody believed that Thoreau is right: In wildness *is* the preservation of the world. If we really believed that, what would we do?
2. Write an essay arguing that "in *tameness* is the preservation of the world." Be serious.
3. Using this selection as your primary source (and using at least one quotation from it), write a two- or three-page "Introduction to Thoreau" that tells new readers whatever you think they need to know in order to read and appreciate what Thoreau has to say.

"GOD'S GRANDEUR"

Gerard Manley Hopkins

> *Gerard Manley Hopkins was a nineteenth-century, English Jesuit priest who wrote a handful of brief, unusual religious poems and one longer work,* The Wreck of the Deutschland. *Partly because of its intense, difficult language, his poetry wasn't published until 1918, almost 30 years after his death. This sonnet, like much of Hopkins's poetry, evokes the presence of God everywhere in nature.*

The world is charged with the grandeur of God.
  It will flame out, like shining from shook foil;°
  It gathers to a greatness, like the ooze of oil°
Crushed. Why do men then now not reck his rod?°
Generations have trod, have trod, have trod;   5
  And all is seared with trade; bleared, smeared with toil;
  And wears man's smudge and shares man's smell: the soil
Is bare now, nor can foot feel, being shod.

And for all this, nature is never spent.
  There lives the dearest freshness deep down things;   10
And though the last lights off the black West went
  Oh, morning, at the brown brink eastward, springs—
Because the Holy Ghost over the bent
  World broods with warm breast and with ah! bright wings.

Reading and Responding

1. Write down the one or two lines you clearly understand or understand the best.
2. Write down one or two lines you don't understand at all, that confuse you, that make no sense.
3. What makes the hard language hard to understand? What's the connection between the easier lines and the hard lines?
4. Why would anyone make a connection between nature and God? Do you think or feel that the two are connected in any way? Write about this for half a page at least.

---

like shining from shook foil: Hopkins was probably thinking of the ways that tinsel or gold foil reflects light, but the image of aluminum foil certainly works here too.
the ooze of oil / Crushed: Don't think of petroleum oil here; think instead of olive oil.
Why do men then now not reck his rod? In other words, why don't people recognize God's rule or discipline?

Working Together

1. Do a five-minute freewrite responding to this question: What's your reaction when you go to the door and the person standing there asks you, "Do you believe that Christ is your personal savior"? Or what's your reaction when you hear a friend talking about religion, trying to get you to attend his or her church? Or what's your reaction when you turn on Sunday morning religious services on television? Briefly share and discuss these freewrites.

2. Take careful notes as your class goes through "God's Grandeur" line by line, paraphrasing Hopkins's basic meaning and explaining the many poetic devices he uses to convey that meaning.

3. In light of the class lecture and discussion, do a second five-minute freewrite answering this question: What's the connection between Hopkins's poem and the opening question about your reaction to religious language? Why should you begin a discussion of Hopkins's poem by first freewriting about this question?

4. Assume that this poem offers a two-part argument, with white space signaling the two parts. As a group, write a two-paragraph summary that captures the argument.

Rethinking and Rewriting

1. Write a paper arguing that the difficult language Hopkins uses is good and necessary, that it's appropriate and effective for expressing this kind of subject. In your analysis, consider the nature of religious language you grew up with and the religious language you hear all around you now.

2. Write about a time or an experience when you felt that nature held more than you could rationally explain.

3. Write an essay that explains why Hopkins's poem speaks for you or why it does not. Quote the poem at least twice to help clarify your discussion.

"CLEAR NIGHT"

Charles Wright

> *A native of Pickwick Dam, Tennessee, Charles Wright is both a translator (of the work of Italian poet Eugenio Montale) and an acclaimed poet. He has been awarded two Fulbrights as well as a fellowship from the Guggenheim Foundation, and his* Country Music: Selected Early Poems *won the 1983 American Book Award in Poetry. The poem reprinted here comes from* China Trace *(1977), a book-long sequence of individual poems addressing our deepest questions of identity and nature.*

As You Read

As you read this poem, assume that the first four lines are "scene setting," the second four are "the request," and the last four are "the response." Pick the section you understand most clearly and summarize it. Write questions that, if answered, would help you understand the other sections.

Clear night, thumb-top of a moon, a back-lit sky.
Moon-fingers lay down their same routine
On the side deck and the threshold, the white keys and the black keys.
Bird hush and bird song. A cassia flower falls.

I want to be bruised by God.   5
I want to be strung up in a strong light and singled out.
I want to be stretched, like music wrung from a dropped seed.
I want to be entered and picked clean.

And the wind says "What?" to me.
And the castor beans, with their little earrings of death, say "What?" to   10
    me.
And the stars start out on their cold slide through the dark.
And the gears notch and the engines wheel.

Reading and Responding

Write about the night sky. Write about a time when you've actually been able to see the Milky Way. Write about the first time you saw it. Or write about the first time you learned where to find the North Star. Or write about how the night sky is just darkness for you, something without any particular meaning or significance.

Working Together

1. Pick out any two lines that hit you hard. Read these two to your group. Once you've all read, talk about how and why you chose as you did.

2. As a group, pretend that you're Charles Wright and you wrote this poem. What prompted you to write it? Why didn't you write an essay? (*Hint:* "I don't know" is not a useful answer. Think about length, think about impact, think about stanzas versus paragraphs, and the like.)

Rethinking and Rewriting

1. Read "Clear Night" and then read "God's Grandeur" (also in this chapter). Next, write a dialogue between Hopkins and Wright; start your dialogue by assuming that they've just read the other's poem. Make sure that the dialogue makes clear what you think they share as well as the ways you think they differ or disagree.
2. If "Clear Night" seems to speak for you and for your experience, write an essay explaining that.
3. If "Clear Night" does not seem to speak for you, rewrite the poem so that it comes closer to doing so. In your rewrite, try to stay with the original cadence and sentence structures. Also turn in a one-page discussion that explains your rewritten version.

"THE OPEN BOAT"

Stephen Crane

Although he died of tuberculosis at only age 28, Stephen Crane wrote hundreds of newspaper articles, stories, and poems, as well as six novels, including The Red Badge of Courage *(1895). Crane's classic short story, "The Open Boat" (1898)—based on his own experience being shipwrecked off the Florida coast—asks whether nature is at all concerned about the fate of human beings.*

As You Read

As you read, mark any place in the story where the narrator steps out and directly tells us what he thinks the story means—any piece of explicit commentary.

A Tale Intended to Be after the Fact:° Being the Experience of Four Men

from the Sunk Steamer Commodore

I

None of them knew the color of the sky. Their eyes glanced level and were fastened upon the waves that swept toward them. These waves were of the hue of slate, save for the tops, which were of foaming white, and all of the men knew the colors of the sea. The horizon narrowed and widened, and dipped and rose, and at all times its edge was jagged with waves that seemed thrust up in points like rocks.

Many a man ought to have a bathtub larger than the boat which here rode upon the sea. These waves were most wrongfully and barbarously abrupt and tall, and each froth-top was a problem in small-boat navigation.

The cook squatted in the bottom, and looked with both eyes at the six inches of gunwale which separated him from the ocean. His sleeves were rolled over his fat forearms, and the two flaps of his unbuttoned vest dangled as he bent to bail out the boat. Often he said, "Gawd! that was a narrow clip." As he remarked it he invariably gazed eastward over the broken sea.

The oiler, steering with one of the two oars in the boat, sometimes raised himself suddenly to keep clear of water that swirled in over the stern. It was a thin little oar, and it seemed often ready to snap.

after the Fact: Crane also published a newspaper account of this experience in the January 7, 1897, issue of the New York *Press.*

The correspondent, pulling at the other oar, watched the waves and   5
wondered why he was there.

The injured captain, lying in the bow, was at this time buried in that
profound dejection and indifference which comes, temporarily at least, to
even the bravest and most enduring when, willy-nilly, the firm fails, the
army loses, the ship goes down. The mind of the master of a vessel is
rooted deep in the timbers of her, though he command for a day or a
decade; and this captain had on him the stern impression of a scene in the
grays of dawn of seven turned faces, and later a stump of a topmast with a
white ball on it, that slashed to and fro at the waves, went low and lower,
and down. Thereafter there was something strange in his voice. Although
steady, it was deep with mourning, and of a quality beyond oration or
tears.

"Keep 'er a little more south, Billie," said he.

"A little more south, sir," said the oiler in the stern.

A seat in his boat was not unlike a seat upon a bucking broncho, and
by the same token a broncho is not much smaller. The craft pranced and
reared and plunged like an animal. As each wave came, and she rose for it,
she seemed like a horse making at a fence outrageously high. The manner
of her scramble over these walls of water is a mystic thing, and, moreover,
at the top of them were ordinarily these problems in white water, the foam
racing down from the summit of each wave requiring a new leap, and a
leap from the air. Then, after scornfully bumping a crest, she would slide
and race and splash down a long incline, and arrive bobbing and nodding
in front of the next menace.

A singular disadvantage of the sea lies in the fact that after successfully   10
surmounting one wave you discover that there is another behind it just as
important and just as nervously anxious to do something effective in the
way of swamping boats. In a ten-foot dinghy one can get an idea of the
resources of the sea in the line of waves that is not probable to the average
experience, which is never at sea in a dinghy. As each slaty wall of water
approached, it shut all else from the view of the men in the boat, and it
was not difficult to imagine that this particular wave was the final outburst
of the ocean, the last effort of the grim water. There was a terrible grace
in the move of the waves, and they came in silence, save for the snarling
of the crests.

In the wan light the faces of the men must have been gray. Their
eyes must have glinted in strange ways as they gazed steadily astern. Viewed
from a balcony, the whole thing would, doubtless, have been weirdly picturesque. But the men in the boat had no time to see it, and if they had
had leisure, there were other things to occupy their minds. The sun swung
steadily up the sky, and they knew it was broad day because the color of
the sea changed from slate to emerald-green streaked with amber lights,
and the foam was like tumbling snow. The process of the breaking day was
unknown to them. They were aware only of this effect upon the color of
the waves that rolled toward them.

In disjointed sentences the cook and the correspondent argued as to
the difference between a life-saving station and a house of refuge. The
cook had said: "There's a house of refuge just north of the Mosquito Inlet
Light, and as soon as they see us they'll come off in their boat and pick
us up."

"As soon as who see us?" said the correspondent.

"The crew," said the cook.

"Houses of refuge don't have crews," said the correspondent. "As I   *15*
understand them, they are only places where clothes and grub are stored
for the benefit of shipwrecked people. They don't carry crews."

"Oh, yes, they do," said the cook.

"No, they don't," said the correspondent.

"Well, we're not there yet, anyhow," said the oiler, in the stern.

"Well," said the cook, "perhaps it's not a house of refuge that I'm
thinking of as being near Mosquito Inlet Light; perhaps it's a life-saving
station."

"We're not there yet," said the oiler in the stern.   *20*

II

As the boat bounced from the top of each wave the wind tore
through the hair of the hatless men, and as the craft plopped her stern
down again the spray slashed past them. The crest of each of these waves
was a hill, from the top of which the men surveyed for a moment a broad
tumultuous expanse, shining and wind-riven. It was probably splendid, it
was probably glorious, this play of the free sea, wild with lights of emerald
and white and amber.

"Bully good thing it's an on-shore wind," said the cook. "If not,
where would we be? Wouldn't have a show."

"That's right," said the correspondent.

The busy oiler nodded his assent.

Then the captain, in the bow, chuckled in a way that expressed   *25*
humor, contempt, tragedy, all in one. "Do you think we've got much of a
show now, boys?" said he.

Whereupon the three were silent, save for a trifle of hemming and
hawing. To express any particular optimism at this time they felt to be
childish and stupid, but they all doubtless possessed this sense of the situation in their minds. A young man thinks doggedly at such times. On the
other hand, the ethics of their condition was decidedly against any open
suggestion of hopelessness. So they were silent.

"Oh, well," said the captain, soothing his children, "we'll get ashore
all right."

But there was that in his tone which made them think; so the oiler
quoth, "Yes! if this wind holds."

The cook was bailing. "Yes! if we don't catch hell in the surf."

Canton-flannel° gulls flew near and far. Sometimes they sat down on *30*
the sea, near patches of brown seaweed that rolled over the waves with a
movement like carpets on a line in a gale. The birds sat comfortably in
groups, and they were envied by some in the dinghy, for the wrath of the
sea was no more to them than it was to a covey of prairie chickens a
thousand miles inland. Often they came very close and stared at the men
with black bead-like eyes. At these times they were uncanny and sinister
in their unblinking scrutiny, and the men hooted angrily at them, telling
them to be gone. One came, and evidently decided to alight on the top of
the captain's head. The bird flew parallel to the boat and did not circle,
but made short sidelong jumps in the air in chicken fashion. His black eyes
were wistfully fixed upon the captain's head. "Ugly brute," said the oiler
to the bird. "You look as if you were made with a jackknife." The cook
and the correspondent swore darkly at the creature. The captain naturally
wished to knock it away with the end of the heavy painter, but he did not
dare do it, because anything resembling an emphatic gesture would have
capsized this freighted boat; and so, with his open hand, the captain gently
and carefully waved the gull away. After it had been discouraged from the
pursuit the captain breathed easier on account of his hair, and others
breathed easier because the bird struck their minds at this time as being
somehow gruesome and ominous.

In the meantime the oiler and the correspondent rowed; and also
they rowed. They sat together in the same seat, and each rowed an oar.
Then the oiler took both oars; then the correspondent took both oars,
then the oiler; then the correspondent. They rowed and they rowed. The
very ticklish part of the business was when the time came for the reclining
one in the stern to take his turn at the oars. By the very last star of truth,
it is easier to steal eggs from under a hen than it was to change seats in the
dinghy. First the man in the stern slid his hand along the thwart and moved
with care, as if he were of Sèvres.° Then the man in the rowing-seat slid
his hand along the other thwart. It was all done with the most extraordinary care. As the two sidled past each other, the whole party kept watchful
eyes on the coming wave, and the captain cried: "Look out, now! Steady,
there!"

The brown mats of seaweed that appeared from time to time were
like islands, bits of earth. They were travelling, apparently, neither one way
nor the other. They were, to all intents, stationary. They informed the
men in the boat that it was making progress slowly toward the land.

The captain, rearing cautiously in the bow after the dinghy soared on
a great swell, said that he had seen the lighthouse at Mosquito Inlet. Presently the cook remarked that he had seen it. The correspondent was at the
oars then, and for some reason he too wished to look at the lighthouse;

Canton-flannel: A type of cotton fabric commonly woven in Canton, China.
Sèvres: A kind of fine porcelain. So the man moves with great carefulness.

but his back was toward the far shore, and the waves were important, and for some time he could not seize an opportunity to turn his head. But at last there came a wave more gentle than the others, and when at the crest of it he swiftly scoured the western horizon.

"See it?" said the captain.

"No," said the correspondent, slowly; "I didn't see anything."   *35*

"Look again," said the captain. He pointed. "It's exactly in that direction."

At the top of another wave the correspondent did as he was bid, and this time his eyes chanced on a small, still thing on the edge of the swaying horizon. It was precisely like the point of a pin. It took an anxious eye to find a lighthouse so tiny.

"Think we'll make it, Captain?"

"If this wind holds and the boat don't swamp, we can't do much else," said the captain.

The little boat, lifted by each towering sea and splashed viciously by   *40* the crests, made progress that in the absence of seaweed was not apparent to those in her. She seemed just a wee thing wallowing, miraculously top up, at the mercy of five oceans. Occasionally a great spread of water, like white flames, swarmed into her.

"Bail her, cook," said the captain, serenely.

"All right, Captain," said the cheerful cook.

III

It would be difficult to describe the subtle brotherhood of men that was here established on the seas. No one said that it was so. No one mentioned it. But it dwelt in the boat, and each man felt it warm him. They were a captain, an oiler, a cook, and a correspondent, and they were friends—friends in a more curiously iron-bound degree than may be common. The hurt captain, lying against the water jar in the bow, spoke always in a low voice and calmly; but he could never command a more ready and swiftly obedient crew than the motley three of the dinghy. It was more than a mere recognition of what was best for the common safety. There was surely in it a quality that was personal and heart-felt. And after this devotion to the commander of the boat, there was this comradeship, that the correspondent, for instance, who had been taught to be cynical of men, knew even at the time was the best experience of his life. But no one said that it was so. No one mentioned it.

"I wish we had a sail," remarked the captain. "We might try my overcoat on the end of an oar, and give you two boys a chance to rest." So the cook and the correspondent held the mast and spread wide the overcoat; the oiler steered; and the little boat made good way with her new rig. Sometimes the oiler had to scull sharply to keep a sea from breaking into the boat, but otherwise sailing was a success.

Meanwhile the lighthouse had been growing slowly larger. It had *45* now almost assumed color, and appeared like a little gray shadow on the sky. The man at the oars could not be prevented from turning his head rather often to try for a glimpse of this little gray shadow.

At last, from the top of each wave, the men in the tossing boat could see land. Even as the lighthouse was an upright shadow on the sky, this land seemed but a long black shadow on the sea. It certainly was thinner than paper. "We must be about opposite New Smyrna," said the cook, who had coasted this shore often in schooners. "Captain, by the way, I believe they abandoned that life-saving station there about a year ago."

"Did they?" said the captain.

The wind slowly died away. The cook and the correspondent were not now obliged to slave in order to hold high the oar. But the waves continued their old impetuous swooping at the dinghy, and the little craft, no longer underway, struggled woundily over them. The oiler or the correspondent took the oars again.

Shipwrecks are *apropos* of nothing. If men could only train for them and have them occur when the men had reached pink condition, there would be less drowning at sea. Of the four in the dinghy none had slept any time worth mentioning for two days and two nights previous to embarking in the dinghy, and in the excitement of clambering about the deck of a foundering ship they had also forgotten to eat heartily.

For these reasons, and for others, neither the oiler nor the correspon- *50* dent was fond of rowing at this time. The correspondent wondered ingenuously how in the name of all that was sane could there be people who thought it amusing to row a boat. It was not an amusement; it was a diabolical punishment, and even a genius of mental aberrations could never conclude that it was anything but a horror to the muscles and a crime against the back. He mentioned to the boat in general how the amusement of rowing struck him, and the weary-faced oiler smiled in full sympathy. Previously to the foundering, by the way, the oiler had worked a double watch in the engine-room of the ship.

"Take her easy, now, boys," said the captain. "Don't spend yourselves. If we have to run a surf you'll need all your strength, because we'll sure have to swim for it. Take your time."

Slowly the land arose from the sea. From a black line it became a line of black and a line of white—trees and sand. Finally the captain said that he could make out a house on the shore. "That's the house of refuge, sure," said the cook. "They'll see us before long, and come out after us."

The distant lighthouse reared high. "The keeper ought to be able to make us out now, if he's looking through a glass," said the captain. "He'll notify the life-saving people."

"None of those other boats could have got ashore to give word of the wreck," said the oiler, in a low voice, "else the life-boat would be out hunting us."

Slowly and beautifully the land loomed out of the sea. The wind   *55*
came again. It had veered from the northeast to the southeast. Finally a
new sound struck the ears of the men in the boat. It was the low thunder
of the surf on the shore. "We'll never be able to make the lighthouse now,"
said the captain. "Swing her head a little more north, Billie."

"A little more north, sir," said the oiler.

Whereupon the little boat turned her nose once more down the wind,
and all but the oarsman watched the shore grow. Under the influence of
this expansion doubt and direful apprehension were leaving the minds of
the men. The management of the boat was still most absorbing, but it could
not prevent a quiet cheerfulness. In an hour, perhaps, they would be ashore.

Their backbones had become thoroughly used to balancing in the
boat, and they now rode this wild colt of a dinghy like circus men. The
correspondent thought that he had been drenched to the skin, but happening to feel in the top pocket of his coat, he found therein eight cigars.
Four of them were soaked with sea-water; four were perfectly scatheless.
After a search, somebody produced three dry matches; and thereupon the
four waifs rode impudently in their little boat and, with an assurance of an
impending rescue shining in their eyes, puffed at the big cigars, and judged
well and ill of all men. Everybody took a drink of water.

IV

"Cook," remarked the captain, "there don't seem to be any signs of
life about your house of refuge."

"No," replied the cook. "Funny they don't see us!"   *60*

A broad stretch of lowly coast lay before the eyes of the men. It was
of low dunes topped with dark vegetation. The roar of the surf was plain,
and sometimes they could see the white lip of a wave as it spun up the
beach. A tiny house was blocked out black upon the sky. Southward, the
slim lighthouse lifted its little gray length.

Tide, wind, and waves were swinging the dinghy northward. "Funny
they don't see us," said the men.

The surf's roar was here dulled, but its tone was nevertheless thunderous and mighty. As the boat swam over the great rollers the men sat
listening to this roar. "We'll swamp sure," said everybody.

It is fair to say here that there was not a life-saving station within
twenty miles in either direction; but the men did not know this fact, and
in consequence they made dark and opprobrious remarks concerning the
eyesight of the nation's life-savers. Four scowling men sat in the dinghy
and surpassed records in the invention of epithets.

"Funny they don't see us."   *65*

The light-heartedness of a former time had completely faded. To their
sharpened minds it was easy to conjure pictures of all kinds of incompetency
and blindness and, indeed, cowardice. There was the shore of the populous
land, and it was bitter and bitter to them that from it came no sign.

"Well," said the captain, ultimately, "I suppose we'll have to make a try for ourselves. If we stay out here too long, we'll none of us have strength left to swim after the boat swamps."

And so the oiler, who was at the oars, turned the boat straight for the shore. There was a sudden tightening of muscles. There was some thinking.

"If we don't all get ashore," said the captain—"if we don't all get ashore, I suppose you fellows know where to send news of my finish?"

They then briefly exchanged some addresses and admonitions. As for   70
the reflections of the men, there was a great deal of rage in them. Perchance they might be formulated thus: "If I am going to be drowned—if I am going to be drowned—if I am going to be drowned, why, in the name of the seven mad gods who rule the sea, was I allowed to come thus far and contemplate sand and trees? Was I brought here merely to have my nose dragged away as I was about to nibble the sacred cheese of life? It is preposterous. If this old ninny-woman, Fate, cannot do better than this, she should be deprived of the management of men's fortunes. She is an old hen who knows not her intention. If she has decided to drown me, why did she not do it in the beginning and save me all this trouble? The whole affair is absurd. . . . But no; she cannot mean to drown me. She dare not drown me. She cannot drown me. Not after all this work." Afterward the man might have had an impulse to shake his fist at the clouds. "Just you drown me, now, and then hear what I call you!"

The billows that came at this time were more formidable. They seemed always just about to break and roll over the little boat in a turmoil of foam. There was a preparatory and long growl in the speech of them. No mind unused to the sea would have concluded that the dinghy could ascend these sheer heights in time. The shore was still afar. The oiler was a wily surfman. "Boys," he said, swiftly, "she won't live three minutes more, and we're too far out to swim. Shall I take her to sea again, Captain?"

"Yes; go ahead!" said the captain.

This oiler, by a series of quick miracles and fast and steady oarsmanship, turned the boat in the middle of the surf and took her safely to sea again.

There was a considerable silence as the boat bumped over the furrowed sea to deeper water. Then somebody in gloom spoke: "Well, anyhow, they must have seen us from the shore by now."

The gulls went in slanting flight up the wind toward the gray, deso-   75
late east. A squall, marked by dingy clouds and clouds brick-red, like smoke from a burning building, appeared from the southeast.

"What do you think of those life-saving people? Ain't they peaches?"

"Funny they haven't seen us."

"Maybe they think we're out here for sport! Maybe they think we're fishin'. Maybe they think we're damned fools."

It was a long afternoon. A changed tide tried to force them southward, but wind and wave said northward. Far ahead, where coast-line, sea, and sky formed their mighty angle, there were little dots which seemed to indicate a city on the shore.

"St. Augustine?"

The captain shook his head. "Too near Mosquito Inlet."

And the oiler rowed, and then the correspondent rowed; then the oiler rowed. It was a weary business. The human back can become the seat of more aches and pains than are registered in books for the composite anatomy of a regiment. It is a limited area, but it can become the theatre of innumerable muscular conflicts, tangles, wrenches, knots, and other comforts.

"Did you ever like to row, Billie?" asked the correspondent.

"No," said the oiler; "hang it!"

When one exchanged the rowing-seat for a place in the bottom of the boat, he suffered a bodily depression that caused him to be careless of everything save an obligation to wiggle one finger. There was cold sea-water swashing to and fro in the boat, and he lay in it. His head, pillowed on a thwart, was within an inch of the swirl of a wave-crest, and sometimes a particularly obstreperous sea came inboard and drenched him once more. But these matters did not annoy him. It is almost certain that if the boat had capsized he would have tumbled comfortably out upon the ocean as if he felt sure that it was a great soft mattress.

"Look! There's a man on the shore!"

"Where?"

"There? See 'im? See 'im?"

"Yes, sure! He's walking along."

"Now he's stopped. Look! He's facing us!"

"He's waving at us!"

"So he is! By thunder!"

"Ah, now we're all right! Now we're all right! There'll be a boat out here for us in half an hour."

"He's going on. He's running. He's going up to that house there."

The remote beach seemed lower than the sea, and it required a searching glance to discern the little black figure. The captain saw a floating stick, and they rowed to it. A bath towel was by some weird chance in the boat, and, tying this on the stick, the captain waved it. The oarsman did not dare turn his head, so he was obliged to ask questions.

"What's he doing now?"

"He's standing still again. He's looking, I think. . . . There he goes again—toward the house. . . . Now he's stopped again."

"Is he waving at us?"

"No, not now; he was, though."

"Look! There comes another man!"

"He's running."

"Look at him go, would you!"

"Why, he's on a bicycle. Now he's met the other man. They're both waving at us. Look!"

"There comes something up the beach."

"What the devil is that thing?" *105*

"Why, it looks like a boat."

"Why, certainly, it's a boat."

"No; it's on wheels."

"Yes, so it is. Well, that must be the life-boat. They drag them along shore on a wagon."

"That's the life-boat, sure." *110*

"No, by God, it's—it's an omnibus."

"I tell you it's a life-boat."

"It is not! It's an omnibus. I can see it plain. See? One of these big hotel omnibuses."

"By thunder, you're right. It's an omnibus, sure as fate. What do you suppose they are doing with an omnibus? Maybe they are going around collecting the life-crew, hey?"

"That's it, likely. Look! There's a fellow waving a little black flag. *115* He's standing on the steps of the omnibus. There come those other two fellows. Now they're all talking together. Look at the fellow with the flag. Maybe he ain't waving it!"

"That ain't a flag, is it? That's his coat. Why, certainly, that's his coat."

"So it is; it's his coat. He's taken it off and is waving it around his head. But would you look at him swing it!"

"Oh, say, there isn't any life-saving station there. That's just a winter-resort hotel omnibus that has brought over some of the boarders to see us drown."

"What's that idiot with the coat mean? What's he signaling, anyhow?"

"It looks as if he were trying to tell us to go north. There must be a *120* life-saving station up there."

"No; he thinks we're fishing. Just giving us a merry hand. See? Ah, there, Willie!"

"Well, I wish I could make something out of those signals. What do you suppose he means?"

"He don't mean anything; he's just playing."

"Well, if he'd just signal us to try the surf again, or to go to sea and wait, or go north, or go south, or go to hell, there would be some reason in it. But look at him! He just stands there and keeps his coat revolving like a wheel. The ass!"

"There come more people." *125*

"Now there's quite a mob. Look! Isn't that a boat?"

"Where? Oh, I see where you mean. No, that's no boat."

"That fellow is still waving his coat."

"He must think we like to see him do that. Why don't he quit it? It don't mean anything."

"I don't know. I think he is trying to make us go north. It must be *130* that there's a life-saving station there somewhere."

"Say, he ain't tired yet. Look at 'im wave!"

"Wonder how long he can keep that up. He's been revolving his coat ever since he caught sight of us. He's an idiot. Why aren't they getting men to bring a boat out? A fishing boat—one of those big yawls—could come out here all right. Why don't he do something?"

"Oh, it's all right now."

"They'll have a boat out here for us in less than no time, now that they've seen us."

A faint yellow tone came into the sky over the low land. The shadows on the sea slowly deepened. The wind bore coldness with it, and the men began to shiver.

135

"Holy smoke!" said one, allowing his voice to express his impious mood, "if we keep on monkeying out here! If we've got to flounder out here all night!"

"Oh, we'll never have to stay here all night! Don't you worry. They've seen us now, and it won't be long before they'll come chasing out after us."

The shore grew dusky. The man waving a coat blended gradually into this gloom, and it swallowed in the same manner the omnibus and the group of people. The spray, when it dashed uproariously over the side, made the voyagers shrink and swear like men who were being branded.

"I'd like to catch the chump who waved the coat. I feel like socking him one, just for luck."

"Why? What did he do?"

140

"Oh, nothing, but then he seemed so damned cheerful."

In the meantime the oiler rowed, and then the correspondent rowed, and then the oiler rowed. Gray-faced and bowed forward, they mechanically, turn by turn, plied the leaden oars. The form of the lighthouse had vanished from the southern horizon, but finally a pale star appeared, just lifting from the sea. The streaked saffron in the west passed before the all-merging darkness, and the sea to the east was black. The land had vanished, and was expressed only by the low and drear thunder of the surf.

"If I am going to be drowned—if I am going to be drowned—if I am going to be drowned, why, in the name of the seven mad gods who rule the sea, was I allowed to come thus far and contemplate sand and trees? Was I brought here merely to have my nose dragged away as I was about to nibble the sacred cheese of life?"

The patient captain, drooped over the water-jar, was sometimes obliged to speak to the oarsman.

"Keep her head up! Keep her head up!"

145

"Keep her head up, sir." The voices were weary and low.

This was surely a quiet evening. All save the oarsman lay heavily and listlessly in the boat's bottom. As for him, his eyes were just capable of noting the tall black waves that swept forward in a most sinister silence, save for an occasional subdued growl of a crest.

The cook's head was on a thwart, and he looked without interest at the water under his nose. He was deep in other scenes. Finally he spoke. "Billie," he murmured, dreamfully, "what kind of pie do you like best?"

V

"Pie!" said the oiler and the correspondent, agitatedly. "Don't talk about those things, blast you!"

"Well," said the cook, "I was just thinking about ham sandwiches, 150 and—"

A night on the sea in an open boat is a long night. As darkness settled finally, the shine of the light, lifting from the sea in the south, changed to full gold. On the northern horizon a new light appeared, a small bluish gleam on the edge of the waters. These two lights were the furniture of the world. Otherwise there was nothing but waves.

Two men huddled in the stern, and distances were so magnificent in the dinghy that the rower was enabled to keep his feet partly warm by thrusting them under his companions. Their legs indeed extended far under the rowing-seat until they touched the feet of the captain forward. Sometimes, despite the efforts of the tired oarsman, a wave came piling into the boat, an icy wave of the night, and the chilling water soaked them anew. They would twist their bodies for a moment and groan, and sleep the dead sleep once more, while the water in the boat gurgled about them as the craft rocked.

The plan of the oiler and the correspondent was for one to row until he lost the ability, and then arouse the other from his sea-water couch in the bottom of the boat.

The oiler plied the oars until his head drooped forward and the overpowering sleep blinded him; and he rowed yet afterward. Then he touched a man in the bottom of the boat, and called his name. "Will you spell me for a little while?" he said meekly.

"Sure, Billie," said the correspondent, awaking and dragging himself 155 to a sitting position. They exchanged places carefully, and the oiler, cuddling down in the sea-water at the cook's side, seemed to go to sleep instantly.

The particular violence of the sea had ceased. The waves came without snarling. The obligation of the man at the oars was to keep the boat headed so that the tilt of the rollers would not capsize her, and to preserve her from filling when the crests rushed past. The black waves were silent and hard to be seen in the darkness. Often one was almost upon the boat before the oarsman was aware.

In a low voice the correspondent addressed the captain. He was not sure that the captain was awake, although this iron man seemed to be always awake. "Captain, shall I keep her making for that light north, sir?"

The same steady voice answered him. "Yes. Keep it about two points off the port bow."

The cook had tied a life-belt around himself in order to get even the warmth which this clumsy cork contrivance could donate, and he seemed almost stove-like when a rower, whose teeth invariably chattered wildly as soon as he ceased his labor, dropped down to sleep.

The correspondent, as he rowed, looked down at the two men sleep-   *160*
ing underfoot. The cook's arm was around the oiler's shoulders, and, with
their fragmentary clothing and haggard faces, they were the babes of the
sea—a grotesque rendering of the old babes in the wood.

Later he must have grown stupid at his work, for suddenly there was
a growling of water, and a crest came with a roar and a swash into the
boat, and it was a wonder that it did not set the cook afloat in his life-belt.
The cook continued to sleep, but the oiler sat up, blinking his eyes and
shaking with the new cold.

"Oh, I'm awful sorry, Billie," said the correspondent, contritely.

"That's all right, old boy," said the oiler, and lay down again and was
asleep.

Presently it seemed that even the captain dozed, and the correspondent thought that he was the one man afloat on all the ocean. The wind
had a voice as it came over the waves, and it was sadder than the end.

There was a long, loud swishing astern of the boat, and a gleaming   *165*
trail of phosphorescence, like blue flame, was furrowed on the black waters. It might have been made by a monstrous knife.

Then there came a stillness, while the correspondent breathed with
open mouth and looked at the sea.

Suddenly there was another swish and another long flash of bluish
light, and this time it was alongside the boat, and might almost have been
reached with an oar. The correspondent saw an enormous fin speed like a
shadow through the water, hurling the crystalline spray and leaving the
long glowing trail.

The correspondent looked over his shoulder at the captain. His face
was hidden, and he seemed to be asleep. He looked at the babes of the sea.
They certainly were asleep. So, being bereft of sympathy, he leaned a little
way to one side and swore softly into the sea.

But the thing did not then leave the vicinity of the boat. Ahead or
astern, on one side or the other, at intervals long or short, fled the long
sparkling streak, and there was to be heard the *whirroo* of the dark fin. The
speed and power of the thing was greatly to be admired. It cut the water
like a gigantic and keen projectile.

The presence of this biding thing did not affect the man with the   *170*
same horror that it would if he had been a picnicker. He simply looked at
the sea dully and swore in an undertone.

Nevertheless, it is true that he did not wish to be alone with the thing.
He wished one of his companions to awake by chance and keep him company with it. But the captain hung motionless over the water-jar and the
oiler and the cook in the bottom of the boat were plunged in slumber.

VI

"If I am going to be drowned—if I am going to be drowned—if
I am going to be drowned, why, in the name of the seven mad gods

who rule the sea, was I allowed to come thus far and contemplate sand and trees?"

During this dismal night, it may be remarked that a man would conclude that it was really the intention of the seven mad gods to drown him, despite the abominable injustice of it. For it was certainly an abominable injustice to drown a man who had worked so hard, so hard. The man felt it would be a crime most unnatural. Other people had drowned at sea since galleys swarmed with painted sails, but still—

When it occurs to a man that nature does not regard him as important, and that she feels she would not maim the universe by disposing of him, he at first wishes to throw bricks at the temple, and he hates deeply the fact that there are no bricks and no temples. Any visible expression of nature would surely be pelleted with his jeers.

Then, if there be no tangible thing to hoot, he feels, perhaps, the   175
desire to confront a personification and indulge in pleas, bowed to one knee, and with hands supplicant, saying, "Yes, but I love myself."

A high cold star on a winter's night is the word he feels that she says to him. Thereafter he knows the pathos of his situation.

The men in the dinghy had not discussed these matters, but each had, no doubt, reflected upon them in silence and according to his mind. There was seldom any expression upon their faces save the general one of complete weariness. Speech was devoted to the business of the boat.

To chime the notes of his emotions, a verse mysteriously entered the correspondent's head. He had even forgotten that he had forgotten this verse, but it suddenly was in his mind.

> A soldier of the Legion lay dying in Algiers;
> There was lack of woman's nursing,
>   there was dearth of woman's tears;
> But a comrade stood beside him,
>   and he took the comrade's hand,
> And he said, "I never more shall see
>   my own, my native land."[1]

In his childhood the correspondent had been made acquainted with the fact that a soldier of the Legion lay dying in Algiers, but he had never regarded it as important. Myriads of his schoolfellows had informed him of the soldier's plight, but the dinning had naturally ended by making him perfectly indifferent. He had never considered it his affair that a soldier of the Legion lay dying in Algiers, nor had it appeared to him as a matter for sorrow. It was less to him than the breaking of a pencil's point.

Now, however, it quaintly came to him as a human, living thing. It   180
was no longer merely a picture of a few throes in the breast of a poet,

---

1. The correspondent is quoting a poem, *Bingen on the Rhine,* by Caroline Norton (1808–1877).

meanwhile drinking tea and warming his feet at the grate; it was an actuality—stern, mournful, and fine.

The correspondent plainly saw the soldier. He lay on the sand with his feet out straight and still. While his pale left hand was upon his chest in an attempt to thwart the going of his life, the blood came between his fingers. In the far Algerian distance, a city of low square forms was set against a sky that was faint with the last sunset hues. The correspondent, plying the oars and dreaming of the slow and slower movements of the lips of the soldier, was moved by a profound and perfectly impersonal comprehension. He was sorry for the soldier of the Legion who lay dying in Algiers.

The thing which had followed the boat and waited had evidently grown bored at the delay. There was no longer to be heard the slash of the cutwater, and there was no longer the flame of the long trail. The light in the north still glimmered, but it was apparently no nearer to the boat. Sometimes the boom of the surf rang in the correspondent's ears, and he turned the craft seaward then and rowed harder. Southward, some one had evidently built a watch-fire on the beach. It was too low and too far to be seen, but it made a shimmering, roseate reflection upon the bluff in back of it, and this could be discerned from the boat. The wind came stronger, and sometimes a wave suddenly raged out like a mountain-cat, and there was to be seen the sheen and sparkle of a broken crest.

The captain, in the bow, moved on his water-jar and sat erect. "Pretty long night," he observed to the correspondent. He looked at the shore. "Those life-saving people take their time."

"Did you see that shark playing around?"

"Yes, I saw him. He was a big fellow, all right."   18.

"Wish I had known you were awake."

Later the correspondent spoke into the bottom of the boat. "Billie!" There was a slow and gradual disentanglement. "Billie, will you spell me?"

"Sure," said the oiler.

As soon as the correspondent touched the cold, comfortable sea-water in the bottom of the boat and had huddled close to the cook's life-belt he was deep in sleep, despite the fact that his teeth played all the popular airs. This sleep was so good to him that it was but a moment before he heard a voice call his name in a tone that demonstrated the last stages of exhaustion. "Will you spell me?"

"Sure, Billie."   19(

The light in the north had mysteriously vanished, but the correspondent took his course from the wide-awake captain.

Later in the night they took the boat farther out to sea, and the captain directed the cook to take one oar at the stern and keep the boat facing the seas. He was to call out if he should hear the thunder of the surf. This plan enabled the oiler and the correspondent to get respite together. "We'll give those boys a chance to get into shape again," said the captain. They curled down and, after a few preliminary chatterings and trembles, slept once more the dead sleep. Neither knew they had bequeathed to the cook the company of another shark, or perhaps the same shark.

As the boat caroused on the waves, spray occasionally bumped over the side and gave them a fresh soaking, but this had no power to break their repose. The ominous slash of the wind and the water affected them as it would have affected mummies.

"Boys," said the cook, with the notes of every reluctance in his voice, "she's drifted in pretty close. I guess one of you had better take her to sea again." The correspondent, aroused, heard the crash of the toppled crests.

As he was rowing, the captain gave him some whiskey-and-water, *195* and this steadied the chills out of him. "If I ever get ashore and anybody shows me even a photograph of an oar—"

At last there was a short conversation.

"Billie! . . . Billie, will you spell me?"

"Sure," said the oiler.

VII

When the correspondent again opened his eyes, the sea and the sky were each of the gray hue of the dawning. Later, carmine and gold was painted upon the waters. The morning appeared finally, in its splendor, with a sky of pure blue, and the sunlight flamed on the tips of the waves.

On the distant dunes were set many little black cottages, and a tall *200* white windmill reared above them. No man, nor dog, nor bicycle appeared on the beach. The cottages might have formed a deserted village.

The voyagers scanned the shore. A conference was held in the boat. "Well," said the captain, "if no help is coming, we might better try a run through the surf right away. If we stay out here much longer we will be too weak to do anything for ourselves at all." The others silently acquiesced in this reasoning. The boat was headed for the beach. The correspondent wondered if none ever ascended the tall wind-tower, and if then they never looked seaward. This tower was a giant, standing with its back to the plight of the ants. It represented in a degree, to the correspondent, the serenity of nature amid the struggles of the individual—nature in the wind, and nature in the vision of men. She did not seem cruel to him then, nor beneficent, nor treacherous, nor wise. But she was indifferent, flatly indifferent. It is, perhaps, plausible that a man in this situation, impressed with the unconcern of the universe, should see the innumerable flaws of his life, and have them taste wickedly in his mind, and wish for another chance. A distinction between right and wrong seems absurdly clear to him, then, in this new ignorance of the grave-edge, and he understands that if he were given another opportunity he would mend his conduct and his words, and be better and brighter during an introduction or at a tea.

"Now, boys," said the captain, "she is going to swamp sure. All we can do is to work her in as far as possible, and then when she swamps, pile out and scramble for the beach. Keep cool now, and don't jump until she swamps sure."

The oiler took the oars. Over his shoulders he scanned the surf. "Captain," he said, "I think I'd better bring her about and keep her head-on to the seas and back her in."

"All right, Billie," said the captain. "Back her in." The oiler swung the boat then, and, seated in the stern, the cook and the correspondent were obliged to look over their shoulders to contemplate the lonely and indifferent shore.

The monstrous inshore rollers heaved the boat high until the men were again enabled to see the white sheets of water scudding up the slanted beach. "We won't get in very close," said the captain. Each time a man could wrest his attention from the rollers, he turned his glance toward the shore, and in the expression of the eyes during this contemplation there was a singular quality. The correspondent, observing the others, knew that they were not afraid, but the full meaning of their glances was shrouded.   *20.*

As for himself, he was too tired to grapple fundamentally with the fact. He tried to coerce his mind into thinking of it, but the mind was dominated at this time by the muscles, and the muscles said they did not care. It merely occurred to him that if he should drown it would be a shame.

There were no hurried words, no pallor, no plain agitation. The men simply looked at the shore. "Now, remember to get well clear of the boat when you jump," said the captain.

Seaward the crest of a roller suddenly fell with a thunderous crash, and the long white comber came roaring down upon the boat.

"Steady now," said the captain. The men were silent. They turned their eyes from the shore to the comber and waited. The boat slid up the incline, leaped at the furious top, bounced over it, and swung down the long back of the wave. Some water had been shipped, and the cook bailed it out.

But the next crest crashed also. The tumbling, boiling flood of white water caught the boat and whirled it almost perpendicular. Water swarmed in from all sides. The correspondent had his hands on the gunwale at this time, and when the water entered at that place he swiftly withdrew his fingers, as if he objected to wetting them.   *21(*

The little boat, drunken with this weight of water, reeled and snuggled deeper into the sea.

"Bail her out, cook! Bail her out!" said the captain.

"All right, Captain," said the cook.

"Now, boys, the next one will do for us sure," said the oiler. "Mind to jump clear of the boat."

The third wave moved forward, huge, furious, implacable. It fairly swallowed the dinghy, and almost simultaneously the men tumbled into the sea. A piece of life-belt had lain in the bottom of the boat, and as the correspondent went overboard he held this to his chest with his left hand.   *21.*

The January water was icy, and reflected immediately that it was colder than he had expected to find it off the coast of Florida. This appeared to his dazed mind as a fact important enough to be noted at the time. The coldness of the water was sad; it was tragic. This fact was somehow mixed and confused with his opinion of his own situation, so that it seemed almost a proper reason for tears. The water was cold.

When he came to the surface he was conscious of little but the noisy water. Afterward he saw his companions in the sea. The oiler was ahead in the race. He was swimming strongly and rapidly. Off to the correspondent's left, the cook's great white and corked back bulged out of the water, and in the rear the captain was hanging with his one good hand to the keel of the overturned dinghy.

There is a certain immovable quality to a shore, and the correspondent wondered at it amid the confusion of the sea.

It seemed also very attractive; but the correspondent knew that it was a long journey, and he paddled leisurely. The piece of life-preserver lay under him, and sometimes he whirled down the incline of a wave as if he were on a hand-sled.

But finally he arrived at a place in the sea where travel was beset with   220
difficulty. He did not pause swimming to inquire what manner of current had caught him, but there his progress ceased. The shore was set before him like a bit of scenery on a stage, and he looked at it and understood with his eyes each detail of it.

As the cook passed, much farther to the left, the captain was calling to him, "Turn over on your back, cook! Turn over on your back and use the oar."

"All right, sir." The cook turned on his back, and, paddling with an oar, went ahead as if he were a canoe.

Presently the boat also passed to the left of the correspondent, with the captain clinging with one hand to the keel. He would have appeared like a man raising himself to look over a board fence if it were not for the extraordinary gymnastics of the boat. The correspondent marvelled that the captain could still hold to it.

They passed on nearer to shore—the oiler, the cook, the captain—and following them went the water-jar, bouncing gaily over the seas.

The correspondent remained in the grip of this strange new enemy,   225
a current. The shore, with its white slope of sand and its green bluff topped with little silent cottages, was spread like a picture before him. It was very near to him then, but he was impressed as one who, in a gallery, looks at a scene from Brittany or Algiers.

He thought: "I am going to drown? Can it be possible? Can it be possible? Can it be possible?" Perhaps an individual must consider his own death to be the final phenomenon of nature.

But later a wave perhaps whirled him out of this small deadly current, for he found suddenly that he could again make progress toward the shore. Later still he was aware that the captain, clinging with one hand to the keel of the dinghy, had his face turned away from the shore and toward him, and was calling his name. "Come to the boat! Come to the boat!"

In his struggle to reach the captain and the boat, he reflected that when one gets properly wearied drowning must really be a comfortable arrangement—a cessation of hostilities accompanied by a large degree of relief; and he was glad of it, for the main thing in his mind for some moments had been horror of the temporary agony; he did not wish to be hurt.

Presently he saw a man running along the shore. He was undressing with most remarkable speed. Coat, trousers, shirt, everything flew magically off him.

"Come to the boat!" called the captain.   230

"All right, Captain." As the correspondent paddled, he saw the captain let himself down to bottom and leave the boat. Then the correspondent performed his one little marvel of the voyage. A large wave caught him and flung him with ease and supreme speed completely over the boat and far beyond it. It struck him even then as an event in gymnastics and a true miracle of the sea. An overturned boat in the surf is not a plaything to a swimming man.

The correspondent arrived in water that reached only to his waist, but his condition did not enable him to stand for more than a moment. Each wave knocked him into a heap, and the undertow pulled at him.

Then he saw the man who had been running and undressing, and undressing and running, come bounding into the water. He dragged ashore the cook, and then waded toward the captain; but the captain waved him away and sent him to the correspondent. He was naked—naked as a tree in winter; but a halo was about his head, and he shone like a saint. He gave a strong pull, and a long drag, and a bully heave at the correspondent's hand. The correspondent, schooled in the minor formulae, said, "Thanks, old man." But suddenly the man cried, "What's that?" He pointed a swift finger. The correspondent said, "Go."

In the shallows, face downward, lay the oiler. His forehead touched sand that was periodically, between each wave, clear of the sea.

The correspondent did not know all that transpired afterward. When   235
he achieved safe ground he fell, striking the sand with each particular part of his body. It was as if he had dropped from a roof, but the thud was grateful to him.

It seems that instantly the beach was populated with men with blankets, clothes, and flasks, and women with coffee-pots and all the remedies sacred to their minds. The welcome of the land to the men from the sea was warm and generous; but a still and dripping shape was carried slowly up the beach, and the land's welcome for it could only be the different and sinister hospitality of the grave.

When it came night, the white waves paced to and fro in the moonlight, and the wind brought the sound of the great sea's voice to the men on the shore, and they felt that they could then be interpreters.

Reading and Responding

After your first reading, quickly summarize the plot.

Working Together

1. What's the moral of this story? How do we know that moral?
2. If this were a television movie, how would the producers change its ending? Why would they do that? What do you think Stephen Crane would say in response to these changes?
3. Construct an alternative interpretation of this story. Accept the facts, but give a different interpretation from the one the narrator gives.
4. What would Gerard Manley Hopkins have said about this story? Henry David Thoreau?

Rethinking and Rewriting

1. Write a short essay simply explaining the theme of this story, illustrating with details from Crane's description of landscape, character, action.
2. Write an essay about a near-death experience or some experience of struggle, hardship, or near-disaster from your own life. In the end, draw some conclusions that seem appropriate to your experience and how you view it now.

"AGAINST NATURE"

Joyce Carol Oates

> *An amazingly prolific writer, Joyce Carol Oates has produced over 25 novels in her career so far, from the realistic to the surrealistic to the gothic— not counting volumes of poetry, essays, and literary criticism. In this striking essay from her 1983 collection,* The Profane Art, *Oates flies in the face of sentimental nature-writing clichés.*

As You Read

When you get to the section beginning "Early Nature memories," stop reading and write for ten minutes on one of your own early memories of nature.

> We soon get through with Nature. She excites an expectation which she cannot satisfy.
>
> THOREAU, *Journal,* 1854

> Sir, if a man has experienced the inexpressible, he is under no obligation to attempt to express it.
>
> SAMUEL JOHNSON

The writer's resistance to Nature.

It has no sense of humor: in its beauty, as in its ugliness, or its neutrality, there is no laughter.

It lacks a moral purpose.

It lacks a satiric dimension, registers no irony.

Its pleasures lack resonance, being accidental; its horrors, even when 5
premeditated, are equally perfunctory, "red in tooth and claw," et cetera.

It lacks a symbolic subtext—excepting that provided by man.

It has no (verbal) language.

It has no interest in ours.

It inspires a painfully limited set of responses in "nature writers"—
REVERENCE, AWE, PIETY, MYSTICAL ONENESS.

It eludes us even as it prepares to swallow us up, books and all.   10

I was lying on my back in the dirt gravel of the towpath beside the Delaware and Raritan Canal, Titusville, New Jersey, staring up at the sky and trying, with no success, to overcome a sudden attack of tachycardia that had come upon me out of nowhere—such attacks are always "out of nowhere," that's their charm—and all around me Nature thrummed with life, the air smelling of moisture and sunlight, the canal reflecting the sky, red-winged blackbirds testing their spring calls; the usual. I'd become the jar in Tennessee, a fictitious center, or parenthesis, aware beyond my erratic heartbeat of the numberless heartbeats of the earth, its pulsing, pumping life, sheer life, incalculable. Struck down in the midst of motion—I'd been jogging a minute before—I was "out of time" like a fallen, stunned boxer, privileged (in an abstract manner of speaking) to be an involuntary witness to the random, wayward, nameless motion on all sides of me.

Paroxysmal tachycardia can be fatal, but rarely; if the heartbeat accelerates to 250–270 beats a minute you're in trouble, but the average attack is about 100–150 beats and mine seemed about average; the trick now was to prevent it from getting worse. Brainy people try brainy strategies, such as thinking calming thoughts, pseudo-mystic thoughts, *If I die now it's a good death,* that sort of thing, *if I die this is a good place and good time;* the idea is to deceive the frenzied heartbeat that, really, you don't care: you hadn't any other plans for the afternoon. The important thing with tachycardia is to prevent panic! you must prevent panic! otherwise you'll have to be taken by ambulance to the closest emergency room, which is not so very nice a way to spend the afternoon, really. So I contemplated the blue sky overhead. The earth beneath my head. Nature surrounding me on all sides; I couldn't quite see it but I could hear it, smell it, sense it, there is something *there,* no mistake about it. Completely oblivious to the predicament of the individual but that's only "natural," after all, one hardly expects otherwise.

When you discover yourself lying on the ground, limp and unresisting, head in the dirt, and, let's face it, helpless, the earth seems to shift forward as a presence; hard, emphatic, not mere surface but a genuine force—there is no other word for it but *presence.* To keep in motion is to keep in time, and to be stopped, stilled, is to be abruptly out of time, in another time dimension perhaps, an alien one, where human language has no resonance. Nothing to be said about it expresses it, nothing touches it, it's an absolute against which nothing human can be measured. . . . Moving through space and time by way of your own volition you inhabit an interior consciousness, a hallucinatory consciousness, it might be said, so long as breath, heartbeat, the body's autonomy hold; when motion is stopped you are jarred out of it. The interior is invaded by the exterior. The outside wants to come in, and only the self's fragile membrane prevents it.

The fly buzzing at Emily's death.

Still, the earth *is* your place. A tidy grave site measured to your size. *15* Or, from another angle of vision, one vast democratic grave.

Let's contemplate the sky. Forget the crazy hammering heartbeat, don't listen to it, don't start counting, remember that there is a clever way of breathing that conserves oxygen as if you're lying below the surface of a body of water breathing through a very thin straw but you *can* breathe through it if you're careful, if you don't panic; one breath and then another and then another, isn't that the story of all lives? careers? Just a matter of breathing. Of course it is. But contemplate the sky, it's there to be contemplated. A mild shock to see it so blank, blue, a thin airy ghostly blue, no clouds to disguise its emptiness. You are beginning to feel not only weight-less but near-bodiless, lying on the earth like a scrap of paper about to be blown off. Two dimensions and you'd imagined you were three! And there's the sky rolling away forever, into infinity—if "infinity" can be "rolled into"—and the forlorn truth is, that's where you're going too. And the lovely blue isn't even blue, is it? isn't even there, is it? a mere optical illusion, isn't it? no matter what art has urged you to believe.

Early Nature memories. Which it's best not to suppress.

. . . Wading, as a small child, in Tonawanda Creek near our house, and afterward trying to tear off, in a frenzy of terror and revulsion, the sticky fat black bloodsuckers that had attached themselves to my feet, par-ticularly between my toes.

. . . Coming upon a friend's dog in a drainage ditch, dead for several days, evidently the poor creature had been shot by a hunter and left to die, bleeding to death, and we're stupefied with grief and horror but can't resist sliding down to where he's lying on his belly, and we can't resist squatting over him, turning the body over.

. . . The raccoon, mad with rabies, frothing at the mouth and tearing at his own belly with his teeth, so that his intestines spill out onto the ground . . . a sight I seem to remember though in fact I did not see. I've been told I did not see.

Consequently, my chronic uneasiness with Nature mysticism; Nature adoration; Nature-as-(moral)-instruction-for-mankind. My doubt that one can, with philosophical validity, address "Nature" as a single coherent noun, anything other than a Platonic, hence discredited, is-ness. My resis-tance to "Nature writing" as a genre, except when it is brilliantly fiction-alized in the service of a writer's individual vision—Thoreau's books and *Journal,* of course, but also, less known in this country, the miniaturist prose poems of Colette (*Flowers and Fruit*) and Ponge (*Taking the Side of Things*)— in which case it becomes yet another, and ingenious, form of storytelling. The subject is *there* only by the grace of the author's language.

Nature has no instructions for mankind except that our pool belea-guered humanist-democratic way of life, our fantasies of the individual's high worth, our sense that the weak, no less than the strong, have a right to survive, are absurd. When Edmund of *King Lear* said excitedly, "Nature, be thou my goddess!" he knew whereof he spoke.

In any case, where *is* Nature, one might (skeptically) inquire. Who   *20* has looked upon her/its face and survived?

But isn't this all exaggeration, in the spirit of rhetorical contentious-ness? Surely Nature is, for you, as for most reasonably intelligent people, a "perennial" source of beauty, comfort, peace, escape from the delirium of civilized life; a respite from the ego's ever-frantic strategies of self-promotion, as a way of ensuring (at least in fantasy) some small measure of immortality? Surely Nature, as it is understood in the usual slapdash way, as human, if not dilettante, *experience* (hiking in a national park, jogging on the beach at dawn, even tending, with the usual comical frustrations, a suburban garden), is wonderfully consoling; a place where, when you go there, it has to take you in?—a palimpsest of sorts you choose to read, layer by layer, always with care, always cautiously, in proportion to your psychological strength?

Nature: as in Thoreau's upbeat Transcendentalist mode ("The indescribable innocence and beneficence of Nature,—such health, such cheer, they afford forever! and such sympathy have they ever with our race, that all Nature would be affected . . . if any man should ever for a just cause grieve"), and not in Thoreau's grim mode ("Nature is hard to be overcome but she must be overcome").

Another way of saying, not *Nature-in-itself* but *Nature-as-experience.*

The former, Nature-in-itself, is, to allude slantwise to Melville, a blankness ten times blank; the latter is what we commonly, or perhaps always, mean, when we speak of Nature as a noun, a single entity—something of *ours.* Most of the time it's just an activity, a sort of hobby, a weekend, a few days, perhaps a few hours, staring out the window at the mind-dazzling autumn foliage of, say, northern Michigan, being rendered speechless—temporarily—at the sight of Mt. Shasta, the Grand Canyon, Ansel Adams's West. Or Nature writ small, contained in the back yard. Nature filtered through our optical nerves, our "senses," our fiercely romantic expectations. Nature that pleases us because it mirrors our souls, or gives the comforting illusion of doing so.

Nature as the self's (flattering) mirror, but not ever, no, never, *25* Nature-in-itself.

Nature is mouths, or maybe a single mouth. Why glamorize it, romanticize it?—well, yes, but we must, we're writers, poets, mystics (of a sort) aren't we, precisely what else are we to do but glamorize and romanticize and generally exaggerate the significance of anything we focus the white heat of our "creativity" upon? And why not Nature, since it's there, common property, mute, can't talk back, allows us the possibility of transcending the human condition for a while, writing prettily of mountain ranges, white-tailed deer, the purple crocuses outside this very window, the thrumming dazzling "life force" we imagine we all support. Why not?

Nature *is* more than a mouth—it's a dazzling variety of mouths. And it pleases the senses, in any case, as the physicists' chill universe of numbers certainly does not.

Oscar Wilde, on our subject:

Nature is no great mother who has borne us. She is our creation. It is in our brain that she quickens to life. Things are because we see them, and what we see, and how we see it, depends on the

Arts that have influenced us. To look at a thing is very different from seeing a thing. . . . At present, people see fogs, not because there are fogs, but because poets and painters have taught them the mysterious loveliness of such effects. There may have been fogs for centuries in London. I dare say there were. But no one saw them. They did not exist until Art had invented them. . . . Yesterday evening Mrs. Arundel insisted on my going to the window and looking at the glorious sky, as she called it. And so I had to look at it. . . . And what was it? It was simply a very second-rate Turner, a Turner of a bad period, with all the painter's worst faults exaggerated and over-emphasized.

"The Decay of Lying," 1889

(If we were to put it to Oscar Wilde that he exaggerates, his reply might well be, "Exaggeration? I don't know the meaning of the word.")

Walden, that most artfully composed of prose fictions, concludes, in the rhapsodic chapter "Spring," with Henry David Thoreau's contemplation of death, decay, and regeneration as it is suggested to him, or to his protagonist, by the spectacle of vultures feeding off carrion. There is a dead horse close by his cabin, and the stench of its decomposition, in certain winds, is daunting. Yet "the assurance it gave me of the strong appetite and inviolable health of Nature was my compensation for this. I love to see that Nature is so rife with life that myriads can be afforded to be sacrificed and suffered to prey upon one another; that tender organizations can be so serenely squashed out of existence like pulp,—tadpoles which herons gobble up, and tortoises and toads run over in the road; and that sometimes it has rained flesh and blood! . . . The impression made on a wise man is that of universal innocence."

Come off it, Henry David. You've grieved these many years for your elder brother, John, who died a ghastly death of lockjaw; you've never wholly recovered from the experience of watching him die. And you know, or must know, that you're fated too to die young of consumption. . . . But this doctrinaire Transcendentalist passage ends *Walden* on just the right note. It's as impersonal, as coolly detached, as the Oversoul itself: a "wise man" filters his emotions through his brain.

Or through his prose.

Nietzsche: "We all pretend to ourselves that we are more simple-minded than we are: that is how we get a rest from our fellow men."

Once out of nature I shall never take
My bodily form from any natural thing,
But such a form as Grecian goldsmiths make
Of hammered gold and gold enamelling
To keep a drowsy Emperor awake;

Or set upon a golden bough to sing
To lords and ladies of Byzantium
Of what is past, or passing, or to come.

> William Butler Yeats, "Sailing to Byzantium"

Yet even the golden bird is a "bodily form [taken from a] natural thing."
No, it's impossible to escape!

The writer's resistance to Nature.

Wallace Stevens: "In the presence of extraordinary actuality, consciousness takes the place of imagination."

Once, years ago, in 1972 to be precise, when I seemed to have been *35* another person, related to the person I am now as one is related, tangentially, sometimes embarrassingly, to cousins not seen for decades—once, when we were living in London, and I was very sick, I had a mystical vision. That is, I "had" a "mystical vision"—the heart sinks: such pretension—or something resembling one. A fever dream, let's call it. It impressed me enormously and impresses me still, though I've long since lost the capacity to see it with my mind's eye, or even, I suppose, to believe in it. There is a statute of limitations on "mystical visions," as on romantic love.

I was very sick, and I imagined my life as a thread, a thread of breath, or heartbeat, or pulse, or light—yes, it was light, radiant light; I was burning with fever and I ascended to that plane of serenity that might be mistaken for (or *is,* in fact) Nirvana, where I had a waking dream of uncanny lucidity:

My body is a tall column of light and heat.
My body is not "I" but "it."
My body is not one but many.

My body, which "I" inhabit, is inhabited as well by other creatures, unknown to me, imperceptible—the smallest of them mere sparks of light.

My body, which I perceive as substance, is in fact an organization of infinitely complex, overlapping, imbricated structures, radiant light their manifestation, the "body" a tall column of light and blood heat, a temporary agreement among atoms, like a high-rise building with numberless rooms, corridors, corners, elevator shafts, windows. . . . In this fantastical structure the "I" is deluded as to its sovereignty, let alone its autonomy in the (outside) world; the most astonishing secret is that the "I" doesn't exist!—but it behaves as if it does, as if it were one and not many.

In any case, without the "I" the tall column of light and heat would die, and the microscopic life particles would die with it . . . will die with it. The "I," which doesn't exist, is everything.

But Dr. Johnson is right, the inexpressible need not be expressed. *40*
And what resistance, finally? There is none.

This morning, an invasion of tiny black ants. One by one they appear, out of nowhere—that's their charm too!—moving single file across the white Parsons table where I am sitting, trying without much success to write a poem. A poem of only three or four lines is what I want, something short, tight, mean; I want it to hurt like a white-hot wire up the nostrils, small and compact and turned in upon itself with the density of a hunk of rock from the planet Jupiter. . . .

But here come the black ants: harbingers, you might say, of spring. One by one by one they appear on the dazzling white table and one by one I kill them with a forefinger, my deft right forefinger, mashing each against the surface of the table and then dropping it into a wastebasket at my side. Idle labor, mesmerizing, effortless, and I'm curious as to how long I can do it—sit here in the brilliant March sunshine killing ants with my right forefinger—how long I, and the ants, can keep it up.

After a while I realize that I can do it a long time. And that I've written my poem.

Reading and Responding

1. What surprises you in this essay? What had you never considered before?
2. What offended you in this essay (if anything did)?
3. Have you ever known anyone who feels the way Oates does? Describe this person.

Working Together

1. Focus on the Oscar Wilde quotation; and as a group, see whether you can phrase what Wilde says (and what Oates seems to agree with) in your own words.
2. Working as a group, decide how Oates sees the connections (if any) between nature and death. Start by finding the mentions of death or threat of death.
3. Explain what for you seems to be the obvious, self-evident, or natural truth about our relationship to the natural world—the truth you've always taken for granted.
    - Explain how Oates affirms or (more likely) challenges that natural, self-evident view.
    - Discuss why this issue isn't black and white, open and shut after all.
    - Consider the consequences of adopting Oates's view on this issue—the consequences if everyone believed what she does. What would the world be like? How would people behave?

Rethinking and Rewriting

1. Write a "Before and After" essay. Before: what you always thought before you read Oates. Then: a description of what Oates says. After:

how you still think what you thought before, but in a new, different, or more complicated way.

2. Write an essay about some miserable, horrible time you had on a campout or a hike or some other trip into the wilderness—bugs, rain, hardship. Use this experience to confirm Oates's thesis. Or admit to all this misery and still deny her thesis.

3. Write an essay in which you have Wordsworth or Thoreau, or both, respond to Oates. What would they say if they'd read the essay and were moved enough to respond?

"NONMORAL NATURE"

Stephen Jay Gould

> *Since 1974, Harvard paleontologist Stephen Jay Gould has written a monthly column for* Natural History *explaining, through example after example, the logic of evolutionary theory. These essays have been collected in a number of books, including* Ever Since Darwin *(1977) and* The Panda's Thumb *(1980), winner of the National Book Award. In this piece Gould again makes his central argument: that the physical world is neutral, indifferent to us, and that humans are therefore responsible for their own behavior.*

When the Right Honorable and Reverend Francis Henry, earl of Bridgewater, died in February, 1829, he left £8,000 to support a series of books "on the power, wisdom and goodness of God, as manifested in the creation." William Buckland, England's first official academic geologist and later dean of Westminster, was invited to compose one of the nine Bridgewater Treatises. In it he discussed the most pressing problem of natural theology: if God is benevolent and the Creation displays his "power, wisdom and goodness," then why are we surrounded with pain, suffering, and apparently senseless cruelty in the animal world?

Buckland considered the depredation of "carnivorous races" as the primary challenge to an idealized world where the lion might dwell with the lamb. He resolved the issue to his satisfaction by arguing that carnivores actually increase "the aggregate of animal enjoyment" and "diminish that of pain." Death, after all, is swift and relatively painless, victims are spared the ravages of decrepitude and senility, and populations do not outrun their food supply to the greater sorrow of all. God knew what he was doing when he made lions. Buckland concluded in hardly concealed rapture:

> The appointment of death by the agency of carnivora, as the ordinary termination of animal existence, appears therefore in its main results to be a dispensation of benevolence; it deducts much from the aggregate amount of the pain of universal death; it abridges, and almost annihilates, throughout the brute creation, the misery of disease, and accidental injuries, and lingering decay; and imposes such salutary restraint upon excessive increase of numbers, that the supply of food maintains perpetually a due ratio to the demand. The result is, that the surface of the land and depths of the waters are ever crowded with myriads of animated beings, the pleasures of whose life are coextensive with its duration; and which throughout the little day of existence that is allotted to them, fulfill with joy the functions for which they were created.

We may find a certain amusing charm in Buckland's vision today, but such arguments did begin to address "the problem of evil" for many of

Buckland's contemporaries—how could a benevolent God create such a world of carnage and bloodshed? Yet this argument could not abolish the problem of evil entirely, for nature includes many phenomena far more horrible in our eyes than simple predation. I suspect that nothing evokes greater disgust in most of us than slow destruction of a host by an internal parasite—gradual ingestion, bit by bit, from the inside. In no other way can I explain why *Alien,* an uninspired, grade-C, formula horror film, should have won such a following. That single scene of Mr. Alien, popping forth as a baby parasite from the body of a human host, was both sickening and stunning. Our nineteenth-century forebears maintained similar feelings. The greatest challenge to their concept of a benevolent deity was not simple predation—but slow death by parasitic ingestion. The classic case, treated at length by all great naturalists, invoked the so-called ichneumon fly. Buckland had sidestepped the major issue.

The "ichneumon fly," which provoked such concern among natural theologians, was actually a composite creature representing the habits of an enormous tribe. The Ichneumonoidea are a group of wasps, not flies, that include more species than all the vertebrates combined (wasps, with ants and bees, constitute the order Hymenoptera; flies, with their two wings—wasps have four—form the order Diptera). In addition, many non-ichneumonid wasps of similar habits were often cited for the same grisly details. Thus, the famous story did not merely implicate a single aberrant species (perhaps a perverse leakage from Satan's realm), but hundreds of thousands—a large chunk of what could only be God's creation.

The ichneumons, like most wasps, generally live freely as adults but *5* pass their larval life as parasites feeding on the bodies of other animals, almost invariably members of their own phylum, the Arthropoda. The most common victims are caterpillars (butterfly and moth larvae), but some ichneumons prefer aphids and others attack spiders. Most hosts are parasitized as larvae, but some adults are attacked, and many tiny ichneumons inject their brood directly into the egg of their host.

The free-flying females locate an appropriate host and then convert it to a food factory for their own young. Parasitologists speak of ectoparasitism when the uninvited guest lives on the surface of its host, and endoparasitism when the parasite dwells within. Among endoparasitic ichneumons, adult females pierce the host with their ovipositor and deposit eggs within. (The ovipositor, a thin tube extending backward from the wasp's rear end, may be many times as long as the body itself.) Usually, the host is not otherwise inconvenienced for the moment, at least until the eggs hatch and the ichneumon larvae begin their grim work of interior excavation.

Among ectoparasites, however, many females lay their eggs directly upon the host's body. Since an active host would easily dislodge the egg, the ichneumon mother often simultaneously injects a toxin that paralyzes the caterpillar or other victim. The paralysis may be permanent, and the caterpillar lies, alive but immobile, with the agent of its future destruction secure on its belly. The egg hatches, the helpless caterpillar twitches, the wasp larva pierces and begins its grisly feast.

Since a dead and decaying caterpillar will do the wasp larva no good, it eats in a pattern that cannot help but recall, in our inappropriate, anthropocentric interpretation, the ancient English penalty for treason—drawing and quartering, with its explicit object of extracting as much torment as possible by keeping the victim alive and sentient. As the king's executioner drew out and burned his client's entrails, so does the ichneumon larva eat fat bodies and digestive organs first, keeping the caterpillar alive by preserving intact the essential heart and central nervous system. Finally, the larva completes its work and kills its victim, leaving behind the caterpillar's empty shell. Is it any wonder that ichneumons, not snakes or lions, stood as the paramount challenge to God's benevolence during the heyday of natural theology?

As I read through the nineteenth- and twentieth-century literature on ichneumons, nothing amused me more than the tension between an intellectual knowledge that wasps should not be described in human terms and a literary or emotional inability to avoid the familiar categories of epic and narrative, pain and destruction, victim and vanquisher. We seem to be caught in the mythic structures of our own cultural sagas, quite unable, even in our basic descriptions, to use any other language than the metaphors of battle and conquest. We cannot render this corner of natural history as anything but story, combining the themes of grim horror and fascination and usually ending not so much with pity for the caterpillar as with admiration for the efficiency of the ichneumon.

I detect two basic themes in most epic descriptions: the struggles of prey and the ruthless efficiency of parasites. Although we acknowledge that we may be witnessing little more than automatic instinct or physiological reaction, still we describe the defenses of hosts as though they represented conscious struggles. Thus, aphids kick and caterpillars may wriggle violently as wasps attempt to insert their ovipositors. The pupa of the tortoiseshell butterfly (usually considered an inert creature silently awaiting its conversion from duckling to swan) may contort its abdominal region so sharply that attacking wasps are thrown into the air. The caterpillars of *Hapalia*, when attacked by the wasp *Apanteles machaeralis*, drop suddenly from their leaves and suspend themselves in air by a silken thread. But the wasp may run down the thread and insert its eggs nonetheless. Some hosts can encapsulate the injected egg with blood cells that aggregate and harden, thus suffocating the parasite.

J. H. Fabre, the great nineteenth-century French entomologist, who remains to this day the preeminently literate natural historian of insects, made a special study of parasitic wasps and wrote with an unabashed anthropocentrism about the struggles of paralyzed victims (see his books *Insect Life* and *The Wonders of Instinct*). He describes some imperfectly paralyzed caterpillars that struggle so violently every time a parasite approaches that the wasp larvae must feed with unusual caution. They attach them-

10

selves to a silken strand from the roof of their burrow and descend upon a safe and exposed part of the caterpillar:

> The grub is at dinner: head downwards, it is digging into the limp belly of one of the caterpillars. . . . At the least sign of danger in the heap of caterpillars, the larva retreats . . . and climbs back to the ceiling, where the swarming rabble cannot reach it. When peace is restored, it slides down [its silken cord] and returns to table, with its head over the viands and its rear upturned and ready to withdraw in case of need.

In another chapter, he describes the fate of a paralyzed cricket:

> One may see the cricket, bitten to the quick, vainly move its antennae and abdominal styles, open and close its empty jaws, and even move a foot, but the larva is safe and searches its vitals with impunity. What an awful nightmare for the paralyzed cricket!

Fabre even learned to feed paralyzed victims by placing a syrup of sugar and water on their mouthparts—thus showing that they remained alive, sentient, and (by implication) grateful for any palliation of their inevitable fate. If Jesus, immobile and thirsting on the cross, received only vinegar from his tormentors, Fabre at least could make an ending bittersweet.

The second theme, ruthless efficiency of the parasites, leads to the opposite conclusion—grudging admiration for the victors. We learn of their skill in capturing dangerous hosts often many times larger than themselves. Caterpillars may be easy game, but psammocharid wasps prefer spiders. They must insert their ovipositors in a safe and precise spot. Some leave a paralyzed spider in its own burrow. *Planiceps hirsutus,* for example, parasitizes a California trapdoor spider. It searches for spider tubes on sand dunes, then digs into nearby sand to disturb the spider's home and drive it out. When the spider emerges, the wasp attacks, paralyzes its victim, drags it back into its own tube, shuts and fastens the trapdoor, and deposits a single egg upon the spider's abdomen. Other psammocharids will drag a heavy spider back to a previously prepared cluster of clay or mud cells. Some amputate a spider's legs to make the passage easier. Others fly back over water, skimming a buoyant spider along the surface.

Some wasps must battle with other parasites over a host's body. *Rhyssella curvipes* can detect the larvae of wood wasps deep within alder wood and drill down to a potential victim with its sharply ridged ovipositor. *Pseudorhyssa alpestris,* a related parasite, cannot drill directly into wood since its slender ovipositor bears only rudimentary cutting ridges. It locates the holes made by *Rhyssella,* inserts its ovipositor, and lays an egg on the host (already conveniently paralyzed by *Rhyssella*), right next to the egg deposited by its relative. The two eggs hatch at about the same time, but the larva of *Pseudorhyssa* has a bigger head bearing much larger mandibles. *Pseudorhyssa* seizes the smaller *Rhyssella* larva, destroys it, and proceeds to feast upon a banquet already well prepared.

Other praises for the efficiency of mothers invoke the themes of early, quick, and often. Many ichneumons don't even wait for their hosts to develop into larvae, but parasitize the egg directly (larval wasps may then either drain the egg itself or enter the developing host larva). Others simply move fast. *Apanteles militaris* can deposit up to seventy-two eggs in a single second. Still others are doggedly persistent. *Aphidius gomezi* females produce up to 1,500 eggs and can parasitize as many as 600 aphids in a single working day. In a bizarre twist upon "often," some wasps indulge in polyembryony, a kind of iterated supertwining. A single egg divides into cells that aggregate into as many as 500 individuals. Since some polyembryonic wasps parasitize caterpillars much larger than themselves and may lay up to six eggs in each, as many as 3,000 larvae may develop within, and feed upon a single host. These wasps are endoparasites and do not paralyze their victims. The caterpillars writhe back and forth, not (one suspects) from pain, but merely in response to the commotion induced by thousands of wasp larvae feeding within.

Maternal efficiency is often matched by larval aptitude. I have already mentioned the pattern of eating less essential parts first, thus keeping the host alive and fresh to its final and merciful dispatch. After the larva digests every edible morsel of its victim (if only to prevent later fouling of its abode by decaying tissue), it may still use the outer shell of its host. One aphid parasite cuts a hole in the bottom of its victim's shell, glues the skeleton to a leaf by sticky secretions from its salivary gland, and then spins a cocoon to pupate within the aphid's shell.

In using inappropriate anthropocentric language for this romp through the natural history of ichneumons, I have tried to emphasize just why these wasps became a preeminent challenge to natural theology—the antiquated doctrine that attempted to infer God's essence from the products of his creation. I have used twentieth-century examples for the most part, but all themes were known and stressed by the great nineteenth-century natural theologians. How then did they square the habits of these wasps with the goodness of God? How did they extract themselves from this dilemma of their own making?

The strategies were as varied as the practitioners; they shared only the theme of special pleading for an a priori doctrine—our naturalists *knew* that God's benevolence was lurking somewhere behind all these tales of apparent horror. Charles Lyell, for example, in the first edition of his epochal *Principles of Geology* (1830–1833), decided that caterpillars posed such a threat to vegetation that any natural checks upon them could only reflect well upon a creating deity, for caterpillars would destroy human agriculture "did not Providence put causes in operation to keep them in due bounds."

The Reverend William Kirby, rector of Barham, and Britain's foremost entomologist, chose to ignore the plight of caterpillars and focused instead upon the virtue of mother love displayed by wasps in provisioning their young with such care.

20

The great object of the female is to discover a proper nidus for her eggs. In search of this she is in constant motion. Is the caterpillar of a butterfly or moth the appropriate food for her young? You see her alight upon the plants where they are most usually to be met with, run quickly over them, carefully examining every leaf, and, having found the unfortunate object of her search, insert her sting into its flesh, and there deposit an egg. . . . The active Ichneumon braves every danger, and does not desist until her courage and address have insured subsistence for one of her future progeny.

Kirby found this solicitude all the more remarkable because the female wasp will never see her child and enjoy the pleasures of parenthood. Yet love compels her to danger nonetheless:

A very large proportion of them are doomed to die before their young come into existence. But in these the passion is not extinguished. . . . When you witness the solicitude with which they provide for the security and sustenance of their future young, you can scarcely deny to them love for a progeny they are never destined to behold.

Kirby also put in a good word for the marauding larvae, praising them for their forbearance in eating selectively to keep their caterpillar alive. Would we all husband our resources with such care!

In this strange and apparently cruel operation one circumstance is truly remarkable. The larva of the Ichneumon, though every day, perhaps for months, it gnaws the inside of the caterpillar, and though at last it has devoured almost every part of it except the skin and intestines, carefully all this time it avoids injuring the vital organs, as if aware that its own existence depends on that of the insect upon which it preys! . . . What would be the impression which a similar instance amongst the race of quadrupeds would make upon us? If, for example, an animal . . . should be found to feed upon the inside of a dog, devouring only those parts not essential to life, while it cautiously left uninjured the heart, arteries, lungs, and intestines,—should we not regard such an instance as a perfect prodigy, as an example of instinctive forbearance almost miraculous? [The last three quotes come from the 1856, and last pre-Darwinian, edition of Kirby and Spence's *Introduction to Entomology*.]

This tradition of attempting to read moral meaning from nature did not cease with the triumph of evolutionary theory in 1859—for evolution could be read as God's chosen method of peopling our planet, and ethical messages might still populate nature. Thus, St. George Mivart, one of Darwin's most effective evolutionary critics and a devout Catholic, argued that "many amiable and excellent people" had been misled by the apparent suffering of animals for two reasons. First, whatever the pain, "physical suffering and moral evil are simply incommensurable." Since beasts are not moral agents, their feelings cannot bear any ethical message. But secondly, lest our visceral sensitivities still be aroused, Mivart assures us that animals must feel little, if any, pain. Using a favorite racist argument of the time— that "primitive" people suffer far less than advanced and cultured folk— Mivart extrapolated further down the ladder of life into a realm of very limited pain indeed: Physical suffering, he argued,

> depends greatly upon the mental condition of the sufferer. Only during consciousness does it exist, and only in the most highly organized men does it reach its acme. The author has been assured that lower races of men appear less keenly sensitive to physical suffering than do more cultivated and refined human beings. Thus only in man can there really be any intense degree of suffering, because only in him is there that intellectual recollection of past moments and that anticipation of future ones, which constitute in great part the bitterness of suffering. The momentary pang, the present pain, which beasts endure, though real enough, is yet, doubtless, not to be compared as to its intensity with the suffering which is produced in man through his high prerogative of self-consciousness [from *Genesis of Species,* 1871].

It took Darwin himself to derail this ancient tradition—and he proceeded in the gentle way so characteristic of his radical intellectual approach to nearly everything. The ichneumons also troubled Darwin greatly and he wrote of them to Asa Gray in 1860:

> I own that I cannot see as plainly as others do, and as I should wish to do, evidence of design and beneficence on all sides of us. There seems to me too much misery in the world. I cannot persuade myself that a beneficent and omnipotent God would have designedly created the Ichneumonidae with the express intention of their feeding within the living bodies of Caterpillars, or that a cat should play with mice.

Indeed, he had written with more passion to Joseph Hooker in 1856: "What a book a devil's chaplain might write on the clumsy, wasteful, blundering, low, and horribly cruel works of nature!"

This honest admission—that nature is often (by our standards) cruel and that all previous attempts to find a lurking goodness behind everything represent just so much special pleading—can lead in two directions. One might retain the principle that nature holds moral messages, but reverse the usual perspective and claim that morality consists in understanding the ways of nature and doing the opposite. Thomas Henry Huxley advanced this argument in his famous essay on *Evolution and Ethics* (1893):

> The practice of that which is ethically best—what we call goodness or virtue—involves a course of conduct which, in all respects,

is opposed to that which leads to success in the cosmic struggle for existence. In place of ruthless self-assertion it demands self-restraint; in place of thrusting aside, or treading down, all competitors, it requires that the individual shall not merely respect, but shall help his fellows. . . . It repudiates the gladiatorial theory of existence. . . . Laws and moral precepts are directed to the end of curbing the cosmic process.

The other argument, radical in Darwin's day but more familiar now, holds that nature simply is as we find it. Our failure to discern a universal good does not record any lack of insight or ingenuity, but merely demonstrates that nature contains no moral messages framed in human terms. Morality is a subject for philosophers, theologians, students of the humanities, indeed for all thinking people. The answers will not be read passively from nature; they do not, and cannot, arise from the data of science. The factual state of the world does not teach us how we, with our powers for good and evil, should alter or preserve it in the most ethical manner.

Darwin himself tended toward this view, although he could not, as a man of his time, thoroughly abandon the idea that laws of nature might reflect some higher purpose. He clearly recognized that specific manifestations of those laws—cats playing with mice, and ichneumon larvae eating caterpillars—could not embody ethical messages, but he somehow hoped that unknown higher laws might exist "with the details, whether good or bad, left to the working out of what we may call chance."

Since ichneumons are a detail, and since natural selection is a law regulating details, the answer to the ancient dilemma of why such cruelty (in our terms) exists in nature can only be that there isn't any answer—and that framing the question "in our terms" is thoroughly inappropriate in a natural world neither made for us nor ruled by us. It just plain happens. It is a strategy that works for ichneumons and that natural selection has programmed into their behavioral repertoire. Caterpillars are not suffering to teach us something; they have simply been outmaneuvered, for now, in the evolutionary game. Perhaps they will evolve a set of adequate defenses sometime in the future, thus sealing the fate of ichneumons. And perhaps, indeed probably, they will not.

Another Huxley, Thomas's grandson Julian, spoke for this position, using as an example—yes, you guessed it—the ubiquitous ichneumons:

Natural selection, in fact, though like the mills of God in grinding slowly and grinding small, has few other attributes that a civilized religion would call divine. . . . Its products are just as likely to be aesthetically, morally, or intellectually repulsive to us as they are to be attractive. We need only think of the ugliness of *Sacculina* or a bladder-worm, the stupidity of a rhinoceros or a stegosaur, the horror of a female mantis devouring its mate or a brood of ichneumon flies slowly eating out a caterpillar.

If nature is nonmoral, then evolution cannot teach any ethical theory *30* at all. The assumption that it can has abetted a panoply of social evils that ideologues falsely read into nature from their beliefs—eugenics and (mis-named) social Darwinism prominently among them. Not only did Darwin eschew any attempt to discover an antireligious ethic in nature, he also expressly stated his personal bewilderment about such deep issues as the problem of evil. Just a few sentences after invoking the ichneumons, and in words that express both the modesty of this splendid man and the compatibility, through lack of contact, between science and true religion, Darwin wrote to Asa Gray,

> I feel most deeply that the whole subject is too profound for the human intellect. A dog might as well speculate on the mind of Newton. Let each man hope and believe what he can.

Postscript

Michele Aldrich sent an even better literary reference than any I had found. Mark Twain, in a biting bit of satire called "Little Bessie Would Assist Providence," chronicles a conversation of mother and daughter—daughter insisting that a benevolent God would not have given her little friend "Billy Norris the typhus" and visited other unjust disasters upon decent people, mother assuring her that there must be a good reason for it all. Bessie's last rejoinder, which summarily ends the essay as you shall see, invokes our old friends, the ichneumons:

> Mr. Hollister says the wasps catch spiders and cram them down into their nests in the ground—alive, mama!—and there they live and suffer days and days and days, and the hungry little wasps chewing their legs and gnawing into their bellies all the time, to make them good and religious and praise God for His infinite mercies. I think Mr. Hollister is just lovely, and ever so kind; for when I asked him if he would treat a spider like that he said he hoped to be damned if he would; and then he—Dear mama, have you fainted!

James W. Tuttleton, chairman of the English department at New York University, sent me a stunning poem by Robert Frost that seems designed as a commentary upon Darwin's last statement that chance may regulate in the small, even if purpose might be found in the large. Or do we even see true purpose in the large? The poem is called, simply, "Design":

> I found a dimpled spider, fat and white,
> On a white heal-all, holding up a moth
> Like a white piece of rigid satin cloth—
> Assorted characters of death and blight
> Mixed ready to begin the morning right,

Like the ingredients of a witches' broth—
A snow-drop spider, a flower like a froth,
And dead wings carried like a paper kite.

What had that flower to do with being white,
The wayside blue and innocent heal-all?
What brought the kindred spider to that height,
Then steered the white moth thither in the night?
What but design of darkness to appall?—
If design govern in a thing so small.

I was so struck by the image of the spider as a drop, the flower as a froth, the moth as a pair of two-dimensional wings. Forms so unlike, yet all white and all brought together in one spot for destruction. Why? Or, as we read the last two lines, may we even ask such a question? I think that we cannot, and I regard this insight as the most liberating theme of Darwin's revolution.

Reading and Responding

1. Make a list of everything you didn't understand in this essay on a first reading.
2. Make a list of everything you did understand in this essay on a first reading.
3. Mark what seems to be the central passage of the essay, the one where Stephen Jay Gould makes his main point.

Working Together

1. In class, combine and collate your lists of responses.
2. Take what you agree is the central passage in the piece and translate it into language a twelve-year-old would understand. Make it as simple and clear as you possibly can, not worrying about awkwardness.
3. Give an example from your own experience of nature of the idea Gould is expressing.
4. Think metaphorically. Assume that this essay is a response to a mental or intellectual disease, an effort to cure some illness in the way people think. What is that disease?

Rethinking and Rewriting

1. Write an essay about a personal experience that runs counter to Gould's claim: some time when nature *did* seem to have moral significance for you. Does Gould force you to rethink that experience?
2. Translate William Buckland's argument (as Gould summarizes it in the opening pages of his essay); write it in clear twentieth-century prose.

Then explain why you agree or disagree with Buckland. Or explain how you disagree with him intellectually, though your actions might suggest that you agree with him.

3. Write an essay comparing and contrasting Gould and Thomas (see "Re-thinking and Rewriting," item 2, at the end of "The Tucson Zoo").

"THE TUCSON ZOO"

Lewis Thomas

Medical doctor and biomedical researcher, Lewis Thomas began writing a column for the New England Journal of Medicine *in 1971. The first of these graceful, informal, personal essays about the wonders of the physical world were eventually collected and published as* The Lives of the Cell, *winner of the 1974 National Book Award. Several other collections followed, including* The Medusa and the Snail *(1979), from which this essay about a brief "epiphany" is taken.*

As You Read

1. In a sentence or two, write down your thoughts and reactions after reading the first paragraph.
2. In a sentence or two, write down your thoughts and reactions after reading the second paragraph. Have your reactions changed? Why?
3. Mark in the margins any place in the essay where the transitions aren't clear to you, where you momentarily aren't sure of Thomas's direction.

Science gets most of its information by the process of reductionism, exploring the details, then the details of the details, until all the smallest bits of the structure, or the smallest parts of the mechanism, are laid out for counting and scrutiny. Only when this is done can the investigation be extended to encompass the whole organism or the entire system. So we say.

Sometimes it seems that we take a loss, working this way. Much of today's public anxiety about science is the apprehension that we may forever be overlooking the whole by an endless, obsessive preoccupation with the parts. I had a brief, personal experience of this misgiving one afternoon in Tucson, where I had time on my hands and visited the zoo, just outside the city. The designers there have cut a deep pathway between two small artificial ponds, walled by clear glass, so when you stand in the center of the path you can look into the depths of each pool, and at the same time you can regard the surface. In one pool, on the right side of the path, is a family of otters; on the other side, a family of beavers. Within just a few feet from your face, on either side, beavers and otters are at play, underwater and on the surface, swimming toward your face and then away, more filled with life than any creatures I have ever seen before, in all my days. Except for the glass, you could reach across and touch them.

I was transfixed. As I now recall it, there was only one sensation in my head: pure elation mixed with amazement at such perfection. Swept off my feet, I floated from one side to the other, swiveling my brain, staring astounded at the beavers, then at the otters. I could hear shouts across my corpus callosum, from one hemisphere to the other. I remember thinking, with what was left in charge of my consciousness, that I wanted no part of the science of beavers and otters; I wanted never to know how they performed their marvels; I wished for no news about the physiology of their breathing, the coordination of their muscles, their vision, their endocrine systems, their digestive tracts. I hoped never to have to think of them as collections of cells. All I asked for was the full hairy complexity, then in front of my eyes, of whole, intact beavers and otters in motion.

It lasted, I regret to say, for only a few minutes, and then I was back in the late twentieth century, reductionist as ever, wondering about the details by force of habit, but not, this time, the details of otters and beavers. Instead, me. Something worth remembering had happened in my mind, I was certain of that; I would have put it somewhere in the brain stem; maybe this was my limbic system at work. I became a behavioral scientist, an experimental psychologist, an ethologist, and in the instant I lost all the wonder and the sense of being overwhelmed. I was flattened.

But I came away from the zoo with something, a piece of news about   5
myself: I am coded, somehow, for otters and beavers. I exhibit instinctive behavior in their presence, when they are displayed close at hand behind glass, simultaneously below water and at the surface. I have receptors for this display. Beavers and otters possess a "release" for me, in the terminology of ethology, and the releasing was my experience. What was released? Behavior. What behavior? Standing, swiveling flabbergasted, feeling exultation and a rush of friendship. I could not, as the result of the transaction, tell you anything more about beavers and otters than you already know. I learned nothing new about them. Only about me, and I suspect also about you, maybe about human beings at large: we are endowed with genes which code out our reaction to beavers and otters, maybe our reaction to each other as well. We are stamped with stereotyped, unalterable patterns of response, ready to be released. And the behavior released in us, by such confrontations, is, essentially, a surprised affection. It is compulsory behavior and we can avoid it only by straining with the full power of our conscious minds, making up conscious excuses all the way. Left to ourselves, mechanistic and autonomic, we hanker for friends.

Everyone says, stay away from ants. They have no lessons for us; they are crazy little instruments, inhuman, incapable of controlling themselves, lacking manners, lacking souls. When they are massed together, all touching, exchanging bits of information held in their jaws like memoranda, they become a single animal. Look out for that. It is a debasement, a loss of individuality, a violation of human nature, an unnatural act.

Sometimes people argue this point of view seriously and with deep thought. Be individuals, solitary and selfish, is the message. Altruism, a jargon word for what used to be called love, is worse than weakness, it is sin, a violation of nature. Be separate. Do not be a social animal. But this is a hard argument to make convincingly when you have to depend on language to make it. You have to print up leaflets or publish books and get them bought and sent around, you have to turn up on television and catch the attention of millions of other human beings all at once, and then you have to say to all of them, all at once, all collected and paying attention: be solitary; do not depend on each other. You can't do this and keep a straight face.

Maybe altruism is our most primitive attribute, out of reach, beyond our control. Or perhaps it is immediately at hand, waiting to be released, disguised now, in our kind of civilization, as affection or friendship or attachment. I don't see why it should be unreasonable for all human beings to have strands of DNA coiled up in chromosomes, coding out instincts for usefulness and helpfulness. Usefulness may turn out to be the hardest test of fitness for survival, more important than aggression, more effective, in the long run, than grabbiness. If this is the sort of information biological science holds for the future, applying to us as well as to ants, then I am all for science.

One thing I'd like to know most of all: when those ants have made the Hill, and are all there, touching and exchanging, and the whole mass begins to behave like a single huge creature, and *thinks,* what on earth is that thought? And while you're at it, I'd like to know a second thing: when it happens, does any single ant know about it? Does his hair stand on end?

Working Together

1. Do a one-page freewriting in class describing some intense, arresting, completely absorbing time in your recent experience, some moment when you felt fully awake and fully engaged, a time when things seemed especially clear or interesting or important to you. (*Hint:* Think in terms of moments of intense action or intense attention.) Describe this moment as clearly and concretely as you can.
2. Talk about your freewrites in groups or in pairs. Read yours aloud if you feel comfortable doing that. Discuss: Why was the moment important to you? What makes it stand out? Can you say for sure?
3. Now, what does any of what you've done in these activities have to do with Lewis Thomas's "The Tucson Zoo"? How does your freewriting and discussion help you understand what Thomas is doing in this essay?

Rethinking and Rewriting

1. Take your in-class freewriting and your thoughts from the discussion and work them into a revised personal essay. It should have this structure: experience itself (for several paragraphs—clear and direct description of the moment); mind-movie (for several paragraphs—just what

you are thinking about at that moment, your thinking aloud about what it means).

2. Write an essay comparing Thomas's "The Tucson Zoo" and Gould's "Nonmoral Nature." On the basis of these two pieces, explain how these two scientists fundamentally disagree about the nature of nature.

"A FIELD OF SILENCE"

Annie Dillard

In this essay from Teaching a Stone to Talk *(1982), Annie Dillard describes what may have been a religious experience. (See also "The Silent Neighborhood" in chapter 6.)*

There is a place called "the farm" where I lived once, in a time that was very lonely. Fortunately I was unconscious of my loneliness then, and felt it only deeply, bewildered, in the half-bright way that a puppy feels pain.

I loved the place, and still do. It was an ordinary farm, a calf-raising, haymaking farm, and very beautiful. Its flat, messy pastures ran along one side of the central portion of a quarter-mile road in the central part of an island, an island in Puget Sound, on the Washington coast, so that from the high end of the road you could look west toward the Pacific, to the sound and its hundred islands, and from the other end—and from the farm—you could see east to the water between you and the mainland, and beyond it the mainland's mountains slicked with snow.

I liked the clutter about the place, the way everything blossomed or seeded or rusted; I liked the hundred half-finished projects, the smells, and the way the animals always broke loose. It is calming to herd animals. Often a regular rodeo breaks out—two people and a clever cow can kill a morning—but still, it is calming. You laugh for a while, exhausted, and silence is restored; the beasts are back in their pastures, the fences are not fixed but disguised as if they were fixed, ensuring the animals' temporary resignation; and a great calm descends, a lack of urgency, a sense of having to invent something to do until the next time you must run and chase cattle.

The farm seemed eternal in the crude way the earth does—extending, that is, a very long time. The farm was as old as earth, always there, as old as the island, the Platonic form of "farm," of human society itself, a piece of land eaten and replenished a billion summers, a piece of land worked on, lived on, grown over, plowed under, and stitched again and again, with fingers or with leaves, in and out and into human life's thin weave. I lived there once.

I lived there once and I have seen, from behind the barn, the long 5
roadside pastures heaped with silence. Behind the rooster, suddenly, I saw the silence heaped on the fields like trays. That day the green hayfields supported silence evenly sown; the fields bent just so under the even pressure of silence, bearing it, palming it aloft: cleared fields, part of a land, a planet, that did not buckle beneath the heel of silence, nor split up scattered to bits, but instead lay secret, disguised as time and matter as though

that were nothing, ordinary—disguised as fields like those which bear the silence only because they are spread, and the silence spreads over them, great in size.

I do not want, I think, ever to see such a sight again. That there is loneliness here I had granted, in the abstract—but not, I thought, inside the light of God's presence, inside his sanction, and signed by his name.

I lived alone in the farmhouse and rented; the owners, in their twenties, lived in another building just over the yard. I had been reading and restless for two or three days. It was morning. I had just read at breakfast an Updike story, "Packed Dirt, Churchgoing, A Dying Cat, A Traded Car," which moved me. I heard our own farmyard rooster and two or three roosters across the street screeching. I quit the house, hoping at heart to see either of the owners, but immediately to watch our rooster as he crowed.

It was Saturday morning late in the summer, in early September, clear-aired and still. I climbed the barnyard fence between the poultry and the pastures; I watched the red rooster, and the rooster, reptilian, kept one alert and alien eye on me. He pulled his extravagant neck to its maximum length, hauled himself high on his legs, stretched his beak as if he were gagging, screamed, and blinked. It was a ruckus. The din came from everywhere, and only the most rigorous application of reason could persuade me that it proceeded in its entirety from this lone and maniac bird.

After a pause, the roosters across the street started, answering the proclamation, or cranking out another round, arhythmically, interrupting. In the same way there is no pattern nor sense to the massed stridulations of cicadas; their skipped beats, enjambments, and failed alterations jangle your spirits, as though each of those thousand insects, each with identical feelings, were stubbornly deaf to the others, and loudly alone.

I shifted along the fence to see if either of the owners was coming or going. To the rooster I said nothing, but only stared. And he stared at me; we were both careful to keep the wooden fence slat from our line of sight, so that his profiled eye and my two eyes could meet. From time to time I looked beyond the pastures to learn if anyone might be seen on the road.

When I was turned away in this manner, the silence gathered and struck me. It bashed me broadside from the heavens above me like yard goods; ten acres of fallen, invisible sky choked the fields. The pastures on either side of the road turned green in a surrealistic fashion, monstrous, impeccable, as if they were holding their breaths. The roosters stopped. All the things of the world—the fields and the fencing, the road, a parked orange truck—were stricken and self-conscious. A world pressed down on their surfaces, a world battered just within their surfaces, and that real world, so near to emerging, had got stuck.

There was only silence. It was the silence of matter caught in the act and embarrassed. There were no cells moving, and yet there were cells. I could see the shape of the land, how it lay holding silence. Its poise and its stillness were unendurable, like the ring of the silence you hear in your skull when you're little and notice you're living, the ring which resumes later in life when you're sick.

There were flies buzzing over the dirt by the henhouse, moving in circles and buzzing, black dreams in chips off the one long dream, the dream of the regular world. But the silent fields were the real world, eternity's outpost in time, whose look I remembered but never like this, this God-blasted, paralyzed day. I felt myself tall and vertical, in a blue shirt, self-conscious, and wishing to die. I heard the flies again; I looked at the rooster who was frozen looking at me.

Then at last I heard whistling, human whistling far on the air, and I was not able to bear it. I looked around, heartbroken; only at the big yellow Charolais farm far up the road was there motion—a woman, I think, dressed in pink, and pushing a wheelbarrow easily over the grass. It must have been she who was whistling and heaping on top of the silence those hollow notes of song. But the slow sound of the music—the beautiful sound of the music ringing the air like a stone bell—was isolate and detached. The notes spread into the general air and became the weightier part of silence, silence's last straw. The distant woman and her wheelbarrow were flat and detached, like mechanized and pink-painted properties for a stage. I stood in pieces, afraid I was unable to move. Something had unhinged the world. The houses and roadsides and pastures were buckling under the silence. Then a Labrador, black, loped up the distant driveway, fluid and cartoonlike, toward the pink woman. I had to try to turn away. Holiness is a force, and like the others can be resisted. It was given, but I didn't want to see it, God or no God. It was as if God had said, "I am here, but not as you have known me. This is the look of silence, and of loneliness unendurable; it too has always been mine, and now will be yours." I was not ready for a life of sorrow, sorrow deriving from knowledge I could just as well stop at the gate.

I turned away, willful, and the whole show vanished. The realness of things disassembled. The whistling became ordinary, familiar; the air above the fields released its pressure and the fields lay hooded as before. I myself could act. Looking to the rooster I whistled to him myself, softly, and some hens appeared at the chicken house window, greeted the day, and fluttered down.

Several months later, walking past the farm on the way to a volleyball game, I remarked to a friend, by way of information, "There are angels in those fields." Angels! That silence so grave and so stricken, that choked and unbearable green! I have rarely been so surprised at something I've said. Angels! What are angels? I had never thought of angels, in any way at all.

From that time I began to think of angels. I considered that sights such as I had seen of the silence must have been shared by the people who said they saw angels. I began to review the thing I had seen that morning.

My impression now of those fields is of thousands of spirits—spirits trapped, perhaps, by my refusal to call them more fully, or by the paralysis of my own spirit at that time—thousands of spirits, angels in fact, almost discernible to the eye, and whirling. If pressed I would say they were three or four feet from the ground. Only their motion was clear (clockwise, if you insist); that, and their beauty unspeakable.

There are angels in those fields, and, I presume, in all fields, and everywhere else. I would go to the lions for this conviction, to witness this fact. What all this means about perception, or language, or angels, or my own sanity, I have no idea.

Reading and Responding

1. Read the first page of Joyce Carol Oates's essay and write six words or phrases (your own) that accurately describe this opening. Then read the first page of Annie Dillard's "A Field of Silence" and write six words or phrases (again your own) that accurately describe this opening.
2. Tell the story of your reading of this piece, in chronological order.
3. Dillard spends the first two-thirds of this essay presenting an experience and the last third telling us what she thinks it means. Describe what's going through your mind as you finish the description itself. Describe what's going through your mind as you read Dillard's interpretation of the experience. Are you surprised?

Working Together

1. On the basis only of your readings of the openings of Oates's essay and Dillard's here, which essay would you choose to continue to read? As a group, decide on your answer to this question, and have at least three good reasons to explain yourselves.
2. Read the first two pages of the essay aloud, or have someone else read them. As you listen, underline any sentences or phrases that seem especially intense, dense, charged, poetic, odd, direct, concrete—somehow different, somehow forcing you to read more slowly or pay attention.
3. Write some of these sentences or phrases on the board. Do they have anything in common? What are they like?
4. Given the subject of this essay, given what Dillard is trying to do, why are these sentences appropriate? How do they reflect the experience the essay describes?

Rethinking and Rewriting

1. Describe an experience of silence. Or arrange to have an experience of silence—say for at least ten minutes. Describe what really happened, how you really responded to the silence, and how you felt.

2. Compare the experience Dillard relates in this essay with the experience Charles Wright relates in "Clear Night." How are these experiences similar, and how are they different? End your discussion by identifying the experience that seems more like your own, and explain why that's the case.
3. Compare Dillard's experience of "angels" with Norris's experience of the Dakota landscape. Are the two writers describing the same experience? Consider, too, their differing styles and voices.

"THE BEAUTIFUL PLACES"

Kathleen Norris

> *Author of two books of poetry,* Falling Off *(1971) and* The Middle of
> the World *(1981), Kathleen Norris has lived for almost twenty years in
> Lemmon, South Dakota. Her life in this landscape is the subject of her recent
> book of creative nonfiction,* Dakota: A Spiritual Geography, *from which
> this essay is taken.*

Before and As You Read
1. This essay begins with an epigraph from *The Wizard of Oz,* a key to
   Kathleen Norris's thesis. Quickly paraphrase the epigraph in a sentence
   or two, and then, as you read, mark two or three key passages where
   Norris makes the same point in her own words.
2. Before you even begin reading, do a half-page freewrite responding to
   these questions: What do you expect from an essay entitled "The Beautiful Places"? What kind of landscape do you assume will be described?

> The Scarecrow sighed. "Of course I cannot understand it,"
> he said. "If your heads were stuffed with straw like
> mine, you would probably all live in the beautiful places,
> and then Kansas would have no people at all. It is
> fortunate for Kansas that you have brains."
>
> —L. FRANK BAUM, *The Wizard of Oz*

The high plains, the beginning of the desert West, often act as a
crucible for those who inhabit them. Like Jacob's angel, the region requires
that you wrestle with it before it bestows a blessing. This can mean driving
through a snowstorm on icy roads, wondering whether you'll have to pull
over and spend the night in your car, only to emerge under tag ends of
clouds into a clear sky blazing with stars. Suddenly you know what you're
seeing: the earth has turned to face the center of the galaxy, and many
more stars are visible than the ones we usually see on our wing of the
spiral.

Or a vivid double rainbow marches to the east, following the wild
summer storm that nearly blew you off the road. The storm sky is gun-
metal gray, but to the west the sky is peach streaked with crimson. The
land and sky of the West often fill what Thoreau termed our "need to
witness our limits transgressed." Nature, in Dakota, can indeed be an experience of the holy.

More Americans than ever, well over 70 percent, now live in urban
areas and tend to see Plains land as empty. What they really mean is devoid

of human presence. Most visitors to Dakota travel on interstate highways that will take them as quickly as possible through the region, past our larger cities to such attractions as the Badlands and the Black Hills. Looking at the expanse of land in between, they may wonder why a person would choose to live in such a barren place, let alone love it. But mostly they are bored: they turn up the car stereo, count the miles to civilization, and look away.

Dakota is a painful reminder of human limits, just as cities and shopping malls are attempts to deny them. This book is an invitation to a land of little rain and few trees, dry summer winds and harsh winters, a land rich in grass and sky and surprises. On a crowded planet, this is a place inhabited by few, and by the circumstance of inheritance, I am one of them. Nearly twenty years ago I returned to the holy ground of my childhood summers; I moved from New York City to the house my mother had grown up in, in an isolated town on the border between North and South Dakota.

More than any other place I lived as a child or young adult—Virginia, Illinois, Hawaii, Vermont, New York—this is my spiritual geography, the place where I've wrestled my story out of the circumstances of landscape and inheritance. The word "geography" derives from the Greek words for earth and writing, and writing about Dakota has been my means of understanding that inheritance and reclaiming what is holy in it. Of course Dakota has always been such a matrix for its Native American inhabitants. But their tradition is not mine, and in returning to the Great Plains, where two generations of my family lived before me, I had to build on my own traditions, those of the Christian West. *5*

When a friend referred to the western Dakotas as the Cappadocia of North America, I was handed an essential connection between the spirituality of the landscape I inhabit and that of the fourth-century monastics who set up shop in Cappadocia and the deserts of Egypt. Like those monks, I made a countercultural choice to live in what the rest of the world considers a barren waste. Like them, I had to stay in this place, like a scarecrow in a field, and hope for the brains to see its beauty. My idea of what makes a place beautiful had to change, and it has. The city no longer appeals to me for the cultural experiences and possessions I might acquire there, but because its population is less homogenous than Plains society. Its holiness is to be found in being open to humanity in all its diversity. And the western Plains now seem bountiful in their emptiness, offering solitude and room to grow.

I want to make it clear that my move did not take me "back to the land" in the conventional sense. I did not strike out on my own to make a go of it with "an acre and a cow," as a Hungarian friend naively imagined. As the homesteaders of the early twentieth century soon found out, it is not possible to survive on even 160 acres in western Dakota. My move was one that took me deep into the meaning of inheritance, as I had to try to fit myself into a complex network of long-established relationships.

My husband and I live in the small house in Lemmon, South Dakota, that my grandparents built in 1923. We moved there after they died because my mother, brother, and sisters, who live in Honolulu, did not want to hold an estate auction, the usual procedure when the beneficiaries of an inheritance on the Plains live far away. I offered to move there and manage the farm interests (land and a cattle herd) that my grandparents left us. David Dwyer, my husband, also a poet, is a New York City native who spent his childhood summers in the Adirondacks, and he had enough sense of adventure to agree to this. We expected to be in Dakota for just a few years.

It's hard to say why we stayed. A growing love of the prairie landscape and the quiet of a small town, inertia, and because as freelance writers, we found we had the survival skills suitable for a frontier. We put together a crazy quilt of jobs: I worked in the public library and as an artist-in-residence in schools in both Dakotas; I also did freelance writing and bookkeeping. David tended bar, wrote computer programs for a number of businesses in the region, and did freelance translation of French literature for several publishers. In 1979 we plunged into the cable television business with some friends, one of whom is an electronics expert. David learned how to climb poles and put up the hardware, and I kept the books. It was a good investment; after selling the company we found that we had bought ourselves a good three years to write. In addition, I still do bookkeeping for my family's farm business: the land is leased to people I've known all my life, people who have rented our land for two generations and also farm their own land and maintain their own cattle herds, an arrangement that is common in western Dakota.

In coming to terms with my inheritance, and pursuing my vocation   10
as a writer, I have learned, as both farmers and writers have discovered before me, that it is not easy to remain on the Plains. Only one of North Dakota's best-known writers—Richard Critchfield, Louise Erdrich, Lois Hudson, and Larry Woiwode—currently lives in the state. And writing the truth about the Dakota experience can be a thankless task. I recently discovered that Lois Hudson's magnificent novel of the Dakota Dust Bowl, *The Bones of Plenty,* a book arguably better than *The Grapes of Wrath,* was unknown to teachers and librarians in a town not thirty miles from where the novel is set. The shame of it is that Hudson's book could have helped these people better understand their current situation, the economic crisis forcing many families off the land. Excerpts from *The Grapes of Wrath* were in a textbook used in the school, but students could keep them at a safe distance, part of that remote entity called "American literature" that has little relation to their lives.

The Plains are full of what a friend here calls "good telling stories," and while our sense of being forgotten by the rest of the world makes it all the more important that we preserve them and pass them on, instead we often neglect them. Perversely, we do not even claim those stories which have attracted national attention. Both John Neihardt and Frederick Manfred have written about Hugh Glass, a hunter and trapper mauled by a grizzly bear in 1823 at the confluence of the Little Moreau and Grand rivers just south of Lemmon. Left for dead by his companions, he crawled and limped some two hundred miles southeast, to the trading post at Fort Kiowa on the Missouri River. Yet when Manfred wanted to give a reading in Lemmon a few years ago, the publicist was dismissed by a high school principal who said, "Who's he? Why would our students be interested?" Manfred's audience of eighty—large for Lemmon—consisted mainly of the people who remembered him from visits he'd made in the early 1950s while researching his novel *Lord Grizzly.*

Thus are the young disenfranchised while their elders drown in details, "story" reduced to the social column of the weekly newspaper that reports on family reunions, card parties, even shopping excursions to a neighboring town. But real story is as hardy as grass, and it survives in Dakota in oral form. Good storytelling is one thing rural whites and Indians have in common. But Native Americans have learned through harsh necessity that people who survive encroachment by another culture need story to survive. And a storytelling tradition is something Plains people share with both ancient and contemporary monks: we learn our ways of being and reinforce our values by telling tales about each other.

One of my favorite monastic stories concerns two fourth-century monks who "spent fifty years mocking their temptations by saying 'After this winter, we will leave here.' When the summer came, they said, 'After this summer, we will go away from here.' They passed all their lives in this way." These ancient monks sound remarkably like the farmers I know in Dakota who live in what they laconically refer to as "next-year country."

We hold on to hopes for next year every year in western Dakota: hoping that droughts will end; hoping that our crops won't be hailed out in the few rainstorms that come; hoping that it won't be too windy on the day we harvest, blowing away five bushels an acre; hoping (usually against hope) that if we get a fair crop, we'll be able to get a fair price for it. Sometimes survival is the only blessing that the terrifying angel of the Plains bestows. Still, there are those born and raised here who can't imagine living anywhere else. There are also those who are drawn here— teachers willing to take the lowest salaries in the nation; clergy with theological degrees from Princeton, Cambridge, and Zurich who want to serve small rural churches—who find that they cannot remain for long. Their professional mobility sets them apart and becomes a liability in an isolated Plains community where outsiders are treated with an uneasy mix of hospitality and rejection.

"Extremes," John R. Milton suggests in his history of South Dakota,   *15*
is "perhaps the key word for Dakota . . . What happens to extremes is that they come together, and the result is a kind of tension." I make no attempt in this book to resolve the tensions and contradictions I find in the Dakotas

between hospitality and insularity, change and inertia, stability and instability, possibility and limitation, between hope and despair, between open
hearts and closed minds.

I suspect that these are the ordinary contradictions of human life, and
that they are so visible in Dakota because we are so few people living in a
stark landscape. We are at the point of transition between East and West in
America, geographically and psychically isolated from either coast, and
unlike either the Midwest or the desert West. South Dakota has been
dubbed both the Sunshine State and the Blizzard State, and both designations have a basis in fact. Without a strong identity we become a mythic
void; "the Great Desolation," as novelist Ole Rolvaag wrote early in this
century, or "The American Outback," as *Newsweek* designated us a few
years ago.

Geographical and cultural identity is confused even within the Dakotas. The eastern regions of both states have more in common with each
other than with the area west of the Missouri, colloquially called the
"West River." Although I commonly use the term "Dakota" to refer to both
Dakotas, most of my experience is centered in this western region, and it
seems to me that especially in western Dakota we live in tension between
myth and truth. Are we cowboys or farmers? Are we fiercely independent
frontier types or community builders? One myth that haunts us is that the
small town is a stable place. The land around us was divided neatly in 160-
acre rectangular sections, following the Homestead Act of 1863 (creating
many section-line roads with 90-degree turns). But our human geography
has never been as orderly. The western Dakota communities settled by
whites are, and always have been, remarkably unstable. The Dakotas have
always been a place to be *from:* some 80 percent of homesteaders left within
the first twenty years of settlement, and our boom-and-bust agricultural
and oil industry economy has kept people moving in and out (mostly out)
ever since. Many small-town schools and pulpits operate with revolving
doors, adding to the instability.

When I look at the losses we've sustained in western Dakota since
1980 (about one fifth of the population in Perkins County, where I live,
and a full third in neighboring Corson County) and at the human cost in
terms of anger, distrust, and grief, it is the prairie descendants of the
ancient desert monastics, the monks and nuns of Benedictine communities
in the Dakotas, who inspire me to hope. One of the vows a Benedictine
makes is *stability:* commitment to a particular community, a particular
place. If this vow is countercultural by contemporary American standards,
it is countercultural in the way that life on the Plains often calls us to be.
Benedictines represent continuity in the boom-and-bust cycles of the
Plains; they incarnate, and can articulate, the reasons people want to stay.

Terrence Kardong, a monk at an abbey in Dakota founded roughly a
thousand years after their European motherhouse, has termed the Great
Plains "a school for humility," humility being one goal of Benedictine life.
He writes, "in this eccentric environment . . . certainly one is made aware

that things are not entirely in control." In fact, he says, the Plains offer constant reminders that "we are quite powerless over circumstance." His abbey, like many Great Plains communities with an agricultural base, had a direct experience of powerlessness, going bankrupt in the 1920s. Then, and at several other times in the community's history, the monks were urged to move to a more urban environment.

Kardong writes, "We may be crazy, but we are not necessarily stupid . . . We built these buildings ourselves. We've cultivated these fields since the turn of the century. We watched from our dining room window the mirage of the Killdeer Mountains rise and fall on the horizon. We collected a library full of local history books and they belong here, not in Princeton. Fifty of our brothers lie down the hill in our cemetery. We have become as indigenous as the cottonwood trees . . . If you take us somewhere else, we lose our character, our history—maybe our soul."   20

A monk does not speak lightly of the soul, and Kardong finds in the Plains the stimulus to develop an inner geography. "A monk isn't supposed to need all kinds of flashy surroundings. We're supposed to have a beautiful inner landscape. Watching a storm pass from horizon to horizon fills your soul with reverence. It makes your soul expand to fill the sky."

Monks are accustomed to taking the long view, another countercultural stance in our fast-paced, anything-for-a-buck society which has corrupted even the culture of farming into "agribusiness." Kardong and many other writers of the desert West, including myself, are really speaking of values when they find beauty in this land no one wants. He writes: "We who are permanently camped here see things you don't see at 55 m.p.h. . . . We see white-faced calves basking in the spring grass like the lilies of the field. We see a chinook wind in January make rivulets run. We see dust-devils and lots of little things. We are grateful."

The so-called emptiness of the Plains is full of such miraculous "little things." The way native grasses spring back from a drought, greening before your eyes; the way a snowy owl sits on a fencepost, or a golden eagle hunts, wings outstretched over grassland that seems to go on forever. Pelicans rise noisily from a lake; an antelope stands stock-still, its tattooed neck like a message in unbreakable code; columbines, their long stems beaten down by hail, bloom in the mud, their whimsical and delicate flowers intact. One might see a herd of white-tailed deer jumping a fence; fox cubs wrestling at the door of their lair; cock pheasants stepping out of a medieval tapestry into windrowed hay; cattle bunched in the southeast corner of a pasture, anticipating a storm in the approaching thunderheads. And above all, one notices the quiet, the near-absence of human noise.

My spiritual geography is a study in contrasts. The three places with which I have the deepest affinity are Hawaii, where I spent my adolescent years; New York City, where I worked after college; and western South Dakota. Like many Americans of their generation, my parents left their small-town roots in the 1930s and moved often. Except for the family home in Honolulu—its yard rich with fruits and flowers (pomegranate, tangerine, lime, mango, plumeria, hibiscus, lehua, ginger, and bird-of-paradise)—and my maternal grandparents' house in a remote village in western Dakota—its modest and hard-won garden offering columbine, daisies and mint—all my childhood places are gone.

When my husband and I moved nearly twenty years ago from New York to that house in South Dakota, only one wise friend in Manhattan understood the inner logic of the journey. Others, appalled, looked up Lemmon, South Dakota (named for George Lemmon, a cattleman and wheeler-dealer of the early 1900s, and home of the Petrified Wood Park—the world's largest—a gloriously eccentric example of American folk art) in their atlases and shook their heads. How could I leave the artists' and writers' community in which I worked, the diverse and stimulating environment of a great city, for such barrenness? Had I lost my mind? But I was young, still in my twenties, an apprentice poet certain of the rightness of returning to the place where I suspected I would find my stories. As it turns out, the Plains have been essential not only for my growth as a writer, they have formed me spiritually. I would even say they have made me a human being.

St. Hilary, a fourth-century bishop (and patron saint against snake bites) once wrote, "Everything that seems empty is full of the angels of God." The magnificent sky above the Plains sometimes seems to sing this truth; angels seem possible in the wind-filled expanse. A few years ago a small boy named Andy who had recently moved to the Plains from Pennsylvania told me he knew an angel named Andy Le Beau. He spelled out the name for me and I asked him if the angel had visited him here. "Don't you know?" he said in the incredulous tone children adopt when adults seem stupefyingly ignorant. "Don't you know?" he said, his voice rising, "*This* is where angels drown."

Andy no more knew that he was on a prehistoric sea bed than he knew what *le beau* means in French, but some ancient wisdom in him had sensed great danger here; a terrifying but beautiful landscape in which we are at the mercy of the unexpected, and even angels proceed at their own risk.

Reading and Responding

Do another freewrite responding to these questions: What kind of landscape is described? How does it differ from the stereotype of a "beautiful" place?

Working Together

1. List the key reasons Norris finds the Dakota landscape beautiful—important, useful, good.
2. Why for Norris is this particular landscape spiritually useful? How in her view is God revealed in this landscape? To put this another way, how does this landscape make it possible for us to experience God's

presence in the world? What's the connection between the Dakota landscape and the Benedictine spirituality Norris also celebrates?

3. Imagine Norris in a panel discussion with Wordsworth, Oates, Hopkins, and Crane. This question has just been put to the panel: "Does God reveal himself in a landscape?" What would Norris say, what would the others say, and how would Norris respond to what the others say? Who would be her allies? Who would she argue against, and how?

Rethinking and Rewriting

1. Describe a landscape, a city, a building—some place that most people pass by without thinking about, a place people actually dislike, or a place people find uninteresting. Praise this place. Argue that it's a good place. Argue that it's a good place *because* most people don't notice it or care about it.

2. Do research on the Benedictine monastic tradition. Write a paper explaining the major tenets of this way of life.

Essay Topics for Chapter 10

1. If you have a strong religious conviction, try to gently and patiently explain that conviction to someone who does not share it. Do this not so much by quoting philosophers or religious books or religious authorities but, rather, by explaining an experience (or set of experiences) you had that helped form your religious convictions. Focus on the experience first; then interpret it for your readers so that they see how the experience has helped form your beliefs. Make sure that the experience itself gets most of your words. If you have no strong religious convictions of any sort, discuss and explain that. If you feel deeply unsure about religious questions, discuss and explain that. Whatever your convictions or questions, end your essay by linking your beliefs to your own view of nature.

2. Compare Stephen Crane's "The Open Boat" and Barry Lopez's "Gone Back into the Earth." Would Crane and Lopez argue about the essence of nature or would they agree? Which author more clearly reflects your own position?

3. Compare Stephen Crane's "The Open Boat" and Kathleen Dean Moore's "Alamo Canyon Creek." Would Crane and Moore agree or disagree? Which author more clearly reflects your own position?

4. Having read both Joyce Carol Oates's "Against Nature" and Lewis Thomas's "The Tucson Zoo," explain how these two essays seem related to you. Quote from both; end by choosing sides and explaining the reasons for your choice.

5. Assume that you are Annie Dillard (author of "A Field of Silence") and you've just this morning read Joyce Carol Oates's essay "Against Nature." As Annie Dillard, write a two-page, single-spaced (or four-

page, double-spaced) letter to Joyce Carol Oates telling her how you're responding to her essay. Assume that you know Oates slightly but only well enough to address her as "Dear Joyce."

6. Assume that you are Joyce Carol Oates (author of "Against Nature") and you've just this morning read Annie Dillard's "A Field of Silence." As Joyce Carol Oates, write a two-page, single-spaced (or four-page, double-spaced) letter to Annie Dillard telling her how you're responding to her essay. Assume that you know Dillard but only well enough to address her as "Dear Annie."

7. Explain your own position on "the nature of nature." Base this essay on your own experience, but also anchor your discussion by using at least three sources outside your own experience. Of these three outside sources at least one should be a selection from this chapter.

8. Argue that Kathleen Norris and Gretel Ehrlich share common values and outlooks. Or argue how different they are. Or do both. Variations: Follow these same directions with other pairs of writers (make sure at least one of them comes from this chapter). For example, pair Kathleen Norris with Joyce Carol Oates, or Mary Oliver with Gerard Manley Hopkins, or Stephen Crane with Annie Dillard.

9. If you are a vegetarian, explain why. If you're not a vegetarian, explain why. Explain what's been important in your decision here (or explain why it's never even been a decision). End by explaining how you think this question is or is not related to your overall view of nature and people's place in nature.

10. We tend to locate our landfills in remote areas whenever we can. Suppose that a waste management company proposed a landfill outside Lemmon, South Dakota, with garbage to be brought in by trains from other places in the Midwest. How would Kathleen Norris react to this proposal? Assume that you are Kathleen Norris and you're going to write a letter to the local newspaper (they have a five-hundred-word limit for letters). What would you say?

11

The Forest

One of the ideas we've been trying to get across so far is that environmental issues are too complex to be reduced to easy oppositions between good guys and bad guys, right and wrong. Even what nature itself is isn't clear and definable once and for all. We know that something good and beautiful and important is out there, beyond us, but what that something means is very much connected to who we are, where we live, and when we live. All of us are biased. All of us are in relationship to the world—which is to say that we can never see the world wholly, purely, completely.

The forest is an ideal subject for organizing and testing these ideas. We know that a forest is beautiful and important, and we know that there are great problems in forestry today—conflicts over how forests should be understood and appreciated. The debate about our forests is at the center of the environmental debate. And that's the point. There are conflicts here. Good people of goodwill can look at a stand of trees and see different things. They see different things because they see differently.

The first white settlers in this country didn't see the forest as a paradise and refuge but as a wilderness to be feared and conquered. A logger might see a clear-cut as evidence of jobs and prosperity and a job well done; an environmentalist might see the same patch of ground as a travesty.

Are old-growth trees "decadent" or "majestic"? And just what is "old-growth" anyway? How much of that "old-growth" is left, exactly?

In the selections that follow we mean to involve you in these questions as a way of encouraging a sense of openness. We want you to resist the slogans and clichés. An awareness of complexity often leads to a feeling of humility, perhaps even charity, and it may be that these are just the feelings we need to break the gridlock in today's discussions of forestry.

"A WILDERNESS CONDITION"

Roderick Nash

> *Roderick Nash's landmark study,* Wilderness and the American Mind, *first appeared in 1967. Since then it has been revised twice in order to discuss new developments in both politics and ecology. In his preface to the most recent edition (1983) Nash notes that wilderness is not a concept Native Americans understood: "As Standing Bear recognized, for his people 'there was no wilderness; since nature was not dangerous but hospitible; not forbidding but friendly.'" In the chapter reprinted here Nash recounts the first settlers' view of the landscape they came to inhabit.*

Before and As You Read

1. Before reading, write several sentences about your first reactions when you see or hear the word *forest.* What do you think of?
2. As you read, annotate the text: Mark the passages that seem most important, write questions in the margin, number what you think are the main points, and point out connections and patterns.

> Looking only a few years through the vista of futurity what a sublime spectacle presents itself! Wilderness, once the chosen residence of solitude and savageness, converted into populous cities, smiling villages, beautiful farms and plantations!
>
> CHILLICOTHE (Ohio) *Supporter,* 1817

Alexis de Tocqueville resolved to see wilderness during his 1831 trip to the United States, and in Michigan Territory in July the young Frenchman found himself at last on the fringe of civilization. But when he informed the frontiersmen of his desire to travel for *pleasure* into the primitive forest, they thought him mad. The Americans required considerable persuasion from Tocqueville to convince them that his interests lay in matters other than lumbering or land speculation. Afterwards he generalized in his journal that "living in the wilds, [the pioneer] only prizes the works of man" while Europeans, like himself, valued wilderness because of its novelty.[1] Expanding the point in *Democracy in America,* Tocqueville concluded: "in Europe people talk a great deal of the wilds of America, but the Americans themselves never think about them; they are

---

1. Alexis de Tocqueville, *Journey to America,* trans. George Lawrence, ed. J. P. Mayer (New Haven, Conn., 1960), p. 335. For the circumstances of the Michigan trip and a slightly different translation see George Wilson Pierson, *Tocqueville in America* (Garden City, N.Y., 1959), pp. 144–99.

insensible to the wonders of inanimate nature and they may be said not to perceive the mighty forests that surround them till they fall beneath the hatchet. Their eyes are fixed upon another sight," he added, "the . . . march across these wilds, draining swamps, turning the course of rivers, peopling solitudes, and subduing nature."[2]

The unfavorable attitude toward wilderness that Tocqueville observed in Michigan also existed on other American frontiers. When William Bradford stepped off the *Mayflower* into a "hideous and desolate wilderness" he started a tradition of repugnance. With few exceptions later pioneers continued to regard wilderness with defiant hatred and joined the Chillicothe *Supporter* in celebrating the advance of civilization as the greatest of blessings. Under any circumstances the necessity of living in close proximity to wild country—what one of Bradford's contemporaries called "a Wilderness condition"—engendered strong antipathy. Two centuries after Bradford, a fur trader named Alexander Ross recorded his despair in encountering a "gloomy," "dreary," and "unhallowed wilderness" near the Columbia River.[3]

Two components figured in the American pioneer's bias against wilderness. On the direct, physical level, it constituted a formidable threat to his very survival. The transatlantic journey and subsequent western advances stripped away centuries. Successive waves of frontiersmen had to contend with wilderness as uncontrolled and terrifying as that which primitive man confronted. Safety and comfort, even necessities like food and shelter, depended on overcoming the wild environment. For the first Americans, as for medieval Europeans, the forest's darkness hid savage men, wild beasts, and still stranger creatures of the imagination. In addition civilized man faced the danger of succumbing to the wildness of his surroundings and reverting to savagery himself. The pioneer, in short, lived too close to wilderness for appreciation. Understandably, his attitude was hostile and his dominant criteria utilitarian. The *conquest* of wilderness was his major concern.

Wilderness not only frustrated the pioneers physically but also acquired significance as a dark and sinister symbol. They shared the long Western tradition of imagining wild country as a moral vacuum, a cursed and chaotic wasteland. As a consequence, frontiersmen acutely sensed that they battled wild country not only for personal survival but in the name of nation, race, and God. Civilizing the New World meant enlightening darkness, ordering chaos, and changing evil into good. In the morality play of westward expansion, wilderness was the villain, and the pioneer, as

---

2. Tocqueville, *Democracy in America*, ed. Phillips Bradley (2 vols. New York 1945), 2, 74.
3. William Bradford, *Of Plymouth Plantation, 1620–1647*, ed. Samuel Eliot Morison (New York, 1952), p. 62; Edward Johnson, *Johnson's Wonder-Working Providence, 1628–1651* (1654), ed. J. Franklin Jameson, Original Narratives of Early American History, 7 (New York, 1910), p. 100; Alexander Ross, *Adventures of the First Settlers on the Oregon or Columbia River* (London, 1849), pp. 143, 146.

hero, relished its destruction. The transformation of a wilderness into civilization was the reward for his sacrifices, the definition of his achievement, and the source of his pride. He applauded his successes in terms suggestive of the high stakes he attached to the conflict.

The discovery of the New World rekindled the traditional European   5
notion that an earthly paradise lay somewhere to the west. As the reports of the first explorers filtered back the Old World began to believe that America might be the place of which it had dreamed since antiquity. One theme in the paradise myth stressed the material and sensual attributes of the new land. It fed on reports of fabulous riches, a temperate climate, longevity, and garden-like natural beauty.[4] Promoters of discovery and colonization embellished these rumors. One Londoner, who likely never set foot in the New World, wrote lyrically of the richness of Virginia's soil and the abundance of its game. He even added: "nor is the present wildernesse of it without a particular beauty, being all over a naturall Grove of Oakes, Pines, Cedars . . . all of so delectable an aspect, that the melanchollyest eye in the World cannot look upon it without contentment, nor content himselfe without admiration."[5] Generally, however, European portrayers of a material paradise in the New World completely ignored the "wildernesse" aspect, as inconsistent with the idea of beneficent nature. Illogically, they exempted America from the adverse conditions of life in other uncivilized places.

Anticipations of a second Eden quickly shattered against the reality of North America. Soon after he arrived the seventeenth-century frontiersman realized that the New World was the antipode of paradise. Previous hopes intensified the disappointment. At Jamestown the colonists abandoned the search for gold and turned, shocked, to the necessity of survival in a hostile environment. A few years later William Bradford recorded his dismay at finding Cape Cod wild and desolate. He lamented the Pilgrims' inability to find a vantage point "to view from this wilderness a more goodly country to feed their hopes."[6] In fact, there was none. The forest stretched farther than Bradford and his generation imagined. For Europeans wild country was a single peak or heath, an island of uninhabited land surrounded by settlement. They at least knew its character and extent. But the seemingly boundless wilderness of the New World was

---

4. Loren Baritz, "The Idea of the West," *American Historical Review, 66* (1961), 618–40; Charles L. Sanford, *The Quest for Paradise* (Urbana, Ill., 1961), pp. 36 ff.; Howard Mumford Jones, *O Strange New World* (New York, 1964), pp. 1–34; Louis B. Wright, *The Dream of Prosperity in Colonial America* (New York, 1965); Leo Marx, *The Machine in the Garden: Technology and the Pastoral Ideal in America* (New York, 1964), pp. 34–72.
5. E[dward] W[illiams], *Virginia . . . Richly and Truly Valued* (1650) in Peter Force, *Tracts and Other Papers* (4 vols. New York, 1947), *3,* No. 11, 11.
6. Bradford, p. 62.

something else. In the face of this vast blankness, courage failed and imagination multiplied fears.

Commenting on the arrival of the Puritans some years after, Cotton Mather indicated the change in attitude that contact with the New World produced. "Lady Arabella," he wrote, left an "earthly *paradise*" in England to come to America and "encounter the sorrows of a wilderness." She then died and "left that *wilderness* for the Heavenly *paradise*."[7] Clearly the American wilderness was not paradise. If men expected to enjoy an idyllic environment in America, they would have to *make* it by conquering wild country. Mather realized in 1693 that "Wilderness" was the stage "thro' which we are passing to the Promised Land."[8] Yet optimistic Americans continued to be fooled. "Instead of a garden," declared one traveler in the Ohio Valley in 1820, "I found a wilderness."[9]

How frontiersmen described the wilderness they found reflected the intensity of their antipathy. The same descriptive phrases appeared again and again. Wilderness was "howling," "dismal," "terrible." In the 1650s John Eliot wrote of going "into a wilderness where nothing appeareth but hard labour [and] wants," and Edward Johnson described "the penuries of a Wildernesse."[10] Cotton Mather agreed in 1702 about the "difficulties of a rough and hard wilderness," and in 1839 John Plumbe, Jr. told about "the hardships and privations of the wilderness" in Iowa and Wisconsin.[11] Invariably the pioneers singled out wilderness as the root cause of their difficulties. For one thing, the physical character of the primeval forest proved baffling and frustrating to settlers. One chronicler of the "Wildernesse-worke" of establishing the town of Concord, Massachusetts portrayed in graphic detail the struggle through "unknowne woods," swamps, and flesh-tearing thickets. The town founders wandered lost for days in the bewildering gloom of the dense forest. Finally came the back-breaking labor of carving fields from the wilderness.[12] Later generations who settled forested regions reported similar hardships. On every frontier obtaining cleared land, the symbol of civilization, demanded tremendous effort.

The pioneers' situation and attitude prompted them to use military metaphors to discuss the coming of civilization. Countless diaries, addresses,

---

7. Mather, *Magnalia Christi Americana* (2 vols. Hartford, Conn., 1853), *I*, 77. The original edition was 1702.

8. Mather, *The Wonders of the Invisible World* (London, 1862), p. 13. Alan Heimert, "Puritanism, the Wilderness, and the Frontier," *New England Quarterly, 26* (1953), 369–70, has commented on this point.

9. Adlard Welby, *A Visit to North America* (London, 1821), p. 65.

10. Eliot, "The Learned Conjectures" (1650) as quoted in Williams, *Wilderness and Paradise,* p. 102; Johnson, p. 75.

11. Mather, *Magnalia, I,* 77; Plumbe, *Sketches of Iowa and Wisconsin* (St. Louis, 1839), p. 21.

12. Johnson, pp. 111–15; For a dramatic portrayal of the forest as obstacle, see Richard G. Lillard, *The Great Forest* (New York, 1947), pp. 65–94.

and memorials of the frontier period represented wilderness as an "enemy" which had to be "conquered," "subdued," and "vanquished" by a "pioneer army." The same phraseology persisted into the present century; an old Michigan pioneer recalled how as a youth he had engaged in a "struggle with nature" for the purpose of "converting a wilderness into a rich and prosperous civilization."[13] Historians of westward expansion chose the same figure: "they conquered the wilderness, they subdued the forests, they reduced the land to fruitful subjection."[14] The image of man and wilderness locked in mortal combat was difficult to forget. Advocates of a giant dam on the Colorado River system spoke in the 1950s of "that eternal problem of subduing the earth" and of "conquering the wilderness" while a President urged us in his 1961 inaugural address to "conquer the deserts." Wilderness, declared a correspondent to the *Saturday Evening Post* in 1965, "is precisely what man has been fighting against since he began his painful, awkward climb to civilization. It is the dark, the formless, the terrible, the old chaos which our fathers pushed back. . . . It is held at bay by constant vigilance, and when the vigilance slackens it swoops down for a melodramatic revenge."[15] Such language animated the wilderness, investing it with an almost conscious enmity toward men, who returned it in full measure.

Along with the obstacle it offered to settlement and civilization, wilderness also confronted the frontier mind with terrifying creatures, both known and imagined. Wild men headed the menagerie. Initially Indians were regarded with pity and instructed in the Gospel, but after the first massacres most of the compassion changed to contempt.[16] Sweeping out of the forest to strike, and then melting back into it, savages were almost always associated with wilderness. When Mary Rowlandson was captured in the 1670s on the Massachusetts frontier, she wrote that she went "mourning and lamenting, leaving farther my own Country, and travelling into the vast and howling Wilderness." The remainder of her account revealed an hysterical horror of her captors and of what she called "this Wilderness-condition." A century later J. Hector St. John Crevecoeur discussed the imminency of Indian attack as one of the chief "distresses" of

10

---

13. General B. M. Cutcheon, "Log Cabin Times and Log Cabin People," *Michigan Pioneer Historical Society Collections, 39* (1901), 611.

14. George Cary Eggleston, *Our First Century* (New York, 1905), p. 255. The representation in late-nineteenth century literature of evil, menacing nature has been discussed in Carleton F. Culmsee, *Malign Nature and the Frontier,* Utah State University Monograph Series, 8, (Logan, Utah, 1959).

15. Ashel Manwaring and Ray P. Greenwood, "Proceedings before the United States Department of the Interior: Hearings on Dinosaur National Monument, Echo Park and Split Mountain Dams," (April 3, 1950), Department of the Interior Library, Washington, D.C., pp. 535, 555; John F. Kennedy, "For the Freedom of Man," *Vital Speeches, 27* (1961), 227; Robert Wernick, "Speaking Out: Let's Spoil the Wilderness," *Saturday Evening Post, 238* (Nov. 6, 1965), 12.

16. Roy Harvey Pearce, *The Savages of America: A Study of the Indian and the Idea of Civilization* (rev. ed., Baltimore, 1965); Jones, *O Strange New World,* pp. 50 ff.

frontier life and described the agony of waiting, gun in hand, for the first arrows to strike his home. "The wilderness," he observed, "is a harbour where it is impossible to find [the Indians] . . . a door through which they can enter our country whenever they please." Imagination and the presence of wild country could multiply fears. Riding through "savage haunts" on the Santa Fe Trail in the 1830s, Josiah Gregg noticed how "each click of a pebble" seemed "the snap of a firelock" and "in a very rebound of a twig [was] the whisk of an arrow."[17]

Wild animals added to the danger of the American wilderness, and here too the element of the unknown intensified feelings. Reporting in 1630 on the "discommodities" of New England, Francis Higginson wrote that "this Countrey being verie full of Woods and Wildernesses, doth also much abound with Snakes and Serpents of strange colours and huge greatnesse." There were some, he added, "that haue [have] Rattles in their Tayles that will not flye from a Man . . . but will flye upon him and sting him so mortally, that he will dye within a quarter of an houre after." Clearly there was some truth here and in the stories that echo through frontier literature of men whom "the savage Beasts had devoured . . . in the Wilderness," but often fear led to exaggeration. Cotton Mather, for instance, warned in 1707 of "the *Evening Wolves,* the rabid and howling *Wolves* of the *Wilderness* [which] would make . . . Havock among you, *and not leave the Bones till the morning.*" Granted this was a jeremiad intended to shock Mather's contemporaries into godly behavior, but his choice of imagery still reflected a vivid conception of the physical danger of wild country. Elsewhere Mather wrote quite seriously about the "Dragons," "Droves of Devils," and "Fiery flying serpents" to be found in the primeval forest.[18] Indeed, legends and folktales from first contact until well into the national period linked the New World wilderness with a host of monsters, witches, and similar supernatural beings.[19]

A more subtle terror than Indians or animals was the opportunity the freedom of wilderness presented for men to behave in a savage or bestial manner. Immigrants to the New World certainly sought release from oppressive European laws and traditions, yet the complete license of the wilderness was an overdose. Morality and social order seemed to stop at the edge of the clearing. Given the absence of restraint, might not the pioneer

---

17. Mary Rowlandson, *Narrative of the Captivity and Restauration* (1682) in *Narratives of the Indian Wars, 1675–1699,* ed. Charles H. Lincoln, Original Narratives of Early American History, 19 (New York, 1913), pp. 126, 131–32; Crevecoeur, *Letters from an American Farmer* (London, 1782), 272; Gregg, *Commerce of the Prairies or the Journal of a Santa Fe Trader* (2 vols. New York, 1845) *I,* 88.

18. Higginson, *New-Englands Plantation* (1630) in Force, *I,* No. 12, 11–12; John Lawson, *Lawson's History of North Carolina* (1714), ed. Frances L. Harriss (Richmond, Va., 1951), p. 29; Cotton Mather, *Frontiers Well-Defended* (Boston, 1707), p. 10; Mather, *Wonders,* pp. 13, 85.

19. Richard M. Dorson, *American Folklore* (Chicago, 1959), pp. 8 ff.; Jones, pp. 61 ff.

succumb to what John Eliot called "wilderness-temptations?"[20] Would not the proximity of wildness pull down the level of all American civilization? Many feared for the worst, and the concern with the struggle against barbarism was widespread in the colonies.[21] Seventeenth-century town "planters" in New England, for instance, were painfully aware of the dangers wilderness posed for the individual. They attempted to settle the northern frontier through the well-organized movement of entire communities. Americans like these pointed out that while liberty and solitude might be desirable to the man in a crowd, it was the gregarious tendency and controlling institutions of society that took precedence in the wilderness.

Yale's president, Timothy Dwight, spoke for most of his generation in regretting that as the pioneer pushed further and further into the wilds he became "less and less a civilized man." J. Hector St. John Crevecoeur was still more specific. Those who lived near "the great woods," he wrote in 1782, tend to be "regulated by the wildness of their neighborhood." This amounted to no regulation at all; the frontiersmen were beyond "the power of example, and check of shame." According to Crevecoeur, they had "degenerated altogether into the hunting state" and became ultimately "no better than carnivorous animals of a superior rank." He concluded that if man wanted happiness, "he cannot live in solitude, he must belong to some community bound by some ties."[22]

The behavior of pioneers frequently lent substance to these fears. In the struggle for survival many existed at a level close to savagery, and not a few joined Indian tribes. Even the ultimate horror of cannibalism was not unknown among the mountain men of the Rockies, as the case of Charles "Big Phil" Gardner proved.[23] Wilderness could reduce men to such a condition unless society maintained constant vigilance. Under wilderness conditions the veneer civilization laid over the barbaric elements in man seemed much thinner than in the settled regions.

It followed from the pioneer's association of wilderness with hardship [15] and danger in a variety of forms, that the rural, controlled, state of nature

---

20. Eliot as quoted in Williams, *Wilderness and Paradise*, p. 102.

21. Oscar Handlin, *Race and Nationality in American Life* (Garden City, N.Y., 1957), p. 114; Louis B. Wright, *Culture on the Moving Frontier* (Indianapolis, 1955), esp. pp. 11–45. Edmund S. Morgan, *The Puritan Dilemma* (Boston, 1958) has used the example of John Winthrop to demonstrate how the Puritan emphasis on the organic community was in part a response to the license of the wilderness. Roy Harvey Pearce contends that "the Indian became important for the English mind, not for what he was in and of himself, but rather for what he showed civilized men they were not and must not be": Pearce, *Savages of America*, p. 5.

22. Timothy Dwight, *Travels in New-England and New-York* (4 vols. New Haven, Conn., 1821–22), 2, 441; Crevecoeur, *Letters*, pp. 55–57, 271.

23. LeRoy R. Hafen, "Mountain Men: Big Phil the Cannibal," *Colorado Magazine, 13* (1936), 53–58. Other examples may be found in Ray A. Billington, *The American Frontiersman: A Case-Study in Reversion to the Primitive* (Oxford, 1954) and Arthur K. Moore, *The Frontier Mind* (Lexington, Ky., 1957), pp. 77 ff.

was the object of his affection and goal of his labor. The pastoral condition seemed closest to paradise and the life of ease and contentment. Americans hardly needed reminding that Eden had been a garden. The rural was also the fruitful and as such satisfied the frontiersman's utilitarian instincts. On both the idyllic and practical counts wilderness was anathema.

Transforming the wild into the rural had Scriptural precedents which the New England pioneers knew well. Genesis 1:28, the first commandment of God to man, stated that mankind should increase, conquer the earth, and have dominion over all living things. This made the fate of wilderness plain. In 1629 when John Winthrop listed reasons for departing "into . . . the wilderness," an important one was that "the whole earth is the lords Garden & he hath given it to the sonnes of men, and with a general Condision, Gen. 1.28: Increase & multiply, replenish the earth & subdue it." Why remain in England, Winthrop argued, and "suffer a whole Continent . . . to lie waste without any improvement."[24] Discussing the point a year later, John White also used the idea of man's God-appointed dominion to conclude that he did not see "how men should make benefit of [vacant land] . . . but by habitation and culture."[25] Two centuries later advocates of expansion into the wilderness used the same rhetoric. "There can be no doubt," declared Lewis Cass, soldier and senator from Michigan, in 1830, "that the Creator intended the earth should be reclaimed from a state of nature and cultivated." In the same year Governor George R. Gilmer of Georgia noted that this was specifically "by virtue of that command of the Creator delivered to man upon his formation—be fruitful, multiply, and replenish the earth, and subdue it."[26] Wilderness was waste; the proper behavior toward it, exploitation.

Without invoking the Bible, others involved in the pioneering process revealed a proclivity for the rural and useful. Wherever they encountered wild country they viewed it through utilitarian spectacles: trees became lumber, prairies farms, and canyons the sites of hydroelectric dams. The pioneers' self-conceived mission was to bring these things to pass. Writing about his experience settling northern New York in the late eighteenth century, William Cooper declared that his "great primary object" was "to cause the Wilderness to bloom and fructify." Another popular expression of the waste-to-garden imagery appeared in an account of how the Iowa farmer "makes the wilderness blossom like the rose." Rural,

---

24. Winthrop, *Conclusions for the Plantation in New England* (1629) in *Old South Leaflets* (9 vols. Boston, 1895), 2, No. 50, 5.
25. White, *The Planters Plea* (1630) in Force, *Tracts*, 2, No. 3, 2. For a discussion of similar rationales which the Puritans used in taking land from the Indians see Chester E. Eisinger, "The Puritans' Justification for Taking the Land," *Essex Institute Historical Collections, 84* (1948), 131–43.
26. Cass, "Removal of the Indians," *North American Review, 30* (1830), 77; Gilmer as quoted in Albert K. Weinberg, *Manifest Destiny: A Study of Nationalist Expansionism in American History* (Baltimore, 1935), p. 83.

garden-like nature was invariably the criterion of goodness to this mentality. A seventeenth-century account of New England's history noted the way a "howling wilderness" had, through the labors of settlers, become "pleasant Land." Speaking of the Ohio country in 1751, Christopher Gist noted that "it wants Nothing but Cultivation to make it a most delightful Country." Wilderness alone could neither please nor delight the pioneer. "Uncultivated" land, as an early nineteenth-century report put it, was "absolutely useless."[27]

At times the adulation of the pastoral became charged with emotion. On a trip to the fringe of settlement in the 1750s Thomas Pownall wrote: "with what an overflowing Joy does the Heart melt, while one views the Banks where rising Farms, new Fields, or flowering Orchards begin to illuminate this Face of Nature; nothing can be more delightful to the Eye, nothing go with more penetrating Sensation to the Heart." Similarly, on his 1806 journey of discovery Zebulon M. Pike conceived of the wild prairies near the Osage River as "the future seats of husbandry" and relished the thought of "the numerous herds of domestic cattle, which are no doubt destined to crown with joy these happy plains." Several decades later, in the Sierra, Zenas Leonard anticipated in a few years even those mountains being "greeted with the enlivening sound of the workman's hammer, and the merry whistle of the ploughboy."[28] Frontiersmen such as these looked through, rather than at, wilderness. Wild country had value as potential civilization.

Enthusiasm for "nature" in America during the pioneering period almost always had reference to the rural state. The frequent celebrations of country life, beginning with Richard Steele's *The Husbandman's Calling* of 1668 and continuing through the more familiar statements of Robert Beverley, Thomas Jefferson, and John Taylor of Caroline, reveal only a contempt for the wild, native landscape as "unimproved" land.[29] When wilderness scenery did appeal, it was not for its wildness but because it

---

27. Cooper, *A Guide in the Wilderness or the History of the First Settlements in the Western Counties of New York with Useful Instructions to Future Settlers* (Dublin, 1810), p. 6; John B. Newhall, *A Glimpse of Iowa in 1846* (Burlington, 1846), ix; Anonymous, *A Brief Relation of the State of New England* (1689) in Force, *Tracts, 4,* No. 11, 4–5; *Christopher Gist's Journals,* ed. William M. Darlington (Pittsburgh, 1893), p. 47; Gabriel Franchere, *Narrative of a Voyage to the Northwest Coast of America,* ed. and trans. J. V. Huntington (New York, 1854), p. 323.
28. Thomas Pownall, *A Topographical Description of . . . Parts of North America* (1776) as *A Topographical Description of the Dominions of the United States of America,* ed. Lois Mulkearn (Pittsburgh, 1949), p. 31; Zebulon Montgomery Pike, *The Expeditions of Zebulon Montgomery Pike,* ed. Elliott Coues (3 vols. New York, 1893), 2, 514; *Adventures of Zenas Leonard: Fur Trader,* ed. John C. Ewers (Normal, Okla., 1959), p. 94.
29. American attraction to the rural is fully discussed in Marx, *Machine in the Garden;* Sanford, *Quest for Paradise;* Henry Nash Smith, *Virgin Land: The American West as Symbol and Myth* (Cambridge, Mass., 1950), pp. 121 ff.; and A. Whitney Griswold, *Farming and Democracy* (New York, 1948).

resembled a "Garden or Orchard in England."[30] The case of Samuel Sewall is instructive, since his 1697 encomium to Plum Island north of Boston has been cited[31] as the earliest known manifestation of love for the New World landscape. What actually appealed to Sewall, however, was not the island's wild qualities but its resemblance to an English countryside. He mentioned cattle feeding in the fields, sheep on the hills, "fruitful marshes," and, as a final pastoral touch, the doves picking up left-over grain after a harvest. In Plum Island Sewall saw the rural idyll familiar since the Greeks, hardly the American wilderness. Indeed, in the same tract, he singled out "a dark Wilderness Cave" as the fearful location for pagan rites.[32]

Samuel Sewall's association of wild country with the ungodly is a   20
reminder that wilderness commonly signified other than a material obstacle or physical threat. As a concept it carried a heavy load of ethical connotations and lent itself to elaborate figurative usage. Indeed, by the seventeenth century "wilderness" had become a favorite metaphor for discussing the Christian situation. John Bunyan's *Pilgrim's Progress* summarized the prevailing viewpoint of wilderness as the symbol of anarchy and evil to which the Christian was unalterably opposed. The book's opening phrase, "As I walk'd through the Wilderness of this World," set the tone for the subsequent description of attempts to keep the faith in the chaotic and temptation-laden existence on earth. Even more pointed in the meaning it attached to wilderness was Benjamin Keach's *Tropologia, or a Key to Open Scripture Metaphor.* In a series of analogies, Keach instructed his readers that as wilderness is "barren" so the world is devoid of holiness; as men lose their way in the wilds so they stray from God in the secular sphere; and as travelers need protection from beasts in wild country, so the Christian needs the guidance and help of God. "A Wilderness," Keach concluded, "is a solitary and dolesom Place: so is this World to a godly Man."[33]

The Puritans who settled New England shared the same tradition regarding wilderness that gave rise to the attitudes of Bunyan and Keach.

---

30. George Percy, "Observations" (1625) in *Narratives of Early Virginia, 1606–1625,* ed. Lyon Gardiner Tyler, Original Narratives of Early American History, 5 (New York, 1907), p. 16. The same rhetoric was employed when pioneers emerged from the heavy, Eastern forest onto the open, garden-like prairies of Indiana and Illinois: James Hall, *Notes on the Western States* (Philadelphia, 1838), p. 56.
31. Perry Miller, in *The American Puritans: Their Prose and Poetry* (Garden City, N.Y., 1956), pp. 213, 295, and in *The New England Mind: From Colony to Province* (Boston, 1961), p. 190, contends that Sewall's "cry of the heart" marked the moment at which the Puritan became an American "rooted in the American soil" and took "delight in the American prospect."
32. Sewall, *Phaenomena . . . or Some Few Lines Towards a Description of the New Haven* (Boston, 1697), pp. 51, 59–60.
33. Bunyan, *The Pilgrim's Progress from this World to That which is to Come,* ed. James Blanton Wharey (Oxford, 1928), [p. 9.]; Keach, *Tropologia* (4 vols. London, 1681–82), 4, 391–92.

In the middle of his 1664 dictionary of the Indian language Roger Williams moralized: "the Wildernesse is a cleer resemblance of the world, where greedie and furious men persecute and devoure the harmlesse and innocent as the wilde beasts pursue and devoure the Hinds and Roes." The Puritans, especially, understood the Christian conception of wilderness, since they conceived of themselves as the latest in a long line of dissenting groups who had braved the wild in order to advance God's cause. They found precedents for coming to the New World in the twelfth-century Waldensians and in still earlier Christian hermits and ascetics who had sought the freedom of deserts or mountains. As enthusiastic practitioners of the art of typology (according to which events in the Old Testament were thought to prefigure later occurrences), the first New Englanders associated their migration with the Exodus. As soon as William Bradford reached Massachusetts Bay, he looked for "Pisgah," the mountain from which Moses had allegedly seen the promised land. Edward Johnson specifically compared the Puritans to "the ancient Beloved of Christ, whom he of old led by the hand from Egypt to Canaan, through that great and terrible Wildernesse." For Samuel Danforth the experience of John the Baptist seemed the closest parallel to the New England situation, although he too likened their mission to that of the children of Israel.[34]

While the Puritans and their predecessors in perfectionism often fled to the wilderness from a corrupt civilization, they never regarded the wilderness itself as their goal. The driving impulse was always to carve a garden from the wilds; to make an island of spiritual light in the surrounding darkness. The Puritan mission had no place for wild country. It was, after all, a *city* on a hill that John Winthrop called upon his colleagues to erect. The Puritans, and to a considerable extent their neighbors in the plantations to the south,[35] went to the wilderness in order to begin the task of redeeming the world from its "wilderness" state. Paradoxically, their sanctuary and their enemy were one and the same.[36]

Recent scholarship has glossed over the strength of the Puritans' intellectual legacy concerning wilderness. Their conception of the American wilderness did not come entirely or even largely "out of that wilderness

34. Williams, *A Key into the Language of America,* ed. J. Hammond Trumbull, Publications of the Narragansett Club, 1 (Providence, R.I., 1866), p. 130; Bradford, *Of Plymouth Plantation,* p. 62; Johnson, *Wonder-Working Providence,* 59; Danforth, *A Brief Recognition of New-England's Errand into the Wilderness* (Cambridge, Mass., 1671), pp. 1, 5, 9.

35. On this point see Perry Miller, "The Religious Impulse in the Founding of Virginia: Religion and Society in the Early Literature," *William and Mary Quarterly,* 5 (1948), 492–522, and Louis B. Wright, *Religion and Empire: The Alliance Between Piety and Commerce in English Expansion, 1558–1625* (Chapel Hill, N.C., 1943).

36. Williams, *Wilderness and Paradise,* pp. 73 ff., explores the meaning of this relationship.

itself," as Alan Heimert alleges.[37] They realized before leaving Europe that they were, as John Winthrop put it in 1629, fleeing "into . . . the wildernesse" to found the true Church.[38] And their Bibles contained all they needed to know in order to hate wilderness. Contact with the North American wilderness only supplemented what the Puritans already believed. In this sense the colonists' conception of the wilderness was more a product of the Old World than of the New.[39]

For the Puritans, of course, wilderness was metaphor as well as actuality. On the frontier the two meanings reinforced each other, multiplying horrors. Seventeenth-century writing is permeated with the idea of wild country as the environment of evil. Just as the Old Testament scribes represented the desert as the cursed land where satyrs and lesser demons roamed, the early New Englanders agreed with Michael Wigglesworth that on the eve of settlement the New World was: "a waste and howling wilderness, / Where none inhabited / But hellish fiends, and brutish men / That Devils worshiped." This idea of a pagan continent haunted the Puritan imagination. Wigglesworth went on to term North America the region of "eternal night" and "grim death" where the "Sun of righteousness" never shone. As a consequence "the dark and dismal Western woods" were "the Devils den." Cotton Mather believed he knew how it got into this condition: Satan had seduced the first Indian inhabitants for the purpose of making a stronghold. From this perspective, the natives were not merely heathens but active disciples of the devil. Mather verged on hysteria in describing "the Indians, whose chief Sagamores are well known unto some of our Captives to have been horrid Sorcerers, and hellish Conjurers and such as Conversed with Daemons."[40] The wilderness that harbored such beings was never merely neutral, never just a physical obstacle.

As self-styled agents of God the Puritan pioneers conceived their mission as breaking the power of evil. This involved an inner battle over

25

---

37. Heimert, "Puritanism, the Wilderness, and the Frontier," 361.

38. Winthrop, *Conclusions,* 5.

39. In comparison to the impulse to redeem the wilderness, I am deliberately minimizing as of secondary and ephemeral significance the notion of some Puritans that the Atlantic Ocean was *their* Sinai desert and that Canaan lay across it in New England. Heimert, 361–62, discusses this position briefly.

Without intending to belittle my debt to him, I am also discounting Perry Miller's contention that the nature of the Puritans' "errand" to the New World changed by the late seventeenth century from leading the Reformation to conquering the American wilderness: *Errand Into the Wilderness* (Cambridge, Mass., 1956), Chapter 1. The latter purpose, I feel, was strong from the beginning and was, moreover, always a necessary part of the former.

40. Wigglesworth, *God's Controversy with New England* (1662) in *Proceedings of the Massachusetts Historical Society,* 12 (1871), pp. 83, 84; Mather, *Magnalia, I,* 42; Mather, *Decennium Luctuosum: An History of Remarkable Occurrences in the Long War which New-England hath had with the Indian Salvages* (1699) in Lincoln, ed., *Narratives,* p. 242. For elaboration on the idea of Indians as devils see Jones, *O Strange New World,* pp. 55–61, and Pearce, *Savages of America,* pp. 19–35.

that "desolate and outgrowne wildernesse of humaine nature,"[41] and on the New England frontier it also meant conquering wild nature. The Puritans seldom forgot that civilizing the wilderness meant far more than profit, security, and worldly comfort. A manichean battle was being waged between "the cleare sunshine of the Gospell" on the one hand and "thick antichristian darkness" on the other.[42] Puritan writing frequently employed this light-and-dark imagery to express the idea that wilderness was ungodly. As William Steele declared in 1652 in regard to missionary work among the Indians, the "first fruits of a barren Wilderness" were obtained when civilization and Christianity succeeded in "shining . . . a beame of Light into the darknesse of another World." Cotton Mather's *Magnalia* concerned the wondrous way that religion "flying . . . to the American Strand" had "irradiated an Indian Wilderness." Those who resisted the "glorious gospel-shine" fled, as might be expected, ever deeper into "forrests wide & great."[43]

In view of the transcendant importance they attached to conquering wilderness the Puritans understandably celebrated westward expansion as one of their greatest achievements. It was a ceaseless wonder and an evidence of God's blessing that wild country should become fruitful and civilized. Edward Johnson's *Wonder-Working Providence* of 1654 is an extended commentary on this transformation. Always it was "Christ Jesus" or "the Lord" who "made this poore barren Wildernesse become a fruitfull Land" or who "hath . . . been pleased to turn one of the most Hideous, boundless, and unknown Wildernesses in the world . . . to a well-ordered Commonwealth." In Boston, for instance, the "admirable Acts of Christ" had in a few decades transformed the "hideous Thickets" where "Wolfes and Beares nurst up their young" into "streets full of Girles and Boys sporting up and downe."[44] Johnson and his contemporaries never doubted that God was on their side in their effort to destroy the wilderness. God's "*blessing* upon their undertakings," the elderly John Higginson wrote in 1697, made it possible that "a *wilderness* was subdued . . . Towns erected, and Churches settled . . . in a place where . . . [there] had been nothing before but *Heathenism, Idolatry, and Devil-worship.*"[45] The New England colonists saw themselves as "Christs Army" or "Souldiers of Christ" in a war against wildness.[46]

---

41. "R.I.," *The New Life of Virginia* (1612) in Force, *Tracts*, 1, No. 7, 7.

42. Thomas Shepard, *The Clear Sunshine of the Gospel Breaking Forth upon the Indians in New-England* (1648) in Joseph Sabin, *Sabin's Reprints* (10 vols. New York, 1865), *10*, 1; Mather, *Magnalia, I*, 64.

43. William Steele, "To the Supreme Authority of this Nation" in Henry Whitfield, *Strength out of Weakness* (1652) in *Sabin's Reprints, 5*, [2]; Mather, *Magnalia, I*, 25; Wigglesworth, *God's Controversy*, p. 84.

44. Johnson, *Wonder-Working Providence*, pp. 71, 108, 248.

45. Higginson, "An Attestation to the Church-History of New-England" in Mather, *Magnalia, I*, 13.

46. Johnson, *Wonder-Working Providence*, pp. 60, 75.

One reason why the Puritan settlers portrayed wilderness as replete with physical hardships and spiritual temptations was to remind later generations of the magnitude of their accomplishment. The credit for this feat, of course, went to God, but the colonists could not hide a strong sense of pride in their own role in breaking the wilderness. One of the first explicit statements appeared in the *Memoirs* of Roger Clap. A member of the group who arrived in New England in 1630, Clap decided in the 1670s to write an account of the early days for the instruction of his children. He detailed the distresses of life in the "then unsubdued wilderness" and the many "wants" of God's servants. Then, directly addressing the second generation, he drew the moral: "you have better food and raiment than was in former times; but have you better hearts than your forefathers had?" In 1671 Joshua Scottow used the same theme when he demanded that the initial colonists' "Voluntary Exile into this Wilderness" be "Recollected, Remembered, and not Forgotten."[47] Implied was a relationship between the dangers of the wilderness and the quality of those who faced them. A few years later John Higginson looked back on his long experience as a pioneer and declared: "our *wilderness-condition* hath been full of *humbling, trying, distressing providences.*" Their purpose, he felt, had been to determine "whether according to our professions, and [God's] expectation we would *keep [H]is* commandments or not."[48] Survival seemed an indication of success in this respect. Portrayed as a harsh and hostile environment, wilderness was a foil that emphasized the predicament and accentuated the achievement of pioneers.

The sinister connotation of wilderness did not end with the seventeenth century. Representatives of later generations, especially those persons who came into direct contact with the frontier, continued to sense the symbolic potency of wild country. While Jonathan Edwards might occasionally derive spiritual joy from, and even perceive beauty in, natural objects such as clouds, flowers, and fields, wilderness was still beyond the pale.[49] For Edwards, as for his Christian predecessors, "the land that we have to travel through [to Heaven] is a wilderness; there are many mountains, rocks, and rough places that we must go over in the way."[50] Following

47. *Memoirs of Capt. Roger Clap* (1731) in Alexander Young, *Chronicles of the First Planters of the Colony of Massachusetts Bay* (Boston, 1846), pp. 351, 353; Scottow, *Old Men's Tears for their own Declensions Mixed with Fears of their and Posterities further falling off from New-England's Primitive Constitution* (Boston, 1691), p. 1. Roger Williams stressed his agony in the Rhode Island wilderness for a similar purpose: Perry Miller, *Roger Williams* (Indianapolis, 1953), p. 52. Secondary commentary on the question may be found in Kenneth B. Murdock, "Clio in the Wilderness: History and Biography in Puritan New England," *Church History, 24* (1955), 221–38.

48. Higginson, "Attestation" in Mather, *Magnalia, I,* 16.

49. For examples of Edwards' appreciation of natural beauty see Alexander V. G. Allen, *Jonathan Edwards* (Boston, 1890), pp. 355–56, and *Images or Shadows of Divine Things by Jonathan Edwards,* ed. Perry Miller (New Haven, 1948), pp. 135–37.

50. "True Christian's Life," *The Works of President Edwards* (4 vols. New York, 1852) *4,* 575.

the Puritans, Americans continued to interpret wilderness in Biblical terms. When Eleazar Wheelock founded Dartmouth College on the upper Connecticut in 1769, he took as his motto "Vox Clamantis in Deserto." The use of "desert" to describe a forest in this and so many other accounts suggests that the Old Testament was even more important than New England actuality in determining reaction to the wilderness. The Dartmouth motto also was reminiscent of John the Baptist, and the initial impulse behind the college was similar: spreading the Word into a pagan realm. Later college founders advanced boldly into the west with a comparable idea of striking the spark that would in time transform darkness into light. Joseph P. Thompson, for instance, closed an 1859 speech before the Society for the Promotion of Collegiate and Theological Education At the West with an exhortation: "go you into the moral wilderness of the West; there open springs in the desert, and build a fountain for the waters of life."[51] Wilderness remained the obstacle to overcome.

Much of the writing of Nathaniel Hawthorne suggests the persistence into the nineteenth century of the Puritan conception of wilderness. For him wild country was still "black" and "howling" as well as a powerful symbol of man's dark and untamed heart. In several of Hawthorne's short stories wilderness dominated the action. Its terrifying qualities in *Roger Malvin's Burial* (1831) prompted a man to shoot his son in retribution for a dark deed the father performed earlier in "the tangled and gloomy forest." The protagonist of *Young Goodman Brown* (1835) also found the wilderness a nightmarish locale of both the devil and devilish tendencies in man. *The Scarlet Letter* (1850) climaxed Hawthorne's experimentation with the wilderness theme. The primeval forest he creates around seventeenth-century Salem represents and accentuates the "moral wilderness" in which Hester Prynne wandered so long. The forest meant freedom from social ostracism, yet Hawthorne left no doubt that such total license would only result in an irresistible temptation to evil. The illegitimate Pearl, "imp of evil, emblem and product of sin" is the only character at home in the wilderness. For Hawthorne and the Puritans a frightening gulf, both literal and figurative, existed between civilization and wilderness.[52]

The increasing tendency to redefine America's mission in secular   30
rather than sacred terms made little difference in regard to antipathy toward wilderness. Insofar as the westward expansion of civilization was thought

---

51. Thompson, *The College as a Religious Institution* (New York, 1859), p. 34. Williams, *Wilderness and Paradise*, pp. 141 ff., discusses the expansion of colleges in terms of the paradise tradition.

52. References are to *The Complete Writings of Nathaniel Hawthorne* (Old Manse ed. 22 vols. New York, 1903). For instruction in Hawthorne's use of wilderness I am indebted to R. W. B. Lewis, *The American Adam: Innocence, Tragedy, and Tradition in the Nineteenth Century* (Chicago, 1955), pp. 111–14; Wilson O. Clough, *The Necessary Earth: Nature and Solitude in American Literature* (Austin, Texas, 1964), pp. 117–25; Edwin Fussell, *Frontier: American Literature and the American West* (Princeton, N.J., 1965), pp. 69–131; and Chester E. Eisinger, "Pearl and the Puritan Heritage," *College English, 52* (1951), 323–29.

good, wilderness was bad. It was construed as much a barrier to progress, prosperity, and power as it was to godliness. On every frontier intense enthusiasm greeted the transformation of the wild into the civilized. Pioneer diaries and reminiscences rang with the theme that what was "unbroken and trackless wilderness" had been "reclaimed" and "transformed into fruitful farms and . . . flourishing cities" which, of course, was "always for the better."[53] Others simply said the wilds had been made "like *Eden*."[54]

This taming of the wilderness gave meaning and purpose to the frontiersman's life. In an age which idealized "progress," the pioneer considered himself its spearhead, performing a worthy cause in the interest of all mankind. While laboring directly for himself and his heirs, pioneers and their spokesmen were ever conscious that greater issues hung in the balance. Orators at state agricultural society gatherings harped on the theme of the beneficent effect of the law of "progressive development or growth" under whose guidance cities sprang "from the bosom of the wilderness." They raised paeans to those who worked "until the wilderness has blossomed with the fruits of their toil, and these once western wilds are vocal with the songs of joy."[55] As the pioneer conceived it, the rewards of this process were far greater than bountiful harvests. Was he not the agent of civilization battling man's traditional foe on behalf of the welfare of the race? After all, it was he who broke "the long chain of savage life" and for "primeval barbarism" substituted "civilization, liberty and law" not to speak of "arts and sciences."[56] Put in these terms, there could be little doubt of the value of destroying wilderness. As Andrew Jackson asked rhetorically in his 1830 inaugural address, "what good man would prefer a country covered with forests and ranged by a few thousand savages to our extensive Republic, studded with cities, towns, and prosperous farms, embellished with all the improvements which art can devise or industry execute."[57] In the vocabulary of material progress, wilderness had meaning only as an obstacle.

---

53. Judge Wilkinson, "Early Recollections of the West," *American Pioneer*, 2 (1843), 161; William Henry Milburn, *The Pioneer Preacher: Rifle, Axe, and Saddle-Bags* (New York, 1858), p. 26; J. H. Colton, *The Western Tourist and Emigrant's Guide* (New York, 1850), p. 25; and Henry Howe, *Historical Collections of the Great West* (2 vols. Cincinnati, 1854), I, 84.
54. As quoted from a 1796 account in Jones, *O Strange New World*, p. 212.
55. A. Constantine Barry, "Wisconsin—Its Condition, Prospects, Etc.: Annual Address Delivered at the State Agricultural Fair," *Transactions of the Wisconsin State Agricultural Society*, 4 (1856), pp. 266, 268.
56. Columbus *Ohio State Journal* (1827) as quoted in Roscoe Carlyle Buley, *The Old Northwest Pioneer Period, 1815–1840* (2 vols. Indianapolis, 1950), 2, 45; *Laws of Indiana* (1824–25) in Buley, 2, 46; Dr. S. P. Hildreth, "Early Emigration," *American Pioneer*, 2 (1843), 134.
57. Andrew Jackson, "Second Annual Message," *A Compilation of the Messages and Papers of the Presidents*, ed. J. D. Richardson (10 vols. Washington, D.C., 1896–99), 2, 521. On the doctrine of progress and its incompatibility with appreciation of wilderness see Arthur A. Ekirch, Jr., *The Idea of Progress in America, 1815–1860* (New York, 1944); Moore, *Frontier Mind*, pp. 139–58; Weinberg, *Manifest Destiny;* and Alan Trachtenberg, *Brooklyn Bridge: Fact and Symbol* (New York, 1965), pp. 7–21.

The nineteenth-century pioneer's emphasis on material progress did not entirely exclude the older idea of conquering wilderness in the name of God. William Gilpin, an early governor of Colorado and trumpeter of America's Manifest Destiny, made clear that "'Progress is God'" and that the "occupation of wild territory . . . proceeds with all the solemnity of a providential ordinance." It was, in fact, the "hand of God" that pushed the nation westward and caused the wilderness to surrender to ax and plow. The frontiersmen never forgot that one of their chief aims was the "extension of pure Christianity": they viewed with satisfaction the replacement of the "savage yell" with the "songs of Zion." Settlement and religion went together. Charles D. Kirk summarized in an 1860 novel the frontier view of the westward march as "the tramp, tramp, steady and slow, but sure, of the advancing hosts of Civilization and Christianity."[58]

Understandably, subjugation of wilderness was the chief source of pioneer pride. Indeed the whole nation considered the settlement of the West its outstanding accomplishment. Timothy Dwight even felt it worthy of comparison with the cultural magnificence of Europe. "*The conversion of a wilderness into a desirable residence for man,*" he declared early in the century, "at least . . . may compensate the want of ancient castles, ruined abbeys, and fine pictures."[59] For a young country, self-conscious about its achievements and anxious to justify independence with success, the conquest of wilderness bolstered the national ego. "What a people we are! What a country is this of ours," chortled Josiah Grinnell in 1845, "which but as yesterday was a wilderness." On a humbler level the individual pioneer felt a glow of pride in clearing the land or breaking the virgin sod. One guidebook for settlers advertised: "you look around and whisper, 'I vanquished this wilderness and made the chaos pregnant with order and civilization, alone I did it.'" The same note often sounds in the rhetoric of a President who takes great pride in the way his family made the "barren" and "forbidding" country in the valley of Texas' Pedernales River "abundant with fruit, cattle, goats and sheep."[60]

Of course, many pioneers deliberately chose to live in the wilderness. Many moved westward to a new homestead, legend has it, when they could see a neighbor's smoke. Love of the wilds, however, did not prompt this behavior but rather a hunger for their destruction. Pioneers welcomed wild country as a challenge. They conceived of themselves as agents in the regenerating process that turned the ungodly and useless into a beneficent

---

58. Gilpin, *Mission of the North American People: Geographical, Social and Political* (Philadelphia, 1873), p. 99; John Reynolds, *The Pioneer History of Illinois* (Belleville, Ill., 1852), p. 228; Hildreth, "Early Emigration," 134; Kirk, *Wooing and Warring in the Wilderness* (New York, 1860), p. 38.
59. Dwight, *Travels, I,* 18.
60. Grinnell, *Sketches of the West* (Milwaukee, 1847), pp. 40–41; Sidney Smith, *The Settlers' New Home: or the Emigrant's Location* (London, 1849), p. 19; Lyndon B. Johnson, "State of the Union: The Great Society," *Vital Speeches, 31* (1965), 197.

civilization. To perform this function wilderness was necessary, hence the westward urge. Only a handful of mountain men and voyageurs were literally absorbed by the forest and ignored the regenerative mission. Reverting to the primitive, in some cases even joining Indian tribes, these exceptions regarded civilization with the antipathy most pioneers reserved for wilderness.[61]

Tocqueville, on the whole, was correct in his analysis that "living in the wilds" produced a bias against them. Constant exposure to wilderness gave rise to fear and hatred on the part of those who had to fight it for survival and success. Although there were a few exceptions, American frontiersmen rarely judged wilderness with criteria other than the utilitarian or spoke of their relation to it in other than a military metaphor. It was their children and grandchildren, removed from a wilderness condition, who began to sense its ethical and aesthetic values. Yet even city dwellers found it difficult to ignore the older attitudes completely. Prejudice against wilderness had the strength of centuries behind it and continued to influence American opinion long after pioneering conditions disappeared. Against this darker background of repugnance more favorable responses haltingly took shape.

35

Reading and Responding

After a first reading, write several sentences about how you think the first American colonists would have responded to seeing or hearing the word *forest*.

Working Together

1. Sitting in a circle with three or four other students, pass your books around to see how the others annotated their text: Pass to the right, read, pass to the right, read—until you get your book back. Discuss these questions: Did you mark the same passages? Why? What are your different styles of annotating? Why annotate? What do your annotations tell you about the nature of Roderick Nash's writing? Can you come to some conclusions about Nash's main points?

---

61. Almost by definition, written accounts of men who completely broke the ties with civilization are practically nonexistent. Moore, *Frontier Mind,* Billington, *American Frontiersman,* Stanley Vestal, *Mountain Men* (Boston, 1937), Sydney Greenbie, *Furs to Furrows: An Epic of Rugged Individualism* (Caldwell, Idaho, 1939), especially Chapter 19, Hiram Chittenden, *The American Fur Trade of the Far West* (3 vols. New York, 1902), *I,* 65 ff., and Grace Lee Nute, *The Voyageur* (New York, 1931) provide illuminating insights. Lewis Mumford, *The Golden Day: A Study in American Experience and Culture* (New York, 1926), pp. 55–56, argues against my interpretation.

2. On one side of the board, write down all your first associations with the word *forest*. On the other side, write down all the associations the Puritans had, according to Nash.
3. Discuss why, according to Nash, the Puritans felt the way they did. What in their culture and material circumstances led to this response? What in your culture and material circumstances leads to the response you have to forests?
4. Record by writing down everything your teacher and your classmates say during this discussion.

Rethinking and Rewriting

1. Reread the Nash piece, annotating again.
2. Drawing on the class discussion and your marginal comments on Nash, write an essay with this title: "A Forest Is Not Just a Forest" or "A Forest Is Never Really Just There." Your thesis should be that the meaning and value of a forest isn't objectively "out there"; it's culturally determined. For evidence, quote both the Nash piece and the comments of your classmates, referring as well to your own experience and reactions.
3. Walk in a forest or in a park with enough trees that it seems like a forest. First, describe what you're seeing and how you're feeling. Next, try to describe what you think a sixteenth- and seventeenth-century American colonist would be seeing and feeling. Draw on Nash. Once you've made your contrasts clear, draw some conclusions.
4. Pay attention to how Nash structures his paragraphs and how they lead one to the next. Once you have a sense of how Nash proceeds as a writer, write a five-hundred-word introduction to "A Wilderness Condition." Give your readers information on Nash's subject, and also give them information on how to read Nash effectively.

"A LIFE IN OUR HANDS"

Keith Ervin

> *Keith Ervin is a freelance writer living in Seattle, Washington. His articles on environmental issues have appeared in* Sierra, Pacific Northwest, Washington, The Oregonian, *and* Seattle Weekly. *The following essay is the first chapter of his 1989 book,* Fragile Majesty: The Battle for North America's Last Great Forest, *the result of over four years of intensive research. The book was published by the Seattle Mountaineers.*

Before and As You Read

1. Preread this piece quickly (five minutes), and write down at least three observations about Keith Ervin's writing. From your prereading, what plans should you make for your more careful reading of this selection?
2. As you read this piece, annotate it, looking for major shifts in topic or subject. Start by putting a 1 in the margin at the beginning (label it "spotted owl"). Then put a new number in the margin each time you come to another topic or shift in the discussion.
3. As you read this piece, annotate it, looking for the important factual material—facts that make a difference to your understanding or facts that seem crucial to anyone's understanding. Mark them with a wiggly line in the margin.
4. Read with a piece of paper or your reading journal nearby and see whether you can outline "A Life in Our Hands" as you read. Look for the introduction of large new ideas as a way to identify this essay's structure.
5. As you read, look for sections, sentences, or even phrases that help you understand Ervin's definition of the word *forest*. Annotate the large sections, and copy out the important phrases.

Its nose twitching, the small mouse makes its way along the narrow branch. The animal's quivering body speaks of caution, yet it remains oblivious to its impending doom.

The owl is perched on a higher branch, his sharp eyes riveted on the prey. Silently, motionlessly, the bird calculates the best method of attack. Suddenly, he swoops down and, with scarcely a pause in his wingbeats, snatches the rodent in his talons. A few thrusts of his powerful wings and the deadly hunter is safely roosting in another tree, savoring his meal.

Watching the northern spotted owl are three other sets of eyes, the eyes of men. Two biologists and I have walked to this patch of woods on the northern edge of Washington State's Olympic Peninsula, in pursuit of the most controversial bird in America. For the spotted owl has become both a powerful symbol and the chief focus in the battle now raging to save North America's last great forest: the "old growth" of the Pacific Northwest.

On our way into the forest, before we heard the owl's first *Hoo-hoo! . . . Hooooooo!,* one of my companions, Stan Sovern, spotted a logging tower in a clearcut on the ridgetop. When Sovern climbed the ridge earlier in the year to band a female owl, the clearcut wasn't there. Sovern and Eric Forsman are after the male today. Their search will be punctuated by the occasional whine of a chain saw and the toot of a whistle on the logging site.

The owl, ready for another mouse, flies to a perch closer to the men.   5
Forsman, the lanky young biologist directing this research sponsored by the U.S. Forest Service, walks slowly toward the bird, carrying a fishing rod with a nooselike loop at the tip. The bird calmly sits on the branch as Forsman slowly raises the pole, slips the loop around its neck, then gently lowers the now-struggling owl to the ground. Sovern takes the owl in his hands and holds the bird's wings tightly as Forsman clips colored metal bands to both legs. The bands will help scientists in their studies of the spotted owl population on the peninsula.

Forsman and Sovern carefully examine each feather on both wings to determine the progress of molting. Then they gently stuff the bird into a bag and weigh him. The men freeze, then sigh, in response to the earthshaking crash of an old-growth tree. The ancient forest is falling.

The biologists release the bird and "mouse" him once again. His second meal in his mouth, the bird watches us from a branch far beyond the reach of Forsman's fishing pole. Finally, tired of these games with humans, the owl flies off.

Walking down the hill, we notice what we had missed in our haste on the way up. A series of yellow markers are stapled to tree trunks. "BOUNDARY CLEAR-CUT," they read. The signs are familiar to those who roam the national forests of the Pacific Northwest. Part of the owl's home was torn down today. The trees in which we saw him roosting will fall soon.

The spotted owl researchers don't mix much with townsfolk here in logging country. Except when they're in the field, they stick close to the Forest Service work station where they sleep in a mobile home and raise mice for trapping owls. Likewise, the Washington Wildlife Department biologists surveying spotted owls on state land don't often leave their cabin to spend time in the nearby town of Forks.

Already, the findings of Forsman and other researchers have inflamed   10
local passions. Logging is by far the biggest industry on the Olympic Peninsula. The nearby town of Forks bills itself, plausibly, as the logging capital of the world. Spotted owl researchers are about as popular here as freedom riders were in the Deep South. The café in Forks sells T-shirts and logging suspenders that read, "SPOTTED OWL HUNTER." A popular float in Forks' Fourth of July parade featured a logger chasing a spotted owl with a

chain saw. Local managers of the Washington Department of Natural Resources—stewards of the state forestlands—drew laughs when they handed
out bogus spotted owl hunting regulations.

The northern spotted owl, *Strix occidentalis caurina,* is a subspecies that
has become symbolic of the battle over the last of this continent's virgin
forests. The bird is unusual, though perhaps not unique, in its specializa-
tion. It doesn't just require forest for its survival. To live and breed at viable
levels, it needs a special kind of forest. Only a conifer forest will do. Only
a forest in the temperate zone of the Pacific Coast between northern
California and southern British Columbia. Only a forest essentially undisturbed by humans. Preferably a forest in which the oldest trees took root
anywhere from 200 to 1,000 years ago. And large enough that a breeding
pair can forage over hundreds or even thousands of acres.

The spotted owl has become a symbol of the fragile ecosystem
unique to the old-growth forests of the Pacific Northwest. It has become
a symbol, too, of the threat that loggers and their families feel in the face
of a growing movement to save the ancient forests. "They're putting people out of work for a danged bird," fumes one logger. "That's just sheer
stupidity." Leaders of the forest-products industry have taken to calling the
spotted owl "the billion-dollar bird."

Though attention has focused on the owl as an emblem for the
forests, it's only one part of a greater issue. An entire ecosystem, one of the
grandest on the planet, is at stake. This ecosystem is home to a yet-
uncatalogued range of plant and animal life. The majestic woods are mostly
gone. Less than one-fifth of the old growth that once covered the landscape of western Oregon and western Washington still stands. No one has
tallied the full dimensions of this loss because no one has made a comprehensive inventory of the remaining old growth, much less figured out how
much has already been cut down.

What remains is going fast. In the national forests alone, 48,000 acres
of virgin forests are being cleared to feed the sawmills and pulp mills of
Oregon and Washington each year. The U.S. Bureau of Land Management
(BLM) is selling off another 22,000 acres. Within fifteen years—barely a
summer's afternoon in the time frame of the forest—the last of the old
growth on state and private lands will be gone.

Then there will be only what's left in the national parks, national   15
forests, and, in Oregon, on land administered by the BLM. To the timber
industry, that's a lot of land. Over a million acres of older forests on federal
land is being preserved in the Douglas fir region west of the Cascade
Range crest for a number of reasons: wilderness and recreation values,
habitat for the spotted owl and other species, or site-specific engineering
problems such as steep and unstable soils or regeneration difficulties. A
million acres that could be providing jobs and profits. A million acres that
timber industry lobbyists claim the spotted owl doesn't even need.

Compared to what once was, a million acres of protected forest is a
pittance. When European settlement began, an estimated 850 million acres

of what are now the lower forty-eight states were covered by virgin forests. The trees were cut or burned down, first to make way for the settlers, then to produce lumber. The forests of the Pacific Coast and the Rockies are all that's left to give us an inkling of what this land may have been like three centuries ago. Even in the Northwest—where settlement began in earnest only 150 years ago—the lowland forests where trees grew to almost unimaginable size in rich alluvial soils have long disappeared.

What's left is being fragmented by patchwork clearcuts into isolated stands that are losing their ability to support spotted owls and other creatures of the ancient forests. The remaining old growth, mostly at higher elevations and on steep hillsides, sometimes is described as "the dregs."

Ah, but what dregs! In biomass alone, the Pacific forests are rivaled by no other forests on earth. The rain forests of the tropics are small things by comparison. Below the Northwest's mantle of tall trees is a unique world of plant and animal life. The Olympic rain forest's rich mantle of mosses, lichens, club mosses, and liverworts is thicker and heavier than that of any other temperate forest in the world. The Northwest forests have been called, justifiably, "the world center of mushroom diversity." Beyond the spotted owl, animals as diverse as bald eagle, red tree vole, and rough-skinned newt find their best habitat in ancient forests. Only now, when this ecosystem is in danger, have scientists come to appreciate the magnificence of these forests.

No one has done more than Jerry Franklin to demonstrate the biological opulence and uniqueness of the Pacific Northwest's old-growth forests. The Forest Service's Pacific Northwest Research Station in Corvallis, Oregon, calls Franklin its chief plant ecologist. The University of Washington's College of Forest Resources calls him professor of ecosystem analysis. Some people simply call him the guru of old growth.

Franklin grew up playing in the second-growth forests near his Camas, Washington, home. Even more special to him than those woods were the old-growth groves of the Gifford Pinchot National Forest, where his family spent vacations camping. Forests were in the family line. Franklin's parents even gave Jerry the fitting middle name of Forest. The mystique of the forest never wore out. Even today, the scientist speaks of the "aura" of old growth and of the "inspiration" he draws from the ancient forests.

The son of a worker in Crown Zellerbach's Camas paper mill, Franklin is no wild-eyed environmental radical. His soft voice and avuncular, down-home manner have only boosted his credibility in the highly politicized atmosphere surrounding the debate over management of the last old-growth forests.

Franklin has been studying the forests of Washington and Oregon since the late 1950s, when he was a forestry graduate student at Oregon State University. It wasn't until 1970, though, that serious research into the old-growth ecosystem was first undertaken. As deputy director of the Coniferous Forest Biome research project, Franklin played a crucial role in obtaining funding from the National Science Foundation and lining up researchers from Oregon State and the University of Washington.

20

"I think the bottom line is we learned the old-growth forest was distinctive in a number of its characteristics from younger forests," Franklin recalls, leaning back from the desk in his university office. "It's not just a younger forest grown up to a larger size. It performs some functions very well, and it has a different kind of structure than a younger forest does and because of that provides habitat for a different set of animals. It was interesting because the Forest Service had stopped doing research on old growth in about 1960 because they felt we had learned everything we needed to know about it—which was basically how to cut it down and regenerate a young forest."

Initially, the researchers weren't investigating old growth per se, rather the coniferous forests of the Douglas fir region. The focus slowly shifted toward ancient forests as it became apparent that the most distinctive features of the Northwest woods were precisely those that took centuries to develop. It was the spectacular biomass and vegetative richness of old growth that stood out in study after study. The biomass accumulated by the big trees in old growth, it turned out, produced a unique set of flora and fauna. By 1981, scientists knew enough about old growth to describe it in a landmark report authored by Franklin and seven associates, *Ecological Characteristics of Old-Growth Douglas-Fir Forests.*

As Franklin explains, big trees are the engine that drives the old-growth ecosystem: "The trees are large, old, the crown structures are very complex, the dead wood component—standing dead trees and logs—is very conspicuous and that's in part because many of the species are quite decay-resistant so that these large woody structures disappear only slowly. And because of the canopies, they modify the environment within the forest incredibly so that the moisture and temperature conditions are totally different than they are outside or even in young forests. And that's one reason why many organisms find it to be a very favorable environment. It's extremely stable, the extremes are highly muted."   25

In the microclimate of the old-growth forest, animals and plants find warmth and shelter from the snow in winter. They find coolness and moisture in summer. From fog and clouds, the crowns of tall trees wring moisture—in some drainages accounting for one-fourth of total precipitation in some watersheds. The wind is still on the forest floor, rarely blowing harder than two miles an hour. The irregular canopy of old growth lets in enough light to support a far richer understory than is found in young forests.

The old-growth ecosystem begins with big trees, both live and dead. Another ecologist, Elliott Norse of The Wilderness Society, says of the forest giants, "These trees are as exceptional in the plant world as whales are in the animal world. Ancient conifers are the whales of the forests." The Pacific Northwest forest range, from northern California to southeast Alaska, produces the biggest conifers in the world. Only the huge eucalyptus-dominated forests of Australia and New Zealand come close to the biomass of the Northwest old growth. On average, the Douglas fir and noble fir forests of Oregon and Washington contain three times the biomass of tropical rain forests. This "huge photosynthetic factory," as Jerry Franklin sometimes calls old growth, accumulates biological mass more efficiently than any ecosystem on earth. Trees simply grow crazy in the Northwest.

Temperate forests typically are deciduous or mixed deciduous–conifer stands. The Pacific Coast, with its distinctive weather patterns, breaks the mold. Conifers overshadow deciduous trees a thousand to one by timber volume. Although there is ample precipitation for trees, rain and snow fall primarily during the winter months. Drought is an annual summer event. Seattle typically receives three inches of rain between June and August. Less than half that amount falls on Medford, Oregon. Deciduous trees can carry on photosynthesis only during the warm months when their leaves are out. If rainfall is inadequate during that critical time, deciduous trees just can't make it. Conifers, able to produce carbohydrates year-round, have a tremendous competitive advantage on the West Coast.

Conifers aren't just unusually plentiful here, they grow like nowhere else. Ten genera of conifers grow in the Northwest; the largest and longest-living species of each is found on the coast. "They have a genetic makeup that simply enables them to persist and grow for very long periods of time," Franklin observes. "Whereas a loblolly pine in the Southeast is pretty much pooping out by the time it gets to be fifty or sixty years old, a Douglas fir is only beginning to get started at that age."

Taken individually, none of the attributes of old growth reported in *Ecological Characteristics* was terribly surprising. Of course an ancient forest is dominated by big trees. Of course standing dead trees are abundant, as are large logs on the ground and in streams. Anyone who looked could see that mushrooms, mosses, lichens, and liverworts grew in profusion. The report galvanized the scientific community, and began to ripple through the national forests' interest groups, because it showed for the first time how the whole system worked and how it differed from other forests.

Franklin and his colleagues pointed out that the deep, irregular crown of an old-growth Douglas fir provides "ideal habitat" for such specialized creatures as the red tree vole, northern flying squirrel, and northern spotted owl. The old-growth canopy provides a home for an estimated 1,500 species of invertebrates. Large logs offer animal habitat and seedbeds for young trees. Nitrogen, often in short supply in forest soils, is built up by lichens in the forest canopy and by bacteria that proliferate in rotting logs. Large logs also provide a home for mammals that spread underground fungi. The food chain, or "energy cycle," of small old-growth streams begins with woody debris rather than green plants. Few plant or animal species are found *only* in old growth, but many find their best habitat there, and some may require a reservoir of old growth for their survival.

Between 175 and 250 years typically are required for old-growth characteristics to develop under natural conditions. Old growth "begins to come into its prime" after 350 years, says biologist Andy Carey. The term "old growth" has been used by foresters for many decades. Yet it wasn't until the mid-1980s that scientists even tried to develop an ecological definition of the term. Before that, foresters and researchers used whatever definition they found most convenient. Those wildly varying definitions generally were based on a single criterion such as tree size or age. Some foresters used the term old growth for anything that had not been cut. In 1986, the Forest Service's Old-Growth Definition Task Group, chaired by Jerry Franklin, proposed a definition that could be applied to a stand by a forester with a tape measure. The definition was both ecological and quantifiable. There had to be a certain mix of species, a certain number of live trees of various sizes per acre, along with a specified number of snags and logs of defined size.

The ecological definition set objective standards by which anyone can determine whether a forest is to be considered old growth. The standards were somewhat arbitrary; there's no magic point at which a forest is suddenly transformed from a "mature" forest into "old growth." Jerry Franklin speaks of "degrees of old-growthedness" and a "continual gradient of old-growth characteristics . . . It becomes a little more sophisticated than a simple yes-or-no answer, 'It is or it ain't.'"

The forest in which Eric Forsman and Stan Sovern captured the spotted owl wouldn't meet the ecological definition of old growth. It had the mix of species and the deep, multilayered canopy characteristic of old growth, but it lacked the requisite number of centuries-old trees to meet the definition. A forest in the process of becoming old growth, it supports a wider range of wildlife than an even-aged tree farm but probably fewer species than true old growth. By 1989, Franklin was urging scientists to supplement the old-growth definition with more flexible measures of a forest's ecological structure.

The either-or definition is the closest thing that exists to a scientific 35 consensus on the minimum standards for old growth. Yet even after the definition was published, national forests continued to release draft management plans that bore no relation to the definition. By continuing to use nonecological definitions, the Forest Service was able to say that millions more acres of old growth remained on its land than the ecological approach indicated.

The scientists who wrote *Ecological Characteristics* warned that the ancient forests were rapidly disappearing. It was true that the Forest Service would be selling old-growth timber for the next forty years and that some of the virgin forest was protected in national parks, wilderness areas, and research natural areas. "Nevertheless," the scientific group reported, "these reserves occupy less than 5 percent of the original landscape, and the end of the unreserved old-growth forests is in sight."

If an old-growth forest were a stage, the principal players would be the big trees. Like the protagonists of a Shakespearean drama, these nobles shape the world in which a host of lesser trees and plants live. Those others play supporting roles. Just as great men and women do much to shape society, so these trees give an ancient forest its structure.

From southern British Columbia to northernmost California, the dominant tree is Douglas fir. During its lifetime of a thousand years or more, this magnificent tree may exceed ten feet in diameter and occasionally pushes to 300 feet in height. The deeply furrowed, reddish-brown bark of old-growth specimens make this monarch instantly recognizable. Its cones are equally distinctive, bearing a sort of forked tongue like that of the serpent that tempted Eve. As a sapling, Douglas fir makes a perfectly proportioned Christmas tree. The crown of the mature tree, whether growing in the forest or in the full sunlight, takes on an irregular and highly individual shape. A single stem or "leader" points straight up from the top of the tree; the fingerlike tip of each major branch aims outward and upward.

Ironically, Douglas fir isn't a fir at all. Its Latin name, *Pseudotsuga menziesii,* identifies it as a false hemlock. Early botanists (including David Douglas himself) mislabeled it variously as pine, hemlock, fir, and spruce. Only in the late nineteenth century, after discovering a related Asian species, did scientists conclude the tree represented a new genus, and the name *Pseudotsuga* stuck.

Nowhere in what foresters call the "Douglas fir region" is the tree a climax species. As a forest grows and matures, its vegetation changes until it reaches its climax, or final stage. Old growth, like the Douglas fir that so often dominates it, is a transitional stage. Intolerant of shade, Douglas fir can't grow in its own shadow; it must give way to more tolerant species. Fir manages to maintain its overall dominance because of its longevity, because thick bark sees it through most fires unscathed, and because it aggressively establishes itself in openings created by fire or other natural events.

Immense forests of giant Douglas fir standing butt to butt are no longer abundant as they were during the days when John Muir visited Puget Sound. Still, his observations on the tree he called Douglas spruce tell us much about a land that could give rise to a profusion of these giants:

> For so large a tree it is astonishing how many find nourishment and space to grow on any given area. The magnificent shafts push their spires into the sky close together with as regular a growth as that of a well-tilled field of grain. And no ground has been better tilled for the growth of trees than that on which these forests are growing. For it has been thoroughly ploughed and rolled by the mighty glaciers from the mountains, and sifted and mellowed and outspread in beds hundreds of feet in depth by the broad streams that issued from their fronts at the time of their recession, after they had long covered the land.

Like Douglas fir, western red cedar (*Thuja plicata*) is something other than what its name implies. An arborvitae rather than a true cedar, this majestic tree belongs to the cypress family. The tree's decay-resistant heartwood is as prized by shake splitters and fence builders today as it was by the Coast Salish natives a millennium ago. Unlike Douglas fir, shade-tolerant red cedar can maintain its forest dominance over the centuries. As long-lived and as massive at the base as fir—but not as tall—western red cedar is distinguished by its scaly leaves, its shaggy fir, and its flared, amoeba-shaped butt. Alaska yellow cedar, a smaller cousin of red cedar, may live up to 3,500 years.

Western hemlock (*Tsuga heterophylla*) had little commercial value until the pulp industry moved into the Northwest. Now used for lumber as well as paper and cellophane products, old-growth hemlock is especially popular in Japan. The pliable tip of hemlock, whether young or old, bends earthward as if in prayer. It's a lovely understory tree; its short needles spread flatly from the stem, forming a fanlike network of lace. This lacework of hemlock is a classic feature of a fir-hemlock forest.

Because this tree doesn't attain the mighty dimensions of Douglas fir or cedar, it's easy to dismiss it. But hemlock is a survivor. If a forest makes it through enough centuries without fire or other environmental catastrophe, this shade-tolerant tree will replace Douglas fir as the dominant tree. Hemlock is the most widespread climax species, ranging from the spruce forests of Alaska to the redwood country of California.

Sitka spruce (*Picea sitchensis*) thrives primarily in the coastal fog belt   45 from southern Alaska to the southern tip of Oregon. Sitka spruce is an extremely fast-growing tree under the proper conditions. One thirteen-foot-thick Olympic rain forest specimen reportedly added a foot to its diameter in less than thirty-five years. Like hemlock, spruce prefers to begin life in the nurturing climate of a nurse log. Once used to build aircraft and now valued as a superior wood for piano sounding boards, Sitka spruce is Alaska's most important timber species.

The mighty coast redwood (*Sequoia sempervirens*) hugs the immediate coastal region from the edge of spruce country in southernmost Oregon south to the San Francisco Bay area. The redwood is the world's tallest tree, exceeded in mass only by the incomprehensibly large giant sequoia (*Sequoiadendron giganteum*) of the Sierra Nevada. Redwood appears to be a climax species—although some scientists question whether it, like cedar, eventually gives way to hemlock through the process of forest succession. Like red cedar, redwood is remarkably resistant to rot. Virgin redwood stands have been reduced to a fraction of their original extent, and heavy logging continues.

Big trees are the key ingredient in building the forest structure that has come to be called old growth. Yet big trees do not, by themselves, add up to an ecosystem. In fact, the trees of old growth are a varied lot. Just about the only thing this ecosystem lacks is uniformity. Its living trees differ by species, by age, by size, by shape and depth of their foliage, and by soundness of their bark and wood. Centuries are required for development of the distinctive multilayered canopy that comes with a mix of young and old trees. With time, older trees die, leaving their large remains for bacteria, fungi, insects, birds, and mammals to forage in and build homes.

Seen from a steep hillside above the forest floor or from a low-flying airplane, the irregular canopy of an ancient forest is striking. In contrast to the uniform, unbroken canopy of a second-growth forest, the old-growth canopy appears random and disordered. The dominant trees vary in height, thickness, and foliage. The tops of some trees are broken; others have lost their foliage and died, still others have fallen. The gaps left by these fallen or humbled comrades allow light to filter through to the understory. The crown of an old-growth tree has been described as resembling a bottle brush—"albeit one with many missing bristles."

Early settlers and loggers, working on level ground, had little opportunity to view the remarkable forest canopy from treetop level. But today, with most of the remaining old growth limited to narrow mountain valleys, the steep mountainsides offer wondrous panoramas. At some point almost every trail through ancient forest ascends to a high point from which it's possible to look through the canopy. The tops of the trees— many of them broken off, some alive, others dead, a few charred by lightning—may seem close enough to touch. To view the canopy from this perspective is as to feel as though one is actually in the canopy. The varying heights of the trees, their irregular spacing, the crowns of every shape and density, the quality of light, all create a more-real-than-real, super-three-dimensional effect.

Draped over the trees of old growth are mosses, lichens, club mosses, 50 and liverworts. These "epiphytes," from the Greek prefix *epi* (upon) and suffix *phyte* (plant), grow nonparasitically atop other plants. Drawing their nutrients directly from rainfall and from particles in the air, epiphytes contribute significantly to the fertility of the forest. More than 130 epiphytic mosses have been identified in the Olympic rain forest alone. Lichens— symbiotic combinations of fungi and algae—may display tiny, delicate-looking branches or they may have a crude crustlike appearance. The most abundant epiphytic lichen is the large, leafy *Lobaria oregana*. As pieces of this and the closely related lungwort (*Lobaria pulmonaria*) break off and fall to the forest floor, they are eaten by browsing animals or they decompose to add valuable nitrogen to the soil. The waxy lungwort is named for its resemblance to the inside of the human lung. These nitrogen-fixing lichens are rare in young forests.

Until recently, it was believed that mosses and lichens had no directly beneficial or harmful effect on their host trees. It turns out, however, that some trees are more than passive hosts for the epiphytes. Nalini M. Nadkarni, a University of Washington graduate student in forest ecology, made a remarkable discovery when she used mountain climbing equipment to propel herself into the canopy of the Olympic rain forest. Weighing the epiphytes, she found three tons of dry plant mass per acre, four times the amount typical of other forests. Peeling back the vegetative mats, Nadkarni found a network of roots running along the branches and trunk of bigleaf maple. These maple roots, ranging from tiny white tips to chunky three-inch-diameter roots, were present only under moss and lichens. "Greatly excited," she wrote in *Natural History,* "I realized that here was a shortcut in the rain forest's nutrient cycling system. Host trees were capable of tapping the arboreal cupboards in their own crowns."

Nadkarni found that other deciduous trees in the Olympic rain forest—vine maple, red alder, and black cottonwood—also took water and nutrients from the organic matter created by epiphytes. Traveling to the cloud forests of Costa Rica and Papua New Guinea, she saw the same phenomenon of trees taking advantage of the nutrient treasure provided by mosses, liverworts, and lichens.

The old-growth canopy, developed to make the most of the sun's energy, has been likened to the ocean's surface. Zoologist Marston Bates put it this way in his classic book, *The Forest and the Sea:* "Most life is near the top, because that is where the sunlight strikes and everything below depends on this surface. Life in both the forest and the sea is distributed in horizontal layers." The crowns of trees are like the pelagic, or surface, layer of the ocean because that is where photosynthesis is concentrated. On the forest floor, as on the benthos, or bottom, of the sea, life depends on "second-hand materials that drift down from above—on fallen leaves, on fallen fruits, on roots and logs. Only a few special kinds of green plants were able to grow in the rather dim light that reached the forest floor."

Because scientists have not had 200 years to watch old-growth forests develop, they must deduce how the process works. The 1984 report of a Society of American Foresters (SAF) task force on old growth recognized these uncertainties. "Can old growth be managed?" the task force asked. The group answered its own question this way:

> Through silviculture, foresters can grow big trees and grow them faster than nature unassisted. Yet there is no evidence that old-growth conditions can be reproduced silviculturally. In fact, the question is essentially moot, as it would take 200 years or more to find an answer. Old-growth management, for the foreseeable future, will be predicated on preservation of existing old-growth stands.

Preservation may not be the most exact word for protecting a living system from destruction. If one fact emerges clearly from the new research on the forest ecosystem, it is that change is its very essence. The forest is forever in the process of *becoming.* Conifers are constantly struggling through the brush layer of a new clearing. Live trees keep being turned into fodder for the fungi that help to grow new trees. Like Sisyphus forever trying to reach the top of the hill, the forest continually struggles toward climax, the final and most stable stage of vegetative succession. Some natural or human-caused event inevitably sets the forest back to an earlier stage of succession, so old growth is constantly being created.

An old-growth forest "preserved" by humans inevitably will change. Old trees will fall and young trees will grow. Openings will be created and then filled with new life. The forest may reach climax. Or it may be

55

completely toppled by windstorm or fire. Over a century, a 600-year-old stand may become a 700-year-old stand or a 100-year-old stand. But along with change, the forest maintains continuity and achieves a kind of stability. The young science of ecology teaches that complexity creates stability. The old-growth forests of the Northwest offer a wonderful laboratory—certainly the best on this continent—for studying the hidden ways in which seemingly independent creatures of the woods support one another.

The SAF task force wasn't saying that *all* old growth should be preserved. The point was that in our hubris we shouldn't assume that we can duplicate a natural process we barely understand. Not surprisingly, one of the eleven members of the task force was Jerry Franklin.

The implications of the new forest research reach far beyond the arcane interests of the scientists. The productivity of tree farms, for example, may depend more on maintaining healthy wildlife populations than on eliminating "pests." Consider the class of fungi known as mycorrhizae. The growth of conifers, like that of many other photosynthetic plants, requires the assistance of these fungi whose name means "fungus root." Unable to make direct use of the sun's energy, a fungus attaches itself to tree roots and helps itself to the sugars produced by the host plant. In return, the fungus absorbs water and nutrients, passing them along to the host tree. Antibiotics in the fungus protect the tree from root-rot pathogens, while the mycorrhizal sheath around the roots creates a physical barrier against some parasites. Tons of mycorrhizae are present in a single acre of old-growth forest, feeding the trees and storing nutrients that otherwise would be washed out of the soil and lost to the forest. The contribution that mycorrhizal fungi make to tree growth and forest fertility can scarcely be overstressed.

The story of the mycorrhiza-tree relationship doesn't end there. What at first seems a *pas de deux* is in fact a *ménage à trois*. For without the small mammals of the forest, the symbiosis would break down. Hypogeous, or underground, fungi depend on mammals for much of the dispersal of their spores. Truffles, the underground fruiting bodies of these fungi, are an important food source for a number of small animals in the old-growth forest. An animal finds a truffle by smell, digs it up, and eats it. All of the truffle is digested—except the spores, which are excreted in the animal's feces. Wherever the animal goes, the fungus goes.

Truffles were the key to a mystery that had long baffled biologists. *60* Biologists knew that bobcats and coyotes preyed on the northern flying squirrel. How do they catch an animal that presumably spent its time in the forest canopy? Analysis of the squirrels' stomach contents provided the answer. During the winter, lichens in tree crowns were the primary food source for flying squirrels. But between spring and fall, when the snow pack melted, the nocturnal animals came down to the ground to dig truffles. That's when their predators caught them. Laboratory studies of truffle-eating squirrels show that they pass nitrogen-fixing bacteria through their bodies along with fungal spores. Hypogeous fungi provide a home and small mammals a transport system for bacteria that add fertility to the forest floor.

The small California red-backed vole, whose tunnels are ubiquitous in the soil around rotting logs, shows a similar preference for truffles. The vole's environment, the Coast Range of southern Oregon and northern California, is ideal; this is one of very few places in the world where hypogeous fungi fruit year-round. If the fungus supply briefly runs short, the vole temporarily switches to lichens. Its favorite food may be *Rhizopogon vinicolor,* a mycorrhizal fungus that fruits mostly in rotten wood. *Rhizopogon* attaches itself to the roots of trees that grow in nurse logs. Forest researchers Chris Maser and James M. Trappe sum up the vole-fungus-tree relationship:

> Thus, there is a tight cycle of interdependence: the vole needs the truffle for food; the truffle depends on the vole for dispersal of spores and on a mycorrhizal tree host for energy; the tree requires mycorrhizal fungi for uptake of nutrients and provides the rotten wood needed by the vole for cover. Moreover, since both voles and *Rhizopogon vinicolor* specialize in rotten wood as habitat, the vole disperses the *Rhizopogon* spores to the kind of substrate in which the fungus thrives.

Are the small truffle-eaters the forester's friend or foe? Townsend's chipmunk and the deer mouse, long cursed as pests that eat conifer seeds, also are eager consumers of truffles. In that second role, they assist the growth of young Douglas fir by bringing mycorrhizal fungi to their roots. Maser, raising one of the critical questions for forestry in the twenty-first century, argues that losses of wildlife and changes in soil chemistry may lead to declines in commercial forest productivity. Already, he believes, there are signs that this has happened in parts of Europe. Other scientists such as Roy R. Silen worry that the genetic diversity of the trees may be narrowed perilously far by clearcutting the virgin forests and replanting "genetically improved" trees.

In the long run, if not the short run, what's good for nature as a whole is good for the human species. The future of the timber industry depends on the hardiness and genetic diversity of the tree kingdom. Mature and old-growth forests are the reservoirs of that diversity. This era of impending climatic change would seem to be the least appropriate time to deliberately narrow the forests' genetic diversity.

More broadly viewed, the genetic variation within a particular species is only one part of the richness of life forms known as biological diversity. The other two elements of biological diversity are a variety of species and a variety of ecosystems. All three elements of genetic diversity are placed at risk as North America's last virgin forests are replaced by the even-aged monoculture of tree farms. What's happening to the forests of the Pacific Northwest mirrors a worldwide phenomenon. Global deforestation may cause the extinction of one-fourth of the earth's five million species over the next several decades. The use of plants from the tropical rain forests as sources of pharmaceuticals has been widely discussed. Only recently has the bark of the Pacific yew been identified as a potent weapon against cancerous tumors in mice. The National Cancer Institute in 1987 contracted for the harvest of 60,000 pounds of the yew's papery red bark to determine whether the taxol derivative is safe for use in humans. The yew, found in old-growth forests, is not grown on tree farms.

Jerry Franklin believes management practices on commercial forestlands may be an even more important factor in maintaining biological diversity than is the amount of old growth that's preserved. No matter how successful environmentalists are in their efforts to save the ancient forests, he points out, commercially managed forests will cover a much greater area. If timber practices on those lands aren't changed, "we're going to effectively lose the war for biologic diversity." His recipe, and that of a growing number of his colleagues, is to keep more old-growth characteristics in the managed forests.

"We've got to quit leaving them in a billiard-table condition," says Franklin. "We have to leave more material behind, leave trees, snags, patches of reproduction, down logs—leaving a lot more heterogeneity in the cutover areas than we've been doing until this point. What we've got to do is leave our Germanic heritage behind us and cherish a little bit of disorder and chaos in our cutover areas."

During the short time that scientists have paid serious attention to the old-growth ecosystem, they have learned that the spotted owl is just one of dozens of vertebrates that are most at home in the ancient forests. They've learned about the tree vole, whose family may live in a single tree for generations; the northern flying squirrel, which feeds on lichens in the winter and truffles in the summer; the goshawk, whose short wings are adapted for flight among the trees; the pileated woodpecker, which excavates its home in large Douglas fir snags; the Olympic salamander, which lays its eggs in the rotting wood of large logs; the marbled murrelet, a seabird that returns each night to its nest in the ancient forest; and the national symbol, the bald eagle, which prefers to build its nest in older woods.

This growing recognition of the uniqueness of the old-growth ecosystem comes at an awkward time. It's awkward for the forest-products industry because the decline of private and state timber inventories leaves the industry more dependent than ever on federal sales of virgin timber. It's awkward for those concerned about the ecosystem because the amount of low-elevation old growth is dwindling fast. We've entered an era of scarcity, and public-policy decisions will be painful. For more than a century, the timber industry has been the leading employer in the Pacific Northwest. Although aerospace-industry employment has inched ahead in Washington and tourism is growing rapidly, the importance of timber can hardly be overstated. More than one-third of Oregon's manufacturing-sector jobs still are in lumber and wood products. . . .

65

The more I have learned about the debate over the old growth, the more I have been struck by the complexity of the issues. We've gained some insight into the ancient forest ecosystem, but we can't quite put our finger on the glue that holds it together. We haven't taken seriously the need of Native Americans for pristine forests to practice their traditional religion. The timber industry contends that its tree farms could support a healthy population of spotted owls, but it still practices the kind of even-aged silviculture that drives owls out.

While independent sawmills are going out of business for lack of logs, two-fifths of Washington's timber harvest is sold abroad unmilled. The forest-products industry clamors for unabated timber sales but, for the most part, remains silent about the understocked second-growth forests and the conversion of the best timberlands to suburban tracts. The continuing loss of jobs in the forest-products industry has far more to do with the automation of sawmills, log exports, and conversion of private timberland than with measures designed to protect the old-growth forests.

We haven't figured out whether the regional economy benefits more from logging an old-growth forest or from promoting the recreational potential of the forest. Nor has anyone quantified the damage done to the Northwest's important salmon-fishing industry by logging and road building. Our growing knowledge about nutrient cycling in old-growth forests has raised disturbing questions about the sustainability of tree farming as currently practiced. Increasingly, it looks as though the future of the timber industry requires that old-growth characteristics be incorporated into tree farms.

The slash burning that typically follows clearcutting throws carbon into the atmosphere, exacerbating the greenhouse effect. Logging of the ancient forests is more than a regional problem. Virgin forests are falling around the world, from Vancouver Island to Indonesia and from the Amazon to Africa. Like the rain forests of the tropics, the temperate forests of Oregon and Washington are being stripped to keep a troubled industry afloat and to satisfy the voracious appetite of Japanese and American consumers for lovely, fine-grained wood.

The fate of the ancient forests has become the premier issue of public land management in the western United States. The basic question confronting the body politic is how much old growth should be cut for the timber industry's benefit and how much preserved. The courts have been asked to resolve the issue, but they appear to be only a detour on the way to Congress. This process may not yield the best results—and certainly won't if the issues remain as poorly understood as they are at present. A recent scene before a congressional subcommittee shouldn't surprise us. An environmentalist had been talking for some time about the importance of old-growth forests when a puzzled congressman interrupted to ask, "Okra? What's this okra you're talking about?"

What ought to concern us even more than the lack of knowledge of a decision-maker from the Southeast is the absence of constructive dialogue among those closest to the situation. Precious little problem-solving has taken place. One Seattle newspaper editor is reported to have thundered, "I hope I never read the word old growth again!" The Forest Service proposes, with none of Solomon's subtlety or wisdom, to carve the remaining old growth in two, giving half to the environmentalists and half to industry. As a solution it won't stick, because neither side is buying into it. When the courts and Congress get through deciding matters, the outcome may not do much to help an endangered ecosystem *or* industry. But an imposed settlement is exactly what's going to happen unless representatives of environmental groups and the timber industry decide there's more to be gained than lost by negotiation. A satisfactory settlement must be more creative than just carving lines through the old growth.

In desperate times, people turn to desperate measures. Environmental 75 radicals have taken to sabotaging logging equipment and "inoculating" old-growth trees with spikes that pose a deadly hazard to mill workers. Not all loggers are kidding when they talk about hunting spotted owls.

Those who earn their livelihood from the forests feel they are under attack by outsiders who understand neither their way of life nor the forests themselves. It's as if Midwestern farmers, struggling to pay their debts, had to fight a powerful political movement bent on turning their farms back into a natural prairie. If environmentalists aren't a cynical elite, then, by golly, they must be naive sentimentalists duped by the Bambi syndrome.

The alleged sentimentality of environmentalists was confronted head-on by Robert Vincent, a wildlife consultant more concerned over the prospect of board feet of timber lost to industry than over the loss of spotted owl habitat. At a conference on old growth, Vincent noted that the richness and diversity of these forests is built on the death and decay of trees. He first likened old growth to a cemetery, then to "a self-centered miser" who buries his fortune in Crisco cans. On the other hand, he continued,

> . . . there are some people who really enjoy old things. The unchanging, the stagnant, the dying. In fact, we almost seem to live in an era of ancestral worship of things. Where do people go to make a visit? Certainly not to Houston or Denver, but to Rome, Venice, Paris, and Brussels where they can see old cathedrals and stagnated cities that haven't been touched for years. In fact, the longer a city stagnates or the longer a ruin stands, the more beautiful it becomes. It's kind of ridiculous, isn't it? . . . I suppose that if we could preserve an automobile junkyard for 1,000 years, it might be considered a thing of beauty.

Ridiculous though it may seem to some, there is something in most of us that looks in awestruck wonder at a forest that has been growing stronger and wilder for a millennium. And, as those in the European tourism business know, people are willing to pay for that feeling of awe. There's money in them thar woods, whether they're chopped down or left standing. Our feelings of wonder at the ancient creations of man and nature go beyond dollars and cents, of course. As we stand at the last corner of our continent gazing at the fast-disappearing old growth, our values are being put to the test.

The determination of people in logging country to preserve their livelihoods is a legitimate desire, one that must be confronted forthrightly. So, too, is the "sentimental" view that the virgin forests are a gift of God, not to be destroyed lightly.

Eric Forsman and Stan Sovern have more work to do. As soon as the   80 spotted owl is banded, they clamber back to the truck and head out on the logging roads toward Forks. They're going to join another member of the research team, Timm Kaminski, who is trying to locate another bird and outfit her with a radio transmitter. If the effort is successful, the scientists will be able to track her movements through the winter and into the next year. The data they collect will add valuable information about the kinds of forest in which these owls nest and forage.

We follow a dirt road over state and private land that has been almost entirely cut over. Finally, we see the distinctive tree line of a natural forest. Most of these woods, Forsman explains, are "Twenty-one Blow." The hurricane that whipped through the west side of the Olympic Peninsula on January 21, 1921, tore down thousands, perhaps millions of old-growth trees. On one part of the peninsula, the 100-mile-an-hour winds left a thirty-foot-deep pile of trees; on another, an entire herd of 200 elk was wiped out by falling timber.

We pull off the road next to Kaminski's pickup. Forsman shouts to Kaminski, but there's no answer. So he shoulders a radio receiver and tunes into the channel on which the male owl's transmitter is broadcasting. By walking in on the male, he hopes to find Kaminski and the female he's after. The woods are remarkably open. Despite the young hemlocks growing beneath their mature elders, there are no impenetrable thickets here. Moss covers the ground, rotting logs support a profusion of new life, and the rotting base of a gigantic dead tree stands as a reminder of the forest that stood here before the Twenty-one Blow. This is not, strictly speaking, old growth. Like the first forest we visited, it's what Forsman calls a "mature" or "mixed stand." In common with old growth, this stand has a deep, multilayered canopy, a mottled pattern of soft sunlight, and an abundance of dead wood both standing and fallen. What it lacks are the very large trees that only centuries can produce. To see true old growth, we would have to cross the creek to a cedar grove with trees seven feet in diameter and larger. It's there, on a privately owned parcel surrounded by state land, that the birds nest.

Forsman picks up strong signals on his radio. Soon he spots Kaminski and sees the female roosting overhead. Sovern and I keep a respectful distance to avoid spooking the bird. Sovern goes through his pack and prepares his gear. The juvenile, which we can't see from our location, is begging its parents for food: *Whhhhhhhhhip! . . . Whhhhhhhhiip!* It sounds something like a preschooler trying to whistle. Forsman and Kaminski trap the female while Sovern continues to prepare the equipment needed to strap the radio to her back. The adult male, pumping his broad wings, flies above our heads toward his mate. The male and the juvenile watch from branches as Forsman makes the capture. The whole family is here.

Sovern and I walk over. Sovern takes hold of the bird. A feisty one, she snaps at Forsman as he painstakingly fits the tiny transmitter on her back and adjusts the thin straps that hold it on. With each snap of her powerful beak she makes a loud cracking sound, like the pop of two wood blocks being slammed together. Once, she manages to get Forsman's finger. The scientists cover her large brown eyes.

Not far away, the juvenile keeps begging for his dinner. The male protests his mate's treatment: *Hooo . . . hooo . . . hooo . . . hooo!*   *85*

The spotted owl is not, to some people's minds, the most intelligent of birds. Certainly it is not the most cautious. One spotted owl, oblivious to the human threat, wound up in Seattle's Woodland Park Zoo after being struck by a logging truck. The female in Sovern's hands has been moused so many times she has become quite tame. Cautious though she may be about crossing a clearcut, where she could become a great horned owl's prey, she fails to appreciate the peril that humans pose. While she lies helplessly, her family can only watch and voice their useless protest.

Perhaps it's best that they don't understand their precarious future. The birds on the branches are no safer than the bird on the ground. Their fate, like that of the forest itself, is in our hands.

Working Together

1. Compare your annotations and see whether you can make a rough, one-page outline of this entire selection.
2. Pool your annotations and reading notes to make one page of notes, phrases, quotations, and paraphrasings that add up to what Ervin means by the word *forest.*
3. Assume that you are members of the "townsfolk here in logging country." How do you define the word *forest?*
4. Looking especially at what Jerry Franklin has to say, work as a group to arrive at a brief definition of *old growth.* Is this definition the same as the one for *forest,* or do these definitions differ?
5. As a group, discuss whether Ervin's piece does or does not argue in favor of "preservation." How does talking about preservation make sense and how does it not, according to Ervin?
6. As a group, discuss the primary approach that Ervin takes in this piece. Think in terms of the departments on your campus. Is Ervin's approach the English department approach? the computer science department approach?

Rethinking and Rewriting

1. In two or three pages, summarize Ervin's argument against "the even-aged monoculture of tree farms." Don't inject your own feelings; just try to accurately present Ervin. Once you've finished, write a page that discusses how easy or difficult it was for you to write this summary.

2. Identify two or three fundamental facts that anchor Ervin's discussion, and then do some additional research to check those facts and to see whether the thinking has changed since this article was written. End by drawing appropriate conclusions based on your research.

3. Take some aspect of forest ecology—the spotted owl or truffles or the class of fungi called mycorrhizae, for example—and do some research to deepen and add to your understanding of it. Approach this topic from the viewpoint of a biologist or someone interested in biology. Assume that you're writing to your classmates and that they're eager to learn more about how a forest works.

4. Assume that Keith Ervin were going to visit your campus. What local issues would interest him? What new facts would he need to understand in order to really appreciate the complexities of these local issues? (If you can limit this to just one issue, so much the better.) Communicate this information in the form of a letter (no more than three pages single-spaced or six pages double-spaced) that you'd send three weeks before Ervin's visit.

5. Argue that what Ervin's concerned about is really just a local issue that ought to be decided only by local input. Or argue that what Ervin's concerned about is really a national issue that ought to be decided on a national basis.

6. Ervin's piece mentions salmon fishing only briefly. Research salmon and salmon fishing and see whether or not they are connected to forest practices. Explain what you discover to those readers who don't know much about salmon.

7. Take the description of the complex interrelationships in an old-growth forest and use these complexities as a metaphor for life, the writing process, relationships, family, school, whatever. How is life (or something else) like an old-growth forest?

"AXE-IN-HAND"

Aldo Leopold

> *A naturalist and wildlife biologist, Aldo Leopold worked for the forest service for nearly twenty years and then was a faculty member at the University of Wisconsin until his death in 1941. As a naturalist, he pioneered the ecological approach to wildlife and land management. As a writer, he is known for* The Sand County Almanac *(1949), a series of journal-like meditations on the natural world and the human need for wilderness. This excerpt is one of those meditations.*

As You Read

As you read, construct two columns on a piece of paper. Label one of them "birch" and the other one "pine," and fill in each column with the appropriate attributes and reasons for cutting it down or saving it.

The Lord giveth, and the Lord taketh away, but He is no longer the only one to do so. When some remote ancestor of ours invented the shovel, he became a giver: he could plant a tree. And when the axe was invented, he became a taker: he could chop it down. Whoever owns land has thus assumed, whether he knows it or not, the divine functions of creating and destroying plants.

Other ancestors, less remote, have since invented other tools, but each of these, upon close scrutiny, proves to be either an elaboration of, or an accessory to, the original pair of basic implements. We classify ourselves into vocations, each of which either wields some particular tool, or sells it, or repairs it, or sharpens it, or dispenses advice on how to do so; by such division of labors we avoid responsibility for the misuse of any tool save our own. But there is one vocation—philosophy—which knows that all men, by what they think about and wish for, in effect wield all tools. It knows that men thus determine, by their manner of thinking and wishing, whether it is worth while to wield any.

* * *

November is, for many reasons, the month for the axe. It is warm enough to grind an axe without freezing, but cold enough to fell a tree in comfort. The leaves are off the hardwoods, so that one can see just how the branches intertwine, and what growth occurred last summer. Without this clear view of treetops, one cannot be sure which tree, if any, needs felling for the good of the land.

I have read many definitions of what is a conservationist, and written not a few myself, but I suspect that the best one is written not with a pen, but with an axe. It is a matter of what a man thinks about while chopping, or while deciding what to chop. A conservationist is one who is humbly aware that with each stroke he is writing his signature on the face of his land. Signatures of course differ, whether written with axe or pen, and this is as it should be.

I find it disconcerting to analyze, *ex post facto,* the reasons behind my own axe-in-hand decisions. I find, first of all, that not all trees are created free and equal. Where a white pine and a red birch are crowding each other, I have an *a priori* bias; I always cut the birch to favor the pine. Why?

Well, first of all, I planted the pine with my shovel, whereas the birch crawled in under the fence and planted itself. My bias is thus to some extent paternal, but this cannot be the whole story, for if the pine were a natural seedling like the birch, I would value it even more. So I must dig deeper for the logic, if any, behind my bias.

The birch is an abundant tree in my township and becoming more so, whereas pine is scarce and becoming scarcer; perhaps my bias is for the underdog. But, what would I do if my farm were further north, where pine is abundant and red birch is scarce? I confess I don't know. My farm is here.

The pine will live for a century, the birch for half that; do I fear that my signature will fade? My neighbors have planted no pines but all have many birches; am I snobbish about having a woodlot of distinction? The pine stays green all winter, the birch punches the clock in October; do I favor the tree that, like myself, braves the winter wind? The pine will shelter a grouse but the birch will feed him; do I consider bed more important than board? The pine will ultimately bring ten dollars a thousand, the birch two dollars; have I an eye on the bank? All of these possible reasons for my bias seem to carry some weight, but none of them carries very much.

So I try again, and here perhaps is something; under this pine will ultimately grow a trailing arbutus, an Indian pipe, a pyrola, or a twin flower, whereas under the birch a bottle gentian is about the best to be hoped for. In this pine a pileated woodpecker will ultimately chisel out a nest; in the birch a hairy will have to suffice. In this pine the wind will sing for me in April, at which time the birch is only rattling naked twigs. These possible reasons for my bias carry weight, but why? Does the pine stimulate my imagination and my hopes more deeply than the birch does? If so, is the difference in the trees, or in me?

The only conclusion I have ever reached is that I love all trees, but I am in love with pines.

As I said, November is the month for the axe, and, as in other love affairs, there is skill in the exercise of bias. If the birch stands south of the pine, and is taller, it will shade the pine's leader in the spring, and thus discourage the pine weevil from laying her eggs there. Birch competition is a minor affliction compared with this weevil, whose progeny kill the pine's leader and thus deform the tree. It is interesting to meditate that this insect's preference for squatting in the sun determines not only her own continuity as a species, but also the future figure of my pine, and my own success as a wielder of axe and shovel.

Again, if a drouthy summer follows my removal of the birch's shade, the hotter soil may offset the lesser competition for water, and my pine be none the better for my bias.

Lastly, if the birch's limbs rub the pine's terminal buds during a wind, the pine will surely be deformed, and the birch must either be removed regardless of other considerations, or else it must be pruned of limbs each winter to a height greater than the pine's prospective summer growth.

Such are the pros and cons the wielder of an axe must foresee, compare, and decide upon with the calm assurance that his bias will, on the average, prove to be something more than good intentions.

The wielder of an axe has as many biases as there are species of trees on his farm. In the course of the years he imputes to each species, from his responses to their beauty or utility, and their responses to his labors for or against them, a series of attributes that constitute a character. I am amazed to learn what diverse characters different men impute to one and the same tree. [15]

Thus to me the aspen is in good repute because he glorifies October and he feeds my grouse in winter, but to some of my neighbors he is a mere weed, perhaps because he sprouted so vigorously in the stump lots their grandfathers were attempting to clear. (I cannot sneer at this, for I find myself disliking the elms whose resproutings threaten my pines.)

Again, the tamarack is to me a favorite second only to white pine, perhaps because he is nearly extinct in my township (underdog bias), or because he sprinkles gold on October grouse (gunpowder bias), or because he sours the soil and enables it to grow the loveliest of our orchids, the showy lady's-slipper. On the other hand, foresters have excommunicated the tamarack because he grows too slowly to pay compound interest. In order to clinch this dispute, they also mention that he succumbs periodically to epizootics of saw-fly, but this is fifty years hence for my tamaracks, so I shall let my grandson worry about it. Meanwhile my tamaracks are growing so lustily that my spirits soar with them, skyward.

To me an ancient cottonwood is the greatest of trees because in his youth he shaded the buffalo and wore a halo of pigeons, and I like a young cottonwood because he may some day become ancient. But the farmer's wife (and hence the farmer) despises all cottonwoods because in June the female tree clogs the screens with cotton. The modern dogma is comfort at any cost.

I find my biases more numerous than those of my neighbors because I have individual likings for many species that they lump under one aspersive category: brush. Thus I like the wahoo, partly because deer, rabbits, and mice are so avid to eat his square twigs and green bark and partly because his cerise berries glow so warmly against November snow. I like the red dogwood because he feeds October robins, and the prickly ash because my woodcock take their daily sunbath under the shelter of his thorns. I like the hazel because his October purple feeds my eye, and because his November catkins feed my deer and grouse. I like the bittersweet because my father did, and because the deer, on the 1st of July of each year, begin suddenly to eat the new leaves, and I have learned to predict this event to my guests. I cannot dislike a plant that enables me, a mere professor, to blossom forth annually as a successful seer and prophet.

It is evident that our plant biases are in part traditional. If your grandfather liked hickory nuts, you will like the hickory tree because your father told you to. If, on the other hand, your grandfather burned a log carrying a poison ivy vine and recklessly stood in the smoke, you will dislike the species, no matter with what crimson glories it warms your eyes each fall. 20

It is also evident that our plant biases reflect not only vocations but avocations, with a delicate allocation of priority as between industry and indolence. The farmer who would rather hunt grouse than milk cows will not dislike hawthorn, no matter if it does invade his pasture. The coonhunter will not dislike basswood, and I know of quail hunters who bear no grudge against ragweed, despite their annual bout with hayfever. Our biases are indeed a sensitive index to our affections, our tastes, our loyalties, our generosities, and our manner of wasting weekends.

Be that as it may, I am content to waste mine, in November, with axe in hand.

Reading and Responding

1. Describe the tone or voice of this piece: Who would play the voice in the movie? What clothes would the voice wear? What other kind of writing, talking, or language is the voice most like?
2. Mark the most quotable passages in this short piece.

Working Together

1. Share the quotable passages you marked. Did you mark similar things? Why or why not? What makes the passages quotable?
2. Describe the language that isn't quotable. What's it doing? How does this language relate to the quotable language?
3. Take a quotable passage and ruin it. Make it unquotable. What have you done?
4. Pool your understanding of pine versus birch, and write a group paragraph that explains the controversy and how it's finally decided.

Rethinking and Rewriting

1. Write an essay with this title: "With _____ in Hand" (power drill, beer can, pencil or pen, shovel, football). Describe what's going through your mind as you handle this object or use this tool. Assume that this tool is your means to a "signature" as Aldo Leopold discusses it.

2. Write an essay giving and explaining your definition of *environmentalist*.
3. Write an essay giving and explaining your definition of some other class of people (college professors, members of sororities and fraternities, writers). Imitate the tone and structure of "Axe-in-Hand."

"UNCHOPPING A TREE"

W. S. Merwin

*W. S. Merwin was born in New York City and has lived for extended
periods in France, Portugal, Spain, England, and Hawaii. A nonfiction
writer and distinguished translator, as well as Pulitzer Prize–winning poet
(for* The Carrier of Ladders, *1970), Merwin has written articles for* The
Nation *and radio scripts for the BBC. In this carefully constructed brief essay
Merwin proceeds from a startling assumption.*

As You Read
1. Briefly record your reaction after reading the first few sentences.
2. Record your reaction in the middle of the piece.
3. Record your reaction at the end.

Start with the leaves, the small twigs, and the nests that have been
shaken, ripped, or broken off by the fall; these must be gathered and
attached once again to their respective places. It is not arduous work, unless
major limbs have been smashed or mutilated. If the fall was carefully and
correctly planned, the chances of anything of the kind happening will have
been reduced. Again, much depends upon the size, age, shape, and species
of the tree. Still, you will be lucky if you can get through this stage without
having to use machinery. Even in the best of circumstances it is a labor
that will make you wish often that you had won the favor of the universe
of ants, the empire of mice, or at least a local tribe of squirrels, and could
enlist their labors and their talents. But no, they leave you to it. They have
learned, with time. This is men's work. It goes without saying that if the
tree was hollow in whole or in part, and contained old nests of bird or
mammal or insect, or hoards of nuts or such structures as wasps or bees
build for their survival, the contents will have to be repaired where necessary, and reassembled, insofar as possible, in their original order, including
the shells of nuts already opened. With spiders' webs you must simply do
the best you can. We do not have the spider's weaving equipment, nor any
substitute for the leaf's living bond with its point of attachment and nourishment. It is even harder to simulate the latter when the leaves have once
become dry—as they are bound to do, for this is not the labor of a moment. Also it hardly needs saying that this is the time for repairing any
neighboring trees or bushes or other growth that may have been damaged
by the fall. The same rules apply. Where neighboring trees were of the
same species it is difficult not to waste time conveying a detached leaf back
to the wrong tree. Practice, practice. Put your hope in that.

Now the tackle must be put into place, or the scaffolding, depending
on the surroundings and the dimensions of the tree. It is ticklish work.

Almost always it involves, in itself, further damage to the area, which will have to be corrected later. But as you've heard, it can't be helped. And care now is likely to save you considerable trouble later. Be careful to grind nothing into the ground.

At last the time comes for the erecting of the trunk. By now it will scarcely be necessary to remind you of the delicacy of this huge skeleton. Every motion of the tackle, every slight upward heave of the trunk, the branches, their elaborately re-assembled panoply of leaves (now dead) will draw from you an involuntary gasp. You will watch for a leaf or a twig to be snapped off yet again. You will listen for the nuts to shift in the hollow limb and you will hear whether they are indeed falling into place or are spilling in disorder—in which case, or in the event of anything else of the kind—operations will have to cease, of course, while you correct the matter. The raising itself is no small enterprise, from the moment when the chains tighten around the old bandages until the bole hangs vertical above the stump, splinter above splinter. Now the final straightening of the splinters themselves can take place (the preliminary work is best done while the wood is still green and soft, but at times when the splinters are not badly twisted most of the straightening is left until now, when the torn ends are face to face with each other). When the splinters are perfectly complementary the appropriate fixative is applied. Again we have no duplicate of the original substance. Ours is extremely strong, but it is rigid. It is limited to surfaces, and there is no play in it. However the core is not the part of the trunk that conducted life from the roots up into the branches and back again. It was relatively inert. The fixative for this part is not the same as the one for the outer layers and the bark, and if either of these is involved in the splintered section they must receive applications of the appropriate adhesives. Apart from being incorrect and probably ineffective, the core fixative would leave a scar on the bark.

When all is ready the splintered trunk is lowered onto the splinters of the stump. This, one might say, is only the skeleton of the resurrection. Now the chips must be gathered, and the sawdust, and returned to their former positions. The fixative for the wood layers will be applied to chips and sawdust consisting only of wood. Chips and sawdust consisting of several substances will receive applications of the correct adhesives. It is as well, where possible, to shelter the materials from the elements while working. Weathering makes it harder to identify the smaller fragments. Bark sawdust in particular the earth lays claim to very quickly. You must find your own ways of coping with this problem. There is a certain beauty, you will notice at moments, in the pattern of the chips as they are fitted back into place. You will wonder to what extent it should be described as natural, to what extent man-made. It will lead you on to speculations about the parentage of beauty itself, to which you will return.

The adhesive for the chips is translucent, and not so rigid as that for the splinters. That for the bark and its subcutaneous layers is transparent and runs into the fibers on either side, partially dissolving them into each other. It does not set the sap flowing again but it does pay a kind of tribute to the preoccupations of the ancient thoroughfares. You could not roll an egg over the joints but some of the mine-shafts would still be passable, no doubt. For the first exploring insect who raises its head in the tight echoless passages. The day comes when it is all restored, even to the moss (now dead) over the wound. You will sleep badly, thinking of the removal of the scaffolding that must begin the next morning. How you will hope for sun and a still day!

The removal of the scaffolding or tackle is not so dangerous, perhaps, to the surroundings, as its installation, but it presents problems. It should be taken from the spot piece by piece as it is detached, and stored at a distance. You have come to accept it there, around the tree. The sky begins to look naked as the chains and struts one by one vacate their positions. Finally the moment arrives when the last sustaining piece is removed and the tree stands again on its own. It is as though its weight for a moment stood on your heart. You listen for a thud of settlement, a warning creak deep in the intricate joinery. You cannot believe it will hold. How like something dreamed it is, standing there all by itself. How long will it stand there now? The first breeze that touches its dead leaves all seems to flow into your mouth. You are afraid the motion of the clouds will be enough to push it over. What more can you do? What more can you do?

But there is nothing more you can do.

Others are waiting.

Everything is going to have to be put back.

Working Together

1. In a few sentences, summarize what you think Merwin's main point is. Put it as bluntly as you can.
2. Discuss why Merwin just doesn't come out and say his point? Why does he make his point in this indirect, odd way?

Rethinking and Rewriting

1. Write an essay with this title, filling in the blanks: "Un_____ing a _____" (Unwriting a Paper, Unreading a Book, Undrinking a Bottle of Wine, Unhurting a Friend, Undriving a Car).
2. Describe any process in reverse.
3. Argue any position or make some point about something without coming out and stating your position. Do it obliquely, through some trick or shift in perspective.

"ELEGY FOR A FOREST CLEAR-CUT BY THE WEYERHAEUSER COMPANY"

David Wagoner

A long-time resident of Seattle and teacher at the University of Washington, David Wagoner has maintained a distinguished career as editor (of Poetry Northwest *and of the notebooks of Theodore Roethke), novelist, and poet. In all, he has published more than fifteen books. The poem reprinted here appeared originally in Wagoner's book* Sleeping in the Woods *(1974).*

Five months after your death, I come like the others
Among the slash and stumps, across the cratered
Three square miles of your graveyard:
Nettles and groundsel first out of the jumble,
Then fireweed and bracken   5
Have come to light where you, for ninety years,
Had kept your shadows.

The creek has gone as thin as my wrist, nearly dead
To the world at the dead end of summer,
Guttering to a pool where the tracks of an earth-mover   10
Showed it the way to falter underground.
Now pearly everlasting
Has grown to honor the deep dead cast of your roots
For a bitter season.

Those water- and earth-led roots decay for winter   15
Below my feet, below the fir seedlings
Planted in your place (one out of ten alive
In the summer drought),
Below the small green struggle of the weeds
For their own ends, below grasshoppers,   20
The only singers now.

The chains and cables and steel teeth have left
Nothing of what you were:
I hold my hands over a stump and remember
A hundred and fifty feet above me branches   25
No longer holding sway. In the pitched battle
You fell and fell again and went on falling
And falling and always falling.

Out in the open where nothing was left standing
(The immoral equivalent of a forest fire),   30
I sit with my anger. The creek will move again,
Come rain and snow, gnawing at raw defiles,

Clear-cutting its own gullies.
As selective as reapers stalking through wheatfields,
Selective loggers go where the roots go.   *35*

Reading and Responding

1. What does the speaker in this poem find alive in the clear-cut? Make a list of these things.
2. What's an elegy sound like? Using this one as an example, write a few sentences about the tone of an elegy. If this were music, what would it sound like?
3. Choose one of the stanzas and copy it word for word and line for line in your own writing. On the basis of that stanza and the experience of writing it out as you have, write two or three sentences that explain the difference between poetry and everyday prose.

Working Together

1. Number each of the stanzas 1 through 5. Then order them in a new way. Once you've decided on your new ordering, be ready to explain that order and whatever you've learned as a result of doing it.
2. As a group, make a list of other places that might provoke in you the same kind of response that Wagoner has in this poem.
3. As a group, assume that you are David Wagoner. Why did you write this poem? What did you hope to accomplish?

Rethinking and Rewriting

1. Using this poem as an example, write two or three pages explaining why you can't stand reading poems or why you find reading poems interesting.
2. Locate another poem by David Wagoner, copy it, and write a two- or three-page explanation of why you like that second poem better than you like "Elegy" or why you prefer "Elegy."
3. Walk to a forest (or forestlike area) or walk to a clear-cut. While you're there, write one page that talks about what you see and what you feel. Polish that page later (make it as clear and error-free as you can), but don't change its primary character.

"OLD GROWTH AND THE MEDIA"

Mark Hatfield

> *After several years as dean of students and a professor of political science at Willamette University, as well as a member of the Oregon legislature, Mark Hatfield served from 1959 to 1967 as the governor of Oregon. Since 1967, as an influential Republican senator from Oregon, he has supported legislation calling for water pollution control, reforestation of public lands, and the development of alternative energy sources. His belief is that comprehensive environmental planning can "integrate our economy and our ecology" in ways that "demonstrate loving stewardship of the whole of creation." Senator Hatfield is also the author of a number of books, including an autobiography,* Not Quite So Simple *(1967),* Conflict of Conscience *(1971),* Between a Rock and a Hard Place *(1976), and, as coauthor,* The Causes of World Hunger *(1982).*

In the fall of 1989, I received a call from a reporter at CBS News. The caller was interested in doing a story on the "deforestation of the Pacific Northwest."

On the surface, anybody who has heard about the spotted owl and the old-growth forests of the Pacific Northwest would not question the premise of the question. By now, we've all heard the horror stories; we've read them in the newspapers and seen the footage on the nightly news. The message is: The loggers in the Northwest have clear-cut the land and there's no more old-growth trees left, right?

Wrong.

While seemingly unassuming, the request from CBS pointed to a significant problem in the ongoing debate over the management of our national forests and, more specifically, in the debate over the northern spotted owl and our old-growth forests.

Throughout this debate, policy-makers have been plagued by several factors, some of which were directly related to the media's coverage of the issue. The problems were just as prevalent in the regional media (which one would expect to have more expertise on details) as they were in the national media.

First, there was a general lack of understanding of what is admittedly an extraordinarily complex issue. But this lack of understanding often led to inaccuracies in reporting and, in some cases, the omission of important information. When theories of forestry are presented as fact, and information provided by special interest groups is presented to the public as gospel without verification, the public is ill-served. Yet that is exactly what has happened in story after story, in broadcast after broadcast.

With the old-growth issue, policy-makers are still operating in an environment of rapidly changing information, scientific and otherwise. At the same time, we have made a supreme effort to base our decisions on the most timely and scientifically defensible information available to us. Given the fact that one of the great challenges of our age is to manage the flood of information thrown at us every hour of the day, this hasn't always been easy.

Unfortunately, we live today in a society of instant gratification. Whether it is going to a fast-food restaurant for a quick meal or buying throw-away diapers or cameras, our lives have become geared to the need for rapid response. Decisions affecting thousands of lives and the future of our planet are increasingly made with an alarming glibness.

Because of this, the responsibility of the nation's elected officials to gather, evaluate and act on rapidly changing information is a daunting one. But the responsibility doesn't stop with Congress.

I believe that the media in a free society has no less an obligation to   10
make sure certain facts are presented accurately and fairly. While there have been exceptions, my view is that just the opposite has been true in the reporting of the "Great Forest Wars."

Additionally, of the hundreds of thousands of column inches written and miles of videotape filmed on this subject, the human dimension of this story has often been downplayed as having less importance than the biological questions—when in fact these factors are inextricably linked. In some cases, the human dimension has been ignored altogether.

The CBS request about the "deforestation of the Pacific Northwest" was a common example of the kind of misinformation being perpetuated by media accounts of the problem. Over time such statements have become part of the nomenclature for reporters and editors alike. There are other examples, such as the statement: "We are about to cut down the last of the old-growth forests." Or a variation: "Only 12 percent of the old-growth forest remains" (or 10 or 5 percent, depending on which interest group the reporter chooses to believe).

Broadcast media in particular has fallen victim to these sweeping generalizations. As any propagandist worth his salt knows, perception often becomes reality, especially if perception is repeated enough. The media, in my view, have been less-than-aggressive in challenging oft-repeated assertions. Many of these claims (the less than 12 percent old growth remaining is a good example) are repeated in the media without being checked with credentialed professionals, and the public is ill-served in the process.

Unfortunately, most facts dealing with forestry (or any area of natural science) often require considerable explanation to develop in context, requiring precious time few broadcast outlets have, and precious space newspapers no longer have. The result is the combination of film or still photos of trees crashing to earth, which inevitably skews the public's understanding of the issue. In the case of the old-growth controversy, such imagery led to thousands of calls and letters to offices of lawmakers who could only respond with clarification, fact or—more often—nothing at all.

Had reporters searching for a story on "the deforestation of the   15
Northwest forests" researched the subject more thoroughly, they would

know that the forests of Oregon and Washington cannot be compared to the Brazilian rainforests. When trees are harvested on public and private land in Oregon and Washington, new trees must be replanted in accordance with federal laws. If reforestation of a site cannot be assured, it cannot be harvested. It's as simple as that.

The result of this policy is that we now have *more* trees growing in Oregon and Washington today than there were in the 1920s. Every year Congress provides funding for the Forest Service to replant millions of seedlings and thousands of acres of forests for the next generation.

The old-growth part of the question is more complex.

There is no single definition of *old growth,* and yet reporters and editors have repeatedly (and inconsistently) used selected definitions—or parts of definitions—for *old growth* without clarification. Any statement about how much old growth remains is necessarily dependent upon which definition is used (there are at least four). To say that only 12 percent, or 10 percent or 5 percent remains, assumes that every acre of forest land was in an old growth condition before humans logged the first tree.

Such a notion is without foundation.

Nature has, without help from humans, destroyed regenerated forests   20
by wind, fire, insects and disease. This has in itself, created forest lands with a variety of ages, classifications and conditions. Forests were never entirely old growth. Most forest ecologists today estimate that the forests have never been more than 20 percent old growth at any point in time. Today, using a definition developed by a Forest Service research report (PNW-447), the Forest Service estimates that there are 3.75 million acres of "old growth" in Oregon and Washington. This is 19.7 percent of the national forest land base—just about the historic average based on the estimates by the forest ecologists.

The point is this: While policy-makers try to work with and make decisions on the best information available, the media has no less an obligation to do the same. With a few exceptions in both the regional and national media, this simply has not happened.

A good case study of this problem was a six-part "in-depth" series analyzing the national forest management controversy in the Portland *Oregonian* last year.

The state's largest newspaper of record had a golden opportunity to provide its readers with a clear and detailed analysis of the issue.

When I learned the story was being written, I hoped that it would be an objective one, perhaps clarifying misconceptions, pointing out problems and errors where warranted. Instead, hundreds of thousands of *Oregonian* readers were treated to one of the longest editorials in the paper's 140-year history.

For example, the *Oregonian* repeatedly used old-growth acreage fig-   25
ures provided by the Wilderness Society. This definition, also valid depending on the forest characteristics being examined, varies considerably from the Forest Service definition. Although mentioning the Forest Ser-

vice definition in passing, the *Oregonian* chose to use the Wilderness Society definition throughout the article to paint, in the reporter's own words, a "far bleaker" picture of the situation.

The *Oregonian* series, "Northwest Forests: A Day of Reckoning," went beyond objective reporting. The series took a good news story idea and turned it into a searing six-part editorial advocating a sharp reduction in forest management activities in the Northwest. In doing so, the *Oregonian* not only did a disservice to its readers, but violated the basic responsibility of the media to report "objectively."

The *Oregonian* also reported that Forest Service supervisors were "under pressure from Northwest lawmakers to meet unsustainable timber sale targets" but offered no proof of any such "pressure." I was a primary target of that accusation, and yet I can state categorically that I never pressured anyone in the Forest Service to cut more than what was sustainable.

What the *Oregonian* did not report is that Congress has actually *lowered* the volume of timber sold each year to levels below what the Forest Service considers sustainable. It is unfortunate that the *Oregonian* reporter further confused the issue by not explaining the distinction between the amount of timber *sold* annually (a level which Congress sets based on information from the Forest Service) and the amount of timber *harvested* annually (which is complicated but can be explained by analyzing the amount of timber held under contract and the requirements of the marketplace, and which *is not* determined by Congress).

The *Oregonian* series emphasized the negative aspects of the issue and in some cases omitted key facts that would have presented a more accurate picture. Nowhere in the article was it mentioned that many of the concerns expressed about public forest management (soil erosion, watershed protection and enhancement, scenic protection, etc.) had been addressed in new forest plans now in place for each of the region's 19 national forests. The fact that 15 years and $230 million worth of work on those forest plans had led to improved forest management was incomprehensibly omitted from the series.

A basic premise of the *Oregonian* series was that Oregon is in the throes 30 of a "painful but long predicted transition from an economy built on wholesale harvesting of its virgin forests to one more complex and diversified," but the statement is misleading. The fact is that Oregon has been steadily diversifying its economy for over 30 years. The problem is that much of the rural part of Oregon—about 70 communities and approximately 500,000 people—remains economically dependent upon forestry, agriculture and fishing. These communities do not have the flexibility to respond to sudden, unplanned change. And because 52 percent of our land base is owned by the federal government, federal decisions can create major shock waves in those towns and communities.

In addition, the *Oregonian* relied heavily on environmental sources and gave only token representation to forest industry sources in an attempt to provide an appearance of fairness. Out of a total of approximately 2,700 column inches of print, only 53 inches, or two percent of the total, cited industry sources, and some of them were contacted only one week before the series ran.

This problem of selective reporting within the context of a news story was elevated to the national arena with a cover story in *Time* magazine, "Owl vs. Man." In what was clearly a major piece for *Time,* reporter Ted Gup spent several days in Oregon talking to industry and environmental sources to get a handle on the story. And yet, in the final analysis, Gup failed to examine in any detail what congressional solution might be offered and instead ended his story with a statement that only reflected the inadequacy of his research:

> In the case of the Northwest, the Federal Government should help retrain loggers and mill workers with grants to spur economic diversification. Congress could also help sustain the Northwest's processing mills by passing legislation aimed at reducing raw-log exports.

Mr. Gup's editorializing missed the point. First of all, Congress has provided and is still providing funds for retraining of mill workers and others displaced by the current crisis. Second, Congress has banned the export of raw logs from federal lands for over 20 years, and just last summer (before the *Time* article was written) it restored the rights of states to ban the export of logs removed from state lands.

And nowhere in the *Time* story (with the exception of a short sidebar) did we see images of displaced workers, of second- or third-generation logging families, or the schools that would close for lack of funds, or local officials who face severe budget restrictions due to the loss of timber receipts.

Instead we got brilliantly composed photographs of a logger making   35 the final cut into a giant tree, of anti-logging protesters, of clear-cuts and of spotted owl juxtaposed with the opening paragraph: "A lumberjack presses his snarling chain saw into the flesh of a Douglas Fir that has held its place against wind and fires, rock slide and flood, for 200 years."

As has been the case in most contemporary reporting about environmental issues, the human dimension was largely ignored in the media until only recently. Stories about shortcomings in the management of the forests by federal agencies, directives from Congress, and the "overcutting" of the forests have almost completely overshadowed the human element.

Rarely have I seen an honest perspective of the human side of this problem. And I have never seen reported the fact that counties in some of the more timber-dependent areas in Oregon receive as much as $1,535 per child from timber receipts, or that tax rates on an average home may skyrocket in some areas if a balanced solution to this problem isn't found.

For the media, it's easy to portray a quick-fix image, but the fact is, there are no simple solutions to the problem.

Certainly, we must continue to work toward true economic diversi-fication, but we cannot define diverisfication as shutting off one economic faucet only to hope another will be turned on in its place. We can't define diversification as building up one sector of the economy at the expense of the other.

In the end, the media's coverage of the old-growth issue, while ex-   *40* tensive, has been lacking in balance. Policy-makers have tried to make decisions using the best available information, and we have tried to look to the long term for reasonable solutions. We have tried to incorporate balance between the need to protect our natural resources and the need to protect a way of life for a large segment of the people whom we represent. It hasn't always been easy.

The media has no less an obligation to do the same.

Reading and Responding

1. How is your reading of this article influenced by your knowledge that Mark Hatfield is a United States senator?
2. How is your reading influenced by your knowledge that Mark Hatfield is a Republican senator?

Working Together

1. Outline this article in class, working in groups. What is the main point? What are the subpoints?
2. List the evidence and support Senator Hatfield uses to back up his claims.
3. Categorize the evidence and support he uses. What kinds of support does he draw on (facts, testimony of others, commonsense reasoning)? Where does this evidence come from: What are the sources, and how are they indicated?
4. Besides evidence, what other strategies does Hatfield use to convince his readers? Consider, in particular, his tone and voice.

Rethinking and Rewriting

1. Write an essay lining up Senator Hatfield's arguments with the infor-mation and arguments of Keith Ervin's "A Life in Our Hands." Be clear and logical about exactly what points the two writers disagree about. What's the main source of the dispute about old-growth forests?
2. Look up both the *Oregonian* and the *Time* articles Hatfield cites. Write a paper agreeing or disagreeing with his assessment, using Ervin's sources of information.
3. Write a response to Hatfield's article. Make sure that your response quotes him at least twice as you work to make your own points.

"TROUBLE IN MILL CITY"

David Seideman

> *David Seideman's* Showdown at Opal Creek *(1993) tells the story of two Mill City, Oregon, friends and antagonists, Tom Hirons, logger, and George Atiyeh, environmentalist. Hirons stands to lose his livelihood in the woods; Atiyeh stands to lose a landscape and ecosystem that has remained mostly unaffected by people. The book is a study in what happens to resource-dependent towns once the resource is depleted. In this selection Seideman (a reporter for* Time*) describes Mill City itself.*

As You Read

1. As you read, copy out a list of words or phrases that seem to you to be particularly accurate descriptions of Mill City as it is now.
2. When you get to the section of this essay discussing Mill City's history, make two lists: one showing the benefits of being a company town, another showing the drawbacks.

Two hours from dawn, on a crisp spring night, darkness cloaks Mill City. Thick mist dripping from a starless sky suspends the promise of sun for the ninth straight day. That's the Pacific Northwest for you. Here on Broadway, the town's older commercial core, Marie and Charley Stewart will open their mom and pop general store at 8:00 a.m. sharp, as they have every day for the past forty-three years, except on Sundays—when the lights go on an hour later—and the big four holidays when they're closed. "If we ain't got it, you don't need it," reads the slogan on Charley's delivery van. He really does sell every item imaginable. Most townspeople will drop by during the day to shop and catch up on gossip.

All is not still at this hour. Down the road, Young and Morgan's plywood mill is bathed in the soaking orange glow of floodlights and plumes of boiler steam. Log trucks on their first runs rumble past the empty storefront once occupied by the Dew Drop Inn Malt Shop. They hook a horseshoe right by the steel bridge carted in sections from Pennsylvania at the turn of the century and inch up the steep hill. A year hardly used to pass without some truck sliding back down and dumping a load. Flatlanders from other parts would be scared helpless, and even Doc Kimmel, a big man around here, once had his car remodeled that way.

Next door to the old railway depot, George Long, the local printer, has already put to bed this week's issue of *The Mill City Enterprise*—circulation, 1,280. An old letterpressman, he is one of the last two printers in the state using offset printing for the timber companies' business cards and stationery. Melting wax and lead perfume the air as he pushes his seventy-year-old linotype machine's pedal to the floor. CLUNK CLUNK. This antique will retire along with George.

The hauls of Mill City's wooden gold keep on coming, trundling down Broadway, past the First Christian Church, where the Pastor Aaron Veach delivers the finest sermons around. On Highway 22, the top timbermen strike deals over breakfast at their favorite hangout, the Dutch End Cafe. They grab pens and pencils from the breast pockets of their plaid shirts to make quick computations. The pancakes at Dutch End are buttermilk, biscuits come with white gravy, and the coffee is drunk black or not at all. Shortly after dawn, students arrive at school by bus or on foot. Just last year, the ultra modern middle school installed a sleek new chemistry lab. Halfway up the hill, renters slip last night's movie through the door of Marlene Hirons's video store. In addition to adventure and romance, her hunting and fishing selections do a brisk business. At the post office around the corner, friends and neighbors don't seem to mind having to pick up mail in person, through the rural delivery system's post office boxes, as it gives them another chance to socialize. Across the street, Girods Hilltop Market unloads fresh shipments of produce. Three years ago Jim Girod established Mill City's first deli department, a radical notion for most customers. Reckoning it sold fancy items, they initially stuck to prepackaged Oscar Mayer cold cuts. Once the idea caught on, though, the deli became one of the store's main attractions.

Mill City is a nice place to call home. Hunkered down in the foothills of the Cascade Range in the heart of North Santiam Canyon, its storybook setting and flavor conjure up a bygone era's flavor. A population of 1,550 enjoys sublime seclusion. Stayton has only three times as many people and is fifteen miles away. Just over 100,000 live in the capital, Salem, thirty-two miles to the northwest. Seventy-five miles to the southeast, 20,000 live in Bend, surrounded by Oregon's High Desert. The sole route to Mill City is east–west, on Highway 22, traversing rolling farmland and forests dotted by the occasional clear-cut. In chilly waters flowing from the mountain's snowcapped peaks, steelhead ply the North Santiam, a fishing line's cast away from Broadway. *5*

In the hamlet's close-knit community people take care of their own in good times and bad. Boys riding their bicycles to the store can park them unlocked outside. They probably learn that from their parents, who leave keys in their cars' ignition while in stores. On warm evenings, families watch television in living rooms with their doors wide open. The television sets splash flickers of light across well-manicured lawns. On July Fourth, the town struts its hospitality by inviting out-of-town guests to delight in fireworks and logging competitions. The fire trucks in the parade belong to the town's crack volunteer fire department, a key part of Mill City's dependable emergency services. The roar of the Life Flight helicopter overhead sends a collective shudder through the canyon—a local logger has been maimed or worse. On a trip from Mill City to Stayton,

Sue Moberg recently accompanied a friend who learned her husband, a logger, had been killed on the job. The victim turned out to be someone else with the same name. Death pulls one and all together as tightly as life itself. When Charley Stewart, Jr., a beloved figure in his father's general store and heir to the family business, died in a car accident last summer, the whole town grieved as an extended family at the funeral and at home.

George Long, the *Mill City Enterprise*'s dyspeptic poet laureate, reserves his sentimental side for "It Ain't All Roses," the weekly column he has penned for the past twenty years since buying the paper. Recently, he ran a test to separate the "genuine certified Mill City old-timer" from the newcomer. Herewith a sampling:

> 1) The pickups in your neighborhood outnumber the cars three to one. 2) You no longer use your turn signals because everyone knows where you are headed. 3) You go out at 10:00 p.m., do the town, and are home by 10:30. 4) Fourth street is the edge of town. 5) You missed church on Sunday and received a get-well card. 6) You've been run off First Street by a chip truck. 7) You forgot your purse (wallet) and didn't discover it until the checker was through with your groceries and they trusted you to come back and pay later. 8) You have received mail addressed something like "the guy who lives four houses south of the post office in Mill City." 9) You drove in to the ditch at least five miles from town and the word got back to town before you did. 10) You have dialed the wrong number but talk for fifteen minutes anyway. 11) Your children have had at least two teachers who also taught you.

Mill City is a small town straight out of the 1950s, beset by 1990s problems. Alcoholism and other social ailments exact financial and human costs. Teenage pregnancy is distressingly high. But all these social maladies pale in comparison these days to the economic disruption sweeping timber-dependent communities with names like Sweet Home, Roseburg, and Humboldt, from northern California to Washington State. Its ultimate impact may dwarf those that occurred in steel and farming country in the 1970s and 1980s. On top of fundamental industrial shifts, the nation is forcing Mill City and its counterparts to grapple with natural resources issues largely beyond their capacity or, for that matter, beyond the comprehension of the "experts" in Washington, D.C.

The latest dip in the traditional boom and bust cycles of timber towns augurs a transition of historical dimensions. Over the past two decades, three national recessions have induced severe housing slumps and lowered demand for lumber, thereby severing the lifelines of the Northwest's local economies. Eighty percent of the Mill City–North Santiam Canyon economy is directly related to the manufacturing of primary wood products. Today's growing sentiment for preserving ancient forests and a dwindling timber supply from years of overcutting may well doom the only way of life most residents have ever known. In the next five years, wood supply will drop in half from historic highs in the 1980s. Asleep, Mill City families writhe in their beds, praying they can make payments to keep the house and the car. In the morning's small hours, they are haunted by nightmares of their town turning into a rural ghetto as bleak as an Appalachian coal town. . . .

In 1909, the sale of the sawmill and most of Mill City to A. B. Hammond ushered in the era of the company town. Hell bent on expanding across the Northwest and beyond, the timber magnate from San Francisco viewed the town and profits as synonymous. "Here is the seat of a busy industry where the Hammond Lumber Company is zealously turning out lumber for the commercial world at the rate of over 250,000 feet daily. The Hammond mill at Mill City is the largest institution of its kind in the Willamette Valley," declared the 1916 Mill City School yearbook. "No mill in the state is better equipped and few on the coast are adapted to make lumber for the finest retail businesses. The machinery is all modern in both the saw and planing mill."

Throughout its twenty-one-year reign, the Hammond Lumber Company suffused every fiber of Mill City's political, economic, and political being. At the outset, the primitive conditions meant no electricity or running water. Hammond quickly brought the town into the twentieth century. First it rigged the mill's stream turbines to power a light and water plant. The shacks that blighted most mill communities came down. On the Santiam's southern bank, Hammond laid out twenty-five neatly trimmed blocks. Families took up residence in the thirty-two modern, comfortable homes, replete with lawns and gardens (most are still standing). Half the crew boarded in the company hotel. In the early teens, a guest plunked down $4.50 a week for board and a double bed, two men to a room. The fine meals were served family-style, all you can eat. Conversation, in a melody of foreign languages, dwelled on their employer's fringe benefits. Private health insurance gave peace of mind. For 75 cents a month, workers enjoyed the services of Doc Ransom on contract with Hammond at his residence-*cum*-hospital across the road from the company's horse barn.

Six days a week, at dawn, the mill's wake-up whistle shrieked for breakfast. The coffee had barely cooled before the final whistle blew at seven o'clock. For the next eleven hours, including a sixty-minute lunch break, a common laborer brought home two dollars, mostly in gold. (A dollar then was roughly the equivalent of eleven today.) The head sawyer, the top man in the mill, earned five dollars a day. Exclaimed a local boy: "Someday I am going to take time off to look at a man who makes that much money." The work was as long as it was hard. Men stacked lumber by hand onto two-wheel carts. Until Model T Fords were modified as tractor units, the men relied on a horse with a long chain fastened to a tree for motor power. When the Santiam crested in the spring, "river rats" rafted the logs down the river, keeping their balance with the finesse of a gymnast on a spinning top. One slip was all it took to be crushed or drowned. On the days when the mill exceeded its target, Hammond passed out free cigars. (The ungrateful recipients complained they came from the company's store's unsold inventory and were too dry even to chew.) Not surprisingly, turnover was heavy. It was said the mill had three crews: "one working, one coming, and one going."

In return for the job security and basic creature comforts, the town submitted absolutely to the company's autocracy. What was good for Hammond was good for Mill City. All lights had to be out in homes from 8:00 p.m. to 5:00 a.m. to preserve power at the mill. Electric ranges and refrigerators were prohibited for the same reason. This being the great Northwest, wood had always been as free as the wind. Yet once Hammond gobbled up 90 percent of the private land around Mill City and put timber off-limits to cutting, it charged whatever it pleased for the main source of fuel and heat. The company store, a prehistoric Stewart's filled with dark wooden and glass cases, sold everything under the sun and then some, from fifteen-cent-a-pound meat—"an old milk cow that had been milked to death . . . and was so tough you couldn't shoot through it"—to seventy-five-cent overalls. Customers made purchases in company-issued script rather than money. Hammond automatically deducted the amount, plus rent and utilities, from paychecks.

Half the year, the bookkeeper's hardbound ledger heaved from the weight of unsettled accounts. From November through March the snows shut down the mill, along with employees' income. In an age before unemployment compensation and welfare benefits, families had to charge groceries all winter long. By the time they finally cleared their credit in July, the long, vicious cycle was four months away from beginning anew. Workers were broke and had to work the next month just to survive.

The monopoly guaranteed that Mill City owed its soul to the company store. The efforts of small entrepreneurs to break off a small piece of business met unhappy fates. Hammond employees caught leaving the upstarts received pink slips the next day. To bring home the message, the company cut off the power supply to an upstart grocer's lights, thereby forcing him to sell. Patronizing businesses elsewhere was virtually impossible for lack of time off and modern transportation.

Hammond owned the railroad, Mill City's sole link to the outside world. The wood-fired *Skunk Train,* so named for the stink it created, arrived from Albany at 10:00 a.m., no sooner or later, occasioning such a social affair that most of the local women dressed up in their Sunday finery to greet it in case someone important happened to be aboard. Many of the passengers had to scrub the pitch off their hands from helping the tired rail crew toss cordwood in the tender every few miles. One Sunday in the first August after Hammond took over the Skunk, workers and their families dug into their hard-earned savings for a special company-arranged excursion. From Yaquina Bay on the coast, a ferry took passengers to Newport Beach. Though disposable income was tight and the long round trip cut into the fun in the sun, the seats were full.

15

No price probably seemed too high to escape Mill City's stifling isolation for a few hours. Day to day, before used Studebakers and Model T's became affordable in the late 1920s, the horizons reached as far as people's feet carried them. When Walter Witt's appendix burst, his uncle and other relatives had to carry him all the way down the hill to Doc Ransom. By contrast, Mrs. Bill Beatram passed away of an unknown illness. The mill suspended operations on the day of her funeral to allow the whole work force to attend. In the procession from her house following the service, the only two autos were the hearse and the car for the next of kin. The rest of the mourners walked the three miles to the cemetery.

Hammond's tightfisted attention to the bottom line kept it remarkably depression proof. When the bottom fell out of the lumber market in 1929, the company's patriarch wanted to close Mill City's operation. His plant manager convinced him that it could remain profitable simply by slashing wages. A series of 10 percent cuts over a number of weeks finally lapped up 70 percent of total pay. The mill dropped to two six-hour shifts per week. At 20 cents an hour, workers ended up averaging $2.50 a week by 1933, about what they earned a day twenty years earlier, when Hammond first arrived on the scene. At least they had jobs. In 1934 the final whistle wailed, not out of deference to the green eye-shaders, but because old man Hammond died. An internecine quarrel among his heirs prompted stockholders back East to send a new man to take over the presidency. He moved swiftly—and, some think in retrospect, unwisely—to liquidate assets. "The mill of the Hammond Lumber Company, which made Mill City, is being dismantled," reported the *Oregonian* in October 1935, "and as this was the only reason for the town's existence it will not be long until there will be no town there at all." A mass exodus ensued among young loggers.

That winter, panic struck the neighbors left behind. Overnight, Hammond had orphaned employees with families and unpaid mortgages. Houses commanded fire-sale prices—from two hundred dollars to five hundred dollars for a well-built house. "When Hammond closed down, everybody thought Mill City was going to be a ghost town," the retired logger Wilbur Harlan recalls. "Boy, they said it would be nothing." Weaned on Hammond's quasi-benevolent despotism, an entire populace suddenly had to fend for itself.

The prospect of perishing concentrated minds wonderfully. Townspeople called a meeting and fifty men, with the help of a Salem lawyer, scraped together eleven thousand dollars to launch a small, cooperative mill. They bought the log pond from Hammond and equipment from Clatskanie, another terminally ill timber town. Since Hammond had logged off most of the timber within reach of three strung-out donkeys (steam engines used for skidding and loading logs), Mill City Manufacturing, the new firm, had to settle for turning out about half of Hammond's top volume. Production peaked at a hundred thousand board feet during World War II, about the same time the doomsayers' predictions about

20

overcutting came true. With private lands already depleted, the timber supply was on the verge of running out.

The nation's peacetime construction boom proved a godsend. Washington, D.C.'s, decision to open the national forests for logging presented a new source of timber and gave birth to dozens of new sawmills and logging companies throughout the North Santiam Canyon. Mill City had one more reason to believe that its feline inclination toward multiple lives would last forever.

For nearly a decade, talk of moribund timber towns always comes back to the sad tale of Valsetz. To woodsmen it represents what Pompeii was for Rome—the death of a small but vibrant civilization. For sixty-two years, Boise Cascade ran Valsetz—Oregon's rainiest community—much like Hammond once did Mill City, except that Boise Cascade owned every square inch of land. On February 24, 1984, however, business was far from usual for the 150 residents tucked away in the heavily forested Coast Ranges, forty miles west of Salem. Valsetz's two streets, Main Street and Cadillac Avenue, bustled with the sluggish foot traffic of heavyhearted locals on their way to and from the post office, cafe, and general store and houses belonging to the company. On this day, Boise Cascade commenced implementing a plan to recoup four straight years of losses by converting Valsetz into a tree farm.

The company went about methodically erasing Valsetz—man, beast, and abode—from the face of the earth. "That's big business," shrugged Cecelia Hutchinson, forty-seven, a cook and waitress at the cafe. "A person's a number now, not a person." Bulldozer's first plowed through the veneer mill's front entrance, reducing the twenty-five-year-old structure to rubble. A lighted match finished off the job. By April, more than a third of the town's sixty houses were pounded into heaps of shattered glass, rafters, and abandoned possessions before succumbing to the torch.

The balance remained standing for the families with children still in school. They had until mid-June, after the term ended, to vacate the premises. "Time will help to ease the bitterness that once flowed so feverishly through our hearts," Anthony Johnson, the eighteen-year-old valedictorian, told his graduating class of nine. "Time is a great healer. In order to survive in this ever-changing world, we cannot let hatred control us." Two weeks later the Valsetz post office made its final delivery and hung a sign on the front door reading "Closed Forever." On her home's garage, Dana Reckard, an eleven-year-old girl in Valsetz's last family to move out, spray-painted the message "Boise Cascade—Hope Your Proud." By the summer, Valsetz had vanished without a trace.

Perhaps only a sentimentalist could blame a conglomerate for ridding itself of an unprofitable venture, oblivious to the sensitivities of faceless victims. The free-enterprise system abounds with comparable tragedies before and since Boise Cascade drew the final curtain on the era of this company's town. Americans, after all, pride themselves on their rootless mobility. Nonetheless, the antiseptic disposal of a home to hundreds of employees and their families for more than half a century—like so many leaf piles in autumn—still sends chills across the Northwest. Timbermen in Mill City and elsewhere speak of their towns "drying up and blowing away like Valsetz," a specter terrifying enough to convert eleven-year-olds into cynics.

"I think Mill City will be like Valsetz," says Chelsea Stewart, a six-teen-year-old junior in Ross Miller's humanities class at the Santiam High School, which incorporates Mill City and nearby Gates. The teacher has invited me to meet the cream of the student body. On a break from their advanced course in history, literature, and philosophy, they have a lot more on their minds today than Homer. Virtually all of the teenagers' fathers work either in the mills or the woods, as their fathers and grandfathers once did. Economics and environmentalism may deprive the fourth gen-eration of the opportunity to follow in their footsteps. Graduates will no longer have the luxury of heading into the mills or the woods. "We have to do our damnedest to make sure kids leave," Miller says. "The huge majority will."

Education, the surest escape, has traditionally ranked as a low priority. Out of this year's senior class, twenty-five, only four will stretch themselves at a four-year college rather than a two-year junior school. Rarely do any of them actually complete the four years. Many in Miller's class admit that after twelve years of school, they lack the motivation to tough out the work load at an institution such as Oregon State, which has raised its grade-point average requirement to almost a B level. From their vantage point on campus, home remains where their hearts are; Mill City doesn't seem so bad after all. "It's a cultural thing," says a peach-fuzzed sophomore. "You don't have the drive. You're just satisfied to be who you are." Parents, few of whom attended college themselves, refrain from exerting pressure.

Students toying with the notion of higher education view a business degree, or its vocation equivalent, as a preferable stepping-stone to a career rather than a liberal arts degree. I, a history and English major, am asked my salary. The students are surprised to learn that, as a journalist with a bachelor's degree in English and history from Georgetown University in Washington, D.C., I earn hardly more income than their fathers in a good year in the mills or woods. Nevertheless, college-educated Americans in general outearn workers with just a high-school diploma by up to forty percent.

In practical terms, the average male adolescent in Mill City can hop from the school bus to crummy on the day of graduation. Four male seniors, out of about fifteen in this year's class, are unable to wait that long and simply drop out. "College is the ultimate deferred gratification," Miller says. With diplomas fresh in hand from the previous year, many male graduates still hang around the high school, showing off their gainful em-ployment's material rewards, after work or during winter downtime. The nineteen-year-old loggers swagger in the fringy and unhemmed jeans, wool socks, and—the uniform's most macho accessory—hickory shirts begging for a needle and thread. Their wheels are high-rider pickups, twelve feet off the ground. These status symbols announce to the world that they have made it. The schoolboy still collecting small change feels small standing in the shadow of woodsmen raking in twelve dollars an hour. The intense peer pressure blinds him to twenty-six-year-olds with bad backs or thirty-year-olds hobbling about on crutches.

He takes solace from a good woman standing by him. A lot of the coeds become premature adults. Nearly half the seniors this year are pregnant. Within the cultural milieu, it is perfectly acceptable for a seventeen-year-old to bring her baby to school. She, like the father in the pickup, enjoys being the center of attention at school. "The babies come to the baseball games," Stewart says. "I don't understand at all what possesses them to do it." A fourteen-year-old too young to marry her ex-love, a mill-worker ten years her senior, lets Mom and Grandmom take care of the baby while she struggles to attend classes. The parents look the other way, as they do in small towns and urban ghettos nationwide. In logging country, the young couples who do wed and have three or four children by their midtwenties must scramble to support them. "We have kids who go away to college and kids who get married and stay," says Pastor Veach, "but the ones that get married and stay, stay in the timber industry."

In Oregon, the educational system is ill equipped for the transition away from its principal source of funding. The U.S. Forest Service returns 25 percent of the revenues from its timber sales to counties within national forests. The counties keep three fourths of the money and give the rest to schools. Portions of timber sales from the federal Bureau of Land Management forests go to counties to offset property taxes for schools and services. Dave Alexander, the ranger in the Detroit District of the U.S. Forest Service, is quick to point this out on a forestry tour he and Hirons lead to observe Earth Day.

Naturally, the Mill City high school eschews any pretense of even-handedness toward the logging crisis. On the Friday of a massive rally orchestrated by the timber industry in support of the cause, students are given the choice of attending it or classes. The administrators offer to provide the schools' own buses for transportation. The industry appreciates the offer but has already rented a fleet and easily fills it with backers of all ages. The young receive strong encouragement from their parents to take the ride. Atiyeh is furious upon discovering that his mischievous son Aziz has seized the opportunity to skip classes that day.

King timber remains writ large on the blackboards. Three months after the spotted owl's listing as a threatened species, marking the beginning of the end of the timber era as Mill City knows it, Santiam High begins the first forestry class ever, the brainchild of Carol Cree. The pleasant and earnest substitute teacher in the district leads the class. Cree is married to a logging company owner and worked in Hirons's CGO office until recently. "Why?" Miller says he asked her. "It doesn't make any sense.

30

Industry got real excited at first, except when it came time to foot the bill." The funds came out of arts and other courses.

The class amounts to a symbolic gesture of solidarity with the timber companies' faded glory. Cree defends the curriculum, from tree identification to logging skills, that she and Hirons have developed as solid vocational training. "There will always be forests and logging," Cree insists, even while acknowledging that there will be fewer jobs. In the classroom a "How a Tree Grows" poster hangs alone, surrounded by posters of yarders and chainsaws.

Outside, fourteen students—all boys, most of whom have fathers in the timber trade—prepare for the past. At the corner of the football field, they throw axes and saw mammoth logs by hand in a scene as surrealistic as blacksmiths fitting horseshoes in a Ford factory. "I want to be out in the brush," says Jeremy Timey, the fifteen-year-old son of a foreman for a local logging company, "but I'm probably going into the service. I'd rather be a farmer. Right now I'm worried about my parents not having a job."

35

Reading and Responding

This selection closes by discussing the fate of Mill City high school students. Freewrite about your reactions to this part. Do these students sound like you in any ways, or was your experience fundamentally different?

Working Together

1. As a group, decide how you would introduce Mill City to an audience that has no knowledge of lumbering or of company towns. What would you have to explain in some detail?

2. Assume that you were a resident in Mill City during the time that it was owned by Hammond Lumber Company. What would daily life be like? How would you feel about Hammond Lumber Company? Write a group paragraph that describes this period. Then skip forward to the present and assume that you're a current resident of Mill City. What's improved since the Hammond Lumber days, and what new worries do you have? Write a second paragraph that describes these issues.

3. As a group, assume that you could advise high school students living in towns like Mill City. What would you say to them?

Rethinking and Rewriting

1. Residents of Mill City might argue that since most of the harvestable timber has been cut and much of the rest has been tied up by court challenges to continued logging, these circumstances make Mill City inhabitants victims of circumstances out of their control. If they cannot log any more, then they want federal funds—your tax dollars—to help

them relocate or retrain in order to get new jobs. Write a letter to the editor of the *Mill City Enterprise* and explain why you think Mill City should get federal funds for these purposes, or write explaining why you're not willing to send your tax dollars to support relocation or retraining programs.

2. Write a glossary to accompany this reading. Write a paragraph that introduces the glossary and explains why it's needed; then list the words—up to twenty, with their definitions—that readers might find unfamiliar.

3. David Seideman's piece brings up the question of vocational training (in Mill City that means learning to work in the woods) versus higher education. What's your view on this? Should students be studying for specific jobs, or should they be concentrating on getting a more fully rounded education? Explain your own feelings. Pretend that you have grown up in Mill City: What kind of education is important to you? How is that education similar to or different from the education you're pursuing now?

"FOREST OF VOICES"

Chris Anderson

A native northwesterner (born and raised in Spokane, Washington), Chris Anderson now teaches at Oregon State University. He has published a book on writing and two books on literary nonfiction; he has also edited or coedited several collections of essays. His most recent book, Edge Effects: Notes from an Oregon Forest *(1993), explores both literally and metaphorically what it means to live with a twelve-thousand-acre research forest (owned by Oregon State University's College of Forestry) as your neighbor.*

The forester had been dozing in the forestry truck, waiting for the satellites to come up. He was parked off the road in the northeast corner of the forest, blocking the gate to a meadow, something like a geiger counter set on a tripod next to the truck. He said there'd be four satellites in another hour—invisible in the afternoon sky—and that by bouncing signals off each he'd be able to establish the corner for a "brass cap survey" for a GIS map of this part of the forest. He showed us the actual brass cap, the size of a cookie, cemented in the ground.

A few minutes later Bob and I walked in the prairie behind him, a remnant of the prairie that covered this land for hundreds of years, most of it taken over now by the forest. It was June, and the wind blew across onion flower, clover, wild sunflower, Hooker's pink. Then: the suggestion of wagon ruts, as if two people had been walking side by side ahead of us—as if the wind were blowing harder in two narrow rows, making faint corridors in the grass. That's the Applegate Trail, Bob said to me, pointing, the southern route of the Oregon Trail. A hundred and forty years ago the horses and oxen and wagons would come up over the hill to the south, he said, curve to the west to avoid the marshy valley floor, then spread out right there, right through where the forestry truck is sitting, on their way north. You can see evidence of the trail in that row of fruit trees and oak over to the right, too, the vegetation patterns uniform and straight seen from the air. Farther down, among ash and cottonwood, we saw even clearer ruts in the widening of a cutbank on Soap Creek.

Waiting for satellites on the Applegate Trail. It's an image that sticks with me not just because of the historical irony, that brief slipping of perspective, but because it suggests how plotted and pieced and inscribed this forest is, how overlaid with the human. Past and present, the forest is everywhere enmeshed in human mapping, human measuring.

The forest in fact is an invader, I learned, the prairie much older and in some sense original. If I had looked up from my wagon 140 years ago I would have seen nothing but waving grass and an occasional isolated oak or fir. The forest I see now is the product of human intervention, existing in this form only because of the ecological impact of the settlers who flowed up this trail and into the valley.

Seen on a map Oregon State University's McDonald-Dunn Research   5
Forest looks like a lopsided wing, the apex pointing east, a ridge line of
hills and small peaks defining the V. The hills are the beginning of the
Coast Range; the wheat and grass fields of the Willamette Valley flatten
out to the east. The lower part of the wing is McDonald Forest, 6,800
acres running southwest to northeast just five miles north of Corvallis. The
upper part is Paul Dunn Forest, 4,073 acres running southeast to northwest. It's a mixed Douglas-fir and hardwood forest now, typical of this side
of the Coast Range, the fir always in the process of crowding out the oak
and maple and madrone. Hazel and oceanspray compete with seedlings in
the underbrush. The College of Forestry began acquiring the land in the
late twenties with money given by Mary McDonald, the elderly widow of
a mining and timber baron in San Francisco, buying up logged-over or
tax-delinquent tracts piece by piece for use as a research laboratory. After
sixty years of management and experimentation the forest is still a "mosaic," medium-sized clearcuts alternating with 15-, 30-, and 50-year-old
plantations up and down the V. A few pieces of 100- to 140-year-old trees
remain, and there are small sections of old-growth on the upper northern
draws.

I didn't know any of this until recently, even after I bought the new
house on the boundary of the forest (at the top of the lower wing, near
the apex). I am a person of atmospheres and moods, not by nature interested in science and historical fact, lacking a sense of topography. The
forest was just a line of timbered hills I could see from town, a place to
hike and brood when life got too complicated. I moved to its boundary
for all the sentimental reasons people move to forests, for silence and solitude and simplicity.

But then the College of Forestry decided to log part of the hillside
behind the house and I suddenly found myself attending that first meeting
of homeowners, listening to scientists and forest managers trying to explain
some of the complexities beneath the beautiful surfaces. There must have
been over a hundred people packed into Peavy Lodge that evening, all of
us in L. L. Bean khaki and flannel, it seemed, and all of us concerned,
uneasy. The scientists and managers talked about "gap dynamics" and "bio-
diversity assessment" and "aesthetic viewsheds," showing us computer-
enhanced photographs of the "targeted" timber "units" before and after
"treatment." Neighborhood environmentalists stood up angrily, reading
from prepared statements arguing for the integrity of the ecosystem. Several other homeowners spoke up for the forestry staff, to scattered applause,
repeating the available clichés on jobs and the timber supply.

I had moved to the forest for silence but found myself immersed in
words. I had moved for experience but found myself struggling with competing theories. I had moved for solitude but suddenly was trying to situate
myself in a tense, divided community. Interviewing forestry faculty, tromp-
ing through the poison oak, or driving the logging roads, I learned over

the course of one summer that the forest I live near is a forest of voices, of language and ideas.

Anxiety motivated my researches at first, the hope that knowledge would bring perspective at least, if not evidence for arguments and strategies for influencing policy. I joined the Sustainable Forestry New Paradigm Working Group at Oregon State, an interdisciplinary faculty research group close to decision-making in the College of Forestry. I started asking around. From the beginning the forest intrigued me as a subject for writing, too. I knew that writing an essay was probably the best way I had of getting people to pay attention to the problem; and more and more the dilemmas and conflicts of forestry began to interest me in themselves, take on a life of their own. If nothing else I knew that writing would help me handle the crisis personally, help me order my feelings. In a sense, I guess, I wanted to harvest the forest myself, exploiting the new resource for sentences and paragraphs—acting out as a writer the same paradoxes of use I kept discovering in my reading and interviews.

The research project that has entirely redesigned the hill behind my   10 house, for example, is entitled "Comparisons of Terrestrial Vertebrate Communities and Tree Regeneration Among Three Silvicultural Systems in the East-Central Coast Range, Oregon." Its authors are John Tappeiner, a tall, bearded silviculturalist in his mid-fifties, and Bill McComb, a thirty-something wildlife biologist, deep-voiced and intense. "Examining scales, intensities, distribution and frequencies of disturbances that once occurred in unmanaged forests," they write, "can provide a basis for designing silvicultural prescriptions that produce a landscape that in structure and composition may imitate 'natural' landscapes." Trees fall over in the wind. Trees die from disease. Small fires break out at intervals. All these create "disturbances" or "gaps" in a naturally developing forest, and this may be the key to managing forests for both timber and other "values." Plants and animals apparently survive such small-scale disturbances. A number of small clear-cuts can create similar gaps—chunks of timber taken out and used—while still leaving "a matrix of mature forest" to provide suitable habitat for certain kinds of wildlife. Large-scale clear-cutting has the opposite effect, according to Tappeiner and McComb, isolating small islands of trees in a sea of disturbance, replicating rarer catastrophic wildfires. Research suggests that many birds and mammals suffer in these big openings, and there's evidence that new trees won't keep growing back rotation after rotation.

Talking with McComb over coffee one day on campus, the murmur and clatter of the commons all around us, I was struck by how academic our conversation was, how abstract and even literary. The forest is like a poem to him, a complex text whose levels he reads. But his and Tappeiner's interpretive metaphors translate into the falling of real trees, the opening of real gaps. Their "licor measurements of percent sky" have determined the amount of twilight I see as I walk the logging roads and trails, the percentage of sunrise. Their use of a "snag recruitment simulator" has left sawed-off trunks where flickers and woodpeckers are beginning to nest. Tappeiner and McComb write the forest, not just write *about* it; their paragraph indentations are new openings in the trees.

Now there are three kinds of cuts on the hill. At the end of one logging road where I often walk is a substantial clearcut with about a dozen large snags distributed across it. That's the experimental control. To the north and west are "two-story" or "shelterwood" stands, pieces where all but a third of the tall trees have been taken off. And then folded into the rest of the forest are dozens of half-acre to acre "patchcuts," the miniclear-cuts that most interest Tappeiner and McComb, replicating blowdown and disease. What are the effects of these different cuttings on mammals and birds? How successful is reforestation in these different openings—what will grow in the partial shade, and how well?

Four-thirty one July morning I went out into the patchcuts with Carol Chambers, one of McComb's graduate students, to help chart the movements of diurnal songbirds. She's a slim, soft-spoken woman from Kentucky, a long blonde braid hanging down the back of her plaid shirt. We would go to a blue- or pink-ribboned stake, sit down in the bedstraw and candy flower, and listen. The forest was alive with bird song, a cacophony of dozens of species calling out, announcing their presence, repeating themselves. Carol would point and say, quietly, "olive-sided flycatcher" or "hermit warbler" or "Swainson's thrush," recording acronyms in a note-book grid and marking approximate distances on a circular target. It was a wonderful morning, the sun coming up orange through the tree trunks, a thousand blended notes in the air. Another day we walked up and down the hills checking live traps for mice and voles. Carol would reach in with a gloved hand, take the animal—usually a deer mouse—by the tail, attach the tail to a pencil-sized scale (the mouse struggling upside down for a minute, its little legs scrambling), clip a toe for marking, and let the specimen go. We talked about nature writing as we went from site to site, sharing our enthusiasm for Annie Dillard and Wendell Berry.

The warm August day I watched part of the logging operation a graduate student from Forest Engineering was doing time and motion studies on the head faller, clocking how long it took him to angle the trees so that they fell clear in the patchcut. Marvin is a precision faller, a friendly and unassuming middle-aged man in suspenders and hard hat. He joked good-naturedly with the research coordinator showing me around, complaining about all the "New Forestry bullshit" and the tricky angles it requires, but you could tell he was proud of his craftsmanship, and he was quick: falling a tree, measuring it, and "bucking" it into two or three pieces in about ten minutes.

Later that day I saw the yarding operation on another site. A high-towered yarder pulled logs to the top of a slope where the swiveling tongs of the "shovel" pinched and whipped them around to a pile. As the "chasers" undid the choker cables and sawed off random limbs, I heard over the sound of their chain saws the foreman shouting about a "serious deflection" problem with the skyline, something about not enough arc between the cable and a ground bulge, a problem sure to be worse on unit ten, next up. My impression was of hugeness and loudness and danger, the swooping and swinging of big logs, though I was told that these 140-year-old trees are nothing compared to the monstrous old-growth the really big machines can yard. The question for the forest engineers on the project is how much this smaller-scale, finesse logging really costs in comparison to conventional clear-cutting (Answer: at least 22 percent more on the first harvest).

Other researchers are involved in the project, too, studying the effects of the cutting on the human community. Becky Johnson, a resource economist, is interested in "the socioeconomic impact of harvesting techniques on residents on the urban fringe." She thinks of the forest, she told me, as a "multiple output commercial asset," and she wants to measure the "non-commodity values" that are a part of that asset, how much people would pay for what they don't currently have to pay for. Questionnaires are going out. One afternoon I participated in an aesthetic-perception survey conducted by Mark Brunson, a graduate student in Forest Resources. He took us to different sites—clearcut, patchcut, old-growth, and so on—and asked us to rate our aesthetic responses on a numerical scale, taking into account sounds, smells, spatial definition, and the possibilities for camping and hiking. We carried the survey form loose as we walked, balancing the sheets awkwardly on our thighs when we wanted to write or using a stump as backing. It was a late autumn day, even the clearcuts soft and full in the fading light.

Not surprisingly, most of us in the study rated the patchcuts as more aesthetically pleasing than clearcuts. From a distance the smaller openings are almost invisible on the more level parts of the hillside. To Mark this suggests that the human habitat can be maintained within the matrix of the mature forest, too, the "viewshed" preserved.

I think of a moment from a tour that summer of the Andrews Research Forest in the Cascades outside Eugene. About thirty of us from OSU's Sustainable Forestry New Paradigm Working Group—foresters and scientists and humanists—were walking single file down a trail through 500-year–old growth, gesturing with our hands, turning around to make points, filling the air with our voices: ". . . reading streams for their level of complexity . . . the role of lichen as nitrogen-fixers in canopy microclimates . . . hierarchical scales . . . complex communities . . . structural diversity."

I think of the plastic ribbons and markers and stakes and trail signs and spray-painted numbers on the trunks of trees everywhere in McDonald Forest, as if the endless studies and reports have begun to show through on the land itself. "Wildlife Tree," one of the latest signs reads, "Please Protect / OSU Research Forests." They're bright red plastic, screwed onto many of the newly created snags, a picture of a pileated woodpecker on the side. And this sentence was tacked to a fir when the harvest began, in the forest behind the house: "The Research Management request that all individuals recreating in the adjacent area please follow these guidelines."

Much of this language infuriates me. Calling a stream "an open-water   20
system," as I heard a hydrologist do the other day, is just silly, and potentially dangerous. The real, concrete particulars get lost in abstractions. If you think of a forest as a multiple-output commercial asset day after day, analyzable only on a spreadsheet, you forget how it smells and what it's like to walk in it in the morning. The important realities are beyond any words. Scientists, of course, don't always use the language of science, don't always view their experience scientifically, but the long-term effects of jargon—like radiation—are sometimes hard to protect against. And sometimes the abstractions are deliberate obscurings. "Treatments" and "prescriptions," after all, are just euphemisms for cutting, for killing. We can't finally trust any of this. Yet at the same time I found myself oddly soothed by the sound of the words I kept hearing, reassured that at least there was some rational method behind what was happening in the forest. Living on the level of abstraction was therapeutic for a while, giving me some perspective and detachment. Deeper than that, hearing the words and models and paradigms over and over again moved me beyond my initial naivete. The language kept showing me that the forest is a complex place, a human place, not just something to look at or find refuge within.

Jeff Garver, the manager of McDonald Forest, is a six-foot-five former track star and Eagle Scout, bearded now and still imposing. I spent two whole days bouncing around in his Chevy Blazer getting the standard tour. He drove left-handed, grabbing for a Big Gulp with his right or talking on one of his two cellular phones, dialing with his thumb. His speech is practiced and unmodulated, its cadences a mixture of law enforcement and public relations, although now and then I'd sense a sharper-edged voice underneath. He kept handing me the keys and making me fumble with the recessed locks on the metal gates blocking the entrances to logging roads.

At the Lewisburg Saddle he looked out at the far view of hills and valley and praised the "gorgeous" plantations we could see from there, their "sharp, tight points" versus the "ratty and beat-up tops" of the narrow strip of old-growth canopy. He noted "the good bird activity" in the clearcut in front of us, and the way the far clearcut, on Forest Peak, blended into the hillside. He designed that clearcut, trying to carve its edges so that they "fit better with the mind's eye." "Straight lines are as ugly as you get. I like the nice rounded contours—like a '51 Ford." Variety, "multiple-use," is what he kept stressing. There were always margins and alternating textures in the scenes he showed me, a quilting of clearcuts and various plantations. In fifty years the same "elements" will be present in these scenes, he said, just in different combinations, as if the forest is a vast temporal playing board, the same squares exchanging position over time.

The patchcuts don't make sense to him, though he's tried to accommodate the scientists. He's doing the best he can in a difficult position, answering to a divided faculty and trying to manage seventy-two separate research projects without the benefit of a coherent long-term management plan. Given public anxiety and involvement, too, he knows he has to practice what another forester I talked with called "sensitive forestry." Still, by the end of our second day, as he seemed to relax more and more, Jeff was calling the New Forestry just "weird science," "deep fungal," the product of computer jockeys and college professors with no real experience working in the woods. He thinks we need to be practical. The brush left by the patchcuts is a fire hazard, there's too much merchantable timber left on the sites, and the trees won't grow back anyway. The goal of the forest should not be research alone but the utilization of the available resources, as in any good commercial operation. Revenue is necessary to sustain the research anyway, and it costs at least a million dollars a year just to keep McDonald-Dunn going.

What Jeff honors is the paradigm of forest management that's dominated the College of Forestry, and all forestry, for two generations. His faith is in the good "site prep" of clearcut ground—poisoning and burning—then the planting of genetically strong seedlings, then judicious thinning over time. "Cut a hundred acres. Plant a hundred acres. Thin a hundred acres. Don't cut more than you grow. You can color that with all sorts of fancy computer models, but it all comes down to this."

But that, of course, is Jeff's model. He, too, reads the forest. He, too, writes it. He sculpts it, changes it over time, putting his ideas into action. His forest is just as complex a place as Tappeiner and McComb's, requiring just as precise a jargon to understand and manipulate (there are "bearing strengths" and "blind leads," "catch points" and "deflection angles," "inslopes" and "tangencies"). What I used to see as simply an expanse of trees, a hillside of fir, is in fact a silvicultural system managed day to day through hard work and insiders' knowledge.

It is a system sustained by a budget, a regular office staff, and up to thirty part-time employees. It is an institution. There are a motor pool and a coffee fund, there are staff meetings and office parties and rows of cabinets preserving old memoranda. Five other foresters—for recreation, reforestation, research, public education, and engineering—branch under Jeff on the organizational chart. There are insiders and outsiders, a pecking order. Each morning people check in at the office, gossip over coffee, return their cups to their pegs, and fan out across the forest to plant seedlings, put up signs, wait for satellites.

The Andrews Forest, coadministered by Oregon State and the Forest Service, is more impressive than McDonald-Dunn. It's only a little bigger than McDonald-Dunn—around 16,000 acres—but it sits in the midst of the Willamette National Forest, miles into the Cascades from Eugene, and it's mostly old-growth, uninterrupted expanses of huge trees set aside for research. It has the old-growth mystique. Walking through its trails you have that sense of being hushed. You're always looking up.

McDonald-Dunn seems small and dull in comparison. It is close to the hubbub of town, an "urban fringe forest" cut up into littler pieces. I've heard it called a "hobby forest," too, significant only because it is convenient. There is very little old-growth except in protected draws where the fires couldn't reach.

And this the single most surprising fact about the forest to me. This is what Bob Zybach taught me that day in June when we startled the napping forester and walked in the ruts of the Applegate Trail: 150 years ago McDonald-Dunn wasn't a forest at all. It was an oak savannah, a prairie extending as far as the eye could see with just a scattering of two or three oak or fir per acre. That's why grass still grows on the forest floor and large stumps are rare. Long branches stick out from the odd big trees in the midst of newer growth, a sign they were once growing in the open, without competition. They're "hooter" trees, savannah oak and fir. Large-scale harvesting wasn't even possible on McDonald-Dunn until the late fifties and early sixties because too few of the trees were big enough. The whole Willamette Valley is the same, the result of "cultural fire"—the seasonal burning practices of the Kalapuya and other Indians.

Early trappers and explorers described the vast expanses of grass and *30* wildflower, and the smoke that obscured them parts of the year when the Indians were burning. For instance, we have these notes from the 1826 journals of David Douglas, a Hudson's Bay botanist who gave his name to the fir:

> 9/27 Country undulating: soil rich, light with beautiful solitary oaks and pines interspersed through it and must have a fine effect, but being burned and not a single blade of grass except on the margins of the rivulets to be seen.

> 9/30 (heading south) . . . Most parts of the country burned; only on little patches in the valleys and on the flats near the low hills that verdure is to be seen.

Other explorers write of choking smoke and the absence of grass for livestock in the fall, the "grand panorama view of prairie," and "the excellent quality of grass abounding" in the spring and summer. All up and down the valley the Indians would burn, every season for perhaps thousands of years, altering the landscape to suit the berries and hazel nuts they fed on, harvesting the roasted tar-weed seeds and herding deer into unburned corners. Even more dramatically than contemporary foresters and managers, the Kalapuya and other tribes made and remade the land, "culturing" countless acres of it from Washington to California.

McDonald-Dunn Forest is the result of "fire suppression" in the 1840's and 50's when the first settlers arrived, which is to say that the Kalapuya quickly died out, victims of malaria and smallpox, and that the Douglas fir, after being restrained for so long, finally claimed the meadows.

Forests are supposed to be old, of course. They're supposed to be permanent, given. But McDonald Forest is actually quite young, even ephemeral, when seen from the perspective of biological and geological time, as Zybach explained to me that day in June, wading ahead of me through the wildflowers. Its Douglas fir are technically "invaders." What I took as solid suddenly seemed fragile, the trees like feathers, like false-fronts.

"Trees are cheap," Bob says. "They're everywhere." Too many in one spot make him nervous, since he's spent most of his life working beneath them. "Do you know how many people get killed by falling trees every year?" he asks, laughing. What he loves are the sweeping vistas, the tall grasses, the wildflowers remaining from the indigenous prairie. If he had his way he'd clear-cut and burn a big part of the forest, returning it to savannah. That would be aesthetically pleasing to him. That would be restoring the forest to its healthy, "natural" state, fire cleansing the forest of pests and undergrowth while returning nutrients to the soil. There were few significant snags or islands of fir in the forest before the settlers came. The Tappeiner and McComb patchcuts, their "New Forestry" snag distributions, are about as natural as a "garden," just another example of "college sense," the "weird shit" of overgrown "college boys."

Bob Zybach is a small, muscular man in his early forties, sandy hair falling to his shoulders, a former logger and private reforester with a passion for history and a contempt for academics and bureaucrats. He's a "taxpayer" more than a "tuition payer," he told me, even though he's been studying forestry at Oregon State since his business failed in the timber bust of the early 80's. A self-taught historian, lifelong student of Indians and pioneers, he was recently commissioned by the dean to compile a "Cultural Resources Inventory" of McDonald Forest. I asked him to show me some of the sites he'd catalogued. When I picked him up the first time he was wearing a "Save the Rain Forest" T-shirt, the second time a "Desert Storm" trucker's cap. He gets carried away when he talks, acknowledges that he can seem "abrasive." He says he's used to shouting at people over chain saws.

It was great fun bombing around the forest with Bob in the old Buick, debating for hours about what's natural and why that matters, what's really true and what's the product of academic self-interest, the money of the funding agencies. Off Homestead Road we gathered shards of blue crockery from the site of the old Tortora place, first settled in the 1870's. We found the rusted body of a stove reservoir there, too, a remnant from the time of World War I. Two sixty-year-old firs grew from a ten-by-fifteen hole left by the original foundation, the sides rounded now from age, and there were century-old pear and apple trees in the pasture. The rest of the homestead, what used to be oak savannah, is covered now by second-growth fir, a little forest stretching down to the bottom of the draw.

It was there, Bob claimed, in the mid-seventies, just down the hill, that Eric Forsman conducted his first spotted owl experiments as an Oregon State graduate student, coaxing the birds from the trees with mice. Consider that, Bob repeated: catching spotted owls—the symbol of old-growth—near the site of a homestead where old-growth has never been recorded, in a young forest rising from the last of a prairie long ago settled by pioneers.

Later we fought our way through vine maple and alder and dense forest to the site of the old Coote sawmill, dating from the 1930's. We passed a giant cottonwood and a very large maple. Then up ahead, sticking out of the creek like a giant rusted fin, was the perpendicular windshield frame of a Model T. Coming closer we could see the circular hole in the back of the cab where the rear window used to be. Near fallen trunks on the other side were scattered fire bricks from a kiln, the remains of a metal water tank, and indentations in the ground indicating a road and a wide staging area. All around us was deep forest, the wildest we had seen that day. "Some industrial site," Bob said, gesturing.

On the way home, by the side of the highway, we stopped and found several "bearing oaks" or "witness oaks" from the 1850's, their trunks blazed with an axe. Early settlers used these trees as fixed points to find their bearings for the first land surveys. One was inscribed with several small circles arranged in an arc. Not far away, in the same stand, were modern bearing trees, precise survey numbers marked on metal plates.

Because the valley floor was often flooded and marshy, the hills and ridges of what is now McDonald-Dunn Forest have always been the site of human habitation and culture. That is why the Kalapuya lived here, following the ridge lines to look out at their fires. That is why the California Trail of the 1820's followed the wide bench against the hillsides, taking Hudson's Bay pack trains north and south through the valley—why the Applegate Trail of the 1850's hugged the hills farther down, near what is now Highway 99, taking settlers to their promised farmlands. Jedediah Smith, the famous mountain man, traveled the California Trail, right behind where my house now stands. Peter Burnett, the first governor of California, the first leader of a wagon train on the Oregon Trail, and my wife's great-great-great-grand uncle, passed by Corvallis on his way south to the Gold Rush. My house was built on what was once the Donation Land Claim of a man named Fuller; we live on his upper pasture. Next to us was the claim of Thomas Reed, the first settler in this part of the valley. His house was framed in 1853 by Bushrod Wilson, a well-known local carpenter, and it became a famous wayside for travelers on the Applegate.

For thousands of years McDonald-Dunn Forest has been crisscrossed and carved out and built on, layer after layer of culture sooner or later sifting down to the forest floor. Its cultural value far outweighs the value

40

of its timber in Bob's mind, timber which exists in the first place precisely because of human intervention. For him the forest is not a mosaic but a "time machine," the past lives of its people recorded in vegetation patterns and old orchards merging now into fir, in hidden wells and pieces of tin, in arrowheads and fragments of flint—lives of ordinary people more admirable than the conspicuously consuming yuppies who now live on the forest edge. He imagines the people of the past living in harmony with the land, quiet and slow, wiser than any computer-generated model.

Walking into Bob's rented house near campus you see piles of old journals and documents on the couch and the coffee table and filling up the corners, maps rolled up everywhere or spread out on the floor and in the kitchen, old history books and transcribed tape recordings spilling out of file cabinets, the blurred mimeographs of family histories. Here are Alexander McLeod's Hudson's Bay journals describing the climate and vegetation of the valley, together with the notes of the Wilkes expedition of 1841. Here are the memoirs of Sarah Cummins:

> Sitting alone and glancing over my past life, long and eventful as it has been, I recall many of its scenes of pioneer adventure that were marvelous manifestations of the power and goodness of God in protecting us in our travels through wild regions, inhabited by savages and the haunt of wild beasts.

Here the day book of Lester Hulin:

> to day 5 of us laid in the bushes to watch for indians we heard them halloo but they kept at a proper distance we think they saw us go in the willows our caravan moved on to a lake, then about 3 ms up it and camped distance about 10 ms

> passed around a large swamp filled with ducks geese and cranes then passing a good spring we came to a lake watered our cattle and passed on over stony roads and at last camped without water good grass in sight of another lake distance about 14 ms

And Bob is in the process of compiling an oral history of the Soap Creek Valley, interviewing elderly residents who remember stories of what the forest was like at the turn of the century, and before:

> You asked about stories on the trail. I only remember one that they told. They come up just looking over a ridge and here was a bunch of stuff waving on ahead. They were ready to group up, and then discovered it was willows instead of a bunch of Indians.

> It snowed and snowed and snowed in 83. Dad used to talk about that. He talked about finally it quit snowing and they decided they wanted to hike over to some friends or family or something for a visit and he said that that old snow was piled up and kind of

slippery on the surface. And Dad was walking with a stick with a nail in the end of it. He got down on the side of a hill and he started slipping and sliding down, he said his mother was standing out there shouting "Jim, Jim, Jim, Jim Jim!"

A forest of voices, of stories.

The Thomas Reed house is still standing, near the entrance to Peavy Arboretum. It's a large yellow house now, expanded over the years. A riding mower and a Rototiller were parked in back, near the garage, the day Bob and I walked up the driveway. Through the front window I could see a microwave on refinished kitchen counters. We knocked on the door, but no one was home. Log trucks geared down Highway 99 behind us.

Driving my daughter to her piano lesson last week, to the top of Vineyard Mountain, I counted six minivans, three BMW's, three mountain bikers, and two pairs of white-shorted joggers. Upscale neighborhoods rim the forest, developments with names like McDonald Forest Estates and Timber Hill and Skyline West. Long, split-level houses are built into hill-sides, hidden in oak and fir, their cedar decks offering views of the valley and the Cascades. Right now a developer is grubbing out a "real estate cut" at the base of Vineyard Mountain, removing the fir and leaving the madrone in preparation for a forty-eight unit housing development. I can hear the Caterpillars powering from here, over the whine of my computer fan. This morning's paper describes a neighborhood protest at the Benton County Planning Commission last night, over a hundred homeowners expressing their worry that still another development on the mountain will severely deplete the already marginal supply of drinking water.

Over 35,000 "recreation days" are spent in the forest each year, accord-ing to a recent Master's thesis. There are mountain bikers and equestrians and hikers on the roads and trails. The Timberhill Harriers run here every weekend. Once we stumbled into a timber carnival over at Cronemiller Lake. High-school timber clubs from across the state were competing in axe throwing and timber cruising and tree climbing. Trucks and campers were parked everywhere. A hotdog stand was set up. Another day we came across a mountain bike competition, the finish line at the lake. Mud-spattered riders came whizzing off the hill, numbers flapping on their jerseys.

Once I was walking with the kids on the 510 Road when I heard *45* jazz guitar seeping through the trees, then lounge music piano. Farther on we saw a wedding reception at Peavy Lodge, tuxedoed young men parking their cars, women hiking up their gowns to climb the steps. We could see a long sheet cake, balloons flying from folding chairs.

It all seems natural to me now. There has always been a "human/forest interface" here, beginning at least as early as the first makeshift shel-ters of the Kalapuya.

Perhaps the central effect of my studying the forest this last year has been to complicate my understanding of the "natural." On the one hand some of the rhetoric of environmentalism seems naive and unconsidered to me now, even foolishly arrogant. We can't ground our arguments for what is right on some sentimental longing for the unspoiled, as if only what is nonhuman is good. That's to be ignorant of history, as well as to misunderstand our own responsibilities. Wendell Berry argues that just as culture depends on wilderness—just as we need to preserve wilderness to survive as a culture, spiritually and physically—wilderness now depends on culture. Setting aside the Andrews Forest to remain as old-growth is a cultural act. It is the drawing of a line, the creating of value. Preserving wilderness means erecting fences, fumbling with locks in metal gates.

But that argument also works another way. Often in my conversations with foresters and scientists a policy or practice would be explained to me as if it were inevitable, as if things had to be done that way, inexorably. Sometimes there was an arrogant privileging of expertise, an invoking of the tropes of objectivity and practicality, as if my concerns with aesthetics and spiritual values were merely subjective, merely personal. But the history of the forest argues something far different. It argues for change, for patterns too shifting and evolving to justify any single practice or claim of ownership. Clear-cutting isn't an ancient, inevitable method: the first settlers didn't have enough trees to cut; selective logging was practiced between the wars; Mary McDonald started giving money to the School of Forestry for the expressed purpose of encouraging reforestation, not harvesting.

We can do anything we want. As a nation we can choose, for example, to pay more for timber. Who's to say that the current price is inevitable, objectively right, that there aren't other values we might pay for other ways? On McDonald-Dunn Forest we can choose to pay a recreational use fee, as some have suggested, to take the financial pressures off the forest. We can decide, as a community, that the first goal of the forest should be education and research, not the generation of revenue—or we can choose to clear-cut and burn all 12,000 acres. Science imposes limits of fact. Trees grow at certain rates in certain soils in certain climates. Ecosystems function according to complex interchanges of energy. But even then these are facts to be interpreted, the basis of policies we need to construct. The history of the forest shows that it has always been cultured, shaped. It has been made. No policy can be justified on the grounds that it is pure.

One evening at the end of the summer I walked to my first meeting 50
of the McDonald Forest Trails Committee, over in the Forestry Club Cabin, a mile or so from the house. It was odd to be walking through the forest to a committee meeting instead of driving to town for one. It almost seemed as if time had fallen away and I was hiking to a gathering at the Reed place for the evening, to catch up on the news and tell stories with my neighbors.

The meeting was a potluck, pasta salad shining under the cabin's new fluorescent lights. The room smelled like a school cafeteria. The agenda was up on a marker board in the front, items listed in ten-minute increments, and by the time I got there discussion of the "Multiple Use Trails Map and Guide" was underway. Representatives of the equestrians were politely complaining to representatives of the mountain bikers while Mary Rellergert, the recreation forester, practiced her conflict-resolution skills. Everyone kept using the term "user group": how do we accommodate the overlapping concerns of these different "user groups"? how can we get the full participation of this or that "user group"?

Two hours later I escaped back into the dark, familiar forest, to the sound of crickets and the smell of smoke from the field burning in the valley. It was early September, still warm, exactly a year since the loggers began their work. The last of the sun glowed over the edge of the shelterwood.

I could have named the different trees I brushed past, explained the theory behind the shelterwood, pointed out where the California Trail came in from the south, following the 510 Road. But I was glad to be walking in the dark, with just the sound of the trees around me. I was glad that the loggers were gone, the forest returned to its own rhythms and silences. After a year of studying and learning and interviewing experts, it's still the surfaces I value, still the feel of things, the smell of blackberry and needle duff, the play of shadow. McDonald Forest may not be as spectacular as the Andrews, but living on and near it through the seasons I have come to feel for it a special affection.

And this is what I want to argue for: for local knowledge, for personal knowledge. After all the terms and ideas and paradigms, what I value most is the sense of familiar ground, of a place I know well enough to find my way home in the dark, and I want to argue for that, just for the feeling of being here, fully, with the heart and the senses. I want to argue for the mind at rest.

The difference is that I know now I will have to *argue* for these things. I will have to fight for them and represent them publicly, and to do that I will have to know something about current silvicultural practices and the ecology of the forest. I will have to attend more potluck meetings at the forestry cabin. To make possible for others the knowing of a forest by heart, I will have to learn to speak the language of "user groups" and "recreationists" and even "multiple-use managers." I will have to make my own voice heard in the forest of voices.

Reading and Responding

1. Notice that Chris Anderson uses blank space to separate the major sections of the essay. Number the sections in the margins of the text, and write a brief one- or two-line summary of each section, perhaps a subtitle. What is the point of each section? What is the main method of development in each section, the main kind of writing?

2. Notice the kinds of information that Anderson uses, the sources of his details. Mark and label them in the margins. What kind of research does he rely on the most?

Working Together

1. In a few sentences, explain the title, "Forest of Voices."
2. Anderson focuses on several individuals in this essay. Does any one of them come out looking better than the others? Is Anderson on the side of one more than the others, or does he treat them all equally? (Notice how much space he devotes to each one, the things he quotes them as saying, how he describes their physical appearance).
3. Explain this statement: "We can do anything we want."
4. Compare this essay to Tom Wolfe's "O Rotten Gotham" or John McPhee's "Duty of Care." What do they have in common?
5. Discuss these questions: How is Anderson's essay different from a traditional term paper? How is it similar?

Rethinking and Rewriting

1. Write an essay about learning something you didn't know before that surprised you, overturned some unconsidered assumption.
2. Do an in-depth profile of a particular piece of ground, area, or ecosystem: a park, a city block, a garden. Write a biography of a place.
3. Write an essay built out of a series of interviews, profiling several individuals associated with an issue or place.
4. Write a term paper as a series of scenes, dialogues, portraits, and stories, grounding your facts and research in your own experience.

Essay Topics for Chapter 11

1. Using all or most of the pieces in this chapter as evidence and support, write a paper with this thesis: that it's absurd and simplistic to reduce the whole debate about forestry in America to a conflict between spotted owls and loggers; that the issue is far too complicated and full of paradoxes and disputed facts for anyone to be arrogant or dogmatic; that, in fact, the issues themselves are a lot like an old-growth forest, complex and interrelated and very hard to reduce to any single solution.
2. Using relevant pieces in this chapter, illustrate this thesis: that our attitudes about the forest are culturally and historically conditioned; that different people in different contexts can—and do—view a forest in different ways.
3. Write a before-and-after paper about walking in a forest. "Before" should describe how you felt walking through a forest before you read the pieces in this chapter. "After" should describe how you feel walking through the same forest after reading these pieces—how the reading

complicates what you see, what's going through your head. Describe the walks themselves, in detail, working in relevant passages from the readings.

4. Do some research on the economic costs associated with the depletion of a resource—the depletion of trees in the Northwest, the depletion of fish off the New England coast, the depletion of salmon in the rivers of Oregon and Washington. Just try to explain one of these in terms of how the depletion affects local economies. Use any reading from this chapter to help you.

5. Update and extend through research one or more of the fact pieces in this chapter. Take Ervin's numbers and show what's happened in the several years since he wrote his article, for instance. Do research on the "New Forestry" in current forestry practices and the scientific studies being done on its effectiveness (Jerry Franklin's name may be useful here). Do research on the federal government's forestry policies and connect them to the readings in this chapter.

6. Do a profile of Jack Ward Thomas (head of the Forest Service in the Clinton administration), relating his life and his statements about forestry to relevant pieces in this chapter.

7. Take a local forestry problem—a conflict over a proposed harvest, a new housing development, or recreational access, for example—and write about that problem in the context of these essays and the issues they raise. This piece can be informative or argumentative.

8. Do some research specifically on clear-cutting. What happens to a clear-cut after five years, after ten years, after thirty years? What does science have to say about clear-cutting?

9. Research new alternatives to wood as a building material (plastic wall studs or park benches, for example). Of the alternatives you discover, which seem particularly promising?

10. Choose a large timber company (Georgia-Pacific and Weyerhaeuser are two, for example) and see whether you can find out what sorts of forestry practices the company now advocates. Have these practices changed in the past ten years?

11. Investigate the Pacific Northwest forest industry (both federal and private). Why is this source of lumber so important? Where does the wood go? Who uses it? Why should people in other parts of the country care about what happens to trees in the Northwest?

12. Suppose you wanted to chop down a tree in your city, a tree planted between the sidewalk and the street. Would you be able to simply rent a chain saw and go to work one Saturday? Find out what rules and regulations govern trees in the city where you live.

12

Nature in Crisis

Though it's true that our understanding of the natural world is always culturally situated—a product of who and where and when we are—there are also facts to be considered. There are physical realities that science can measure and to some degree verify. And what science has measured in the past few decades is a crisis. The consensus among scientists is that the world is running out of things—water, wood fiber, minerals—and that much of what remains is becoming fouled, contaminated, ruined almost beyond renewal. Most scientists agree that the earth—whatever our cultural biases, whatever our point of view—is in deep trouble.

In the selections that follow we present several of the most famous and influential warnings about this global crisis as well as several pieces exploring particular dimensions of the crisis—global warming, the shortage of water, disappearing species.

But here, too, there is controversy. Even the facts are contested, as several of these pieces make clear. Though the scientific consensus is gloomy, some scientists disagree, citing errors in the research and offering different interpretations of the data. That changes are happening is beyond question. But what those changes really mean isn't necessarily clear.

"SOOTFALL AND FALLOUT"

E. B. White

In this essay from The Points of My Compass *(1962), E. B. White takes a global environmental problem and sees it as his problem, something happening in his own backyard, here and now. (See also the headnote for "Once More to the Lake" in chapter 9.)*

Turtle Bay, October 18, 1956

This is a dark morning in the apartment, but the block is gay with yellow moving vans disgorging Mary Martin's belongings in front of a house a couple of doors east of here, into which (I should say from the looks of things) she is moving. People's lives are so exposed at moments like this, their possessions lying naked in the street, the light of day searching out every bruise and mark of indoor living. It is an unfair exposé—end tables with nothing to be at the end of, standing lamps with their cords tied up in curlers, bottles of vermouth craning their long necks from cartons of personal papers, and every wastebasket carrying its small cargo of miscellany. The vans cause a stir in the block. Heads appear in the windows of No. 230, across the way. Passers-by stop on the sidewalk and stare brazenly into the new home through the open door. I have a mezzanine seat for the performance; like a Peeping Tom, I lounge here in my bathrobe and look down, held in the embrace of a common cold, before which scientists stand in awe although they have managed to split the atom, infect the topsoil with strontium 90, break the barrier of sound, and build the Lincoln Tunnel.

What a tremendous lot of stuff makes up the cumulus called "the home"! The trivet, the tiny washboard, the fire tools, the big copper caldron large enough to scald a hog in, the metal filing cabinets, the cardboard filing cabinets, the record player, the glass and the china invisible in their barrels, the carpet sweeper. (I wonder whether Miss Martin knows that she owns an old-fashioned carpet sweeper in a modern shade of green.) And here comes a bright little hacksaw, probably the apple of Mr. Halliday's eye. When a writing desk appears, the movers take the drawers out, to lighten the load, and I am free to observe what a tangle Mary Martin's stationery and supplies are in—like my wife's, everything at sixes and sevens. And now the bed, under the open sky above Forty-eighth Street. And now the mattress. A wave of decency overtakes me. I avert my gaze.

The movers experience the worst trouble with two large house plants, six-footers, in their great jars. The jars, on being sounded, prove to be a third full of water and have to be emptied into the gutter. Living things are always harder to lift, somehow, than inanimate objects, and I think any mover would rather walk up three flights with a heavy bureau than go into a waltz with a rubber plant. There is really no way for a man to put his arms around a big house plant and still remain a gentleman.

Out in back, away from the street, the prospect is more pleasing. The yellow cat mounts the wisteria vine and tries to enter my bedroom, stirred by dreams of a bullfinch in a cage. The air is hazy, smoke and fumes being pressed downward in what the smog reporter of the *Times* calls "a wigwam effect." I don't know what new gadget the factories of Long Island are making today to produce such a foul vapor—probably a new jet applicator for the relief of nasal congestion. But whatever it is, I would swap it for a breath of fresh air. On every slight stirring of the breeze, the willow behind Mary Martin's wigwam lets drop two or three stylish yellow leaves, and they swim lazily down like golden fish to where Paul, the handyman, waits with his broom. In the ivy border along the wall, watchful of the cat, three thrushes hunt about among the dry leaves. I can't pronounce "three thrushes," but I can see three thrushes from this window, and this is the first autumn I have ever seen three at once. An October miracle. I think they are hermits, but the visibility is so poor I can't be sure.

This section of Manhattan boasts the heaviest sootfall in town, and the United States of America boasts the heaviest fallout in the world, and when you take the sootfall and the fallout and bring smog in on top of them, I feel I am in a perfect position to discuss the problem of universal pollution. The papers, of course, are full of the subject these days, as they follow the presidential campaigners around the nation from one contaminated area to another.

I have no recent figures on sootfall in the vicinity of Third Avenue, but the *Times* last Saturday published some figures on fallout from Dr. Willard F. Libby, who said the reservoir of radioactive materials now floating in the stratosphere from the tests of all nations was roughly twenty-four billion tons. That was Saturday. Sunday's *Times* quoted Dr. Laurence H. Snyder as saying, "In assessing the potential harm [of weapons-testing], statements are always qualified by a phrase such as 'if the testing of weapons continues at the present rate . . .' This qualification is usually obsolete by the time the statement is printed." I have an idea the figure twenty-four billion tons may have been obsolete when it appeared in the paper. It may not have included, for instance, the radioactive stuff from the bomb the British set off in Australia a week or two ago. Maybe it did, maybe it didn't. The point of Dr. Snyder's remark is clear; a thermonuclear arms race is, as he puts it, self-accelerating. Bomb begets bomb. A begets H. Anything you can build, I can build bigger.

"Unhappily," said Governor Harriman the other night, "we are still thinking in small, conventional terms, and with unwarranted complacency."

The habit of thinking in small, conventional terms is, of course, not limited to us Americans. You could drop a leaflet or a Hubbard squash on the head of any person in any land and you would almost certainly hit a brain that was whirling in small, conventional circles. There is something about the human mind that keeps it well within the confines of the parish, and only one outlook in a million is nonparochial. The impression one gets from campaign oratory is that the sun revolves around the earth, the earth revolves around the United States, and the United States revolves around whichever city the speaker happens to be in at the moment. This is what a friend of mine used to call the Un-Copernican system. During a presidential race, candidates sometimes manage to create the impression that their thoughts are ranging widely and that they have abandoned conventional thinking. I love to listen to them when they are in the throes of these quadrennial seizures. But I haven't heard much from either candidate that sounded unconventional—although I have heard some things that sounded sensible and sincere. A candidate could easily commit political suicide if he were to come up with an unconventional thought during a presidential tour.

I think man's gradual, creeping contamination of the planet, his sending up of dust into the air, his strontium additive in our bones, his discharge of industrial poisons into rivers that once flowed clear, his mixing of chemicals with fog on the east wind add up to a fantasy of such grotesque proportions as to make everything said on the subject seem pale and anemic by contrast. I hold one share in the corporate earth and am uneasy about the management. Dr. Libby said there is new evidence that the amount of strontium reaching the body from topsoil impregnated by fallout is "considerably less than the 70 percent of the topsoil concentration originally estimated." Perhaps we should all feel elated at this, but I don't. The correct amount of strontium with which to impregnate the topsoil is *no* strontium. To rely on "tolerances" when you get into the matter of strontium 90, with three sovereign bomb testers already testing, independently of one another, and about fifty potential bomb testers ready to enter the stratosphere with their contraptions, is to talk with unwarranted complacency. I belong to a small, unconventional school that believes that *no* rat poison is the correct amount to spread in the kitchen where children and puppies can get at it. I believe that *no* chemical waste is the correct amount to discharge into the fresh rivers of the world, and I believe that if there is a way to trap the fumes from factory chimneys, it should be against the law to set these deadly fumes adrift where they can mingle with fog and, given the right conditions, suddenly turn an area into another Donora, Pa.

"I have seen the smoky fury of our factories—rising to the skies," said President Eisenhower pridefully as he addressed the people of Seattle last night. Well, I can see the smoky fury of our factories drifting right into this room this very minute; the fury sits in my throat like a bundle of needles, it explores my nose, chokes off my breath, and makes my eyes burn. The room smells like a slaughterhouse. And the phenomenon gets a brief mention in the morning press.

One simple, unrefuted fact about radioactive substances is that scientists do not agree about the "safe" amount. All radiation is harmful, all of

10

it shortens life, all is cumulative, nobody keeps track of how much he gets in the form of X-rays and radio therapy, and all of it affects not only the recipient but his heirs. Both President Eisenhower and Governor Stevenson have discussed H-bomb testing and the thermonuclear scene, and their views differ. Neither of them, it seems to me, has quite told the changing facts of life on earth. Both tend to speak of national security as though it were still capable of being dissociated from universal well-being; in fact, sometimes in these political addresses it sounds as though this nation, or any nation, through force of character or force of arms, could damn well rise *above* planetary considerations, as though we were greater than our environment, as though the national verve somehow transcended the natural world.

"Strong we shall stay free," said President Eisenhower in Pittsburgh. And Governor Stevenson echoed the statement in Chicago: ". . . only the strong can be free."

This doctrine of freedom through strength deserves a second look. It would have served nicely in 1936, but nobody thought of it then. Today, with the H-bomb deterring war, we are free and we are militarily strong, but the doctrine is subject to a queer, embarrassing amendment. Today it reads, "Strong we shall stay free, *provided we do not have to use our strength.*" That's not quite the same thing. What was true in 1936, if not actually false today, is at best a mere partial, or half truth. A nation wearing atomic armor is like a knight whose armor has grown so heavy he is immobilized; he can hardly walk, hardly sit his horse, hardly think, hardly breathe. The H-bomb is an extremely effective deterrent to war, but it has little virtue as a *weapon* of war, because it would leave the world uninhabitable.

For a short while following the release of atomic energy, a strong nation was a secure nation. Today, no nation, whatever its thermonuclear power, is a strong nation in the sense that it is a fully independent nation. All are weak, and all are weak from the same cause: each depends on the others for salvation, yet none likes to admit this dependence, and there is no machinery for interdependence. The big nations are weak because the strength has gone out of their arms—which are too terrifying to use, too poisonous to explode. The little nations are weak because they have always been relatively weak and now they have to breathe the same bad air as the big ones. Ours is a balance, as Mr. Stevenson put it, not of power but of terror. If anything, the H-bomb rather favors small nations that don't as yet possess it; they feel slightly more free to jostle other nations, having discovered that a country can stick its tongue out quite far these days without provoking war, so horrible are war's consequences.

The atom, then, is a proper oddity. It has qualified the meaning of 15 national security, it has very likely saved us from a third world war, it has given a new twist to the meaning of power, and it has already entered our bones with a cancer-producing isotope. Furthermore, it has altered the concept of personal sacrifice for moral principle. Human beings have always been willing to shed their blood for what they believed in. Yesterday this was clear and simple; we would pay in blood because, after the price was exacted, there was still a chance to make good the gain. But the modern price tag is not blood. Today our leaders and the leaders of other nations are, in effect, saying, "We will defend our beliefs not alone with our blood—by God, we'll defend them, if we have to, with our genes." This is bold, resolute talk, and one can't help admiring the spirit of it. I admire the spirit of it, but the logic of it eludes me. I doubt whether any noble principle—or any ignoble principle, either, for that matter—can be preserved at the price of genetic disintegration.

The thing I watch for in the speeches of the candidates is some hint that the thermonuclear arms race may be bringing people nearer together, rather than forcing them farther apart. I suspect that because of fallout we may achieve a sort of universality sooner than we bargained for. Fallout may compel us to fall in. The magic-carpet ride on the mushroom cloud has left us dazed—we have come so far so fast. There is a passage in Anne Lindbergh's book *North to the Orient* that captures the curious lag between the mind and the body during a plane journey, between the slow unfolding of remembered images and the swift blur of modern flight. Mrs. Lindbergh started her flight to the Orient by way of North Haven, her childhood summer home. "The trip to Maine," she wrote, "used to be a long and slow one. There was plenty of time in the night, spattered away in the sleeper, in the morning spent ferrying across the river at Bath, in the afternoon syncopated into a series of calls on one coast town after another—there was plenty of time to make the mental change coinciding with our physical change. . . . But on this swift flight to North Haven in the *Sirius* my mind was so far behind my body that when we flew over Rockland Harbor the familiar landmarks below me had no reality."

Like the girl in the plane, we have arrived, but the familiar scene lacks reality. We cling to old remembered forms, old definitions, old comfortable conceptions of national coziness, national self-sufficiency. The Security Council meets solemnly and takes up Suez, eleven sovereign fellows kicking a sovereign ditch around while England threatens war to defend her "lifelines," when modern war itself means universal contamination, universal deathlines, and the end of ditches. I would feel more hopeful, more *secure,* if the councilmen suddenly changed their tune and began arguing the case for mud turtles and other ancient denizens of ponds and ditches. That is the thing at stake now, and it is what will finally open the canal to the world's ships in perfect concord.

Candidates for political office steer clear of what Mrs. Luce used to call "globaloney," for fear they may lose the entire American Legion vote and pick up only Norman Cousins. Yet there are indications that supranational ideas are alive in the back of a few men's minds. Through the tangle of verbiage, the idea of "common cause" skitters like a shy bird. Mr. Dulles uses the word "interdependent" in one sentence, then returns promptly to the more customary, safer word "independent." We give aid to Yugoslavia to assure her "independence," and the very fact of the gift is proof that neither donor nor recipient enjoys absolute independence anymore; the two are locked in mortal *inter*dependence. Mr. Tito says he is for "new forms and new laws." I haven't the vaguest notion of what he means by that, and I doubt whether he has, either. Certainly there are no *old* laws, if by "laws" he means enforceable rules of conduct by which the world community is governed. But I'm for new forms, all right. Governor Stevenson, in one of his talks, said, "Nations have become so accustomed to living in the dark that they find it hard to learn to live in the light." What light? The light of government? If so, why not say so? President Eisenhower ended a speech the other day with the phrase "a peace of justice in a world of law." Everything else in his speech dealt with a peace of justice in a world of anarchy.

The riddle of disarmament, the riddle of peace, seems to me to hang on the interpretation of these conflicting and contradictory phrases—and on whether or not the men who use them really mean business. Are we independent or interdependent? We can't possibly be both. Do we indeed seek a peace of justice in a world of law, as the President intimates? If so, when do we start, and how? Are we for "new forms," or will the old ones do? In 1945, after the worst blood bath in history, the nations settled immediately back into old forms. In its structure, the United Nations reaffirms everything that caused the Second World War. At the end of a war fought to defeat dictators, the U.N. welcomed Stalin and Perón to full membership, and the Iron Curtain quickly descended to put the seal of authority on this inconsistent act. The drafters of the Charter assembled in San Francisco and defended their mild, inadequate format with the catchy phrase "Diplomacy is the art of the possible." Meanwhile, a little band of physicists met in a squash court and said, "The hell with the art of the possible. Watch this!"

The world organization debates disarmament in one room and, in the next room, moves the knights and pawns that make national arms imperative. This is not justice and law, and this is not light. It is not new forms. The U.N. is modern in intent, old-fashioned in shape. In San Francisco in 1945, the victor nations failed to create a constitution that placed a higher value on principle than on sovereignty, on common cause than on special cause. The world of 1945 was still 100 percent parochial. The world of 1956 is still almost 100 percent parochial. But at last we have a problem that is clearly a community problem, devoid of nationality—the problem of the total pollution of the planet.

We have, in fact, a situation in which the deadliest of all weapons, the H-bomb, together with its little brother, the A-bomb, is the latent source of great agreement among peoples. The bomb is universally hated, and it is universally feared. We cannot escape it with collective security; we shall have to face it with united action. It has given us a few years of grace without war, and now it offers us a few millenniums of oblivion. In a paradox of unbelievable jocundity, the shield of national sovereignty suddenly becomes the challenge of national sovereignty. And, largely because of events beyond our control, we are able to sniff the faint stirring of a community ferment—something every man can enjoy.

The President speaks often of "the peaceful uses of atomic energy," and they are greatly on his mind. I believe the peaceful use of atomic energy that should take precedence over all other uses is this: stop it from contaminating the soil and the sea, the rain and the sky, and the bones of man. This is elementary. It comes ahead of "good-will" ships and it comes ahead of cheap power. What good is cheap power if your child already has an incurable cancer?

The hydrogen-garbage-disposal program unites the people of the earth in a common antilitterbug drive for salvation. Radioactive dust has no nationality, is not deflected by boundaries; it falls on Turk and Texan impartially. The radio-strontium isotope finds its way into the milk of Soviet cow and English cow with equal ease. This simple fact profoundly alters the political scene and calls for political leaders to echo the physicists and say, "Never mind the art of the possible. Watch this!"

To me, living in the light means an honest attempt to discover the germ of common cause in a world of special cause, even against the almost insuperable odds of parochialism and national fervor, even in the face of the dangers that always attend political growth. Actually, nations are already enjoying little pockets of unity. The European coal-steel authority is apparently a success. The U.N., which is usually impotent in political disputes, has nevertheless managed to elevate the world's children and the world's health to a community level. The trick is to encourage and hasten this magical growth, this benign condition—encourage it and get it on paper, while children still have healthy bones and before we have all reached the point of no return. It will not mean the end of nations; it will mean the true beginning of nations.

Paul-Henri Spaak, addressing himself to the Egyptian government   25
the other day, said, "We are no longer at the time of the absolute sovereignty of states." We are not, and we ought by this time to know we are not. I just hope we learn it in time. In the beautiful phrase of Mrs. Lindbergh's, there used to be "plenty of time in the night." Now there is hardly any time at all.

Well, this started out as a letter and has turned into a discourse. But I don't mind. If a candidate were to appear on the scene and come out for the dignity of mud turtles, I suppose people would hesitate to support him, for fear he had lost his reason. But he would have my vote, on the theory that in losing his reason he had kept his head. It is time men allowed their imagination to infect their intellect, time we all rushed headlong into the wilder regions of thought where the earth again revolves around the sun instead of around the Suez, regions where no individual and no group can blithely assume the right to sow the sky with seeds of mischief, and where the sovereign nation at last begins to function as the true friend and guardian of sovereign man.

P.S. (May 1962). The dirty state of affairs on earth is getting worse, not better. Our soil, our rivers, our seas, our air carry an ever-increasing load of industrial wastes, agricultural poisons, and military debris. The seeds of mischief are in the wind—in the warm sweet airs of spring. Contamination continues in greater force and new ways, and with new excuses: the Soviet tests last autumn had a double-barreled purpose—to experiment and to intimidate. This was the first appearance of the diplomacy of dust; the breaking of the moratorium by Russia was a high crime, murder in the first degree. President Kennedy countered with the announcement that he would reply in kind unless a test-ban agreement could be reached by the end of April. None was reached, and our tests are being conducted. One more nation, France, has joined the company of testers. If Red China learns the trick, we will probably see the greatest pyrotechnic display yet, for the Chinese love fireworks of all kinds.

I asked myself what I would have done, had I been in the President's shoes, and was forced to admit I would have taken the same course—test. The shattering of the moratorium was for the time being the shattering of our hopes of good nuclear conduct. In a darkening and dirt-ridden world the course of freedom must be maintained even by desperate means, while there is a time of grace, and the only thing worse than being in an arms race is to be in one and not compete. The President's decision to resume testing in the atmosphere was, I believe, a correct decision, and I think the people who protest by lying down in the street have not come up with an alternative course that is sensible and workable. But the time of grace will run out, sooner or later, for all nations. We are in a vast riddle, all of us—dependence on a strength that is inimical to life—and what we are really doing is fighting a war that uses the lives of future individuals, rather than the lives of existing young men. The President did his best to lighten the blow by pointing out that fallout isn't as bad as it used to be, that our tests would raise the background radiation by only one percent. But this is like saying that it isn't dangerous to go in the cage with the tiger because the tiger is taking a nap. I am not calmed by the news of fallout's mildness, or deceived by drowsy tigers. The percentages will increase, the damage will mount steadily unless a turn is made somehow. Because our adversary tests, we test; because we test, they test. Where is the end of this dirty habit? I think there is no military solution, no economic solution, only a political solution, and this is the area to which we should give the closest attention and in which we should show the greatest imaginative powers.

These nuclear springtimes have a pervasive sadness about them, the virgin earth having been the victim of rape attacks. This is a smiling morning; I am writing where I can look out at our garden piece, which has been newly harrowed, ready for planting. The rich brown patch of ground used to bring delight to eye and mind at this fresh season of promise. For me the scene has been spoiled by the maggots that work in the mind. Tomorrow we will have rain, and the rain falling on the garden will carry its cargo of debris from old explosions in distant places. Whether the amount of this freight is great or small, whether it is measurable by the farmer or can only be guessed at, one thing is certain: the character of rain has changed, the joy of watching it soak the waiting earth has been diminished, and the whole meaning and worth of gardens has been brought into question.

Reading and Responding

1. This piece is dated October 18, 1956. What effect does this dating have on your reading as you begin? What expectations do you have? Why would E. B. White want to locate the essay in this way?
2. Mark passages or phrases that seem dated to you, unfamiliar, historically distant. What would you have to know and what kind of research would you have to do to better understand these passages?
3. Mark passages that seem contemporary, that could have been written today. What makes them seem contemporary?

Working Together

1. Do a quick page of writing to start a discussion. Assume that you're White and that you've just finished writing the first draft of this essay this morning. Why did you want to write the essay? What thoughts and feelings led to the writing? What did you want to accomplish? How do you feel now, with the first draft done?
2. Share these ideas in class.
3. You're still White. Give a quick tour of the piece you've written, pointing out the two or three passages you're most proud of and why. Point out the places you're still unsure of.

Rethinking and Rewriting

1. Broadly imitating White, write an essay describing your own backyard, in detail; then connect this one, small piece of ground to some larger environmental problem. What global problem involves your own plot of ground? What visible or invisible environmental crisis is right now taking place in the air or in the soil? What is the larger context for where you find yourself right now?
2. Imitating the letter format of White's essay, write a letter back to White explaining your responses to what he's written and updating the problems he's described. Have other problems taken the place of the ones that worried him? Have things gotten better, or worse?

"ELIXIRS OF DEATH"

Rachel Carson

Well known for The Sea Around Us, *which won the 1952 National Book Award, Rachel Carson went on to write* Silent Spring *(1962), which focused world attention on the growing use of pesticides in the production of food, an issue that remains as current today as it was three decades ago. Carson was for many years the editor in chief of publications for the U.S. Fish and Wildlife Service. The selection here is chapter 3 from* Silent Spring.

For the first time in the history of the world, every human being is now subjected to contact with dangerous chemicals, from the moment of conception until death. In the less than two decades of their use, the synthetic pesticides have been so thoroughly distributed throughout the animate and inanimate world that they occur virtually everywhere. They have been recovered from most of the major river systems and even from streams of groundwater flowing unseen through the earth. Residues of these chemicals linger in soil to which they may have been applied a dozen years before. They have entered and lodged in the bodies of fish, birds, reptiles, and domestic and wild animals so universally that scientists carrying on animal experiments find it almost impossible to locate subjects free from such contamination. They have been found in fish in remote mountain lakes, in earthworms burrowing in soil, in the eggs of birds—and in man himself. For these chemicals are now stored in the bodies of the vast majority of human beings, regardless of age. They occur in the mother's milk, and probably in the tissues of the unborn child.

All this has come about because of the sudden rise and prodigious growth of an industry for the production of man-made or synthetic chemicals with insecticidal properties. This industry is a child of the Second World War. In the course of developing agents of chemical warfare, some of the chemicals created in the laboratory were found to be lethal to insects. The discovery did not come by chance: insects were widely used to test chemicals as agents of death for man.

The result has been a seemingly endless stream of synthetic insecticides. In being man-made—by ingenious laboratory manipulation of the molecules, substituting atoms, altering their arrangement—they differ sharply from the simpler inorganic insecticides of prewar days. These were derived from naturally occurring minerals and plant products—compounds of arsenic, copper, lead, manganese, zinc, and other minerals, pyrethrum from the dried flowers of chrysanthemums, nicotine sulphate from some of the relatives of tobacco, and rotenone from leguminous plants of the East Indies.

What sets the new synthetic insecticides apart is their enormous biological potency. They have immense power not merely to poison but to enter into the most vital processes of the body and change them in sinister and often deadly ways. Thus, as we shall see, they destroy the very enzymes whose function is to protect the body from harm, they block the oxidation processes from which the body receives its energy, they prevent the normal functioning of various organs, and they may initiate in certain cells the slow and irreversible change that leads to malignancy.

Yet new and more deadly chemicals are added to the list each year and new uses are devised so that contact with these materials has become practically worldwide. The production of synthetic pesticides in the United States soared from 124,259,000 pounds in 1947 to 637,666,000 pounds in 1960—more than a fivefold increase. The wholesale value of these products was well over a quarter of a billion dollars. But in the plans and hopes of the industry this enormous production is only a beginning.

A Who's Who of pesticides is therefore of concern to us all. If we are going to live so intimately with these chemicals—eating and drinking them, taking them into the very marrow of our bones—we had better know something about their nature and their power.

Although the Second World War marked a turning away from inorganic chemicals as pesticides into the wonder world of the carbon molecule, a few of the old materials persist. Chief among these is arsenic, which is still the basic ingredient in a variety of weed and insect killers. Arsenic is a highly toxic mineral occurring widely in association with the ores of various metals, and in very small amounts in volcanoes, in the sea, and in spring water. Its relations to man are varied and historic. Since many of its compounds are tasteless, it has been a favorite agent of homicide from long before the time of the Borgias to the present. Arsenic was the first recognized elementary carcinogen (or cancer-causing substance), identified in chimney soot and linked to cancer nearly two centuries ago by an English physician. Epidemics of chronic arsenical poisoning involving whole populations over long periods are on record. Arsenic-contaminated environments have also caused sickness and death among horses, cows, goats, pigs, deer, fishes, and bees; despite this record arsenical sprays and dusts are widely used. In the arsenic-sprayed cotton country of southern United States beekeeping as an industry has nearly died out. Farmers using arsenic dusts over long periods have been afflicted with chronic arsenic poisoning; livestock have been poisoned by crop sprays or weed killers containing arsenic. Drifting arsenic dusts from blueberry lands have spread over neighboring farms, contaminating streams, fatally poisoning bees and cows, and causing human illness. "It is scarcely possible . . . to handle arsenicals with more utter disregard of the general health than that which has been practiced in our country in recent years," said Dr. W. C. Hueper, of the National Cancer Institute, an authority on environmental cancer. "Anyone who has watched the dusters and sprayers of arsenical insecticides at work must have been impressed by the almost supreme carelessness with which the poisonous substances are dispensed."

Modern insecticides are still more deadly. The vast majority fall into one of two large groups of chemicals. One, represented by DDT, is known as the "chlorinated hydrocarbons." The other group consists of the organic phosphorus insecticides, and is represented by the reasonably familiar malathion and parathion. All have one thing in common. As mentioned above, they are built on a basis of carbon atoms, which are also the indispensable building blocks of the living world, and thus classed as "organic." To understand them, we must see of what they are made, and how, although linked with the basic chemistry of all life, they lend themselves to the modifications which make them agents of death.

The basic element, carbon, is one whose atoms have an almost infinite capacity for uniting with each other in chains and rings and various other configurations, and for becoming linked with atoms of other substances. Indeed, the incredible diversity of living creatures from bacteria to the great blue whale is largely due to this capacity of carbon. The complex protein molecule has the carbon atom as its basis, as have molecules of fat, carbohydrates, enzymes, and vitamins. So, too, have enormous numbers of nonliving things, for carbon is not necessarily a symbol of life.

Some organic compounds are simply combinations of carbon and   *10* hydrogen. The simplest of these is methane, or marsh gas, formed in nature by the bacterial decomposition of organic matter under water. Mixed with air in proper proportions, methane becomes the dreaded "fire damp" of coal mines. Its structure is beautifully simple, consisting of one carbon atom to which four hydrogen atoms have become attached:

Chemists have discovered that it is possible to detach one or all of the hydrogen atoms and substitute other elements. For example, by substituting one atom of chlorine for one of hydrogen we produce methyl chloride:

Take away three hydrogen atoms and substitute chlorine and we have the anesthetic chloroform:

Substitute chlorine atoms for all of the hydrogen atoms and the result is carbon tetrachloride, the familiar cleaning fluid:

In the simplest possible terms, these changes rung upon the basic molecule of methane illustrate what a chlorinated hydrocarbon is. But this illustration gives little hint of the true complexity of the chemical world of the hydrocarbons, or of the manipulations by which the organic chemist creates his infinitely varied materials. For instead of the simple methane molecule with its single carbon atom, he may work with hydrocarbon molecules consisting of many carbon atoms, arranged in rings or chains, with side chains or branches, holding to themselves with chemical bonds not merely simple atoms of hydrogen or chlorine but also a wide variety of chemical groups. By seemingly slight changes the whole character of the substance is changed; for example, not only what is attached but the place of attachment to the carbon atom is highly important. Such ingenious manipulations have produced a battery of poisons of truly extraordinary power.

DDT (short for dichloro-diphenyl-trichloro-ethane) was first synthesized by a German chemist in 1874, but its properties as an insecticide were not discovered until 1939. Almost immediately DDT was hailed as a means of stamping out insect-borne disease and winning the farmers' war against crop destroyers overnight. The discoverer, Paul Müller of Switzerland, won the Nobel Prize.

DDT is now so universally used that in most minds the product takes on the harmless aspect of the familiar. Perhaps the myth of the harmlessness of DDT rests on the fact that one of its first uses was the wartime dusting of many thousands of soldiers, refugees, and prisoners, to combat lice. It is widely believed that since so many people came into extremely intimate contact with DDT and suffered no immediate ill effects the chemical must certainly be innocent of harm. This understandable misconception arises from the fact that—unlike other chlorinated hydrocarbons—DDT *in powder form* is not readily absorbed through the skin. Dissolved in oil, as it usually is, DDT is definitely toxic. If swallowed, it is absorbed slowly through the digestive tract; it may also be absorbed through the lungs. Once it has entered the body it is stored largely in organs rich in fatty substances (because DDT itself is fat-soluble) such as the adrenals, testes, or thyroid. Relatively large amounts are deposited in the liver, kidneys, and the fat of the large, protective mesenteries that enfold the intestines.

This storage of DDT begins with the smallest conceivable intake of the chemical (which is present as residues on most foodstuffs) and continues until quite high levels are reached. The fatty storage depots act as biological magnifiers, so that an intake of as little as $\frac{1}{10}$ of 1 part per million in the diet results in storage of about 10 to 15 parts per million, an increase of one hundredfold or more. These terms of reference, so commonplace to the chemist or the pharmacologist, are unfamiliar to most of us. One part in a million sounds like a very small amount—and so it is. But such substances are so potent that a minute quantity can bring about vast changes in the body. In animal experiments, 3 parts per million has been found to inhibit an essential enzyme in heart muscle; only 5 parts per million has brought about necrosis or disintegration of liver cells; only 2.5 parts per million of the closely related chemicals dieldrin and chlordane did the same.

This is really not surprising. In the normal chemistry of the human   *15*
body there is just such a disparity between cause and effect. For example, a quantity of iodine as small as two ten-thousandths of a gram spells the difference between health and disease. Because these small amounts of pesticides are cumulatively stored and only slowly excreted, the threat of chronic poisoning and degenerative changes of the liver and other organs is very real.

Scientists do not agree upon how much DDT can be stored in the human body. Dr. Arnold Lehman, who is the chief pharmacologist of the Food and Drug Administration, says there is neither a floor below which DDT is not absorbed nor a ceiling beyond which absorption and storage ceases. On the other hand, Dr. Wayland Hayes of the United States Public Health Service contends that in every individual a point of equilibrium is reached, and that DDT in excess of this amount is excreted. For practical purposes it is not particularly important which of these men is right. Storage in human beings has been well investigated, and we know that the average person is storing potentially harmful amounts. According to various studies, individuals with no known exposure (except the inevitable dietary one) store an average of 5.3 parts per million to 7.4 parts per million; agricultural workers 17.1 parts per million; and workers in insecticide plants as high as 648 parts per million! So the range of proven storage is quite wide and, what is even more to the point, the minimum figures are above the level at which damage to the liver and other organs or tissues may begin.

One of the most sinister features of DDT and related chemicals is the way they are passed on from one organism to another through all the links of the food chains. For example, fields of alfalfa are dusted with DDT; meal is later prepared from the alfalfa and fed to hens; the hens lay eggs which contain DDT. Or the hay, containing residues of 7 to 8 parts per million, may be fed to cows. The DDT will turn up in the milk in the amount of about 3 parts per million, but in butter made from this milk the concentration may run to 65 parts per million. Through such a process of transfer, what started out as a very small amount of DDT may end as a heavy concentration. Farmers nowadays find it difficult to obtain uncontaminated fodder for their milk cows, though the Food and Drug Administration forbids the presence of insecticide residues in milk shipped in interstate commerce.

The poison may also be passed on from mother to offspring. Insecticide residues have been recovered from human milk in samples tested by Food and Drug Administration scientists. This means that the breast-fed human infant is receiving small but regular additions to the load of toxic chemicals building up in his body. It is by no means his first exposure, however: there is good reason to believe this begins while he is still in the womb. In experimental animals the chlorinated hydrocarbon insecticides freely cross the barrier of the placenta, the traditional protective shield between the embryo and harmful substances in the mother's body. While the quantities so received by human infants would normally be small, they are not unimportant because children are more susceptible to poisoning than adults. This situation also means that today the average individual almost certainly starts life with the first deposit of the growing load of chemicals his body will be required to carry thenceforth.

All these facts—storage at even low levels, subsequent accumulation, and occurrence of liver damage at levels that may easily occur in normal diets—caused Food and Drug Administration scientists to declare as early as 1950 that it is "extremely likely the potential hazard of DDT has been underestimated." There has been no such parallel situation in medical history. No one yet knows what the ultimate consequences may be.

Chlordane, another chlorinated hydrocarbon, has all the unpleasant   20
attributes of DDT plus a few that are peculiarly its own. Its residues are long persistent in soil, on foodstuffs, or on surfaces to which it may be applied, yet it is also quite volatile and poisoning by inhalation is a definite risk to anyone handling or exposed to it. Chlordane makes use of all available portals to enter the body. It penetrates the skin easily, is breathed in as vapor, and of course is absorbed from the digestive tract if residues are swallowed. Like all other chlorinated hydrocarbons, its deposits build up in the body in cumulative fashion. A diet containing such a small amount of chlordane as 2.5 parts per million may eventually lead to storage of 75 parts per million in the fat of experimental animals.

So experienced a pharmacologist as Dr. Lehman has described chlordane as "one of the most toxic of insecticides—anyone handling it could be poisoned." Judging by the carefree liberality with which dusts for lawn treatments by suburbanites are laced with chlordane, this warning has not been taken to heart. The fact that the suburbanite is not instantly stricken has little meaning, for the toxins may sleep long in his body, to become manifest months or years later in an obscure disorder almost impossible to trace to its origins. On the other hand, death may strike quickly. One victim who accidentally spilled a 25 per cent solution on his skin developed symptoms of poisoning within 40 minutes and died before medical help could be obtained. No reliance can be placed on receiving advance warning which might allow treatment to be had in time.

Heptachlor, one of the constituents of chlordane, is marketed as a separate formulation. It has a particularly high capacity for storage in fat. If the diet contains as little as ⅒ of 1 part per million there will be measurable amounts of heptachlor in the body. It also has the curious ability to undergo change into a chemically distinct substance known as heptachlor epoxide. It does this in soil and in the tissues of both plants and animals. Tests on birds indicate that the epoxide that results from this change is about four times as toxic as the original chemical, which in turn is four times as toxic as chlordane.

As long ago as the mid-1930's a special group of hydrocarbons, the chlorinated naphthalenes, was found to cause hepatitis, and also a rare and almost invariably fatal liver disease in persons subjected to occupational exposure. They have led to illness and death of workers in electrical industries; and more recently, in agriculture, they have been considered a cause of a mysterious and usually fatal disease of cattle. In view of these antecedents, it is not surprising that three of the insecticides that belong to this group are among the most violently poisonous of all the hydrocarbons. These are dieldrin, aldrin, and endrin.

Dieldrin, named for a German chemist, Diels, is about 5 times as toxic as DDT when swallowed but 40 times as toxic when absorbed through the skin in solution. It is notorious for striking quickly and with terrible effect at the nervous system, sending the victims into convulsions. Persons thus poisoned recover so slowly as to indicate chronic effects. As with other chlorinated hydrocarbons, these long-term effects include severe damage to the liver. The long duration of its residues and the effective insecticidal action make dieldrin one of the most used insecticides today, despite the appalling destruction of wildlife that has followed its use. As tested on quail and pheasants, it has proved to be about 40 to 50 times as toxic as DDT.

There are vast gaps in our knowledge of how dieldrin is stored or   25
distributed in the body, or excreted, for the chemists' ingenuity in devising insecticides has long ago outrun biological knowledge of the way these poisons affect the living organism. However, there is every indication of long storage in the human body, where deposits may lie dormant like a slumbering volcano, only to flare up in periods of physiological stress when the body draws upon its fat reserves. Much of what we do know has been learned through hard experience in the antimalarial campaigns carried out by the World Health Organization. As soon as dieldrin was substituted for DDT in malaria-control work (because the malaria mosquitoes had become resistant to DDT), cases of poisoning among the spraymen began to occur. The seizures were severe—from half to all (varying in the different programs) of the men affected went into convulsions and several died. Some had convulsions as long as *four months* after the last exposure.

Aldrin is a somewhat mysterious substance, for although it exists as a separate entity it bears the relation of alter ego to dieldrin. When carrots are taken from a bed treated with aldrin they are found to contain residues of dieldrin. This change occurs in living tissues and also in soil. Such alchemistic transformations have led to many erroneous reports, for if a chemist, knowing aldrin has been applied, tests for it he will be deceived into thinking all residues have been dissipated. The residues are there, but they are dieldrin and this requires a different test.

Like dieldrin, aldrin is extremely toxic. It produces degenerative changes in the liver and kidneys. A quantity the size of an aspirin tablet is enough to kill more than 400 quail. Many cases of human poisonings are on record, most of them in connection with industrial handling.

Aldrin, like most of this group of insecticides, projects a menacing shadow into the future, the shadow of sterility. Pheasants fed quantities too small to kill them nevertheless laid few eggs, and the chicks that hatched soon died. The effect is not confined to birds. Rats exposed to aldrin had fewer pregnancies and their young were sickly and short-lived. Puppies born of treated mothers died within three days. By one means or another, the new generations suffer for the poisoning of their parents. No one knows whether the same effect will be seen in human beings, yet this chemical has been sprayed from airplanes over suburban areas and farmlands.

Endrin is the most toxic of all the chlorinated hydrocarbons. Although chemically rather closely related to dieldrin, a little twist in its molecular structure makes it 5 times as poisonous. It makes the progenitor of all this group of insecticides, DDT, seem by comparison almost harmless. It is 15 times as poisonous as DDT to mammals, 30 times as poisonous to fish, and about 300 times as poisonous to some birds.

In the decade of its use, endrin has killed enormous numbers of fish, has fatally poisoned cattle that have wandered into sprayed orchards, has poisoned wells, and has drawn a sharp warning from at least one state health department that its careless use is endangering human lives.

30

In one of the most tragic cases of endrin poisoning there was no apparent carelessness; efforts had been made to take precautions apparently considered adequate. A year-old child had been taken by his American parents to live in Venezuela. There were cockroaches in the house to which they moved, and after a few days a spray containing endrin was used. The baby and the small family dog were taken out of the house before the spraying was done about nine o'clock one morning. After the spraying the floors were washed. The baby and dog were returned to the house in midafternoon. An hour or so later the dog vomited, went into convulsions, and died. At 10 p.m. on the evening of the same day the baby also vomited, went into convulsions, and lost consciousness. After that fateful contact with endrin, this normal, healthy child became little more than a vegetable—unable to see or hear, subject to frequent muscular spasms, apparently completely cut off from contact with his surroundings. Several months of treatment in a New York hospital failed to change his condition or bring hope of change. "It is extremely doubtful," reported the attending physicians, "that any useful degree of recovery will occur."

The second major group of insecticides, the alkyl or organic phosphates, are among the most poisonous chemicals in the world. The chief and most obvious hazard attending their use is that of acute poisoning of people applying the sprays or accidentally coming in contact with drifting spray, with vegetation coated by it, or with a discarded container. In Florida, two children found an empty bag and used it to repair a swing. Shortly thereafter both of them died and three of their playmates became ill. The bag had once contained an insecticide called parathion, one of the organic phosphates; tests established death by parathion poisoning. On another occasion two small boys in Wisconsin, cousins, died on the same night. One had been playing in his yard when spray drifted in from an adjoining field where his father was spraying potatoes with parathion; the other had run playfully into the barn after his father and had put his hand on the nozzle of the spray equipment.

The origin of these insecticides has a certain ironic significance. Although some of the chemicals themselves—organic esters of phosphoric acid—had been known for many years, their insecticidal properties remained to be discovered by a German chemist, Gerhard Schrader, in the late 1930's. Almost immediately the German government recognized the value of these same chemicals as new and devastating weapons in man's war against his own kind, and the work on them was declared secret. Some became the deadly nerve gases. Others, of closely allied structure, became insecticides.

The organic phosphorus insecticides act on the living organism in a peculiar way. They have the ability to destroy enzymes—enzymes that perform necessary functions in the body. Their target is the nervous system, whether the victim is an insect or a warm-blooded animal. Under normal conditions, an impulse passes from nerve to nerve with the aid of a "chemical transmitter" called acetylcholine, a substance that performs an essential function and then disappears. Indeed, its existence is so ephemeral that medical researchers are unable, without special procedures, to sample it before the body has destroyed it. This transient nature of the transmitting chemical is necessary to the normal functioning of the body. If the acetylcholine is not destroyed as soon as a nerve impulse has passed, impulses continue to flash across the bridge from nerve to nerve, as the chemical exerts its effects in an ever more intensified manner. The movements of the whole body become uncoordinated: tremors, muscular spasms, convulsions, and death quickly result.

This contingency has been provided for by the body. A protective enzyme called cholinesterase is at hand to destroy the transmitting chemical once it is no longer needed. By this means a precise balance is struck and the body never builds up a dangerous amount of acetylcholine. But on contact with the organic phosphorus insecticides, the protective enzyme is destroyed, and as the quantity of the enzyme is reduced that of the transmitting chemical builds up. In this effect, the organic phosphorus compounds resemble the alkaloid poison muscarine, found in a poisonous mushroom, the fly amanita.

Repeated exposures may lower the cholinesterase level until an individual reaches the brink of acute poisoning, a brink over which he may be pushed by a very small additional exposure. For this reason it is considered important to make periodic examinations of the blood of spray operators and others regularly exposed.

Parathion is one of the most widely used of the organic phosphates. It is also one of the most powerful and dangerous. Honeybees become "wildly agitated and bellicose" on contact with it, perform frantic cleaning movements, and are near death within half an hour. A chemist, thinking to learn by the most direct possible means the dose acutely toxic to human beings, swallowed a minute amount, equivalent to about .00424 ounce. Paralysis followed so instantaneously that he could not reach the antidotes he had prepared at hand, and so he died. Parathion is now said to be a favorite instrument of suicide in Finland. In recent years the State of California has reported an average of more than 200 cases of accidental parathion poisoning annually. In many parts of the world the fatality rate from parathion is startling: 100 fatal cases in India and 67 in Syria in 1958, and an average of 336 deaths per year in Japan.

Yet some 7,000,000 pounds of parathion are now applied to fields and orchards of the United States—by hand sprayers, motorized blowers and dusters, and by airplane. The amount used on California farms alone could, according to one medical authority, "provide a lethal dose for 5 to 10 times the whole world's population."

One of the few circumstances that save us from extinction by this means is the fact that parathion and other chemicals of this group are decomposed rather rapidly. Their residues on the crops to which they are applied are therefore relatively short-lived compared with the chlorinated hydrocarbons. However, they last long enough to create hazards and produce consequences that range from the merely serious to the fatal. In Riverside, California, eleven out of thirty men picking oranges became violently ill and all but one had to be hospitalized. Their symptoms were typical of parathion poisoning. The grove had been sprayed with parathion some two and a half weeks earlier; the residues that reduced them to retching, half-blind, semiconscious misery were sixteen to nineteen days old. And this is not by any means a record for persistence. Similar mishaps have occurred in groves sprayed a month earlier, and residues have been found in the peel of oranges six months after treatment with standard dosages.

The danger to all workers applying the organic phosphorus insecticides in fields, orchards, and vineyards, is so extreme that some states using these chemicals have established laboratories where physicians may obtain aid in diagnosis and treatment. Even the physicians themselves may be in some danger, unless they wear rubber gloves in handling the victims of poisoning. So may a laundress washing the clothing of such victims, which may have absorbed enough parathion to affect her.

Malathion, another of the organic phosphates, is almost as familiar to the public as DDT, being widely used by gardeners, in household insecticides, in mosquito spraying, and in such blanket attacks on insects

40

as the spraying of nearly a million acres of Florida communities for the Mediterranean fruit fly. It is considered the least toxic of this group of chemicals and many people assume they may use it freely and without fear of harm. Commercial advertising encourages this comfortable attitude.

The alleged "safety" of malathion rests on rather precarious ground, although—as often happens—this was not discovered until the chemical had been in use for several years. Malathion is "safe" only because the mammalian liver, an organ with extraordinary protective powers, renders it relatively harmless. The detoxification is accomplished by one of the enzymes of the liver. If, however, something destroys this enzyme or interferes with its action, the person exposed to malathion receives the full force of the poison.

Unfortunately for all of us, opportunities for this sort of thing to happen are legion. A few years ago a team of Food and Drug Administration scientists discovered that when malathion and certain other organic phosphates are administered simultaneously a massive poisoning results—up to 50 times as severe as would be predicted on the basis of adding together the toxicities of the two. In other words, $\frac{1}{100}$ of the lethal dose of each compound may be fatal when the two are combined.

This discovery led to the testing of other combinations. It is now known that many pairs of organic phosphate insecticides are highly dangerous, the toxicity being stepped up or "potentiated" through the combined action. Potentiation seems to take place when one compound destroys the liver enzyme responsible for detoxifying the other. The two need not be given simultaneously. The hazard exists not only for the man who may spray this week with one insecticide and next week with another; it exists also for the consumer of sprayed products. The common salad bowl may easily present a combination of organic phosphate insecticides. Residues well within the legally permissible limits may interact.

The full scope of the dangerous interaction of chemicals is as yet little   45
known, but disturbing findings now come regularly from scientific laboratories. Among these is the discovery that the toxicity of an organic phosphate can be increased by a second agent that is not necessarily an insecticide. For example, one of the plasticizing agents may act even more strongly than another insecticide to make malathion more dangerous. Again, this is because it inhibits the liver enzyme that normally would "draw the teeth" of the poisonous insecticide.

What of other chemicals in the normal human environment? What, in particular, of drugs? A bare beginning has been made on this subject, but already it is known that some organic phosphates (parathion and malathion) increase the toxicity of some drugs used as muscle relaxants, and that several others (again including malathion) markedly increase the sleeping time of barbiturates.

In Greek mythology the sorceress Medea, enraged at being supplanted by a rival for the affections of her husband Jason, presented the new bride with a robe possessing magic properties. The wearer of the robe immediately suffered a violent death. This death-by-indirection now finds its counterpart in what are known as "systemic insecticides." These are chemicals with extraordinary properties which are used to convert plants or animals into a sort of Medea's robe by making them actually poisonous. This is done with the purpose of killing insects that may come in contact with them, especially by sucking their juices or blood.

The world of systemic insecticides is a weird world, surpassing the imaginings of the brothers Grimm—perhaps most closely akin to the cartoon world of Charles Addams. It is a world where the enchanted forest of the fairy tales has become the poisonous forest in which an insect that chews a leaf or sucks the sap of a plant is doomed. It is a world where a flea bites a dog, and dies because the dog's blood has been made poisonous, where an insect may die from vapors emanating from a plant it has never touched, where a bee may carry poisonous nectar back to its hive and presently produce poisonous honey.

The entomologists' dream of the built-in insecticide was born when workers in the field of applied entomology realized they could take a hint from nature: they found that wheat growing in soil containing sodium selenate was immune to attack by aphids or spider mites. Selenium, a naturally occurring element found sparingly in rocks and soils of many parts of the world, thus became the first systemic insecticide.

What makes an insecticide a systemic is the ability to permeate all   *50* the tissues of a plant or animal and make them toxic. This quality is possessed by some chemicals of the chlorinated hydrocarbon group and by others of the organophosphorus group, all synthetically produced, as well as by certain naturally occurring substances. In practice, however, most systemics are drawn from the organophosphorus group because the problem of residues is somewhat less acute.

Systemics act in other devious ways. Applied to seeds, either by soaking or in a coating combined with carbon, they extend their effects into the following plant generation and produce seedlings poisonous to aphids and other sucking insects. Vegetables such as peas, beans, and sugar beets are sometimes thus protected. Cotton seeds coated with a systemic insecticide have been in use for some time in California, where 25 farm laborers planting cotton in the San Joaquin Valley in 1959 were seized with sudden illness, caused by handling the bags of treated seeds.

In England someone wondered what happened when bees made use of nectar from plants treated with systemics. This was investigated in areas treated with a chemical called schradan. Although the plants had been sprayed before the flowers were formed, the nectar later produced contained the poison. The result, as might have been predicted, was that the honey made by the bees also was contaminated with schradan.

Use of animal systemics has concentrated chiefly on control of the cattle grub, a damaging parasite of livestock. Extreme care must be used in order to create an insecticidal effect in the blood and tissues of the host without setting up a fatal poisoning. The balance is delicate and government veterinarians have found that repeated small doses can gradually deplete an animal's supply of the protective enzyme cholinesterase, so that without warning a minute additional dose will cause poisoning.

There are strong indications that fields closer to our daily lives are being opened up. You may now give your dog a pill which, it is claimed, will rid him of fleas by making his blood poisonous to them. The hazards discovered in treating cattle would presumably apply to the dog. As yet no one seems to have proposed a human systemic that would make us lethal to a mosquito. Perhaps this is the next step.

So far . . . we have been discussing the deadly chemicals that are 55 being used in our war against the insects. What of our simultaneous war against the weeds?

The desire for a quick and easy method of killing unwanted plants has given rise to a large and growing array of chemicals that are known as herbicides, or, less formally, as weed killers. . . . The question that here concerns us is whether the weed killers are poisons and whether their use is contributing to the poisoning of the environment.

The legend that the herbicides are toxic only to plants and so pose no threat to animal life has been widely disseminated, but unfortunately it is not true. The plant killers include a large variety of chemicals that act on animal tissue as well as on vegetation. They vary greatly in their action on the organism. Some are general poisons, some are powerful stimulants of metabolism, causing a fatal rise in body temperature, some induce malignant tumors either alone or in partnership with other chemicals, some strike at the genetic material of the race by causing gene mutations. The herbicides, then, like the insecticides, include some very dangerous chemicals, and their careless use in the belief that they are "safe" can have disastrous results.

Despite the competition of a constant stream of new chemicals issuing from the laboratories, arsenic compounds are still liberally used, both as insecticides (as mentioned above) and as weed killers, where they usually take the chemical form of sodium arsenite. The history of their use is not reassuring. As roadside sprays, they have cost many a farmer his cow and killed uncounted numbers of wild creatures. As aquatic weed killers in lakes and reservoirs they have made public waters unsuitable for drinking or even for swimming. As a spray applied to potato fields to destroy the vines they have taken a toll of human and nonhuman life.

In England this latter practice developed about 1951 as a result of a shortage of sulfuric acid, formerly used to burn off the potato vines. The Ministry of Agriculture considered it necessary to give warning of the hazard of going into the arsenic-sprayed fields, but the warning was not understood by the cattle (nor, we must assume, by the wild animals and birds) and reports of cattle poisoned by the arsenic sprays came with monotonous regularity. When death came also to a farmer's wife through arsenic-contaminated water, one of the major English chemical companies (in 1959) stopped production of arsenical sprays and called in supplies already in the hands of dealers, and shortly thereafter the Ministry of Agriculture announced that because of high risks to people and cattle restrictions on the use of arsenites would be imposed. In 1961, the Australian government announced a similar ban. No such restrictions impede the use of these poisons in the United States, however.

Some of the "dinitro" compounds are also used as herbicides. They are rated as among the most dangerous materials of this type in use in the United States. Dinitrophenol is a strong metabolic stimulant. For this reason it was at one time used as a reducing drug, but the margin between the slimming dose and that required to poison or kill was slight—so slight that several patients died and many suffered permanent injury before use of the drug was finally halted.

A related chemical, pentachlorophenol, sometimes known as "penta," is used as a weed killer as well as an insecticide, often being sprayed along railroad tracks and in waste areas. Penta is extremely toxic to a wide variety of organisms from bacteria to man. Like the dinitros, it interferes, often fatally, with the body's source of energy, so that the affected organism almost literally burns itself up. Its fearful power is illustrated in a fatal accident recently reported by the California Department of Health. A tank truck driver was preparing a cotton defoliant by mixing diesel oil with pentachlorophenol. As he was drawing the concentrated chemical out of a drum, the spigot accidentally toppled back. He reached in with his bare hand to regain the spigot. Although he washed immediately, he became acutely ill and died the next day.

While the results of weed killers such as sodium arsenite or the phenols are grossly obvious, some other herbicides are more insidious in their effects. For example, the now famous cranberry-weed-killer aminotriazole, or amitrol, is rated as having relatively low toxicity. But in the long run its tendency to cause malignant tumors of the thyroid may be far more significant for wildlife and perhaps also for man.

Among the herbicides are some that are classified as "mutagens," or agents capable of modifying the genes, the materials of heredity. We are rightly appalled by the genetic effects of radiation; how then, can we be indifferent to the same effect in chemicals that we disseminate widely in our environment?

Reading and Responding

1. In the margins, mark any passages you don't understand, and be prepared to talk about them in class.

2. From these passages and others, come up with two or three questions to begin and focus a class discussion. From your first reading of this article, what are the issues, problems, and ideas the class should discuss?

Working Together

1. Share your questions, issues, and discussion topics with others. Write them all on the board, or working in groups, record them on a single sheet of paper.
2. Do the questions overlap? Are there one or two main questions being asked in different ways? Can you find a central, thesis question that organizes the rest—that the rest can be placed under, made subordinate to?
3. Discuss strategies for answering these questions. Organize your second reading.

Rethinking and Rewriting

1. Consider these questions as the basis for follow-up research on the problems Rachel Carson describes. Write a paper summarizing and synthesizing your research.
   - What's happened since this book was published?
   - When was DDT banned?
   - What led to the ban?
   - What effects of DDT persist?
   - What were the positive effects of the ban?
   - Where is DDT still used worldwide?
2. Write an essay that begins by describing the chemicals you use every day. If you use chemicals on a lawn or in a garden, stay with those. If you use chemicals to kill insects, focus on those. If you have a closet full of chemicals, focus on those. Start by describing them briefly by brand name and intended use. Then look for any caution statements on the label (often in small print). From this inventory and set of descriptions, choose one of these products and see what you can find out about its ingredients. What's this product made of? What does it do, and how does it do so? What kind of safety testing is required for this product, and who requires it? If you can find information on the actual results of the testing of this product, include that as well. Consider your essay as a report to people who also buy and use this product, and end with a recommendation. Tell your readers whether they should continue to purchase this product. If you have a negative recommendation, can you suggest a better alternative?
3. Consider a fresh food you enjoy eating all year even though it's really a seasonal food. For example, tomatoes are available year-round in many areas, as are various kinds of grapes and other fruits and vegetables.

Focus on one of these foods and see whether you can find out where this food comes from when it's not being harvested locally. Once you've identified the origin of the food, see whether you can find out what rules govern the use of pesticides there. Consider your essay as a report to people who buy this fresh food even though it's out of season.

"SHIPS IN THE DESERT"

Al Gore

> *Vice President Al Gore graduated from Harvard in 1969, served as an army reporter in Vietnam, and for seven years was a reporter for the Nashville Tennessean. In 1976, after attending Vanderbilt Law School, he began the first of his three terms as a Democratic congressman, and in 1984 he was elected to the United States Senate. In 1988 he made an unsuccessful bid for the Democratic nomination for president, partly, he says—in the moving, highly personal introduction to his* Earth in the Balance *(1992)—to "elevate the importance of the [environmental] crisis as a political issue." He notes that he had become "increasingly impatient with the status quo, with conventional wisdom, with the lazy assumption that we can always muddle through." Since 1992 he has served as vice president of the United States. In "Ships in the Desert," the first chapter of his book, Gore surveys the ecological problems facing the planet.*

Before and As You Read

1. Before you begin reading, answer this question: Does it matter to you that this piece is written by a politician? If yes, why? If no, why? Once you've finished reading, come back to this same question and answer it again.
2. This chapter from Al Gore's book *Earth in the Balance* is a kind of tour of the environmental crisis, an overview of the major problems facing the planet. As you read, number in the margins the problems that Gore surveys, and write a short title or subheading for each.

I was standing in the sun on the hot steel deck of a fishing ship capable of processing a fifty-ton catch on a good day. But it wasn't a good day. We were anchored in what used to be the most productive fishing site in all of central Asia, but as I looked out over the bow, the prospects of a good catch looked bleak. Where there should have been gentle blue-green waves lapping against the side of the ship, there was nothing but hot dry sand—as far as I could see in all directions. The other ships of the fleet were also at rest in the sand, scattered in the dunes that stretched all the way to the horizon.

Oddly enough, it made me think of a fried egg I had seen back in the United States on television the week before. It was sizzling and popping the way a fried egg should in a pan, but it was in the middle of a sidewalk in downtown Phoenix. I guess it sprang to mind because, like the ship on which I was standing, there was nothing wrong with the egg itself. Instead, the world beneath it had changed in an unexpected way that made the egg seem—through no fault of its own—out of place. It was illustrating the newsworthy point that at the time Arizona wasn't having an especially good day, either, because for the second day in a row temperatures had reached a record 122 degrees.

As a camel walked by on the dead bottom of the Aral Sea, my thoughts returned to the unlikely ship of the desert on which I stood, which also seemed to be illustrating the point that its world had changed out from underneath it with sudden cruelty. Ten years ago the Aral was the fourth-largest inland sea in the world, comparable to the largest of North America's Great Lakes. Now it is disappearing because the water that used to feed it has been diverted in an ill-considered irrigation scheme to grow cotton in the desert. The new shoreline was almost forty kilometers across the sand from where the fishing fleet was now permanently docked. Meanwhile, in the nearby town of Muynak the people were still canning fish—brought not from the Aral Sea but shipped by rail through Siberia from the Pacific Ocean, more than a thousand miles away.

I had come to the Aral Sea in August 1990 to witness at first hand the destruction taking place there on an almost biblical scale. But during the trip I encountered other images that also alarmed me. For example, the day I returned to Moscow from Muynak, my friend Alexei Yablokov, possibly the leading environmentalist in the Soviet Union, was returning from an emergency expedition to the White Sea, where he had investigated the mysterious and unprecedented death of several *million* starfish, washed up into a knee-deep mass covering many miles of beach. That night, in his apartment, he talked of what it was like for the residents to wade through the starfish in hip boots, trying to explain their death.

Later investigations identified radioactive military waste as the likely   5
culprit in the White Sea deaths. But what about all of the other mysterious mass deaths washing up on beaches around the world? French scientists recently concluded that the explanation for the growing number of dead dolphins washing up along the Riviera was accumulated environmental stress, which, over time, rendered the animals too weak to fight off a virus. This same phenomenon may also explain the sudden increase in dolphin deaths along the Gulf Coast in Texas as well as the mysterious deaths of 12,000 seals whose corpses washed up on the shores of the North Sea in the summer of 1988. Of course, the oil-covered otters and seabirds of Prince William Sound a year later presented less of a mystery to science, if no less an indictment of our civilization.

As soon as one of these troubling images fades, another takes its place, provoking new questions. What does it mean, for example, that children playing in the morning surf must now dodge not only the occasional jellyfish but the occasional hypodermic needle washing in with the waves? Needles, dead dolphins, and oil-soaked birds—are all these signs that the shores of our familiar world are fast eroding, that we are now standing on some new beach, facing dangers beyond the edge of what we are capable of imagining?

With our backs turned to the place in nature from which we came, we sense an unfamiliar tide rising and swirling around our ankles, pulling at the sand beneath our feet. Each time this strange new tide goes out, it leaves behind the flotsam and jetsam of some giant shipwreck far out at sea, startling images washed up on the sands of our time, each a fresh warning of hidden dangers that lie ahead if we continue on our present course.

My search for the underlying causes of the environmental crisis has led me to travel around the world to examine and study many of these images of destruction. At the very bottom of the earth, high in the Trans-Antarctic Mountains, with the sun glaring at midnight through a hole in the sky, I stood in the unbelievable coldness and talked with a scientist in the late fall of 1988 about the tunnel he was digging through time. Slipping his parka back to reveal a badly burned face that was cracked and peeling, he pointed to the annual layers of ice in a core sample dug from the glacier on which we were standing. He moved his finger back in time to the ice of two decades ago. "Here's where the U.S. Congress passed the Clean Air Act," he said. At the bottom of the world, two continents away from Washington, D.C., even a small reduction in one country's emissions had changed the amount of pollution found in the remotest and least accessible place on earth.

But the most significant change thus far in the earth's atmosphere is the one that began with the industrial revolution early in the last century and has picked up speed ever since. Industry meant coal, and later oil, and we began to burn lots of it—bringing rising levels of carbon dioxide (CO_2), with its ability to trap more heat in the atmosphere and slowly warm the earth. Fewer than a hundred yards from the South Pole, upwind from the ice runway where the ski plane lands and keeps its engines running to prevent the metal parts from freeze-locking together, scientists monitor the air several times every day to chart the course of that inexorable change. During my visit, I watched one scientist draw the results of that day's measurements, pushing the end of a steep line still higher on the graph. He told me how easy it is—there at the end of the earth—to see that this enormous change in the global atmosphere is still picking up speed.

Two and a half years later I slept under the midnight sun at the other end of our planet, in a small tent pitched on a twelve-foot-thick slab of ice floating in the frigid Arctic Ocean. After a hearty breakfast, my companions and I traveled by snowmobiles a few miles farther north to a rendezvous point where the ice was thinner—only three and a half feet thick—and a nuclear submarine hovered in the water below. After it crashed through the ice, took on its new passengers, and resubmerged, I talked with scientists who were trying to measure more accurately the thickness of the polar ice cap, which many believe is thinning as a result of global

10

warming. I had just negotiated an agreement between ice scientists and the U.S. Navy to secure the release of previously top secret data from submarine sonar tracks, data that could help them learn what is happening to the north polar cap. Now, I wanted to see the pole itself, and some eight hours after we met the submarine, we were crashing through that ice, surfacing, and then I was standing in an eerily beautiful snowscape, windswept and sparkling white, with the horizon defined by little hummocks, or "pressure ridges" of ice that are pushed up like tiny mountain ranges when separate sheets collide. But here too, CO_2 levels are rising just as rapidly, and ultimately temperatures will rise with them—indeed, global warming is expected to push temperatures up much more rapidly in the polar regions than in the rest of the world. As the polar air warms, the ice here will thin; and since the polar cap plays such a crucial role in the world's weather system, the consequences of a thinning cap could be disastrous.

Considering such scenarios is not a purely speculative exercise. Six months after I returned from the North Pole, a team of scientists reported dramatic changes in the pattern of ice distribution in the Arctic, and a second team reported a still controversial claim (which a variety of data now suggest) that, overall, the north polar cap has thinned by 2 percent in just the last decade. Moreover, scientists established several years ago that in many land areas north of the Arctic Circle, the spring snowmelt now comes earlier every year, and deep in the tundra below, the temperature of the earth is steadily rising.

As it happens, some of the most disturbing images of environmental destruction can be found exactly halfway between the North and South poles—precisely at the equator in Brazil—where billowing clouds of smoke regularly blacken the sky above the immense but now threatened Amazon rain forest. Acre by acre, the rain forest is being burned to create fast pasture for fast-food beef; as I learned when I went there in early 1989, the fires are set earlier and earlier in the dry season now, with more than one Tennessee's worth of rain forest being slashed and burned each year. According to our guide, the biologist Tom Lovejoy, there are more different species of birds in each square mile of the Amazon than exist in all of North America—which means we are silencing thousands of songs we have never even heard.

But for most of us the Amazon is a distant place, and we scarcely notice the disappearance of these and other vulnerable species. We ignore these losses at our peril, however. They're like the proverbial miners' canaries, silent alarms whose message in this case is that living species of animals and plants are now vanishing around the world *one thousand times faster* than at any time in the past 65 million years (see illustration).

To be sure, the deaths of some of the larger and more spectacular animal species now under siege do occasionally capture our attention. I have also visited another place along the equator, East Africa, where I

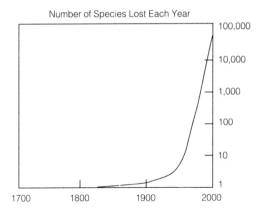

Number of Species Lost Each Year

This graph portrays the estimated loss of living species from 1700 to 1992. The normal or "background"
rate of extinction remained essentially unchanged for
the last 65 million years—from the disappearance of
the dinosaurs along with countless other species at the
end of the Cretaceous era until the present century.

encountered the grotesquely horrible image of a dead elephant, its head
mutilated by poachers who had dug out its valuable tusks with chain saws.
Clearly, we need to change our purely aesthetic consideration of ivory,
since its source is now so threatened. To me, its translucent whiteness
seems different now, like evidence of the ghostly presence of a troubled
spirit, a beautiful but chill apparition, inspiring both wonder and dread.

A similar apparition lies just beneath the ocean. While scuba diving   15
in the Caribbean, I have seen and touched the white bones of a dead coral
reef. All over the earth, coral reefs have suddenly started to "bleach" as
warmer ocean temperatures put unaccustomed stress on the tiny organisms
that normally live in the skin of the coral and give the reef its natural
coloration. As these organisms—nicknamed "zooks"—leave the membrane of the coral, the coral itself becomes transparent, allowing its white
limestone skeleton to shine through—hence its bleached appearance. In
the past, bleaching was almost always an occasional and temporary phenomenon, but repeated episodes can exhaust the coral. In the last few
years, scientists have been shocked at the sudden occurrence of extensive
worldwide bleaching episodes from which increasing numbers of coral
reefs have failed to recover. Though dead, they shine more brightly than
before, haunted perhaps by the same ghost that gives spectral light to an
elephant's tusk.

But one doesn't have to travel around the world to witness humankind's assault on the earth. Images that signal the distress of our global

environment are now commonly seen almost anywhere. A few miles from the Capitol, for example, I encountered another startling image of nature out of place. Driving in the Arlington, Virginia, neighborhood where my family and I live when the Senate is in session, I stepped on the brake to avoid hitting a large pheasant walking across the street. It darted between the parked cars, across the sidewalk, and into a neighbor's backyard. Then it was gone. But this apparition of wildness persisted in my memory as a puzzle: Why would a pheasant, let alone such a large and beautiful mature specimen, be out for a walk in my neighborhood? Was it a much wilder place than I had noticed? Were pheasants, like the trendy Vietnamese potbellied pigs, becoming the latest fashion in unusual pets? I didn't solve the mystery until weeks later, when I remembered that about three miles away, along the edge of the river, developers were bulldozing the last hundred acres of untouched forest in the entire area. As the woods fell to make way for more concrete, more buildings, parking lots, and streets, the wild things that lived there were forced to flee. Most of the deer were hit by cars; other creatures—like the pheasant that darted into my neighbor's backyard—made it a little farther.

Ironically, before I understood the mystery, I felt vaguely comforted to imagine that perhaps this urban environment, so similar to the one in which many Americans live, was not so hostile to wild things after all. I briefly supposed that, like the resourceful raccoons and possums and squirrels and pigeons, all of whom have adapted to life in the suburbs, creatures as wild as pheasants might have a fighting chance. Now I remember that pheasant when I take my children to the zoo and see an elephant or a rhinoceros. They too inspire wonder and sadness. They too remind me that we are creating a world that is hostile to wildness, that seems to prefer concrete to natural landscapes. We are encountering these creatures on a path we have paved—one that ultimately leads to their extinction.

On some nights, in high northern latitudes, the sky itself offers another ghostly image that signals the loss of ecological balance now in progress. If the sky is clear after sunset—and if you are watching from a place where pollution hasn't blotted out the night sky altogether—you can sometimes see a strange kind of cloud high in the sky. This "noctilucent cloud" occasionally appears when the earth is first cloaked in the evening darkness; shimmering above us with a translucent whiteness, these clouds seem quite unnatural. And they should: noctilucent clouds have begun to appear more often because of a huge buildup of methane gas in the atmosphere. (Also called natural gas, methane is released from landfills, from coal mines and rice paddies, from billions of termites that swarm through the freshly cut forestland, from the burning of biomass and from a variety of other human activities.) Even though noctilucent clouds were sometimes seen in the past, all this extra methane carries more water vapor into the upper atmosphere, where it condenses at much higher altitudes to form more clouds that the sun's rays still strike long after sunset has brought the beginning of night to the surface far beneath them.

What should we feel toward these ghosts in the sky? Simple wonder or the mix of emotions we feel at the zoo? Perhaps we should feel awe for our own power: just as men tear tusks from elephants' heads in such quantity as to threaten the beast with extinction, we are ripping matter from its place in the earth in such volume as to upset the balance between daylight and darkness. In the process, we are once again adding to the threat of global warming, because methane has been one of the fastest-growing greenhouse gases, and is third only to carbon dioxide and water vapor in total volume, changing the chemistry of the upper atmosphere. But, without even considering that threat, shouldn't it startle us that we have now put these clouds in the evening sky which glisten with a spectral light? Or have our eyes adjusted so completely to the bright lights of civilization that we can't see these clouds for what they are—a physical manifestation of the violent collision between human civilization and the earth?

Even though it is sometimes hard to see their meaning, we have by now all witnessed surprising experiences that signal the damage from our assault on the environment—whether it's the new frequency of days when the temperature exceeds 100 degrees, the new speed with which the sun burns our skin, or the new constancy of public debate over what to do with growing mountains of waste. But our response to these signals is puzzling. Why haven't we launched a massive effort to save our environment? To come at the question another way: Why do some images startle us into immediate action and focus our attention on ways to respond effectively? And why do other images, though sometimes equally dramatic, produce instead a kind of paralysis, focusing our attention not on ways to respond but rather on some convenient, less painful distraction? [20]

In a roundabout way, my visit to the North Pole caused me to think about these questions from a different perspective and gave them a new urgency. On the submarine, I had several opportunities to look through the periscope at the translucent bottom of the ice pack at the North Pole. The sight was not a little claustrophobic, and at one point I suddenly thought of the three whales that had become trapped under the ice of the Beaufort Sea a couple of years earlier. Television networks from four continents came to capture their poignant struggle for air and in the process so magnified the emotions felt around the world that soon scientists and rescue workers flocked to the scene. After several elaborate schemes failed, a huge icebreaker from the Soviet Union cut a path through the ice for the two surviving whales. Along with millions of others, I had been delighted to see them go free, but there on the submarine it occurred to me that if we are causing 100 extinctions each day—and many scientists believe we are—approximately 2,000 living species had disappeared from the earth during the whales' ordeal. They disappeared forever—unnoticed.

Similarly, when a little girl named Jessica McClure fell into a well in Texas, her ordeal and subsequent rescue by a legion of heroic men and women attracted hundreds of television cameras and journalists who sent the story into the homes and minds of hundreds of millions of people. Here, too, our response seems skewed: during the three days of Jessica's ordeal, more than 100,000 boys and girls her age or younger died of preventable causes—mostly starvation and diarrhea—due to failures of both crops and politics. As they struggled for life, none of these children looked into a collection of television cameras, anxious to send word of their plight to a waiting world. They died virtually unnoticed. Why?

Perhaps one part of the answer lies in the perceived difficulty of an effective response. If the problem portrayed in the image is one whose solution appears to involve more effort or sacrifice than we can readily imagine, or if even maximum effort by any one individual would fail to prevent the tragedy, we are tempted to sever the link between stimulus and moral response. Then, once a response is deemed impossible, the image that briefly caused us to consider responding becomes not just startling but painful. At that point, we begin to react not to the image but to the pain it now produces, thus severing a more basic link in our relationship to the world: the link between our senses and our emotions. Our eyes glaze over as our hearts close. We look but we don't see. We hear but refuse to listen.

Still, there are so many distressing images of environmental destruction that sometimes it seems impossible to know how to absorb or comprehend them. Before considering the threats themselves, it may be helpful to classify them and thus begin to organize our thoughts and feelings so that we may be able to respond appropriately.

A useful system comes from the military, which frequently places a conflict in one of three different categories, according to the theater in which it takes place. There are "local" skirmishes, "regional" battles, and "strategic" conflicts. This third category is reserved for struggles that can threaten a nation's survival and must be understood in a global context.

Environmental threats can be considered in the same way. For example, most instances of water pollution, air pollution, and illegal waste dumping are essentially local in nature. Problems like acid rain, the contamination of underground aquifers, and large oil spills are fundamentally regional. In both of these categories, there may be so many similar instances of particular local and regional problems occurring simultaneously all over the world that the pattern appears to be global, but the problems themselves are still not truly strategic because the operation of the global environment is not affected and the survival of civilization is not at stake.

However, a new class of environmental problems does affect the global ecological system, and these threats are fundamentally strategic. The 600 percent increase in the amount of chlorine in the atmosphere during the last forty years has taken place not just in those countries producing the chlorofluorocarbons responsible but in the air above every country, above Antarctica, above the North Pole and the Pacific Ocean—all the way from the surface of the earth to the top of the sky. The increased levels of chlorine disrupt the global process by which the earth regulates

25

the amount of ultraviolet radiation from the sun that is allowed through the atmosphere to the surface; and if we let chlorine levels continue to increase, the radiation levels will also increase—to the point that all animal and plant life will face a new threat to their survival.

Global warming is also a strategic threat. The concentration of carbon dioxide and other heat-absorbing molecules has increased by almost 25 percent since World War II, posing a worldwide threat to the earth's ability to regulate the amount of heat from the sun retained in the atmosphere. This increase in heat seriously threatens the global climate equilibrium that determines the pattern of winds, rainfall, surface temperatures, ocean currents, and sea level. These in turn determine the distribution of vegetative and animal life on land and sea and have a great effect on the location and pattern of human societies.

In other words, the entire relationship between humankind and the earth has been transformed because our civilization is suddenly capable of affecting the entire global environment, not just a particular area. All of us know that human civilization has usually had a large impact on the environment; to mention just one example, there is evidence that even in prehistoric times, vast areas were sometimes intentionally burned by people in their search for food. And in our own time we have reshaped a large part of the earth's surface with concrete in our cities and carefully tended rice paddies, pastures, wheatfields, and other croplands in the countryside. But these changes, while sometimes appearing to be pervasive, have, until recently, been relatively trivial factors in the global ecological system. Indeed, until our lifetime, it was always safe to assume that nothing we did or could do would have any lasting effect on the global environment. But it is precisely that assumption which must now be discarded so that we can think strategically about our new relationship to the environment.

Human civilization is now the dominant cause of change in the   *30* global environment. Yet we resist this truth and find it hard to imagine that our effect on the earth must now be measured by the same yardstick used to calculate the strength of the moon's pull on the oceans or the force of the wind against the mountains. And if we are now capable of changing something so basic as the relationship between the earth and the sun, surely we must acknowledge a new responsibility to use that power wisely and with appropriate restraint. So far, however, we seem oblivious of the fragility of the earth's natural systems.

This century has witnessed dramatic changes in two key factors that define the physical reality of our relationship to the earth: a sudden and startling surge in human population, with the addition of one China's worth of people every ten years, and a sudden acceleration of the scientific and technological revolution, which has allowed an almost unimaginable magnification of our power to affect the world around us by burning, cutting, digging, moving, and transforming the physical matter that makes up the earth.

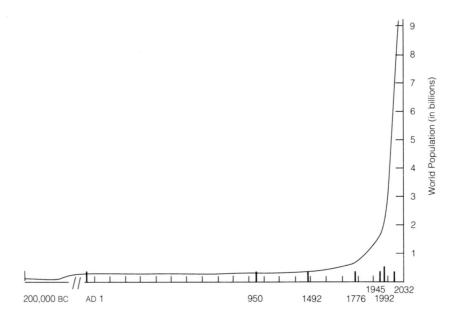

World population, after remaining stable for most of history, began to grow gradually after the agricultural revolution a few thousand years ago. This slow rate of increase continued until the onset of the industrial revolution, when the curve began sloping upward. In this century, the rate of increase has accelerated so rapidly that an extra billion people are being added to the population each decade. By the beginning of 1992, the population had climbed to almost 5.5 billion. By the year 2032, it is expected to reach 9 billion.

The surge in population is both a cause of the changed relationship and one of the clearest illustrations of how startling the change has been, especially when viewed in a historical context. From the emergence of modern humans 200,000 years ago until Julius Caesar's time, fewer than 250 million people walked on the face of the earth. When Christopher Columbus set sail for the New World 1,500 years later, there were approximately 500 million people on earth. By the time Thomas Jefferson wrote the Declaration of Independence in 1776, the number had doubled again, to 1 billion. By midway through this century, at the end of World War II, the number had risen to just above 2 billion people.

In other words, from the beginning of humanity's appearance on earth to 1945, it took more than ten thousand generations to reach a world population of 2 billion people. Now, in the course of one human lifetime—mine—the world population will increase from 2 to more than 9 billion, and it is already more than halfway there (see the graph on the following pages).

Like the population explosion, the scientific and technological revolution began to pick up speed slowly during the eighteenth century. And this ongoing revolution has also suddenly accelerated exponentially. For example, it is now an axiom in many fields of science that more new and important discoveries have taken place in the last ten years than in the entire previous history of science. While no single discovery has had the kind of effect on our relationship to the earth that nuclear weapons have had on our relationship to warfare, it is nevertheless true that taken together, they have completely transformed our cumulative ability to exploit the earth for sustenance—making the consequences of unrestrained exploitation every bit as unthinkable as the consequences of unrestrained nuclear war.

Now that our relationship to the earth has changed so utterly, we   *35* have to see that change and understand its implications. Our challenge is to recognize that the startling images of environmental destruction now occurring all over the world have much more in common than their ability to shock and awaken us. They are symptoms of an underlying problem broader in scope and more serious than any we have ever faced. Global warming, ozone depletion, the loss of living species, deforestation—they all have a common cause: the new relationship between human civilization and the earth's natural balance.

There are actually two aspects to this challenge. The first is to realize that our power to harm the earth can indeed have global and even permanent effects. The second is to realize that the only way to understand our new role as a co-architect of nature is to see ourselves as part of a complex system that does not operate according to the same simple rules of cause and effect we are used to. The problem is not our effect *on* the environment so much as our relationship *with* the environment. As a result, any solution to the problem will require a careful assessment of that relationship as well as the complex interrelationship among factors within civilization and between them and the major natural components of the earth's ecological system.

There is only one precedent for this kind of challenge to our thinking, and again it is military. The invention of nuclear weapons and the subsequent development by the United States and the Soviet Union of many thousands of strategic nuclear weapons forced a slow and painful recognition that the new power thus acquired forever changed not only the relationship between the two superpowers but also the relationship of humankind to the institution of warfare itself. The consequences of all-out war between nations armed with nuclear weapons suddenly included the possibility of the destruction of both nations—completely and simultaneously. That sobering realization led to a careful reassessment of every aspect of our mutual relationship to the prospect of such a war. As early as 1946 one strategist concluded that strategic bombing with missiles "may well tear away the veil of illusion that has so long obscured the reality of the change in warfare—from a fight to a process of destruction."

Nevertheless, during the earlier stages of the nuclear arms race, each of the superpowers assumed that its actions would have a simple and direct effect on the thinking of the other. For decades, each new advance in weaponry was deployed by one side for the purpose of inspiring fear in the other. But each such deployment led to an effort by the other to leapfrog the first one with a more advanced deployment of its own. Slowly, it has become apparent that the problem of the nuclear arms race is not primarily caused by technology. It is complicated by technology, true; but it arises out of the relationship between the superpowers and is based on an obsolete understanding of what war is all about.

The eventual solution to the arms race will be found, not in a new deployment by one side or the other of some ultimate weapon or in a decision by either side to disarm unilaterally, but rather in new understandings and in a mutual transformation of the relationship itself. This transformation will involve changes in the technology of weaponry and the denial of nuclear technology to rogue states. But the key changes will be in the way we think about the institution of warfare and about the relationship between states.

The strategic nature of the threat now posed *by* human civilization   40
to the global environment and the strategic nature of the threat *to* human civilization now posed by changes in the global environment present us with a similar set of challenges and false hopes. Some argue that a new ultimate technology, whether nuclear power or genetic engineering, will solve the problem. Others hold that only a drastic reduction of our reliance on technology can improve the conditions of life—a simplistic notion at best. But the real solution will be found in reinventing and finally healing the relationship between civilization and the earth. This can only be accomplished by undertaking a careful reassessment of all the factors that led to the relatively recent dramatic change in the relationship. The transformation of the way we relate to the earth will of course involve new technologies, but the key changes will involve new ways of thinking about the relationship itself.

Reading and Responding

How much of this information did you already know? How much was unfamiliar to you? Write about this for at least half a page.

Working Together

1. In a few sentences, record your reaction to the disasters Gore catalogues. How did you feel when you were finished with this piece?
2. Who do you think Gore had in mind as his audience? What effect did he want to have on his audience?
3. Consider Gore's major strategies and their effects on you and others in the class: the use of personal experience and narrative writing; the use of graphs and charts and statistics; and particularly the tone of the

writing, its voice. Identify two parts of this writing that seem to you particularly effective, and give two reasons to account for their impact.

4. Imagine your mother or father reading this piece, or your uncle, or your next-door neighbor back home, or your best friend. What would they think about the environmental crisis before reading? What would they think of Vice President Al Gore? How would they feel during and after the reading?

Rethinking and Rewriting

1. Take one of the problems Gore catalogues and accept his statistics as reliable. Assume, furthermore, that you've been convinced by these readings, that you weren't worried about the issue before but that Gore persuaded you that the problem is real. Write a letter home to your mother or father or some other relative or friend willing to listen to you speak seriously, someone you know who hasn't thought much about these things, someone who might even resist such talk. Do your best to explain the problem. Try to change the person's mind, make him or her receptive and concerned.

2. Take any one of the problems Gore discusses and update his research in a research paper. Check out his sources first, decide if they're reliable, and then fill in with information gathered in the years since his book was published. Are his predictions true? Have things gotten better or worse?

3. Consider Gore's essay as an effort at persuasion. Was this piece successful (did it persuade you)? On the basis of your answer here, explain the features of writing that successfully persuades you (or would successfully persuade you) on a subject like this one.

"UNDER THE SUN"

Samuel W. Matthews

A senior assistant editor for National Geographic, *Samuel Matthews here gathers together considerable data as well as information from an impressive list of experts in order to help readers understand the dynamics and issues of what has become known as "global warming" or "the greenhouse effect." This article, reprinted from the October 1990 issue, suggests both the ambition and the limitations of current science.*

Before You Read

Preread this piece and note five words or phrases that seem to describe it. From your prereading, give yourself two pieces of useful advice about how to read this selection. Write them down briefly.

The road up earth's most massive mountain—Mauna Loa on the Big Island of Hawaii—is a narrow, twisting strip of tar, laid by prison labor through raw, jagged lava fields. You can drive it—with great caution and constant awe—to a small cluster of white and blue huts standing more than two miles high in the clear, cool Pacific sky.

Here for 32 years the level of carbon dioxide in the earth's atmosphere has been recorded daily at the Mauna Loa Observatory by Charles David Keeling of the Scripps Institution of Oceanography and by scientists from the National Oceanic and Atmospheric Administration (NOAA). And for 32 years the level has risen, in a wavy curve of spring-fall variations . . . , from 315 parts per million (ppm) in 1958 to more than 355 in mid-1990.

That steadily climbing CO_2 level (air locked in glacial ice a century ago held only about 280 ppm—25 percent less) is an incontrovertible measure of what man and his machines have done to the atmosphere of the earth in scarcely one lifetime. Because of it, say many scientists who study the climate, our planet is bound to become warmer—has already warmed—as more and more energy from the sun is caught and held in the thin blanket of air around us.

"As Pogo put it, the enemy is us," said Elmer Robinson, director of Mauna Loa Observatory, while we drove together up the desolate slope of the volcano. "By burning more and more fossil fuel—gasoline, natural gas, coal, peat—even ordinary firewood, we are putting into the air more of the gases that act much like a globe of glass around the planet. That's what's called the greenhouse effect.

"Up here we measure not only CO_2," he went on, as he led me through a laboratory jammed with humming recorders and glowing computer terminals. "We also read methane, chlorofluorocarbons, nitrous ox-   *5* ide, and ozone, all of which add to the warming. We see and measure dust of various sizes in the troposphere, the weather layer of the atmosphere."

Such data, recorded by NOAA here and at American Samoa in mid-Pacific, at Point Barrow in Alaska, and at the South Pole, form the hard evidence on which climatologists base widely varying and controversial visions of the future. Average temperature worldwide, by careful calculations, has gone up about half a degree Celsius—one degree Fahrenheit—since the late 1800s.

In this century, the decade of the 1980s saw the six warmest years in weather records. Yet there are some researchers and statisticians who argue this apparent warming of the planet may be only a temporary blip, that natural warming periods have occurred before, without man's intervention, and that there is as yet no sure evidence of long-term change.

All this was in my mind under the blaze of sunlight that beautiful winter day atop Mauna Loa. Through a small occulting telescope maintained there by the National Center for Atmospheric Research at Boulder, Colorado, I stared at the darkened face of the sun, ringed by its glowing, gauzy corona.

From that blazing disk high in the Hawaiian sky comes the endless power that drives and rules all life on earth: its plant growth and the food chains of all its creatures; the winds, rains, and churning weather of the planet; the ocean currents, forests, prairies, and deserts.

Our home star in the heavens burns steadily, almost without varia- 10 tion. It is the "almost," coupled with what man's activities are doing to the atmosphere, that this story is about. It is becoming more and more apparent that the effects of the sun upon our planet are changing. Our one and only home may be in harm's way, and we can scarcely sense just what is happening—or know what to do about it.

That burning energy of our sun works the miracle on earth called photosynthesis. Powered by sunlight, plants green with chlorophyll combine carbon dioxide from the air with water from soil or sea into energy-rich carbohydrates, releasing into the atmosphere the oxygen we need to breathe.

It is the same process by which primitive bacteria of ocean shallows, more than two billion years ago, first produced enough oxygen to permit other life on earth to develop. And it is the same process—still imperfectly understood—that grows the corn of Iowa, the grass of your lawn, the rain forests of Brazil, the floating plankton that sustains life in the seas.

"Without carbon dioxide in the atmosphere, life as we know it would be impossible," Elmer Robinson had said on Mauna Loa. "We couldn't exist if it weren't for greenhouse warming."

About half of the radiant energy reaching earth from the sun, because of its short wavelengths, can pass through the atmosphere to the earth's surface. But the longer waves of heat that radiate back toward space are absorbed and reradiated by water vapor, carbon dioxide, other gases, and clouds, and the atmosphere warms.

"That's the greenhouse effect," Elmer had said. "Without it, earth   *15*
would be frozen—at least 60 degrees Fahrenheit colder—and there would
be no more life here than on Mars. But if it were to increase. . . . Well,
some climatologists say we face temperatures three to nine degrees higher
in the next century."

Back in the last glacial age, some 20,000 years ago, world temperature
averaged about nine degrees colder than today. The carbon dioxide level
was only 190 to 200 parts per million, ancient ice samples from Greenland
and Antarctica show. As the ice melted back, the CO_2 level gradually rose
to about 280 ppm by the beginning of the industrial age.

"By the middle of the coming century—in our children's lifetime,"
Elmer had said, "the level will reach 550 or even 600 at its current rate
of rise."

The prospect of doubled CO_2—and even more rapid rise of other
gases, such as methane, which together equal the warming effect of CO_2 in
the atmosphere—is what has atmospheric scientists urgently refining their
computer models of the climate. World population also is predicted to double by the middle of the next century, from five billion people to ten. And
as all nations become more developed and use more fuel to support those
people, the release of carbon dioxide and other gases to the air is bound to
keep increasing—despite the care taken or which fuels are burned.

With more warmth and more CO_2, some ask, would not more crops
grow, in wider areas than today? Would we not benefit from a warmer world?

Perhaps, in some areas. The more CO_2 in the air, the more produc-   *20*
tive some plants become. But the biggest unknown is what changes would
occur in the planet's weather patterns.

Most climate models show that in some regions—northern Scandi-
navia, Siberia, and Canada, for example—more rain would fall and more
trees and crops grow. But in today's great mid-continent breadbasket
regions, warming would lead to the drying of soil in summer. Destructive
droughts, such as that of 1988 in North America, would strike more often,
until the Great Plains and Ukraine turn semidesert. Storms such as hurri-
canes and tornadoes might become more violent. Forests would decline
and change under the temperature rise, and wildlife would have to migrate—if it could—or perish. The permafrost under Arctic tundra would
thaw, deep peatlands would decompose, and vast new amounts of carbon
dioxide and methane could be released.

And just as inevitably, as ocean waters warm and expand and the ice on
Greenland and Antarctica melts back, the seas would creep higher onto the
edges of the continents. Large parts of such low countries as Bangladesh—
already swept by ruinous floods and typhoons—would be submerged; cities
like Miami, Venice, even New York, would cower behind dikes.

"If a rise of one to three feet, as the models have predicted, seems
extreme," says environmental scientist Stephen Leatherman of the University of Maryland, "keep in mind that the oceans rose more than 300 feet
after the last ice age—all in only a few thousand years."

If the ice cap on the island of Greenland were to melt completely, glaciologists estimate the oceans would rise another 20 feet. Sea level in the eastern United States has already risen a foot in this century alone, and it is predicted to go up at least another foot in the century ahead. With that one-foot rise, Leatherman says, the high-water line at Ocean City, Maryland, will move inland 100 to 200 feet; in Florida, 200 to 1,000 feet; in Louisiana, several miles.

Yet paradoxically, say other glaciologists, the huge ice domes on both Greenland and Antarctica may not be shrinking but growing. The paradox is that this too may be a sign of global warming. As the atmosphere warms, it holds more water vapor from evaporation of oceans and soil; hence more snow falls in the polar regions, hence more ice and possibly lower sea levels. But the warmer seas eventually will melt back the fringes of the polar ice, and the oceans will creep inexorably higher.

Foretelling what may happen to the world if it should warm by even one or two degrees is the toughest problem facing climatologists today. Even though there have been times in the dim geologic past when temperatures were warmer—with no ice at all on the polar regions—there are vast differences today. No one knows whether the "wild card" of human activity will disrupt or make more extreme the cycles ordained by nature.

To try to predict the effects of human intervention, scientists mathematically simulate the weather systems of the globe. Their equations, called general circulation models (GCMs), are so complex that only a few of today's supercomputers can solve them.

The equations relate such things as the balance of radiation to and from the planet, air circulation, evaporation and rainfall, ice cover, sea-surface temperature—then try to assess what might happen if the sun were to become brighter by a tiny amount or if the carbon dioxide in the atmosphere gradually doubles as expected. The computers then calculate and map the changes in the weather of future days, weeks, seasons—or centuries.

One key to their accuracy lies in how finely they divide the planet's surface, the blanket of the atmosphere, and the seas. Most now divide the globe into blocks of at least five degrees of latitude and five of longitude: 300 nautical miles on a side, roughly the size and shape of Colorado. The best models then divide the atmosphere into as many as 20 layers and add in the oceans' currents and multiple layers. The computations are so formidable that a supercomputer might take a week to run a single change of input to determine its effect.

On a high shelf of Colorado's Front Range, where deer roam in the open above the university town of Boulder, stand the sand-hued buildings of the National Center for Atmospheric Research (NCAR), one of the principal climate-modeling centers in the nation. The others are NASA's Goddard Institute for Space Studies (GISS) on upper Broadway in New

York City and NOAA's Geophysical Fluid Dynamics Laboratory (GFDL) in Princeton, New Jersey.

The computer room at NCAR, its floor carpeted with bright red squares, is a futuristic assemblage of multicolored cabinets, computer terminals, and blinking panels of lights. The chief of the center, Bill Buzbee, showed me two red-and-black cylinders, each about five feet in diameter and five feet high, with segments seemingly cut out of them like huge wedges of cheese.

"Those are our Cray supercomputers," Bill said. "Not many exist in the world. If you'd like to buy one, it might cost you about 20 million bucks. And it would not be powerful enough for much of the modeling we're asked to do."

"If our global grid were reduced to two and a half degrees on a side and the number of vertical layers increased," I had heard Jerry Mahlman, director of GFDL, say, "it would multiply the demand on the computer 16-fold; at one degree square, which might be necessary to forecast weather and climate accurately for local regions on the globe, the order of complexity—and computer time—would go up at least 500 times."

I began to appreciate what these machines do. They reduce inconceivably complicated systems of the atmosphere and oceans to logical, mathematical predictions of what might happen if man or nature changes the ways things are with the world.

All the most advanced GCMs, fed a doubling of carbon dioxide, come up with similar results: The world will warm by the middle of the next century by two to five degrees Celsius—three to nine degrees Fahrenheit—with even greater warming in the subpolar latitudes. The differences between the models show up in regional effects . . . exactly where drying or more rainfall may occur, whether the Northern and Southern Hemispheres may react differently. *35*

The modelers acknowledge they may be as much as a decade away from full confidence in their results. At GFDL they have been trying for 20 years to couple ocean circulation to the atmosphere. Syukuro Manabe, one of GFDL's most noted modelers . . . , admits that in the early days "all sorts of crazy things happened [in the computer] . . . sea ice covered the tropical oceans, for example."

Another noted climate modeler—and spokesman for potential trouble—is James Hansen, director of NASA's Goddard Institute (GISS) in New York City. . . . During the scorching hot, dry summer of 1988 he captured international attention when he testified before a Senate subcommittee.

"The world is getting warmer," he said bluntly. "We can state with 99 percent confidence that current temperatures represent a real global warming trend, rather than a chance fluctuation. We will surely have more years like this—more droughts and many more days above a hundred degrees—in the 1990s."

He repeated these predictions in subsequent scientific meetings and climate symposiums—upsetting colleagues who felt he should hedge his concerns with more qualifications and maybes. But that is not Jim Hansen's way.

Some have heard and heeded what he and others have been saying. 40 Senator Albert Gore, Jr., of Tennessee, one of the most outspoken politicians calling for action in the face of world warming, has said bluntly: "The greenhouse effect is the most important environmental problem we have ever faced. [It threatens] loss of forests, widespread drought and famine, loss of wild species . . . topsoil, stratospheric ozone. . . . Do we have the capacity, the will, to change habits of millennia in a generation?"

Stephen H. Schneider of NCAR, an intense, curly-haired prophet of the future, has been deeply involved in climate research for more than 20 years. He writes, speaks, and travels incessantly; he is one of the worried scientists to whom policy-makers listen carefully.

"I agree with Jim Hansen and others that the world has gotten warmer over the past century—faster than ever since about 1975," he told me. "I'm not so quick to say it's entirely due to the greenhouse effect—though that's certainly there. Natural climate variations may be at work too, reinforcing—or at other times masking—the greenhouse forcing. In coming decades some years and some parts of the world may be cooler, but others will be much warmer than normal.

"The 1988 drought in North America, for example, has been linked by colleagues at NCAR with the El Niño phenomenon of the tropical Pacific Ocean. A shift in the jet stream, caused by massive ocean-atmosphere interactions in the Pacific, was the likely cause of that hot, extremely dry summer.

"But whatever the local and temporary weather changes, the world can't wait for proof of warming before trying to do something about it. We're engaged in a huge experiment, using our earth as the laboratory, and the experiment is irreversible. By the time we find the greenhouse warming *has* damaged earth's ability to feed its people, it will be too late to do much about it."

What would he have us do about it now? Try to slow the release of 45 greenhouse gases—by more rigorous energy conservation and changes in fuel use (natural gas releases half as much CO_2 as coal); by reducing the burning of rain forests, which increases the level of CO_2 in the air; and by planting many more trees, wherever possible.

"Keep in mind, it's not only carbon dioxide that's at fault," Steve Schneider points out. "Methane, which is released from decomposing tundra and marshes, rice fields, termites, and the guts of cattle, is increasing in the atmosphere faster than CO_2, at something like one percent a year. And molecule for molecule it has 20 to 30 times the greenhouse effect of CO_2. Nitrogen gases, from fertilizers as well as car exhausts and factory smokestacks, chlorofluorocarbons (CFCs) and other industrial products—all the other gases we're pouring into the air—are already doubling the warming potential of CO_2 alone.

"We can hope to reduce some of them, such as the CFCs that attack stratospheric ozone," he said. "But the others go with the industrial development of the world; all we can realistically hope is to slow their release, to gain time to cope with the results.

"If we can delay a 2°C increase of global temperature from 2025 to 2050, we will have more time to develop alternate energy sources: Nuclear—possibly fusion—is one option, despite its problems. But tapping the sun directly, by solar heat plants and converting sunlight directly into electricity, is both possible and coming down in cost."

I was to see his future in California, at the Rancho Seco nuclear plant outside Sacramento, flanked by 20 acres of solar panels slowly swinging with the sun across the sky; at a pioneering solar-cell factory near Los Angeles, where a breakthrough in "thin-film" technology was closing in on conventional electric power costs; and on a treeless mountain pass above Oakland, where a seemingly endless array of propellers taps the sun's energy from the winds sweeping in off the Pacific. . . .

Computer forecasting of climate is uncertain for reasons other than the sheer complexity of the equations. There are variables and feedbacks that even the best of the models barely approach. 50

The oceans are the chief reservoir of heat, controlling weather over the entire globe. As currents such as the Gulf Stream carry the heat from the tropics to high latitudes, cold water from the polar regions sinks and flows toward the Equator, overturning the seas about every thousand years.

"The tropical oceans are the driving mechanism of the climate," says climatologist Eric J. Barron of Pennsylvania State University. "The oceans are the memory of the climate system," adds Kirk Bryan of GFDL at Princeton. Yet until recently even the most advanced mathematical models treated the oceans only as vast, shallow swamps.

Carbon dioxide is absorbed by seawater, some of it incorporated into the shells of tiny marine creatures that die and become carbonate sediments on the bottom. Scientists estimate that a significant part of the seven billion metric tons of carbon released into the air each year is taken up in the seas. Oddly, the colder the water, the more CO_2 it can hold. As the oceans warm under the effect of more CO_2 in the atmosphere, there is great uncertainty about how much of that new CO_2 will be absorbed. Is there a limit to how much carbon can be locked away? Have the oceans already reached their holding capacity?

World-famed geochemist Wallace S. Broecker of Columbia University's Lamont-Doherty Geological Observatory worries that rapid switches in ocean circulation might occur under relatively small changes in global climate. Ice and seafloor core samples show that there have been sudden climate changes in the past, he says, from warming conditions to marked glaciation and back in as little time as a century. It could happen again.

As the seas and air warm, more water evaporates into the atmosphere,   *55*
creating more clouds and another great enigma to the mathematical modelers. Much is yet unknown about the net effects of clouds on global weather.

"Clouds are the window shades of the planet," says Steve Schneider of NCAR. "They may be even more important than the oceans or the greenhouse gases in regulating the heat received from the sun."

In daylight low thick clouds reflect sunlight back into space and have a cooling effect. At night they hold in heat radiated from the surface and thus warm the atmosphere. High thin clouds, such as cirrus, may act differently, also adding to the greenhouse effect. Storm clouds transport and release vast amounts of heat.

The incredibly complicated interactions of the atmosphere, land, and oceans lead many scientists to doubt that local and regional weather patterns can ever be accurately predicted for more than a few days into the future. Listening to atmospheric physicists discuss the new mathematical science called chaos is a form of mental mugging; they speak of random walks, strange attractors, and climatic ripples such as the "butterfly effect"—the notion put forward by MIT meteorologist Edward Lorenz that the flap of a butterfly's wings in Peru could lead to a tornado in Kansas. Yet these are today's frontiers of understanding.

The limit of that understanding leads Eric Barron of Penn State to quote Mark Twain's famous droll remark: "The researches of many commentators have already thrown much darkness on this subject, and it is probable that, if they continue, we shall soon know nothing at all about it."

Feedbacks—the relationships between the natural forces that control   *60*
climate—will be the crucial key, most modelers agree: clouds affecting surface temperatures; rainfall and droughts changing soil moisture, vegetation, and evaporation; snow and ice melting from ice caps and glaciers, changing the reflectivity of the planet and raising the level of the seas.

More volcanic eruptions, throwing fine dust and gases high into the stratosphere, might operate against the greenhouse, cooling the earth temporarily. But the best computer models suggest that to bring on marked cooling, volcanic explosions far more violent than those of Mount St. Helens in 1980 or Krakatoa in 1883 would have to occur every five years for as long as a century. The resulting dirty air and acid rain would be worse for life on earth than global warming.

If a return to ice-age conditions rather than greenhouse warming sounds farfetched, it was thought a serious possibility as recently as the mid-1970s. The nine major interglacial periods of the past million years have each lasted scarcely 10,000 years before the cold returned—and it has now been longer than that since the last great continental ice sheets melted back. And even though global temperature has been rising since the start of the industrial age, from 1940 until 1970 it leveled and even declined slightly in the Northern Hemisphere.

J. Murray Mitchell, Jr., senior climate researcher of the U.S. Weather Bureau and later of NOAA's Environmental Data Service, was one of those who documented that downward drift. Now retired, he told me recently: "We thought natural forces, such as volcanic activity or perhaps variation in the sun's radiance, might be at work. But we still don't know whether it was a real change or just a quarter-century-long twitch in the climate cycle."

Does the sun blaze absolutely uniformly, sending always the same amount of light, heat, and other radiation into space? Is its total radiance constant, as has long been assumed, or does the energy received by the earth vary, even minutely? The question is crucial in today's climate studies.

From astrophysical evidence the sun is thought to have been 25 to 30 percent dimmer when the earth was young—three and a half billion years ago. Pondering how life could have developed under this "faint young sun," earth scientists postulate that a super-greenhouse effect must have been at work, with 100 to 1,000 times as much CO_2 in the atmosphere. Otherwise the surface of the planet would have been frozen solid, and photosynthesis impossible. Yet it indeed occurred, absorbing much of the carbon dioxide and producing the oxygen in the atmosphere necessary for the evolution of life.

In the time of modern science the sun's radiation has seemed absolutely steady. Astronomers have tried for more than a century to detect any change in the "solar constant." It was only in the past decade that they succeeded.

The answer lay in taking solar instruments above the unsteady window of earth's atmosphere, into the black clarity of space. That goal was reached in February 1980 with the launch of the Solar Maximum Mission (SMM) satellite, dubbed Solar Max. It went into space to read solar output just as the number of sunspots—the dark areas on the sun's face that signal changes in its magnetic activity—had reached a peak in their 11-year cycle.

By 1985 Solar Max showed a real, though very slight, decline in the sun's brightness. The drop was only about one-tenth of one percent, but to solar physicists such as Richard Willson of the Jet Propulsion Laboratory, a principal scientist of the project, it was startling. If there is an actual fluctuation of the sun's output of even that small amount, it might have a long-term, measurable effect on global weather.

In 1986 the number of sunspots reached a minimum, as predicted. Shortly after, there began a rapid increase in sunspots—greater than in any previous solar cycle of this century. Scientists expected the upturn to continue until the next peak in 1990 or '91, but an unforeseen hazard put the Solar Max project in peril.

As the sun's activity increased, it warmed the outermost fringe of earth's atmosphere slightly, causing it to expand. The added drag began to slow the satellite, and it dropped in its orbit by a few kilometers. Instead of circling the planet at least until 1991, Solar Max began tumbling in August 1989, and by early December ended its life as a fireball of blazing metal in the sky.

"Even without the Solar Max readings—long before this century, in fact—we've known that changes occur in the sun," I heard from John A. Eddy of the Office for Interdisciplinary Earth Studies in Boulder. He is one of the world's leading solar historians.

"Chinese, Korean, and Japanese court astronomers recorded spots on the sun at least 2,000 years ago. Galileo saw them in his first telescope in 1610. The fact that the spots varied on a regular cycle wasn't recognized until 1843, by a German amateur astronomer, Heinrich Schwabe. Their number and position changed, and in some years there were more of them, in other years and decades, many fewer.

"We know today," Jack Eddy went on, "that the spots not only are real but also indicate massive changes going on in the sun. As the spots cross its face—moving with the rotating body—they affect the total energy the sun sends out into space."

As outward evidence of magnetic disturbances on the sun, the spots sometimes herald solar storms or flares, which can disrupt short-wave radio communications on earth or with satellites and cause destructive surges in high-voltage power networks. In March 1989 a massive solar flare disrupted the electric-power grid of much of eastern Canada and produced spectacular shimmering lights in the ionosphere. . . . The pulsating red, green, and white curtains called the aurora borealis, or northern lights, were seen as far south as Florida and Texas.

Do sunspots affect the planet's weather and climate? There have been 75 times in past centuries when sunspots were very scarce—or missing entirely, if lack of any record of them can be believed. One notable period was between 1645 and 1715, the so-called Maunder Minimum, named for a British solar astronomer of the 19th century. The coincidence of their absence with the particularly cold period of the Little Ice Age, which gripped Europe from the 1400s to the 1800s, has long intrigued solar scientists.

Eddy and other astrophysicists point to the Maunder and a sequence of earlier minimums as the clearest evidence of long-term change in the sun's total activity, perhaps in cycles longer than the principal periods of 11 and 22 years, and of a possible connection between sunspots and the earth's climate.

The evidence remains circumstantial. "But there can be little doubt," Eddy has written, "that variability is a real feature of the sun. The challenge now is to understand it."

One clue to sunspots and their effects on the earth lies in an unlikely repository—the record of weather changes locked in the growth rings of trees. At the Laboratory of Tree-Ring Research of the University of

Arizona at Tucson, director Malcolm Hughes and others showed me the 8,500-year consecutive tree-ring record acquired by that pioneering laboratory in decades of work in the U.S. Southwest. Periods of faster and slower growth in tree rings since the 17th century have been linked to wet periods and droughts—and possibly to the sunspot cycle.

"There is clear variability in much of this tree-ring record, in a pulse close to 20 years," Hughes said. "Scientists such as Murray Mitchell and my colleague Charles Stockton see this pulse as a combination of the sunspot cycle and a lunar cycle of 18.6 years and relate it to cyclical droughts in the West, such as the 1930s Dust Bowl.

"More than that, varying amounts of a carbon isotope in the tree rings—carbon 14—may be a clue to long-term changes in solar radiation and its effect on the earth's atmosphere," Hughes told me.   80

"The irregularities in the carbon-14 production rate are known as the Suess wiggles, for Hans E. Suess, their discoverer. They are extremely important in calibrating and correcting the carbon-14 calendar used to date ancient events from remnants of organic materials, such as ancient wood or bones."

Other theories of sunspot-climate relationships have come and gone, but no true "smoking gun" had been found—until the mid-1980s. Then a German atmospheric physicist, Karin Labitzke of the Free University of Berlin, together with Harry van Loon of NCAR in Boulder, published a remarkable fit between reversing winds in the stratosphere, polar air temperatures, and the sunspot cycle. If their discovery is confirmed, it will indicate a direct link between sunspots and the atmosphere of earth—a possibly crucial connection. The work has been cited as among the most significant now being pursued at NCAR.

One connection may be a better understanding of the ozone hole in the so-called polar vortex over Antarctica each winter, a giant whirlpool of stratospheric winds.

In the mid-1980s the world became suddenly aware that the protective ozone shield in the atmosphere was in danger—was, in fact, greatly depleted in a huge "hole" over the frozen wastes of Antarctica. The mysterious stuff called ozone, which until then was known to the public chiefly as an acrid, lung-burning element of smog in overcrowded cities, was being destroyed in the stratosphere by chemicals made and released in the 20th century by humans.

Ozone is a variant form of oxygen—the most life-sustaining gas of   85
all. Under the intense ultraviolet bombardment from the sun at the upper reaches of the earth's atmosphere, normal two-atom molecules of oxygen are split into single atoms—O rather than O_2, in chemists' terms. Some of these single oxygen atoms rejoin with O_2 molecules to form ozone—O_3. The amount in the stratosphere is very scant, less than ten parts per million (at sea level the layer would be about as thick as a pane of window glass), but that layer is enough to stop most of the sun's

dangerous ultraviolet rays from reaching the earth's surface, 10 to 30 miles below.

The possibility of ozone destruction by man-made chemicals had been predicted as early as 1974 by two farsighted researchers, F. Sherwood Rowland and Mario J. Molina, at the University of California at Irvine.

Certain industrial gases dubbed CFCs—chlorofluorocarbons—are so highly stable and inert that they do not react with other substances in nature. Thus they have long been used as the coolants in refrigerators and air conditioners, as the propellants in aerosol cans, in making foam-plastic objects such as coffee cups and fast-food containers, and as solvents for cleaning electronic circuit boards and computer chips. But there could be great danger, warned Rowland and Molina, when those same long-lived gases drift to the upper layers of the atmosphere.

In that same region where ozone is created by solar bombardment, the CFCs could break apart, they postulated, freeing chlorine atoms that could attack and destroy ozone molecules by the billions. If this were to deplete the ozone layer around the whole world, it would put all mankind at risk.

The hazard was judged serious enough for the United States to ban CFCs from aerosol cans in the late 1970s. But CFCs are still produced for other uses, and millions of tons more lie waiting to be freed from scrapped refrigerators and air conditioners.

Then came the first startling report by British scientists in 1985 of an 90 Antarctic ozone hole, and a rash of scare stories blossomed in the world's press. Emergency field studies of the stratosphere above Antarctica were mounted by U.S. science agencies, led by NASA, NOAA, and the National Science Foundation. In 1987 an ER-2 aircraft, capable of flying to 70,000 feet in the stratosphere, and a DC-8 jammed with instruments flew from Punta Arenas, Chile, near the tip of South America, out across the ice-locked Antarctic continent.

The hole was real; the ozone had dropped by 50 percent. . . . Its destruction was confined within the rotating swirl of winds in the polar vortex. And it was caused by a chemical reaction, not some unfathomed atmospheric phenomenon. The reaction seemed to occur in the presence of thin polar ice clouds that form in the intense cold of late winter, just before the sun returns to strike the polar latitudes.

Less than a year later, in September 1987, more than 40 nations sent delegates to Montreal, Canada. The industrialized countries agreed to reduce production of CFCs by 50 percent by 1998. A June 1990 revision called for a 100 percent ban by the year 2000, with a ten-year time lag for less developed nations.

Does another ozone hole develop over the Arctic in its winter? If the Northern Hemisphere, far more populous than the Southern, is also being depleted of its ozone umbrella, it might pose a far more serious emergency.

The same team of atmospheric scientists and computer experts, including Robert Watson of NASA and Adrian Tuck and Susan Solomon of

NOAA, spent 45 cold, bleak days in January and February 1989 in the North Sea port of Stavanger, Norway. There the same ER-2 and DC-8 flew 28 missions, from the northernmost airstrip that could safely be used, to take readings from the air of the polar Arctic.

It took a year to analyze all the data. In March 1990 the scientists *95* published their answer. The polar vortex and ice clouds existed also in the northern stratosphere, though not to the same extent as in the southern. Ozone was being depleted in the Arctic as well, by as much as 15 to 17 percent at some altitudes.

Over the heavily populated mid-latitudes of the globe, the researchers believe, winter ozone levels may have dropped in the past decade by as much as 4 to 6 percent. And even if all CFC production worldwide were to be halted—an unlikely possibility even to the signers of the Montreal Protocol—the amount already existing and waiting to be released to the atmosphere would mean a continuing ozone drop for decades to come.

The worry is that stratospheric ozone forms the earth's principal shield against dangerous ultraviolet radiation from the sun. This short wavelength light, below the range of human visibility, kills many forms of life—bacteria, for example, which is why it is used for sterilizing surgical instruments and protecting many foods. But ultraviolet also kills beneficial forms of life, and it can affect the life cycle of many plants, both on land and in the seas.

Middle and long wavelengths of UV cause not just tanning and extreme sunburn in human skin but the most prevalent forms of skin cancer. They also can cause cataracts in the eyes and injure the immune responses of skin, which protect us from many harmful, even deadly diseases.

The Environmental Protection Agency issued a risk assessment in 1987, predicting that for every one percent drop in global ozone, there would be a one to three percent increase in skin cancers. Global ozone has dropped at least 2 percent in the past ten years, EPA said, leading to possibly four million added cases of skin cancer. In the past ten years alone, dangerous skin cancers have risen by 50 percent. Because of the long latency periods after exposure, doctors believe that case numbers will escalate even faster in coming decades.

As the public and bodies politic become ever more aware of these *100* issues and hazards to our home planet, the fundamental question remains: What can be done to safeguard our future?

Much is being proposed, both in this country and in international conferences and discussions among heads of state. Some scientists worry that not enough is yet known about the atmosphere and climate systems to justify spartan proposals of sacrifice and denial. Others counter that *something* must be done before it is too late.

One ambitious effort is the International Geosphere-Biosphere Programme (IGBP). In 1992 it will begin a 10-to-20-year study of the planet, a massive, coordinated follow-up to the historic International Geophysical Year of the mid-1950s.

In this country, planning has been taken on by the National Academy of Sciences and a federal committee whose members include NASA, NOAA, the Environmental Protection Agency, the Departments of Energy, Agriculture, and Defense, the National Science Foundation, and other agencies. Each has its own projects, such as NASA's Mission to Planet Earth, a proposed 15-to-20-billion-dollar program to study the planet from space platforms to be launched beginning in 1998. The President's budget for fiscal 1991 includes an additional billion dollars for pursuing such research efforts.

NASA's chief scientist for global change, Ichtiaque Rasool, in mid-1989 cited to me some of the basic hard facts on which the world's climatologists largely agree:

• The trace gases in the atmosphere—carbon dioxide, methane, nitrous oxide, CFCs—are rising rapidly. They are already at the highest levels of the past 160,000 years.

• These gases incontrovertibly alter the earth's radiation balance through the greenhouse effect.

• Average global temperature has risen about one degree Fahrenheit in the past century, though not steadily.

But will this unusual warmth continue? Or will cooler-than-normal *105* seasons or years return? And what is "normal"?

It is the central uncertainty about natural versus man-made forces in the climate system that causes scientists and politicians alike to hedge their concerns. It is tempting to ask: If nature will correct what we do to the atmosphere, must we give up our profligate ways?

As evidence mounts, the answer seems increasingly clear: We are the wild card in nature, in our ever increasing numbers. "Humankind has become a more important agent of environmental change than nature," Frank Press, president of the U.S. National Academy of Sciences, said bluntly at an international meeting of the Group of Seven industrial nations in Paris in mid-1989.

And what we are doing to the earth's atmosphere, to the blue planet on which we live, is not merely ominous. It may already be beyond correction.

Reading and Responding

1. Write down all the numbers and statistics that seem most important to you in this piece.
2. Look now at your list. Circle the most important fact or statistic, the one that explains the most or bothers you the most.

Working Together

1. Share, as a class, the statistics, numbers, and facts that seemed most central. Write them on the board. Does one number or fact stand out to everyone? Are there different numbers and facts striking the class? Are the numbers and facts related, one set contained in another?
2. Translate those numbers into words; that is, summarize, in your own words, the main point of this essay.
3. Describe the way you felt after reading all these statistics.

Rethinking and Rewriting

1. Write an essay about any subject in which you rely heavily on numbers, facts, and statistics.
2. Summarize Samuel Matthews's piece, drawing on the guidelines in chapter 3, "Writing Summaries."
3. Explain why you view this selection as primarily an objective report, aiming to inform readers. Show what Matthews does to make it an objective report. Or argue that this piece is really an argument, that it means to persuade readers of some truth or move readers to take some action. Or explain why the distinction between objective reporting and persuasion is blurred here and difficult to untangle.

"THE END OF NATURE"

Bill McKibben

> *Here is an excerpt, adapted by the author for this anthology, from Bill McKibben's 1989 book* The End of Nature. *Several sections of the book were first published in the* New Yorker. *This piece records McKibben's personal, emotional reactions to the kinds of science and statistics Matthews reports in "Under the Sun"—it's an elegy for the world lost to the greenhouse effect. (See also the headnote for "Daybreak" in chapter 7.)*

Before and As You Read

1. Read only the first paragraph of this selection and then respond to it with a paragraph of your own. Are you with Bill McKibben? Is his experience radically different from yours? Does his sense of nature as "a world apart" make sense to you? Once you've written this paragraph, go back and keep reading.
2. As you read, mark the passage you like the best, that seems most beautiful or moving.

Almost every day, I hike up the hill out my back door. Within a hundred yards the woods swallows me up, and there is nothing to remind me of human society—no trash, no stumps, no fence, not even a real path. Looking out from the high places, you can't see road or house; it is a world apart from man. But once in a while someone will be cutting wood farther down the valley, and the snarl of a chain saw will fill the woods. It is harder on those days to get caught up in the timeless meaning of the forest, for man is nearby. The sound of the chain saw doesn't blot out all the noises of the forest or drive the animals away, but it does drive away the feeling that you are in another, separate, timeless, wild sphere.

Now that we have changed the most basic forces around us, the noise of that chain saw will always be in the woods. We have changed the atmosphere, and that will change the weather. The temperature and rainfall are no longer to be entirely the work of some separate, uncivilizable force, but instead in part a product of our habits, our economies, our ways of life. Even in the most remote wilderness, where the strictest laws forbid the felling of a single tree, the sound of that saw will be clear, and a walk in the woods will be changed—tainted—by its whine. The world outdoors will mean much the same thing as the world indoors, the hill the same thing as the house.

An idea, a relationship, can go extinct, just like an animal or a plant. The idea in this case is "nature," the separate and wild province, the world apart from man to which he adapted, under whose rules he was born and died. In the past, we spoiled and polluted parts of that nature, inflicted environmental "damage." But that was like stabbing a man with toothpicks: though it hurt, annoyed, degraded, it did not touch vital organs, block the path of the lymph or blood. We never thought that we had wrecked nature. Deep down, we never really thought we could: it was too big and too old; its forces—the wind, the rain, the sun—were too strong, too elemental.

But, quite by accident, it turned out that the carbon dioxide and other gases we were producing in our pursuit of a better life—in pursuit of warm houses and eternal economic growth and of agriculture so productive it would free most of us from farming—*could* alter the power of the sun, could increase its heat. And that increase *could* change the patterns of moisture and dryness, breed storms in new places, breed deserts. Those things may or may not have yet begun to happen, but it is too late to altogether prevent them from happening. We have produced the carbon dioxide—we are ending nature.

We have not ended rainfall or sunlight; in fact, rainfall and sunlight   5 may become more important forces in our lives. It is too early to tell exactly how much harder the wind will blow, how much hotter the sun will shine. That is for the future. But the *meaning* of the wind, the sun, the rain—of nature—has already changed. Yes, the wind still blows—but no longer from some other sphere, some inhuman place.

In the summer, my wife and I bike down to the lake nearly every afternoon for a swim. It is a dogleg Adirondack lake, with three beaver lodges, a blue heron, some otter, a family of mergansers, the occasional loon. A few summer houses cluster at one end, but mostly it is surrounded by wild state land. During the week we swim across and back, a trip of maybe forty minutes—plenty of time to forget everything but the feel of the water around your body and the rippling, muscular joy of a hard kick and the pull of your arms.

But on the weekends, more and more often, someone will bring a boat out for waterskiing, and make pass after pass up and down the lake. And then the whole experience changes, changes entirely. Instead of being able to forget everything but yourself, and even yourself except for the muscles and the skin, you must be alert, looking up every dozen strokes to see where the boat is, thinking about what you will do if it comes near. It is not so much the danger—few swimmers, I imagine, ever die by Evinrude. It's not even so much the blue smoke that hangs low over the water. It's that the motorboat gets in your mind. You're forced to think, not feel—to think of human society and of people. The lake is utterly different on these days, just as the planet is utterly different now.

The idea of nature will not survive the new global pollution—the carbon dioxide and the CFCs and the like. This new rupture with nature is different not only in scope but also in kind from salmon tins in an English stream. We have changed the atmosphere, and thus we are changing the weather. By changing the weather, we make every spot on earth man-made and artificial. We have deprived nature of its independence, and that is fatal to its meaning. Nature's independence *is* its meaning; without it there is nothing but us.

If you travel by plane and dog team and snowshoe to the farthest corner of the Arctic and it is a mild summer day, you will not know whether the temperature is what it is "supposed" to be, or whether, thanks to the extra carbon dioxide, you are standing in the equivalent of a heated room. If it is twenty below and the wind is howling—perhaps absent man it would be forty below. Since most of us get to the North Pole only in our minds, the real situation is more like this: if in July there's a heat wave in London, it won't be a natural phenomenon. It will be a man-made phenomenon—an amplification of what nature intended or a total invention. Or, at the very least, it *might* be a man-made phenomenon, which amounts to the same thing. The storm that might have snapped the hot spell may never form, or may veer off in some other direction, not by the laws of nature but by the laws of nature as they have been rewritten, blindly, crudely, but effectively, by man. If the sun is beating down on you, you will not have the comfort of saying, "Well, that's nature." Or if the sun feels sweet on the back of your neck, that's fine, but it isn't nature. A child born now will never know a natural summer, a natural autumn, winter, or spring. Summer is going extinct, replaced by something else that will be called "summer." This new summer will retain some of its relative characteristics—it will be hotter than the rest of the year, for instance, and the time of year when crops grow—but it will not be summer, just as even the best prosthesis is not a leg.

And, of course, climate determines an enormous amount of the rest 10 of nature—where the forests stop and the prairies or the tundra begins, where the rain falls and where the arid deserts squat, where the wind blows strong and steady, where the glaciers form, how fast the lakes evaporate, where the seas rise. As John Hoffman, of the Environmental Protection Agency, noted in the *Journal of Forestry,* "trees planted today will be entering their period of greatest growth when the climate has already changed." A child born today might swim in a stream free of toxic waste, but he won't ever see a natural stream. If the waves crash up against the beach, eroding dunes and destroying homes, it is not the awesome power of Mother Nature. It is the awesome power of Mother Nature as altered by the awesome power of man, who has overpowered in a century the processes that have been slowly evolving and changing of their own accord since the earth was born.

Those "record highs" and "record lows" that the weathermen are always talking about—they're meaningless now. It's like comparing pole vaults between athletes using bamboo and those using fiberglass poles, or dash times between athletes who've been chewing steroids and those who've stuck to Wheaties. They imply a connection between the past and the present which doesn't exist. The comparison is like hanging Rembrandts next to Warhols; we live in a postnatural world. Thoreau once said he could walk for half an hour and come to "some portion of the earth's surface where man does not stand from one year's end to another, and there, consequently, politics are not, for they are but the cigar-smoke of a man." Now you could walk half a year and not reach such a spot. Politics— our particular way of life, our ideas about how we should live—now blows its smoke over every inch of the globe.

About a half mile from my house, right at the head of the lake, the town has installed a streetlight. It is the only one for miles, and it is undeniably useful—without it, a car or two each summer would undoubtedly miss the turn and end up in the drink. Still, it intrudes on the dark. Most of the year, once the summer people have left, there is not another light to be seen. On a starry night the Milky Way stands out like a marquee; on a cloudy night you can walk in utter pitch-black, unable to see even the dog trotting at your side. But then, around the corner, there is the streetlamp, and soon you are in its sodium-vapor circle, a circle robbed of mystery by its illumination. It's true that the bugs love the lamp; on a June night there is more wildlife buzzing around it than in any square acre of virgin forest. But it breaks up the feeling of the night. And now it is as if we had put a huge lamp in the sky, and cast that same prosaic sterile light at all times on all places.

While I was stacking wood one morning last fall I noticed a lot of ash floating through the air. "Did you make a fire?" I asked my wife through the window. "No," she said. I wandered off down the road to see if it was coming from the nearest occupied house—but that's quite a way off. I finally stopped long enough to trap a piece of the ash in my fist so I could look at it. It turned out to be a bug I had never seen before—a blackflylike creature with a gray, woolly clump of something on its back that certainly looked like ash. Not man! Nature!

If only that were the case with most of the changes around us—if only all the analogies were just analogies. If only they were all figments, and the world were the same old place it had always been. But the world, the whole world, is touched by our work, even when that work is invisible.

In a famous essay, "Sootfall and Fallout," which was written at the height of the atmospheric atomic testing in the early 1960s, E. B. White says that the joy he always took in his newly dug garden patch "has been spoiled by the maggots that work in the mind. Tomorrow we will have rain, and the rain falling on the garden will carry its cargo of debris from old explosions in distant places. Whether the amount of this freight is great or small, whether it is measurable by the farmer or can only be guessed at, one thing is certain: the character of rain has changed, the joy of watching it soak the waiting earth has been diminished, and the whole meaning and worth of gardens has been called into question." Happily, we have ceased atmospheric atomic testing. Unhappily, White's words still hold true; only, now the culprits—carbon dioxide, methane, nitrous oxide, chlorofluorocarbons—are the result not of some high and distant drama, a few grand explosions, but of a billion explosions of a hundred million pistons every second, near and far and insidiously common.

We will have a hard time believing this new state of affairs. Even the most farseeing naturalists of an earlier day couldn't comprehend that the atmosphere, the climate, could be dramatically altered. Thoreau, complaining about the logging that eventually destroyed virtually every stand of virgin timber between the Atlantic and the Mississippi, said that soon the East "would be so bald that every man would have to grow whiskers to hide its nakedness, but, thank God, the sky was safe." And John Muir, the Scottish-born explorer of Yosemite, wrote one day in his diary about following a herd of grazing sheep through the valley: "Thousands of feet trampling leaves and flowers, but in this mighty wilderness they seem but a feeble band, and a thousand gardens should escape their blighting touch. They cannot hurt the trees, though some of the seedlings suffer, and should the woolly locusts be greatly multiplied, as on account of dollar value they are likely to be, then the forests too, in time, may be destroyed. Only the sky will then be safe." George Perkins Marsh, the first modern environmentalist, knew a century ago that cutting down forests was a horrible idea, yet he said, "The revolutions of the seasons, with their alterations of temperatures, and of length of day and night, the climate of different zones, and the general conditions and movements of the atmosphere and seas, depend upon causes for the most part cosmical, and, of course, beyond our control."

And even as it dawns on us what we have done, there will be plenty of opportunity to forget, at least for a while, that anything has changed. For it isn't natural *beauty* that is ended; in fact, in the same way that the smog breeds spectacular sunsets, there may appear new, unimagined beauties. What will change is the meaning that beauty carries, for when we look at a sunset, we see, or think we see, many things beyond a particular arrangement of orange and purple and rose.

There is also another emotional response—one that corresponds to the cry "What will I do without him?" when someone vital dies.

I took a day's hike last fall, walking Mill Creek from the spot where it runs by my door to the place where it crosses the main county road near Wevertown. It's a distance of maybe nine miles as the car flies, but rivers are far less efficient, and endlessly follow pointless, time-wasting, uneconomical meanders and curves. Mill Creek cuts some fancy figures, and so I was able to feel a bit exploratory—a budget Bob Marshall. In a strict sense, it wasn't much of an adventure. I stopped at the store for a liverwurst sandwich at lunchtime, the path was generally downhill, the temperature stuck at an equable 55 degrees, and since it was the week before the hunting season opened I didn't have to sing as I walked to keep from getting shot. On the other hand, I had made an arbitrary plan—to follow the creek—and, as a consequence, I spent hours stumbling through overgrown marsh, batting at ten-foot saplings and vines, emerging only every now and then, scratched and weary, into the steeper wooded sections. When Thoreau was on Katahdin, nature said to him, "I have never made this soil for thy feet, this air for thy breathing, these rocks for they neighbors. I cannot pity nor fondle thee there, but forever relentlessly drive thee hence to where I *am* kind. Why seek me where I have not called thee, and then complain because you find me but a stepmother?" Nature said this to me on Mill Creek, or at least it said, "Go home and tell your wife you walked to Wevertown." I felt I should have carried a machete, or employed a macheteist. (The worst thing about battling through brake and bramble of this sort is that it's so anonymous—gray sticks, green stalks with reddish thorns, none of them to be found in any of the many guides and almanacs on my shelf.) And though I started the day with eight dry socks, none saw noon in that pleasant state.

If it was all a little damp and in a minor key, the sky was nonetheless *20* bright blue, and rabbits kept popping out from my path, and pheasants fired up between my legs, and at each turning some new gift appeared: a vein of quartz, or a ridge where the maples still held their leaves, or a pine more than three feet in diameter that beavers had gnawed all the way around and halfway through and then left standing—a forty-foot sculpture. It was October, so there weren't even any bugs. And always the plash of the stream in my ear. It isn't Yosemite, the Mill Creek Valley, but its small beauties are absorbing, and one can say with Muir on his mountaintop, "Up here all the world's prizes seem as nothing."

And so what if it isn't nature primeval? One of our neighbors has left several kitchen chairs along his stretch of the bank, spaced at fifty-yard intervals for comfort in fishing. At one old homestead, a stone chimney stands at either end of a foundation now filled by a graceful birch. Near the one real waterfall, a lot of rusty pipe and collapsed concrete testifies to the old mill that once stood there. But these aren't disturbing sights— they're almost comforting, reminders of the way that nature has endured and outlived and with dignity reclaimed so many schemes and disruptions of man. (A mile or so off the creek, there's a mine where a hundred and fifty years ago a visionary tried to extract pigment for paint and pack it out on mule and sledge. He rebuilt after a fire; finally an avalanche convinced him. The path in is faint now, but his chimney, too, still stands, a small Angkor Wat of free enterprise.) Large sections of the area were once farmed; but the growing season is not much more than a hundred days, and the limits established by that higher authority were stronger than the (powerful) attempts of individual men to circumvent them, and so the farms returned to forest, with only a dump of ancient bottles or a section of stone wall as a memorial. (Last fall, though, my wife and I found, in one abandoned meadow, a hop vine planted at least a century before. It was still flowering, and with its blossoms we brewed beer.) These ruins are humbling sights, reminders of the negotiations with nature that have established the world as we know it.

Changing socks (soaking for merely clammy) in front of the waterfall, I thought back to the spring before last, when a record snowfall melted in only a dozen or so warm April days. A little to the south, an inflamed stream washed out a highway bridge, closing the New York Thruway for months. Mill Creek filled till it was a river, and this waterfall, normally one of those diaphanous-veil affairs, turned into a cataract. It filled me with awe to stand there then, on the shaking ground and think, This is what nature is capable of.

But as I sat there this time, and thought about the dry summer we'd just come through, there was nothing awe-inspiring or instructive, or even lulling, in the fall of the water. It suddenly seemed less like a waterfall than like a spillway to accommodate the overflow of a reservoir. That didn't decrease its beauty, but it changed its meaning. It has begun or will soon begin to rain and snow when the particular mix of chemicals we've injected into the atmosphere adds up to rain or snow—when they make it hot enough over some tropical sea to form a cloud and send it this way. I had no more control, in one sense, over this process than I ever did. But it felt different, and lonelier. Instead of a world where rain had an independent and mysterious existence, the rain had become a subset of human activity: a phenomenon like smog or commerce or the noise from the skidder towing logs on Cleveland Road—all things over which I had no control, either. The rain bore a brand; it was a steer, not a deer. And that was where the loneliness came from. There's nothing there except us. There's no such thing as nature anymore—that other world that isn't business and art and breakfast is now not another world, and there is nothing except us alone.

At the same time that I felt lonely, though, I also felt crowded, without privacy. We go to the woods in part to escape. But now there is nothing except us and so there is no escaping other people. As I walked in the autumn woods I saw a lot of sick trees. With the conifers, I suspected acid rain. (At least I have the luxury of only suspecting; in too many places, they *know*). And so who walked with me in the woods? Well, there were the presidents of the Midwest utilities who kept explaining why they had to burn coal to make electricity (cheaper, fiduciary responsibility, no *proof* it kills trees) and then there were the congressmen who couldn't bring themselves to do anything about it (personally favor but politics the art of compromise, very busy with the war on drugs) and before long the whole human race had arrived to explain its aspirations. We like to drive, they said, air conditioning is a necessity nowadays, let's go to the mall. By this point, the woods were pretty densely populated. As I attempted to escape, I slipped on another rock, and in I went again. Of course, the person I was fleeing most fearfully was myself, for I drive (I drove forty thousand miles one year), and I'm burning a collapsed barn behind the house next week because it is much the cheapest way to deal with it, and I live on about four hundred times what Thoreau conclusively proved was enough, so I've done my share to take this independent, eternal world and turn it into a science-fair project (and not even a good science-fair project but a cloddish one, like pumping poison into an ant farm and "observing the effects").

The walk along Mill Creek, or any stream, or up any hill, or through any woods, is changed forever—changed as profoundly as when it shifted from pristine and untracked wilderness to mapped and deeded and cultivated land. Our local shopping mall now has a club of people who go "mall walking" every day. They circle the shopping center en masse—Caldor to Sears to J. C. Penney, circuit after circuit with an occasional break to shop. This seems less absurd to me now than it did at first. I like to walk in the outdoors not solely because the air is cleaner but because outdoors we venture into a sphere larger than ourselves. Mall walking involves too many other people, and too many purely human sights, ever to be more than good-natured exercise. But now, out in the wild, the sunshine on one's shoulders is a reminder that man has cracked the ozone, that, thanks to us, the atmosphere absorbs where once it released.

The greenhouse effect is a more apt name than those who coined it imagined. The carbon dioxide and trace gases act like the panes of glass on a greenhouse—the analogy is accurate. But it's more than that. We have built a greenhouse, *a human creation,* where once there bloomed a sweet and wild garden.

Reading and Responding

In a few sentences, summarize what McKibben means by "the end of nature."

Working Together

1. Read aloud, as a class, the passages you marked. What do they all have in common?
2. Share your summaries of the main argument. Discuss. Then write a new summary of several sentences in light of the discussion.
3. Write a group paragraph explaining this reading to class members who had to miss a week of school (they're choir members or orchestra members on tour; or they're members of a sports team competing at the regional or national level; or they've been on a weeklong field trip). In your paragraph, include the word *postnatural* as part of your explanation.

Rethinking and Rewriting

1. Write an essay illustrating the idea of "the end of nature" from your own experience. Take one or two examples, imitating McKibben's personal style.

2. Write an essay in which you admit that nature is, in fact, dead, at least in one sense; but that isn't a problem for you, there's nothing wrong with that as far as you're concerned; and in any event we've got to move on and make do, since there's nothing we can do about it anyway. Or write an essay arguing that that is precisely the wrong response we should have to McKibben's "The End of Nature."
3. Write a letter to McKibben, responding to his essay.

"GREENHOUSE EARTH"

Dixy Lee Ray

> *In a long and varied political career Dixy Lee Ray was chairman of the Atomic Energy Commission, assistant secretary of state in the U.S. Bureau of Oceans, and governor of Washington State. She was also a member of the zoology faculty at the University of Washington. In this excerpt from* Trashing the Planet: How Science Can Help Us Deal with Acid Rain, Depletion of the Ozone, and Nuclear Waste (Among Other Things) *(1990), written with the help of journalist Lou Guzzo, Ray argued that recent warnings about the destruction of the earth are hysterical exaggerations based on faulty science. Her last book, also written with Guzzo, is entitled* Environmental Overkill: Whatever Happened to Common Sense? *(1993).*

Before and As You Read

1. Notice in the first paragraph of this article that Dixy Lee Ray uses the phrase "environmental hysteria." What's the tone of this phrase? What does it imply about environmentalism? As you read, underline or bracket every phrase like this that you find. What's the cumulative effect of such language?
2. You should know in advance that Ray is setting out here to dispute the factual basis of the environmental crisis that worries Gore, Matthews, and McKibben. As you read, carefully mark, number, and title Ray's major chunks of research, information, and argument.

The year 1988 ended on a high note of environmental hysteria about global warming, fueled by an unusually hot, dry summer (in the United States). Testifying at a Senate hearing, NASA's James Hansen claimed that the high temperatures presaged the onset of the long debated "greenhouse effect" caused by increased carbon dioxide (CO_2) in the atmosphere.

Forgotten was the harsh winter of 1982, or of 1978, when, for example, barges carrying coal and heating oil froze in river ice and more than 200 people lost their lives in the cold weather.

Only days after *Time* magazine featured a doomed, overheated Earth as its "man of the year" for 1988, Alaska experienced the worst cold in its history. The freezing weather set in on January 12, 1989. Twenty different locations in our most northerly state recorded their lowest-ever temperatures, mainly in the range of −50 to −65 degrees Fahrenheit. At Tanana, near Fairbanks, −75 degrees Fahrenheit was reached. (The all-time low recorded anywhere in Alaska was −80 degrees in January 1971 at a Prospect Creek pipeline station.) The cold persisted; it did not moderate and begin to move south until the first week of February. Old-timers agreed that no such cold had ever been experienced before, and they expressed amazement that the temperature remained a chilly −16 degrees Fahrenheit along the coast even with an 81-knot wind blowing. This was unheard of, since usually it is coldest when the wind is quiet. In early February, the cold seeped down from Alaska along both sides of the Rocky Mountains, bringing near-record lows both to the Pacific Northwest and throughout the Midwest south to Texas and eventually to the mid-Atlantic and New England states. Proponents of the "greenhouse-is-here-global-warming-has-begun" theory were very quiet during these weeks.

To be fair, even if the projected greenhouse warming should occur, no one would expect it to happen all at once or without intervening cold spells. So let's examine the situation more closely.

Of course, the earth, with its enveloping blanket of atmosphere, con-   5 stitutes a "greenhouse." This fact has never been at issue. Indeed, were it not for the greenhouse function of air, the earth's surface might be like the moon, bitterly cold (−270 degrees Fahrenheit) at night and unbearably hot (+212 degrees Fahrenheit) during the day. Although the amount of solar energy reaching the moon is essentially the same as that reaching earth, the earth's atmosphere acts like a filter. Of the incoming solar radiation, about 20 percent is absorbed in the atmosphere, about 50 percent reaches and warms the earth's surface, and the rest is reflected back into space. As the earth's surface is warmed up, infrared radiation is emitted. It is the presence of CO_2 (and water vapor, methane, hydrocarbon, and a few other gases) in the atmosphere that absorbs the long wavelength infrared radiation, thereby producing the warming "greenhouse effect." This accounts for a net warming of the earth's atmosphere system of about 55 degrees Fahrenheit. Without this natural greenhouse, it would be difficult to sustain life on this planet.

All the important "greenhouse gases" are produced in nature, as well as by humans. For example, CO_2 comes naturally from the respiration of all living organisms and from decaying vegetation. It is also injected into the atmosphere by volcanoes and forest and grass fires. Carbon dioxide from man-made sources comes primarily from burning fossil fuels for home and building heat, for transportation, and for industrial processes. The amount of CO_2 released into the atmosphere is huge and it is commonly believed that it is divided about evenly between natural and man-made sources.

Hydrocarbons come from growing plants, especially coniferous trees, such as fir and pine, and from various industries. In the transportation arena, hydrocarbons result from incomplete oxidation of gasoline. Both hydrocarbons and methane also enter the atmosphere through the metabolism of cows and other ruminants. It is estimated that American cows produce about 50 million tons of these gases per year—and there is no control technology for such emissions. Methane seeps into the air from swamps, coal mines, and rice paddies; it is often "flared" from oil wells. The largest source of greenhouse gas may well be termites, whose digestive activities are responsible for about 50 billion tons of CO_2 and methane annually. This is 10 times more than the present world production of CO_2 from burning fossil fuel. Methane may be oxidized in the atmosphere, leading to an estimated one billion tons of carbon monoxide per year. All in all, the atmosphere is a grand mixture of gases, in a constant state of turbulence, and yet maintained in an overall state of dynamic balance.

But now this balance appears to be disturbed as CO_2 and the other major greenhouse gases are on the rise, increasing their concentration in the air at a rate of about one percent per year. CO_2 is responsible for about half of the increase. Analysis of air bubbles trapped in glacial ice and of carbon isotopes in tree rings and ocean sediment cores indicate that CO_2 levels hovered around 260 to 280 parts per million from the end of the last ice age (10,000 years ago) till the mid-nineteenth century, except for an anomolous rise 300 years ago. And these measurements also show that CO_2 concentrations have varied widely (by 20 percent) as the earth has passed through glacial and interglacial periods. While today's 25 percent increase in CO_2 can be accounted for by the burning of fossil fuels, what caused the much greater increases in the prehistoric past?

The present increase has brought the CO_2 level to 340 parts per million, up about 70 parts per million. If we add the greater amounts of methane, hydrocarbons, and so forth, there is now a total of about 407 parts per million of greenhouse gases. This is large enough so that from the greenhouse effect alone we should have experienced a global warming of about two to four degrees Fahrenheit. But this has not happened.

The observed and recorded temperature pattern since 1880 does not   10
fit with the CO_2 greenhouse warming calculations. During the 1880s, there was a period of cooling, followed by a warming trend. The temperature rose by one degree Fahrenheit during 1900 to 1940, then fell from 1940 to 1965, and then began to rise again, increasing by about 0.3 degrees Fahrenheit since 1975. When all these fluctuations are analyzed, it appears unlikely that there has been any overall warming in the last 50 years. And if the temperature measurements taken in the northern hemisphere are corrected for the urban effect—the so-called "heat island" that exists over cities due mainly to the altered albedo from removing vegetation—then it is probable that not only has there been no warming; there may have been a slight cooling. It all depends on whose computer model you choose to believe.

Clearly, there is still something that is not understood about global conditions and about the weather links between the oceans and the atmosphere. Have the experts fully taken into account the role of the sea as a sink or reservoir for CO_2, including the well known fact that much more CO_2 dissolves in cold water than in warm? Interest in the greenhouse gases and projections of global warming has stimulated greater interest in the role that the oceans play in influencing moderately or even drastically changing global climate. The oceans hold more CO_2 than does the atmosphere, 60 times more. Complex circulation patterns that involve waters of different temperature, together with the activities of marine organisms that deposit carbonate in their skeletons, carry carbon dioxide to the depths of the ocean.

Recall that all the public furor about global warming was triggered in June 1988, when NASA scientist James Hansen testified in the U.S. Senate that the greenhouse effect is changing the climate now! He said he was 99 percent sure of it, and that "1988 would be the warmest year on record, unless there is some remarkable, improbable cooling in the remainder of the year." Well, there was. Almost while Dr. Hansen was testifying, the eastern tropical Pacific Ocean underwent a remarkable, improbable cooling—a sudden drop in temperature of seven degrees. No one knows why. But the phenomenon is not unknown; it is called La Nina to distinguish it from the more commonly occurring El Nino, or warm current, and it has happened 19 times in the last 102 years.

Dr. Hansen did not consider the possibility of La Nina, because his computer program does not take sea temperatures into account. Yet the oceans cover 73 percent of the earth's surface.

When people, including scientists, talk "global," it is hard to believe that they can ignore 73 percent of the globe, but obviously they sometimes do. It is all the more astonishing to ignore ocean-atmosphere interactions, especially in the Pacific, when it is well established that El Nino has profound and widespread effects on weather patterns and temperatures; does it not follow that La Nina may also? Indeed, some atmospheric scientists credit the severely cold winter of 1988–89 to the earlier temperature drop in the tropical Pacific.

Once again, since the greenhouse gases are increasing, what's keeping   15
the earth from warming up? There are a number of possible explanations. Perhaps there is some countervailing phenomenon that hasn't been taken into account; perhaps the oceans exert greater lag than expected and the warming is just postponed; perhaps the sea and its carbonate-depositing inhabitants are a much greater sink than some scientists believe; perhaps the increase in CO_2 stimulates more plant growth and removal of more CO_2 than calculated; perhaps there is some other greenhouse gas, like water vapor, that is more important than CO_2; perhaps varying cloud cover provides a greater feedback and self-correcting mechanism than has been taken into account; perhaps. . . . The fact is, there is simply not enough good data on most of these processes to know for sure what is happening in these enormous, turbulent, interlinked, dynamic systems like atmosphere and oceanic circulation. The only thing that can be stated with certainty is that they do affect the weather. So also do forces outside the planet, and in a moment we'll look at the sun in this regard.

First, we must acknowledge that some zealots in the greenhouse issue make much of deforestation, especially in the tropical rain forests, but this topic is marked more by emotion bordering on hysteria than on solid scientific data. Good measurements on CO_2 uptake and oxygen production in tropical rain forests are lacking. Such information could be critical, because we know that in temperate climates mature trees and climax forests add little in the way of photosynthetic activity and consequent CO_2 removal from the atmosphere. Mature trees, like all living things, metabolize more slowly as they grow old. A forest of young, vigorously growing trees will remove five to seven tons more CO_2 per acre per year than old growth. There are plenty of good reasons to preserve old growth forests, but redressing the CO_2 balance is not one of them. If we are really interested (as we should be) in reducing atmospheric CO_2, we should be vigorously pursuing reforestation and the planting of trees and shrubs, including in urban areas, where local impacts on the atmosphere are greatest.

Reforestation *has* been going on through enlightened forestry practices on private lands by timber companies and as a result of changes in agriculture and land use. In the United States, the average annual wood growth is now more than three times what it was in 1920, and the growing stock has increased 18 percent from 1952 to 1977. Forests in America continue to increase in size, even while supplying a substantial fraction of the world's timber needs.

Finally, it should be kept in mind that when a tree is cut for timber, it will no longer remove CO_2 from the atmosphere, but it won't release its stored carbon either—until or unless it is burned or totally decayed. In the whole deforestation question, it would be interesting to try to determine what effect the deforestation of Europe had on temperature and climate in the nineteenth century, and, similarly, what the effect was of the earlier deforestation of the Mediterranean area and the Middle East.

If we study history, we find that there is no good or widely accepted explanation for why the earth's temperature and climate were as they were at any particular time in the past, including the recurring ice ages and the intervening warm periods. What caused the "little ice age" of the late seventeenth century and why was it preceded by 800 years of relative warmth? Is all this really due to human activity? What about natural phenomena? Recent studies of major deep sea currents in the Atlantic ocean suggest a causative relation to the onset of ice ages. Occasional unusual actions by nature can release great quantities of CO_2 and other greenhouse gases to the atmosphere.

I received my lesson in humility, my respect for the size and vast power of natural forces on May 18, 1980. For those who might not instantly recognize that date, it was a Sunday, a beautiful spring morning when at 8:31 Mount St. Helens erupted with the force of more than 500 atomic bombs. Gases and particulate matter were propelled 80,000 feet, approximately 15 miles, into the stratosphere and deposited above the ozone layer. The eruption continued for nearly 12 hours and more than four billion tons of earth were displaced.

Because Mount St. Helens is relatively accessible, there were many studies conducted and good data are available on the emissions—at least those that occurred after May 18. For the remaining seven months of 1980,

Mount St. Helens released 910,000 metric tons of CO_2, 220,000 metric tons of sulfur dioxide, and unknown amounts of aerosols into the atmosphere. Many other gases, including methane, water vapor, carbon monoxide, and a variety of sulfur compounds were also released, and emissions still continue to seep from the crater and from fumaroles and crevices.

Gigantic as it was, Mount St. Helens was not a large volcanic eruption. It was dwarfed by Mount St. Augustine and Mount Redoubt in Alaska in 1976 and 1989 and El Chicon in Mexico in 1982. El Chicon was an exceptionally sulfurous eruption. The violence of its explosion sent more than 100 million tons of sulfur gases high into the stratosphere. Droplets of sulfuric acid formed; these continue to rain down onto the earth's surface. The earth, at present, appears to be in a period of active volcanism, with volcanic eruptions occurring at a rate of about 100 per year. Most of these are in remote locations, where accurate measurement of the gaseous emissions is not possible, but they must be considerable. Some estimates from large volcanic eruptions in the past suggest that all of the air polluting materials produced by man since the beginning of the industrial revolution do not begin to equal the quantities of toxic materials, aerosols, and particulates spewed into the air from just three volcanoes: Krakatoa in Indonesia in 1883, Mount Katmai in Alaska in 1912, and Hekla in Iceland in 1947. Despite these prodigious emissions, Krakatoa, for example, produced some chilly winters, spectacular sunsets, and a global temperature drop of 0.3 degrees Centigrade, but no climate change. From written records, we also know that the famous "year without a summer" that followed the eruption of Mount Tambora in 1816 meant that the summer temperature in Hartford, Connecticut, did not exceed 82 degrees Fahrenheit. No doom.

We can conclude from these volcanic events that the atmosphere is enormous and its capacity to absorb and dilute pollutants is also very great. This is no excuse, of course, to pollute the air deliberately, which would be an act of folly. But it does give us some perspective on events.

So far, we have considered only those phenomena that occur on earth that might influence global temperature, weather, and eventually the climate. "Weather" means the relatively short-term fluctuations in temperature, precipitation, winds, cloudiness, and so forth, that shift and change over periods of hours, days, or weeks. Weather patterns may be cyclic, more or less repeating themselves every few years. The "climate," on the other hand, is generally accepted to be the mean of weather changes over a period of about 30 years. Weather may change rapidly, but the climate may remain essentially the same over thousands of years, as it probably has for the last 8,000 years.

Now, what about the effects on weather of extraterrestrial phenomena? After all, it is the sun that determines the climate on earth—but the role of the sun, with its ever-shifting solar radiation, is generally ignored as being inconsequential in affecting shorter-term weather patterns. But is this really so?

Consider: the earth shifts in its position relative to the sun. Its orbit is eccentric, varying over a period of 97,000 years. The inclination of the earth's axis shifts with respect to the ecliptic over a cycle of 41,000 years, and the precession of the equinox varies over a period of 21,000 years. How do these shifts affect the amount of solar radiation reaching the earth? Some astronomers believe that at least for the last 500,000 to one million years, these phenomena are related to the initiation and dissipation of glacial and interglacial intervals.

Although it may seem to us that the sun is stable and stationary, it is in fact whirling through the Milky Way galaxy, taking its family of planets with it. Activity on the sun itself goes through periods of relative quiet and then erupts into flares and protuberances, sunspots, and gigantic upheavals that "rain" solar material out into space. One recent solar storm was measured at 43,000 miles across. This produced the largest solar flare ever recorded. Some of the increased solar radiation from such storms reaches the earth and disrupts radio communication and television transmission and increases the aurora borealis. Solar activity in the form of storms seen as sunspots has a span of roughly 11 years. It seems that the sunspots whirl clockwise for about 11 years, then reverse and go counterclockwise for another 11 years. This interval is an average and may vary from 7 to 17 years. The controlling mechanism for this reversal is unknown.

Then there is another variable. The sun "flickers"; that is, it dims and brightens slightly over a period of about 70 years. When it dims, the sunspots attain lower maxima. When the sun brightens, the sunspots have higher maxima than "normal." Although this dimming and brightening has been suspected for some time, the first actual measurement of such a "flicker" was made on April 4, 1980, when a satellite measuring solar radiation outside the earth's atmosphere recorded a 0.2 percent drop in radiation. Changes in solar radiation are now routinely measured.

Coupled with the activity of the sun, there is the moon's gravitational force, to which the earth's waters respond daily and in 28-day cycles of tides. Also, there are 20-year and 60-year tidal cycles, as well as longer ones. Moreover, the solid land also responds to the moon's gravitational force, but because we move with the ground, we do not feel it. Recently, a 556-year variation in the moon's orbit around the earth was analyzed; some meteorologists believe that the occasional confluence of all these sun-and-moon cycles may trigger dramatic changes in ocean currents and temperatures. And it is now widely acknowledged that the oceans are a major influence on the climate. There is also a 500-to-600-year cycle in volcanic activity, which appears to be near a peak at the present time.

Let's consider again. Does all this variability in solar activity really have anything to do with weather or climate? No one knows for certain. But studies are continuing, and Dr. John Eddy of the National Center for Atmospheric Research has found an interesting correlation between decades of low sunspot activity and cold periods, such as the "little ice age" of the seventeenth century, when there was a virtual absence of sunspot

30

activity between 1645 and 1715, and decades of high sunspot activity with warm temperatures on earth.

Since the sunspot cycle is not perfectly regular and varies considerably, how do scientists determine the extent of sunspot activity that occurred decades or centuries ago? This is a neat piece of scientific detective work that merits a brief explanation. It involves another extraterrestrial phenomenon—cosmic radiation.

Cosmic rays consist of high energy particles that enter the earth's atmosphere from outer space. These energetic particles split the nuclei of atmospheric gases, giving rise to some of the background radiation to which all living organisms are exposed. Among the fission products are Potassium-40 and Carbon-14, which get into the food chain and are eaten (by animals) or absorbed (by plants), and that is one of the reasons that the bodies of all living organisms are radioactive. Of these two fission products, it is Carbon-14 that is the most interesting for tracing events in the past.

C-14, whose half-life is a relatively short 5,570 years, is being produced continuously in the atmosphere (through interaction with cosmic rays) and is continuously taken up by *living* organisms, but not by dead ones. Therefore, by measuring the amount of C-14 in dead or fossil material, one can infer the date of death. This is called carbon-dating. C-14 is a very good but not perfect clock of history, because the assumption is that the formation of C-14 is not only continuous but also that it occurs at a steady rate. But what Dr. Eddy has determined is that the rate of formation varies with the amount of cosmic radiation, which, in turn, varies with the amount of sunspot activity, because high solar activity also creates more solar wind that can compress the earth's magnetic field. This stronger field is more effective in shielding cosmic rays from the earth's atmosphere, which means that less C-14 is formed during periods of high sunspot activity. Less C-14 equates with warmer periods on earth.

Taking advantage of these phenomena, Dr. Eddy measured the C-14 radioactivity in tree rings in trees that are up to 5,000 years old. Keep in mind that the years (rings) of low C-14 equate with years of high solar activity and warm temperatures. Dr. Eddy recorded 12 prolonged periods with either unusually cold or unusually mild winters over the last 5,000 years. These correlations between solar activity and weather on earth seem good; his measurements identified the terrible winter of 1683–84, also recorded in the novel *Lorna Doone,* when trees in Somerset, England, froze and many exploded from the buildup of internal ice.

If Dr. Eddy's work and theory hold up, the mid-twentieth century was an unusually warm period, and the earth may be set soon to enter a slow return to cooler temperatures. Besides, in geologically recent times, ice ages recur about every 11,000 to 12,000 years, and it is now 11,000 years since the last one. How do all these complications interact with the greenhouse effect? Again, no one really knows. All we can say with confidence is that it is probably more complicated than many environmentalists seem to believe.

35

When we consider all of the complex geophysical phenomena that might affect the weather and climate on earth, from changes in ocean temperatures and currents, volcanic eruptions, solar storms, and cyclic movements of heavenly bodies, it is clear that none of these is under human control or could be influenced by human activity. Is the "greenhouse effect" and its theoretical enhancement by increases in atmospheric CO_2 from human sources more powerful or capable of overshadowing all other planetary influences? Until the supporters of the man-produced-CO_2-caused-global-warming-theory can explain warm and cold episodes in the past, we should remain skeptical. What caused the 80 parts per million increase in CO_2 during a 100-year period 300 years ago and the high peak—many times anything measured since—of 130,000 years ago?

The alteration of the chemical content of the air by *human* production of greenhouse gases, however, is something that man *can* control. And because no one knows what the ultimate consequences of heightened CO_2 might be, it is reasonable and responsible to reduce human contribution wherever possible.

Fortunately, there are ways to accomplish this. For starters, we can phase out the use of fossil fuel for making electricity and turn to the established and proven technology that has no adverse impact on the atmosphere—nuclear power. The energy of the atom now produces 20 percent of the electricity in the United States—more than the total of all electricity used in 1950. The number of nuclear power plants can be increased.

Second, we can shift to an essentially all-electric economy, utilizing electricity for direct heating of buildings and homes and extending the use of electric processes in industry. With enough electricity available, it can also be used to desalinate sea water and purify the fresh water sources that have become polluted. It can also be used to split water and obtain hydrogen, which has great potential as a clean fuel for transportation. Its "burning" produces only water vapor.

And we can turn, once again, to electric buses and trains, and even-   *40*
tually to electric automobiles.

None of these shifts away from fossil fuels will be easy or fast, but if we have an abundance of electricity from nuclear power plants, it can be done. That would leave fossil fuels for the important synthetics and plastics industries, and for the manufacture of medicinals, pesticides, and fertilizers.

There are also two important caveats; though steps to reduce CO_2 production may be possible for an advanced, highly technical, industrialized society with plenty of electricity, the infrastructure to make use of it, and money to spend, the story is different in the nonindustrialized world. In China, for example, 936 million metric tons of coal were burned in 1987. Who is going to tell China to stop or to change? What alternative do the Chinese have? No matter what we in the Western world do, the amount of CO_2 arising from human use of fossil fuel will not be significantly reduced.

The second caveat is to remember that draconian measures intended to make rapid and large decreases in CO_2 formation won't do much good if they are so costly that they seriously impede the economy and degrade our standard of living without achieving the desired result. Certainly the level of atmospheric CO_2 is increasing, but nothing in all our knowledge of weather and climate guarantees that global warming will inevitably occur. It may, or it may not; the uncertainties are legion. The computer models are too simplistic and include too many estimates and guesses and too little about the role of the hydrosphere, both water vapor and the oceans.

Notwithstanding all this, deliberate, reasoned steps can and should be taken to lower CO_2 emissions; responsible stewardship of the planet demands no less.

Finally, let's suppose that a worst case scenario does develop and that global warming does occur. If the warming caused polar ice to melt, only that on land, as in the Antarctic continent (or the glaciers of Greenland), would materially affect global sea level. When ice floats, as in the Arctic ocean, it already displaces approximately the same amount of water that would result if it were to melt. (There would be some slight thermal expansion.) Whether Arctic ice stays solid or melts would no more cause the sea level to rise than ice cubes melting would cause a full glass of ice water to overflow.

Analysis of sea level data since 1900 indicates that the oceans may be rising at a rate of 10 to 25 centimeters per century (about 0.1 inch per year). The data are very sketchy and uncertain. The sea rise, if it is real, is not uniform and other phenomena, such as land subsidence or upthrust, the building and erosion of beaches by weather, and the variation of inshore currents, could all affect the few measurements that are available.

Some scientists postulate that the west Antarctic ice sheet, which is anchored on bedrock below sea level, could melt and add enough water to raise the world sea level by six or seven meters. This would be disastrous for most coastlines, but if it should happen, it would probably take several hundred years, and there is currently neither observational evidence nor scientific measurements to indicate that it is under way. In fact, new measurements show that the glaciers in Antarctica are growing, not melting.

Air temperatures in Antarctica average −40 degrees Centigrade. A five-degree rise in air temperature to −35 degrees Centigrade is certainly not enough to melt ice. But somewhat warmer sea water (above one degree Centigrade) might get under the ice sheet and start it slipping into the sea; then it would float and displace an enormous volume of water, causing the sea level to rise. But this is also a very unlikely "what if?" with no evidence to support it.

Now, what about ozone in the stratosphere; how significant are the "holes" measured above Antarctica? Are we humans destroying our protective cover? Quite a few people seem to think so.

But let me start with a quotation from an analysis of the ozone prob-   *50*
lem published in the 1987–88 Annual Report of the Rand Corporation:

> The extent of ozone depletion and the severity of the consequences
> of projected emission levels are extremely uncertain. Projections of
> future depletion are based on complex simulation models that have
> not been reconciled with the limited available measurements. . . .
>
> Because of pervasive uncertainty about the likely extent of
> future ozone depletion, its relationship to the quantity of potential
> ozone depleters emitted, its effect on the biosphere, and the ap-
> propriate valuation of these consequences, it is not currently pos-
> sible to choose the level of emission-limiting regulations that will
> maximize welfare by optimally balancing costs of environmental
> damage against those of emission control. Policymakers must act
> in the face of this uncertainty.

Is that all perfectly clear? What the writer is trying to say, diplo-
matically, I think, is that nobody knows how much ozone depletion has
really taken place or what effect, if any, that ozone loss may have on the
environment or on living creatures. The Rand Corporation writer em-
phasizes that present knowledge of ozone layer thickness is full of uncertainty and that the conclusions that have been drawn are based on
incomplete computer models. There is little reliable, accurate, direct
measurement. Nevertheless, he says, "policymakers must act. . . ." Why?
Because some doom-predicting scientists say that "irreversible damage
may occur"? What is their evidence?

Given the media hoopla and hysteria surrounding the ozone issue,
surely it is time to examine the whole question with some sober common
sense.

We know that the earth's ozone layer is turbulent. It undergoes periodic changes in thickness. Natural fluctuations are about 15 percent and
it quickly returns to equilibrium. Changes appear to be both seasonal and
latitudinal. Seasonal changes above Antarctica are largest when measured at
the end of winter. The changes in ozone layer thickness in Antarctica have
now been measured in the Arctic, as well. (No one looked until recently.)

The best measurement data indicate that the ozone layer increased in
average thickness during the 1960s and decreased during 1979–86. The
decreases were comparable in magnitude to the increases of the 1960s.

The term, ozone "hole," is misleading, since it persists for only a few   *55*
weeks. The Antarctic ozone "hole" grew during the early 1980s, becoming large in 1985, smaller in 1986, and reaching its greatest size in 1987.
In 1988, the "hole" did not appear as expected. It was finally discovered—
only 15 percent as large as predicted and displaced over the ocean.

The changes in the amount of ozone appear to be related to complex
chloride chemistry and the presence of nitrous oxide. Although there is
widespread belief that the necessary chloride ion comes from chlorofluo-
rocarbon (CFC) this has not been unequivocally established. On the other

hand, the eruption of Mount St. Augustine (Alaska) in 1976 injected 289 billion kilograms of hydrochloric acid directly into the stratosphere. That amount is 570 times the total world production of chlorine and fluorocarbon compounds in the year 1975. Mount Erebus, which is located just 15 kilometers upwind from McMurdo Sound, has been erupting, constantly, for the last 100 years, ejecting more than 1,000 tons of chlorine per day. Since the world production of CFC peaked at 1.1 million tons per year—equivalent to 750,000 tons of chlorine, and 300 million tons of chlorine reach the atmosphere each year through evaporation of sea water alone—we cannot be sure where the stratospheric chloride comes from, and whether humans have any effect upon it.

So much is known. Most atmospheric scientists also agree that ozone molecules are being created and destroyed naturally by very short wavelengths of ultraviolet light from the sun. Since the same narrow band of ultraviolet light that breaks down chlorofluorocarbons (CFCs) to destroy ozone also breaks down oxygen to create ozone, the result is a balance between these two processes, a competition between CFC and O_2 for the necessary solar energy. Moreover, the result depends on the relative abundance of the two gases (CFC and O_2) in the ozone layer, and data from the National Oceanic and Atmospheric Administration (NOAA) show 60,000 ozone molecules created for every one destroyed by chlorine from a CFC molecule. It is quite possible that overall depletion of ozone is *not* occurring and indeed the NOAA data from measurements taken at the surface of the earth indicate that the total amount of ozone above the United States is actually increasing. In addition, it is known that interaction of solar wind with the earth's magnetic field, which causes the auroras, can also destroy stratospheric ozone. Solar wind comes from solar flares and these are increasing in the present period of sunspot maxima.

So is the sky falling? Still being debated among atmospheric scientists is whether the recently measured ozone changes have been occurring all along or whether they are a new phenomenon sparked by human activity or perhaps a combination of both. To quote a January 1989 summary published in *Science* (Vol. 239), "the recent losses may be natural and may result from long-term fluctuations of the general circulation of the atmosphere." Some researchers, pointing out that atmospheric dynamics can cause big changes in ozone, describe a 48-hour period at the beginning of September 1988, when the ozone decreased 10 percent over a 3 million square kilometer area. Robert T. Watson, head of NASA's upper atmospheric research program, said, "In our opinion, all provisional, we do not believe that change can be chemical [that is, caused by CFCs]. It is strong evidence that *meteorological processes alone* can effectively depress areas of ozone over the Antarctic continent." Direct evidence has yet to be produced, and Robert Watson of NASA reported that the optical diffuser plate on the Nimbus satellite had deteriorated so rapidly in space that its ozone depletion measurements are "useless garbage."

Against this background of uncertainty and the conviction of some respected scientists that natural processes may account for ozone "holes," how can public officials and governmental representatives seriously consider taking drastic action—for example, to ban CFCs—as if that would "cure" the problem, if indeed there is a problem?

Consider that in the United States economy alone, CFCs, mainly freon, are used in 100 million refrigerators, 90 million cars and trucks, 40,000 supermarket display cases, and 100,000 building air conditioners. It is estimated that banning CFCs would mean changing or replacing capital equipment valued at $135 billion. And all the proposed substitutes have problems; none is in production, most of them are toxic, and many are flammable. Of course, we could always return to using toxic ammonia and sulfur dioxide! Note that one of the biggest users of freon is refrigeration, and the most important reason for refrigeration is food preservation. If the proponents of banning CFC are so anxious to reduce its use, why aren't they out campaigning for irradiating food as a substitute for refrigeration? Food irradiation is an available technology used by all our astronauts and in hospitals for patients that require a sterile environment.

We are told that the ozone hole is important because the ozone blanket blocks much of the ultraviolet light in sunshine, which, if it penetrates to the earth's surface, could cause skin cancer, eye problems, and plant damage. This could be worrisome, except that actual records from a network of recording instruments set up in 1974 to measure ultraviolet light reaching the earth's surface have shown a continuously decreasing penetration of from 0.5 percent to 1.1 percent per year. If the theories about ozone depletion were correct, ultraviolet radiation should have been increasing, not decreasing.

Furthermore, the form of skin cancer caused by ultraviolet radiation is relatively harmless, though irritating and unsightly, and 99 percent of the cases can be cured if treated in time. On the other hand, malignant melanoma, another unrelated type of skin cancer, is generally fatal. Its appearance is not related to ultraviolet radiation; its cause is unknown. Tragically, it is increasing, by 800 percent since 1935. As for plants, most are protected by several mechanisms that function to repair damage caused by ultraviolet light. The conclusion is hard to avoid: that the claims of skin cancer due to ozone loss are simply a widely repeated scare tactic.

The historian Hans Morgenthau wrote in 1946:

Two moods determine the attitude of our civilization to the social world: confidence in the power of reason, as represented by modern science, to solve the social problems of the age, and despair at the ever renewed failure of scientific reason to solve them.

The intellectual and moral history of mankind is the story of inner insecurity, of the anticipation of impending doom, of metaphysical anxieties.

John Maddox, editor of the prestigious British journal *Nature* has said that "these days there also seems to be an underlying cataclysmic sense among people. Scientists don't seem to be immune to this."

Well, they ought to be. And we ought to remember that using our   65
technology will go a long way toward averting those cataclysmic events and the "doom-is-almost-here" philosophy that seems to have so much appeal. Scientists owe it to society to show the way to a better life and an improved environment—through quality technology.

Working Together

1. As a class or in groups, line up, in opposing columns, the major facts and claims about facts in Matthews's "Under the Sun" and in Ray's piece.
   - What are the major issues in dispute?
   - What are the major ways that each writer supports his or her claims?
2. How can the average reader judge which writer (see item 1) is most believable or reliable? As you look at Matthews's and Ray's writing, what strategies or intellectual moves or phrasings inspire confidence, and which ones make you suspicious?
3. Consider the larger context outside the article itself. For example, Ray was the conservative governor of Washington State and before that head of the Atomic Energy Commission, the government agency in charge of nuclear power plants. Matthews's piece was published in *National Geographic* magazine. What agendas are implicit here, for both writers; what axes to grind?
4. How do your own biases and predispositions enter in? What are your own politics and beliefs? How do they affect your response to Ray's argument?

Rethinking and Rewriting

1. Do research on the life and career of Dixy Lee Ray and write a profile, putting this chapter from her book *Trashing the Planet* in its larger context.
2. Do research on how *Trashing the Planet* was reviewed in major newspapers and magazines. Be aware of the political orientation of the publications you look at. In the end, draw some tentative conclusions about the nature of "scientific fact" and the relationship of facts and politics.

"A SEMIDESERT WITH A DESERT HEART"

Marc Reisner

> *A 1970 graduate of Earlham College (Richmond, Indiana), Marc Reisner was a staff writer for the National Resources Defense Council until 1979, when he was awarded a fellowship to research the problem of water in the American West. The following excerpt is the first chapter of the book that resulted from this long research,* Cadillac Desert: The American West and Its Disappearing Water *(1986).*

One late November night in 1980 I was flying over the state of Utah on my way back to California. I had an aisle seat, and since I believe that anyone who flies in an airplane and doesn't spend most of his time looking out the window wastes his money, I walked back to the rear door of the airplane and stood for a long time at the door's tiny aperture, squinting out at Utah.

Two days earlier, a fierce early blizzard had gone through the Rocky Mountain states. In its wake, the air was pellucid. The frozen fire of a winter's moon poured cold light on the desert below. Six inches away from the tip of my nose the temperature was, according to the pilot, minus sixty-five, and seven miles below it was four above zero. But here we were, two hundred highly inventive creatures safe and comfortable inside a fat winged cylinder racing toward the Great Basin of North America, dozing, drinking, chattering, oblivious to the frigid emptiness outside.

Emptiness. There was nothing down there on the earth—no towns, no light, no signs of civilization at all. Barren mountains rose duskily from the desert floor; isolated mesas and buttes broke the wind-haunted distance. You couldn't see much in the moonlight, but obviously there were no forests, no pastures, no lakes, no rivers; there was no fruited plain. I counted the minutes between clusters of lights. Six, eight, nine, eleven— going nine miles a minute, that was a lot of uninhabited distance in a crowded century, a lot of emptiness amid a civilization whose success was achieved on the pretension that natural obstacles do not exist.

Then the landscape heaved upward. We were crossing a high, thin cordillera of mountains, their tops already covered with snow. The Wasatch Range. As suddenly as the mountains appeared, they fell away, and a vast gridiron of lights appeared out of nowhere. It was clustered thickly under the aircraft and trailed off toward the south, erupting in ganglionic clots that winked and shimmered in the night. Salt Lake City, Orem, Draper, Provo: we were over most of the population of Utah.

That thin avenue of civilization pressed against the Wasatches, intimidated by a fierce desert on three sides, was a poignant sight. More startling

5

than its existence was the fact that it had been there only 134 years, since Brigham Young led his band of social outcasts to the old bed of a drying desert sea and proclaimed, "This is the place!" *This* was the place? Someone in that first group must have felt that Young had become unhinged by two thousand horribly arduous miles. Nonetheless, within hours of ending their ordeal, the Mormons were digging shovels into the earth beside the streams draining the Wasatch Range, leading canals into the surrounding desert which they would convert to fields that would nourish them. Without realizing it, they were laying the foundation of the most ambitious desert civilization the world has seen. In the New World, Indians had dabbled with irrigation, and the Spanish had improved their techniques, but the Mormons attacked the desert full-bore, flooded it, subverted its dreadful indifference—moralized it—until they had made a Mesopotamia in America between the valleys of the Green River and the middle Snake. Fifty-six years after the first earth was turned beside City Creek, the Mormons had six million acres under full or partial irrigation in several states. In that year—1902—the United States government launched its own irrigation program, based on Mormon experience, guided by Mormon laws, run largely by Mormons. The agency responsible for it, the U.S. Bureau of Reclamation, would build the highest and largest dams in the world on rivers few believed could be controlled—the Colorado, the Sacramento, the Columbia, the lower Snake—and run aqueducts for hundreds of miles across deserts and over mountains and through the Continental Divide in order to irrigate more millions of acres and provide water and power to a population equal to that of Italy. Thanks to irrigation, thanks to the Bureau—an agency few people know—states such as California, Arizona, and Idaho became populous and wealthy; millions settled in regions where nature, left alone, would have countenanced thousands at best; great valleys and hemispherical basins metamorphosed from desert blond to semitropic green.

On the other hand, what has it all amounted to?

Stare for a while at a LANDSAT photograph of the West, and you will see the answer: not all that much. Most of the West is still untrammeled, unirrigated, depopulate in the extreme. Modern Utah, where large-scale irrigation has been going on longer than anywhere else, has 3 percent of its land area under cultivation. California has twelve hundred major dams, the two biggest irrigation projects on earth, and more irrigated acreage than any other state, but its irrigated acreage is not much larger than Vermont. Except for the population centers of the Pacific Coast and the occasional desert metropolis—El Paso, Albuquerque, Tucson, Denver—you can drive a thousand miles in the West and encounter fewer towns than you would crossing New Hampshire. Westerners call what they have established out here a civilization, but it would be more accurate to call it a beachhead. And if history is any guide, the odds that we can sustain it would have to be regarded as low. Only one desert civilization, out of dozens that grew up in antiquity, has survived uninterrupted into modern times. And Egypt's approach to irrigation was fundamentally different from all the rest.

If you begin at the Pacific rim and move inland, you will find large cities, many towns, and prosperous-looking farms until you cross the Sierra Nevada and the Cascades, which block the seasonal weather fronts moving in from the Pacific and wring out their moisture in snows and drenching rains. On the east side of the Sierra-Cascade crest, moisture drops immediately—from as much as 150 inches of precipitation on the western slope to as little as four inches on the eastern—and it doesn't increase much, except at higher elevations, until you have crossed the hundredth meridian, which bisects the Dakotas and Nebraska and Kansas down to Abilene, Texas, and divides the country into its two most significant halves—the one receiving at least twenty inches of precipitation a year, the other generally receiving less. Any place with less than twenty inches of rainfall is hostile terrain to a farmer depending solely on the sky, and a place that receives seven inches or less—as Phoenix, El Paso, and Reno do—is arguably no place to inhabit at all. Everything depends on the manipulation of water—on capturing it behind dams, storing it, and rerouting it in concrete rivers over distances of hundreds of miles. Were it not for a century and a half of messianic effort toward that end, the West as we know it would not exist.

The word "messianic" is not used casually. Confronted by the desert, the first thing Americans want to do is change it. People say that they "love" the desert, but few of them love it enough to live there. I mean in the real desert, not in a make-believe city like Phoenix with exotic palms and golf-course lawns and a five-hundred-foot fountain and an artificial surf. Most people "love" the desert by driving through it in air-conditioned cars, "experiencing" its grandeur. That may be some kind of experience, but it is living in a fool's paradise. To *really* experience the desert you have to march right into its white bowl of sky and shape-contorting heat with your mind on your canteen as if it were your last gallon of gas and you were being chased by a carload of escaped murderers. You have to imagine what it would be like to drink blood from a lizard or, in the grip of dementia, claw bare-handed through sand and rock for the vestigial moisture beneath a dry wash.

Trees, because of their moisture requirements, are our physiological counterparts in the kingdom of plants. Throughout most of the West they begin to appear high up on mountainsides, usually at five or six thousand feet, or else they huddle like cows along occasional streambeds. Higher up the rain falls, but the soil is miserable, the weather is extreme, and human efforts are under siege. Lower down, in the valleys and on the plains, the weather, the soil, and the terrain are more welcoming, but it is almost invariably too dry. A drought lasting three weeks can terrorize an eastern farmer; a drought of five months is, to a California farmer, a normal state of affairs. (The lettuce farmers of the Imperial Valley don't even *like* rain; it is so hot in the summer it wilts the leaves.) The Napa Valley of California receives as much Godwater—a term for rain in the arid West—as Illinois, but almost all of it falls from November to March; a weather front between May and September rates as much press attention as a meteor shower. In Nevada you see rainclouds, formed by orographic updrafts over the mountains, almost every day. But rainclouds in the desert seldom mean rain, because the heat reflected off the earth and the ravenous dryness can vaporize a shower in midair, leaving the blackest-looking cumulonimbus trailing a few pathetic ribbons of moisture that disappear before reaching the ground. And if rain does manage to fall to earth, there is nothing to hold it, so it races off in evanescent brown torrents, evaporating, running to nowhere.

One does not really conquer a place like this. One inhabits it like an occupying army and makes, at best, an uneasy truce with it. New England was completely forested in 1620 and nearly deforested 150 years later; Arkansas saw nine million acres of marsh and swamp forest converted to farms. Through such Promethean effort, the eastern half of the continent was radically made over, for better or worse. The West never can be. The only way to make the region over is to irrigate it. But there is too little water to begin with, and water in rivers is phenomenally expensive to move. And even if you succeeded in moving every drop, it wouldn't make much of a difference. John Wesley Powell, the first person who clearly understood this, figured that if you evenly distributed all the surface water flowing between the Columbia River and the Gulf of Mexico, you would *still* have a desert almost indistinguishable from the one that is there today. Powell failed to appreciate the vast amount of water sitting in underground aquifers, a legacy of the Ice Ages and their glacial melt, but even this water, which has turned the western plains and large portions of California and Arizona green, will be mostly gone within a hundred years—a resource squandered as quickly as oil.

At first, no one listened to Powell when he said the overwhelming portion of the West could never be transformed. People figured that when the region was settled, rainfall would magically increase, that it would "follow the plow." In the late 1800s, such theories amounted to Biblical dogma. When they proved catastrophically wrong, Powell's irrigation ideas were finally embraced and pursued with near fanaticism, until the most gigantic dams were being built on the most minuscule foundations of economic rationality and need. Greening the desert became a kind of Christian ideal. In May of 1957, a very distinguished Texas historian, Walter Prescott Webb, wrote an article for *Harper's* entitled "The American West, Perpetual Mirage," in which he called the West "a semidesert with a desert heart" and said it had too dark a soul to be truly converted. The greatest national folly we could commit, Webb argued, would be to exhaust the Treasury trying to make over the West in the image of Illinois—a folly which, by then, had taken on the appearance of national policy. The editors of *Harper's* were soon up to their knees in a flood of vitriolic mail from westerners condemning Webb as an infidel, a heretic, a doomsayer.

Desert, semidesert, call it what you will. The point is that despite heroic efforts and many billions of dollars, all we have managed to do in the arid West is turn a Missouri-size section green—and that conversion has been wrought mainly with nonrenewable groundwater. But a goal of many westerners and of their federal archangels, the Bureau of Reclamation and Corps of Engineers, has long been to double, triple, quadruple the amount of desert that has been civilized and farmed, and now these same people say that the future of a hungry world depends on it, even if it means importing water from as far away as Alaska. What they seem not to understand is how difficult it will be just to hang on to the beachhead they have made. Such a surfeit of ambition stems, of course, from the remarkable record of success we have had in reclaiming the American desert. But the same could have been said about any number of desert civilizations throughout history—Assyria, Carthage, Mesopotamia; the Inca, the Aztec, the Hohokam—before they collapsed.

And it may not even have been drought that did them in. It may have been salt.

The Colorado River rises high in the Rockies, a trickle of frigid snowmelt bubbling down the west face of Longs Peak, and begins its fifteen-hundred-mile, twelve-thousand-foot descent to the Gulf of California. Up there, amid mountain fastnesses, its waters are sweet. The river swells quickly, taking in the runoff of most of western Colorado, and before long becomes a substantial torrent churning violently through red canyons down the long west slope of the range. Not far from Utah, at the threshold of the Great Basin, the rapids die into riffles and the Colorado River becomes, for a stretch of forty miles, calm and sedate. It has entered the Grand Valley, a small oasis of orchards and cows looking utterly out of place in a landscape where it appears to have rained once, about half a million years ago. The oasis is man-made and depends entirely on the river. Canals divert a good share of the flow and spread it over fields, and when the water percolates through the soil and returns to the river it passes through thick deposits of mineral salts, a common phenomenon in the West. As the water leaves the river, its salinity content is around two hundred parts per million; when it returns, the salinity content is sixty-five hundred parts per million.

The Colorado takes in the Gunnison River, whose waters have also filtered repeatedly through irrigated, saline earth, and disappears into the canyonlands of Utah. Near the northernmost tentacle of Lake Powell, where the river backs up for nearly two hundred miles behind Glen Canyon Dam, it receives its major tributary, the Green River. The land along the upper Green is heavily irrigated, and so is the land beside its two major tributaries, the Yampa and the White. Some of *their* tributaries, which come out of the Piceance Basin, are saltier than the ocean. In Lake Powell, the water spreads exposing vast surface acreage to the sun, which evaporates several feet each year, leaving all the salts behind. Released by

15

Glen Canyon Dam, the Colorado takes in the Little Colorado, Kanab Creek, the Muddy, and one of the more misnamed rivers on earth, the Virgin. It pools again in Lake Mead, again in Lake Mojave, and again in Lake Havasu; it takes in the Gila River and its oft-used tributaries, the Salt and the Verde, all turbid with alkaline leachate. A third of its flow then goes to California, where some of it irrigates the Imperial Valley and the rest allows Los Angeles and San Diego to exist. By then, the water is so salty that restaurants often serve it with a slice of lemon. If you pour it on certain plants, they will die.

Along the Gila River in Arizona, the last tributary of the Colorado, is a small agricultural basin which Spaniards and Indians tried to irrigate as early as the sixteenth century. It has poor drainage—the soil is underlain by impermeable clays—so the irrigation water rose right up to the root zones of the crops. With each irrigation, it became saltier, and before long everything that was planted died. The Spaniards finally left, and the desert took the basin back; for a quarter of a millennium, it remained desert. Then, in the 1940s, the Bureau of Reclamation reclaimed it again, building the Welton-Mohawk Project and adding an expensive drainage system to collect the sumpwater and carry it away. Just above the Mexican border, the drain empties into the Colorado River.

In 1963, the Bureau closed the gates of Glen Canyon Dam. As Lake Powell filled, the flow of fresh water below it was greatly reduced. At the same time, the Welton-Mohawk drain was pouring water with a salinity content of sixty-three hundred parts per million directly into the Colorado. The salinity of the river—what was left of it—soared to fifteen hundred parts per million at the Mexican border. The most important agricultural region in all of Mexico lies right below the border, utterly dependent on the Colorado River; we were giving the farmers slow liquid death to pour over their fields.

The Mexicans complained bitterly, to no avail. By treaty, we had promised them a million and a half acre-feet of water. But we hadn't promised them *usable* water. By 1973, Mexico was in a state of apoplexy. The ruin of its irrigated agricultural lands along the lower Colorado was the biggest issue in the campaign of presidential candidate Luis Echeverría, who was elected by a wide margin in that year. Still, the United States continued to do nothing. But 1973 also saw the arrival of OPEC. Some new geologic soundings in the Bay of Campeche indicated that Mexico might soon become one of the greatest oil-exporting nations in the world. When Echeverría threatened to drag the United States before the World Court at The Hague, Richard Nixon sent his negotiators down to work out a salinity-control treaty. It was signed within a few months.

Once we agreed to give Mexico water of tolerable quality, we had to decide how to do it. Congress's solution was to authorize a desalination plant ten times larger than any in existence that will clean up the Colorado River just as it enters Mexico. What it will cost nobody knows; the official 20 estimate in 1985 was $300 million, not counting the 40,000 kilowatts of electricity required to run it. Having done that, Congress wrote what amounts to a blank check for a welter of engineered solutions farther upriver, whose exact nature is still under debate. Those could cost another $600 million, probably more. One could easily achieve the same results by buying out the few thousand acres of alkaline and poorly drained land that contribute most to the problem, but there, once again, one runs up against the holiness of the blooming desert. Western Congressmen, in the 1970s, were perfectly willing to watch New York City collapse when it was threatened with bankruptcy and financial ruin. After all, New York was a profligate and sinful place and probably deserved such a fate. But they were not willing to see one acre of irrigated land succumb to the forces of nature, regardless of cost. So they authorized probably $1 billion worth of engineered solutions to the Colorado salinity problem in order that a few hundred upstream farmers could go on irrigating and poisoning the river. The Yuma Plant will remove the Colorado's salt—actually just enough of it to fulfill our treaty obligations to Mexico—at a cost of around $300 per acre-foot of water. The upriver irrigators buy the same amount from the Bureau for $3.50.

Nowhere is the salinity problem more serious than in the San Joaquin Valley of California, the most productive farming region in the entire world. There you have a shallow and impermeable clay layer, the residual bottom of an ancient sea, underlying a million or so acres of fabulously profitable land. During the irrigation season, temperatures in the valley fluctuate between 90 and 110 degrees; the good water evaporates as if the sky were a sponge, the junk water goes down, and the problem gets worse and worse. Very little of the water seeps through the Corcoran Clay, so it rises back up into the root zones—in places, the clay is only a few feet down—waterlogs the land, and kills the crops. A few thousand acres have already gone out of production—you can see the salt on the ground like a dusting of snow. In the next few decades, as irrigation continues, that figure is expected to increase almost exponentially. To build a drainage system for the valley—a giant network of underground pipes and surface canals that would intercept the junk water and carry it off—could cost as much as a small country's GNP. In 1985, the Secretary of the Interior put forth a figure of $5 billion for the Westlands region, and Westlands is only half the problem. Where would the drainwater go? The Westlands' drainwater, temporarily stored in a huge sump which was christened a wildlife preserve, has been killing thousands of migrating waterfowl; the water contains not just salts but selenium, pesticides, and God knows what else. There is one logical terminus: San Francisco Bay. As far as northern Californians are concerned, the farmers stole all this water from them; now they want to ship it back full of crud.

As is the case with most western states, California's very existence is premised on epic liberties taken with water—mostly water that fell as rain on the north and was diverted to the south, thus precipitating the state's longest-running political wars. With the exception of a few of the rivers draining the remote North Coast, virtually every drop of water in the state is put to some economic use before being allowed to return to the sea. Very little of this water is used by people, however. Most of it is used for irrigation—85 percent of it, to be exact. That is a low percentage, by western standards. In Arizona, 90 percent of the water consumed goes to irrigation; in Colorado and New Mexico, the figure is almost as high. In Kansas, Nevada, Nebraska, North Dakota, South Dakota, Oklahoma, Texas, Wyoming, Montana; even in Washington, Oregon, and Idaho—in all of those states, irrigation accounts for nearly all of the water that is consumptively used.

By the late 1970s, there were 1,251 major reservoirs in California, and every significant river—save one—had been dammed at least once. The Stanislaus River is dammed fourteen times on its short run to the sea. California has some of the biggest reservoirs in the country; its rivers, seasonally swollen by the huge Sierra snowpack, carry ten times the runoff of Colorado's. And yet all of those rivers and reservoirs satisfy only 60 percent of the demand. The rest of the water comes from under the ground. The rivers are infinitely renewable, at least until the reservoirs silt up or the climate changes. But a lot of the water being pumped out of the ground is as nonrenewable as oil.

Early in the century, before the federal government got into the business of building dams, most of the water used for irrigation in California was groundwater. The farmers in the Central Valley (which comprises both the Sacramento and the San Joaquin) pumped it out so relentlessly that by the 1930s the state's biggest industry was threatened with collapse. The growers, by then, had such a stranglehold on the legislature that they convinced it, in the depths of the Depression, to authorize a huge water project—by far the largest in the world—to rescue them from their own greed. When the bonds to finance the project could not be sold, Franklin Delano Roosevelt picked up the unfinished task. Today, the Central Valley Project is still the most mind-boggling public works project on five continents, and in the 1960s the state built its own project, nearly as large. Together, the California Water Project and the Central Valley Project have captured enough water to supply eight cities the size of New York. But the projects brought into production far more land than they had water to supply, so the growers had to supplement their surface water with tens of thousands of wells. As a result, the groundwater overdraft, instead of being alleviated, has gotten worse.

In the San Joaquin Valley, pumping now exceeds natural replenish-   25
ment by more than half a trillion gallons a year. By the end of the century it could rise to a trillion gallons—a mining operation that, in sheer volume, beggars the exhaustion of oil. How long it can go on, no one knows. It depends on a lot of things, such as the price of food and the cost of energy and the question whether, as carbon dioxide changes the world's climate, California will become drier. (It is expected to become much drier.) But

it is one reason you hear talk about redirecting the Eel and the Klamath and the Columbia and, someday, the Yukon River.

The problem in California is that there is absolutely no regulation over groundwater pumping, and, from the looks of things, there won't be any for many years to come. The farmers loathe the idea, and in California "the farmers" are the likes of Exxon, Tenneco, and Getty Oil. Out on the high plains, the problem is of a different nature. There, the pumping of groundwater is regulated. But the states have all decided to regulate their groundwater out of existence.

The vanishing groundwater in Texas, Kansas, Colorado, Oklahoma, New Mexico, and Nebraska is all part of the Ogallala aquifer, which holds two distinctions: one of being the largest discrete aquifer in the world, the other of being the fastest-disappearing aquifer in the world. The rate of withdrawal over natural replenishment is now roughly equivalent to the flow of the Colorado River. This was the region called the Dust Bowl, the one devastated by the Great Drought; that was back before anyone knew there was so much water underfoot, and before the invention of the centrifugal pump. The prospect that a region so plagued by catastrophe could become rich and fertile was far too tantalizing to resist; the more irrigation, everyone thought, the better. The states knew the groundwater couldn't last forever (even if the farmers thought it would), so, like the Saudis with their oil, they had to decide how long to make it last. A reasonable period, they decided, was twenty-five to fifty years.

"What are you going to do with all that water?" asks Felix Sparks, the former head of the Colorado Water Conservation Board. "Are you just going to leave it in the ground?" Not necessarily, one could reply, but fifty years or a little longer is an awfully short period in which to exhaust the providence of half a million years, to consume as much nonrenewable water as there is in Lake Huron. "Well," says Sparks, "when we use it up, we'll just have to get more water from somewhere else."

Stephen Reynolds, Sparks's counterpart in New Mexico—as state engineer, the man in charge of water, he may be the most powerful person in the state—says much the same thing: "We made a conscious decision to mine out our share of the Ogallala in a period of twenty-five to forty years." In the portions of New Mexico that overlie the Ogallala, according to Reynolds, some farmers withdraw as much as five feet of water a year, while nature puts back a quarter of an inch. What will happen to the economy of Reynolds's state when its major agricultural region turns to dust? "Agriculture uses about 90 percent of our water, and produces around 20 percent of the state's income, so it wouldn't necessarily be a knockout economic blow," he answers. "Of course, you are talking about drastic changes in the whole life and culture of a very big region encompassing seven states.

"On the other hand," says Reynolds, half-hopefully, "we may decide   30
as a matter of national policy that all this agriculture is too important to lose. We can always decide to build some more water projects."

More water projects. During the first and only term of his presidency, Jimmy Carter decided that the age of water projects had come to a deserved end. As a result, he drafted a "hit list" on which were a couple of dozen big dams and irrigation projects, east and west, which he vowed not to fund. Carter was merely stunned by the reaction from the East; he was blown over backward by the reaction from the West. Of about two hundred western members of Congress, there weren't more than a dozen who dared to support him. One of the projects would return five cents in economic benefits for every taxpayer dollar invested; one offered irrigation farmers subsidies worth more than $1 million each; another, a huge dam on a middling California river, would cost more than Hoover, Shasta, Glen Canyon, Bonneville, and Grand Coulee combined. But Carter's hit list had as much to do with his one-term presidency as Iran.

Like millions of easterners who wonder how such projects get built, Jimmy Carter had never spent much time in the West. He had never driven across the country and watched the landscape turn from green to brown at the hundredth meridian, the threshold of what was once called the Great American Desert—but which is still wet compared to the vast ultramontane basins beyond. In southern Louisiana, water is the central fact of existence, and a whole culture and set of values have grown up around it. In the West, lack of water is the central fact of existence, and a whole culture and set of values have grown up around it. In the East, to "waste" water is to consume it needlessly or excessively. In the West, to waste water is *not* to consume it—to let it flow unimpeded and undiverted down rivers. Use of water is, by definition, "beneficial" use—the term is right in the law—even if it goes to Fountain Hills, Arizona, and is shot five hundred feet into 115-degree skies; even if it is sold, at vastly subsidized rates, to farmers irrigating crops in the desert which their counterparts in Mississippi or Arkansas are, at that very moment, being paid not to grow. To easterners, "conservation" of water usually means protecting rivers from development; in the West, it means building dams.

More water projects. In the West, nearly everyone is for them. Politicians of every stripe have sacrificed their most sacred principles on the altar of water development. Barry Goldwater, scourge of welfare and champion of free enterprise, has been a lifelong supporter of the Central Arizona Project, which comes as close to socialism as anything this country has ever done (the main difference being that those who are subsidized are well-off, even rich). Former Governor Jerry Brown of California attended the funeral of E. F. Schumacher, the English economist who wrote *Small Is Beautiful,* then flew back home to lobby for a water project that would cost more than it did to put a man on the moon. Alan Cranston, the leading liberal in the U.S. Senate, the champion of the poor and the oppressed, successfully lobbied to legalize illegal sales of subsidized water to big corporate farmers, thus denying water—and farms—to thousands of the poor and oppressed.

In the West, it is said, water flows uphill toward money. And it literally does, as it leaps three thousand feet across the Tehachapi Mountains in gigantic siphons to slake the thirst of Los Angeles, as it is shoved a thousand feet out of Colorado River canyons to water Phoenix and Palm Springs and the irrigated lands around them. It goes 444 miles (the distance from Boston to Washington) by aqueduct from the Feather River to south of L.A. It goes in man-made rivers, in siphons, in tunnels. In a hundred years, actually less, God's riverine handiwork in the West has been stood on its head. A number of rivers have been nearly dried up. One now flows backward. Some flow through mountains into other rivers' beds. There are huge reservoirs where there was once desert; there is desert, or cropland, where there were once huge shallow swamps and lakes.

It still isn't enough.   *35*

In 1971, the Bureau of Reclamation released a plan to divert six million acre-feet from the lower Mississippi River and create a river in reverse, pumping the water up a staircase of reservoirs to the high plains in order to save the irrigation economy of West Texas and eastern New Mexico, utterly dependent on groundwater, from collapse. Since the distance the water would have to travel is a thousand miles, and the elevation gain four thousand feet, and since six million acre-feet of water weigh roughly 16.5 trillion pounds, a lot of energy would be required to pump it. The Bureau figured that six nuclear plants would do, and calculated the cost of the power at one mill per kilowatt-hour, a tiny fraction of what it costs today. The whole package came to $20 billion, in 1971 dollars; the benefit-cost ratio would have been .27 to 1. For each dollar invested, twenty-seven cents in economic productivity would be returned. "That's kind of discouraging," says Stephen Reynolds. "But when you consider our balance-of-payments deficits, you have to remember that we send $100 billion out of this country each year just to pay for imported oil. The main thing we export is food. The Ogallala region produces a very large share of our agricultural exports."

More water projects. In the early 1960s, the Ralph M. Parsons Corporation, a giant engineering firm based in Pasadena, California, released a plan to capture much of the flow of the Yukon and Tanana rivers and divert it two thousand miles to the Southwest through the Rocky Mountain Trench. The proposal, called the North American Water and Power Alliance, wasn't highly regarded by Canada, which was the key to the "alliance," but in the West it was passionately received. Ten years later, as environmentalism and inflation both took root, NAWAPA seemed destined for permanent oblivion. But then OPEC raised the price of oil 1,600 percent, and Three Mile Island looked as if it might seal fission's doom. California was hit by the worst drought in its history; had it lasted one more year, its citizens might have begun migrating back east, their mattresses strapped to the tops of their Porsches and BMWs. All of a sudden the hollowness of our triumph over nature hit home with striking effect.

With hydroelectricity now regarded by many as salvation, and with nearly half the irrigated farmland in the West facing some kind of doom—drought, salt, or both combined—NAWAPA, in the early 1980s, began to twitch again. The cost had doubled, from $100 billion to $200 billion, but by then we were spending that much in a single year on defense. The project could produce 100,000 megawatts of electricity; it could rescue California, the high plains, and Arizona and still have enough water left to turn half of Nevada green. The new Romans were now saying that it wasn't a matter of *whether* NAWAPA would be built, but when.

Perhaps they are right. Perhaps, despite the fifty thousand major dams we have built in America; despite the fact that federal irrigation has, for the most part, been a horribly bad investment in free-market terms; despite the fact that the number of free-flowing rivers that remain in the West can be counted on two hands; perhaps, despite all of this, the grand adventure of playing God with our waters will go on. Perhaps it will be consummated on a scale of which our forebears could scarcely dream. By encouraging millions of people to leave the frigid Northeast, we could save a lot of imported oil; by doubling our agricultural exports, we could pay for the oil we import today. As the ancient, leaking water systems and infrastructure of the great eastern cities continue to decay, we may see an East-West alliance develop: you give us our water projects, we'll give you yours. Perhaps, in some future haunted by scarcity, the unthinkable may be thinkable after all.

In the West, of course, where water is concerned, logic and reason have never figured prominently in the scheme of things. As long as we maintain a civilization in a semidesert with a desert heart, the yearning to civilize more of it will always be there. It is an instinct that followed close on the heels of food, sleep, and sex, predating the Bible by thousands of years. The instinct, if nothing else, is bound to persist.

The lights of Salt Lake City began to fade, an evanescent shimmer 40 on the rear horizon. A few more minutes and the landscape was again a black void. We were crossing the Great Basin, the arid heart of the American West. The pilot announced that the next glow of civilization would be Reno, some six hundred miles away. I remembered two things about Reno. The annual precipitation there is seven inches, an amount that Florida and Louisiana and Virginia have received in a day. But even though gambling and prostitution are legal around Reno, water metering, out of principle, was for a long time against the law.

Reading and Responding

1. Freewrite a paragraph summary of this article.
2. Reread; in the margins, mark which slot from the TRIAC scheme (see chapter 2) Marc Reisner is filling at which points: where he's illustrating (I), analyzing (A), restating his thesis (R), and so on.

3. Freewrite about where your water comes from when you open the tap. If you know where it comes from, talk about that. If you don't know, guess. Then write about how you'd find out for sure.

Working Together

1. Outline this piece on the board, using TRIAC.
2. Between major sections, insert transitional words or phrases: *because, since, but, and, for instance, on the other hand,* and the like.
3. What's the function of the blank space Reisner uses in the article?
4. Identify the major paragraph "blocs" here: Find a topic sentence in one paragraph that governs a number of other paragraphs—that is, one paragraph that controls a group of others that may or may not have their own topic sentences.

Rethinking and Rewriting

1. Write a paper on any subject imitating the structure of Reisner's article.
2. Do research on the water system in your community. Where does the water come from, how much is there, how is the water purified, have there been any problems with the system? If you live in the West, how is your situation related to the problems Reisner describes? If you live in other parts of the country, how is your situation different?
3. Keep a water diary for three days. Record *every* use you make of water. Then combine this personal experience with your reading of Reisner. What do these two sources teach you? What would you like to know more about? If you were going to do a research project on some aspect of water use, what questions would you want to answer?

"SAVE THE WHALES,
SCREW THE SHRIMP"

Joy Williams

> *Recipient of fellowships from both the National Endowment for the Arts and the Guggenheim Foundation, Joy Williams is best known as a fiction writer, and she has recently been selected to receive the Strauss Living Award from the American Academy of Arts and Letters. In this essay, which originally appeared in* Esquire, *Williams gives readers a monologue with an attitude. Listen to it as you read—or better yet, read parts of it aloud.*

Before You Read

Read only the first long paragraph of this piece. Then see whether you can define the "you" that Joy Williams seems to be addressing. List the attributes of this "you." Once you've listed them, ask yourself whether you fit this description. That is, in what ways is Williams's "you" actually like you? Write about that for a paragraph.

I don't want to talk about *me*, of course, but it seems as though far too much attention has been lavished on *you* lately—that your greed and vanities and quest for self-fulfillment have been catered to far too much. You just want and want and want. You haven't had a mandala dream since the eighties began. To have a mandala dream you'd have to instinctively know that it was an attempt at self-healing on the part of Nature, and you don't believe in Nature anymore. It's too isolated from you. You've abstracted it. It's so messy and damaged and sad. Your eyes glaze as you travel life's highway past all the crushed animals and the Big Gulp cups. You don't even take pleasure in looking at nature photographs these days. Oh, they can be just as pretty, as always, but don't they make you feel increasingly . . . anxious? Filled with more trepidation than peace? So what's the point? You see the picture of the baby condor or the panda munching on a bamboo shoot, and your heart just sinks, doesn't it? A picture of a poor old sea turtle with barnacles on her back, all ancient and exhausted, depositing her five gallons of doomed eggs in the sand hardly fills you with joy, because you realize, quite rightly, that just outside the frame falls the shadow of the condo. What's cropped from the shot of ocean waves crashing on a pristine shore is the plastics plant, and just beyond the dunes lies a parking lot. Hidden from immediate view in the butterfly-bright meadow, in the dusky thicket, in the oak and holly wood, are the surveyors' stakes, for someone wants to build a mall exactly there—some gas stations and supermarkets, some pizza and video shops, a health club, maybe a bulimia treatment center. Those lovely pictures of leopards and herons and wild rivers, well, you just know they're going to be accompanied by a text that will serve only to bring you down. You don't want to think about it! It's all so uncool. And you don't want to feel guilty either. Guilt is uncool. Regret maybe you'll consider. *Maybe*. Regret is a possibility, but don't push me, you say. Nature photographs have become something of a problem, along with almost everything else. Even though they leave the bad stuff out—maybe because you *know* they're leaving all the bad stuff out—such pictures are making you increasingly aware that you're a little too late for Nature. Do you feel that? Twenty years too late, maybe only ten? Not *way* too late, just a little too late? Well, it appears that you are. And since you are, you've decided you're just not going to attend this particular party.

Pascal said that it is easier to endure death without thinking about it than to endure the thought of death without dying. This is how you manage to dance the strange dance with that grim partner, nuclear annihilation. When the U.S. Army notified Winston Churchill that the first atom bomb had been detonated in New Mexico, it chose the code phrase BABIES SATISFACTORILY BORN. So you entered the age of irony, and the strange double life you've been leading with the world ever since. Joyce Carol Oates suggests that the reason writers—*real* writers, one assumes—don't write about Nature is that it lacks a sense of humor and registers no irony. It just doesn't seem to be of the times—these slick, sleek, knowing, objective, indulgent times. And the word *Environment*. Such a bloodless word. A flat-footed word with a shrunken heart. A word increasingly disengaged from its association with the natural world. Urban planners, industrialists, economists, and developers use it. It's a lost word, really. A cold word, mechanistic, suited strangely to the coldness generally felt toward Nature. It's their word now. You don't mind giving it up. As for *Environmentalist,* that's one that can really bring on the yawns, for you've tamed and tidied it, neutered it quite nicely. An environmentalist must be calm, rational, reasonable, and willing to compromise, otherwise you won't listen to him. Still, his beliefs are *opinions* only, for this is the age of radical subjectivism. Not long ago, Barry Commoner spoke to the Environmental Protection Agency. He scolded them. They loved it. The way they protect the environment these days is apparently to find an "acceptable level of harm from a pollutant and then issue rules allowing industry to pollute to that level." Commoner suggested that this was inappropriate. An EPA employee suggested that any other approach would place limits on economic growth and implied that Commoner was advocating this. Limits on economic growth! Commoner vigorously denied this. Oh, it was a healthy exchange of ideas, healthier certainly than our air and water. We needed that little spanking, the EPA felt. It was refreshing. The agency has recently lumbered into action in its campaign to ban dinoseb. You seem to have liked your dinoseb. It's been a popular weed killer, even though it has been directly linked with birth defects. You must hate weeds a lot. Although the

EPA appears successful in banning the poison, it will still have to pay the disposal costs and compensate the manufacturers for the market value of the chemicals they still have in stock.

That's ironic, you say, but farmers will suffer losses, too, oh dreadful financial losses, if herbicide and pesticide use is restricted.

Farmers grow way too much stuff anyway. They grow surplus crops with subsidized water created by turning rivers great and small into a plumbing system of dams and canals. Rivers have become *systems*. Wetlands are increasingly being referred to as *filtering systems*—things deigned *useful* because of their ability to absorb urban run-off, oil from roads, et cetera.

We know that. We've known that for years about farmers. We know   5
a lot these days. We're very well informed. If farmers aren't allowed to make a profit by growing surplus crops, they'll have to sell their land to developers, who'll turn all that *arable land* into office parks. Arable land isn't Nature anyway, and besides, we like those office parks and shopping plazas, with their monster supermarkets open twenty-four hours a day with aisle after aisle after aisle of *products*. It's fun. Products are fun.

Farmers like their poisons, but ranchers like them even more. There are well-funded predominantly federal and cooperative programs like the Agriculture Department's Animal Damage Control Unit that poison, shoot, and trap several thousand animals each year. This unit loves to kill things. It was created to kill things—bobcats, foxes, black bears, mountain lions, rabbits, badgers, countless birds—all to make this great land safe for the string bean and the corn, the sheep and the cow, even though you're not consuming as much cow these days. A burger now and then, but burgers are hardly cows at all, you feel. They're not all *our* cows in any case, for some burger matter is imported. There's a bit of Central American burger matter in your bun. Which is contributing to the conversion of tropical rain forest into cow pasture. Even so, you're getting away from meat these days. You're eschewing cow. It's seafood you love, shrimp most of all. And when you love something, it had better watch out, because you have a tendency to love it to death. Shrimp, shrimp, shrimp. It's more common on menus than chicken. In the wilds of Ohio, far, far from watery shores, four out of the six entrées on a menu will be shrimp, for some modest sum. Everywhere, it's all the shrimp you can eat or all you *care* to eat, for sometimes you just don't feel like eating all you *can*. You are intensively *harvesting* shrimp. Soon there won't be any left and then you can stop. It takes that, often, to make you stop. Shrimpers shrimp, of course. That's their *business*. They put out these big nets and in these nets, for each pound of shrimp, they catch more than ten times that amount of fish, turtles, and dolphins. These, quite the worse for wear, they dump back in. There is an object called TED (Turtle Excluder Device), which would save thousands of turtles and some dolphins from dying in the nets, but the shrimpers are loath to use TEDs, as they say it would cut the size of their shrimp catch.

We've heard about TED, you say.

They want you, all of you, to have all the shrimp you can eat and more. At Kiawah Island, off the coast of South Carolina, visitors go out on Jeep "safaris" through the part of the island that hasn't been developed yet. ("Wherever you see trees," the guide says, "really, that's a lot.") The safari comprises six Jeeps, and these days they go out at least four times a day, with more trips promised soon. The tourists drive their own Jeeps and the guide talks to them by radio. Kiawah has nice beaches, and the guide talks about turtles. When he mentions the shrimpers' role in the decline of the turtle, the shrimpers, who share the same frequency, scream at him. Shrimpers and most commercial fishermen (many of them working with drift and gill nets anywhere from six to thirty miles long) think of themselves as an *endangered species.* A recent newspaper headline said, "Shrimpers Spared Anti-Turtle Devices." Even so, with the continuing wanton depletion of shrimp beds, they will undoubtedly have to find some other means of employment soon. They might, for instance, become part of that vast throng laboring in the *tourist industry.*

Tourism has become an industry as destructive as any other. You are no longer benign in your traveling somewhere to look at the scenery. You never thought there was much gain in just looking anyway, you've always preferred to *use* the scenery in some manner. In your desire to get away from what you've got, you've caused there to be no place to get away *to.* You're just all bumpered up out there. Sewage and dumps have become prime indicators of America's lifestyle. In resort towns in New England and the Adirondacks, measuring the flow into the sewage plant serves as a business barometer. Tourism is a growth industry. You believe in growth. *Controlled* growth, of course. Controlled exponential growth is what you'd really like to see. You certainly don't want to put a moratorium or a cap on anything. That's illegal, isn't it? Retro you're not. You don't want to go back or anything. Forward. Maybe ask directions later. Growth is *desirable* as well as being *inevitable.* Growth is the one thing you seem to be powerless before, so you try to be realistic about it. Growth is—it's weird—it's like cancer or something.

Recently you, as tourist, have discovered your national parks and are   *10* quickly *overburdening* them. Spare land and it belongs to you! It's exotic land too, not looking like all the stuff around it that looks like everything else. You want to take advantage of this land, of course, and use it in every way you can. Thus the managers—or *stewards,* as they like to be called— have developed *wise* and *multiple-use* plans, keeping in mind exploiters' interests (for they have their needs, too) as well as the desires of the backpackers. Thus mining, timbering, and ranching activities take place in the national forests, where the Forest Service maintains a system of logging roads eight times larger than the interstate highway system. The national parks are more of a public playground and are becoming increasingly Europeanized in their look and management. Lots of concessions and motels.

You deserve a clean bed and a hot meal when you go into the wilderness. At least your stewards think that you do. You keep your stewards busy. Not only must they cater to your multiple and conflicting desires, they have to manage your wildlife *resources*. They have managed wildfowl to such an extent that the reasoning has become, If it weren't for hunters, ducks would disappear. Duck stamps and licensing fees support the whole rickety duck-management system. Yes! If it weren't for the people who killed them, wild ducks wouldn't exist! Managers are managing all wild creatures, not just those that fly. They track and tape and tag and band. They relocate, restock, and reintroduce. They cull and control. It's hard to keep it all straight. Protect or poison? Extirpate or just mostly eliminate? Sometimes even the stewards get mixed up.

This is the time of machines and models, hands-on management and master plans. Don't you ever wonder as you pass that billboard advertising another MASTER-PLANNED COMMUNITY just what master they are actually talking about? Not the Big Master, certainly. Something brought to you by one of the tiny masters, of which there are many. But you like these tiny masters and have even come to expect and require them. In Florida they've just started a ten-thousand-acre city in the Everglades. It's a *megaproject,* one of the largest ever in the state. Yes, they must have thought you wanted it. No, what you thought of as the Everglades, the Park, is only a little bitty part of the Everglades. Developers have been gnawing at this irreplaceable, strange land for years. It's like they just *hate* this ancient sea of grass. Maybe you could ask them about this sometime. Roy Rogers is the senior vice president of strategic planning, and the old cowboy says that every tree and bush and inch of sidewalk in the project has been planned. Nevertheless, because the whole thing will take twenty-five years to complete, the plan is going to be constantly changed. You can understand this. The important thing is that there be a blueprint. You trust a blueprint. The tiny masters know what you like. You like *a secure landscape* and *access to services.* You like grass—that is, lawns. The ultimate lawn is the golf course, which you've been told has "some ecological value." You believe this! Not that it really matters, you just like to play golf. These golf courses require a lot of watering. So much that the more inspired of the masters have taken to watering them with effluent, *treated* effluent, but yours, from all the condos and villas built around the stocked artificial lakes you fancy.

I really don't want to think about sewage, you say, but it sounds like progress.

It is true that the masters are struggling with the problems of your incessant flushing. Cuisine is also one of their concerns. Advances in sorbets—sorbet intermezzos—in their clubs and fine restaurants. They know what you want. You want A HAVEN FROM THE ORDINARY WORLD. If you're A NATURE LOVER in the West you want to live in a $200,000 home in A WILD ANIMAL HABITAT. If you're eastern and consider yourself more hip, you want to live in new towns—brand-new reconstructed-from-scratch towns—in a house of NINETEENTH-CENTURY DESIGN. But in these new towns the masters are building, getting around can be confusing. There is an abundance of curves and an infrequency of through streets. It's the new wilderness without any trees. You can get lost, even with all the "mental bread crumbs" the masters scatter about as visual landmarks—the windmill, the water views, the various groupings of landscape "material." You *are* lost, you know. But you trust a Realtor will show you the way. There are many more Realtors than tiny masters, and many of them have to make do with less than a loaf—that is, trying to sell stuff that's already been built in an environment already "enhanced" rather than something being planned—but they're everywhere, willing to show you the path. If Dante returned to Hell today, he'd probably be escorted down by a Realtor, talking all the while about how it was just another level of Paradise.

When have you last watched a sunset? Do you remember where you were? With whom? At Loews Ventana Canyon Resort, the Grand Foyer will provide you with that opportunity through lighting which is computerized to diminish with the approaching sunset!

The tiny masters are willing to arrange Nature for you. They will compose it into a picture that you can look at at your leisure, when you're not doing work or something like that. Nature becomes scenery, a prop. At some golf courses in the Southwest, the saguaro cacti are reported to be repaired with green paste when balls blast into their skin. The saguaro can attempt to heal themselves by growing over the balls, but this takes time, and the effect can be somewhat . . . baroque. It's better to get out the pastepot. Nature has become simply a visual form of entertainment, and it had better look snappy.   15

Listen, you say, we've been at Ventana Canyon. It's in the desert, right? It's very, very nice, a world-class resort. A totally self-contained environment with everything that a person could possibly want, on more than a thousand acres in the middle of zip. It sprawls but nestles, like. And they've maintained the integrity of as much of the desert ecosystem as possible. Give them credit for that. *Great* restaurant, too. We had baby bay scallops there. Coming into the lobby there are these two big hand-carved coyotes, mutely howling. And that's the way we like them, *mute.* God, why do those things howl like that?

Wildlife is a personal matter, you think. The attitude is up to you. You can prefer to see it dead or not dead. You might want to let it mosey about its business or blow it away. Wild things exist only if you have the graciousness to allow them to. Just outside Tucson, Arizona, there is a brand-new structure modeled after a French foreign legion outpost. It's the *International Wildlife Museum,* and it's full of dead animals. Three hundred species are there, at least a third of them—the rarest ones—killed and collected by one C. J. McElroy, who enjoyed doing it and now shares what's left with you. The museum claims to be educational because you can watch a taxidermist at work or touch a lion's tooth. You can get real close to these dead animals, closer than you can in a zoo. Some of you prefer zoos, however, which are becoming bigger, better, and bioclimatic. New-age zoo designers want the animals to *flow right out into your space.* In Dallas there will soon be a Wilds of Africa exhibit; in San Diego there's a simulated rain forest, where you can thread your way "down the side of a lush canyon, the air filled with a fine mist from 300 high-pressure nozzles"; in New Orleans you've constructed a swamp, the real swamp not far away on the verge of disappearing. Animals in these places are abstractions— wandering relics of their true selves, but that doesn't matter. Animal behavior in a zoo is nothing like natural behavior, but that doesn't really matter, either. Zoos are pretty, contained, and accessible. These new habitats can contain one hundred different species—not more than one or two of each thing, of course—on seven acres, three, one. You don't want to see *too much* of anything, certainly. An *example* will suffice. Sort of like a biological Crabtree & Evelyn basket selected with *you* in mind. You like things reduced, simplified. It's easier to take it all in, park it in your mind. You like things inside better than outside anyway. You are increasingly looking at and living in proxy environments created by substitution and simulation. *Resource economists* are a wee branch in the tree of tiny masters, and one, Martin Krieger, wrote, "Artificial prairies and wildernesses have been created, and there is no reason to believe that these artificial environments need be unsatisfactory for those who experience them. . . . We will have to realize that the way in which we experience nature is conditioned by our society—which more and more is seen to be receptive to responsible intervention."

Nature has become a world of appearances, a mere source of materials. You've been editing it for quite some time; now you're in the process of deleting it. Earth is beginning to look like not much more than a launching pad. Back near Tucson, on the opposite side of the mountain from the dead-animal habitat, you're building Biosphere II (as compared with or opposed to Biosphere I, more commonly known as Earth)—a $2\frac{1}{2}$- acre terrarium, an artificial ecosystem that will include a rain forest, a desert, a thirty-five-foot ocean, and several thousand species of life (lots of microbes), including eight human beings, who will cultivate a bit of farmland. You think it would be nice to colonize other worlds after you've made it necessary to leave this one.

Hey, that's pretty good, you say, all that stuff packed into just $2\frac{1}{2}$ acres. That's only about three times bigger than my entire *house.*

It's small all right, but still not small enough to be, apparently, useful. For the purposes of NASA, say, it would have to be smaller, oh much smaller, and energy-efficient too. Fiddle, fiddle, fiddle. You support fiddling, as well as meddling. This is how you learn. Though it's quite apparent the environment has been grossly polluted and the natural world 20 abused and defiled, you seem to prefer to continue pondering effects rather than preventing causes. You want proof, you insist on proof. A Dr. Lave from Carnegie-Mellon—and he's an expert, an economist, and an environmental *expert*—says that scientists will have to prove to you that you will suffer if you don't become less of a "throwaway society." *If you really want me to give up my car or my air conditioner, you'd better prove to me first that the earth would otherwise be uninhabitable,* Dr. Lave says. *Me* is *you,* I presume, whereas *you* refers to them. You as in me—that is, *me, me, me*—certainly strike a hard bargain. Uninhabitable the world has to get before you rein in your requirements. You're a consumer after all, *the* consumer upon whom so much attention is lavished, the ultimate user of a commodity that has become, these days, everything. To try to appease your appetite for proof, for example, scientists have been leasing for experimentation forty-six pristine lakes in Canada.

They don't want to *keep* them, they just want to *borrow* them.

They've been intentionally contaminating many of the lakes with a variety of pollutants dribbled into the propeller wash of research boats. *It's one of the boldest experiments in lake ecology ever conducted.* They've turned these remote lakes into huge *real-world test tubes.* They've been doing this since 1976! And what they've found so far in these *preliminary* studies is that pollutants are really destructive. The lakes get gross. Life in them ceases. It took about eight years to make this happen in one of them, everything carefully measured and controlled all the while. Now the scientists are slowly reversing the process. But it will take hundreds of years for the lakes to recover. They think.

Remember when you used to like rain, the sound of it, the feel of it, the way it made the plants and trees all glisten. We needed that rain, you would say. It looked pretty too, you thought, particularly in the movies. Now it rains and you go, Oh-oh. A nice walloping rain these days means *overtaxing our sewage treatment plants.* It means *untreated waste discharged directly into our waterways.* It means . . .

Okay. Okay.

Acid rain! And we all know what this is. Or most of us do. People of power in government and industry still don't seem to know what it is. Whatever it is, they say, they don't want to curb it, but they're willing to study it some more. Economists call air and water pollution "externalities" anyway. Oh, acid rain. You do get so sick of hearing about it. The words have already become a white-noise kind of thing. But you think in terms of *mitigating* it maybe. As for *the greenhouse effect,* you think in terms of *countering* that. One way that's been discussed recently is the planting of new forests, not for the sake of the forests alone, oh my heavens, no. Not for the sake of majesty and mystery or of Thumper and Bambi, are you kidding me, but because, as every schoolchild knows, trees absorb carbon dioxide. They just soak it up and store it. They just love it. So this is the plan: you plant millions of acres of trees, and you can go on doing pretty

25

much whatever you're doing—driving around, using staggering amounts of energy, keeping those power plants fired to the max. Isn't Nature remarkable? So willing to serve? You wouldn't think it had anything more to offer, but it seems it does. Of course these "forests" wouldn't exactly be forests. They would be more like trees. *Managed* trees. The Forest Service, which now manages our forests by cutting them down, might be called upon to evolve in their thinking and allow these trees to grow. They would probably be patented trees after a time. Fast-growing, uniform, genetically-created-to-be-toxin-eating *machines.* They would be *new-age* trees, because the problem with planting the old-fashioned variety to *combat* the greenhouse effect, which is caused by pollution, is that they're already dying from it. All along the crest of the Appalachians from Maine to Georgia, forests struggle to survive in a toxic soup of poisons. They can't *help* us if we've killed them, now can they?

All right, you say, wow, lighten up will you? Relax. Tell about yourself.

Well, I say, I live in Florida . . .

Oh my God, you say. Florida! Florida is a joke! How do you expect us to take you seriously if you still live there! Florida is crazy, it's pink concrete. It's paved, it's over. And a little girl just got eaten by an alligator down there. It came out of some swamp next to a subdivision and just carried her off. That set your Endangered Species Act back fifty years, you can bet.

I . . .

Listen, we don't want to hear any more about Florida. We don't want   *30*
to hear about Phoenix or Hilton Head or California's Central Valley. If our wetlands—our *vanishing* wetlands—are mentioned one more time, we'll scream. And the talk about condors and grizzlies and wolves is becoming too de trop. We had just managed to get whales out of our minds when those three showed up under the ice in Alaska. They even had *names.* Bone is the dead one, right? It's almost the twenty-first century! Those last condors are *pathetic.* Can't we just get this over with?

Aristotle said that all living things are ensouled and striving to participate in eternity.

Oh, I just bet he said that, you say. That doesn't sound like Aristotle. He was a humanist. We're all humanists here. This is the age of humanism. And it has been for a long time.

You are driving with a stranger in the car, and it is the stranger behind the wheel. In the back seat are your pals for many years now—DO WHAT YOU LIKE and his swilling sidekick, WHY NOT. A deer, or some emblematic animal, something from that myriad natural world you've come from that you now treat with such indifference and scorn—steps from the dimming woods and tentatively upon the highway. The stranger does not decelerate or brake, not yet, maybe not at all. The feeling is that whatever it is *will get out of the way.* Oh, it's a fine car you've got, a fine machine, and oddly you don't mind the stranger driving it, because in a way, everything has gotten too complicated, way, way out of your control. You've given the wheel to the masters, the managers, the comptrollers. Something is wrong, *maybe,* you feel a little sick, *actually,* but the car is luxurious and fast and you're *moving,* which is the most important thing by far.

Why make a fuss when you're so comfortable? Don't make a fuss, make a baby. Go out and get something to eat, build something. Make *another* baby. Babies are cute. Babies show you have faith in the future. Although faith is perhaps too strong a word. They're everywhere these days, in all the crowds and traffic jams, there are the babies too. You don't seem to associate them with the problems of population increase. They're just babies! And you've come to believe in them again. They're a lot more tangible than the afterlife, which, of course, you haven't believed in in ages. At least not for yourself. The afterlife now belongs to plastics and poisons. Yes, plastics and poisons will have a far more extensive afterlife than you, that's known. A disposable diaper, for example, which is all plastic and wood pulp—you like them for all those babies, so easy to use and toss—will take around four centuries to degrade. Almost all plastics do, centuries and centuries. In the sea, many marine animals die from ingesting or being entangled in discarded plastic. In the dumps, plastic squats on more than 25 percent of dump space. But your heart is disposed toward plastic. Someone, no doubt the plastics industry, told you it was convenient. This same industry is now looking into recycling in an attempt to get the critics of their nefarious, multifarious products off their backs. That should make you feel better, because *recycling* has become an honorable word, no longer merely the hobby of Volvo owners. The fact is that people in plastics are born obscurants. Recycling (practically impossible) won't solve the plastic glut, only reduction of production will, and the plastics industry isn't looking into that, you can be sure. Waste is not just the stuff you throw away, of course, it's the stuff you use to excess. With the exception of *hazardous waste,* which you do worry about from time to time, it's even thought you have a declining sense of emergency about the problem. Builders are building bigger houses because you want bigger. You're trading up. Utility companies are beginning to worry about your constantly rising consumption. Utility companies! You haven't entered a new age at all but one of upscale nihilism, deluxe nihilism.

In the summer, particularly in *the industrial Northeast,* you did get a *35* little excited. The filth cut into your fun time. Dead stuff floating around. Sludge and bloody vials. Hygienic devices—appearing not quite so hygienic out of context—all coming in on the tide. The air smelled funny, too. You tolerate a great deal, but the summer of '88 was truly creepy. It was even thought for a moment that the environment would become a political issue. But it didn't. You didn't want it to be, preferring instead to continue in your politics of subsidizing and advancing avarice. The issues were the same as always—jobs, defense, the economy, maintaining and improving the standard of living in this greedy, selfish, expansionistic, industrialized society.

You're getting a little shrill here, you say.

You're pretty well off. You expect to be better off soon. You do. What does this mean? More software, more scampi, more square footage? You have created an ecological crisis. The earth is infinitely variable and alive, and you are killing it. It seems safer this way. But you are not safe. You want to find wholeness and happiness in a land increasingly damaged and betrayed, and you never will. More than material matters. You must change your ways.

What is this? *Sinners in the Hands of an Angry God?*

The ecological crisis cannot be resolved by politics. It cannot be solved by science or technology. It is a crisis caused by culture and character, and a deep change in personal consciousness is needed. Your fundamental attitudes toward the earth have become twisted. You have made only brutal contact with Nature, you cannot comprehend its grace. You must change. Have few desires and simple pleasures. Honor nonhuman life. Control yourself, become more authentic. Live lightly upon the earth and treat it with respect. Redefine the word *progress* and dismiss the managers and masters. Grow inwardly and with knowledge become truly wiser. Make connections. Think differently, behave differently. For this is essentially a moral issue we face and moral decisions must be made.

A *moral issue!* Okay, this discussion is now toast. A *moral* issue . . .   40
And who's this *we* now? Who are *you* is what I'd like to know. You're not me, anyway. I admit, someone's to blame and something should be done. But I've got to go. It's getting late. That's dusk out there. That is dusk, isn't it? It certainly doesn't look like any dawn I've ever seen. Well, take care.

Reading and Responding

1. Tell the story of your reading, from start to finish, paying particular to attention the issue of Williams's tone, her voice. How do you feel at the end of your first reading?
2. Why do you think we (the editors) put this particular piece at the end of this chapter? What's its relationship to the other selections?

Working Together

1. Use metaphors to describe the voice of this essay: What's the weather, the clothing, the music? Who would play the writer in the movie? And so on.
2. In a plain, matter-of-fact, straightforward way, summarize the main point Williams is making.

3. Discuss these questions: Why doesn't Williams simply come out and make her point? Why go about it in this indirect, oblique way? What does her tone and approach accomplish?

4. Working as a class or in a group, write a portrait of the kind of person Williams is satirizing in this piece, the target of her satire. How old is this person? What does he or she wear? How much money does he or she make? Where does the person live? Do you know anybody like this? Describe the person. Are you like this? Why?

5. Respond to Williams: "Wait a minute, what right have you to . . . ?"

Rethinking and Rewriting

1. Watch a sunset and describe it, using Williams's essay as justification—a defense for why this isn't a silly, stupid thing to do after all.

2. Write an essay about growing up with all the ecological doomsaying and catastrophic science Williams alludes to. You've heard all these warnings and predictions all your life. How has that affected your outlook on life and the things you do day to day. Has "the end of nature" made you callous and self-centered, as Williams argues? Assume that's true and that you've changed, that you want others to change. How do you move people out of this frame of mind? What can be done?

Essay Topics for Chapter 12

1. Compare Bill McKibben's "The End of Nature" with any selection in chapter 10, "The Nature of Nature." Explain how McKibben's perspective changes your reading of this selection.

2. Look at Melissa Greene's "No Rms, Jungle Vu," and Joy Williams's "Save the Whales, Screw the Shrimp." From what these two writers have to say about zoos, and from your own experience with zoos, defend one of these positions.

   a. Zoos inevitably present inaccurate pictures of wildlife (the life in zoos is, by definition, contained, *not* wild). Therefore, you'll not visit a zoo again.

   b. Zoos offer many of us the only personal experience we'll have with some animals. However inadequate, this experience is also valuable. Therefore, you'll continue to visit zoos.

   c. Your own alternative position on zoos.

3. Using one of the readings in this chapter as a primary focus, consider the ways that population increases affect the problem discussed. Use your chosen reading as a source, but also extend the discussion (and your understanding) via research. End your discussion by identifying any strategies or practices (other than legislating the birthrate) that we could follow that would lessen the problem.

4. Localize any of the issues brought up in any of the readings in this chapter. For example, if you live in the West, you could talk about

water use in your locale. Or if you live in a farming community, you could investigate the various ways that local farms control weeds and insects.

5. Identify one of the readings in this chapter that really persuades you it's telling the truth. Discuss how it manages to be so persuasive. Identify the writing strategies—the intellectual moves—that make for successful persuasion. A variation is to add to your discussion a selection that you really do not trust and do not find persuasive. Use this second selection to identify the strategies and intellectual moves that do not work, do not persuade.

6. Write a two-page "Introduction to Readers" to any of these readings. Get readers interested, and tell them what they need to know in order to get the most from their reading.

7. Assume the identity of one of the writers in chapter 10 or 11, and as that person, write a letter to one of the writers in this chapter. Assume that in your identity as one of the chapter 10 or 11 writers, you have just read the essay by the writer you've chosen from this chapter. So, for example, you could decide to be Kathleen Norris and choose to write a letter to Joy Williams about her essay "Save the Whales, Screw the Shrimp." Or you could be Charles Wright writing to Bill McKibben, or W. S. Merwin writing to Dixy Lee Ray, or Gerard Manley Hopkins writing to Rachel Carson, and so on.

8. Write a personal essay that says you know you should be more environmentally conscious, but the whole business seems too big—too much outside your control. Make this feeling seem real and substantial and not stupid or selfish. Then shift the discussion 180 degrees and write about how the first part of your essay is wrong. Make this second half at least as truthful and convincing as the first half. Use at least two selections from this chapter to help you make your points.

9. Using any of the problems identified in this chapter, write an essay that argues the importance of good science when it comes to an accurate understanding of this problem. Show the ways that various scientific disciplines and approaches all need to contribute to a full understanding of the problem and its complexities.

10. Using any of the problems identified in this chapter, write an essay explaining how an environmental problem always becomes a political problem, too. Show how politics plays a part in the way the problem is discussed, and show how politics affects what can be done about the problem. If you can also use local examples to illustrate your points here, so much the better.

13

Land Ethics

What is nature for? Who is nature for? Do plants and animals and water and air have value apart from us? Does nature have rights? Or is the issue, finally, what we can make from the world around us—money, artifacts, recreation, culture?

Even if the environment were not depleted and threatened and under seige, we would still have to decide our relationship to the land—we would still have to decide what to do with the land. What is right and proper: to cut down all the trees now, or to leave them alone? To strip a mine of its minerals and abandon the hole, or to work slowly and gradually, husbanding the resource? Clearly, we are always faced with the question of how to use what we've been given. Answering that question inevitably involves us in ethics—the consideration of values, of use in the deepest sense. And it's because natural resources are fast disappearing that the current ethical debate has sharpened, deepened, become more urgent. More is at stake because less remains.

In this chapter we assemble a series of pieces exploring these and related issues, the issues at the heart of the environmental movement. These selections provide both a history of the debate about use and value and a representative sample of the available positions. Divisions will become apparent, and these divisions are real: They lead to decisions that affect both the land and all of us who depend on it.

We mean the previous six chapters to prepare you for this debate—to school you a little in the complexities and crosscurrents, the shades of meaning, the history. We thought that if we started with this chapter right away, too many readers would simply fall back on their first, unconsidered reactions, arguing out of instinct and bias. But if you've read enough of the pieces in this book in anything like the order in which we presented them, and if you've done some of the brainstorming and writing and rewriting we've encouraged, you may be less inclined toward the pat answers and more willing to engage in discussion rather than join a battle.

"PROSPERITY"

Gifford Pinchot

After serving as governor of Pennsylvania, Gifford Pinchot became the first chief of the U.S. Forest Service. In The Fight for Conservation *(1910) (from which the following selection comes), as in his public service, Pinchot argues that the forests are important not primarily for aesthetic and spiritual reasons but as a renewable source of raw materials.*

As You Read

As you read, note any words or phrases that seem old-fashioned or out of date, and also note whatever assertions now seem less true than they might once have been.

The most prosperous nation of to-day is the United States. Our unexampled wealth and well-being are directly due to the superb natural resources of our country, and to the use which has been made of them by our citizens, both in the present and in the past. We are prosperous because our forefathers bequeathed to us a land of marvellous resources still unexhausted. Shall we conserve those resources, and in our turn transmit them, still unexhausted, to our descendants?

Unless we do, those who come after us will have to pay the price of misery, degradation, and failure for the progress and prosperity of our day. When the natural resources of any nation become exhausted, disaster and decay in every department of national life follow as a matter of course. Therefore the conservation of natural resources is the basis, and the only permanent basis, of national success. There are other conditions, but this one lies at the foundation.

Perhaps the most striking characteristic of the American people is their superb practical optimism; that marvellous hopefulness which keeps the individual efficiently at work. This hopefulness of the American is, however, as short-sighted as it is intense. As a rule, it does not look ahead beyond the next decade or score of years, and fails wholly to reckon with the real future of the Nation. I do not think I have often heard a forecast of the growth of our population that extended beyond a total of two hundred millions, and that only as a distant and shadowy goal. The point of view which this fact illustrates is neither true nor farsighted. We shall reach a population of two hundred millions in the very near future, as time is counted in the lives of nations, and there is nothing more certain than that this country of ours will some day support double or triple or five times that number of prosperous people if only we can bring ourselves so to handle our natural resources in the present as not to lay an embargo on the prosperous growth of the future.

We, the American people, have come into the possession of nearly four million square miles of the richest portion of the earth. It is ours to use and conserve for ourselves and our descendants, or to destroy. The fundamental question which confronts us is, What shall we do with it?

That question cannot be answered without first considering the con-   5
dition of our natural resources and what is being done with them to-day. As a people, we have been in the habit of declaring certain of our resources to be inexhaustible. To no other resource more frequently than coal has this stupidly false adjective been applied. Yet our coal supplies are so far from being inexhaustible that if the increasing rate of consumption shown by the figures of the last seventy-five years continues to prevail, our supplies of anthracite coal will last but fifty years and of bituminous coal less than two hundred years. From the point of view of national life, this means the exhaustion of one of the most important factors in our civilization within the immediate future. Not a few coal fields have already been exhausted, as in portions of Iowa and Missouri. Yet, in the face of these known facts, we continue to treat our coal as though there could never be an end of it. The established coal-mining practice at the present date does not take out more than one-half the coal, leaving the less easily mined or lower grade material to be made permanently inaccessible by the caving in of the abandoned workings. The loss to the Nation from this form of waste is prodigious and inexcusable.

The waste in use is not less appalling. But five per cent. of the potential power residing in the coal actually mined is saved and used. For example, only about five per cent. of the power of the one hundred and fifty million tons annually burned on the railways of the United States is actually used in traction; ninety-five per cent. is expended unproductively or is lost. In the best incandescent electric lighting plants but one-fifth of one per cent. of the potential value of the coal is converted into light.

Many oil and gas fields, as in Pennsylvania, West Virginia, and the Mississippi Valley, have already failed, yet vast amounts of gas continue to be poured into the air and great quantities of oil into the streams. Cases are known in which great volumes of oil were systematically burned in order to get rid of it.

The prodigal squandering of our mineral fuels proceeds unchecked in the face of the fact that such resources as these, once used or wasted, can never be replaced. If waste like this were not chiefly thoughtless, it might well be characterized as the deliberate destruction of the Nation's future.

Many fields of iron ore have already been exhausted, and in still more, as in the coal mines, only the higher grades have been taken from the mines, leaving the least valuable beds to be exploited at increased cost or not at all. Similar waste in the case of other minerals is less serious only because they are less indispensable to our civilization than coal and iron. Mention should be made of the annual loss of millions of dollars worth of by-products from coke, blast, and other furnaces now thrown into the air, often not merely without benefit but to the serious injury of the community. In other countries these by-products are saved and used.

We are in the habit of speaking of the solid earth and the eternal hills *10* as though they, at least, were free from the vicissitudes of time and certain to furnish perpetual support for prosperous human life. This conclusion is as false as the term "inexhaustible" applied to other natural resources. The waste of soil is among the most dangerous of all wastes now in progress in the United States. In 1896, Professor Shaler, than whom no one has spoken with greater authority on this subject, estimated that in the upland regions of the states south of Pennsylvania three thousand square miles of soil had been destroyed as the result of forest denudation, and that destruction was then proceeding at the rate of one hundred square miles of fertile soil per year. No seeing man can travel through the United States without being struck with the enormous and unnecessary loss of fertility by easily preventable soil wash. The soil so lost, as in the case of many other wastes, becomes itself a source of damage and expense, and must be removed from the channels of our navigable streams at an enormous annual cost. The Mississippi River alone is estimated to transport yearly four hundred million tons of sediment, or about twice the amount of material to be excavated from the Panama Canal. This material is the most fertile portion of our richest fields, transformed from a blessing to a curse by unrestricted erosion.

The destruction of forage plants by overgrazing has resulted, in the opinion of men most capable of judging, in reducing the grazing value of the public lands by one-half. This enormous loss of forage, serious though it be in itself, is not the only result of wrong methods of pasturage. The destruction of forage plants is accompanied by loss of surface soil through erosion; by forest destruction; by corresponding deterioration in the water supply; and by a serious decrease in the quality and weight of animals grown on overgrazed lands. These sources of loss from failure to conserve the range are felt to-day. They are accompanied by the certainty of a future loss not less important, for range lands once badly overgrazed can be restored to their former value but slowly or not at all. The obvious and certain remedy is for the Government to hold and control the public range until it can pass into the hands of settlers who will make their homes upon it. As methods of agriculture improve and new dry-land crops are introduced, vast areas once considered unavailable for cultivation are being made into prosperous homes; and this movement has only begun.

The single object of the public land system of the United States, as President Roosevelt repeatedly declared, is the making and maintenance of prosperous homes. That object cannot be achieved unless such of the public lands as are suitable for settlement are conserved for the actual home-maker. Such lands should pass from the possession of the Government directly and only into the hands of the settler who lives on the land. Of all forms of conservation there is none more important than that of holding the public lands for the actual home-maker.

It is a notorious fact that the public land laws have been deflected from their beneficent original purpose of home-making by lax administration, short-sighted departmental decisions, and the growth of an unhealthy public sentiment in portions of the West. Great areas of the public domain have passed into the hands, not of the home-maker, but of large individual or corporate owners whose object is always the making of profit and seldom the making of homes. It is sometimes urged that enlightened self-interest will lead the men who have acquired large holdings of public lands to put them to their most productive use, and it is said with truth that this best use is the tillage of small areas by small owners. Unfortunately, the facts and this theory disagree. Even the most cursory examination of large holdings throughout the West will refute the contention that the intelligent self-interest of large owners results promptly and directly in the making of homes. Few passions of the human mind are stronger than land hunger, and the large holder clings to his land until circumstances make it actually impossible for him to hold it any longer. Large holdings result in sheep or cattle ranges, in huge ranches, in great areas held for speculative rise in price, and not in homes. Unless the American homestead system of small free-holders is to be so replaced by a foreign system of tenantry, there are few things of more importance to the West than to see to it that the public lands pass directly into the hands of the actual settler instead of into the hands of the man who, if he can, will force the settler to pay him the unearned profit of the land speculator, or will hold him in economic and political dependence as a tenant. If we are to have homes on the public lands, they must be conserved for the men who make homes.

The lowest estimate reached by the Forest Service of the timber now standing in the United States is 1,400 billion feet, board measure; the highest, 2,500 billion. The present annual consumption is approximately 100 billion feet, while the annual growth is but a third of the consumption, or from 30 to 40 billion feet. If we accept the larger estimate of the standing timber, 2,500 billion feet, and the larger estimate of the annual growth, 40 billion feet, and apply the present rate of consumption, the result shows a probable duration of our supplies of timber of little more than a single generation.

Estimates of this kind are almost inevitably misleading. For example, it is certain that the rate of consumption of timber will increase enormously in the future, as it has in the past, so long as supplies remain to draw upon. Exact knowledge of many other factors is needed before closely accurate results can be obtained. The figures cited are, however, sufficiently reliable to make it certain that the United States has already crossed the verge of a timber famine so severe that its blighting effects will be felt in every household in the land. The rise in the price of lumber which marked the opening of the present century is the beginning of a vastly greater and more rapid rise which is to come. We must necessarily begin to suffer from the scarcity of timber long before our supplies are completely exhausted.

It is well to remember that there is no foreign source from which we can draw cheap and abundant supplies of timber to meet a demand per capita so large as to be without parallel in the world, and that the suffering which will result from the progressive failure of our timber has been but faintly foreshadowed by temporary scarcities of coal.

What will happen when the forests fail? In the first place, the business of lumbering will disappear. It is now the fourth greatest industry in the United States. All forms of building industries will suffer with it, and the occupants of houses, offices, and stores must pay the added cost. Mining will become vastly more expensive; and with the rise in the cost of mining there must follow a corresponding rise in the price of coal, iron, and other minerals. The railways, which have as yet failed entirely to develop a satisfactory substitute for the wooden tie (and must, in the opinion of their best engineers, continue to fail), will be profoundly affected, and the cost of transportation will suffer a corresponding increase. Water power for lighting, manufacturing, and transportation, and the movement of freight and passengers by inland waterways, will be affected still more directly than the steam railways. The cultivation of the soil, with or without irrigation, will be hampered by the increased cost of agricultural tools, fencing, and the wood needed for other purposes about the farm. Irrigated agriculture will suffer most of all, for the destruction of the forests means the loss of the waters as surely as night follows day. With the rise in the cost of producing food, the cost of food itself will rise. Commerce in general will necessarily be affected by the difficulties of the primary industries upon which it depends. In a word, when the forests fail, the daily life of the average citizen will inevitably feel the pinch on every side. And the forests have already begun to fail, as the direct result of the suicidal policy of forest destruction which the people of the United States have allowed themselves to pursue.

It is true that about twenty per cent. of the less valuable timber land in the United States remains in the possession of the people in the National Forests, and that it is being cared for and conserved to supply the needs of the present and to mitigate the suffering of the near future. But it needs no argument to prove that this comparatively small area will be insufficient to meet the demand which is now exhausting an area four times as great, or to prevent the suffering I have described. Measures of greater vigor are imperatively required.

The conception that water is, on the whole, the most important natural resource has gained firm hold in the irrigated West, and is making rapid progress in the humid East. Water, not land, is the primary value in the Western country, and its conservation and use to irrigate land is the first condition of prosperity. The use of our streams for irrigation and for domestic and manufacturing uses is comparatively well developed. Their use for power is less developed, while their use for transportation has only begun. The conservation of the inland waterways of the United States for these great purposes constitutes, perhaps, the largest single task which now confronts the Nation. The maintenance and increase of agriculture, the supply of clear water for domestic and manufacturing uses, the development of electrical power, transportation, and lighting, and the creation of a system of inland transportation by water whereby to regulate freight-rates by rail and to move the bulkier commodities cheaply from place to place, is a task upon the successful accomplishment of which the future of the Nation depends in a peculiar degree.

We are accustomed, and rightly accustomed, to take pride in the   20
vigorous and healthful growth of the United States, and in its vast promise for the future. Yet we are making no preparation to realize what we so easily foresee and glibly predict. The vast possibilities of our great future will become realities only if we make ourselves, in a sense, responsible for that future. The planned and orderly development and conservation of our natural resources is the first duty of the United States. It is the only form of insurance that will certainly protect us against the disasters that lack of foresight has in the past repeatedly brought down on nations since passed away.

Reading and Responding

1. How would you describe the voice of this piece? What other kind of writing or speaking does it sound like to you?
2. Gifford Pinchot says that "the conservation of natural resources is the basis, and the only permanent basis, of national success." Freewrite about that. What do you think Pinchot means? Do you think he's right?

Working Together

1. Write a page teaching the main ideas of this article to someone not in the class, someone who doesn't know anything about the history of environmentalism or the work you've been doing in this class.
2. How have the issues changed since Pinchot wrote this article? How do developments in the past 20 years, in particular, challenge or confirm his claims? What would he say if he were alive today and read, for example, the pieces in chapter 11, in particular, Keith Ervin's "A Life in Our Hands"?
3. As a group, take ten minutes and make a short definition of the word *conservation* as you understand its use today. Then look through Pinchot's article together and see what kind of definition Pinchot would give to the word. Finally, compare your two definitions. On the basis of these comparisons, what conclusions can you draw?

Rethinking and Rewriting

1. Take any significant numbers and statistics from this piece and update them for an essay entitled "Gifford Pinchot Reconsidered." Use the numbers to argue that Pinchot's views no longer apply, do apply, or have to be modified.
2. Write a short biographical sketch of Gifford Pinchot, drawing on library research. Put this article in the context of his life and career.

"HETCH HETCHY VALLEY"

John Muir

> *A naturalist and explorer, John Muir hiked and camped through much of the American West in the mid- to late nineteenth century, recording what he saw and felt and arguing for the preservation of wilderness in such books as* The Mountains of California *(1894) and* Our National Parks *(1901). He was the founder of the Sierra Club, still our country's most powerful environmental lobby. Muir's advocacy helped move the federal government to establish 148 million acres of forest reserves, including both Yosemite and Sequoia national parks in California. What follows is a good example of his efforts at persuasion, a passionate (and finally unsuccessful) attempt to save California's Hetch Hetchy Valley from the effects of dam building.*

As You Read

1. As you read, mark John Muir's main argument, and number the various points he makes to support that argument.
2. As you read, mark words and phrases that seem particularly charged, powerful, loaded, or intense.

Yosemite is so wonderful that we are apt to regard it as an exceptional creation, the only valley of its kind in the world; but Nature is not so poor as to have only one of anything. Several other yosemites have been discovered in the Sierra that occupy the same relative positions on the Range and were formed by the same forces in the same kind of granite. One of these, the Hetch Hetchy Valley, is in the Yosemite National Park about twenty miles from Yosemite and is easily accessible to all sorts of travelers by a road and trail that leaves the Big Oak Flat road at Bronson Meadows a few miles below Crane Flat, and to mountaineers by way of Yosemite Creek basin and the head of the middle fork of the Tuolumne.

It is said to have been discovered by Joseph Screech, a hunter, in 1850, a year before the discovery of the great Yosemite. After my first visit to it in the autumn of 1871, I have always called it the "Tuolumne Yosemite," for it is a wonderfully exact counterpart of the Merced Yosemite, not only in its sublime rocks and waterfalls but in the gardens, groves and meadows of its flowery park-like floor. The floor of Yosemite is about 4000 feet above the sea; the Hetch Hetchy floor about 3700 feet. And as the Merced River flows through Yosemite, so does the Tuolumne through Hetch Hetchy. The walls of both are of gray granite, rise abruptly from the floor, are sculptured in the same style and in both every rock is a glacier monument.

Standing boldly out from the south wall is a strikingly picturesque rock called by the Indians, Kolana, the outermost of a group 2300 feet high, corresponding with the Cathedral Rocks of Yosemite both in relative position and form. On the opposite side of the Valley, facing Kolana, there is a counterpart of the El Capitan that rises sheer and plain to a height of 1800 feet, and over its massive brow flows a stream which makes the most graceful fall I have ever seen. From the edge of the cliff to the top of an earthquake talus it is perfectly free in the air for a thousand feet before it is broken into cascades among talus boulders. It is in all its glory in June, when the snow is melting fast, but fades and vanishes toward the end of summer. The only fall I know with which it may fairly be compared is the Yosemite Bridal Veil; but it excels even that favorite fall both in height and airy-fairy beauty and behavior. Lowlanders are apt to suppose that mountain streams in their wild career over cliffs lose control of themselves and tumble in a noisy chaos of mist and spray. On the contrary, on no part of their travels are they more harmonious and self-controlled. Imagine yourself in Hetch Hetchy on a sunny day in June, standing waist-deep in grass and flowers (as I have often stood), while the great pines sway dreamily with scarcely perceptible motion. Looking northward across the Valley you see a plain, gray granite cliff rising abruptly out of the gardens and groves to a height of 1800 feet, and in front of it Tueeulala's silvery scarf burning with irised sun-fire. In the first white outburst at the head there is abundance of visible energy, but it is speedily hushed and concealed in divine repose, and its tranquil progress to the base of the cliff is like that of a downy feather in a still room. Now observe the fineness and marvelous distinctness of the various sun-illumined fabrics into which the water is woven; they sift and float from form to form down the face of that grand gray rock in so leisurely and unconfused a manner that you can examine their texture, and patterns and tones of color as you would a piece of embroidery held in the hand. Toward the top of the fall you see groups of booming, comet-like masses, their solid, white heads separate, their tails like combed silk interlacing among delicate gray and purple shadows, ever forming and dissolving, worn out by friction in their rush through the air. Most of these vanish a few hundred feet below the summit, changing to varied forms of cloud-like drapery. Near the bottom the width of the fall has increased from about twenty-five feet to a hundred feet. Here it is composed of yet finer tissues, and is still without a trace of disorder—air, water and sunlight woven into stuff that spirits might wear.

So fine a fall might well seem sufficient to glorify any valley; but here, as in Yosemite, Nature seems in nowise moderate, for a short distance to the eastward of Tueeulala booms and thunders the great Hetch Hetchy Fall, Wapama, so near that you have both of them in full view from the same standpoint. It is the counterpart of the Yosemite Fall, but has a much greater volume of water, is about 1700 feet in height, and appears to be nearly vertical, though considerably inclined, and is dashed into huge outbounding bosses of foam on projecting shelves and knobs. No two falls could be more unlike—Tueeulala out in the open sunshine descending like thistledown; Wapama in a jagged, shadowy gorge roaring and thundering, pounding its way like an earthquake avalanche.

Besides this glorious pair there is a broad, massive fall on the main *5* river a short distance above the head of the Valley. Its position is something like that of the Vernal in Yosemite, and its roar as it plunges into a surging trout-pool may be heard a long way, though it is only about twenty feet high. On Rancheria Creek, a large stream, corresponding in position with the Yosemite Tenaya Creek, there is a chain of cascades joined here and there with swift flashing plumes like the one between the Vernal and Nevada Falls, making magnificent shows as they go their glacier-sculptured way, sliding, leaping, hurrahing, covered with crisp clashing spray made glorious with sifting sunshine. And besides all these a few small streams come over the walls at wide intervals, leaping from ledge to ledge with bird-like song and watering many a hidden cliff-garden and fernery, but they are too unshowy to be noticed in so grand a place.

The correspondence between the Hetch Hetchy walls in their trends, sculpture, physical structure, and general arrangement of the main rock-masses and those of the Yosemite Valley has excited the wondering admiration of every observer. We have seen that the El Capitan and Cathedral rocks occupy the same relative positions in both valleys; so also do their Yosemite points and North Domes. Again, that part of the Yosemite north wall immediately to the east of the Yosemite Fall has two horizontal benches, about 500 and 1500 feet above the floor, timbered with golden-cup oak. Two benches similarly situated and timbered occur on the same relative portion of the Hetch Hetchy north wall, to the east of Wapama Fall, and on no other. The Yosemite is bounded at the head by the great Half Dome. Hetch Hetchy is bounded in the same way, though its head rock is incomparably less wonderful and sublime in form.

The floor of the Valley is about three and a half miles long, and from a fourth to half a mile wide. The lower portion is mostly a level meadow about a mile long, with the trees restricted to the sides and the river banks, and partially separated from the main, upper, forested portion by a low bar of glacier-polished granite across which the river breaks in rapids.

The principal trees are the yellow and sugar pines, digger pine, incense cedar, Douglas spruce, silver fir, the California and golden-cup oaks, balsam cottonwood, Nuttall's flowering dogwood, alder, maple, laurel, tumion, etc. The most abundant and influential are the great yellow or silver pines like those of Yosemite, the tallest over two hundred feet in height, and the oaks assembled in magnificent groves with massive rugged trunks four to six feet in diameter, and broad, shady, wide-spreading heads. The shrubs forming conspicuous flowery clumps and tangles are manzanita, azalea, spiræa, brier-rose, several species of ceanothus, calycanthus, philadelphus, wild cherry, etc.; with abundance of showy and fragrant herbaceous plants growing about them or out in the open in beds by themselves—lilies, Mariposa tulips, brodiaeas, orchids, iris, spraguea, draperia, collomia, collinsia, castilleja, nemophila, larkspur, columbine, goldenrods, sunflowers, mints of many species, honeysuckle, etc. Many fine ferns dwell here also, especially the beautiful and interesting rock-ferns—pellaea, and cheilanthes of several species—fringing and rosetting dry rock-piles and ledges; woodwardia and asplenium on damp spots with fronds six or seven feet high; the delicate maidenhair in mossy nooks by the falls, and the sturdy, broad-shouldered pteris covering nearly all the dry ground beneath the oaks and pines.

It appears, therefore, that Hetch Hetchy Valley, far from being a plain, common, rock-bound meadow, as many who have not seen it seem to suppose, is a grand landscape garden, one of Nature's rarest and most precious mountain temples. As in Yosemite, the sublime rocks of its walls seem to glow with life, whether leaning back in repose or standing erect in thoughtful attitudes, giving welcome to storms and calms alike, their brows in the sky, their feet set in the groves and gay flowery meadows, while birds, bees, and butterflies help the river and waterfalls to stir all the air into music—things frail and fleeting and types of permanence meeting here and blending, just as they do in Yosemite, to draw her lovers into close and confiding communion with her.

Sad to say, this most precious and sublime feature of the Yosemite National Park, one of the greatest of all our natural resources for the uplifting joy and peace and health of the people, is in danger of being dammed and made into a reservoir to help supply San Francisco with water and light, thus flooding it from wall to wall and burying its gardens and groves one or two hundred feet deep. This grossly destructive commercial scheme has long been planned and urged (though water as pure and abundant can be got from outside of the people's park, in a dozen different places), because of the comparative cheapness of the dam and of the territory which it is sought to divert from the great uses to which it was dedicated in the Act of 1890 establishing the Yosemite National Park.

The making of gardens and parks goes on with civilization all over the world, and they increase both in size and number as their value is recognized. Everybody needs beauty as well as bread, places to play in and pray in, where Nature may heal and cheer and give strength to body and soul alike. This natural beauty-hunger is made manifest in the little window-sill gardens of the poor, though perhaps only a geranium slip in a broken cup, as well as in the carefully tended rose and lily gardens of the rich, the thousands of spacious city parks and botanical gardens, and in our magnificent National Parks—the Yellowstone, Yosemite, Sequoia, etc.—Nature's sublime wonderlands, the admiration and joy of the world. Nevertheless, like anything else worth while, from the very beginning, however well guarded, they have always been subject to attack by despoiling gainseekers and mischief-makers of every degree from Satan to Senators, eagerly trying to make everything immediately and selfishly commercial, with schemes disguised in smug-smiling philanthropy, industriously, sham-piously crying, "Conservation, conservation, panutilization," that man and beast may be fed and the dear Nation made great. Thus long ago a few enterprising merchants utilized the Jerusalem temple as a place of business instead of a place of prayer, changing money, buying and selling cattle and sheep and doves; and earlier still, the first forest reservation, including only one tree, was likewise despoiled. Ever since the establishment of the Yosemite National Park, strife has been going on around its borders and I suppose this will go on as part of the universal battle between right and wrong, however much its boundaries may be shorn, or its wild beauty destroyed.

The first application to the Government by the San Francisco Supervisors for the commercial use of Lake Eleanor and the Hetch Hetchy Valley was made in 1903, and on December 22nd of that year it was denied by the Secretary of the Interior, Mr. Hitchcock, who truthfully said:

> Presumably the Yosemite National Park was created such by law because of the natural objects of varying degrees of scenic importance located within its boundaries, inclusive alike of its beautiful small lakes, like Eleanor, and its majestic wonders, like Hetch Hetchy and Yosemite Valley. It is the aggregation of such natural scenic features that makes the Yosemite Park a wonderland which the Congress of the United States sought by law to reserve for all coming time as nearly as practicable in the condition fashioned by the hand of the Creator—a worthy object of national pride and a source of healthful pleasure and rest for the thousands of people who may annually sojourn there during the heated months.

In 1907 when Mr. Garfield became Secretary of the Interior the application was renewed and granted; but under his successor, Mr. Fisher, the matter has been referred to a Commission, which as this volume goes to press still has it under consideration.

The most delightful and wonderful camp-grounds in the Park are its three great valleys—Yosemite, Hetch Hetchy, and Upper Tuolumne; and they are also the most important places with reference to their positions relative to the other great features—the Merced and Tuolumne Cañons, and the High Sierra peaks and glaciers, etc., at the head of the rivers. The main part of the Tuolumne Valley is a spacious flowery lawn four or five miles long, surrounded by magnificent snowy mountains, slightly separated from other beautiful meadows, which together make a series about twelve miles in length, the highest reaching to the feet of Mount Dana, Mount Gibbs, Mount Lyell and Mount McClure. It is about 8500 feet above the sea, and forms the grand central High Sierra camp-ground from which excursions are made to the noble mountains, domes, glaciers, etc.; across the Range to the Mono Lake and volcanoes and down the Tuolumne Cañon to Hetch Hetchy. Should Hetch Hetchy be submerged for a reservoir, as proposed, not only would it be utterly destroyed, but the sublime cañon way to the heart of the High Sierra would be hopelessly blocked and the great camping-ground, as the watershed of a city drinking system, virtually would be closed to the public. So far as I have learned, few of all the thousands who have seen the Park and seek rest and peace in it are in favor of this outrageous scheme.

One of my later visits to the Valley was made in the autumn of 1907 *15* with the late William Keith, the artist. The leaf-colors were then ripe, and the great god-like rocks in repose seemed to glow with life. The artist, under their spell, wandered day after day along the river and through the groves and gardens, studying the wonderful scenery; and, after making about forty sketches, declared with enthusiasm that although its walls were less sublime in height, in picturesque beauty and charm Hetch Hetchy surpassed even Yosemite.

That any one would try to destroy such a place seems incredible; but sad experience shows that there are people good enough and bad enough for anything. The proponents of the dam scheme bring forward a lot of bad arguments to prove that the only righteous thing to do with the people's parks is to destroy them bit by bit as they are able. Their arguments are curiously like those of the devil, devised for the destruction of the first garden—so much of the very best Eden fruit going to waste; so much of the best Tuolumne water and Tuolumne scenery going to waste. Few of their statements are even partly true, and all are misleading.

Thus, Hetch Hetchy, they say, is a "low-lying meadow." On the contrary, it is a high-lying natural landscape garden, as the photographic illustrations show.

"It is a common minor feature, like thousands of others." On the contrary it is a very uncommon feature; after Yosemite, the rarest and in many ways the most important in the National Park.

"Damming and submerging it 175 feet deep would enhance its beauty by forming a crystal-clear lake." Landscape gardens, places of recreation and worship, are never made beautiful by destroying and burying them. The beautiful sham lake, forsooth, would be only an eyesore, a dismal blot on the landscape, like many others to be seen in the Sierra. For, instead of keeping it at the same level all the year, allowing Nature centuries of time to make new shores, it would, of course, be full only a month or two in the spring, when the snow is melting fast; then it would be gradually drained, exposing the slimy sides of the basin and shallower parts of the bottom, with the gathered drift and waste, death and decay of the upper basins, caught here instead of being swept on to decent natural burial along the banks of the river or in the sea. Thus the Hetch Hetchy dam-lake would be only a rough imitation of a natural lake for a few of the spring months, an open sepulcher for the others.

"Hetch Hetchy water is the purest of all to be found in the Sierra, *20* unpolluted, and forever unpollutable." On the contrary, excepting that of the Merced below Yosemite, it is less pure than that of most of the other Sierra streams, because of the sewerage of camp-grounds draining into it, especially of the Big Tuolumne Meadows camp-ground, occupied by hundreds of tourists and mountaineers, with their animals, for months every summer, soon to be followed by thousands from all the world.

These temple destroyers, devotees of ravaging commercialism, seem to have a perfect contempt for Nature, and, instead of lifting their eyes to the God of the mountains, lift them to the Almighty Dollar.

Dam Hetch Hetchy! As well dam for water-tanks the people's cathedrals and churches, for no holier temple has ever been consecrated by the heart of man.

Working Together

1. Outline Muir's argument on the board, and consider his main ways of supporting that argument.
2. Consider Muir's other strategies of persuasion, particularly word choice and imagery.
3. In a quick, concluding freewrite, imitate Muir's voice and tone. Argue for something local in that tone, with that approach: say, that the old cedars in the quad on campus shouldn't be cut down or that a new shopping center shouldn't be built. Ham it up. Exaggerate.

Rethinking and Rewriting

1. Do a profile of John Muir, drawing on library research, and put this particular essay in the context of his life and career.
2. Research the fate of the Hetch Hetchy Valley. What is it like today?
3. Imitate Muir: Make a similar argument for some comparable local site threatened by development.

"A STATEMENT OF SAN FRANCISCO'S SIDE OF THE HETCH-HETCHY RESERVOIR MATTER"

Marsden Manson

> *Marsdon Manson served as San Francisco's city engineer from 1907 to 1912. As such, he was personally and professionally convinced that San Francisco's need for additional water could only be met by damming the Tuolumne River and creating a reservoir. Notice that even the title of his argument assumes there will be a reservoir, though at the time this piece was written the reservoir was a plan, not a fact. Manson's statement is really a reply to John Muir and his piece "Hetch Hetchy Valley," written earlier in the controversy (and reprinted just before this selection).*

As You Read

1. Marsden Manson begins by immediately making an argument. After you've read two or three pages, stop and write your response to the argument. What kind of argument is it? On what is it based? Why do you think Manson uses this kind of argument?
2. Annotate this piece as you read, and pay special attention to marking the transitions, the places where Manson moves to a new part of his argument or challenges a counterargument.

To the Members of the Sierra Club:

There has been sent out a ballot for an election on the Hetch-Hetchy question, to be held on Saturday, January 29, 1910. This ballot presents two questions apparently worded to draw out a vote for or against the use of the Hetch-Hetchy Valley as a reservoir. Both of these propositions are speciously arranged, and neither presents the question in its true light.

> *Proposition 1:* "I desire that the Hetch-Hetchy Valley shall remain intact and unaltered as a part of the Yosemite National Park and oppose its use as a reservoir for a water supply for San Francisco, unless an impartial federal commission shall determine that it is absolutely necessary for such use."

The facts regarding this proposition are that San Francisco made an application under the law of February 15, 1901, for the use of this reservoir space for the storage of water for domestic purposes. Such use is pointed out by the U.S. Geological Survey in the 21st Annual Report, Part IV, pages 450–453. This survey was conducted during the years 1897–99, specifically making an estimate of the volumes of water possible to store in this reservoir and of the character of the dam and work necessary for its utilization as such. Congress, acting upon the results of this work, formally made it possible to file upon this and other reservoirs in Yosemite National Park, and other parks and reservations; and *under this formal dedication to public uses of the reservoir spaces within the Yosemite National Park, and other parks and reservations* named in the law of February, 1901, made it possible for individuals, corporations and municipalities to utilize the natural resources originating in these parks, which resources had been previously prohibited by the provisions of the law of October 1, 1890, defining the limits and setting aside the Yosemite Reservation.

Lying within the floor of this reservoir are comparatively level lands, some 800 to 900 acres, of which *San Francisco owns in fee simple 720 acres under patent issued prior to the Act of October 1, 1890.* The area of the water surface when raised to about 150 feet above the level of the lower end of the Valley is about 1200 acres, which embraces quite a considerable area of gravelly and rocky soil at the upper end of the valley and the sloping sides thereof up to the level above named. The application made by San Francisco in 1901 for this permit was denied by the then Secretary of the Interior, and again denied upon a rehearing, the denial being based upon the ground that he was not authorized to make such grant. He used as the basis of his action the prior law of October, 1890, and refused to recognize the modifying effects of the subsequent law of February 15, 1901. Upon the reference of this question to the Attorney-General of the United States, the Acting Attorney-General, Judge Purdy, decided that full authority rested in the Secretary of the Interior under the law of February 15, 1901, and the then Secretary, Mr. Garfield, ultimately made the grant for the use of the remaining lands in the Hetch-Hetchy Reservoir site on May 11, 1908.

The question submitted under Proposition 1 on the ballot is therefore misleading in the extreme, and is not one that under any plea of either law or equity that can be referred to a so-called "impartial federal commission." It is misleading again in the fact that this commission is to determine that the use as a reservoir "is absolutely necessary."

By reference to the grant of May, 1908, under Stipulation No. 3, it will be observed that Lake Eleanor must first be developed to its full capacity before the development of Hetch-Hetchy shall be begun, which shall be undertaken only when the City and County of San Francisco, and adjacent cities, may require such further development. It is manifest, therefore, that the calling into effect of an "impartial federal commission" to determine what has already been determined is not making a just and equitable presentation to the members of the Sierra Club of the question at issue.

> *Proposition 2:* "I favor the use of Hetch-Hetchy Valley as a reservoir for a future water supply for San Francisco and I favor a present dedication by Congress of the right to such use without further investigation."

From the preceding discussion and statement of the facts, it will be seen that San Francisco already holds the right, under the laws of Congress as interpreted by the Attorney-General of the United States and administered by its executive officers, to use that portion of the floor of this valley which remains in the park for a reservoir after having developed Lake Eleanor to its full capacity and upon finding *that the additional supply is necessary.* So far as the laws of Congress can make this dedication, and so far as a conservative and just administrative officer of the government can guard public interests, this dedication has already been made by Congress, accepted by the people of the city under the terms imposed by the executive branch of the government, and no dedication of Congress whatever is needed, nor is asked for.

It is manifest from the above simple recital of the facts with reference to the laws and the actions taken thereunder, that neither of the propositions submitted on the ballot for the election of January 29, 1910, are fairly and equitably stated. This is made still more manifest by the re-issuance by Mr. John Muir, under date of November, 1909, of a pamphlet of some twenty odd pages of garbled quotations and specious statements protesting against the "unnecessary destruction of Hetch-Hetchy Valley." In this it is made to appear on page 3 that the Sierra Club of California formally joins in the protest against the "alleged unnecessary destruction of Hetch-Hetchy Valley." It is claimed by the undersigned that no destruction of the Valley is contemplated even in the remote future, when the use of this valley as a water supply for the homes of the cities about the bay shall become imperative. A reference to the pictures upon the latter pages of this pamphlet will make this perfectly manifest. There are nine of these pictures, and they will be referred to in order of their occurrence in the pamphlet, the pages on which they are printed not being numbered.

The first picture presents a very beautiful view of a portion of the valley opposite the falls known as Wapama. The highest level of the proposed reservoir will not reach the base of these falls. Therefore but little of the base of the granite sides of the valley will be flooded. The floor to be covered is owned in fee simple by San Francisco to the extent heretofore named, or about 720 acres. All of the floor of the valley within the limits of this picture is so owned.

In picture No. 2 the same remarks are true. Neither of the falls will be affected in any way.

Picture No. 3, the same is true.

In picture No. 4 it may be observed that San Francisco again owns the greater portion or all of the floor of the valley within sight, and that the great granite mass of Kolana will be flooded at its base by the highest dam about 10 per cent of its height.

Of pictures Nos. 5 and 6, no features will be affected except the floor of the valley, which again in these pictures embraces areas owned by San Francisco. The falls shown in these two pictures will not be affected in the least.

10

Pictures 7 and 8 represent landscapes in that portion of the valley owned by San Francisco. The general view given in No. 9 will be covered up to a point some fifty feet below the lowest portion of the ledge on the left side of the picture.

This pamphlet is devoted principally to three arguments: First, *that the flooding of the valley floor will destroy the scenic beauty of the Hetch-Hetchy.* The most striking natural features about the valley are all above the highest level to which it is proposed a quarter of a century or more hence to raise the level of the water. The cliffs rise to a height of more than 2500 feet above the valley floor, and as the reservoir will not in any case be more than 275 to 300 feet deep the apparent decrease in the height of the walls will not be perceptible to the eye of the ordinary observer. All of these peaks and cliffs, with their varied markings and color, will remain as now, and will be reflected in the waters of the lake, as are the cliffs surrounding the other lakes in the Sierras. Both of the falls strike the slopes of the bluffs above the level of the highest reservoir surface, and will therefore be in no way altered. The lake which will be formed in the valley by the construction of the dam will be as beautiful as the other lakes which add charm to the landscapes of the Sierras. The floor of the valley owned by San Francisco in its greater portion and for the highest purposes for which it can be used, will be flooded, and this substitution of a lake for the trees and meadows is the measure of the alleged "unnecessary destruction of the Hetch-Hetchy Valley."

It is also true that for about two months in the year the floor of this valley is a "paradise for campers," but it must be remembered that the greater portion of this paradise is owned by San Francisco for the exclusive purpose of making the homes of tens of thousands of families that will never have the opportunity of visiting this "paradise for campers" a source of health and happiness, by introducing into those homes the greatest element of health, namely, the purest water from the most available source.

Secondly: *That the use of the reservoir will make it necessary to exclude the public from the 480 square miles of watershed above it.*

It is not true that the flooding of the valley will shut out visitors from the watershed tributary thereto, for this region is not reasonably accessible for only about three and a half months, during which time the same precautions now taken in Yosemite Valley itself will be ample for many decades, and probably centuries, to keep Tuolumne Meadows clean. Even when these simple precautions shall prove inadequate, no such drastic steps as are proposed in this pamphlet, namely, the shutting out of the public from the watershed, will be necessary, as may be seen by referring to the views of an eminent authority in sanitary engineering, Prof. C. D. Marx, who, on page 341 of the Transactions of the Commonwealth Club, of November 1909, reviews and gives definite proof that there will be absolutely no necessity for in any way restricting the use of the drainage area, and that the simple precautionary measures which are deemed sufficient to protect the supplies of Boston and other cities would be sufficient, and that if the supply shall be suspected of contamination modern methods will remedy this at very small cost and without the drastic measures urged by the opponents to the use of this reservoir.

The character of the watershed above the Hetch-Hetchy is such that it is absurd to suppose that it will be necessary to shut out travel from it. This travel reaches it only in the late summer and early autumn, when dangerous germs are exposed, if upon the surface, to the glaring sun of California skies, one hour of which is fatal to any known pathogenic germ; later to the severe frosts of October, and then to the snows from November to June, and finally to the oxidizing influences in the twenty miles of foaming torrents between the meadows and Hetch-Hetchy, and to the further influences of long storage in the reservoir. When even these great natural safeguards have been overcome as pointed out by Prof. Marx, very simple remedial measures can then be applied.

Thirdly: *That there are many other sources from which San Francisco can draw its water supply, thirteen of them being named.*

The statements that other sources of supply are open to the city as alleged on pages 4, 5 and 6 of Mr. Muir's pamphlet do not present the facts as they stand at present. None of the supplies named on these pages is comparable in availability, abundance, nor purity. Moreover, the pleadings that San Francisco be turned over to the tender mercies of the individuals and corporations owning all of the other Sierra supplies are specious and misleading in the extreme and serve only as a screen behind which the avariciousness and selfishness of corporate greed can be used against the interests of San Francisco and the Bay municipalities. All of these sources have been fully considered, and rejected, by the engineers employed by San Francisco, and this rejection concurred in by Secretary Garfield, who points out in his very able review of the matter that it is not for him, for Congress, nor other authority to determine for San Francisco what source she should select, and it ill becomes the members of the Sierra Club to put themselves in a position in which, whether intending it or not, they are the mere screen for the selfishness of corporations and those who hold "rights to water and power" which have been secured without opposition from those who so earnestly and persistently opposed San Francisco's rights. It is suggested that the city take water from one of these companies after it has been used in their power stations. It is well known that at this elevation it cannot flow by gravity to San Francisco, and will require pumping, and that to pump this to the elevations required for delivery in San Francisco will ultimately require a yearly expenditure of $1,000,000, or a capital investment of about $25,000,000, and the plea that San Francisco accept or acquire these supplies without the necessary power to pump it over the Coast Range and to the higher elevations of the city will play into the hands of the great electrical power monopoly to the extent above named. No wonder, therefore, that if the existing monopoly of these water and power companies be appealed to to furnish funds to oppose San Francisco in the acquisition of rights, which will furnish the water as well as pump it to the homes of the city, that they would be inclined to generously contribute.

20

Mr. John D. Galloway, an able engineer and member of the American Society of Civil Engineers, with a thorough acquaintance with the entire field, and after going into detail over the various possible sources, says, in the Transactions of the Commonwealth Club above referred to, "As a matter of fact, the development of long distance transmission of electric power started first in California, and there is not now a single large river within two hundred miles of San Francisco except the Tuolumne and the Merced which has not one or more electric power plants upon it. Without the Hetch-Hetchy supply the city will indeed be at a loss as to where to go."

The Commonwealth Club of California, an organization formed of broad-minded citizens who take up and have presented to them both sides of the great civic problems which are brought before them, took up the question of this Hetch-Hetchy supply at its meetings of September and November, 1909. At the meeting of the latter month the "Society for the Preservation of National Parks" put the following question: "If you decide that a National Park shall be the last resort, then you must require a complete and thorough showing that no other like utility is reasonably available." To which the Club replied that it was not necessarily the first or the last resort in a municipality in need of water, and "In such a case as that of Hetch-Hetchy it should be shown that no other like utility is available under reasonable conditions of engineering, extinguishment of adverse claims, cost, etc. The city of San Francisco has fulfilled this requirement to the satisfaction of eminent engineers in and out of the city's employment, and to that of Secretary Garfield. Your committee is unwilling to pass upon the statements of those who believe that the city's investigations of other sources have not been sufficiently exhaustive. But, as the Federal authorities have, after examining the data presented by the city's engineers, approved the conclusions of the San Francisco authorities, it would seem only just that those who assert that other sources are available under reasonable conditions should set forth with equal detail the facts on which they base their opinions."

It is manifest, therefore, that the statements made in this pamphlet are only apparently substantiated by the garbled quotations presented therein, and are not in reality based upon true and correct facts, but upon a partisan presentation of selected and misleading quotations to which the city's representative is forced to take this means of refuting. These garbled quotations are grossly misleading, in that they are separated out and arranged to masquerade as the unqualified opinions of those from whom they are quoted, when in many instances the opinions are the exact opposite of the impression which this pamphlet undertakes to scatter broadcast.

As showing the trend of the best minds in San Francisco, for which we think the Commonwealth Club can fairly be said to stand, it may be noted that the Club, after sending a committee to visit the Hetch-Hetchy and make its report (the report was a most elaborate and careful document), and after devoting two evenings to a discussion of the subject, at which Mr. George Edwards, of the Society for the Preservation of National Parks, and Mr. E. T. Parsons, one of the Directors of the Sierra Club, addressed the Club, by a vote of eight to one endorsed the proposition of the immediate development of the Hetch-Hetchy water supply for San Francisco.

The City and County of San Francisco must provide for a supply in   25
the future of at least two hundred million gallons a day. Its present plans include the acquisition of the local supply, which can economically be developed to forty million gallons a day; the building of a reservoir at Lake Eleanor, which can develop a supply of sixty million gallons a day, possibly a supply of one hundred and twenty million gallons a day, which will carry the city along for a period of thirty or forty years' development. When these sources have reached their ultimate development, it is then planned to develop the Hetch-Hetchy supply. By this development it will be a generation or longer before the Hetch-Hetchy supply will be touched. The beauties of this Valley will therefore, under this arrangement, be preserved to the present generation and perhaps to the one that follows it. Should the privileges be taken away from the city, we may well doubt whether such a source of water and power as is presented by the Hetch-Hetchy proposition can be saved for an equal length of time from acquisition by private corporations, which would use them for their own instead of the public use.

We therefore urge that the efforts of San Francisco to acquire and use this source of water for the highest purpose to which water can be devoted should receive the support of the members of the Sierra Club.

The actual reservoir areas to which this grant by Secretary Garfield applies are by no means the entire areas of the reservoirs: In the first one to be developed, Lake Eleanor, all the very desirable meadow lands are privately owned, and San Francisco is acquiring these. The remainder, *less than a square mile at the highest development, is in the Park, and constitutes less than one twelve-hundredth (1/1200) part of the Park area.*

In the second one to be developed, Hetch-Hetchy, San Francisco owns 720 acres, and the *grant of reservoir rights of way again applies to less than a square mile, or to another one twelve-hundredth (1/1200) part of the Park.*

THE GRANT THEREFORE ONLY APPLIES TO LESS THAN ONE SIX-HUNDREDTH (1/600) PART OF THE PARK AREA, and to the use of this small fraction in conjunction with the greater areas owned by the city, for the highest purpose for which they can ever be used, the Sierra Club is asked to protest in the face of a use made available and possible by Congress in the law of February 15, 1901, granted in accordance with this law and accepted by San Francisco by a vote of over six to one.

You are therefore respectfully requested and urged to vote in favor of   30
Proposition No. 2, with the mental reservation that you do not advocate a dedication by Congress of the right to such use without further investigation, for the reason that so far as Congressional action is concerned, such dedication was made by the Act of February 15, 1901, after due and careful

consideration of all the facts by a Scientific Bureau of our country, and that this supply was open to San Francisco, and if denied must inevitably be put to use for some of the great necessities of the human race, and probably through the instrumentality of some selfish corporation.

Working Together

1. From your individual reading, draw up a group outline of Manson's argument.
2. Designate one group "Manson Allies" and another group "Friends of Muir." The Manson Allies are charged with summarizing Manson's argument and adding to it. They should think of themselves as residents of San Francisco—workers, shopkeepers, manufacturers, men, women, children. Why does San Francisco need more water? Why this particular water? In contrast, the Friends of Muir should summarize Muir's argument and add to it. They should think of themselves as the current members of the Sierra Club. Each group should be prepared to speak for ten minutes to give a summary of their position. Ultimately, the whole class has this assignment: to draft a one-page land ethics statement that accurately represents the Manson Allies and a one-page statement that accurately represents the Friends of Muir. Both statements should carry this title: "What Is the Land For?"

Rethinking and Rewriting

1. Write an essay that explains why the issue of damming or not damming a river can be complicated. Use Muir's and Manson's arguments as sources. Or extend this discussion to some local decision that's similar. Explain why the decision is difficult to make.
2. Write an essay explaining how Muir's and Manson's essays represent two different ways of approaching and arguing a question. Which method of argument seems most appealing and convincing to you, and why?
3. Write a three- to five-page statement of your own land ethic. Use Muir and Manson as sources, and add any other sources you wish.

"THE LAND ETHIC"

Aldo Leopold

> *In this section of the* Sand County Almanac *(1949), Leopold sets out his philosophy of land management, his belief that how we manage the land, the trees, and the water is finally a question not of economics but of ethics, of right and wrong, of responsibility and selfishness. (See also the headnote for "Axe-in-Hand" in chapter 11.)*

Before and As You Read

1. Preread this piece, and write two or three sentences that tell you how to proceed with this reading.
2. As you read, stop every page or so (you decide where exactly) and write a one- or two-sentence informal summary of what you've just read. Try to translate Aldo Leopold's words into your own.
3. Though it's simplistic to do so, read this essay thinking just in terms of opposites or dualities. Annotate as you read, using a straight line in the margin for stuff Leopold likes, a wiggly line in the margin for stuff Leopold dislikes.

When God-like Odysseus returned from the wars in Troy, he hanged all on one rope a dozen slave-girls of his household whom he suspected of misbehavior during his absence.

This hanging involved no question of propriety. The girls were property. The disposal of property was then, as now, a matter of expediency, not of right and wrong.

Concepts of right and wrong were not lacking from Odysseus' Greece: witness the fidelity of his wife through the long years before at last his black-prowed galleys clove the wine-dark seas for home. The ethical structure of that day covered wives, but had not yet been extended to human chattels. During the three thousand years which have since elapsed, ethical criteria have been extended to many fields of conduct, with corresponding shrinkages in those judged by expediency only.

The Ethical Sequence

This extension of ethics, so far studied only by philosophers, is actually a process in ecological evolution. Its sequences may be described in ecological as well as in philosophical terms. An ethic, ecologically, is a limitation on freedom of action in the struggle for existence. An ethic, philosophically, is a differentiation of social from anti-social conduct. These are two definitions of one thing. The thing has its origin in the tendency of interdependent individuals or groups to evolve modes of co-operation.

The ecologist calls these symbioses. Politics and economics are advanced symbioses in which the original free-for-all competition has been replaced, in part, by co-operative mechanisms with an ethical content.

The complexity of co-operative mechanisms has increased with pop-   *5* ulation density, and with the efficiency of tools. It was simpler, for example, to define the anti-social uses of sticks and stones in the days of the mastodons than of bullets and billboards in the age of motors.

The first ethics dealt with the relation between individuals; the Mosaic Decalogue is an example. Later accretions dealt with the relation between the individual and society. The Golden Rule tries to integrate the individual to society; democracy to integrate social organization to the individual.

There is as yet no ethic dealing with man's relation to land and to the animals and plants which grow upon it. Land, like Odysseus' slave-girls, is still property. The land-relation is still strictly economic, entailing privileges but not obligations.

The extension of ethics to this third element in human environment is, if I read the evidence correctly, an evolutionary possibility and an ecological necessity. It is the third step in a sequence. The first two have already been taken. Individual thinkers since the days of Ezekiel and Isaiah have asserted that the despoliation of land is not only inexpedient but wrong. Society, however, has not yet affirmed their belief. I regard the present conservation movement as the embryo of such an affirmation.

An ethic may be regarded as a mode of guidance for meeting ecological situations so new or intricate, or involving such deferred reactions, that the path of social expediency is not discernible to the average individual. Animal instincts are modes of guidance for the individual in meeting such situations. Ethics are possibly a kind of community instinct in-the-making.

The Community Concept

All ethics so far evolved rest upon a single premise: that the individ-   *10* ual is a member of a community of interdependent parts. His instincts prompt him to compete for his place in the community, but his ethics prompt him also to co-operate (perhaps in order that there may be a place to compete for).

The land ethic simply enlarges the boundaries of the community to include soils, waters, plants, and animals, or collectively: the land.

This sounds simple: do we not already sing our love for and obligation to the land of the free and the home of the brave? Yes, but just what and whom do we love? Certainly not the soil, which we are sending helter-skelter downriver. Certainly not the waters, which we assume have no function except to turn turbines, float barges, and carry off sewage. Certainly not the plants, of which we exterminate whole communities without batting an eye. Certainly not the animals, of which we have already extirpated many of the largest and most beautiful species. A land ethic of course cannot prevent the alteration, management, and use of these "resources," but it does affirm their right to continued existence, and, at least in spots, their continued existence in a natural state.

In short, a land ethic changes the role of *Homo sapiens* from conqueror of the land-community to plain member and citizen of it. It implies respect for his fellow-members, and also respect for the community as such.

In human history, we have learned (I hope) that the conqueror role is eventually self-defeating. Why? Because it is implicit in such a role that the conqueror knows, *ex cathedra,* just what makes the community clock tick, and just what and who is valuable, and what and who is worthless, in community life. It always turns out that he knows neither, and this is why his conquests eventually defeat themselves.

In the biotic community, a parallel situation exists. Abraham knew   15 exactly what the land was for: it was to drip milk and honey into Abraham's mouth. At the present moment, the assurance with which we regard this assumption is inverse to the degree of our education.

The ordinary citizen today assumes that science knows what makes the community clock tick; the scientist is equally sure that he does not. He knows that the biotic mechanism is so complex that its workings may never be fully understood.

That man is, in fact, only a member of a biotic team is shown by an ecological interpretation of history. Many historical events, hitherto explained solely in terms of human enterprise, were actually biotic interactions between people and land. The characteristics of the land determined the facts quite as potently as the characteristics of the men who lived on it.

Consider, for example, the settlement of the Mississippi valley. In the years following the Revolution, three groups were contending for its control: the native Indian, the French and English traders, and the American settlers. Historians wonder what would have happened if the English at Detroit had thrown a little more weight into the Indian side of those tipsy scales which decided the outcome of the colonial migration into the cane-lands of Kentucky. It is time now to ponder the fact that the cane-lands, when subjected to the particular mixture of forces represented by the cow, plow, fire, and axe of the pioneer, became bluegrass. What if the plant succession inherent in this dark and bloody ground had, under the impact of these forces, given us some worthless sedge, shrub, or weed? Would Boone and Kenton have held out? Would there have been any overflow into Ohio, Indiana, Illinois, and Missouri? Any Louisiana Purchase? Any transcontinental union of new states? Any Civil War?

Kentucky was one sentence in the drama of history. We are commonly told what the human actors in this drama tried to do, but we are seldom told that their success, or the lack of it, hung in large degree on the reaction of particular soils to the impact of the particular forces exerted by their occupancy. In the case of Kentucky, we do not even know where the bluegrass came from—whether it is a native species, or a stowaway from Europe.

Contrast the cane-lands with what hindsight tells us about the South-   *20*
west, where the pioneers were equally brave, resourceful, and persevering.
The impact of occupancy here brought no bluegrass, or other plant fitted
to withstand the bumps and buffetings of hard use. This region, when
grazed by livestock, reverted through a series of more and more worthless
grasses, shrubs, and weeds to a condition of unstable equilibrium. Each
recession of plant types bred erosion; each increment to erosion bred a
further recession of plants. The result today is a progressive and mutual
deterioration, not only of plants and soils, but of the animal community
subsisting thereon. The early settlers did not expect this: on the ciénegas
of New Mexico some even cut ditches to hasten it. So subtle has been its
progress that few residents of the region are aware of it. It is quite invisible
to the tourist who finds this wrecked landscape colorful and charming (as
indeed it is, but it bears scant resemblance to what it was in 1848).

This same landscape was "developed" once before, but with quite different results. The Pueblo Indians settled the Southwest in pre-Columbian
times, but they happened *not* to be equipped with range livestock. Their
civilization expired, but not because their land expired.

In India, regions devoid of any sod-forming grass have been settled,
apparently without wrecking the land, by the simple expedient of carrying
the grass to the cow, rather than vice versa. (Was this the result of some
deep wisdom, or was it just good luck? I do not know.)

In short, the plant succession steered the course of history; the pioneer simply demonstrated, for good or ill, what successions inhered in the
land. Is history taught in this spirit? It will be, once the concept of land as
a community really penetrates our intellectual life.

The Ecological Conscience

Conservation is a state of harmony between men and land. Despite
nearly a century of propaganda, conservation still proceeds at a snail's pace;
progress still consists largely of letterhead pieties and convention oratory.
On the back forty we still slip two steps backward for each forward stride.

The usual answer to this dilemma is "more conservation education."   *25*
No one will debate this, but is it certain that only the *volume* of education
needs stepping up? Is something lacking in the *content* as well?

It is difficult to give a fair summary of its content in brief form, but,
as I understand it, the content is substantially this: obey the law, vote right,
join some organizations, and practice what conservation is profitable on
your own land; the government will do the rest.

Is not this formula too easy to accomplish anything worth-while? It
defines no right or wrong, assigns no obligation, calls for no sacrifice,
implies no change in the current philosophy of values. In respect of land-
use, it urges only enlightened self-interest. Just how far will such education
take us? An example will perhaps yield a partial answer.

By 1930 it had become clear to all except the ecologically blind that southwestern Wisconsin's topsoil was slipping seaward. In 1933 the farmers were told that if they would adopt certain remedial practices for five years, the public would donate CCC labor to install them, plus the necessary machinery and materials. The offer was widely accepted, but the practices were widely forgotten when the five-year contract period was up. The farmers continued only those practices that yielded an immediate and visible economic gain for themselves.

This led to the idea that maybe farmers would learn more quickly if they themselves wrote the rules. Accordingly the Wisconsin Legislature in 1937 passed the Soil Conservation District Law. This said to farmers, in effect: *We, the public, will furnish you free technical service and loan you specialized machinery, if you will write your own rules for land-use. Each county may write its own rules, and these will have the force of* law. Nearly all the counties promptly organized to accept the proffered help, but after a decade of operation, *no county has yet written a single rule.* There has been visible progress in such practices as strip-cropping, pasture renovation, and soil liming, but none in fencing woodlots against grazing, and none in excluding plow and cow from steep slopes. The farmers, in short, have selected those remedial practices which were profitable anyhow, and ignored those which were profitable to the community, but not clearly profitable to themselves.

When one asks why no rules have been written, one is told that the community is not yet ready to support them; education must precede rules. But the education actually in progress makes no mention of obligations to land over and above those dictated by self-interest. The net result is that we have more education but less soil, fewer healthy woods, and as many floods as in 1937. 30

The puzzling aspect of such situations is that the existence of obligations over and above self-interest is taken for granted in such rural community enterprises as the betterment of roads, schools, churches, and baseball teams. Their existence is not taken for granted, nor as yet seriously discussed, in bettering the behavior of the water that falls on the land, or in the preserving of the beauty or diversity of the farm landscape. Land-use ethics are still governed wholly by economic self-interest, just as social ethics were a century ago.

To sum up: we asked the farmer to do what he conveniently could to save his soil, and he has done just that, and only that. The farmer who clears the woods off a 75 per cent slope, turns his cows into the clearing, and dumps its rainfall, rocks, and soil into the community creek, is still (if otherwise decent) a respected member of society. If he puts lime on his fields and plants his crops on contour, he is still entitled to all the privileges and emoluments of his Soil Conservation District. The District is a beautiful piece of social machinery, but it is coughing along on two cylinders because we have been too timid, and too anxious for quick success, to tell the farmer the true magnitude of his obligations. Obligations have no meaning without conscience, and the problem we face is the extension of the social conscience from people to land.

No important change in ethics was ever accomplished without an internal change in our intellectual emphasis, loyalties, affections, and convictions. The proof that conservation has not yet touched these foundations of conduct lies in the fact that philosophy and religion have not yet heard of it. In our attempt to make conservation easy, we have made it trivial.

Substitutes for a Land Ethic

When the logic of history hungers for bread and we hand out a stone, we are at pains to explain how much the stone resembles bread. I now describe some of the stones which serve in lieu of a land ethic.

One basic weakness in a conservation system based wholly on economic motives is that most members of the land community have no economic value. Wildflowers and songbirds are examples. Of the 22,000 higher plants and animals native to Wisconsin, it is doubtful whether more than 5 per cent can be sold, fed, eaten, or otherwise put to economic use. Yet these creatures are members of the biotic community, and if (as I believe) its stability depends on its integrity, they are entitled to continuance. 35

When one of these non-economic categories is threatened, and if we happen to love it, we invent subterfuges to give it economic importance. At the beginning of the century songbirds were supposed to be disappearing. Ornithologists jumped to the rescue with some distinctly shaky evidence to the effect that insects would eat us up if birds failed to control them. The evidence had to be economic in order to be valid.

It is painful to read these circumlocutions today. We have no land ethic yet, but we have at least drawn nearer the point of admitting that birds should continue as a matter of biotic right, regardless of the presence or absence of economic advantage to us.

A parallel situation exists in respect of predatory mammals, raptorial birds, and fish-eating birds. Time was when biologists somewhat overworked the evidence that these creatures preserve the health of game by killing weaklings, or that they control rodents for the farmer, or that they prey only on "worthless" species. Here again, the evidence had to be economic in order to be valid. It is only in recent years that we hear the more honest argument that predators are members of the community, and that no special interest has the right to exterminate them for the sake of a benefit, real or fancied, to itself. Unfortunately this enlightened view is still in the talk stage. In the field the extermination of predators goes merrily on: witness the impending erasure of the timber wolf by fiat of Congress, the Conservation Bureaus, and many state legislatures.

Some species of trees have been "read out of the party" by economics-minded foresters because they grow too slowly, or have too low a sale value to pay as timber crops: white cedar, tamarack, cypress, beech, and hemlock are examples. In Europe, where forestry is ecologically more advanced, the non-commercial tree species are recognized as members of the native forest community, to be preserved as such, within reason. Moreover some (like beech) have been found to have a valuable function in building up soil fertility. The interdependence of the forest and its constituent tree species, ground flora, and fauna is taken for granted.

Lack of economic value is sometimes a character not only of species or groups, but of entire biotic communities: marshes, bogs, dunes, and "deserts" are examples. Our formula in such cases is to relegate their conservation to government as refuges, monuments, or parks. The difficulty is that these communities are usually interspersed with more valuable private lands; the government cannot possibly own or control such scattered parcels. The net effect is that we have relegated some of them to ultimate extinction over large areas. If the private owner were ecologically minded, he would be proud to be the custodian of a reasonable proportion of such areas, which add diversity and beauty to his farm and to his community.

In some instances, the assumed lack of profit in these "waste" areas has proved to be wrong, but only after most of them had been done away with. The present scramble to reflood muskrat marshes is a case in point.

There is a clear tendency in American conservation to relegate to government all necessary jobs that private landowners fail to perform. Government ownership, operation, subsidy, or regulation is now widely prevalent in forestry, range management, soil and watershed management, park and wilderness conservation, fisheries management, and migratory bird management, with more to come. Most of this growth in governmental conservation is proper and logical, some of it is inevitable. That I imply no disapproval of it is implicit in the fact that I have spent most of my life working for it. Nevertheless the question arises: What is the ultimate magnitude of the enterprise? Will the tax base carry its eventual ramifications? At what point will governmental conservation, like the mastodon, become handicapped by its own dimensions? The answer, if there is any, seems to be in a land ethic, or some other force which assigns more obligation to the private landowner.

Industrial landowners and users, especially lumbermen and stockmen, are inclined to wail long and loudly about the extension of government ownership and regulation to land, but (with notable exceptions) they show little disposition to develop the only visible alternative: the voluntary practice of conservation on their own lands.

When the private landowner is asked to perform some unprofitable act for the good of the community, he today assents only with outstretched palm. If the act costs him cash this is fair and proper, but when it costs only fore-thought, open-mindedness, or time, the issue is at least debatable. The overwhelming growth of land-use subsidies in recent years must be ascribed, in large part, to the government's own agencies for conservation education: the land bureaus, the agricultural colleges, and the extension services. As far as I can detect, no ethical obligation toward land is taught in these institutions.

To sum up: a system of conservation based solely on economic self-interest is hopelessly lopsided. It tends to ignore, and thus eventually to eliminate, many elements in the land community that lack commercial value, but that are (as far as we know) essential to its healthy functioning. It assumes, falsely, I think, that the economic parts of the biotic clock will function without the uneconomic parts. It tends to relegate to government many functions eventually too large, too complex, or too widely dispersed to be performed by government.

An ethical obligation on the part of the private owner is the only visible remedy for these situations.

The Land Pyramid

An ethic to supplement and guide the economic relation to land presupposes the existence of some mental image of land as a biotic mechanism. We can be ethical only in relation to something we can see, feel, understand, love, or otherwise have faith in.

The image commonly employed in conservation education is "the balance of nature." For reasons too lengthy to detail here, this figure of speech fails to describe accurately what little we know about the land mechanism. A much truer image is the one employed in ecology: the biotic pyramid. I shall first sketch the pyramid as a symbol of land, and later develop some of its implications in terms of land-use.

Plants absorb energy from the sun. This energy flows through a circuit called the biota, which may be represented by a pyramid consisting of layers. The bottom layer is the soil. A plant layer rests on the soil, an insect layer on the plants, a bird and rodent layer on the insects, and so on up through various animal groups to the apex layer, which consists of the larger carnivores.

The species of a layer are alike not in where they came from, or in what they look like, but rather in what they eat. Each successive layer depends on those below it for food and often for other services, and each in turn furnishes food and services to those above. Proceeding upward, each successive layer decreases in numerical abundance. Thus, for every carnivore there are hundreds of his prey, thousands of their prey, millions of insects, uncountable plants. The pyramidal form of the system reflects this numerical progression from apex to base. Man shares an intermediate layer with the bears, raccoons, and squirrels which eat both meat and vegetables.

The lines of dependency for food and other services are called food chains. Thus soil-oak-deer-Indian is a chain that has now been largely converted to soil-corn-cow-farmer. Each species, including ourselves, is a link in many chains. The deer eats a hundred plants other than oak, and the cow a hundred plants other than corn. Both, then, are links in a hundred chains. The pyramid is a tangle of chains so complex as to seem disorderly, yet the stability of the system proves it to be a highly organized structure. Its functioning depends on the co-operation and competition of its diverse parts.

In the beginning, the pyramid of life was low and squat; the food chains short and simple. Evolution has added layer after layer, link after link. Man is one of thousands of accretions to the height and complexity of the pyramid. Science has given us many doubts, but it has given us at least one certainty: the trend of evolution is to elaborate and diversify the biota.

Land, then, is not merely soil; it is a fountain of energy flowing through a circuit of soils, plants, and animals. Food chains are the living channels which conduct energy upward; death and decay return it to the soil. The circuit is not closed; some energy is dissipated in decay, some is added by absorption from the air, some is stored in soils, peats, and long-lived forests; but it is a sustained circuit, like a slowly augmented revolving fund of life. There is always a net loss by downhill wash, but this is normally small and offset by the decay of rocks. It is deposited in the ocean and, in the course of geological time, raised to form new lands and new pyramids.

The velocity and character of the upward flow of energy depend on the complex structure of the plant and animal community, much as the upward flow of sap in a tree depends on its complex cellular organization. Without this complexity, normal circulation would presumably not occur. Structure means the characteristic numbers, as well as the characteristic kinds and functions, of the component species. This interdependence between the complex structure of the land and its smooth functioning as an energy unit is one of its basic attributes.

When a change occurs in one part of the circuit, many other parts must adjust themselves to it. Change does not necessarily obstruct or divert the flow of energy; evolution is a long series of self-induced changes, the net result of which has been to elaborate the flow mechanism and to lengthen the circuit. Evolutionary changes, however, are usually slow and local. Man's invention of tools has enabled him to make changes of unprecedented violence, rapidity, and scope.

One change is in the composition of floras and faunas. The larger predators are lopped off the apex of the pyramid; food chains, for the first time in history, become shorter rather than longer. Domesticated species from other lands are substituted for wild ones, and wild ones are moved to new habitats. In this world-wide pooling of faunas and floras, some species get out of bounds as pests and diseases, others are extinguished. Such effects are seldom intended or foreseen; they represent unpredicted and often untraceable readjustments in the structure. Agricultural science is largely a race between the emergence of new pests and the emergence of new techniques for their control.

Another change touches the flow of energy through plants and animals and its return to the soil. Fertility is the ability of soil to receive, store, and release energy. Agriculture, by overdrafts on the soil, or by too radical a substitution of domestic for native species in the superstructure, may derange the channels of flow or deplete storage. Soils depleted of their storage, or of the organic matter which anchors it, wash away faster than they form. This is erosion.

Waters, like soil, are part of the energy circuit. Industry, by polluting waters or obstructing them with dams, may exclude the plants and animals necessary to keep energy in circulation.

Transportation brings about another basic change: the plants or animals grown in one region are now consumed and returned to the soil in another. Transportation taps the energy stored in rocks, and in the air, and uses it elsewhere; thus we fertilize the garden with nitrogen gleaned by the guano birds from the fishes of seas on the other side of the Equator. Thus the formerly localized and self-contained circuits are pooled on a worldwide scale.

The process of altering the pyramid for human occupation releases *60* stored energy, and this often gives rise, during the pioneering period, to a deceptive exuberance of plant and animal life, both wild and tame. These releases of biotic capital tend to becloud or postpone the penalties of violence.

* * *

This thumbnail sketch of land as an energy circuit conveys three basic ideas:

1. That land is not merely soil.
2. That the native plants and animals kept the energy circuit open; others may or may not.
3. That man-made changes are of a different order than evolutionary changes, and have effects more comprehensive than is intended or foreseen.

These ideas, collectively, raise two basic issues: Can the land adjust itself to the new order? Can the desired alterations be accomplished with less violence?

Biotas seem to differ in their capacity to sustain violent conversion. Western Europe, for example, carries a far different pyramid than Caesar found there. Some large animals are lost; swampy forests have become meadows or plowland; many new plants and animals are introduced, some of which escape as pests; the remaining natives are greatly changed in distribution and abundance. Yet the soil is still there and, with the help of imported nutrients, still fertile; the waters flow normally; the new structure seems to function and to persist. There is no visible stoppage or derangement of the circuit.

Western Europe, then, has a resistant biota. Its inner processes are tough, elastic, resistant to strain. No matter how violent the alterations, the pyramid, so far, has developed some new *modus vivendi* which preserves its habitability for man, and for most of the other natives.

Japan seems to present another instance of radical conversion without 65 disorganization.

Most other civilized regions, and some as yet barely touched by civilization, display various stages of disorganization, varying from initial symptoms to advanced wastage. In Asia Minor and North Africa diagnosis is confused by climatic changes, which may have been either the cause or the effect of advanced wastage. In the United States the degree of disorganization varies locally; it is worst in the Southwest, the Ozarks, and parts of the South, and least in New England and the Northwest. Better land-uses may still arrest it in the less advanced regions. In parts of Mexico, South America, South Africa, and Australia a violent and accelerating wastage is in progress, but I cannot assess the prospects.

This almost world-wide display of disorganization in the land seems to be similar to disease in an animal, except that it never culminates in complete disorganization or death. The land recovers, but at some reduced level of complexity, and with a reduced carrying capacity for people, plants, and animals. Many biotas currently regarded as "lands of opportunity" are in fact already subsisting on exploitative agriculture, i.e. they have already exceeded their sustained carrying capacity. Most of South America is overpopulated in this sense.

In arid regions we attempt to offset the process of wastage by reclamation, but it is only too evident that the prospective longevity of reclamation projects is often short. In our own West, the best of them may not last a century.

The combined evidence of history and ecology seems to support one general deduction: the less violent the man-made changes, the greater the probability of successful readjustment in the pyramid. Violence, in turn, varies with human population density; a dense population requires a more violent conversion. In this respect, North America has a better chance for permanence than Europe, if she can contrive to limit her density.

This deduction runs counter to our current philosophy, which as- 70 sumes that because a small increase in density enriched human life, that an indefinite increase will enrich it indefinitely. Ecology knows of no density relationship that holds for indefinitely wide limits. All gains from density are subject to a law of diminishing returns.

Whatever may be the equation for men and land, it is improbable that we as yet know all its terms. Recent discoveries in mineral and vitamin nutrition reveal unsuspected dependencies in the up-circuit: incredibly minute quantities of certain substances determine the value of soils to plants, of plants to animals. What of the down-circuit? What of the vanishing species, the preservation of which we now regard as an esthetic luxury? They helped build the soil; in what unsuspected ways may they be essential to its maintenance? Professor Weaver proposes that we use prairie flowers to reflocculate the wasting soils of the dust bowl; who knows for what purpose cranes and condors, otters and grizzlies may some day be used?

Land Health and the A-B Cleavage

A land, ethic, then, reflects the existence of an ecological conscience, and this in turn reflects a conviction of individual responsibility for the health of the land. Health is the capacity of the land for self-renewal. Conservation is our effort to understand and preserve this capacity.

Conservationists are notorious for their dissensions. Superficially these seem to add up to mere confusion, but a more careful scrutiny reveals a single plane of cleavage common to many specialized fields. In each field one group (A) regards the land as soil, and its function as commodity-production; another group (B) regards the land as a biota, and its function as something broader. How much broader is admittedly in a state of doubt and confusion.

In my own field, forestry, group A is quite content to grow trees like cabbages, with cellulose as the basic forest commodity. It feels no inhibition against violence; its ideology is agronomic. Group B, on the other hand, sees forestry as fundamentally different from agronomy because it employs natural species, and manages a natural environment rather than creating an artificial one. Group B prefers natural reproduction on principle. It worries on biotic as well as economic grounds about the loss of species like chestnut, and the threatened loss of the white pines. It worries about a whole series of secondary forest functions: wildlife, recreation, watersheds, wilderness areas. To my mind, Group B feels the stirrings of an ecological conscience.

In the wildlife field, a parallel cleavage exists. For Group A the basic commodities are sport and meat; the yardsticks of production are ciphers of take in pheasants and trout. Artificial propagation is acceptable as a permanent as well as a temporary recourse—if its unit costs permit. Group B, on the other hand, worries about a whole series of biotic side-issues. What is the cost in predators of producing a game crop? Should we have further recourse to exotics? How can management restore the shrinking species, like prairie grouse, already hopeless as shootable game? How can management restore the threatened rarities, like trumpeter swan and whooping crane? Can management principles be extended to wildflowers? Here again it is clear to me that we have the same A-B cleavage as in forestry.

In the larger field of agriculture I am less competent to speak, but there seem to be somewhat parallel cleavages. Scientific agriculture was actively developing before ecology was born, hence a slower penetration of ecological concepts might be expected. Moreover the farmer, by the very nature of his techniques, must modify the biota more radically than the forester or the wildlife manager. Nevertheless, there are many discontents in agriculture which seem to add up to a new vision of "biotic farming."

Perhaps the most important of these is the new evidence that poundage or tonnage is no measure of the food-value of farm crops; the products of fertile soil may be qualitatively as well as quantitatively superior. We can bolster poundage from depleted soils by pouring on imported fertility, but we are not necessarily bolstering food-value. The possible ultimate ramifications of this idea are so immense that I must leave their exposition to abler pens.

The discontent that labels itself "organic farming," while bearing some of the earmarks of a cult, is nevertheless biotic in its direction, particularly in its insistence on the importance of soil flora and fauna.

The ecological fundamentals of agriculture are just as poorly known to the public as in other fields of land-use. For example, few educated people realize that the marvelous advances in technique made during recent decades are improvements in the pump, rather than the well. Acre for acre, they have barely sufficed to offset the sinking level of fertility.

In all of these cleavages, we see repeated the same basic paradoxes: *80* man the conqueror *versus* man the biotic citizen; science the sharpener of his sword *versus* science the searchlight on his universe; land the slave and servant *versus* land the collective organism. Robinson's injunction to Tristram may well be applied, at this juncture, to *Homo sapiens* as a species in geological time:

> Whether you will or not
> You are a King, Tristram, for you are one
> Of the time-tested few that leave the world,
> When they are gone, not the same place it was.
> Mark what you leave.

The Outlook

It is inconceivable to me that an ethical relation to land can exist without love, respect, and admiration for land, and a high regard for its value. By value, I of course mean something far broader than mere economic value; I mean value in the philosophical sense.

Perhaps the most serious obstacle impeding the evolution of a land ethic is the fact that our educational and economic system is headed away from, rather than toward, an intense consciousness of land. Your true modern is separated from the land by many middlemen, and by innumerable physical gadgets. He has no vital relation to it; to him it is the space between cities on which crops grow. Turn him loose for a day on the land, and if the spot does not happen to be a golf links or a "scenic" area, he is bored stiff. If crops could be raised by hydroponics instead of farming, it would suit him very well. Synthetic substitutes for wood, leather, wool, and other natural land products suit him better than the originals. In short, land is something he has "outgrown."

Almost equally serious as an obstacle to a land ethic is the attitude of the farmer for whom the land is still an adversary, or a taskmaster that keeps him in slavery. Theoretically, the mechanization of farming ought to cut the farmer's chains, but whether it really does is debatable.

One of the requisites for an ecological comprehension of land is an understanding of ecology, and this is by no means co-extensive with "education"; in fact, much higher education seems deliberately to avoid ecological concepts. An understanding of ecology does not necessarily originate in courses bearing ecological labels; it is quite as likely to be labeled geography, botany, agronomy, history, or economics. This is as it should be, but whatever the label, ecological training is scarce.

The case for a land ethic would appear hopeless but for the minority   85
which is in obvious revolt against these "modern" trends.

The "key-log" which must be moved to release the evolutionary process for an ethic is simply this: quit thinking about decent land-use as solely an economic problem. Examine each question in terms of what is ethically and esthetically right, as well as what is economically expedient. A thing is right when it tends to preserve the integrity, stability, and beauty of the biotic community. It is wrong when it tends otherwise.

It of course goes without saying that economic feasibility limits the tether of what can or cannot be done for land. It always has and it always will. The fallacy the economic determinists have tied around our collective neck, and which we now need to cast off, is the belief that economics determines *all* land-use. This is simply not true. An innumerable host of actions and attitudes, comprising perhaps the bulk of all land relations, is determined by the land-users' tastes and predilections, rather than by his purse. The bulk of all land relations hinges on investments of time, forethought, skill, and faith rather than on investments of cash. As a land-user thinketh, so is he.

I have purposely presented the land ethic as a product of social evolution because nothing so important as an ethic is ever "written." Only the most superficial student of history supposes that Moses "wrote" the Decalogue; it evolved in the minds of a thinking community, and Moses wrote a tentative summary of it for a "seminar." I say tentative because evolution never stops.

The evolution of a land ethic is an intellectual as well as emotional process. Conservation is paved with good intentions which prove to be futile, or even dangerous, because they are devoid of critical understanding either of the land, or of economic land-use. I think it is a truism that as the ethical frontier advances from the individual to the community, its intellectual content increases.

The mechanism of operation is the same for any ethic: social appro-   90
bation for right actions: social disapproval for wrong actions.

By and large, our present problem is one of attitudes and implements. We are remodeling the Alhambra with a steam-shovel, and we are proud of our yardage. We shall hardly relinquish the shovel, which after all has many good points, but we are in need of gentler and more objective criteria for its successful use.

Working Together

1. Divide this essay into sections, one to each group in the class. In your group, work to condense your section into five (or fewer) core statements. Write them in your own words.
2. Once the groups are ready, combine these core statements to form a whole-class summary of Leopold's "The Land Ethic."

Rethinking and Rewriting

1. Once you're fairly sure that you understand what Leopold argues for in "The Land Ethic," write about why you agree with him or disagree.
2. Write a 500–750-word introduction to "The Land Ethic." Tell readers whatever you think they need to hear in order to make their reading less difficult, easier and richer.
3. Choose a page or less in "The Land Ethic," a page that seems to you to present the very heart of what Leopold has to say. Write an essay that gives a close reading of just this section, quoting it often and leading readers through it slowly, carefully, so that they understand this section as fully and completely as you do.
4. Make some connection between "The Land Ethic" and any other course you've had or are taking now. Show how the material in the other course adds to your understanding or prompts you to think about Leopold in a new way.

"A WHITE HERON"

Sarah Orne Jewett

Born in South Berwick, Maine, in 1849, Sarah Orne Jewett was an active, successful short story writer, friend to both Henry James and Willa Cather. She is perhaps best known today for her collection The Country of the Pointed Firs, *published in 1896. "A White Heron" was the title story for her sixth book of stories and was published in 1886. We've included this story because in its way it presents an alternate form of argument and because we want to continue to show that the root questions of land ethics are not just twentieth-century questions.*

As You Read

1. Read up to the first break in this story (indicated by white space). Write a few sentences describing Sylvia. Don't worry about being too obvious; just write what you know about her, and include your first impressions of what you think about her.
2. Read up to the end of section I. Write a few sentences about the setting of this story. Just explain to yourself where the story takes place. Talk about the kind of world that Sarah Orne Jewett creates.
3. As you read section II, pay attention to what happens to Sylvia as she climbs the tree and attains a new perspective. See if you can determine whether the climb changes her in any way.

I

The woods were already filled with shadows one June evening, just before eight o'clock, though a bright sunset still glimmered faintly among the trunks of the trees. A little girl was driving home her cow, a plodding, dilatory, provoking creature in her behavior, but a valued companion for all that. They were going away from whatever light there was, and striking deep into the woods, but their feet were familiar with the path, and it was no matter whether their eyes could see it or not.

There was hardly a night the summer through when the old cow could be found waiting at the pasture bars; on the contrary, it was her greatest pleasure to hide herself away among the huckleberry bushes, and though she wore a loud bell she had made the discovery that if one stood perfectly still it would not ring. So Sylvia had to hunt for her until she found her, and call Co'! Co'! with never an answering Moo, until her childish patience was quite spent. If the creature had not given good milk and plenty of it, the case would have seemed very different to her owners. Besides, Sylvia had all the time there was, and very little use to make of it. Sometimes in pleasant weather it was a consolation to look upon the cow's pranks as an intelligent attempt to play hide and seek, and as the child had no playmates she lent herself to this amusement with a good deal of zest. Though this chase had been so long that the wary animal herself had given an unusual signal of her whereabouts, Sylvia had only laughed when she came upon Mistress Moolly at the swampside, and urged her affectionately homeward with a twig of birch leaves. The old cow was not inclined to wander farther, she even turned in the right direction for once as they left the pasture, and stepped along the road at a good pace. She was quite ready to be milked now, and seldom stopped to browse. Sylvia wondered what her grandmother would say because they were so late. It was a great while since she had left home at half-past five o'clock, but everybody knew the difficulty of making this errand a short one. Mrs. Tilley had chased the hornéd torment too many summer evenings herself to blame any one else for lingering, and was only thankful as she waited that she had Sylvia, nowadays, to give such valuable assistance. The good woman suspected that Sylvia loitered occasionally on her own account; there never was such a child for straying about out-of-doors since the world was made! Everybody said that it was a good change for a little maid who had tried to grow for eight years in a crowded manufacturing town, but as for Sylvia herself, it seemed as if she never had been alive at all before she came to live at the farm. She thought often with wistful compassion of a wretched geranium that belonged to a town neighbor.

"'Afraid of folks,'" old Mrs. Tilley said to herself, with a smile, after she had made the unlikely choice of Sylvia from her daughter's houseful of children, and was returning to the farm. "'Afraid of folks,' they said! I guess she won't be troubled no great with 'em up to the old place!" When they reached the door of the lonely house and stopped to unlock it, and the cat came to purr loudly, and rub against them, a deserted pussy, indeed, but fat with young robins, Sylvia whispered that this was a beautiful place to live in, and she never should wish to go home.

The companions followed the shady woodroad, the cow taking slow steps and the child very fast ones. The cow stopped long at the brook to drink, as if the pasture were not half a swamp, and Sylvia stood still and waited, letting her bare feet cool themselves in the shoal water, while the great twilight moths struck softly against her. She waded on through the brook as the cow moved away, and listened to the thrushes with a heart that beat fast with pleasure. There was a stirring in the great boughs overhead. They were full of little birds and beasts that seemed to be wide awake, and going about their world, or else saying goodnight to each other in sleepy twitters. Sylvia herself felt sleepy as she walked along. However, it was not much farther to the house, and the air was soft and sweet. She was not often in the woods so late as this, and it made her feel as if she were a part of the gray shadows and the moving leaves. She was just thinking how long it seemed since she first came to the farm a year ago, and wondering if everything went on in the noisy town just the same as when she was there; the thought of the great red-faced boy who used to chase and frighten her made her hurry along the path to escape from the shadow of the trees.

Suddenly this little woods-girl is horror-stricken to hear a clear whis-   5
tle not very far away. Not a bird's-whistle, which would have a sort of friendliness, but a boy's whistle, determined, and somewhat aggressive. Sylvia left the cow to whatever sad fate might await her, and stepped discreetly aside into the brushes, but she was just too late. The enemy had discovered her, and called out in a very cheerful and persuasive tone, "Halloa, little girl, how far is it to the road?" and trembling Sylvia answered almost inaudibly, "A good ways."

She did not dare to look boldly at the tall young man, who carried a gun over his shoulder, but she came out of her bush and again followed the cow, while he walked alongside.

"I have been hunting for some birds," the stranger said kindly, "and I have lost my way, and need a friend very much. Don't be afraid," he added gallantly. "Speak up and tell me what your name is, and whether you think I can spend the night at your house, and go out gunning early in the morning."

Sylvia was more alarmed than before. Would not her grandmother consider her much to blame? But who could have foreseen such an accident as this? It did not seem to be her fault, and she hung her head as if the stem of it were broken, but managed to answer "Sylvy," with much effort when her companion again asked her name.

Mrs. Tilley was standing in the doorway when the trio came into view. The cow gave a loud moo by way of explanation.

"Yes, you'd better speak up for yourself, you old trial! Where'd she   10
tucked herself away this time, Sylvy?" But Sylvia kept an awed silence; she knew by instinct that her grandmother did not comprehend the gravity of the situation. She must be mistaking the stranger for one of the farmer-lads of the region.

The young man stood his gun beside the door, and dropped a lumpy game-bag beside it; then he bade Mrs. Tilley good-evening, and repeated his wayfarer's story, and asked if he could have a night's lodging.

"Put me anywhere you like," he said. "I must be off early in the morning, before day; but I am very hungry, indeed. You can give me some milk at any rate, that's plain."

"Dear sakes, yes," responded the hostess, whose long slumbering hospitality seemed to be easily awakened. "You might fare better if you went out to the main road a mile or so, but you're welcome to what we've got. I'll milk right off, and you make yourself at home. You can sleep on husks or feathers," she proffered graciously. "I raised them all myself. There's good pasturing for geese just below here towards the ma'sh. Now step round and set a plate for the gentleman, Sylvy!" And Sylvia promptly stepped. She was glad to have something to do, and she was hungry herself.

It was a surprise to find so clean and comfortable a little dwelling in this New England wilderness. The young man had known the horrors of its most primitive housekeeping, and the dreary squalor of that level of society which does not rebel at the companionship of hens. This was the best thrift of an old-fashioned farmstead, though on such a small scale that it seemed like a hermitage. He listened eagerly to the old woman's quaint talk, he watched Sylvia's pale face and shining gray eyes with ever growing enthusiasm, and insisted that this was the best supper he had eaten for a month, and afterward the new-made friends sat down in the door-way together while the moon came up.

Soon it would be berry-time, and Sylvia was a great help at picking. The cow was a good milker, though a plaguy thing to keep track of, the hostess gossiped frankly, adding presently that she had buried four children, so Sylvia's mother, and a son (who might be dead) in California were all the children she had left. "Dan, my boy, was a great hand to go gunning," she explained sadly. "I never wanted for pa'tridges or gray squer'ls while he was to home. He's been a great wand'rer, I expect, and he's no hand to write letters. There, I don't blame him, I'd ha' seen the world myself if it had been so I could."

"Sylvy takes after him," the grandmother continued affectionately, after a minute's pause. "There ain't a foot o' ground she don't know her way over, and the wild creaturs counts her one o' themselves. Squer'ls she'll tame to come an' feed right out o' her hands, and all sorts o' birds. Last winter she got the jay-birds to bangeing here, and I believe she'd 'a' scanted herself of her own meals to have plenty to throw out amongst 'em, if I had n't kep' watch. Anything but crows, I tell her, I'm willin' to help support—though Dan he had a tamed one o' them that did seem to have reason same as folks. It was round here a good spell after he went away. Dan an' his father they didn't hitch,—but he never held up his head ag'in after Dan had dared him an' gone off."

The guest did not notice this hint of family sorrows in his eager interest in something else.

"So Sylvy knows all about birds, does she?" he exclaimed, as he looked round at the little girl who sat, very demure but increasingly sleepy, in the moonlight. "I am making a collection of birds myself. I have been at it every since I was a boy." (Mrs. Tilley smiled.) "There are two or three very rare ones I have been hunting for these five years. I mean to get them on my own ground if they can be found."

"Do you cage 'em up?" asked Mrs. Tilley doubtfully, in response to this enthusiastic announcement.

"Oh no, they 're stuffed and preserved, dozens and dozens of them," said the ornithologist, "and I have shot or snared every one myself. I caught a glimpse of a white heron a few miles from here on Saturday, and I have followed it in this direction. They have never been found in this district at all. The little white heron, it is," and he turned again to look at

15

20

Sylvia with the hope of discovering that the rare bird was one of her acquaintances.

But Sylvia was watching a hop-toad in the narrow footpath.

"You would know the heron if you saw it," the stranger continued eagerly. "A queer tall white bird with soft feathers and long thin legs. And it would have a nest perhaps in the top of a high tree, made of sticks, something like a hawk's nest."

Sylvia's heart gave a wild beat; she knew that strange white bird, and had once stolen softly near where it stood in some bright green swamp grass, away over at the other side of the woods. There was an open place where the sunshine always seemed strangely yellow and hot, where tall, nodding rushes grew, and her grandmother had warned her that she might sink in the soft black mud underneath and never be heard of more. Not far beyond were the salt marshes just this side the sea itself, which Sylvia wondered and dreamed much about, but never had seen, whose great voice could sometimes be heard above the noise of the woods on stormy nights.

"I can't think of anything I should like so much as to find that heron's nest," the handsome stranger was saying. "I would give ten dollars to anybody who could show it to me," he added desperately, "and I mean to spend my whole vacation hunting for it if need be. Perhaps it was only migrating, or had been chased out of its own region by some bird of prey."

Mrs. Tilley gave amazed attention to all this, but Sylvia still watched the toad, not divining, as she might have done at some calmer time, that the creature wished to get to its hole under the door-step, and was much hindered by the unusual spectators at that hour of the evening. No amount of thought, that night, could decide how many wished-for treasures the ten dollars, so lightly spoken of, would buy.

The next day the young sportsman hovered about the woods, and Sylvia kept him company, having lost her first fear of the friendly lad, who proved to be most kind and sympathetic. He told her many things about the birds and what they knew and where they lived and what they did with themselves. And he gave her a jack-knife, which she thought as great a treasure as if she were a desert-islander. All day long he did not once make her troubled or afraid except when he brought down some unsuspecting singing creature from its bough. Sylvia would have liked him vastly better without his gun; she could not understand why he killed the very birds he seemed to like so much. But as the day waned, Sylvia still watched the young man with loving admiration. She had never seen anybody so charming and delightful; the woman's heart, asleep in the child, was vaguely thrilled by a dream of love. Some premonition of that great power stirred and swayed these young creatures who traversed the solemn woodlands with soft-footed silent care. They stopped to listen to a bird's song; they pressed forward again eagerly, parting the branches—speaking to each other rarely and in whispers; the young man going first and Sylvia following, fascinated, a few steps behind, with her gray eyes dark with excitement.

25

She grieved because the longed-for white heron was elusive, but she did not lead the guest, she only followed, and there was no such thing as speaking first. The sound of her own unquestioned voice would have terrified her—it was hard enough to answer yes or no when there was need of that. At last evening began to fall, and they drove the cow home together, and Sylvia smiled with pleasure when they came to the place where she heard the whistle and was afraid only the night before.

II

Half a mile from home, at the farther edge of the woods, where the land was highest, a great pine-tree stood, the last of its generation. Whether it was left for a boundary mark, or for what reason, no one could say; the woodchoppers who had felled its mates were dead and gone long ago, and a whole forest of sturdy trees, pines and oaks and maples, had grown again. But the stately head of this old pine towered above them all and made a landmark for sea and shore miles and miles away. Sylvia knew it well. She had always believed that whoever climbed to the top of it could see the ocean; and the little girl had often laid her hand on the great rough trunk and looked up wistfully at those dark boughs that the wind always stirred, no matter how hot and still the air might be below. Now she thought of the tree with a new excitement, for why, if one climbed it at break of day could not one see all the world, and easily discover from whence the white heron flew, and mark the place, and find the hidden nest?

What a spirit of adventure, what wild ambition! What fancied triumph and delight and glory for the later morning when she could make known the secret! It was almost too real and too great for the childish heart to bear.

All night the door of the little house stood open and the whippoor- 30 wills came and sang upon the very step. The young sportsman and his old hostess were sound asleep, but Sylvia's great design kept her broad awake and watching. She forgot to think of sleep. The short summer night seemed as long as the winter darkness, and at last when the whippoorwills ceased, and she was afraid the morning would after all come too soon, she stole out of the house and followed the pasture path through the woods, hastening toward the open ground beyond, listening with a sense of comfort and companionship to the drowsy twitter of a half-awakened bird, whose perch she had jarred in passing. Alas, if the great wave of human interest which flooded for the first time this dull little life should sweep away the satisfactions of an existence heart to heart with nature and the dumb life of the forest!

There was the huge tree asleep yet in the paling moonlight, and small and silly Sylvia began with utmost bravery to mount to the top of it, with tingling, eager blood coursing the channels of her whole frame, with her bare feet and fingers, that pinched and held like bird's claws to the monstrous ladder reaching up, up, almost to the sky itself. First she must mount the white oak tree that grew alongside, where she was almost lost among the dark branches and the green leaves heavy and wet with dew; a bird fluttered off its nest, and a red squirrel ran to and fro and scolded pettishly at the harmless housebreaker. Sylvia felt her way easily. She had often climbed there, and knew that higher still one of the oak's upper branches chafed against the pine trunk, just where its lower boughs were set close together. There, when she made the dangerous pass from one tree to the other, the great enterprise would really begin.

She crept out along the swaying oak limb at last, and took the daring step across into the old pine-tree. The way was harder than she thought; she must reach far and hold fast, the sharp dry twigs caught and held her and scratched her like angry talons, the pitch made her thin little fingers clumsy and stiff as she went round and round the tree's great stem, higher and higher upward. The sparrows and robins in the woods below were beginning to wake and twitter to the dawn, yet it seemed much lighter there aloft in the pine-tree, and the child knew she must hurry if her project were to be of any use.

The tree seemed to lengthen itself out as she went up, and to reach farther and farther upward. It was like a great main-mast to the voyaging earth; it must truly have been amazed that morning through all its ponderous frame as it felt this determined spark of human spirit wending its way from higher branch to branch. Who knows how steadily the least twigs held themselves to advantage this light, weak creature on her way! The old pine must have loved his new dependent. More than all the hawks, and bats, and moths, and even the sweet voiced thrushes, was the brave, beating heart of the solitary gray-eyed child. And the tree stood still and frowned away the winds that June morning while the dawn grew bright in the east.

Sylvia's face was like a pale star, if one had seen it from the ground, when the last thorny bough was past, and she stood trembling and tired but wholly triumphant, high in the treetop. Yes, there was the sea with the dawning sun making a golden dazzle over it, and toward that glorious east flew two hawks with slow-moving pinions. How low they looked in the air from that height when one had only seen them before far up, and dark against the blue sky. Their gray feathers were as soft as moths; they seemed only a little way from the tree, and Sylvia felt as if she too could go flying away among the clouds. Westward, the woodlands and farms reached miles and miles into the distance; here and there were church steeples, and white villages, truly it was a vast and awesome world!

The birds sang louder and louder. At last the sun came up bewilder- 35 ingly bright. Sylvia could see the white sails of ships out at sea, and the clouds that were purple and rose-colored and yellow at first began to fade away. Where was the white heron's nest in the sea of green branches, and was this wonderful sight and pageant of the world the only reward for having climbed to such a giddy height? Now look down again, Sylvia,

where the green marsh is set among the shining birches and dark hemlocks; there where you saw the white heron once you will see him again;
look, look! a white spot of him like a single floating feather comes up from
the dead hemlock and grows larger, and rises, and comes close at last, and
goes by the landmark pine with steady sweep of wing and outstretched
slender neck and crested head. And wait! wait! do not move a foot or a
finger, little girl, do not send an arrow of light and consciousness from
your two eager eyes, for the heron has perched on a pine bough not far
beyond yours, and cries back to his mate on the nest and plumes his
feathers for the new day!

The child gives a long sigh a minute later when a company of shouting cat-birds comes also to the tree, and vexed by their fluttering and
lawlessness the solemn heron goes away. She knows his secret now, the
wild, light, slender bird that floats and wavers, and goes back like an arrow
presently to his home in the green world beneath. Then Sylvia, well satisfied, makes her perilous way down again, not daring to look far below the
branch she stands on, ready to cry sometimes because her fingers ache and
her lamed feet slip. Wondering over and over again what the stranger
would say to her, and what he would think when she told him how to
find his way straight to the heron's nest.

"Sylvy, Sylvy!" called the busy old grandmother again and again, but
nobody answered, and the small husk bed was empty and Sylvia had
disappeared.

The guest waked from a dream, and remembering his day's pleasure hurried to dress himself that might it sooner begin. He was sure
from the way the shy little girl looked once or twice yesterday that she
had at least seen the white heron, and now she must really be made to
tell. Here she comes now, paler than ever, and her worn old frock is
torn and tattered, and smeared with pine pitch. The grandmother and
the sportsman stand in the door together and question her, and the
splendid moment has come to speak of the dead hemlock-tree by the
green marsh.

But Sylvia does not speak after all, though the old grandmother
fretfully rebukes her, and the young man's kind, appealing eyes are looking
straight in her own. He can make them rich with money; he has promised
it, and they are poor now. He is so well worth making happy, and he waits
to hear the story she can tell.

No, she must keep silence! What is it that suddenly forbids her and   40
makes her dumb? Has she been nine years growing and now, when the
great world for the first time puts out a hand to her, must she thrust it
aside for a bird's sake? The murmur of the pine's green branches is in
her ears, she remembers how the white heron came flying through the
golden air and how they watched the sea and the morning together, and
Sylvia cannot speak; she cannot tell the heron's secret and give its life
away.

Dear loyalty, that suffered a sharp pang as the guest went away disappointed later in the day, that could have served and followed him and loved him as a dog loves! Many a night Sylvia heard the echo of his whistle haunting the pasture path as she came home with the loitering cow. She forgot even her sorrow at the sharp report of his gun and the sight of thrushes and sparrows dropping silent to the ground, their songs hushed and their pretty feathers stained and wet with blood. Were the birds better friends than their hunter might have been,—who can tell? Whatever treasures were lost to her, woodlands and summer-time, remember! Bring your gifts and graces and tell your secrets to this lonely country child!

1886

Working Together

1. As a group, write four major questions that your group members have about what happens in this story and/or why it happens. Phrase your questions clearly and rank them #1 for most important to #4 for least important. Then turn your questions over to another group and take its list. Start with that group's most important question and try to answer it. If you can't answer it, be ready to explain why you're having trouble. Continue in this fashion answering the other group's four questions.
2. In your group, discuss what kind of land ethic Jewett would approve of. From your collective reading, try to identify three aspects of that land ethic.
3. As a group, decide how you would argue that telling a story is actually a better, more effective way to make an argument for a land ethic. Explain why the story works more persuasively than an essay or manifesto. Or decide how you would argue that telling a story doesn't work very well as a way to make an argument. Explain why an essay or manifesto works more persuasively than a story.

Rethinking and Rewriting

1. From your reading of "A White Heron," explain your understanding of Jewett's views on nature and how people ought to act toward nature. Keep this piece to no more than 600 words.
2. From your group discussions (or just from your own thinking, if you've not discussed this as a group), argue either that a story is an effective, persuasive way to get readers to consider questions of land ethics or that an essay or manifesto more persuasively affects readers. Use "A White Heron" as the story example.
3. In the end the story doesn't really explain Sylvia's actions. So you try to. Write an "Afterward" that works to account for what Sylvia does

and doesn't do. Use the story itself for evidence, and then (if necessary) speculate on the basis of your sense of the spirit of the story.

4. Argue that whatever this story seems to mean, its impact is unavoidably lessened by the fact that Sylvia is only nine years old, a child. Or argue that the fact that Sylvia is only nine years old actually adds force to the story and increases its impact. Either way, make sure that you explain yourself carefully.

"IS NATURE TOO GOOD FOR US?"

William Tucker

> *William Tucker began his career as a journalist at the Nyack, New Jersey,* Journal News *and other small local newspapers; then he went on to write articles for* Atlantic, *the* New Republic, *the* Wall Street Journal, *the* New York Times, *and other national publications. He was a contributing editor to* Harper's *magazine and is currently a contributing editor to* Forbes. *He is also the author of four book-length studies of American social issues:* Progress and Privilege: America in the Age of Environmentalism *(1982);* Vigilante: The Backlash Against Crime in America *(1985);* The Excluded Americans: Homelessness and Housing Polcies *(1989);* and Zoning, Rent Control, and Affordable Housing *(1991). "As a journalistic entrepreneur," he writes, "I am constantly looking for circumstances where there is a wide gap between what is actually happening and what people think* should *be happening." The following is an excerpt from* Progress and Privilege.

As You Read

As you read, mark the arguments that seem the most reasonable and persuasive. Similarly, mark those arguments that seem *least* persuasive.

Probably nothing has been more central to the environmental movement than the concept of wilderness. "In wildness is the preservation of the world," wrote Thoreau, and environmental writers and speakers have intoned his message repeatedly. Wilderness, in the environmental pantheon, represents a particular kind of sanctuary in which all true values—that is, all nonhuman values—are reposited. Wildernesses are often described as "temples," "churches," and "sacred ground"—refuges for the proposed "new religion" based on environmental consciousness. Carrying the religious metaphor to the extreme, one of the most famous essays of the environmental era holds the Judeo-Christian religion responsible for "ecological crisis."

The wilderness issue also has a political edge. Since 1964, longstanding preservation groups like the Wilderness Society and the Sierra Club have been pressuring conservation agencies like the National Forest Service and the Bureau of Land Management to put large tracts of their holdings into permanent "wilderness designations," countering the "multiple use" concept that was one of the cornerstones of the Conservation Era of the early 1900s.

Preservation and conservation groups have been at odds since the end of the last century, and the rift between them has been a major controversy of environmentalism. The leaders of the Conservation Movement—

most notably Theodore Roosevelt, Gifford Pinchot, and John Wesley Powell—called for rational, efficient development of land and other natural resources: multiple use, or reconciling competing uses of land, and also "highest use," or forfeiting more immediate profits from land development for more lasting gains. Preservationists, on the other hand, the followers of California woodsman John Muir, have advocated protecting land in its natural state, setting aside tracts and keeping them inviolate. "Wilderness area" battles have become one of the hottest political issues of the day, especially in western states—the current "Sagebrush Revolt" comes to mind—where large quantities of potentially commercially usable land are at stake.

The term "wilderness" generally connotes mountains, trees, clear streams, rushing waterfalls, grasslands, or parched deserts, but the concept has been institutionalized and has a careful legal definition as well. The one given by the 1964 Wilderness Act, and that most environmentalists favor, is that wilderness is an area "where man is a visitor but does not remain." People do not "leave footprints there," wilderness exponents often say Wildernesses are, most importantly, areas in which *evidence of human activity is excluded;* they need not have any particular scenic, aesthetic, or recreational value. The values, as environmentalists usually say, are "ecological"—which means, roughly translated, that natural systems are allowed to operate as free from human interference as possible.

The concept of excluding human activity is not to be taken lightly. One of the major issues in wilderness areas has been whether or not federal agencies should fight forest fires. The general decision has been that they should not, except in cases where other lands are threatened. The federal agencies also do not fight the fires with motorized vehicles, which are prohibited in wilderness areas except in extreme emergencies. Thus in recent years both the National Forest Service and the National Park Service have taken to letting forest fires burn unchecked, to the frequent alarm of tourists. The defense is that many forests require periodic leveling by fire in order to make room for new growth. There are some pine trees, for instance, whose cones will break open and scatter their seeds only when burned. This theoretical justification has won some converts, but very few in the timber companies, which bridle at watching millions of board-feet go up in smoke when their own "harvesting" of mature forests has the same effect in clearing the way for new growth and does less damage to forest soils.

The effort to set aside permanent wilderness areas on federal lands began with the National Forest Service in the 1920s. The first permanent reservation was in the Gila National Forest in New Mexico. It was set aside by a young Forest Service officer named Aldo Leopold, who was later to write *A Sand County Almanac,* which has become one of the bibles of the wilderness movement. Robert Marshall, another Forest Service officer, continued the program, and by the 1950s nearly 14 million of the National

Forest System's 186 million acres had been administratively designated wilderness preserves.

Leopold and Marshall had been disillusioned by one of the first great efforts at "game management" under the National Forest Service, carried out in the Kaibab Plateau, just north of the Grand Canyon. As early as 1906 federal officials began a program of "predator control" to increase the deer population in the area. Mountain lions, wolves, coyotes, and bobcats were systematically hunted and trapped by game officials. By 1920, the program appeared to be spectacularly successful. The deer population, formerly numbering 4,000, had grown to almost 100,000. But it was realized too late that it was the range's limited food resources that would threaten the deer's existence. During two severe winters, in 1924–26, 60 percent of the herd died, and by 1939 the population had shrunk to only 10,000. Deer populations (unlike human populations) were found to have no way of putting limits on their own reproduction. The case is still cited as the classic example of the "boom and bust" disequilibrium that comes from thoughtless intervention in an ecological system.

The idea of setting aside as wilderness areas larger and larger segments of federally controlled lands began to gain more support from the old preservationists' growing realizations, during the 1950s, that they had not won the battle during the Conservation Era, and that the national forests were not parks that would be protected forever from commercial activity.

Pinchot's plan for practicing "conservation" in the western forests was to encourage a partnership between the government and large industry. In order to discourage overcutting and destructive competition, he formulated a plan that would promote conservation activities among the larger timber companies while placing large segments of the western forests under federal control. It was a classic case of "market restriction," carried out by the joint efforts of larger businesses and government. Only the larger companies, Pinchot reasoned, could generate the profits that would allow them to cut their forest holdings *slowly* so that the trees would have time to grow back. In order to ensure these profit margins, the National Forest Service would hold most of its timber lands out of the market for some time. This would hold up the price of timber and prevent a rampage through the forests by smaller companies trying to beat small profit margins by cutting everything in sight. Then, in later years, the federal lands would gradually be worked into the "sustained yield" cycles, and timber rights put up for sale. It was when the national forests finally came up for cutting in the 1950s that the old preservation groups began to react.

The battle was fought in Congress. The 1960 Multiple Use and Sustained Yield Act tried to reaffirm the principles of the Conservation Movement. But the wilderness groups had their day in 1964 with the passing of the Wilderness Act. The law required all the federal land-management agencies—the National Forest Service, the National Park Service, and the Fish and Wildlife Service—to review all their holdings, keeping in mind

10

that "wilderness" now constituted a valid alternative in the "multiple use" concept—even though the concept of wilderness is essentially a rejection of the idea of multiple use. The Forest Service, with 190 million acres, and the Park Service and Fish and Wildlife Service, each with about 35 million acres, were all given twenty years to start designating wilderness areas. At the time, only 14.5 million acres of National Forest System land were in wilderness designations.

The results have been mixed. The wilderness concept appears valid if it is recognized for what it is—an attempt to create what are essentially "ecological museums" in scenic and biologically significant areas of these lands. But "wilderness," in the hands of environmentalists, has become an all-purpose tool for stopping economic activity as well. This is particularly crucial now because of the many mineral and energy resources available on western lands that environmentalists are trying to push through as wilderness designations. The original legislation specified that lands were to be surveyed for valuable mineral resources before they were put into wilderness preservation. Yet with so much land being reviewed at once, these inventories have been sketchy at best. And once land is locked up as wilderness, it becomes illegal even to explore it for mineral or energy resources.

Thus the situation in western states—where the federal government still owns 68 percent of the land, counting Alaska—has in recent years become a race between mining companies trying to prospect under severely restricted conditions, and environmental groups trying to lock the doors to resource development for good. This kind of permanent preservation—the antithesis of conservation—will probably have enormous effects on our future international trade in energy and mineral resources.

At stake in both the national forests and the Bureau of Land Management holdings are what are called the "roadless areas." Environmentalists call these lands "de facto wilderness," and say that because they have not yet been explored or developed for resources they should not be explored and developed in the future. The Forest Service began its Roadless Area Resources Evaluation (RARE) in 1972, while the Bureau of Land Management began four years later in 1976, after Congress brought its 174 million acres under jurisdiction of the 1964 act. The Forest Service is studying 62 million roadless acres, while the BLM is reviewing 24 million.

In 1974 the Forest Service recommended that 15 million of the 50 million acres then under study be designated as permanent wilderness. Environmental groups, which wanted much more set aside, immediately challenged the decision in court. Naturally, they had no trouble finding flaws in a study intended to cover such a huge amount of land, and in 1977 the Carter administration decided to start over with a "RARE II" study, completed in 1979. This has also been challenged by a consortium of environmental groups that includes the Sierra Club, the Wilderness Society, the National Wildlife Federation, and the Natural Resources Defense

Council. The RARE II report also recommended putting about 15 million acres in permanent wilderness, with 36 million released for development and 11 million held for further study. The Bureau of Land Management is not scheduled to complete the study of its 24 million acres until 1991.

The effects of this campaign against resource development have been powerful. From 1972 to 1980, the price of a Douglas fir in Oregon increased 500 percent, largely due to the delays in timber sales from the national forests because of the battles over wilderness areas. Over the decade, timber production from the national forests declined slightly, putting far more pressure on the timber industry's own lands. The nation has now become an importer of logs, despite the vast resources on federal lands. In 1979, environmentalists succeeded in pressuring Congress into setting aside 750,000 acres in Idaho as the Sawtooth Wilderness and National Recreational Area. A resource survey, which was not completed until *after* the congressional action, showed that the area contained an estimated billion dollars' worth of molybdenum, zinc, silver, and gold. The same tract also contained a potential source of cobalt, an important mineral for which we are now dependent on foreign sources for 97 percent of what we use.

Perhaps most fiercely contested are the energy supplies believed to be lying under the geological strata running through Colorado, Wyoming, and Montana just east of the Rockies, called the Overthrust Belt. Much of this land is still administered by the Bureau of Land Management for multiple usage. But with the prospect of energy development, environmental groups have been rushing to try to have these high-plains areas designated as wilderness areas as well (cattle grazing is still allowed in wilderness tracts). On those lands permanently withdrawn from commercial use, mineral exploration will be allowed to continue until 1983. Any mines begun by then can continue on a very restricted basis. But the exploration in "roadless areas" is severely limited, in that in most cases there can be no roads constructed (and no use of off-roads vehicles) while exploration is going on. Environmentalists have argued that wells can still be drilled and test mines explored using helicopters. But any such exploration is likely to be extraordinarily expensive and ineffective. Wilderness restrictions are now being drawn so tightly that people on the site are not allowed to leave their excrement in the area.

Impossible Paradises

What is the purpose of all this? The standard environmental argument is that we have to "preserve these last few wild places before they all disappear." Yet it is obvious that something more is at stake. What is being purveyed is a view of the world in which human activity is defined as "bad" and natural conditions are defined as "good." What is being preserved is evidently much more than "ecosystems." What is being preserved is an *image* of wilderness as a semisacred place beyond humanity's intrusion.

It is instructive to consider how environmentalists themselves define the wilderness. David Brower, former director of the Sierra Club, wrote in his introduction to Paul Ehrlich's *The Population Bomb* (1968):

> Whatever resources the wilderness still held would not sustain (man) in his old habits of growing and reaching without limits. Wilderness could, however, provide answers for questions he had not yet learned how to ask. He could predict that the day of creation was not over, that there would be wiser men, and they would thank him for leaving the source of those answers. Wilderness would remain part of his geography of hope, as Wallace Stegner put it, and could, merely because wilderness endured on the planet, prevent man's world from becoming a cage.

The wilderness, he suggested, is a source of peace and freedom. Yet setting wilderness aside for the purposes of solitude doesn't always work very well. Environmentalists have discovered this over and over again, much to their chagrin. Every time a new "untouched paradise" is discovered, the first thing everyone wants to do is visit it. By their united enthusiasm to find these "sanctuaries," people bring the "cage" of society with them. Very quickly it becomes necessary to erect bars to keep people *out*—which is exactly what most of the "wilderness" legislation has been all about.

In 1964, for example, the Sierra Club published a book on the relatively "undiscovered" paradise of Kauai, the second most westerly island in the Hawaiian chain. It wasn't long before the island had been overrun with tourists. When *Time* magazine ran a feature on Kauai in 1979, one unhappy island resident wrote in to convey this telling sentiment: "We're hoping the shortages of jet fuel will stay around and keep people away from here." The age of environmentalism has also been marked by the near overrunning of popular national parks like Yosemite (which now has a full-time jail), intense pressure on woodland recreational areas, full bookings two and three years in advance for raft trips through the Grand Canyon, and dozens of other spectacles of people crowding into isolated areas to get away from it all. Environmentalists are often critical of these inundations, but they must recognize that they have at least contributed to them.

I am not arguing against wild things, scenic beauty, pristine landscapes, and scenic preservation. What I am questioning is the argument that wilderness is a value against which every other human activity must be judged, and that human beings are somehow unworthy of the landscape. The wilderness has been equated with freedom, but there are many different ideas about what constitutes freedom. In the Middle Ages, the saying was that "city air makes a man free," meaning that the harsh social burdens of medieval feudalism vanished once a person escaped into the heady anonymity of a metropolitan community. When city planner Jane Jacobs, author of *The Death and Life of Great American Cities,* was asked by an interviewer if "overpopulation" and "crowding into large cities" weren't making social prisoners of us all, her simple reply was: "Have you ever lived in a small town?"

It may seem unfair to itemize the personal idiosyncrasies of people who feel comfortable only in wilderness, but it must be remembered that the environmental movement has been shaped by many people who literally spent years of their lives living in isolation. John Muir, the founder of the National Parks movement and the Sierra Club spent almost ten years living alone in the Sierra Mountains while learning to be a trail guide. David Brower, who headed the Sierra Club for over a decade and later broke with it to found the Friends of the Earth, also spent years as a mountaineer. Gary Snyder, the poet laureate of the environmental movement, has lived much of his life in wilderness isolation and has also spent several years in a Zen monastery. All these people far outdid Thoreau in their desire to get a little perspective on the world. There is nothing reprehensible in this, and the literature and philosophy that merge from such experiences are often admirable. But it seems questionable to me that the ethic that comes out of this wilderness isolation—and the sense of ownership of natural landscapes that inevitably follows—can serve as the basis for a useful national philosophy.

That Frontier Spirit

The American frontier is generally agreed to have closed down physically in 1890, the year the last Indian Territory of Oklahoma was opened for the settlement. After that, the Conservation Movement arose quickly to protect the remaining resources and wilderness from heedless stripping and development. Along with this came a significant psychological change in the national character, as the "frontier spirit" diminished and social issues attracted greater attention. The Progressive Movement, the Social Gospel among religious groups, Populism, and Conservation all arose in quick succession immediately after the "closing of the frontier." It seems fair to say that it was only after the frontier had been settled and the sense of endless possibilities that came with open spaces had been constricted in the national consciousness that the country started "growing up."

Does this mean the new environmental consciousness has arisen because we are once again "running out of space"? I doubt it. Anyone taking an airplane across almost any part of the country is inevitably struck by how much greenery and open territory remain, and how little room our towns and cities really occupy. The amount of standing forest in the country, for example, has not diminished appreciably over the last fifty years, and is 75 percent of what it was in 1620. In addition, as environmentalists constantly remind us, trees are "renewable resources." If they continue to be handled intelligently, the forests will always grow back. As farming has moved out to the Great Plains of the Middle West, many eastern areas that were once farmed have reverted back to trees. Though mining operations can permanently scar hillsides and plains, they are usually very limited in scope (and as often as not, it is the roads leading to these mines that environmentalists find most objectionable).

It seems to be that the wilderness ethic has actually represented an   *25* attempt psychologically to reopen the American frontier. We have been desperate to maintain belief in unlimited, uncharted vistas within our borders, a preoccupation that has eclipsed the permanent shrinking of the rest of the world outside. Why else would it be so necessary to preserve such huge tracts of "roadless territory" simply because they are now roadless, regardless of their scenic, recreational, or aesthetic values? The environmental movement, among other things, has been a rather backward-looking effort to recapture America's lost innocence.

The central figure in this effort has been the backpacker. The backpacker is a young, unprepossessing person (inevitably white and upper middle class) who journeys into the wilderness as a passive observer. He or she brings his or her own food, treads softly, leaves no litter, and has no need to make use of any of the resources at hand. Backpackers bring all the necessary accouterments of civilization with them. All their needs have been met by the society from which they seek temporary release. The backpacker is freed from the need to support itself in order to enjoy the aesthetic and spiritual values that are made available by this temporary *removal* from the demands of nature. Many dangers—raging rivers or precipitous cliffs, for instance—become sought-out adventures.

Yet once the backpacker runs out of supplies and starts using resources around him—cutting trees for firewood, putting up a shelter against the rain—he is violating some aspect of the federal Wilderness Act. For example, one of the issues fought in the national forests revolves around tying one's horse to a tree. Purists claim the practice should be forbidden, since it may leave a trodden ring around the tree. They say horses should be hobbled and allowed to graze instead. In recent years, the National Forest Service has come under pressure from environmental groups to enforce this restriction.

Wildernesses, then, are essentially parks for the upper middle class. They are vacation reserves for people who want to rough it—with the assurance that few other people will have the time, energy, or means to follow them into the solitude. This is dramatically highlighted in one Sierra Club book that shows a picture of a professorial sort of individual backpacking off into the woods. The ironic caption is a quote from Julius Viancour, an official of the Western Council of Lumber and Sawmill Workers: "The inaccessible wilderness and primitive areas are off limits to most laboring people. We must have access. . . ." The implication for Sierra Club readers is: "What do these beer-drinking, gun-toting, working people want to do in *our* woods?"

This class-oriented vision of wilderness as an upper-middle-class preserve is further illustrated by the fact that most of the opposition to wilderness designations comes not from industry but from owners of off-road vehicles. In most northern rural areas, snowmobiles are now regarded as the greatest invention since the automobile, and people are ready to fight rather than stay cooped up all winter in their houses. It seems ludicrous to them that snowmobiles (which can't be said even to endanger the ground) should be restricted from vast tracts of land so that the occasional city visitor can have solitude while hiking past on snowshoes.

The recent Boundary Waters Canoe Area controversy in northern *30* Minnesota is an excellent example of the conflict. When the tract was first designated as wilderness in 1964, Congress included a special provision that allowed motorboats into the entire area. By the mid-1970s, outboards and inboards were roaming all over the wilderness, and environmental groups began asking that certain portions of the million-acre preserve be set aside exclusively for canoes. Local residents protested vigorously, arguing that fishing expeditions, via motorboats, contributed to their own recreation. Nevertheless, Congress eventually excluded motorboats from 670,000 acres to the north.

A more even split would seem fairer. It should certainly be possible to accommodate both forms of recreation in the area, and there is as much to be said for canoeing in solitude as there is for making rapid expeditions by powerboat. The natural landscape is not likely to suffer very much from either form of recreation. It is not absolute "ecological" values that are really at stake, but simply different tastes in recreation.

Not Entirely Nature

At bottom, then, the mystique of the wilderness has been little more than a revival of Rousseau's Romanticism about the "state of nature." The notion that "only in wilderness are human beings truly free," a credo of environmentalists, is merely a variation on Rousseau's dictum that "man is born free, and everywhere he is in chains." According to Rousseau, only society could enslave people, and only in the "state of nature" was the "noble savage"—the preoccupation of so many early explorers—a fulfilled human being.

The "noble savage" and other indigenous peoples, however, have been carefully excised from the environmentalists' vision. Where environmental efforts have encountered primitive peoples, these indigenous residents have often proved one of the biggest problems. One of the most bitter issues in Alaska is the efforts by environmentalists groups to restrict Indians in their hunting practices.

At the same time, few modern wilderness enthusiasts could imagine, for example, the experience of the nineteenth-century artist J. Ross Browne, who wrote in *Harper's New Monthly Magazine* after visiting the Arizona territories in 1864:

> Sketching in Arizona is . . . rather a ticklish pursuit. . . . I never before traveled through a country in which I was compelled to pursue the fine arts with a revolver strapped around my body, a

double-barreled shot-gun lying across my knees, and half a dozen soldiers armed with Sharpe's carbines keeping guard in the distance. Even with all the safeguards . . . I am free to admit that on occasions of this kind I frequently looked behind to see how the country appeared in its rear aspect. An artist with an arrow in his back may be a very picturesque object . . . but I would rather draw him on paper than sit for the portrait myself.

Wilderness today means the land *after* the Indians have been cleared away but *before* the settlers have arrived. It represents an attempt to hold that particular moment forever frozen in time, that moment when the visionary American settler looked out on the land and imagined it as an empty paradise, waiting to be molded to our vision.

In the absence of the noble savage, the environmentalist substitutes himself. The wilderness, while free of human dangers, becomes a kind of basic-training ground for upper-middle-class values. Hence the rise of "survival" groups, where college kids are taken out into the woods for a week or two and let loose to prove their survival instincts. No risks are spared on these expeditions. Several people have died on them, and a string of lawsuits has already been launched by parents and survivors who didn't realize how seriously these survival courses were being taken.

The ultimate aim of these efforts is to test upper-middle-class values against the natural environment. "Survival" candidates cannot hunt, kill, or use much of the natural resources available. The true test is whether their zero-degree sleeping bags and dried-food kits prove equal to the hazards of the tasks. What happens is not necessarily related to nature. One could as easily test survival skills by turning a person loose without money or means in New York City for three days.

I do not mean to imply that these efforts do not require enormous amounts of courage and daring—"survival skills." I am only suggesting that what the backpacker or survival hiker encounters is not entirely "nature," and that the effort to go "back to nature" is one that is carefully circumscribed by the most intensely civilized artifacts. Irving Babbitt, the early twentieth-century critic of Rousseau's Romanticism, is particularly vigorous in his dissent from the idea of civilized people going "back to nature." This type, he says, is actually "the least primitive of all beings":

> We have seen that the special form of unreality encouraged by the aesthetic romanticism of Rousseau is the dream of the simple life, the return to a nature that never existed, and that this dream made its special appeal to an age that was suffering from an excess of artificiality and conventionalism.

Babbitt notes shrewdly that our concept of the "state of nature" is actually one of the most sophisticated productions of civilization. Most primitive peoples, who live much closer to the soil than we do, are repelled by wilderness. The American colonists, when they first encountered the un-spoiled landscape, saw nothing but a horrible desert, filled with savages.

What we really encounter when we talk about "wilderness," then, is one of the highest products of civilization. It is a reserve set up to keep people *out,* rather than a "state of nature" in which the inhabitants are "truly free." The only thing that makes people "free" in such a reservation is that they can leave so much behind when they enter. Those who try to stay too long find out how spurious this "freedom" is. After spending a year in a cabin in the north Canadian woods, Elizabeth Arthur wrote in *Island Sojourn:* "I never felt so completely tied to *objects,* resources, and the tools to shape them with."

What we are witnessing in the environmental movement's obsession with purified wilderness is what has often been called the "pastoral im-pulse." The image of nature as unspoiled, unspotted wilderness where we can go to learn the lessons of ecology is both a product of a complex, technological society and an escape from it. It is this undeniable paradox that forms the real problem of setting up "wildernesses." Only when we have created a society that gives us the leisure to appreciate it can we go out and experience what we imagine to be untrammeled nature. Yet if we lock up too much of our land in these reserves, we are cutting into our resources and endangering the very leisure that allows us to enjoy nature.

The answer is, of course, that we cannot simply let nature "take over" 40 and assume that because we have kept roads and people out of huge tracts of land, then we have absolved ourselves of a national guilt. The concept of stewardship means taking responsibility, not simply letting nature take its course. Where tracts can be set aside from commercialism at no great cost, they should be. Where primitive hiking and recreation areas are ap-pealing, they should be maintained. But if we think we are somehow appeasing the gods by *not* developing resources where they exist, then we are being very shortsighted. Conservation, not preservation, is once again the best guiding principle.

The cult of wilderness leads inevitably in the direction of religion. Once again, Irving Babbitt anticipated this fully.

> When pushed to a certain point the nature cult always tends to-ward sham spirituality. . . . Those to whom I may seem to be treating the nature cult with undue severity should remember that I am treating it only in its pseudo-religious aspect. . . . My quarrel is only with the asthete who assumes an apocalyptic pose and gives forth as a profound philosophy what is at best only a holiday or weekend view of existence. . . .

It is often said the environmentalism could or should serve as the basis of a new religious consciousness, or a religious "reawakening." This religious trend is usually given an Oriental aura. E. F. Schumacher has a chapter on Buddhist economics in his classic *Small Is Beautiful.* Primitive animisms are also frequently cited as attitudes toward nature that are more "environmentally sound." One book on the environment states baldly that "the American Indian lived in almost perfect harmony with nature." Anthropologist Marvin Harris has even put forth the novel view that primitive man is an environmentalist, and that many cultural habits are unconscious efforts to reduce the population and conserve the environment. He says that the Hindu prohibition against eating cows and the Jewish tradition of not eating pork were both efforts to avoid the ecological destruction that would come with raising these grazing animals intensively. The implication in these arguments is usually that science and modern technology have somehow dulled our instinctive "environmental" impulses, and that Western "non-spiritual" technology puts us out of harmony with the "balance of nature."

Perhaps the most daring challenge to the environmental soundness of current religious tradition came early in the environmental movement, in a much quoted paper by Lynn White, professor of the history of science at UCLA. Writing in *Science* magazine in 1967, White traced "the historical roots of our ecological crisis" directly to the Western Judeo-Christian tradition in which "man and nature are two things, and man is master." "By destroying pagan animism," he wrote, "Christianity made it possible to exploit nature in a mood of indifference to the feelings of natural objets." He continued:

> Especially in its Western form, Christianity is the most anthropocentric religion the world has seen. . . . Christianity, in absolute contrast to ancient paganism and Asia's religions (except, perhaps, Zoroastrianism), not only established a dualism of man and nature but also insisted that it is God's will that man exploit nature for his proper ends. . . . In antiquity every tree, every spring, every stream, every hill had its own *genius loci*, its guardian spirit. . . . Before one cut a tree, mined a mountain, or dammed a brook, it was important to placate the spirit in charge of that particular situation, and keep it placated.

But the question here is not whether the Judeo-Christian tradition is worth saving in and of itself. It would be more than disappointing if we canceled the accomplishments of Judeo-Christian thought only to find that our treatment of nature had not changed a bit.

There can be no question that White is onto a favorite environmental theme here. What he calls the "Judeo-Christian tradition" is what other writers often term "Western civilization." It is easy to go through environmental books and find long outbursts about the evils that "civilization and progress" have brought us. The long list of Western achievements and advances, the scientific men of genius, are brought to task for creating our "environmental crisis." Sometimes the condemnation is of our brains, pure and simple. Here, for example, is the opening statement from a book about pesticides, written by the late Robert van den Bosch, an outstanding environmental advocate:

> Our problem is that we are too smart for our own good, and for that matter, the good of the biosphere. The basic problem is that our brain enables us to evaluate, plan, and execute. Thus, while all other creatures are programmed by nature and subject to her whims, we have our own gray computer to motivate, for good or evil, our chemical engine. . . . Among living species, we are the only one possessed of arrogance, deliberate stupidity, greed, hate, jealousy, treachery, and the impulse to revenge, all of which may erupt spontaneously or be turned on at will.

At this rate, it can be seen that we don't even need religion to lead us astray. We are doomed from the start because we are not creatures of *instinct,* programmed from the start "by nature."

This type of primitivism has been a very strong, stable undercurrent in the environmental movement. It runs from the kind of fatalistic gibberish quoted above to the Romanticism that names primitive tribes "instinctive environmentalists," from the pessimistic predictions that human beings cannot learn to control their own numbers to the notion that only by remaining innocent children of nature, untouched by progress, can the rural populations of the world hope to feed themselves. At bottom, as many commentators have pointed out, environmentalism is reminiscent of the German Romanticism of the nineteenth century, which sought to shed Christian (and Roman) traditions and revive the Teutonic gods because they were "more in touch with nature."

But are progress, reason, Western civilization, science, and the cerebral cortex really at the root of the "environmental crisis?" Perhaps the best answer comes from an environmentalist himself, Dr. Rene Dubos, a world-renowned microbiologist, author of several prize-winning books on conservation and a founding member of the Natural Resources Defense Council. Dr. Dubos takes exception to the notion that Western Christianity has produced a uniquely exploitative attitude toward nature:

> Erosion of the land, destruction of animal and plant species, excessive exploitation of natural resources, and ecological disasters are not peculiar to the Judeo-Christian tradition and to scientific technology. At all times, and all over the world, man's thoughtless interventions into nature have had a variety of disastrous consequences or at least have changed profoundly the complexity of nature.

Dr. Dubos has catalogued the non-Western or non-Christian cultures that have done environmental damage. Plato observed, for instance, that the hills in Greece had been heedlessly stripped of wood, and erosion had been the result; the ancient Egyptians and Assyrians exterminated large numbers of wild animal species; Indian hunters presumably caused the extinction of many large paleolithic species in North America; Buddhist monks building temples in Asia contributed largely to deforestation. Dubos notes:

> All over the globe and at all times . . . men have pillaged nature and disturbed the ecological equilibrium . . . nor did they have a real choice of alternatives. If men are more destructive now . . . it is because they have at their command more powerful means of destruction, not because they have been influenced by the Bible. In fact, the Judeo-Christian peoples were probably the first to develop on a large scale a pervasive concern for land management and an ethic of nature.

The concern that Dr. Dubos cites is the same one we have rescued out of the perception of environmentalism as a movement based on aristocratic conservatism. That is the legitimate doctrine of *stewardship* of the land. In order to take this responsibility, however, we must recognize the part we play in nature—that "the land is ours." It will not do simply to worship nature, to create a cult of wilderness in which humanity is an eternal intruder and where human activity can only destroy.

"True conservation," writes Dubos, "means not only protecting na- 50
ture against human misbehavior but also developing human activities which favor a creative, harmonious relationship between man and nature." This is a legitimate goal for the environmental movement.

Reading and Responding

Do any of William Tucker's arguments surprise you—seem more reasonable than you might have expected? For example, if you think of yourself as a strong environmentalist, someone who supports preservation efforts, you might find yourself agreeing with some of what Tucker says, despite yourself, or at least considering his ideas seriously. Or if you think of yourself as already agreeing with the kind of stance Tucker takes here, you might be surprised by a new, more powerful argument than you'd thought of before. In other words, what does Tucker make you pause and consider that you haven't paused and considered before?

Working Together

1. Divide into three groups: a Tucker Group, a Leopold Group, and a Mediator Group. The Mediator Group is in charge of the proceedings.

   - Take some local controversy about preservation—land to be set aside as a park or a green belt, for example, or an old building people want to save—or take some national preservation controversy currently in the news, something that everyone in the class knows about. Imagine that the Mediator Group has called a meet-

ing of both sides to negotiate a compromise action on this issue.
The Tucker Group summarizes his main arguments and applies
these arguments to this particular issue, arguing for a certain action.
The Mediators write these arguments on one side of the board,
simply recording what is said.

- The Leopold Group then counters each argument, point by point,
  with ideas and reasoning drawn from John Muir, Aldo Leopold,
  and others—argues, in other words, "the other side"—and uses
  these arguments to propose a different action. Mediators write
  these arguments on the board.
- The Mediators then take charge of the meeting, working to find
  common ground in these two positions, areas of overlap, possible
  agreement as a way of brokering a compromise solution. The
  group might list on the board, for example, any way, however
  broad or apparently trivial, that the two sides fundamentally agree.

2. In the end a document should be drawn up representing the compromise and signed by all concerned parties.

Rethinking and Rewriting

1. Write an essay describing and reflecting on the negotiation process that's
   taken place in class. The paper can focus on the issues—summarizing
   the two sides and then explaining the compromise—or it can focus on
   the process of negotiation, the issues of rhetoric, argument, and
   relationship.
2. Use Tucker's arguments to argue against the preservation of a certain
   local landmark or piece of ground.
3. Write a letter to Tucker politely questioning his positions and proposing
   alternatives. Disagree with him. Try to persuade him that he's wrong.
4. Write a personal essay in response to Tucker's argument. Describe a
   relevant experience, something that might illustrate his ideas, counter
   them, or at least complicate them. You don't need to come to a conclusion. Tell the story in as much detail as you can and conclude with
   questions and concerns.

"RETHINKING ENVIRONMENTALISM"

Ron Arnold

> *A native of Texas, Ron Arnold graduated from the University of Washington with a degree in business administration and went on to write over three hundred articles in national magazines on business and environmental issues. His series "The Environmental Battle" won the 1980 American Business Press Award for best magazine series and made him a national spokesman for the "wise use" movement in land management. It also became the basis for his book* Ecology Wars *(1987), from which this excerpt is taken. Arnold is currently president of Northwoods Studios, a media consulting firm in Bellevue, Washington, and executive vice president for the Center for the Defense of Free Enterprise, publisher of both* Ecology Wars *and a second book, written with Alan Gottlieb,* Trashing the Economy: How Runaway Environmentalism Is Wrecking America *(1993).*

As You Read

As you read, note the many facts and statistics Ron Arnold uses to support his arguments. Mark the facts that seem the most important to his claims.

Student to logger: "What have you got against trees?"

Logger to student: "What have you got against people?"

This exchange overheard in a small northern California cafe symbolizes our ecology wars. When it comes to the environment, emotions flare, discussions of specific problems in specific places stop, and minds grab the closest stereotype for support. It's profit-mad developers against tree-hugging little old ladies in tennis shoes. From the Allagash to Waimea Canyon, personalities and individual belief systems are fully engaged. From the North Slope to the Everglades, the gulf of economic/ecologic misunderstanding is enormous and unbridgeable. In short, ideology, not reason, rules American ecology wars.

And yet everybody is an environmentalist of one kind or another. Long before ecology became a fashionable in-word, environmental awareness glimmered through our very language—think of such timeworn phrases as "don't foul your own nest," for example. But during the 1960s environmental awareness grew to the stature of a mass movement, a cultural change of significant proportions. Sensitivity to nature became first a public virtue, then a requirement, then a fetish. By itself this might have been admirable, or at least amusing or tedious at worst. But America's new-found sensitivity to nature came packaged in a strongly anti-industry, anti-people wrapper. It came with a gut feeling that people are no damn good, that everything we do damages nature and that we must be stopped before we totally destroy the earth. The more radical ecology warriors even thought about shutting down industry for good and all, but the more even-tempered settled for big-government regulation of private industry—and they won in Congress and the courts.

Of course, the private sector didn't like regulation much and fought the "command and control" approach to environmental protection tooth and nail. The more enlightened captains of industry felt that there had to be a way to protect nature without damaging free enterprise, that there were market-oriented solutions to pollution, and that people could live in harmony with nature even in the midst of high-growth industrial civilization. Their ideas were not heard. Organized environmentalists didn't want the public distracted from their big-government regulatory proposals and the media did not sympathize with corporate capitalists. The best that some corporate capitalists could do was try to co-opt the environmental movement with massive foundation grants that in fact only sold rope to the hangmen. And so we got ecology wars. We still have them.

For the past fifteen years I've struggled to understand these wars between environmentalists and industry, perhaps harder than most. For up to the time in 1968 when Redwood National Park was carved from private property—the first time such a thing happened in United States history—I had been a staunch proponent of the conservation movement. But ten years later when the Redwood National Park *Expansion* bill took *more* private property from supposedly free enterprises, I found myself firmly advocating the industry viewpoint. To my surprise, I realized that in the ten-year interval *I* had not changed, the *movement* had.

Environmentalism's "New Look"

The original conservation movement with its message of wise use had evolved into the environmental movement with its activism for endless regulation. In the tumultuous and sometimes bitter journey between these two polarized outlooks I encountered many environmental activists, politicians, and industry managers. I have seen both sides of many issues, been torn between loyalties, and made many hard decisions. Most importantly, as a writer I turned for information to natural scientists who dispassionately studied ecology and to social scientists who dispassionately studied mass movements. I can now lay claim to some understanding of the conflict.

The time has come to explode some of the environmental myths that I myself helped create, because they have gone too far: they now constitute a clear and present danger to the survival and well-being of our national economy and our open society. In the past fifteen years, more than a hundred environmental regulatory laws have been passed that focus primarily on social rather than economic results—and the public is not aware of either the laws themselves or of the tremendous costs they levy in higher prices, reduced industrial vigor and outright business failures. Even in the middle of the Reagan administration's first term, in 1982, regulations cost the American economy over $125 billion. Of this amount, 83 percent was spent on compliance with "social engineering" objectives, on bureaucrats playing doctor with natural resources and human lives.

That same year, 1982, even under a conservative Republican president, the United States imported 28 percent of its oil at a cost of $62 billion—a contributing factor to U.S. trade deficits that have made us a debtor nation for the first time in half a century. Ironically, experts estimate that 50 percent of all America's known energy reserves, coal, oil and natural gas, lie under "public" lands, government property that is being methodically sealed off from economic use by overzealous preservationists in the name of "wilderness" and "national parks"—and again, the public is not aware of what's going on. How many people, for example, realize that America will never achieve energy independence as long as the environmental lobby holds sway over Congress?

By 1985, the environmental lobby—a lobby, incidentally, with some *10* of the biggest "clout" in Washington—had pressured Congress to lock up more than 80 million acres of America in federal wilderness areas, with an additional 77 million acres in federal parks. Since the environmental movement began, most of these "preserved" areas were formed not as traditional national parks and reserves were, from existing federal lands, but were seized by government force from private property owners by Act of Congress, a silent scandal that threatens the very roots of American property rights and civil rights.

Even outdoor recreation has been damaged by overrestrictive environmental laws. Dozens of impact-tolerant areas have been placed off-limits to motorized vehicles, 4-wheel-drive clubs have been banned from public lands, trail bikes and snowmobiles prohibited from perfectly acceptable places, float planes from long-used lakes, motor boats from federalized rivers, and the motoring public totally denied access to any federal wilderness area whatsoever—all because of the lobbying power of the environmental movement.

The Impact of Conflict

Let's examine the impact of ecology wars on a specific industry: forest products. Of the 3.6 million square miles that make up the United States, 32 percent, or nearly one-third, are covered with forests—a grand total of 1.13 million square miles of trees, living organisms perfectly adapted to capture solar energy by photosynthesis and store it in the form of wood. This huge genetic reservoir contains 865 species, 61 varieties and 101 hybrids (yet only 120 species have any commercial value) that combine into about 146 forest types in 6 major regions. About one-third of the American forest has no commercial value.

Here's a profile of the two-thirds of our forests that *do* have commercial value: Twenty-eight percent of all commercial forests are publicly owned—17 percent in national forests and 9 percent in state and local forests. Seventy-two percent of the commercial timberland in the U.S. is privately owned, with the bulk held not by big business, but by small individual woodlot owners. Only 14 percent of all private forests (3 percent of the total land area of the U.S.) is owned by the forest industry. Yet this small 14 percent of the working forest produces 28 percent of all the wood grown in America, because of free enterprise and market-oriented management practices.

Lest we fail to see the forest for the trees, we should realize that *land,* not trees, is *the* basic forest resource, which we shall emphasize in a few paragraphs. As foresters are fond of pointing out, trees may come and go, but the land remains to grow new forests. In other words, land is the basic means of production of forests. Since there is only so much land in America that will grow trees, which cannot be significantly enlarged, and since there are more users and uses for the land than there is land to go around, conflicts and competition are inevitable. Therefore, all specific forest environmental disputes such as those over clearcutting, use of herbicides, wilderness preservation, protection of endangered species and so on, can be best understood as *disputes between people who want to use forests for different purposes.*

Two significant problems have been created for the public at large by this Wilderness blitz: First, the majority of the recreational public that has thrown its support behind wilderness proposals did so without being aware of the restrictions that this designation entails. They actually wanted recreation areas that allowed various degrees of development from pure Wilderness to backcountry with primitive hiking shelters to "frontcountry" with hostels containing amenities for hikers to regularly developed car camping sites. According to surveys, the public really doesn't mind timber harvest when properly managed along with recreational values, but they're getting neither the kind of recreation areas they want nor the benefits of the timber that could have been converted into useful products on the same lands.

Second, when an area is designated as official Wilderness, it acts like a mating call to the true wilderness lover, and hordes of people rush to share solitude together. This both ruins the wilderness experience (I know, I've suffered from this "Intrusion Factor"), and puts an unbearable load on the area's natural carrying capacity, trampling endemic wildflowers and frightening away endangered species with armies of nature lovers. The truth is, the American wilderness is being loved to death by its friends. As Colin Fletcher, high priest of backpacking, said in 1971, "The woods are overrun and sons of bitches like me are half the problem." The other half of the problem is the hiker who won't admit being a problem.

Some "wildernists" (a social scientist's neologism for "wilderness-purist," not name-calling on my part) think they can solve the problem by setting aside ever-increasing amounts of wilderness, and capitalize on the scarcity angle in their propaganda. More thoughtful conservationists realize that some kind of regulation on wilderness entry is essential to save the wilderness from its saviors. Socialist arrangements have a habit of cutting both ways. When the regulatory shoe is on his own foot, however, the wildernist finds regulation to be ugly.

A rather unexpected wilderness constituency has come into being by the work of such authors as Colin Fletcher, with a large impact on the vote count in these showdowns: the armchair advocate. These people seldom or never use wilderness themselves, and some have never even seen an official Wilderness. They find peace of mind in the symbolism, in simply knowing that wild places are still preserved out there somewhere in the great world.

Regulationism

In the early 1970s, *regulation* joined wilderness exclusions as a major threat to American industry, both on federal and private lands. Regulation, however, does not produce the instant dramatic changes that wilderness withdrawals do. It quietly makes everyday life more complicated and ultimately more expensive for the whole nation. Restrictions on harvesting methods such as clearcutting, on petroleum drilling methods, on the use of pesticides on farmlands, on manufacturing industries concerning air and water pollution, occupational health and safety factors, and many others add costs and lower the productivity of industrial enterprises. In rare instances, such as regulations that entail recovery of useful materials from wasteful processes, the benefits are real. In most cases, however, the benefits are questionable: The Occupational Safety and Health Administration's vast bureaucracy has produced *no* detectable reduction in industrial injuries or accidents—it's simply costly and worthless government interference with free enterprise.

Many victims of regulation are socially invisible. For example, when the forest products industry operating on federal lands is required to use "landscape management" methods to protect "viewsheds" by shaping clearcuts as if they were natural openings in the forest, we reduce the social "cost" to hikers and tourists who want "natural"-looking scenery, but in cases where the added labor costs can be directly passed on to the consumer, we never get an accounting of the social costs to the thousands of hopeful young home-buying couples who are forced out of the market by spiraling prices.

In trying to fight the growing Regulation State, American industry was bucking a major historical trend. Since the first federal water pollution law was passed in 1948, industry has pushed for incentives rather than controls, and where controls were inevitable, for flexible rather than rigid ones. In one strangling loss after another, American industry has seen Congress give itself authority to regulate air, water, noise, health and safety, wildlife, timber harvest, and dozens of other factors. With the passage of the Resources Conservation and Recovery Act and the Toxic Substances Control Act of 1976 and the Comprehensive Environmental Response, Compensation, and Liability Act of 1980 (CERCLA, also known as the

"Superfund"), all the loopholes had been closed: Congress had authority to regulate literally every substance in existence.

While wilderness issues have been fought primarily in Congress, a substantial part of the regulatory battle has been fought in the courts. In a chart prepared by the editors of *The Wilson Quarterly/summer 1977,* industry lost 7 of the 8 cases selected as landmark decisions. Observers who have noted that the industry spends a great deal of money both lobbying and litigating conclude that the dollars of industry are heavily discounted while those of the environmentalists are highly inflated when measured by the results.

Regulatory disputes have not been confined to federal lands, either. Since the 1949 U.S. Supreme Court decision affirming the constitutionality of state regulation of private land, industrial forests have come in for a heavy burden of regulation as well.

The impact of regulation on American industry and its consuming public is enormous but poorly understood. Consider: to begin with, the metals, trees and petroleum kept from use by restrictive regulations are essential to our civilization. Not just helpful, and not just enjoyable. Essential. Of the 99 sectors listed in the *Scientific American* chart of the input-output structure of the United States economy, all 99 are affected by metals, timber and paper, and petroleum; forest products alone affect all but 11 sectors, or over 85 percent of the total economy. The infrastructure of our knowledge-based "post-industrial" society would collapse instantly without the simple commodity of paper.

Without the forest products industry, we would not miss just the obvious things we get from trees, such as lumber and plywood. Communications would have poorer eyesight and hearing without trees: photographic film and recording tape are made from wood chemicals, but who thinks of them as forest products? Fabrics (rayons and acetates), flavorings (vanillin), fragrances (the versatile turpenes enhance a huge range of products from cosmetics to cleansers), foods (maple syrup and stabilizers for mayonnaise, ice cream and other foods), and thousands of other products ranging from explosives to medicines begin in our forests.

25

The Cumulative Impact of Regulations

Forest regulations themselves take many forms: you can't harvest timber here because it's an archaeological site (two arrowheads were found nearby); there are spotted owls in this forest and you must leave a thousand acres of standing timber for each known mating pair; logging technology cannot get the timber across this creek without dropping bark fragments into the water, so it's off-limits; a local tribe uses this area as a Native American Religious Site, so you can't cut trees nearby; the costs of road-building into this timber are too high to justify logging; the elevation and soil type here are too risky for growing new trees so you can't cut the ones that are here now; there has to be a buffer strip of standing trees left for

200 feet on each side of this stream to keep the solar loading factor from raising water temperatures too high for salmon spawning.

More than 200 *different kinds* of restrictions add up to thousands of specific restrictions on U.S. Forest Service lands alone. Each of these non-timber designations no doubt has a legitimate purpose. But an endless stream of annually increasing restrictive regulations means less land in commercial forests means declining supply in the face of steady (or rising) demand means sharply higher prices (ask any home buyer or office supply house), for Congress has not yet managed to repeal the law of supply and demand.

The impact of regulation can be pernicious. Increased red tape, labor, and time always mean higher internal costs, but these costs cannot always be passed on to the consumer. Wood, remember, is a commodity. One piece (of a given grade) is much like any other piece, and pure price competition prevails over any other market force. Commodity brokers will simply go to the best price available. Timber firms must therefore frequently eat the higher costs from regulation, which means lower profits and dividends, less ability to form capital and expand, or in some cases even to remain competitive.

Worst of all, once Congress has given some bureaucracy a regulatory mandate in law, environmental lobbyists find it easy to pressure the bureaucracy to constantly tighten regulatory provisions and to increase the gross number of regulations—and Congress, having gone on to other matters, isn't even aware of the devastation those cancerous regulations wreak in logging communities as one mill after another goes under. Then, adding insult to injury, environmental lobbyists say, "Oh, it wasn't environmental regulations that did it, it was just a shift in the economy caused by other forces." When you're squeezed out of the market because of regulatory restrictions on supply, your business is not only more sensitive to such economic forces as interest rates, but your economic sector also *influences* them by pushing investment capital into other sectors and other countries.

Perhaps most ominous for the future of regulation, certain leaders of 30 the environmental movement see themselves as the vanguard for a "new society." The new environmental society is not clearly defined in environmentalists' own minds, but it obviously cannot be realized in a world structured by industrial capitalism, as pointed out by historian Donald Worster in *The Journal of Forest History* of January, 1986. For many years I have made this assertion, which has been greeted by derisive denials of environmentalists. However, in 1984, Prof. Lester W. Milbrath of the State University of New York published *Environmentalists: Vanguard for a New Society.* His book and his passionate advocacy for an environmental revolution to change the basic economic structure of America is the best clincher my argument could have.

It is time to look under the hood of this engine of social destruction, for that is exactly what the environmental movement has become, before it does irreparable harm to *both* our economic system *and* our natural heritage. The stakes are high. The outcome will affect the work, the purchasing power, the play, and the general peace of mind of every living American, as we shall see.

Why Ecology Wars?

Conflict over the environment is nothing new. As a little reading in American history will reveal, the fundamental disagreements between environmentalists and industry have been smouldering for well over a hundred years. They flared up during Teddy Roosevelt's era as The Conservation Movement, a landmark coming-to-grips with the new reality that the American frontier had closed, that the nation faced an age of increasing land scarcity, and therefore, increasing resource scarcity. The Rough Rider himself declared in 1905 that the object of land policy was "to consider how best to combine use with preservation." But the environmental movement of today, with its new twists of ecological awareness, its land ethic, and its reliance on big government to enact and enforce its programs, has blossomed only in the last two decades. In the span of a few short years during the mid-1960s and early '70s, a sizeable portion of the public's whim of steel swung away from its traditional focus on material well-being and toward the blue-jeaned counterculture's urge to throw out the industrial baby with the polluted bathwater and go back to Nature, whatever that was conceived to be.

These great shifts in our society have for the most part baffled the leaders of American industry. I've heard many an angry manager ask, "Why do these environmentalists want to destroy our free enterprise system?" And it's not just the leaders who are worried. I've heard down-home miners and loggers ask, "Are they communists?" I've heard ranchers and farmers ask, "What do they want?" But even industry's best experts can't seem to get a grip on environmentalism. While industrial leaders have developed excellent material technology, they have suffered absolutely terrible public relations, and in the political arena were push comes to shove, they've been losing hands down.

Part of the problem is that American industry is just too busy minding the store to keep up on fast-changing issues. Associations such as the National Association of Manufacturers, the American Petroleum Refiners Association, the National Cattlemens Association, the National Forest Products Association, the National Mining Congress, the National Agricultural Chemical Association, the National Ocean Industries Association, and enough others to fill a dozen pages in the District of Columbia telephone directory, all struggle valiantly to put out one environmental brush fire after another. In the pandemonium, they often chart unworkable strategy, as measured in the vote count in Congress and decisions from U.S. Circuit Courts of Appeal and the U.S. Supreme Court. A significant part of this failure, in my assessment, lies in the simple fact that American industry does not understand environmentalism, and therefore does not grasp the true nature of the conflict.

There are, of course, other powerful reasons why American industry   35 has few friends in the general public and is losing many of its political battles. For one thing, industry has few friends in the media. As Mobil Oil vice president for public affairs Herbert Schmertz wrote in a 1984 issue of *Washington Journalism Review,* many "newspersons see crime in the suites. This is not hyperbole. Morley Safer of '60 Minutes' said that, 'No businessman who has made a success for himself is entirely clean, probably.' And, according to the nonprofit Media Institute, 'almost half of all work activities performed by businessmen' on prime-time TV series 'involve illegal acts.' The report added that 'Television almost never portrays business as a socially useful or economically productive activity.'" In fact, the media, both electronic and print, display sufficiently regular hostility to free enterprise that citizen watchdog organizations have arisen to combat the problem, such as Reed Irvine's Accuracy In Media (AIM). Media power is a substantial factor in industry public relations.

For another thing, as Daniel Bell pointed out in his *The Coming of Post-Industrial Society,* the largest part of our employment since 1955 has been increasingly in the service sector. Why is this important to ecology wars? Because it means that most Americans are thereby comfortably buffered from and unaware of the hurly-burly realities of basic resource extraction and conversion in our mines, forests, rangelands, oceans, farms and factories. The total goods sector tends to appear only as a source of pollution to those in the service sector when it is visible at all. This out-of-sight, out-of-mind factor combines with other forces.

The Post-Materialist Blues

The new generation of affluent young citizens now taking over the economy's reins, as noted by Ronald Inglehart in his massive study *The Silent Revolution,* was unscarred by The Great Depression and World War II. They have never known dire want or monstrous physical insecurity. These "post-materialists," as Inglehart dubs them, are less obsessed with success and security than their parents were. They are more oriented toward personal autonomy, needs for love and a sense of belonging, and intellectual and aesthetic pursuits. They do not fully realize how crucial the well-being of industry is to their own well-being, and haven't the faintest notion of industry's needs. They tend to despise crass commercialism, and are politically very liberal and very active. This New American Society, a large minority consisting of perhaps 25 percent of the total population of this country, forms a ready-made base of support for environmentalist causes, and a potent one. We will have more to say about "post-materialists" later.

The two major philosophical views about land use planning are *the free enterprise approach* that relies on markets and enlightened self-interest to allocate scarce resources and *the statist approach* that relies on government control in one form or another to determine land uses.

The major disputes in the forest environmental battle are those that pit private commercial forest firms using market-oriented management practices against governmental restrictions on commercial use. Forest conflict has centered around the two major fronts of our ecology wars: wilderness preservation (removal of federal forests from commodity use), and regulation of commercial forests by legislative and bureaucratic fiat. These two issues of wilderness and regulation are so complex that they can be understood only when viewed in their historical contexts.

Roots of Conflict

At the dawn of the new environmental era, Congress, in The Multiple Use-Sustained Yield Act of 1960, directed the Forest Service to give equal consideration to outdoor recreation, range, timber, watershed, wildlife and fisheries resources. The idea was to provide something for everyone. By and large, foresters throughout the industry approved of the new policy with such responses as "We've been practicing multiple use all along." 40

Multiple use is basically a simple idea, to give the greatest good to the greatest number, but it is exceedingly complicated to put into practice. And it is most definitely and emphatically a statist approach: Multiple use applies only to government forests, and the mere existence of government forests is itself a completely socialist arrangement, although we seldom think of it as such. Sound far out to call American national forests *socialist?* Think it through. The essence of socialism is government ownership of the means of production—virtually every thinking person will grant that basic definition. Land is the basic means of *every kind of production* and land is obviously the basic means of production of forests, as we noted above. The U.S. government owns one-third of the total land area of America. It's true. A third of our nation, including a substantial fraction of our forests, is held in a socialist arrangement. We seem content to let things be that way, but the fact should be kept in mind every time we think of environmental conflict.

Similarly, sustained yield, the concept of cutting no more timber in a given year than grows back in the same time so that you never run out of trees, is easy to say but complex to administer in the forest. Sustained yield is less an inherently statist approach to forest management than multiple use, because private firms may wish to manage their own fee-title timberlands under sustained yield principles. But within the firmly rooted socialist framework of our national forests, back in 1960 sustained yield as a government policy made good sense to the industry and became its major rallying cry in the ecology wars that were to follow.

Wilderness, at first blush, has a wholesome ring in modern America, and it is one of history's perversities that such horrendous controversy has arisen over it. A good part of the reason for such controversy is that Wilderness (capital W) is not wilderness (small w). A 1978 survey by Opinion Research, Inc., found that more than 75 percent of all Americans still didn't realize the difference between just any woodsy recreation spot and officially designated wilderness. The difference is monumental. The Wilderness Act of 1964, which created the National Wilderness Preservation System, mandated that Wilderness is an area of at least 5,000 federally-owned acres and defined it thus:

"A Wilderness, in contrast to those areas where man and his works dominate the landscape, is hereby recognized as an area where the earth and its community of life are untrammeled by man, where man himself is a visitor who does not remain."

In practical terms, that means no roads, no buildings, no motorized 45
vehicles, no timber harvest, no watershed management, severely restricted fire, insect, disease, and wildlife management, and in most places not even toilets. It's the law. But the average American never even heard of it.

To many industries this new law amounted to institutionalizing a confiscatory single use on federal lands in violation of the intent of the earlier Multiple Use–Sustained Yield Act. However, when institutions are built around socialist arrangements such as federal lands, this type of rude political shock is to be expected. To the successful conservation movement, led by the Wilderness Society and Sierra Club, it was a triumph of ecological sensitivity over "Multiple Abuse," as they had come to call timber harvest and other extractive uses of forest land such as mining and petroleum production.

The passage of the Wilderness Act of 1964 marked the watershed in thinking about the American forest, and resource industries have never really been able to cope with it. In one Wilderness showdown after another—the Alpine Lakes Wilderness Area, the Mineral King Recreation Development, RARE I (Roadless Area Review and Evaluation process involving 56 million acres of inventory and 12 million acres of study areas), the Endangered Wilderness Act of 1977, and various Wilderness packages of the 1980s—American industry has gone down to defeat in Congress and the courts. Industry has lost three out of four of its congressional lobbying campaigns since 1960. The great lobbying power of the "Timber Barons" and the "Oil Monopoly" and the "Mining Kings" is one of the more ironic of our quaint public myths today. Businesses, because they exist for profit, are immediately suspect in the lobbies of Congress, regardless of the merit of their argument. Environmental lobbyists are seen by legislators and the bureaucracy as proponents of the common good regardless of the absurdity of their argument.

This pattern is merely the new form of an old struggle, for since John Muir fought for the establishment of Yosemite National Park in the 1880s and the Forest Service in 1924 set aside the world's first official Wilderness Area in New Mexico's Gila National Forest, environmentalists have successfully lobbied more than 77 million acres into the National Park Service's preservation programs and more than 80 million acres into Wilderness (or similar "Primitive Area" designations). By 1985, more than 5 percent of America's total land area (nearly twice as much as is owned by the forest industry) had been set aside in some kind of federally-controlled non-commercial status. The figure is climbing every year as Congress steadily eats away at our basic resource areas. If every study and proposal now on the books were to be taken into account, just to give you an idea of the grandeur of the wilderness mystique, restricted use of some kind is envisioned for *all* federal areas, which, remember, occupy *one-third of America's land.*

All these factors affect employment levels, and we should not forget that the combined Lumber & Plywood and Pulp & Paper sectors feed more than $65 billion annually into our economy and their 1.2 million workers represent 6.6 percent of all U.S. manufacturing employment. However, contrast this with the 4.5 million members of the National Wildlife Federation alone out of the top 10 environmental groups, and you will see how overwhelmed a single industry in modern America can get in the political arena. It is obvious that American industry needs a grass-roots citizen support movement like the environmental movement if our economy is to regain its full vigor and grow at proper rates again.

There's no denying that a new member has come to America's power   *50*
elite: The environmental establishment. Multi-million-dollar non-profit environmental organizations are quite a force unto themselves, but the federal environmental bureaucracy entrenched in such agencies as the Environmental Protection Agency, the President's Council on Environmental Quality, the Department of the Interior, and Department of Agriculture, among many others, commands power that is potentially crushing.

Government's Battle Front

Government today forms a very significant third corner complicating the industry/environmentalist contest. Not only does government make the basic rules of the natural resource game, it also owns a sizeable chunk of the playing field. The federal government alone owns 762 million of the 2.27 billion acre total land area of the United States—and that's not counting state, county and municipal land. As I've repeatedly noted, the feds own one-third of the entire nation, or an area equal to all America's forested land. Government is supposed to act as a mediator on behalf of all its citizens, but too frequently slips into an adversary third-party role with priorities of its own. Then the age-old question arises, "Who will guard the guards?"

The late master strategist and futurologist Herman Kahn of the prestigious Hudson Institute put his finger on this problem when he warned of the "Health and Safety Fascists." This element, Kahn wrote, "has been singularly unreflective about its advocacy of strict, no-compromise controls on business and the environment regarding health, safety, and ecological matters. It has been unaware of its irrational prejudice against both business and the middle class, and consequently of the extent to which its regulatory zeal, from the viewpoint of both those it wants to regulate and of the general public, smacks of the dictatorial."

Ecology Wars Are Here to Stay

Some analysts feel that we are witnessing in the 1980s the maturity of the environmental movement, but I don't think so. I believe that what we have seen is only the first phase, the setting in place of all the laws and court decisions. In the next decade or two we are likely to see several things, first, the screws of wilderness withdrawal and regulation tightening a little here, a little there, despite the legacy of the Reagan administration. Then the revolutionary efforts of the "Vanguard for a New Society" in the form of eco-terrorism will become more widespread. A political agenda will appear that tries to strip our federal lands of *all* extractive resource use, ranging from livestock grazing to petroleum drilling. Then the "Vanguard" will attempt a genuine political takeover, through the ballot box and Political Action Committees if possible and by direct action, to use Professor Milbrath's words, if the democratic process fails.

The day will come when the flexibility of our market economy can no longer bear the strain, and our open society no longer survive in its present form. We may well see the day when regulation grows so vast that totalitarian measures seem both necessary and acceptable to a large public. If this seems too melodramatic, read ecologist William Ophuls' *Ecology and the Politics of Scarcity*, which maintains that modern civilization has outlived its usefulness and must be governed by "implacable ecological imperatives."

American industry has a moral obligation to protect itself from environmentalist attacks. All industry must come to grips with environmentalism, learn what it is, what motivates its actions, what the shape of its history is, how its propaganda works, how to combat it to the fullest extent possible. . . . 55

This is the message America must get: As crass as business tends to be, it is still an essential part of the whole, a vital part of the human ecosystem. And, as sensitive as the environmental movement tends to be, it is now in a position to wield colossally blundering economic power. It was Oscar Wilde who defined a cynic as one who knows the price of everything but the value of nothing. We must be warned that the environmentalist is one who knows the value of everything, but the price of nothing.

Reading and Responding

Mark the passage that most clearly and succinctly expresses Arnold's main argument.

Working Together

1. Do a freewrite recording your first thoughts and reactions when you hear words like *business* or *industry* or phrases like *big business* or *economic realities.* Draw on your personal experience. Admit your biases. Discuss them.

2. As Arnold says in his introduction, emotions always flare when people discuss the environment, facts giving way to stereotypes. Given your biases and predispositions, make a list of words and phrases in this piece that push buttons or ring bells for you, the buzz words or telling language in Arnold's writing that create either a positive or a negative reaction in you (the "myths of environmentalism," for example, or "The Regulation State"). Talk about the language itself, its qualities and structure. Explain what in your background causes you to respond the way you do. Are different students in the class responding to the same words and phrases in different ways? Has Arnold escaped the problem he describes? Is it possible to escape that problem?

3. Make a list of the major facts and statistics Arnold cites to support his arguments. Which evidence do you trust the most or least? why? Where does Arnold's information come from, and how does he cite his sources?

4. Note any of Arnold's claims that you think are not sufficiently backed up or proven—any major argument that seems to be asserted rather than actually grounded in evidence. Note any of his claims that seem to you especially well backed up and illustrated.

Rethinking and Rewriting

1. Check out and confirm one significant assertion, piece of information, research, or statistical claim Arnold uses in this article. For example, research Arnold's claim that 14 percent of the working forest in America produces 28 percent of all the wood grown in America *because* of "free enterprise and market-oriented management practices." Or see what examples you can find to support or refute Arnold's assertions that government regulations only add costs and lower industrial productivity. Write an essay reporting your research, confirming or denying part of Arnold's claims.

2. Arnold claims that free-enterprise market capitalism can best handle the environmental crisis. Find an example, and do a research paper describing one "market-oriented solution" created and applied by a particular business or industry, perhaps by a business in your own area. For example, what's the market-oriented solution to pesticide use? What's the market-oriented solution to a declining resource like fish or timber? Study the history and response to the project through newspapers, magazines, interviews, and so on. Ask the company for its literature on the project. Report what you find, and in the end, return to Arnold's

argument. Is this project one proof that Arnold is right and that business is not always the enemy? Does this project suggest that Arnold is wrong, at least in this case? Or are the facts mixed?

3. Do a profile of Arnold and the "wise use" movement he helped to start. Research the Center for the Defense of Free Enterprise that he directs—write to them for information; see what's been written about them. In light of what you find, revisit Arnold's arguments in this essay. What have you discovered about his motives and aims? How does the person behind the arguments help explain the arguments? Knowing what you know, do you trust Arnold more or less?

"WOMEN, HOME, AND COMMUNITY: THE STRUGGLE IN AN URBAN ENVIRONMENT"

Cynthia Hamilton

> *Cynthia Hamilton is an associate professor in the Pan African Studies Department at California State University, Los Angeles. She received her PhD in political science from Boston University. A grassroots organizer for many years, she helped halt construction of a solid waste incinerator in Los Angeles, an effort she describes in the following essay, first published in Re-weaving the World: The Emergence of Ecofeminism (1990), edited by Irene Diamond and Gloria Feman Orenstein.*

Before You Read

1. Among the several perspectives in this book, Cynthia Hamilton's offers a consciously feminist approach to environmental questions. Do a short freewrite before you start reading, recording all your immediate associations with the word *feminist*—ideas, images, experiences, biases.
2. Read only the first paragraph of this piece, then write a few sentences about the fact that this selection doesn't focus on rural or wilderness issues but focuses instead on a neighborhood in Los Angeles. Do you think of environmental issues as primarily rural/wilderness issues? Do you think of them as urban issues?

In 1956, WOMEN IN SOUTH AFRICA began an organized protest against the pass laws. As they stood in front of the office of the prime minister, they began a new freedom song with the refrain "now you have touched the women, you have struck a rock." This refrain provides a description of the personal commitment and intensity women bring to social change. Women's actions have been characterized as "spontaneous and dramatic," women in action portrayed as "intractable and uncompromising."[1] Society has summarily dismissed these as negative attributes. When in 1986 the City Council of Los Angeles decided that a 13-acre incinerator called LANCER (for Los Angeles City Energy Recovery Project), burning 2,000 tons a day of municipal waste, should be built in a poor residential, Black, and Hispanic community, the women there said "No." Officials had indeed dislodged a boulder of opposition. According to Charlotte Bullock, one of the protestors, "I noticed when we first started fighting the issue

---

1. See Cynthia Cockburn, "When Women Get Involved in Community Action," in Marjorie Mayo (ed.), *Women in the Community* (London: Routledge & Kegan Paul, 1977).

how the men would laugh at the women . . . they would say, 'Don't pay no attention to them, that's only one or two women . . . they won't make a difference.' But now since we've been fighting for about a year the smiles have gone."[2]

Minority communities shoulder a disproportionately high share of the by-products of industrial development: waste, abandoned factories and warehouses, leftover chemicals and debris. These communities are also asked to house the waste and pollution no longer acceptable in White communities, such as hazardous landfills or dump sites. In 1987, the Commission of Racial Justice of the United Church of Christ published *Toxic Wastes and Race*. The commission concluded that race is a major factor related to the presence of hazardous wastes in residential communities throughout the United States. Three out of every five Black and Hispanic Americans lives in communities with uncontrolled toxic sites; 75 percent of the residents in rural areas in the Southwest, mainly Hispanics, are drinking pesticide-contaminated water; more than 2 million tons of uranium tailings are dumped on Native American reservations each year, resulting in Navajo teenagers having seventeen times the national average of organ cancers; more than 700,000 inner city children, 50 percent of them Black, are said to be suffering from lead poisoning, resulting in learning disorders. Working-class minority women are therefore motivated to organize around very pragmatic environmental issues, rather than those associated with more middle-class organizations. According to Charlotte Bullock, "I did not come to the fight against environmental problems as an intellectual but rather as a concerned mother. . . . People say, 'But you're not a scientist, how do you know it's not safe?' I have common sense. I know if dioxin and mercury are going to come out of an incinerator stack, somebody's going to be affected."

When Concerned Citizens of South Central Los Angeles came together in 1986 to oppose the solid waste incinerator planned for the community, no one thought much about environmentalism or feminism. These were just words in a community with a 78 percent unemployment rate, an average income ($8,158) less than half that of the general Los Angeles population, and a residential density more than twice that of the whole city. In the first stages of organization, what motivated and directed individual actions was the need to protect home and children; for the group this individual orientation emerged as a community-centered battle. What was left in this deteriorating district on the periphery of the central business and commercial district had to be defended—a "garbage dump" was the final insult after years of neglect, watching downtown flourish while residents were prevented from borrowing enough to even build a new roof.

---

2. All of the quotes from Charlotte Bullock and Robin Cannon are personal communications, 1986.

The organization was never gender restricted but it became apparent after a while that women were the majority. The particular kind of organization the group assumed, the actions engaged in, even the content of what was said, were all a product not only of the issue itself, the waste incinerator, but also a function of the particular nature of women's oppression and what happens as the process of consciousness begins.

Women often play a primary part in community action because it is about things they know best. Minority women in several urban areas have found themselves part of a new radical core as the new wave of environmental action, precipitated by the irrationalities of capital-intensive growth, has catapulted them forward. These individuals are responding not to "nature" in the abstract but to the threat to their homes and to the health of their children. Robin Cannon, another activist in the fight against the Los Angeles incinerator, says, "I have asthma, my children have asthma, my brothers and sisters have asthma, there are a lot of health problems that people living around an incinerator might be subjected to and I said, 'They can't do this to me and my family.'"

Women are more likely than men to take on these issues precisely because the home has been defined and prescribed as a woman's domain. According to British sociologist Cynthia Cockburn, "In a housing situation that is a health hazard, the woman is more likely to act than the man because she lives there all day and because she is impelled by fear for her children. Community action of this kind is a significant phase of class struggle, but it is also an element of women's liberation."[3]

This phenomenon was most apparent in the battle over the Los Angeles incinerator. Women who had no history of organizing responded as protectors of their children. Many were single parents, others were older women who had raised families. While the experts were convinced that their smug dismissal of the validity of the health concerns these women raised would send them away, their smugness only reenforced the women's determination. According to Charlotte Bullock:

> People's jobs were threatened, ministers were threatened . . . but I said, "I'm not going to be intimidated." My child's health comes first, . . . that's more important than my job.
>
> In the 1950s the city banned small incinerators in the yard and yet they want to build a big incinerator . . . the Council is going to build something in my community which might kill my child. . . . I don't need a scientist to tell me that's wrong.

None of the officials were prepared for the intensity of concern or the consistency of agitation. In fact, the consultants they hired had concluded

3. Cockburn, "When Women," p. 62.

that these women did not fit the prototype of opposition. The consultants had concluded:

> Certain types of people are likely to participate in politics, either by virtue of their issue awareness or their financial resources, or both. Members of middle or higher socioeconomic strata (a composite index of level of education, occupational prestige, and income) are more likely to organize into effective groups to express their political interests and views. All socioeconomic groupings tend to resent the nearby siting of major facilities, but the middle and upper socioeconomic strata possess better resources to effectuate their opposition. Middle and higher socioeconomic strata neighborhoods should not fall at least within the one mile and five mile radii of the proposed site.
>
>   . . . although environmental concerns cut across all subgroups, people with a college education, young or middle aged, and liberal in philosophy are most likely to organize opposition to the siting of a major facility. Older people, with a high school education or less, and those who adhere to a free market orientation are least likely to oppose a facility.[4]

The organizers against the incinerator in South Central Los Angeles are the antithesis of the prototype: they are high school educated or less, above middle age and young, nonprofessionals and unemployed and low-income, without previous political experience. The consultants and politicians thus found it easy to believe that opposition from this group could not be serious.

The intransigence of the City Council intensified the agitation, and the women became less willing to compromise as time passed. Each passing month gave them greater strength, knowledge, and perseverance. The council and its consultants had a more formidable enemy than they had expected, and in the end they have had to compromise. The politicians have backed away from their previous embrace of incineration as a solution to the trash crisis, and they have backed away from this particular site in a poor, Black and Hispanic, residential area. While the issues are far from resolved, it is important that the willingness to compromise has become the official position of the city as a result of the determination of "a few women."

The women in South Central Los Angeles were not alone in their battle. They were joined by women from across the city, White, middle-class, and professional women. As Robin Cannon puts it, "I didn't know we all had so many things in common . . . millions of people in the city had something in common with us—the environment." These two groups

10

---

4. Cerrell Associates, *Political Difficulties Facing Waste to Energy Conversion Plant Siting* (Los Angeles: California Waste Management Board, 1984), pp. 42–43.

of women, together, have created something previously unknown in Los Angeles—unity of purpose across neighborhood and racial lines. According to Charlotte Bullock, "We are making a difference . . . when we come together as a whole and stick with it, we can win because we are right."

This unity has been accomplished by informality, respect, tolerance of spontaneity, and decentralization. All of the activities that we have been told destroy organizations have instead worked to sustain this movement. For example, for a year and a half the group functioned without a formal leadership structure. The unconscious acceptance of equality and democratic process resulted practically in rotating the chair's position at meetings. Newspeople were disoriented when they asked for the spokesperson and the group responded that everyone could speak for the neighborhood.

It may be the case that women, unlike men, are less conditioned to see the value of small advances.[5] These women were all guided by their vision of the possible: that it *was* possible to completely stop the construction of the incinerator, that it is possible in a city like Los Angeles to have reasonable growth, that it is possible to humanize community structures and services. As Robin Cannon says, "My neighbors said, 'You can't fight City Hall . . . and besides, you work there.' I told them I would fight anyway."

None of these women was convinced by the consultants and their traditional justifications for capital-intensive growth: that it increases property values by intensifying land use, that it draws new businesses and inventment to the area, that it removes blight and deterioration—and the key argument used to persuade the working class—that growth creates jobs. Again, to quote Robin Cannon, "They're not bringing real development to our community. . . . They're going to bring this incinerator to us, and then say 'We're going to *give* you fifty jobs when you get this plant.' Meanwhile they're going to shut down another factory [in Riverside] and eliminate two hundred jobs to buy more pollution rights. . . . They may close more shops."

Ironically, the consultants' advice backfired. They had suggested that emphasizing employment and a gift to the community (of $2 million for a community development fund for park improvement) would persuade the opponents. But promises of heated swimming pools, air-conditioned basketball courts and fifty jobs at the facility were more insulting than encouraging. Similarly, at a public hearing, an expert witness' assurance that health risks associated with dioxin exposure were less than those associated with "eating peanut butter" unleashed a flurry of derision.

The experts' insistence on referring to congenital deformities and cancers as "acceptable risks" cut to the hearts of women who rose to speak of a child's asthma, or a parent's influenza, or the high rate of cancer, heart disease, and pneumonia in this poverty-stricken community. The callous

15

---

5. See Cockburn, "When Women," p. 63.

disregard of human concerns brought the women closer together. They came to rely on each other as they were subjected to the sarcastic rebuffs of men who referred to their concerns as "irrational, uninformed, and disruptive." The contempt of the male experts was directed at professionals and the unemployed, at Whites and Blacks—all the women were castigated as irrational and uncompromising. As a result, new levels of consciousness were sparked in these women.

The reactions of the men backing the incinerator provided a very serious learning experience for the women, both professionals and nonprofessionals, who came to the movement without a critique of patriarchy. They developed their critique in practice. In confronting the need for equality, these women forced the men to a new level of recognition—that working-class women's concerns cannot be simply dismissed.

Individual transformations accompanied the group process. As the struggle against the incinerator proceeded to take on some elements of class struggle, individual consciousness matured and developed. Women began to recognize something of their own oppression as women. This led to new forms of action not only against institutions but to the transformation of social relations in the home as well. As Robin Cannon explains:

> My husband didn't take me seriously at first either. . . . He just saw a whole lot of women meeting and assumed we wouldn't get anything done. . . . I had to split my time . . . I'm the one who usually comes home from work, cooks, helps the kids with their homework, then I watch a little TV and go to bed to get ready for the next morning. Now I would rush home, cook, read my materials on LANCER . . . now the kids were on their own . . . I had my own homework. . . . My husband still wasn't taking me seriously. . . . After about 6 months everyone finally took me seriously. My husband had to learn to allocate more time for baby sitting. Now on Saturdays, if they went to the show or to the park, I couldn't attend . . . in the evening there were hearings . . . I was using my vacation time to go to hearings during the workday.

As parents, particularly single parents, time in the home was strained for these women. Children and husbands complained that meetings and public hearings had taken priority over the family and relations in the home. According to Charlotte Bullock, "My children understand, but then they don't want to understand. . . . They say, 'You're not spending time with me.'" Ironically, it was the concern for family, their love of their families, that had catapulted these women into action to begin with. But, in a pragmatic sense, the home did have to come second in order for health and safety to be preserved. These were hard learning experiences. But meetings in individual homes ultimately involved children and spouses alike—everyone worked and everyone listened. The transformation of relations continued as women spoke up at hearings and demonstrations and husbands transported children, made signs, and looked on with pride and support at public forums.

The critical perspective of women in the battle against LANCER went far beyond what the women themselves had intended. For these women, the political issues were personal and in that sense they became feminist issues. These women, in the end, were fighting for what they felt was "right" rather than what men argued might be reasonable. The coincidence of the principles of feminism and ecology that Carolyn Merchant explains in *The Death of Nature* (San Francisco: Harper & Row, 1981) found expression and developed in the consciousness of these women: the concern for Earth as a home, the recognition that all parts of a system have equal value, the acknowledgment of process, and, finally, that capitalist growth has social costs. As Robin Cannon says, "This fight has really turned me around, things are intertwined in ways I hadn't realized. . . . All these social issues as well as political and economic issues are really intertwined. Before, I was concerned only about health and then I began to get into the politics, decision making, and so many things."

In two years, what started as the outrage of a small group of mothers has transformed the political climate of a major metropolitan area. What these women have aimed for is a greater level of democracy, a greater level of involvement, not only in their organization but in the development process of the city generally. They have demanded accountability regarding land use and ownership, very subversive concerns in a capitalist society. In their organizing, the group process, collectivism, was of primary importance. It allowed the women to see their own power and potential and therefore allowed them to consolidate effective opposition. The movement underscored the role of principles. In fact, we citizens have lived so long with an unquestioning acceptance of profit and expediency that sometimes we forget that our objective is to do "what's right." Women are beginning to raise moral concerns in a very forthright manner, emphasizing that experts have left us no other choice but to follow our own moral convictions rather than accept neutrality and capitulate in the face of crisis.

The environmental crisis will escalate in this decade and women are sure to play pivotal roles in the struggle to save our planet. If women are able to sustain for longer periods some of the qualities and behavioral forms they have displayed in crisis situations (such as direct participatory democracy and the critique of patriarchal bureaucracy), they may be able to reintroduce equality and democracy into progressive action. They may also reintroduce the value of being moved by principle and morality. Pragmatism has come to dominate all forms of political behavior and the results have often been disastrous. If women resist the "normal" organizational thrust to barter, bargain, and fragment ideas and issues, they may help set new standards for action in the new environmental movement. 20

Reading and Responding

At the end of your first reading, do a second short freewrite recording your impressions of Hamilton now: Does she confirm your expectations or does she surprise you? And have your views on environmental issues widened (or did they already include urban concerns)?

Working Together

1. Do an in-class freewrite, quickly paraphrasing the following passage and reflecting on what it means: "For these women, the political issues were personal and in that sense they become feminist issues. These women, in the end, were fighting for what they felt was 'right' rather than what men argued might be reasonable." Just try to say this in your own words.
2. Discuss in what sense personal issues are also feminist issues. What's the difference between the right and the reasonable? How do men and women see these issues differently?
3. Share experiences in your own life in which a political issue also became a personal issue—or a time when you fought for the right as opposed to the reasonable.

Rethinking and Rewriting

1. Research and report on the experience Hamilton describes, using newspaper and magazines indexes for the time of the event and looking, too, at letters to the editor, editorials, and so on. What were the other points of view? Did others see this same situation differently? What other facts can you discover about the event?
2. Write an essay about a time in your own life when political issues also became personal issues. Be clear and specific enough that readers will feel the same shift from personal to political or political to personal.
3. Write an essay with this thesis: "If taking the political personally is feminist, then I'm a feminist."

"GETTING ALONG WITH NATURE"

Wendell Berry

Wendell Berry lives and writes on a small farm along the Kentucky River near where his grandparents and great-grandparents farmed before him. He works the land with draft horses and raises crops organically, acting out in his own life the philosophy of agriculture and land management he has advocated in a series of measured, eloquent books of essays, including The Unsettling of America *(1977) and* Home Economics *(1987), from which this essay is taken. Berry is also a novelist, poet, and critic.*

As You Read

1. As you read, mark the major paragraph blocs: groups of paragraphs that seem organized around a single theme. Simply put a line or asterisk in the margins where you think one bloc ends and another begins. Underline, too, the major transitional phrases that signal the beginning of new blocs.
2. Write a subtitle or subheading for each of the blocs identified in item 1, a word or phrase that indicates the major subject or point of that section.

The defenders of nature and wilderness—like their enemies the defenders of the industrial economy—sometimes sound as if the natural and the human were two separate estates, radically different and radically divided. The defenders of nature and wilderness sometimes seem to feel that they must oppose any human encroachment whatsoever, just as the industrialists often apparently feel that they must make the human encroachment absolute or, as they say, "complete the conquest of nature." But there is danger in this opposition, and it can be best dealt with by realizing that these pure and separate categories are pure ideas and do not otherwise exist.

Pure nature, anyhow, is not good for humans to live in, and humans do not want to live in it—or not for very long. Any exposure to the elements that lasts more than a few hours will remind us of the desirability of the basic human amenities: clothing, shelter, cooked food, the company of kinfolk and friends—perhaps even of hot baths and music and books.

It is equally true that a condition that is *purely* human is not good for people to live in, and people do not want to live for very long in it. Obviously, the more artificial a human environment becomes, the more the word "natural" becomes a term of value. It can be argued, indeed, that the conservation movement, as we know it today, is largely a product of the industrial revolution. The people who want clean air, clear streams, and wild forests, prairies, and deserts are the people who no longer have them.

People cannot live apart from nature; that is the first principle of the conservationists. And yet, people cannot live in nature without changing it. But this is true of *all* creatures; they depend upon nature, and they change it. What we call nature is, in a sense, the sum of the changes made by all the various creatures and natural forces in their intricate actions and influences upon each other and upon their places. Because of the woodpeckers, nature is different from what it would be without them. It is different also because of the borers and ants that live in tree trunks, and because of the bacteria that live in the soil under the trees. The making of these differences is the making of the world.

Some of the changes made by wild creatures we would call beneficent: beavers are famous for making ponds that turn into fertile meadows; trees and prairie grasses build soil. But sometimes, too, we would call natural changes destructive. According to early witnesses, for instance, large areas around Kentucky salt licks were severely trampled and eroded by the great herds of hoofed animals that gathered there. The buffalo "streets" through hilly country were so hollowed out by hoof-wear and erosion that they remain visible almost two centuries after the disappearance of the buffalo. And so it can hardly be expected that humans would not change nature. Humans, like all other creatures, must make a difference; otherwise, they cannot live. But unlike other creatures, humans must make a choice as to the kind and scale of the difference they make. If they choose to make too small a difference, they diminish their humanity. If they choose to make too great a difference, they diminish nature, and narrow their subsequent choices; ultimately, they diminish or destroy themselves. Nature, then, is not only our source but also our limit and measure. Or, as the poet Edmund Spenser put it almost four hundred years ago, Nature, who is the "greatest goddesse," acts as a sort of earthly lieutenant of God, and Spenser represents her as both a mother and judge. Her jurisdiction is over the relations between the creatures; she deals "Right to all . . . indifferently," for she is "the equall mother" of all "And knittest each to each, as brother unto brother." Thus, in Spenser, the natural principles of fecundity and order are pointedly linked with the principle of justice, which we may be a little surprised to see that he attributes also to nature. And yet in his insistence on an "indifferent" natural justice, resting on the "brotherhood" of *all* creatures, not just of humans, Spenser would now be said to be on sound ecological footing.

In nature we know that wild creatures sometimes exhaust their vital sources and suffer the natural remedy: drastic population reductions. If lynxes eat too many snowshoe rabbits—which they are said to do repeatedly—then the lynxes starve down to the carrying capacity of their habitat. It is the carrying capacity of the lynx's habitat, not the carrying capacity of the lynx's stomach, that determines the prosperity of lynxes. Similarly, if humans use up too much soil—which they have often done and are doing—then they will starve down to the carrying capacity of *their* habitat. This is nature's "indifferent" justice. As Spenser saw in the sixteenth cen-

5

tury, and as we must learn to see now, there is no appeal from this justice. In the hereafter, the Lord may forgive our wrongs against nature, but on earth, so far as we know, He does not overturn her decisions.

One of the differences between humans and lynxes is that humans can see that the principle of balance operates between lynxes and snowshoe rabbits, as between humans and topsoil; another difference, we hope, is that humans have the sense to act on their understanding. We can see, too, that a stable balance is preferable to a balance that tilts back and forth like a seesaw, dumping a surplus of creatures alternately from either end. To say this is to renew the question of whether or not the human relationship with nature is necessarily an adversary relationship, and it is to suggest that the answer is not simple.

But in dealing with this question and in trying to do justice to the presumed complexity of the answer, we are up against an American convention of simple opposition to nature that is deeply established both in our minds and in our ways. We have opposed the primeval forests of the East and the primeval prairies and deserts of the West, we have opposed man-eating beasts and crop-eating insects, sheep-eating coyotes and chicken-eating hawks. In our lawns and gardens and fields, we oppose what we call weeds. And yet more and more of us are beginning to see that this opposition is ultimately destructive even of ourselves, that it does not explain many things that need explaining—in short, that it is untrue.

If our proper relation to nature is not opposition, then what is it? This question becomes complicated and difficult for us because none of us, as I have said, wants to live in a "pure" primeval forest or in a "pure" primeval prairie; we do not want to be eaten by grizzly bears; if we are gardeners, we have a legitimate quarrel with weeds; if, in Kentucky, we are trying to improve our pastures, we are likely to be enemies of the nodding thistle. But, do what we will, we remain under the spell of the primeval forests and prairies that we have cut down and broken; we turn repeatedly and with love to the thought of them and to their surviving remnants. We find ourselves attracted to the grizzly bears, too, and know that they and other great, dangerous animals remain alive in our imaginations as they have been all through human time. Though we cut down the nodding thistles, we acknowledge their beauty and are glad to think that there must be some place where they belong. (They may, in fact, not always be out of place in pastures; if, as seems evident, overgrazing makes an ideal seedbed for these plants, then we must understand them as a part of nature's strategy to protect the ground against abuse by animals.) Even the ugliest garden weeds earn affection from us when we consider how faithfully they perform an indispensable duty in covering the bare ground and in building humus. The weeds, too, are involved in the business of fertility.

We know, then, that the conflict between the human and the natural estates really exists and that it is to some extent necessary. But we are learning, or relearning, something else, too, that frightens us: namely, that 10 this conflict often occurs at the expense of *both* estates. It is not only possible but altogether probable that by diminishing nature we diminish ourselves, and vice versa.

The conflict comes to light most suggestively, perhaps, when advocates for the two sides throw themselves into absolute conflict where no absolute difference can exist. An example of this is the battle between defenders of coyotes and defenders of sheep, in which the coyote-defenders may find it easy to forget that the sheep ranchers are human beings with some authentic complaints against coyotes, and the sheep-defenders find it easy to sound as if they advocate the total eradication of both coyotes and conservationists. Such conflicts—like the old one between hawk-defenders and chicken-defenders—tend to occur between people who use nature indirectly and people who use it directly. It is a dangerous mistake, I think, for either side to pursue such a quarrel on the assumption that victory would be a desirable result.

The fact is that people need both coyotes and sheep, need a world in which both kinds of life are possible. Outside the heat of conflict, conservationists probably know that a sheep is one of the best devices for making coarse foliage humanly edible and that wool is ecologically better than the synthetic fibers, just as most shepherds will be aware that wild nature is of value to them and not lacking in interest and pleasure.

The usefulness of coyotes is, of course, much harder to define than the usefulness of sheep. Coyote fur is not a likely substitute for wool, and, except as a last resort, most people don't want to eat coyotes. The difficulty lies in the difference between what is ours and what is nature's: What is ours is ours because it is directly useful. Coyotes are useful *indirectly*, as part of the health of nature, from which we and our sheep alike must live and take our health. The fact, moreover, may be that sheep and coyotes need each other, at least in the sense that neither would prosper in a place totally unfit for the other.

This sort of conflict, then, does not suggest the possibility of victory so much as it suggests the possibility of a compromise—some kind of peace, even an alliance, between the domestic and the wild. We know that such an alliance is necessary. Most conservationists now take for granted that humans thrive best in ecological health and that the test or sign of this health is the survival of a diversity of wild creatures. We know, too, that we cannot imagine ourselves apart from those necessary survivals of our own wildness that we call our instincts. And we know that we cannot have a healthy agriculture apart from the teeming wilderness in the topsoil, in which worms, bacteria, and other wild creatures are carrying on the fundamental work of decomposition, humus making, water storage, and drainage. "In wildness is the preservation of the world," as Thoreau said, may be a spiritual truth, but it is also a practical fact.

On the other hand, we must not fail to consider the opposite proposition—that, so long at least as humans are in the world, in human culture is the preservation of wildness—which is equally, and more demandingly,

15

true. If wildness is to survive, then *we* must preserve it. We must preserve it by public act, by law, by institutionalizing wildernesses in some places. But such preservation is probably not enough. I have heard Wes Jackson of the Land Institute say, rightly I think, that if we cannot preserve our farmland, we cannot preserve the wilderness. That said, it becomes obvious that if we cannot preserve our cities, we cannot preserve the wilderness. This can be demonstrated practically by saying that the same attitudes that destroy wildness in the topsoil will finally destroy it everywhere; or by saying that if *everyone* has to go to a designated public wilderness for the necessary contact with wildness, then our parks will be no more natural than our cities.

But I am trying to say something more fundamental than that. What I am aiming at—because a lot of evidence seems to point this way—is the probability that nature and human culture, wildness and domesticity, are not opposed but are interdependent. Authentic experience of either will reveal the need of one for the other. In fact, examples from both past and present prove that a human economy and wildness can exist together not only in compatibility but to their mutual benefit.

One of the best examples I have come upon recently is the story of two Sonora Desert oases in Gary Nabhan's book, *The Desert Smells Like Rain*. The first of these oases, A'al Waipia, in Arizona, is dying because the park service, intending to preserve the natural integrity of the place as a bird sanctuary for tourists, removed the Papago Indians who had lived and farmed there. The place was naturally purer after the Indians were gone, but the oasis also began to shrink as the irrigation ditches silted up. As Mr. Nabhan puts it, "an odd thing is happening to their 'natural' bird sanctuary. They are losing the heterogeneity of the habitat, and with it, the birds. The old trees are dying. . . . These riparian trees are essential for the breeding habitat of certain birds. Summer annual seed plants are conspicuously absent. . . . Without the soil disturbance associated with plowing and flood irrigation, these natural foods for birds and rodents no longer germinate."

The other oasis, Ki:towak, in old Mexico, still thrives because a Papago village is still there, still farming. The village's oldest man, Luis Nolia, is the caretaker of the oasis, cleaning the springs and ditches, farming, planting trees: "Luis . . . blesses the oasis," Mr. Nabhan says, "for his work keeps it healthy." An ornithologist who accompanied Mr. Nabhan found twice as many species of birds at the farmed oasis as he found at the bird sanctuary, a fact that Mr. Nabhan's Papago friend, Remedio, explained in this way: "That's because those birds, they come where the people are. When the people live and work in a place, and plant their seeds and water their trees, the birds go live with them. They like those places, there's plenty to eat and that's when we are friends to them."

Another example, from my own experience, is suggestive in a somewhat different way. At the end of July 1981, while I was using a team of horses to mow a small triangular hillside pasture that is bordered on two sides by trees, I was suddenly aware of wings close below me. It was a young red-tailed hawk, who flew up into a walnut tree. I mowed on to the turn and stopped the team. The hawk then glided to the ground not twenty feet away. I got off the mower, stood and watched, even spoke, and the hawk showed no fear. I could see every feather distinctly, claw and beak and eye, the creamy down of the breast. Only when I took a step toward him, separating myself from the team and mower, did he fly. While I mowed three or four rounds, he stayed near, perched in trees or standing erect and watchful on the ground. Once, when I stopped to watch him, he was clearly watching me, stooping to see under the leaves that screened me from him. Again, when I could not find him, I stooped, saying to myself, "This is what he did to look at me," and as I did so I saw him looking at me.

Why had he come? To catch mice? Had he seen me scare one out of the grass? Or was it curiosity?   *20*

A human, of course, cannot speak with authority of the motives of hawks. I am aware of the possibility of explaining the episode merely by the hawk's youth and inexperience. And yet it does not happen often or dependably that one is approached so closely by a hawk of any age. I feel safe in making a couple of assumptions. The first is that the hawk came because of the conjunction of the small pasture and its wooded borders, of open hunting ground and the security of trees. This is the phenomenon of edge or margin that we know to be one of the powerful attractions of a diversified landscape, both to wildlife and to humans. The human eye itself seems drawn to such margins, hungering for the difference made in the countryside by a hedgy fencerow, a stream, or a grove of trees. And we know that these margins are biologically rich, the meeting of two kinds of habitat. But another difference also is important here: the difference between a large pasture and a small one, or, to use Wes Jackson's terms, the difference between a field and a patch. The pasture I was mowing was a patch—small, intimate, nowhere distant from its edges.

My second assumption is that the hawk was emboldened to come so near because, though he obviously recognized me as a man, I was there with the team of horses, with whom he familiarly and confidently shared the world.

I am saying, in other words, that this little visit between the hawk and me happened because the kind and scale of my farm, my way of farming, and my technology *allowed* it to happen. If I had been driving a tractor in a hundred-acre cornfield, it would not have happened.

In some circles I would certainly be asked if one can or should be serious about such an encounter, if it has any value. And though I cannot produce any hard evidence, I would unhesitatingly answer yes. Such encounters involve another margin—the one between domesticity and wildness—that attracts us irresistibly; they are among the best rewards of outdoor work and among the reasons for loving to farm. When the scale of farming grows so great and obtrusive as to forbid them, the *life* of farming is impoverished.

But perhaps we do find hard evidence of a sort when we consider that *all* of us—the hawk, the horses, and I—were there for our benefit and, to some extent, for our *mutual* benefit: The horses live from the pasture and maintain it with their work, grazing, and manure; the team and I together furnish hunting ground to the hawk; the hawk serves us by controlling the field-mouse population.

These meetings of the human and the natural estates, the domestic and the wild, occur invisibly, of course, in any well-farmed field. The wilderness of a healthy soil, too complex for human comprehension, can yet be husbanded, can benefit from human care, and can deliver incalculable benefits in return. Mutuality of interest and reward is a possibility that can reach to any city backyard, garden, and park, but in any place under human dominance—which is, now, virtually everyplace—it is a possibility that is *both* natural and cultural. If humans want wildness to be possible, then they have to make it possible. If balance is the ruling principle and a stable balance the goal, then, for humans, attaining this goal requires a consciously chosen and deliberately made partnership with nature.

In other words, we can be true to nature only by being true to human nature—to our animal nature as well as to cultural patterns and restraints that keep us from acting like animals. When humans act like animals, they become the most dangerous of animals to themselves and other humans, and this is because of another critical difference between humans and animals: Whereas animals are usually restrained by the limits of physical appetites, humans have mental appetites that can be far more gross and capacious than physical ones. Only humans squander and hoard, murder and pillage because of notions.

The work by which good human and natural possibilities are preserved is complex and difficult, and it probably cannot be accomplished by raw intelligence and information. It requires knowledge, skills, and restraints, some of which must come from our past. In the hurry of technological progress, we have replaced some tools and methods that worked with some that do not work. But we also need culture-borne instructions about who or what humans are and how and on what assumptions they should act. The Chain of Being, for instance—which gave humans a place between animals and angels in the order of Creation—is an old idea that has not been replaced by any adequate new one. It was simply rejected, and the lack of it leaves us without a definition.

Lacking that ancient definition, or any such definition, we do not know at what point to restrain or deny ourselves. We do not know how ambitious to be, what or how much we may safely desire, when or where to stop. I knew a barber once who refused to give a discount to a bald client, explaining that his artistry consisted, not in the cutting off, but in the knowing when to stop. He spoke, I think, as a true artist and a true

25

human. The lack of such knowledge is extremely dangerous in and to an individual. But ignorance of when to stop is a modern epidemic; it is the basis of "industrial progress" and "economic growth." The most obvious practical result of this ignorance is a critical disproportion of scale between the scale of human enterprises and their sources in nature.

The scale of the energy industry, for example, is too big, as is the   *30* scale of the transportation industry. The scale of agriculture, from a technological or economic point of view, is too big, but from a demographic point of view, the scale is too small. When there are enough people on the land to use it but not enough to husband it, then the wildness of the soil that we call fertility begins to diminish, and the soil itself begins to flee from us in water and wind.

If the human economy is to be fitted into the natural economy in such a way that both may thrive, the human economy must be built to proper scale. It is possible to talk at great length about the difference between proper and improper scale. It may be enough to say here that that difference is *suggested* by the difference between amplified and unamplified music in the countryside, or the difference between the sound of a motorboat and the sound of oarlocks. A proper human sound, we may say, is one that allows other sounds to be heard. A properly scaled human economy or technology allows a diversity of other creatures to thrive.

"The proper scale," a friend wrote to me, "confers freedom and simplicity . . . and doubtless leads to long life and health." I think that it also confers joy. The renewal of our partnership with nature, the rejoining of our works to their proper places in the natural order, reshaped to their proper scale, implies the reenjoyment both of nature and of human domesticity. Though our task will be difficult, we will greatly mistake its nature if we see it as grim, or if we suppose that it must always be necessary to suffer at work in order to enjoy ourselves in places specializing in "recreation."

Once we grant the possibility of a proper human scale, we see that we have made a radical change of assumptions and values. We realize that we are less interested in technological "breakthroughs" than in technological elegance. Of a new tool or method we will no longer ask: Is it fast? Is it powerful? Is it a labor saver? How many workers will it replace? We will ask instead: Can we (and our children) afford it? Is it fitting to our real needs? Is it becoming to us? Is it unhealthy or ugly? And though we may keep a certain interest in innovation and in what we may become, we will renew our interest in what we have been, realizing that conservationists must necessarily conserve *both* inheritances, the natural and the cultural.

To argue the necessity of wildness to, and in, the human economy is by no means to argue against the necessity of wilderness. The survival of wilderness—of places that we do not change, where we allow the existence even of creatures we perceive as dangerous—is necessary. Our sanity probably requires it. Whether we go to those places or not, we need to know that they exist. And I would argue that we do not need just the great public wildernesses, but millions of small private or semiprivate ones. Every farm should have one; wildernesses can occupy corners of factory grounds and city lots—places where nature is given a free hand, where no human work is done, where people go only as guests. These places function, I think, whether we intend them to or not, as sacred groves—places we respect and leave alone, not because we understand well what goes on there, but because we do not.

We go to wilderness places to be restored, to be instructed in the natural economies of fertility and healing, to admire what we cannot make. Sometimes, as we find to our surprise, we go to be chastened or corrected. And we go in order to return with renewed knowledge by which to judge the health of our human economy and our dwelling places. As we return from our visits to the wilderness, it is sometimes possible to imagine a series of fitting and decent transitions from wild nature to the human community and its supports: from forest to woodlot to the "two-story agriculture" of tree crops and pasture to orchard to meadow to grainfield to garden to household to neighborhood to village to city—so that even when we reached the city we would not be entirely beyond the influence of the nature of that place.

What I have been implying is that I think there is a bad reason to go to the wilderness. We must not go there to escape the ugliness and the dangers of the present human economy. We must not let ourselves feel that to go there is to escape. In the first place, such an escape is now illusory. In the second place, if, even as conservationists, we see the human and the natural economies as necessarily opposite or opposed, we subscribe to the very opposition that threatens to destroy them both. The wild and the domestic now often seem isolated values, estranged from one another. And yet these are not exclusive polarities like good and evil. There can be continuity between them, and there must be.

What we find, if we weight the balance too much in favor of the domestic, is that we involve ourselves in dangers both personal and public. Not the least of these dangers is dependence on distant sources of money and materials. Farmers are in deep trouble now because they have become too dependent on corporations and banks. They have been using methods and species that enforce this dependence. But such a dependence is not safe, either for farmers or for agriculture. It is not safe for urban consumers. Ultimately, as we are beginning to see, it is not safe for banks and corporations—which, though they have evidently not thought so, are dependent upon farmers. Our farms are endangered because—like the interstate highways or modern hospitals or modern universities—they cannot be inexpensively used. To be usable at all they require great expense.

When the human estate becomes so precarious, our only recourse is to move it back toward the estate of nature. We undoubtedly need better plant and animal species than nature provided us. But we are beginning to see that they can be too much better—too dependent on us and on "the economy," too expensive. In farm animals, for instance, we want good commercial quality, but we can see that the ability to produce meat or milk can actually be a threat to the farmer and to the animal if not accompanied by qualities we would call natural: thriftiness, hardiness, physical vigor, resistance to disease and parasites, ability to breed and give birth without assistance, strong mothering instincts. These natural qualities decrease care, work, and worry; they also decrease the costs of production. They save feed and time; they make diseases and cures exceptional rather than routine.

We need crop and forage species of high productive ability also, but we do not need species that will not produce at all without expensive fertilizers and chemicals. Contrary to the premise of agribusiness advertisements and of most expert advice, farmers do not thrive by production or by "skimming" a large "cash flow." They cannot solve their problems merely by increasing production or income. They thrive, like all other creatures, according to the difference between their income and their expenses.

One of the strangest characteristics of the industrial economy is the 40 ability to increase production again and again without ever noticing—or without acknowledging—the *costs* of production. That one Holstein cow should produce 50,000 pounds of milk in a year may appear to be marvelous—a miracle of modern science. But what if her productivity is dependent upon the consumption of a huge amount of grain (about a bushel a day), and therefore upon the availability of cheap petroleum? What if she is too valuable (and too delicate) to be allowed outdoors in the rain? What if the proliferation of her kind will again drastically reduce the number of dairy farms and farmers? Or, to use a more obvious example, can we afford a bushel of grain at a cost of five to twenty bushels of topsoil lost to erosion?

"It is good to have Nature working for you," said Henry Besuden, the dean of American Southdown breeders. "She works for a minimum wage." That is true. She works at times for almost nothing, requiring only that we respect her work and give her a chance, as when she maintains—indeed, improves—the fertility and productivity of a pasture by the natural succession of clover and grass or when she improves a clay soil for us by means of the roots of a grass sod. She works for us by preserving health or wholeness, which for all our ingenuity we cannot make. If we fail to respect her health, she deals out her justice by withdrawing her protection against disease—which we *can* make, and do.

To make this continuity between the natural and the human, we have only two sources of instruction: nature herself and our cultural tradition. If we listen only to the apologists for the industrial economy, who respect neither nature nor culture, we get the idea that it is somehow our goodness that makes us so destructive: The air is unfit to breathe, the water is unfit to drink, the soil is washing away, the cities are violent and the countryside neglected, all because we are intelligent, enterprising, industrious, and generous, concerned only to feed the hungry and to "make a better future for our children." Respect for nature causes us to doubt this, and our cultural tradition confirms and illuminates our doubt: No good thing is destroyed by goodness; good things are destroyed by wickedness. We may identify that insight as Biblical, but it is taken for granted by both the Greek and the Biblical lineages of our culture, from Homer and Moses to William Blake. Since the start of the industrial revolution, there have been voices urging that this inheritance may be safely replaced by intelligence, information, energy, and money. No idea, I believe, could be more dangerous.

Reading and Responding

Mark three to five passages that seem the most important to you, the most central to the meaning of the essay.

Working Together

1. Share the passages you marked as significant. What are the passages saying? Are you reading the same passages as classmates or different ones? If different, are these passages related to each other—restatements of the same idea, statements of further ideas and implications of the essay's central point? Record the major ideas of the discussion in your reading journal.
2. Use the TRIAC scheme to explore the shape and connections of paragraphs within one of the paragraph blocs you marked on a first reading. How are these paragraphs related? Then use the TRIAC scheme to chart the movement of the whole essay across the different blocs. Notice, in particular, how many times the T (theme) slot is repeated and how often Wendell Berry turns to examples (the I slot).

Rethinking and Rewriting

1. Take one of the passages the class agreed was central to the piece and write an essay exploring the implications of that idea in your own experience. Describe a single experience that substantiates Berry's point—or that contradicts it or doesn't seem to fit it. Or imagine how your life would be different if it were organized in keeping with Berry's ideas.
2. Write a 750-word summary of this essay.
3. Drawing on Berry's discussion of "edges" and "margins," write an essay about an edge or margin in your own life, some border where things suddenly become mixed, interesting, productive. At some point in the essay, explain what Berry means when he talks about edges and how your experience illustrates that idea.
4. Write an essay relating Berry to two or three other writers in this section. What would he say, for example, to Arnold or Tucker? How is

Berry responding to Leopold in this piece? What would Leopold or Tucker say about Berry's position as he outlines it here?

5. Write an essay exploring this idea in your own experience or with examples from others: "The proper scale confers joy."

6. Use this essay by Berry as the basis for an argumentative essay asserting that Watson (chapter 14) and Foreman (chapter 14) are wrong—or that Leopold is wrong.

Essay Topics for Chapter 13

1. Identify another course you've had or are taking now, one that adds to (or complicates) your understanding of the term *land ethics*. Explain what the course taught, and show how it adds to or complicates one of the readings in this chapter.

2. Using one or more of the readings in this chapter as your starting point, extend the notion of land ethics to another major resource: freshwater ethics, air ethics, or sea ethics. Explain how the principles that underpin praiseworthy land ethics might apply to this other area. End by discussing what would have to change if we actually lived by this new set of ethics.

3. Focus on two readings in this chapter and explain how they overlap and agree as well as how they differ. Once you've done this objective analysis, start a new section that tells readers (and yourself) how you respond to these two readings now that you know them so well. If your response is clear and certain, explain that clarity and certainty. If your response is still uncertain, that's fine too; work to explain the contradictions or conflicting claims even if you cannot fully resolve them.

4. Take any one of the readings in this chapter and look for an ally in any of the earlier chapters. For example, you could take Muir's essay and look for someone, perhaps Lopez in "Gone Back into the Earth," who would be inclined to agree with Muir. Or you could take Leopold's essay in this chapter and argue that Carson in "Elixirs of Death" would agree with him. Whoever you choose, explain why the two would be allies; explain why you think they would agree. Make sure that your essay quotes both writers at least once.

5. Using any two of the selections in this chapter as sources, write your own version of land ethics. Use your two readings, but also draw on your own life and your own immediate experience.

6. You're a landowner who's paid a considerable sum to purchase fifty acres of trees. A stream passes through part of this acreage. Market prices for timber are high right now, and you could make a healthy profit by logging the entire fifty acres. Hire one of the authors in this chapter as a consultant. From the ethical principles implied in this author's essay, decide what your author/consultant would tell you to do with your fifty acres of trees. Write an essay that explains what you

think this consultant would tell you and why you think your consultant would make these recommendations. Variation: To extend the length and complexity of this assignment, add a last section that explains carefully whether you'd accept the advice of your consultant. Make sure your reasons are clear.

7. Investigate the land use (or zoning) laws in your area (focus on an urban area if you wish, or focus on rural land). What actions to these laws allow, and what actions do they prohibit or restrict? What principles of land ethics seem to provide the foundations for these laws?

8. Imagine Berry in a panel discussion with Leopold and Arnold. Arrange this discussion as a script or interview, with each speaker taking turns. The subject is, "Nature: Do We Use It or Lose It?" Represent Leopold's and Arnold's positions first; then have Berry respond. What would he say?

9. Take any two selections in this chapter (except for "A White Heron") and assume that instead of talking about land, these authors are discussing your own backyard. Translate each argument in terms of your backyard. Be as literal and specific as you can. Then end your essay by discussing what this comparison has taught you. A variation is to assume that instead of talking about your backyard, these authors are talking about your campus.

10. Use "A White Heron" and any other piece in this chapter to discuss two very different ways to make an argument and persuade readers. Explain how "A White Heron" makes its argument, contrast that with the ways your second selection makes its argument, and close by discussing the advantages and disadvantages of each.

11. Using three or more of the selections in this chapter, write an essay that puts together your responses to the following questions.

   • Identify the position on land ethics that has always seemed obvious, natural, or self-evident to you.

   • Explain what in your upbringing and experience makes this position seem so obvious and reasonable.

   • Using three or more of the readings in this grouping, make a list of reasons to doubt this answer. Why would others doubt your answer. Come to think of it, why should *you?*

   • Using other selections from the chapter, make a list of all the reasons you can think of to believe in this position, after all.

   • Explain why this isn't a black-and-white issue, why it is actually more complex than you realized.

   • Explain the consequences of persuading your readers to accept one or the other position.

   Feel free to organize the essay in exactly this order or to sequence your responses in some other way.

12. Write an "As I See It" essay for your local or campus newspaper arguing a position on some local environmental issue. Use at least one quotation from at least three of the writers in this chapter.

13. Using just the material included in this chapter—assuming that it's representative and complete—write a brief history of the environmental movement. How has it developed? What are its major submovements and its major oppositions?

14. Write an essay tracing the influence of any figure presented in this chapter on any other. For example, show how the ideas of Muir are echoed in Leopold and Berry; or how Leopold is an influence on Berry. Be specific. Quote the texts.

15. Write an autobiographical essay reflecting on the implicit land ethics in use when you grew up. Given the way you lived—the kind of house you lived in, the kind of car your parents drove and the work they did, the way you used raw materials and treated the landscape— what were your land ethics (whether or not you were aware of them)? Which of the writers in this chapter comes closest to expressing this implicit, perhaps unconscious set of values? How have your values changed, if they have, and why?

14

Taking Action

If you've read many of the selections in this book—and especially if you've read them and written about them—then in one sense you've already taken significant action: You've broadened and deepened your own understanding. You've added to your education. And by now you know our main point: that environmental issues are complicated; that things are not always what they seem; that good people of goodwill can disagree. Easy slogans won't do. All of us have to think harder and deeper about the ecology of the earth than we sometimes have in the past, and writing and reading is one way of doing that hard thinking. In writing and reading we learn complexity. We learn revision—we learn reseeing.

But even so, even with all this awareness of the layers and paradoxes, we have to act. We have to make decisions, however messy and unclear the data and however valid the conflicting points of view. Scientists may disagree about the facts; the special-interest groups may see the ethical questions differently (and we all belong to one special-interest group or another). But almost no one disputes that the earth is under greater pressure, and collectively we're the cause. There are more people, more cars, more roads, more houses, more created things in the world; and there are fewer trees, fewer raw minerals, less clean water, less ozone. The situation has reached its crisis point. Something must be done.

In this chapter we present different ways of thinking about decision making and action, different ways of thinking about responsibility. The readings in this book should move us all to action in the world and for the world. But what might those actions be? What are our responsibilities, and how do we exercise those responsibilities? What's possible or reasonable? How do we balance all these conflicting claims—and not just in the abstract, but in our individual lives, here and now, today?

"TRAVELING THROUGH THE DARK"

William Stafford

> *A native of Hutchinson, Kansas, William Stafford lived most of his adult life in Portland, Oregon, where he taught until his retirement from Lewis and Clark College. Stafford's poetry brought him many honors. His book* Traveling Through the Dark *won the National Book Award in 1962, he served as consultant in poetry for the Library of Congress, and he was recipient of the Award in Literature of the American Academy and Institute of Arts and Letters. His most recent books before his death in 1993 include* Passwords, My Name Is William Tell, *and* An Oregon Message. *The following poem suggests that we cannot predict when we might be called on to take action.*

Traveling through the dark I found a deer
dead on the edge of the Wilson River road.
It is usually best to roll them into the canyon:
that road is narrow; to swerve might make more dead.

By glow of the tail-light I stumbled back of the car   5
and stood by the heap, a doe, a recent killing;
she had stiffened already, almost cold.
I dragged her off; she was large in the belly.

My fingers touching her side brought me the reason—
her side was warm; her fawn lay there waiting,   10
alive, still, never to be born.
Beside that mountain road I hesitated.

The car aimed ahead its lowered parking lights;
under the hood purred the steady engine.
I stood in the glare of the warm exhaust turning red;   15
around our group I could hear the wilderness listen.

I thought hard for us all—my only swerving—,
then pushed her over the edge into the river.

Reading and Responding

1. Imagine this poem rewritten as prose—the line breaks taken out and the sentences arranged in one or two paragraphs. How would it read? Would any particular lines or phrases stand out as poetic?
2. Which lines stand out as especially "unpoetic"? Why? Are they really? What do *poetic* and *unpoetic* mean, anyway?

3. Why is this poem included in this book, in a chapter entitled "Taking Action"? Freewrite an answer, and don't worry if you start by saying "I don't know" or "I'm not sure."

Working Together

Here are several possible interpretations of this poem. Divide up into groups, and have each group take an interpretation, finding details in the poem to support it.

- The poem is about the inevitable conflict between technology and the natural world, a conflict that always results in the destruction of nature.

- The poem is about the poet's guilt, his struggling with an insoluble moral problem.

- The poem is about the poet's midlife crisis.

- The poem is about the moral dilemma of abortion.

- The poem isn't about any of these other things; it's just about pushing a deer over the edge of the canyon.

Rethinking and Rewriting

1. Write an essay about a difficult, insoluble moral choice—some decision you felt you had to make at the time but that still troubles you, still feels unresolved.

2. Write an essay that speculates about how William Stafford uses the phrase "—my only swerving—" in this poem. What is this "swerving," and how does it explain (or not explain) the action in the last line. Don't feel that you have to be sure here (though if you feel sure, that's fine, too).

3. Tell the story this poem tells, but tell it as though it actually happened to you and you actually did it all. That is, tell the story using *I*. As you tell the story—your story—include any useful commentary about what you were thinking or feeling at the time (that night) and what you feel now.

4. Write an essay arguing that learning to read poetry is good training for the critical thinking required in all reading—and in life.

"OUT OF YOUR CAR, OFF YOUR HORSE"

Wendell Berry

> *In this essay from the February 1991 issue of* Atlantic, *Wendell Berry makes a series of very practical, very challenging suggestions for how each of us can contribute to the saving of the planet. (See also "Getting Along with Nature" in chapter 13.)*

I. Properly speaking, global thinking is not possible. Those who have "thought globally" (and among them the most successful have been imperial governments and multinational corporations) have done so by means of simplifications too extreme and oppressive to merit the name of thought. Global thinkers have been, and will be, dangerous people. National thinkers tend to be dangerous also; we now have national thinkers in the northeastern United States who look upon Kentucky as a garbage dump.

II. Global thinking can only be statistical. Its shallowness is exposed by the least intention to do something. Unless one is willing to be destructive on a very large scale, one cannot do something except locally, in a small place. Global thinking can only do to the globe what a space satellite does to it: reduce it, make a bauble of it. Look at one of those photographs of half the earth taken from outer space, and see if you recognize your neighborhood. If you want to *see* where you are, you will have to get out of your space vehicle, out of your car, off your horse, and walk over the ground. On foot you will find that the earth is still satisfyingly large, and full of beguiling nooks and crannies.

III. If we could think locally, we would do far better than we are doing now. The right local questions and answers will be the right global ones. The Amish question "What will this do to our community?" tends toward the right answer for the world.

IV. If we want to put local life in proper relation to the globe, we must do so by imagination, charity, and forbearance, and by making local life as independent and self-sufficient as we can—not by the presumptuous abstractions of "global thought."

V. If we want to keep our thoughts and acts from destroying the globe, then we must see to it that we do not ask too much of the globe or of any part of it. To make sure that we do not ask too much, we must learn to live at home, as independently and self-sufficiently as we can. That is the only way we can keep the land we are using, and its ecological limits, always in sight.

VI. The only sustainable city—and this, to me, is the indispensable ideal and goal—is a city in balance with its countryside: a city, that is, that would live off the *net* ecological income of its supporting region, paying as it goes all its ecological and human debts.

VII. The cities we now have are living off ecological principal, by economic assumptions that seem certain to destroy them. They do not live at home. They do not have their own supporting regions. They are out of balance with their supports, wherever on the globe their supports are.

VIII. The balance between city and countryside is destroyed by industrial machinery, "cheap" productivity in field and forest, and "cheap" transportation. Rome destroyed the balance with slave labor; we have destroyed it with "cheap" fossil fuel.

IX. Since the Civil War, perhaps, and certainly since the Second World War, the norms of productivity have been set by the fossil-fuel industries.

X. Geographically, the sources of the fossil fuels are rural. Technically, however, the production of these fuels is industrial and urban. The facts and integrities of local life, and the principle of community, are considered as little as possible, for to consider them would not be quickly profitable. Fossil fuels have always been produced at the expense of local ecosystems and of local human communities. The fossil-fuel economy is the industrial economy par excellence, and it assigns no value to local life, natural or human.

XI. When the industrial principles exemplified in fossil-fuel production are applied to field and forest, the results are identical: local life, both natural and human, is destroyed.

XII. Industrial procedures have been imposed on the countryside pretty much to the extent that country people have been seduced or forced into dependence on the money economy. By encouraging this dependence, corporations have increased their ability to rob the people of their property and their labor. The result is that a very small number of people now own all the usable property in the country, and workers are increasingly the hostages of their employers.

XIII. Our present "leaders"—the people of wealth and power—do not know what it means to take a place seriously: to think it worthy, for its own sake, of love and study and careful work. They cannot take any place seriously because they must be ready at any moment, by the terms of power and wealth in the modern world, to destroy any place.

XIV. Ecological good sense will be opposed by all the most powerful economic entities of our time, because ecological good sense requires the reduction or replacement of those entities. If ecological good sense is to prevail, it can do so only through the work and the will of the people and of the local communities.

XV. For this task our currently prevailing assumptions about knowledge, information, education, money, and political will are inadequate. All our institutions with which I am familiar have adopted the organizational patterns and the quantitative measures of the industrial corporations. *Both* sides of the ecological debate, perhaps as a consequence, are alarmingly abstract.

XVI. But abstraction, of course, is what is wrong. The evil of the industrial economy (capitalist or communist) is the abstractness inherent in its procedures—its inability to distinguish one place or person or creature from another. William Blake saw this two hundred years ago. Anyone can see it now in almost any of our common tools and weapons.

XVII. Abstraction is the enemy *wherever* it is found. The abstractions of sustainability can ruin the world just as surely as the abstractions of industrial economics. Local life may be as much endangered by "saving the planet" as by "conquering the world." Such a project calls for abstract purposes and central powers that cannot know, and so will destroy, the integrity of local nature and local community.

XVIII. In order to make ecological good sense for the planet, you must make ecological good sense locally. You can't act locally by thinking globally. If you want to keep your local acts from destroying the globe, you must think locally.

XIX. No one can make ecological good sense for the planet. Everyone can make ecological good sense locally, *if* the affection, the scale, the knowledge, the tools, and the skills are right.

XX. The right scale in work gives power to affection. When one works beyond the reach of one's love for the place one is working in, and for the things and creatures one is working with and among, then destruction inevitably results. An adequate local culture, among other things, keeps work within the reach of love.

XXI. The question before us, then, is an extremely difficult one: How do we begin to remake, or to make, a local culture that will preserve our part of the world while we use it? We are talking here not just about a kind of knowledge that *involves* affection but also about a kind of knowledge that comes from or with affection—knowledge that is unavailable to the unaffectionate, and that is unavailable to anyone as what is called information.

XXII. What, for a start, might be the economic result of local affection? We don't know. Moreover, we are probably never going to know in any way that would satisfy the average dean or corporate executive. The ways of love tend to be secretive and, even to the lovers themselves, somewhat inscrutable.

XXIII. The real work of planet-saving will be small, humble, and humbling, and (insofar as it involves love) pleasing and rewarding. Its jobs will be too many to count, too many to report, too many to be publicly noticed or rewarded, too small to make anyone rich or famous.

XXIV. The great obstacle may be not greed but the modern hankering after glamour. A lot of our smartest, most concerned people want to come up with a big solution to a big problem. I don't think that planet-saving, if we take it seriously, can furnish employment to many such people.

XXV. When I think of the kind of worker the job requires, I think   25
of Dorothy Day (if one can think of Dorothy Day herself, separate from the publicity that came as a result of her rarity), a person willing to go down and down into the daunting, humbling, almost hopeless local presence of the problem—to face the great problem one small life at a time.

XXVI. Some cities can never be sustainable, because they do not have a countryside around them, or near them, from which they can be sustained. New York City cannot be made sustainable, nor can Phoenix. Some cities in Kentucky or the Midwest, on the other hand, might reasonably hope to become sustainable.

XXVII. To make a sustainable city, one must begin somehow, and I think the beginning must be small and economic. A beginning could be made, for example, by increasing the amount of food bought from farmers in the local countryside by consumers in the city. As the food economy became more local, local farming would become more diverse; the farms would become smaller, more complex in structure, more productive; and some city people would be needed to work on the farms. Sooner or later, as a means of reducing expenses both ways, organic wastes from the city would go out to fertilize the farms of the supporting region; thus city people would have to assume an agricultural responsibility, and would be properly motivated to do so both by the wish to have a supply of excellent food and by the fear of contaminating that supply. The increase of economic intimacy between a city and its sources would change minds (assuming, of course, that the minds in question would stay put long enough to be changed). It would improve minds. The locality, by becoming partly sustainable, would produce the thought it would need to become more sustainable.

Reading and Responding

1. Mark the three propositions that are the clearest to you, that you like the best, or that seem the most powerful.
2. Mark the three propositions you don't understand, that you don't agree with, or that don't seem to fit for whatever reason.
3. Do a freewrite at the end of your first reading: Record anything in your mind at that moment—thoughts, images, questions, observations, experiences.

Working Together

1. Work to agree on the three propositions that seem to your group the best or most powerful. Then write a group paragraph that explains your rationale.
2. Arrange related propositions. Put them in categories and label the categories. How many categories are there? How are they connected?
3. Determine the logical relationships between these propositions, and insert transitional words and phrases between each of them. (Sample transition words and phrases include *that is, in other words, for example, on the other hand, to repeat.*
4. Find a proposition that summarizes the theme for all the rest. Where is it positioned, and why do you think it is positioned there?
5. Which propositions could be deleted without taking away from the meaning of the essay (if any)? What are these propositions doing in the essay—what do they contribute?
6. What would you have to do to make this list of propositions into an essay? What would have to be added or deleted?

Rethinking and Rewriting

1. In an essay, discuss the effect on you as a reader of these separate and discrete units of meaning. How do they force you to read and reflect? What are the advantages and disadvantages of arranging ideas in this way?
2. Write a paper composed of twenty-seven propositions—on any subject. Arrange it exactly as Wendell Berry does this essay.
3. Write an essay illustrating this idea from your own experience and reading, applying it to some particular subject or question: "Abstraction is the enemy *wherever* it is found."
4. Write an essay explaining how the notion presented in item 3 applies to the writing of papers. How is abstraction "the enemy" in writing?

5. Take this statement and apply it to your life right now, particularly in light of the amount of homework you have to do for school: "The right scale in work gives power to affection."
6. Use at least three readings from other parts of this book to illustrate this statement: "Both sides of the ecological debate are alarmingly abstract." Or use examples from recent or local newspapers, letters to the editor, and magazines.

"DUTY OF CARE"

John McPhee

A staff writer for the New Yorker *magazine and a professor of journalism at Princeton University, John McPhee has written over twenty books of creative or literary nonfiction on subjects ranging from oranges to birch bark canoes to geology. His abiding interest has been in environmental themes—for example, in* Encounters with the Archdruid *(1972), a book about David Brower, then director of the Sierra Club; and in* Coming into the Country *(1977), a book about McPhee's experiences in the Alaska wilderness. In this article published recently in the* New Yorker, *McPhee has done his usual intensive, in-depth research into the facts of an issue or problem and then brought these facts alive with his signature literary techniques—scenes, dialogues, portraits, stories, and the careful crafting of sentences.*

As You Read

1. As you read, keep track of all the kinds of research John McPhee must have done for this article. Establish these categories:
   - in-person interviews
   - travel
   - phone interviews
   - general reading
   - library research: journals, technical reports, government reports, magazines, or others

   Under each category, list several facts and pieces of information from the article.
2. As you read, look for McPhee's main point (or main points) and mark it (them) in the margin.

The world's largest pile of scrap tires is not visible from Interstate 5, in Stanislaus County, California. But it's close. Below Stockton, in the region of Modesto and Merced, the highway follows the extreme western edge of the flat Great Central Valley, right next to the scarp where the Coast Ranges are territorially expanding as fresh unpopulated hills. The hills conceal the tires from the traffic. If you were to abandon your car three miles from the San Joaquin County line and make your way on foot southwest one mile, you would climb into steeply creased terrain that in winter is jade green and in summer straw brown, and, any time at all, you would come upon a black vista. At rest on sloping ground, the tires are so deep that they form their own topography—their own escarpments, their own overhanging cliffs. Deposited from a ridgeline, they border a valley for nearly half a mile. When you first glimpse them, you are not sure what they are. From the high ground on the opposite side, the individual tires appear to be grains of black sand. They look like little eggstones—oolites—each a bright yolk ringed in black pearl. Close to them, you walk in tire canyons. In some places, they are piled six stories high, compressing themselves, densifying: at the top, tires; at the bottom, pucks. From the highest elevations of this thick and drifted black mantle, you can look east a hundred miles and see snow on the Sierra.

The tires are from all sides of the bays of San Francisco and up and down the Great Central Valley from Bakersfield to Sacramento. Even before the interstate was there, a tire jockey named Ed Filbin began collecting them—charging dealers and gas stations "tipping fees" of so much per passenger tire and so much per truck tire, as tire jockeys everywhere do. This was long before people began to worry, with regard to used tires, about mosquitoes, fires, landfills, and compounding environmental concerns, or to look upon old tires as a minable resource. Filbin's pile just grew, and he made enough money to diversify, becoming, as he is today, the largest sheep rancher in Nevada. Meanwhile, his tire ranch near Modesto continued to broaden and thicken, until no one, including Filbin, knew how many tires were there. Eventually, the state took notice—and county zoning authorities—and Filbin felt harassed. When I called him one day in Nevada, he sketched these people as "dirty rotten bureaucrats" and said, "I told them to go jump in a crick. I had grandfather rights." With those words, he cradled his telephone, refusing to say more.

There have been many estimates of the number of tires in the great California pile, but the figures tend to be high or low in direct proportion to the appraiser's economic interest or environmental bias. The variations can be absurd, missing agreement with one another by factors as high as five. Not long ago, while I was at the University of California, Davis, working on something else, I began to muse about the tire pile and the problem of counting its contents. In the university library I found David Lundquist, the map librarian, and asked for his suggestions. The pile does not appear on the 7.5-minute Solyo Quadrangle of the United States Geological Survey, and I thought he might have a more sophisticated map of equally ample scale. He said he had recent low-altitude aerial photographs made by the federal Agricultural Stabilization and Conservation Service that amounted to an eyeball-to-earth mosaic of the state. The prints were nine by ten and were in several map-cabinet drawers. Comparing map and photograph indexes, he rummaged through stacks of pictures. When No. 507-52 was at last before us, a shape in black Rorschach, sharply defined, stood out like a mountain lake. The terrain was veiny with clear draws and ridgelines, which made relatively simple the task of re-creating the dark shape on a copy of the Solyo topographic map. To help determine the acreage covered, a Davis geologist gave me a piece of graph paper whose squares were so small that four thousand four hundred and twenty-two of them covered one square mile on the map. Having seen the great pile and moved around it close, I could assign it an average thickness. Jack Waggoner, of Sacramento, who has spent his career as a distributor of tire-retreading and tire-shredding equipment, supplied figures for average densities of tires compressed by their own weight. On its side, a tire occupies about four square feet. A calculator blended these facts. While I had read or been given estimates of eight, nine, fifteen, twenty-five, forty-two, and forty-four, the calculator was reporting that in the world's largest known pile there are thirty-four million tires.

You don't have to stare long at that pile before the thought occurs to you that those tires were once driven upon by the Friends of the Earth. They are not just the used tires of bureaucrats, ballplayers, and litter-strewing rock-deafened ninja-teen-aged nyrds. They are everybody's tires. They are Environmental Defense Fund tires, Rainforest Action Network tires, Wilderness Society tires. They are California Natural Resources Federation tires, Save San Francisco Bay Association tires, Citizens for a Better Environment tires. They are Greenpeace tires, Sierra Club tires, Earth Island Institute tires. They are Earth First! tires! No one is innocent of scrapping those tires. They who carry out what they carry in have not carried out those tires. Of the problem the tire pile represents, everybody is the cause, and the problem, like the pile, has been increasing. (The California Integrated Waste Management Board has referred to the state's "growing tire population.") Most landfills across the country are refusing tires now, because most landfills are filling up, and, moreover, tires "float." They won't stay covered up. They work their way to the surface like glacial rocks. Intended by their manufacturers to be reliable and durable, they most emphatically are. Nothing about an automobile is safer than its tires, whose ultimate irony is that when they reach the end of their intended lives they are all but indestructible. When they are thrown away, they are just as tough as they were when they felt Kick 1. On the surface or underground or on the beds of rivers, they don't decay. They are one per cent of all municipal solid waste and symbol of the other ninety-nine. Locked into the chemistry of each passenger tire is more than two and a half gallons of recoverable petroleum. California by itself discards twenty million tires a year. The United States throws away two hundred and fifty million tires a year. Strewn about the country at last count are something like three billion trashed tires. A hundred and seventy-eight million barrels of oil.

In southern Connecticut, beside a meander bend of the Quinnipiac   5 River, a large privately owned landfill includes a thirty-acre body of water known as the Tire Pond. It was once a quarry, a clay pit. The town line between Hamden and North Haven runs through it. For a decade or so, the tire jockey Joe Farricielli has been tipping tires into the water there. He collects from more than two hundred customers, almost all in Connecticut, who pay him sixty-five cents to take an ordinary tire and as much as five dollars to be rid of a large one. The Tire Pond, now about half full, contains fifteen million tires.

When I made a visit there, the place was managed by Jim Rizzo, vice-president of the Tire Pond. His office was a small brick structure landscaped with young spruce that were standing in the centers of tires. Rizzo was an easy-talking, slightly burly man with a dark and radial mustache, who would not have looked amiss teaching paleontology at Harvard. He was wearing bluejeans and a gray Lacoste pullover. It was an April morning, and out toward the pond we drove in his pickup past trailers newly arrived. Men were grading the tires in them—looking for "high treads," Rizzo said, to be resold. Up the road, the company used to have a retail outlet called Second Time Around. It was not a big success, but they still sell high treads for fifteen dollars at the pond. For California, Mexico is the second time around. California tire jockeys sell more than a million discarded tires in Mexico each year, where they are mounted on Mexicans' cars.

Now Rizzo and I were on a dirt road in what appeared to be a field of dry tires, eye high. There was open water beyond. He said that the tires were protruding above the surface of the pond and were resting on other tires, which went all the way to the bottom. They were standing in water as deep as or deeper than most of the Atlantic Ocean dump sites in the New York bight. In fact, if we were to go down the Quinnipiac and across Long Island Sound and across Long Island to the ocean, we would have to go twenty miles out to sea to find a depth greater than the Tire Pond's. "After the tires get to be five or six feet above water, they are covered with geotextile fabric, and the fabric is then covered with clean fill—concrete, sand, stone, soil—two to three feet thick," Rizzo said. "That is the covering. Everything below that down to the bottom of the pond is tires. That covering is firm. In fact, you and I are now *on* the pond. We are driving on tires."

A large dump truck carrying seven hundred and fifty tires had also driven out upon the pond. It had stopped close to the rubber shoreline. A long stainless hydraulic shaft lifted one end of the bed. Seven hundred and fifty tires slid into the water. They looked like black ice cubes. Rizzo said that when tires are added they do not raise the level of the water. The excess just goes away. A tip is a place where material is dumped, as from wagons. This tip was what was left of the Stiles Brick Company, which in the nineteenth century and on into the twentieth had dug out two hundred thousand cubic yards of clay. The pond was a hundred and forty feet deep. No mosquitoes. No pests. No fires.

Soon after Joe Farricielli bought the landfill, in the middle nineteen-seventies, he experienced a tire fire, and that is what drew his attention to the potentialities of the pond. A tire fire sends off billows of stinking black acidulous smoke, which, drifting downwind full of polynuclear aromatic hydrocarbons, benzene, and other toxic pollutants, attracts the attention of neighbors, zoning boards, and departments of environmental protection. Tire jockeys can recite by heart the roll call of the great fires: Platteville,

Colorado, 1987, where the pile burned for four days; Hagersville, Ontario, 1990, where the pile burned for seventeen days; Palmetto, Georgia, 1992, where the fire burned for five weeks; Winchester, Virginia, 1983–84, where the pile burned continuously for nine months. In the Virginia fire, seven million tires were involved. Tire-pile fires are usually the result of arson. In the pile at Sid's in Norton, Ohio, four fires occurred within six months. Typically, the arsonist fills tires with newspapers. The Tire Pond was beyond the reach of the New Haven *Register,* the Hartford *Courant,* and even the incendiary New York *Times.*

To the Hagersville fire, outside Toronto, in February of 1990, the   10
London Fire Brigade sent an observer. He noted the efficacy of sand and chemicals, and the inadvisability of fighting such fires with water, which augments the toxic spill. Where not much oxygen is involved, a burning tire will decompose into carbon black, gas, and oil. A tire fire oozes oil. If water is used to fight the fire, the oil travels with it. The fluid then contaminates groundwater, surface water, and soil. In Winchester, Virginia, where the tire fire burned for two hundred and seventy-five days, the runoff was collected. It included six hundred and ninety thousand gallons of oil, which was sold for a hundred and eighty-four thousand dollars.

Mosquitoes? A tire that is under water is not breeding mosquitoes. A tire with a little rain in it is a near-perfect mosquito incubator, as any reader of *Mosquito News* or the *Journal of the American Mosquito Control Association* can tell you. Almost any old tire, dumped legally or not, can help disseminate vector-borne viral diseases—for example, La Crosse virus, dengue fever, Sepik fever, Ross River fever, Japanese encephalitis, St. Louis encephalitis. The concern is not just domestic. In the complexities of international economics, the United States annually imports three million used tires. About a quarter of them contain a little water and, often, some mosquito larvae. The tires are, in large part, for recapping and reshipping to other parts of the world, but some are rejected for retreading. They go into scrap heaps, and the mosquitoes stay here. Most of the worn tires that arrive in ships come from Asian countries where *Aedes albopictus* is indigenous—a mosquito that can serve as a viral vector but by nature does not migrate and has a lifetime flight range of less than a thousand yards. In other words, this mosquito goes nowhere on its own. Used tires have dispersed it throughout the Western Hemisphere.

The State of Connecticut has checked the Tire Pond and found no *Aedes albopictus,* Rizzo said. Tires, moreover, are not exactly soluble; they don't affect the water. Since the pond's inception as a tire fill, it has had a water-compliance permit from the Department of Environmental Protection. As if to emphasize the tenor of Rizzo's presentation, two alabaster swans came into view, swimming on the Tire Pond. We were now beyond the filled area and beside the open water. We paused on the pond's eastern shore, on the isthmus that separated it from the Quinnipiac River. The view to the west was multilaminate and somewhat surreal. In the background, against the sky, was a hillside green with shade trees over spread-out suburban homes. The New Haven Country Club was up there somewhere, and Quinnipiac College, and Lake Whitney. The next layer, below, consisted of the light industries of State Street and a lengthy ribbon of a sign that said "Volkswagen, New and Used Cars." The stratum below that was Amtrak—New Haven to the left, Hartford to the right. The bottom layer was the Tire Pond, on its surface the Wagnerian swans, a couple of mallards, a few dozen gulls, and the black-sparkling ice-cube tires drifting about in the wind.

I was growing suspicious of Rizzo. The thought was occurring to me that he and Farricielli had imported the swans. In the bright sun, the birds seemed to blaze white. "We are members of the Audubon Society," Rizzo was saying. "People from Audubon come here to count the birds. Those ducks nest in the tires."

A day or two later, I would talk on the telephone with Milan Bull, director of field studies and ornithology, Connecticut Audubon Society, who said that he always goes to the Tire Pond at Christmas and at one or two other times during the year. "Open spaces attract birds," he explained. "They like the weeds there. Song sparrows, savanna sparrows, brushy-type birds. Meadowlarks. Occasional bobolinks. Open-field birds. Orange-crowned warblers. The Tire Pond is hit regularly during the Christmas count. Maybe two hundred people go there a year. Birds are right in the surface tires. Nests are in the tires—song sparrows', American goldfinches', I guess. We see mallards, pied-billed grebes, wood ducks, the mute swans. Mute swans are an increasing species in Connecticut. There has been a dramatic increase in ten years. There are about four thousand across the state now. The swans don't nest in the Tire Pond, but probably along the Quinnipiac River."

I also met Anne Evans at the Tire Pond. Jack Waggoner, in California, had strongly suggested that I call on her. Born into the tire trade, in Middletown, Connecticut, she had taken charge of her family's business at the age of twenty-two, selling and mounting new tires and paying the Middletown landfill to carry the old ones away. When she was twenty-nine, she had become president of the New England Association of Independent Tire Dealers. But now, at thirty-seven, she had long since given up retailing tires in order to concern herself full time with what might be done to get rid of them—specifically, to develop profitable ways of using them after they have fulfilled their initial purpose. As a convenience to me, she had proposed meeting at the pond to talk tires, and had said that no matter what she might say to me it would not ruffle Jim Rizzo, because he had heard it all before. "The tire industry is really, really, really, really tiny," she had said. "We're a small industry. We all know one another. And we stick together."

Now, on that spring morning, as her dark bright eyes swept over Rizzo's establishment, she said, "At least it's not going to burn." She wore a blue-gray suit over an aquamarine blouse. Her dark glasses, tilted upward, nested in her short black hair. She wore gold earrings, a gold necklace, a sapphire bracelet, and a ring with a diamond as big as a tire. "This place is a blight on the earth," she went on. "They're making a fortune. They bought the clay pit for next to nothing. Their overhead is almost nothing. While other people are spending millions of dollars on equipment for recycling, they've got a hole. The tires will sit in the hole forever. To me it's just something so incredible that thirteen million tires are in a hole and no one cares!"

Someone muttered, "Fifteen million."

"This is the way things went for a long time," she continued. "Tires were just dumped, and no attempt was made to do something with them." The Tire Pond, like the rubber alp in California, had been what she called a "regional solution"—an innovative response to the choking of local land-fills. "I guess this pond is not as bad as a pile of tires in a ravine," she concluded. "On the other hand, tires in a ravine can be removed. These are here for an eternity."

If I wanted to meet an authentic pioneer in doing something about tires, she said, I should go to Baltimore and look up Norman Emanuel. She added reverently, "He mastered the early shredding machines. He sells to energy users. He's done very, very well. And he's still in overalls."

My dialogue with Anne Evans was by no means exhausted, and her widespread insights and personal history would in various ways inform much of the rest of these notes. Meanwhile, I did as I was told. I went to inner Baltimore, just west of Amtrak, and found Bentalou Street, where—seeking, as I was, the preëminent tire shredder of eastern America—I expected to see begrimed industrial structures of the sort that are every-where framed in the begrimed windows of Amtrak. Bentalou was a shade street, though, of maples, sycamores, ash, elms, lindens, flowering cherries. Its row houses had small lawns and covered fieldstone porches—an obvious escalation from the signature marble steps that spill with such perspective symmetry to wide sidewalks of Baltimore. On Bentalou were greening hedges, blossoming azaleas, and, between a cemetery and the railroad tracks, a driveway that led to the Emanuel Tire Company. Mostly open to the sky, it was laid out something like a lumberyard, and Norman Emanuel was off to one side, sitting in his office before a mural map. Hardly a word had passed between us before he sat me down opposite and began to fulminate about officials of the state and the city, not to mention the county. "They haven't found anything that I've done right, but the things I've been doing, they're eliminating that," he said. He was a big beefy dark-haired handsome tan-faced man with the build of a linebacker. He did not look urban, there in the middle of the middle of the city. He looked farm. Direct as he was, he was not always easy to understand. "Burl" equalled "barrel," as in "burl stacking"—the conventional way to stack tires. The form of water that drives turbines was "stame." He wore rubber boots, and his overalls were blue. His shirt was composed of rectan-gular checks of red, yellow, and black. On the forehead of his greenvisored cap was the name of a company in North Carolina that had shown interest in burning Emanuel tire shreds to power machines that chip wood. "We collect three million tires a year," Emanuel continued. "We'd be up to six or eight million now, but the state, they've cut my growth terribly."

It was growth that began in the nineteen-fifties, when he was nineteen years old and, while staying with a relative, found a job in a Baltimore Chevrolet plant. He was from Red Springs, in Robeson County, on the North Carolina coastal plain, where he grew up farming corn, cotton, wheat, and soybeans. In the Chevrolet cafeteria, he overheard a man saying that he had built a house on money he made collecting used tires and selling them for retreads. Norman Emanuel straightaway went to a service station and left with eight old tires. He sold three for three dollars apiece, and the Emanuel Tire Company had shown its first profit. Then he picked up thirty-one more. He sold thirty, and he never looked back.

To his eleven acres in Baltimore he brings tires from Florida, Georgia, South Carolina, North Carolina, Kentucky, Oklahoma, Virginia, West Virginia, Delaware, Pennsylvania, New Jersey, New York, and, of course, Maryland—each tire for a fee. "In 1978, when landfilling was phasing out, I knew I'd have to start making changes," he said. "I was the second person in the United States to have a tire shredder—after Pacific Energy, in Oregon. For a while, I landfilled the shreds."

Outside the office, a shredder was shredding. It was a squarish machine about twelve feet high with a couple of steel ladders and catwalks. Emanuel said, "Go ahead, go up and have a look." Tires were riding a conveyor to the top, and then falling into a hopperlike chamber whose bottom was a pair of rollers with steel teeth. Like the wringer on an old clothes washer, the rollers rolled toward each other, and when a tire fell on them it got caught in the crease. Slowly, quietly, the tire torqued, twisted, writhed—like a snake caught up in a combine, attacked by the steel teeth, squeezed, folded, crushed, chopped, in a few seconds torn to shreds. (At a tire-shredding operation in Sacramento, not long ago, an employee was shredded on his first day of work. For a time, no one missed him. He had left the machine in half-inch cubes.) Emanuel Tire has fourteen shredders, which make two-inch chips and smaller grades, on down to a quarter of an inch. Steel belt wire, like fish bones, protruded from the chips. The most concentrated steel in a tire is in the beads—the two hoops of cable in the rim-touching sides. Emanuel picked up a truck tire, put it on his debeader, and sliced out a bead. The hoop's braided steel was an inch in diameter.

Up the street in another lot were a couple of acres of shredded tires—plains and hills of shredded tires, a terrain that felt underfoot like a well-filled waterbed. To achieve such resiliency, all tires still contain some natural rubber. A big orthopterous machine—its narrow discharge conveyors reaching out like antennae—was chewing chopped tires and spewing product in three directions, forming conical mounds: chips fell to the left, steel forward, crumbs to the right. The chips were one-inch bits of tire. In a couple of days, the machine had piled up thirty tons of steel. Gesturing toward a modest mound of crumbs—a rubber drumlin not much higher than our heads—Emanuel said it represented ten thousand tires. It consisted of quarter-inch bits that felt in the hand like granola.

Emanuel's business has evolved so far away from landfills that nowadays, on principle, he said, he would sell shreds at a loss, if he had to, rather than put them in the ground. Over time, he has developed a roster of customers that is as varied as it is far-flung. He is reluctant to reveal who and where they are, but he will say that some of them are as far away from Baltimore as are St. Louis, Indianapolis, and Chicago. In some instances, he is more specific. He let it drop that the University of Virginia wanted forty tons of quarter-inch material for playing surfaces. For more than a decade, a rubber company in Trenton, New Jersey, had been making boots and gloves from shredded Emanuel tires. A good deal of crumb rubber goes for something he calls "reclaim," accenting the first syllable: running tracks, rubberized asphalt, railroad crossings.

In 1982, he began shipping shredded rubber to Spring Grove, Pennsylvania, for use as boiler fuel at a paper mill. Other paper mills followed, and now about a third of Emanuel's product "goes to burn for energy." One automobile tire, burning, will release about two hundred and fifty thousand British thermal units of energy—enough to heat fourteen hundred pounds of ice water to a boil. A tire contains considerably more energy than an equivalent weight of bituminous coal. United States paper mills, cement plants, and five hundred power plants currently burn bituminous coal. According to the California Integrated Waste Management Board, tires produce less ash and contain less sulphur than many commonly used types of coal, and with "no significant differences in emissions."

It has crossed Norman Emanuel's mind that he could keep the rubber he shreds and make use of it himself. He dreams sometimes of his own 1.5-megawatt power plant, and also of his own vegetable cannery, using "tires as fuel to make that stame." He says, "I see now that I could be almost self-sufficient."

He has in his stockpiles at any given time, in addition to shredded material, more than five hundred thousand tires graded to be sold for use on the road. Of the three million discarded tires that he annually collects, about seven hundred and fifty thousand are in good to excellent condition. One of his warehouses was half again as large as a football field. It was filled with tires that, by and large, were not burl stacked, one upon another, but densely laced, cross-bedded, adroitly assembled in converging angles by a method he called windrowing. The great room was as clean and tidy as a yarn shop.

"I hate a mess," he said. "I hate dirt."

On an amazing percentage of the inventory the treads were so high that the tires seemed new. He exports them all over the world. He sent a hundred thousand tires to Russia last year.

"Russia's a good market but you can't get no money."

Trade is brisk right there on Bentalou, where Baltimore bluebloods often cluster.

"People with Mercedes, people with Jaguars come here to buy tires. I mean, the economy's in bad shape."

His tall slender wife, Dafene, who is also from Robeson County, North Carolina, runs the office. She tries to keep up with the proliferating regulations that inhibit and threaten their business, and she appears to be a good deal cooler than he. A new state law limits them to fifteen thousand cubic feet of inventory, or about five truckloads of shredded material—the practical equivalent of nothing in a nation that throws away two hundred and fifty million tires a year and has about as many Norman Emanuels as congressmen from Alaska. Constricting regulations are what caused him to say, "They haven't found anything that I've done right, but the things I've been doing, they're eliminating that." He likes to let tire chips sit in weather for two to three years, so that oxidation will remove protruding steel—a process too passive to survive regulation. To date, he and Dafene have paid three hundred thousand dollars in legal fees in their effort to come to terms with the state. "The thing is simple: What can you do with tires? Landfill them or shred them. Why does the state want it gone from the face of the earth?" he asks, evidently asserting that the state wants the tires and the shreds to vanish but is not practically considering how that might happen. He grumbles that Texas and North Carolina are the only states that don't create problems for people who collect tires. He summarizes Maryland as follows: "The state says you've got to take tires to an approved place, but there's no place they approve. The State of Maryland, they stuff all their stuff into other states they can." He continues, "Everybody in this country is worried about a vote instead of doing what's right. They've forgot the difference between right and wrong. When I'm dead, everybody will know that I made a difference in solving this tire problem. I'll make it happen. You only live once in your life."

Aerial crop dusters use burning tires as wind socks. To attract fish, tires are piled in oceans as artificial reefs. Tires are amassed around harbors as porous breakwaters. In Guilford, Connecticut, Sally Richards grows mussels on tires. Tires are used on dairy farms to cover the tarps that cover silage. They stabilize the shoulders of highways, the slopes of drainage canals. They are set up as crash barriers, dock bumpers, fences, and playground tunnels and swings. At Churchill Downs, the paving blocks of the paddock are made of scrap tires. Used tires are used to fashion silent stairs. They weigh down ocean dragnets. They become airplane shock absorbers. They become sandals. Crumbed and granulated tires become mud flaps, hockey pucks, running tracks, carpet padding, and office-floor anti-fatigue mats. Australians make crumb rubber by freezing and then crushing tire chips. Japanese have laid railroad track on crumbed tires. Dirt racetracks seeded with crumbed tires are easier on horses. Crumbed tires added to soil will increase porosity and allow more oxygen to reach down to grass

35

roots. Twelve thousand crumbed tires will treat one football field. In Colorado, corn was planted in soil that had been laced with crumbed tires. The corn developed large, strong roots. A mighty windstorm came and went, and the tire-treated field was the only corn left standing in that part of Colorado. All such uses, though, as imaginative and practical as they may be, draw down such a small fraction of the tires annually piled as scrap that while they address the problem they essentially do not affect it.

Retreads don't help much, either, in holding down the national pile, although Air Force One lands on retreads, the jets of the Blue Angels land on retreads, and when H. Norman Schwarzkopf touched down in Saudi Arabia he touched down on retreads. Almost all commercial airliners roll on retreaded tires. Most buses—including school buses—and most taxis are on retreads, and so are ten thousand Frito-Lay trucks and thirty-six thousand U.P.S. trucks. A company sensitive to costs per mile will retread its casings three times. A retread is in no way inferior to a new tire, but new tires are affordable, and the retreaded passenger tire has descended to the status of a clip-on tie. Not long ago, twenty-four million passenger tires were retreaded every year, but the number has declined nearly seventy per cent, swelling the volume of discards. Pilot plants have been erected to decompose tires through pyrolysis (destructive distillation, thermal degradation) in an attempt to recycle some of the fifteen million barrels of oil that are thrown away in tires in the United States each year. The process has not shown a profit. Tire chips go into rubber-modified asphalt concrete. RUMAC, as it is known, absorbs more heat than other surfaces do, gets rid of ice and snow, reduces glare, and makes a quiet road, a resilient road, a deformation-resistant road. A mile of RUMAC thirty-six feet wide and three inches thick uses sixteen thousand tires. The road lasts twice as long as ordinary asphalt. But ordinary asphalt is recycled, and that is hard to do if there is rubber in it. Few miles of American road are RUMAC.

When Jack Waggoner, of Sacramento, first wrote to me about the great tire pile of California, he mentioned that all the scrap tires now strewn about the American landscape would make a stack a hundred and forty-two thousand miles high. If you want to get rid of something like that, you don't try to do it by making lacrosse balls. The technological need is for consumption of old whole tires in a major useful way, and that, he said, was now going on at the big pile. Waggoner is an easygoing, ocean-fishing man in his fifties who has been in some aspect of the tire business all his adult life. In 1957, he was working in a Flying A service station in Lodi, near Stockton, when a customer said to him, "You do a hell of a job washing windshields. Come to work for me." The customer was impressive. Suit, tie, vest, hat, furled umbrella, he "looked like he should be calling on heads of state," but he was actually the sales manager of Super Mold, the largest manufacturer of tire-retreading machinery in the world. For years, Waggoner's territory included Japan, the Philippines, Indonesia, Ceylon, and islands of the South Pacific. He was "real heavy into Vietnam," where eight hundred truck tires were retreaded every day.

Eventually, he started his own company, and when the retread business declined he augmented sales by distributing shredders. Driving south on I-5 toward the big pile, he said, "Once you get rubber in your veins, you can never get it out." I asked him why he, a purveyor of shredding machines, was interested in whole-tire recycling. He said, "Because it's the right thing to do."

On a dirt road behind a truck stop, we soon came to a guardhouse and a platinum-haired security man in a black leather jacket with a huge silver star. Waggoner was grata. No cameras allowed. We made our way into the range. On the hilltop opposite the tires was an electric plant with two Standardkessel boilers and a fueling technology of German design— taller than it was broad, like a castle by the Neckar or the Rhine. From the bottom of the valley rose a moving conveyor at least four hundred feet long. Tires were riding upward, and we climbed five stories of steel steps to watch them arrive. Producing stame, the structure was now and again fogged by its own swirling cloud, which blew off and revealed the creased hills. At the top of the conveyor was a carrousel that accepted the tires, carried them around, and watched them with electric eyes. When air-lock chambers were ready to receive them, fingers of steel came up through the carrousel and shoved them to one side. They went into the air-lock chambers, and then fell to a reciprocating grate—a nickel-chromium stoker grate—which looked something like a stairway, with accordion steps that contracted and expanded and advanced the tire toward the core of conflagration. You could watch this through a window, two inches in diameter. Scarcely had a new tire landed on the grate when—count one, count two—it burst into wild flame, at upward of twenty-five hundred degrees. At the far side of the fire chamber, where the fuel compacted and the heat was most intense, a peephole looked in at the climax of the burning. What appeared there resembled the cliff-like snout of a glacier, white in a bath of auroran red, with white particulate flying like snow, and lumps and bumps and moguls.

The plant was supplying enough power to Pacific Gas & Electric to fulfill the daily requirements of fifteen thousand homes. Among dedicated waste-to-energy fuels, tires have two to three times as many B.T.U.s as municipal solid waste, refuse-derived fuel, or biomass. Generally operating around the clock, the plant was burning seventeen thousand tires a day. It burns five million tires a year.

Filbin the Tire Jockey—having been paid, say, an average of a quarter 40 of a dollar for collecting each of the many millions of tires he had stored here—was now selling them to the Oxford Energy Company, owners of the plant, for slightly more. Doug Tomison, Oxford's plant manager, mentioned "a royalty arrangement on a sliding scale," and the scale had to do with how many million tires were in the great pile. Tomison's rough estimate came in one digit. Tomison was a young handsome dark-haired man on crutches. All in four weeks, he had hit a school bus with his motorcycle, a bee had stung him on the motorcycle, and a cow had kicked him off it, too. But that level of misfortune was painless compared with the kicking he was getting from the tire jockey. "He's killing us," Tomison said. "We're making a profit and giving it to him." By burning whole tires, the company saves a shredding cost of twenty-five dollars a ton, but not even that can turn the thing around. Oxford was paying Filbin over a million dollars a year.

Oxford Energy has been described by Anne Evans as "four or five guys with an idea," and at one point she was one of the guys. As a director of the National Tire Dealers and Retreaders Association, she encouraged Oxford from the beginning. They hired her as a consultant. In Sterling, Connecticut, Oxford has a plant that consumes more tires than the one in California. These are the only power plants in the United States that burn whole tires. By 1995, Oxford hopes to have four plants on line, annually consuming thirty-one million tires. The California plant was dedicated in 1987. On a wall in its trailer-office is a framed citation featuring a large letter "E": "1988 Environmental Protection Award for outstanding achievement by industry in the protection of our natural environment. Awarded by Power Magazine to Oxford Energy Company, Modesto, California. The E stands for environment and is a symbol of concern for the purity of our nation's air and water." And next to that is a 1988 United States Department of Energy "Special Award for Energy Innovation. . . . Presented to the Oxford Energy Company in recognition of a significant contribution to our nation's energy efficiency."

The Attorney General of California has shown professional interest in the tire pile. One of many considerations is that if a smoldering fire were to spread far through it a river of oil would go out of the hills and into the California Aqueduct. Los Angeles' femoral artery, the California Aqueduct is close by Interstate 5, a few thousand yards from the tires and three hundred feet below them. Looking across the valley, we could see in the rolling black dunes tiny figures moving. They were people, carrying tires. One tire at a time, the people were shifting tens of thousands of tires—by hand, the only way to do it—creating fire lanes to satisfy the government.

In the power-plant compound, the second-largest structure was the bag house, full of Gore-Tex bags hung up like balloons. They remove fine ash down to three microns. Burning tires emit nitrogen and sulphur oxides (known as Nox and Sox), carbon monoxide, particulate matter, hydrocarbons, arsenic, cadmium, chromium, lead, zinc, dioxins and furans, polycyclic aromatic hydrocarbons, polychlorinated biphenyls, and benzene. These pollutants are also emitted by coal. About seventy-five per cent of the ash is a rocklike slag of ferrous oxide, which falls into a hopper with a steel-belted thud and hardly requires a filter. A process called Thermal DeNox deals with nitrogen oxides. There is a limestone-slurry spray scrubber to remove sulphur. The fly ash is largely zinc, which is the major pollutant, and it is trapped in the Gore-Tex bags. Computers by the roomful operate the machines. The pollution-control equipment cost Oxford seven million dollars. Well over half of the Nox gets away. Of the Sox, two per cent escapes, as do smaller amounts of carbon monoxide.

As the limestone slurry reacts with the sulphur dioxide, gypsum results—as much as twelve tons a day. Gypsum can be used as a "soil amendment." Farmers buy it all. Zinc is recovered as zinc. The iron oxide, for the most part, is stored, looking for a customer, but some is sold as gravel for use in cement.

The country over-all would do well to burn whole tires in making cement. Flanking Interstate 5 near Redding—two hundred miles north of Filbin's pile—are a limestone quarry and a cement plant. Powdered limestone and shale are fed into a cylindrical precalcining furnace—a ten-story tower—up the side of which runs a chain-conveyor with steel hooks. From each hook hangs a tire. The tires enter from chutes about halfway up the tower, and, as they drop, flash in fire. The mixture of stone and burning tires moves on into a huge revolving drum that is slightly inclined from the horizontal, spins two times a minute, and extends more than two hundred yards. The Fahrenheit temperature rises within it to twenty-six hundred degrees. As the rock, revolving, roasts, the tires supply not only heat but also the iron oxide indispensable to cement. The ash residue of the tires becomes a part of the chemistry of the cement. The tires disappear absolutely. Their steel is completely oxidized. The heat causes the limestone's calcium carbonate and carbon dioxide to separate, leaving calcium oxide, or quicklime. Then quicklime reacts with silica and alumina (in the shale) to form calcium silicates and aluminates, which leave the kiln as clinker in pieces the size of eggs. The clinker is ground with gypsum, and that is cement. No ash, no slag. In Germany and Japan, about twenty per cent of the fuel for cement plants is whole tires. The kiln in Redding—at the Calaveras Cement Company—consumes more than two hundred tires an hour. It has a bag house and other state-of-the-art pollution-control equipment. California has eleven cement plants, ten of which are close to cities, where the tires are. Those eleven plants could consume all of the twenty million tires annually discarded in California and dispose of five million additional tires as well. California cement plants require thirty-four trillion B.T.U.s a year, and ninety per cent of that energy is supplied by coal. In words of the California Integrated Waste Management Board, "The cement manufacturing industry could use all of the waste tires generated in the state as well as the existing stockpiles. . . . From an energy perspective, use of tires as a supplemental fuel in cement kilns displaces fossil fuels and results in no wastes and no significant differences in emissions." A cement plant near Santa Cruz applied for a permit to use tires but gave up because of the cost of fighting environmentalists. Cement plants alone could solve the scrap-tire dilemma. There are enough cement plants in the United States to use three billion tires a year.

In 1989, Anne Evans was invited by Great Britain's Department of Trade and Industry to develop in England a dedicated waste-to-energy

45

tire-burning power plant like the one in California. She was thirty-three years old then. While still in her twenties, she had started a tire export-import business that operated in many countries around the world, including England, and her profits were very large. Always—in a shifting, chronic manner—tires became overstocked or understocked in this place and that. What she did was move them from supply to demand, meanwhile watching currency fluctuations, which she rode like thermals. "If you work very hard at that and don't get a lot of sleep, and if you understand letters of credit, you do very well," she told me. "The idea is to close a deal within twenty-four hours. You make a good relationship with a freight forwarder, and your life gets very simple. Be honest. Do a good job. Don't be greedy. And you'll do well."

Her distributors were involved not only with new tires but with old ones, and the problem of how to dispose of the old ones was everywhere increasing. She remembers her grandfather saying, "He who figures out what to do with these tires is going to make a million"—her grandfather Tony DiGiandomenico, who started the family's Firestone dealership and retreading company in Middletown. Her father, Mario Salemi, had rubber in his veins, too. His parents, and Tony DiGiandomenico's mother, came from Melilli, near Syracuse, in Sicily, as did so many other citizens of Middletown that they built an exact copy of Melilli's ornate and gilded Church of San Sebastiano. To this day, almost anybody from Middletown can cash a personal check in Melilli. It may be a little easier if your name is DiGiandomenico. Anne, at twenty-two and with scarcely any more business training than any other recent product of Newton College of the Sacred Heart, was working in Washington for the National Republican Congressional Campaign Committee when her father fell ill and she went home to take over the tires.

Now she commutes from Connecticut, where her husband is a real-estate broker, to Wolverhampton, in the West Midlands, home of her Elm Energy & Recycling. Wolverhampton is twelve miles from Birmingham. The plant occupies six acres, surrounded by quiet streets and private sub-urban homes. Except for its exhaust stack, it is an unobtrusive ground-hugging structure, in which tires are not stockpiled but arrive instead in a continuous stream of lorries. Michelin, Pirelli, Goodyear, Dunlop—all the big tire companies operate their own retail stores in England. They will pay the haulers, who, in turn, will pay Elm. All their waste tires will go to Wolverhampton. The plant is capable of producing thirty megawatts, but will sell no more than twenty-five. The rest of the power is needed to run the anti-pollution equipment. The site was dedicated in a tent in April of 1992, in ceremonies overhung by chandeliers and enriched by a cello. The pneumatic Michelin man was outside, the chairman of Pirelli was inside. The plant will soon be receiving twenty-five per cent of all tires discarded in the United Kingdom.

"We are the cleanest power station in England," she told me when we talked in Connecticut. "We're green. We're the best thing since peanut butter." She was obviously undaunted by her discovery that, as she put it, "the English are not receptive to women." She said, "There might as well be a sign at Heathrow: 'If you are a woman doing business, go home.'"

She went on to say, "Energy is a good thing for tires. Landfilling   50
should not happen. That's a total waste—of land, of material. But energy may be just another step in the evolution." She thinks that tires themselves will change. She imagines them somehow being made differently, so that the disposal problem will take care of itself. "Tires will change as cars change. Now they hold the shock. That may be put somewhere else. Tires may be different. A different material. Who knows what?" Meanwhile, she was much impressed by a research scientist for a German tire company who studied tires-to-energy and said, "Maybe we can take something out of the tire to make it easier to burn."

"The consumer has got to be willing to pay mandated disposal fees," she concluded. "It costs money to do it right. Every bit of material should be used to its fullest extent. A tire in its first life is a tire. It needs to be used for something further. Unless we do that, we're wasteful. The reality of life is that we can't afford to be wasteful anymore. Let's do something else with this material when we're finished with it, and we'll be in good shape in the next generation. That takes an industrial commitment. It's not a legislative matter. You can't legislate people to feel a certain way. It's got to be in them to say, 'We've got to do this as a society.' When governments raise tipping fees, illegal dumping rises. In England, when someone takes tires away for fifteen pence a tire and dumps them in a vacant lot, it is known as fly tipping. That is why there is a law in England called Duty of Care: you need a waste-management license; you have to know exactly what happens to your waste. The tire stores have to know."

"Do we have such a law?"

"Of course not."

Reading and Responding

In a short freewrite, brainstorm a local environmental problem—perhaps having to do with waste disposal or recycling—that you would be interested in investigating.

Working Together

1. Discuss the ending of the article. Why does McPhee end it like this?
2. What is McPhee's main point in this article? When you do know what his main point is? How does he make that point—with what descriptive details or explicit statements? How many explicit statements does McPhee actually make? In the absence of explicit statements, how do you know what McPhee wants you to think about this subject or what his aim in writing is?

3. Analyze the various kinds of knowledge that McPhee draws on for his article. Think about the various majors and degree programs on your campus. How many of them can you find represented in this selection? List them and jot down a brief explanation for each.
4. Form a research team of three to five students.

- Share possible research topics. Decide on one.
- Divide the research responsibilities among you: one person for interviews, one person for library research, and so on; or one person to interview a particular expert, another to interview another expert, and so on. Distribute the work equally.
- Decide, as a group, how you want to record and share your information: notebooks, reports, index cards.
- Set a schedule.
- Meet and discuss your research and the organization of your papers.

Rethinking and Rewriting

1. Drawing on the information from your research group, write your own paper with the title "Duty of Care." Imitate the style and form of McPhee's article.
2. Working with the other members of your group, write a collaborative paper entitled "Duty of Care," pooling not just your research but also your writing and revising. Submit the paper as a group.
3. Write a personal essay with the title "Duty of Care." This piece may or may not focus on an environmental issue. (It might, for example, be about the act of writing.)
4. Write a letter to the editor of your local or school newspaper arguing that old tires in your area should be recycled or disposed of in one of the ways McPhee describes.
5. At one point, McPhee says, "They are everybody's tires." Write an essay that speaks about some other ecological situation as "everybody's"— everybody's air, everybody's water, everybody's soil. With this new view in mind, discuss how this notion of shared responsibility and shared ownership might change some aspect of your immediate life—how you or your family cares for your own house, or how your institution cares for its campus.

"SHEPHERDS OF THE LABRADOR FRONT"

Paul Watson

At sixteen Paul Watson ran away from his home in New Brunswick, Canada, first riding the rails to Vancouver and then becoming a merchant seaman. In his early twenties he helped form the environmental action group Greenpeace and led many of their early expeditions to interfere with Soviet and Japanese whaling, piloting small rubber rafts between the whales and the harpooners and even ramming a whaling ship with his own boat, The Sea Shepherd. *In 1973 he also joined Native Americans in Wounded Knee, South Dakota, in their armed resistance to government forces. No longer convinced that nonviolent action is always effective in the protection of the environment, Watson left Greenpeace in the late 1970s to form his own group, The Sea Shepherd Society. With the help of journalist Warren Rogers he published his life story in* Sea Shepherd: My Fight for Whales and Seals *(1982); with fellow activist Robert Hunter he wrote a second book,* Cry Wolf! *(1985), about his fight to save the North American wolf. The following piece, first published in* Greenpeace Chronicles, *describes one of Watson's adventures on the high seas.*

Before and As You Read

1. Before you start reading this piece, write down everything you know or have heard about the Greenpeace Foundation. Write down everything you know or have heard about the killing of baby seals and the efforts of Greenpeace and others to stop that killing. What are your biases and feelings before you start reading?
2. Preread this selection. Write two or three sentences noting what you find, and make the last one a direction to yourself about how to read this piece effectively.
3. As you read, mark any passages that confirm your expectations or that surprise you.

Monday morning March 15th. The first day of the seal kill. Our two helicopters lift off from the frozen lichen encrusted barrens of Belle Isle, a lonely forsaken chunk of rock between the island province of Newfoundland and the cold rocky coastline of Labrador. We have made of the island an advance base in order to extend our air range over the ice and sea.

On a north easterly course, the vast expanse of salt ice sweeps by a thousand feet beneath us. Within twenty minutes two ships are spotted. The Norwegian owned Canadian registered sealing vessels, "Martin Karlsen" and "Theron." Plunging through the ice, not yet to the whelping grounds.

We change course following the headings of the ships below, rapidly leaving them behind.

Upon the horizon a black speck appears, then another and another. The fleet with eight ships lies before us.

As the ships loom larger their activity is obvious. No longer a blinding white the ice is flowing crimson in blood. Long gashing streams of seal blood, babies blood, coming from all directions and converging into a grotesque pile-up of carcasses. A constellation of scarlet stars tortuously stained into the hard bluish white of granite hard pack ice.

We circle. We land. Two miles from the nearest ship. It will be a long walk. In an effort to halt our protest, the Canadian Ministry of Fisheries passed a series of new regulations aimed specifically at stopping the intended actions of the Greenpeace Foundation. Our present legal barrier being that no aircraft without the permission of the minister of state for fisheries shall fly lower than 2000 feet over or land less than one half mile from any seal.

The new regulations were incredible. In a rather strange Orwellian way, they were referred to by the government as amendments to the Seal Protection Act. The Federal Minister of Fisheries M. Romeo Le blanc had vowed to stop us. By way of an order in council he achieved the means. He would simply have us arrested. It did not matter to him that Canada has no jurisdiction in International waters. He simply assumed jurisdiction. The Canadian government supported him. Other nations said nothing.

Earlier we had planned to disrupt the hunt by arming ourselves with spray cans containing a green organic dye. Our intention was to destroy the commercial value of the seal pelt by applying an irremoveable green cross to each and every baby whitecoat. It was a good tactic, one that attracted much publicity and cries of outrage from the Fisheries department. The plan did however have one basic flaw, we should have kept it secret. Little did we dream that in Canada, "the true north strong and free," that our government would fabricate special laws to stop us, laws that became effective only days before we could put into effect a plan perfectly legal at its inception.

The government had in addition spread false information to the effect that Greenpeace would kill the seals with the dye. Natural predators would find them, their mothers would reject them, they would freeze to death were among the charges they used to justify the new improved Seal Protection Act. Their own research had employed dyes for twenty years. Federal Fisheries Scientists like Dr. H. Dean Fisher and Dr. David Sergeant had advised us that such was the case and the dye would not harm the seals. The only predators were humans and an occasional Orca. The first predator being unnatural, the second a mammal that locates its prey by other means than sight.

When we arrived in Newfoundland we were greeted by open hostility from the people and the media of that province. We were greeted by the Federal leader of the New Democratic Party who denounced us nationally. We entered Newfoundland at Port aux Basques without the support of any political party and without public or media resistance to the new laws brought down in a dictatorial manner.

We were faced with the fact that if we employed the dye we would immediately be apprehended for a violation of a Federal Fishery Regulation. Our dye would be confiscated, our helicopters seized. The seals would have continued to die. We believe that we made the best possible decision under the circumstances. In fact rather than surrendering, we decided to employ a different tactic. The government had succeeded in turning the majority of the people of Newfoundland against us. We made an attempt to cut off that support and we were successful. We gave up our dyeing plans, asked for and received the support and endorsement of the 9000 member Newfoundland Fisherman, Food and Allied Workers Union. We appealed to the fisherman in the name of conservation, a cause that fishermen are generally sympathetic to. The fact is that the commercial fleets owned by Norwegian companies are wiping out the seal herds. The fact is that the Norwegians destroyed three great herds of seals prior to starting on the Labrador herds in 1947. The fact is that the commercial fleets take only the pelts, leaving the meat on the ice, while the fishermen and Eskimo of Newfoundland and Labrador do eat the meat. With a conservation stand the seals could have a chance. The fishermen are now exerting pressure on the Fisheries to stop the hunt. We siezed the opportunity to grasp a stronger tactic at the cost of sacrificing a weaker now illegal tactic.

On the ice with us now are Newfoundlanders. Across the drifting floes, our crew heads in the direction of the nearest ship. The ice is treacherous and difficult to cross. Baby seals are all around us, beautiful beyond expectation, each a personification of new born perfection. Chubby little bundles of soft white fur, large tear-filled ebony eyes and a cry practically indistinguishable from its human counterpart.

Ahead, the crying is giving way to frightened screaming and the irregular whack and thud of the seal slayer's club.

Norwegians clutching vicious looking hak-a-piks are dispatching the pups in a manner coldly efficient. The ominous hak-a-pik, a club with a dull iron spike on the end, lifts and falls. Each time it descends a vision of innocence is horribly deprived of life, expiring painfully and in many cases slowly.

The Norwegians swear at us. They threaten us. But they do little   15
else. They have been thoroughly lectured. Al Johnson blocks the path of a burly Norwegian, he falls over the sealers intended victim, shielding its little body with his own. The sealers turn away. He approaches another innocent victim. David Garrick cuts him off. Frustrated the sealer returns to his ship.

I pick up a small pup from the ice. Behind me the vessel "Melshorn" rips her way through the ice towards the pup and myself. Each year thousands of seals are crushed by the ships, their numbers not included in the quotas.

With the surprisingly heavy white bundle in my arms, I run to avoid the rampaging steel bow. We are soon safe the baby and I. Finding an isolated area with no sealers about, we part.

It is not a parting without effect. It is now no longer simply a protest of principle on my part. It has suddenly become personal. I had saved that particular pup's life, held its warm body against my own, carried it in my arms.

On all our faces, the tears and the pain of frustrations are obvious. We do all we can and then retreat to our aircraft before dusk descends. Over our heads a Fisheries helicopter and an airplane buzz us and the seals, flying as low as fifty feet overhead.

Friday, March 19th

For three days we have been grounded. An emerging blizzard had   20
heralded the morning of the 16th. We hurriedly evacuated our base camp at Belle Isle. The winds at that time gusted to 40 mph. Returning to the town of St. Anthony we patiently waited out the natural obstacle. Friday, this morning brought calm winds, clear visibility and a rude surprise on return to Belle Isle. Our tents, our personal effects and our equipment had been swept off the island by the storm and out to sea.

Once more, we fly across the floes, now mangled with rafting ice and leads spanning meters of inky black insurpassable North Atlantic chop.

We have chosen a course some thirty miles southward from our last encounter. Instinct is our guide. The position of the sealing fleet is known only to the Fisheries department, a department with a habit of withholding its information.

It was a shot in the dark but it paid off. After eighty miles the fleet once more lay before us. We land. We walk. We encounter a group of Canadian sealers. I try to talk with them but find it unnerving. The man that I'm addressing holds a seal-skinning knife poised a mere three inches from my belly. The knife drips blood. His face and hands are encrusted with the rusty redness of dried blood.

The sealers have been advised by the fisheries officers to not kill seals if any cameras are in the area. They stop and stand around. All about us at a distance other sealers are going about the bloody trade.

Walking on, I find another sealer. Beneath his feet a pup lies slashed   25
open from throat to hind flippers. The heart is exposed expelling steam into the frigid air. The heart still beats weakly.

"Are you proud of your handiwork?" I ask him.

"No bye," a Newfoundlander by his accent, "naught proud t'all, it be me furst year a swiling, I hav nay hart fer it."

This sealer now tells us that he will kill no more seals. He is the only one, the others continue. There are so many of them, so few of us. Another course of action is needed. Perhaps we can stop the ships from moving through the ice. We move across the ice towards an oncoming sealing vessel.

Bob Hunter and myself find a seal twenty feet before the monstrous scarlet ice crushing bow of the "Arctic Endeavor." We hold our position with our backs to the ship.

On the starboard side of the vessel, a crewman is busily attaching and securing winch lines to a bundle of blood soaked pelts. He yells out to us, "Ya betta move b'yes, the ole man a 'int one ta tink twice bout running ya inta the ice."

Bob yells back, "Tell the old bastard to do what he wants, we're not moving."

The ship backs away. We think we've won this round. Then the unexpected. The "Arctic Endeavor" plunges forward picking up speed. Still we look ahead. We feel her coming. We hear her coming. The vibrations of the powerful diesel engines disturb the chilly air and tingle the soles of our feet through our boots. The ice trembles and cracks. Blocks of chunky ice tumble forward before the bow and nudge our feet.

The crewman on the ice screams to the ship's bridge. We can make out his words clearly, "Stop er Cap, stop er, the stupid asses ain't a moving."

The engines are cut and reversed. The ship slowly grinds to a halt, five feet behind our backs.

I pick up the baby whitecoat to remove it to safety. My way is blocked by a uniformed fisheries officer. He takes my picture. He pulls some papers from his pocket and begins to read me the amendments to the Seal Protection Act. "Section 21(B) states that it is a Federal offense to remove a seal from one location to another, it is an offense to pick a live seal up from the ice, you are in violation of this regulation."

Incredibly I listen to this man charged with enforcing the Seal Protection Act. "Do you mean to tell me" I ask, "that I'm supposed to leave this baby to be crushed by that ship."

"That's no business of yours," he replies, "the law is the law, I don't make the laws, I just have to enforce them." He leaves me no choice, I ignore the law, I ignore him and carry the seal to safety. I am still amazed that the government of Canada can presume to have jurisdiction within International waters. But the government is the government and the cards both financial and legal are stacked in favour of the Fisheries Ministry.

Once again the approaching evening forces us to retreat to the land. One of our helicopters, low on fuel, battles the strong head winds and just manages to make it back to base with seven gallons of fuel to spare. Captain Jack Wallace tells us that he has never cut it so close in terms of fuel.

Saturday, March 20th

The coldest morning yet. We find the fleet again. The same ships as yesterday. We circle the fleet at 2500 feet, searching for a place where we can land without violating the regulations. After twenty five minutes in the air, we locate a spot. There's not a seal in sight.

As we begin to descend, we are approached by three Fisheries helicopters. They have been waiting for us. We land. They land. An officer approaches our pilot and informs him that he is in violation of the regulation. He claims we flew lower than 2000 feet and that we are presently only a quarter of a mile from a seal. When we inquire as to the location of this seal we are told that it was on the ice when we landed, but that it has now gone back into the water.

The officers are not interested in arguing, they tell us that their word is final. We are told that our helicopters will be seized when we return to base. Too bad, but the law is the law, they tell us.

We leave our pilots to hassle out the regulations with the Fisheries officers. Our crew sets off across the ice in pursuit of the sealers.

We are now about a mile behind and in the wake of the ship "Arctic Explorer." The ship and her crew of deep-sea butchers have left a source of horrific desolation. We follow the edges of the lead opened up by the ship.

We pass hundreds of slaughtered corpses, the skin stripped from their little bodies. The glazed unseeing eyes are hauntingly disturbing us. In many places the bluish white of the snow and ice has all but disappeared under a coating of crimson. The ice is pitted by the heat of the blood as it spilled from the bodies, melted into the floe, coagulated and frozen in puddles.

We approach closer to the ship, greeted occasionally by a single sad-   45
eyed baby survivor. The survivors whimper and attempt to hide their heads in the snow. The ship looms larger.

As we close in, the weather takes a turn. An instant whiteout. Our helicopters come roaring over the ice to pick us up. The Fisheries officers granted them permission to rescue us. The first helicopter lands. Four crew members jump aboard and the aircraft ascends and speeds across the ice headed toward land. The rest of us jump aboard the second machine. The blizzard becomes more dense, more intense. The wind currents thrash us around. As last the welcome cliffs of Newfoundland are in sight.

Ottawa

Saturday, March 20th was the last day we saw the sealing fleets. We could have located the ships on the 21st and the 22nd, but the Fisheries Department had placed a Royal Canadian Mounted Police guard around our machines and grounded them until our pilots could appear before a magistrate on Tuesday morning.

We paid a bond of $10,000 on each helicopter. A trial date was set for May 18th, and the aircraft were free.

Both helicopters took to the sky before noon on Tuesday. We searched for four hours and found nothing. When we returned to St. Anthony for the last time, the superintendent for fisheries told us that he knew before we left that the fleet would be out of range. We had done all that we were physically capable of doing. We were tired and we had more work to do in Ottawa.

Friday, March 26th. The National Press Building across from the   50
Houses of Parliament. A press conference. The Minister of State for Fish-

eries is invited. He sends two representatives in his stead. He sends Dr. Arthur May, the Director General of the Resource Branch of the Marine and Fisheries Division of the Ministry of Fisheries and Charles Friend, a public relations official to the Fisheries Department.

Dr. May accuses Greenpeace of not doing their homework, and says that the information in regards to harp and hood seal stocks has always been available to the public. Greenpeace states that this is not true. Many requests for information were made, even from the Minister himself. All requests were denied.

Greenpeace ecologist Dr. Patrick Moore presents a statement to the press and the government officials in attendance. The statement reads:

"The Greenpeace Foundation has found that the Minister of Fisheries and his officers have acted in a manner that is unfitting to persons who have been charged with the responsibility of conserving our natural resources. The policy of the Department of Fisheries has consistently discriminated against the interests of Canadians and in favour of foreign commercial interests. They have misled and misinformed the public in such a way as to reduce the effectiveness of our efforts to preserve a species that is defenseless against the onslaught of man's technological might.

We of the Greenpeace Foundation, demand the immediate resignation of the Minister of Fisheries, M. Romeo Le blanc, on the grounds that he has been negligent in providing leadership in the conservation of Canada's marine resources. We also demand that Canada unilaterally declare a 200 mile limit in order to preserve the integrity of the marine resources on the continental shelf. We further demand that the report on harp seal populations presented to the Department of Fisheries in October of 1975 be made public immediately and that all other information regarding the seal herds be released."

It is time that we realize the inevitability of the crisis that now faces 55 the living ecosystem of our small and fragile planet.

As human power and population expands, the other species are diminished. The balance of nature has become chaotic and this is due, primarily, to human technology and human institutions. It is becoming increasingly obvious that we must correct this imbalance ourselves or accept responsibility for leaving a ruined planet to our children. It is they who will finally judge whether we have betrayed them in search of our own short-term gains, our pleasures and our vanity, or whether we conscientiously concerned ourselves with the welfare of future generations. Our children will be lucky enough to avoid the pangs of hunger, let alone enjoy the luxuries of the present era.

Working Together

1. Share the story of your reading in "Before and After" terms: what you thought about Greenpeace and environmental activism before you read this piece; what you thought when you finished. Did your feelings or ideas change? why or why not?

2. Consider this essay for style and form, its sentence rhythms, word choice, and use of detail. How do these strategies succeed or fail in creating certain responses in you as a reader? What response do you think Paul Watson wants to create?

3. Describe the voice of this piece. What do you imagine, just on the basis of the words, about Paul Watson the person? Who would play the writer in the movie? What clothes is he wearing? What does he look like? What other kinds of writing or talking does this piece remind you of?

Rethinking and Rewriting

1. Write an essay giving at least three reasons why you think Watson's action was right and justified. Or write an essay giving at least three reasons why you think his action was wrong, misguided, or ineffective. Or write an essay arguing that Watson's essay doesn't give us the whole story and therefore we have to enlarge the discussion before drawing conclusions.

2. Do a research essay on the fate of the baby seals in the past 20 years. What's the situation now?

3. Do a research essay on some environmental action taken by the Green-peace Foundation in the past year. Focus on a particular action in a particular place. Tell readers the story.

4. Do a long research essay on the Greenpeace Foundation, its history, its effectiveness, and how it's changed.

5. Do a biography of Watson, focusing on his eventual break with the Greenpeace Foundation. Why did he break? What is he doing now?

6. Write an essay in journal form, as Watson does, describing an exciting and important action you've taken in response to crisis, something adventurous, dangerous, or at least unusual. Focus on an action that was an attempt to solve a problem or resolve a crisis or handle an emergency. Or do the opposite: Write the same kind of essay, but about an ordinary, quiet event, something not spectacular. Or write the same kind of essay about a time when you had a chance to act bravely or responsibly or go on an adventure and didn't take that chance.

"EARTH FIRST!"

Dave Foreman

> *After working for The Wilderness Society in the 1970s, Dave Foreman cofounded his own environmental activist group, EARTH FIRST!, and served as editor of The EARTH FIRST! Journal until 1988. He is currently editor of a new conservation magazine, Wild Earth, and owner of a conservation mail-order bookstore. He is the coeditor of Ecodefense (1985), coauthor of The Big Outside: A Descriptive Inventory of the Big Wilderness Areas of the United States (1989), and author of Confessions of an Eco-Warrior (1991). The following declaration of principles was first published in the October 1981 issue of the Progressive.*

Before and As You Read

1. Write down everything you've heard about "Earth First!" and your initial biases, feelings, and expectations. If you haven't heard about "Earth First!," write about your reactions to environmental activism in general: how you feel about people who publically protest and interfere with logging or development. Before reading, what do you expect to find?
2. As you read, mark one passage that seems to you eminently reasonable, something you can agree with.
3. Mark one passage that seems to you too extreme, something you can't go along with.

. . . Maybe—some of us began to feel, even before Reagan's election—it was time for a new joker in the deck: a militant, uncompromising group unafraid to say what needed to be said or to back it up with stronger actions than the established organizations were willing to take. This idea had been kicking around for a couple of years; finally last year several of us (including, among others, Susan Morgan, formerly educational director for the Wilderness Society: Howie Wolke, former Wyoming representative for Friends of the Earth: Bart Koehler, former Wyoming representative for the Wilderness Society, and myself) decided that the time for talk was past. We formed a new national group. EARTH FIRST! We set out to be radical in style, positions, philosophy, and organization in order to be effective and to avoid the pitfalls of co-option and moderation which we had already experienced.

What, we asked ourselves as we sat around a campfire in the Wyoming mountains, were the advantages, the reasons for environmental radicalism?

- To state honestly the views held by many conservationists.

- To demonstrate that the Sierra Club and its allies were raging moderates, believers in the system, and to refute the Reagan/Watt contention that they were "extremist environmentalists."

- To balance such anti-environmental radicals as the Grand County commission and provide a broader spectrum of viewpoints.

- To return some vigor, joy, and enthusiasm to the allegedly tired environmental movement.

- To keep the established groups honest. By stating a pure, noncompromise pro-Earth position, we felt EARTH FIRST! could help keep the other groups from straying too far from their philosophical base.

- To give an outlet to many hard-line conservationists who were no longer active because of disenchantment with compromise politics and the co-option of environmental organizations.

- To provide a productive fringe since it seems that ideas, creativity, and energy spring up on the fringe and later spread into the middle.

- To inspire others to carry out activities straight from the pages of *The Monkey Wrench Gang* even though EARTH FIRST!, we agreed, would itself be ostensibly law-abiding.

- To question the system; to help develop a new world view, a biocentric paradigm, an Earth philosophy. To fight, with uncompromising passion, for Mother Earth.

The name—EARTH FIRST!—was chosen deliberately because it succinctly summed up the one thing on which we could all agree: That in *any* decision, consideration for the health of the Earth must come first, or, as Aldo Leopold said, "A thing is right when it tends to preserve the integrity, stability, and beauty of the biotic community. It is wrong when it tends otherwise."

In a true Earth-radical group, concern for wilderness preservation must be the keystone. The idea of wilderness, after all, is the most radical in human thought—more radical than Paine, than Marx, than Mao. Wilderness says: Human beings are not dominant, Earth is not for *Homo sapiens* alone, human life is but one life form on the planet and has no right to take exclusive possession. Yes, wilderness for its own sake, without any need to justify it for human benefit. Wilderness for wilderness. For grizzlies and whales and titmice and rattlesnakes and stink bugs. And . . . wilderness for human beings. Because it is the laboratory of three million years of human evolution—and because it is home.

It is not enough to protect our few remaining bits of wilderness. The only hope for Earth (and humanity for that matter) is to withdraw huge areas as inviolate natural sanctuaries from the depredations of modern industry and technology. Keep Cleveland, Los Angeles. Contain them. Try to make them habitable. But identify areas—big areas—that can be restored to a semblance of natural conditions, reintroduce the griz and wolf and prairie grasses, and declare them off limits to modern civilization.

In the United States pick an area for each of our major ecosystems and recreate the American wilderness—not in little pieces of a thousand acres but in chunks of a million or ten million. Move out the people and cars. Reclaim the roads and plowed land. It is not enough any longer to say no more dams on our wild rivers. We must begin tearing down some dams already built—beginning with Glen Canyon, Hetch Hetchy, Tellico, and New Melones—and freeing shackled rivers.

This emphasis on wilderness is not to ignore other environmental issues or to abandon the people who suffer because of them. In the United States blacks and Chicanos of the inner cities are the ones most affected by air and water pollution, the ones most trapped by the unnatural confines of urbanity. So we decided that not only should ecomilitants be concerned with these human environmental problems; we should also make common ground with other progressive elements of society whenever possible.

Obviously, for a group more committed to Gila monsters and mountain lions than to people, there will not be a total alliance with the other social movements. But there are issues where Earth radicals can cooperate with feminist, Indian rights, anti-nuke, peace, civil rights, and civil liberties groups. The inherent conservatism of the conservation community has made it wary of snuggling too close to these questionable (in their minds) leftist organizations. We hoped that the way might be paved for better cooperation from the entire conservation movement.

We believed that new tactics were needed—something more than commenting on dreary environmental impact statements and writing letters to members of Congress. Politics in the streets. Civil disobedience. Media stunts. Holding the villains up to ridicule. Using music to charge the cause.

Action is the key. Action is more important than philosophical hair- 10 splitting or endless refining of dogma (for which radicals are so well known). Let our actions set the finer points of our philosophy. And let us recognize that diversity is not only the spice of life, it is also the strength. All that would be required to join us, we decided, was a belief in Earth first. Apart from that, EARTH FIRST! would be big enough to contain street poets and cowboy bar bouncers, agnostics and pagans, vegetarians and raw steak eaters, pacifists and those who think that turning the other cheek is a good way to get a sore face.

Radicals frequently verge toward a righteous seriousness. But we felt that if we couldn't laugh at ourselves we would be merely another bunch of dangerous fanatics who should be locked up (like the oil companies). Not only does humor preserve individual and group sanity, it retards hubris, a major cause of environmental rape, and it is also an effective weapon. Additionally, fire, passion, courage, and emotionalism are called for. We have been too reasonable, too calm, too understanding. It's time to get angry, to cry, to let rage flow at what the human cancer is doing to Mother Earth, to be uncompromising. For EARTH FIRST! it is all or nothing. Win or lose. No truce or cease fire. No surrender. No partitioning of the territory.

Ever since the Earth goddesses of ancient Greece were supplanted by the macho Olympians, repression of women and Earth has gone hand in hand with imperial organization. EARTH FIRST! decided to be nonorganizational: no officers, no bylaws or constitution, no incorporation, no tax status; just a collection of women and men committed to the Earth. At the turn of the century William Graham Sumner wrote a famous essay entitled "The Conquest of the United States by Spain." His thesis was that Spain had ultimately won the Spanish-American War because the United States took on the imperialism and totalitarianism of Spain as a result. We felt that if we took on the organization of the industrial state, we would soon accept their anthropocentric paradigm (much as Audubon and the Sierra Club already had).

In keeping with that view, EARTH FIRST! took the shape of a circle, a group of thirteen women and men around the country who more or less direct the movement, and a collection of regional contacts. We also have local affiliates (so far in Alaska, Montana, Wyoming, Colorado, Arizona, New Mexico, Utah, Arkansas, Maine, and Virginia). We publish a newsletter eight times a year and are developing position papers on a range of issues from automobiles to overgrazing. We also send out press releases. Membership is free, although we do encourage members to kick in ten bucks or more, if they can afford it, to help with expenses. We have not sought any grants or funding with strings attached, nor do we plan to have paid staff (although we hope to have field organizers receiving expenses in the tradition of the Wobblies).

And, when we are inspired, we *act*.

Massive, powerful, like some creation of Darth Vader's. Glen Canyon   15
Dam squats in the canyon of the Colorado River on the Arizona-Utah border and backs the cold dead waters of Lake Powell some 180 miles upstream, drowning the most awesome and magical canyon on Earth. More than any other single entity, Glen Canyon Dam is the symbol of the destruction of wilderness, of the technological rape of the West. The finest fantasy of *eco*-warriors in the West is the destruction of the dam and the liberation of the Colorado. So it was only proper that on March 21, 1981—on the Spring Equinox, the traditional time of rebirth—EARTH FIRST! held its first national gathering at Glen Canyon Dam.

On that morning, seventy-five members of EARTH FIRST! lined the walkway of the Colorado River Bridge 700 feet above the once free river and watched five compatriots busy at work with an awkward black bundle on the massive dam just upstream. Those on the bridge carried placards reading "Damn Watt, Not Rivers," "Free the Colorado," and "Let It Flow." The four men and one woman on the dam attached ropes to a grill on the dam, shouted out "Earth first!" and let 300 feet of black plastic unfurl down the side of the dam, creating the impression of a growing crack. Those on the bridge returned the cheer.

A few minutes later, Edward Abbey, author of *The Monkey Wrench Gang,* a novel of environmental sabotage in the Southwest, told the protesters of the "green and living wilderness" that was Glen Canyon only nineteen years ago:

"And they took it away from us. The politicians of Arizona, Utah, New Mexico, and Colorado, in cahoots with the land developers, city developers, industrial developers of the Southwest, stole this treasure from us in order to pursue and promote their crackpot ideology of growth, profit, and power—growth for the sake of power, power for the sake of growth."

Speaking toward the future, Abbey offered this advice: "Oppose. Oppose the destruction of our homeland by these alien forces from Houston, Tokyo, Manhattan, Washington, D.C., and the Pentagon. And if opposition is not enough, we must resist. And if resistance is not enough, then subvert."

Abbey than launched a nationwide petition campaign demanding the dismantling of Glen Canyon Dam. Hardly had he finished speaking when Park Service police and Coconino County sheriff's deputies arrived on the scene. While they questioned the organizers of the illegal assembly and tried to disperse it, outlaw country singer Johnny Sagebrush led the demonstrators in song for another twenty minutes.   20

The Glen Canyon Dam caper brought EARTH FIRST! an unexpected degree of media attention. Membership in our group has spiraled to more than a thousand with members from Maine to Hawaii. Even the Government is interested—according to reliable reports, the FBI dusted the entire Glen Canyon Dam crack for fingerprints!

Last Fourth of July more than 200 EARTH FIRST!ers gathered in Moab, Utah, for the first Sagebrush Patriot Rally to express support for Federal public lands and to send a message to anti-Earth fanatics that there are Americans who are patriotic about *their* wilderness.

When a few of us kicked off EARTH FIRST! we sensed a growing environmental radicalism in the country but we did not expect the response we have received. Maybe EARTH FIRST! is in the right place at the right time. Tom Turner, editor of Friends of the Earth's *Not Man Apart,* recently wrote to us to say:

"Russ Train once said, 'Thank God for Dave Brower—he makes it so easy for the rest of us to appear reasonable.' Youze guys are about to make Dave Brower look reasonable, and more power to you!"

The cynical may smirk. "But what can you really accomplish? How can you fight Exxon, Coors, David Rockefeller, Japan, and the other great corporate giants of the Earth? How, indeed, can you fight the dominant dogmas of Western Civilization?"   25

Perhaps it *is* a hopeless quest. But is that relevant? Is that important? No, what is important is that one who loves Earth can do no less. Maybe a species will be saved or a forest will go uncut or a dam will be torn down. Maybe not. A monkey wrench thrown into the gears of the machine may not stop it. But it might delay it. Make it cost more. And it feels good to put it there.

Working Together

1. Share the passages you thought were reasonable. Write them on the board. Discuss the question of what makes them seem reasonable to you. Style? Content? What in your own background or beliefs makes you respond the way you do?

2. Write on the board the passages you don't think are reasonable, that you distrust, that make you uncomfortable. Discuss the question of what makes them seem unreasonable or problematic. What in your own background or beliefs makes you respond the way you do?

3. Rewrite several of the sentences you find problematic. Change the style without changing the content. Do the sentences have the same effect? Have they become acceptable? Why or why not?

4. Just on the basis of the words, phrases, and sentences here, describe Dave Foreman the person. What does he look like? How does he dress? How old is he? What other kind of writing or talk is this language like? Who would play Foreman in the movie? Is there any relation between the way this piece is written and its ideas—does it *sound* like what it talks about? Would you like to have lunch with Foreman?

5. Working in groups, make a list of the beliefs, intentions, and basic aims of the writing class you find yourself in right now. Write the kind of declaration or constitution Foreman writes here, but write about the class: what students should dedicate themselves to if they want to get good grades in the class and learn to write well. Make at least three statements, and arrange them in a list, the phrasing parallel. As a class, merge and blend the statements of the groups until you come up with a class "mission statement."

Rethinking and Rewriting

1. Write an essay describing the way your town or community would be different if everyone accepted Foreman's principles—if he succeeded in convincing everyone that he is right. How would the landscape change? How would people behave? What would they do?

2. Assume that you're convinced by Foreman's declarations, that you agree with him. Write an essay describing one thing you would have to do, one problem or issue you'd have to take on. You can write this essay as if you've already accomplished the task and are looking back on it. What did you do?

3. Write an essay attempting to persuade a friend or relative to give money to the Earth First! organization or some other similar organization. Use this document as a source.

4. Write a statement of the beliefs, intentions, or basic aims of some group or community you belong to—a class, a sorority or fraternity, a study group, a basketball team. Write them as a series of parallel statements, in the form of a list, each statement separated with a dot or bullet, just as Foreman does here. Before and after this list, explain the context, elaborate, and extend.

"FORESTERS WITHOUT DIPLOMAS"

Wangari Maathai

A biologist educated in America, Wangari Maathai is now an associate professor at the University of Nairobi, the first woman to achieve such a rank in that part of Africa. She has received many awards for her environmental activism, including the Woman of the World Award and the Africa Prize for Leadership. In the following article from the March/April 1991 issue of MS, *Maathai describes the Green Belt movement she began in Kenya as a way of illustrating her belief that "one person can make a difference."*

The Green Belt movement started in my backyard. I was involved in a political campaign with a man I was married to; I was trying to see what I could do for the people who were helping us during our campaign, people who came from the poor communities. I decided to create jobs for them—cleaning their constituency, planting trees and shrubs, cleaning homes of the richer people in the communities, and getting paid for those services. That never worked, because poor people wanted support right away, and I didn't have money to pay them before the people we were working for had paid *me*. So I dropped the project but stayed with the idea. Then, in 1976—two years after the first backyard idea—I was invited to join the National Council of Women of Kenya.

We were into the U.N.'s "women's decade," and I got exposed to many of the problems women were facing—problems of firewood, malnutrition, lack of food and adequate water, unemployment, soil erosion. Quite often what we see in the streets of our cities, in the rural areas, in the slums, are manifestations of mistakes we make as we pretend we are "developing," as we pursue what we are now calling *mal*development.

And so we decided to go to the women. Why? Well, I am a woman. I was in a women's organization. Women are the ones most affected by these problems. Women are concerned about children, about the future.

So we went to the women and talked about planting trees and overcoming, for example, such problems as the lack of firewood and building and fencing materials, stopping soil erosion, protecting water systems. The women agreed, although they didn't know how to do it.

The next few months we spent teaching them how to do it. We first   5
called the foresters to come and show the women how you plant trees. The foresters proved to be very complicated because they have diplomas, they have complicated ways of dealing with a very simple thing like looking for seeds and planting trees. So eventually we taught the women to just do it using common sense. And they did. They were able to look for seeds in the neighborhood, and learn to recognize seedlings as they germinate when seeds fall on the ground. Women do not have to wait for anybody to grow trees. They are really foresters without a diploma.

We started on World Environment Day, June 5, 1977; that's when we planted the first seven trees. Now, only two are still standing. They are beautiful *nandi* flame trees. The rest died. But by 1988, when we counted according to the records women sent back to us, we had *10 million trees surviving.* Many had already matured to be used by the women. But the most important thing is that the women were now independent; had acquired knowledge, techniques; had become empowered. They have been teaching each other. We started with one tree nursery in the backyard of the office of the National Council of Women. Today we have over 1,500 tree nurseries, 99 percent run by women.

The women get a very small payment for every seedling that survives. The few men who come are extremely poor, so poor that they don't mind working with women. Women do a lot of work that requires caring. And I don't believe that it is solely indoctrination. Women started the environmental movement, and now it has become a movement that even financial donors see they should put money in, because the efforts are providing results. But the minute money is in, the men come in. I would not be surprised that eventually the more successful the Green Belt movement becomes, the more infiltrated it will be by men, who will be there more for the economic benefit than the commitment.

Although men are not involved in the planting at the nursery, they are involved in the planting of trees on farms. These are small-scale farmers. In our part of Africa, men own land; in some communities they own separate titles to the land; in others there is still communal ownership, which is the tradition in Africa. We are most successful in communities where women are involved in land farming.

In Kenya, as in so much of the African continent, 80 percent of the farmers—and the fuel gatherers—are women. Women also keep animals. A large population of Kenyans are nomadic communities: the Maasai, the Samburu, the Somalis, most of the northern communities. We have been unsuccessful there. Yet this is where trees are much needed. Areas that are green now will soon be a desert if not cared for.

We have been approached by other countries, and in 1987–88 we launched what we hoped would become an effort to initiate Green Belt—like activities in other African countries. Unfortunately, we have not been able to follow up. We started having our own problems in Kenya because of our having criticized the government for wanting to put up a big building in a Nairobi public park. But we are encouraging an establishment of a Green Belt Center in Nairobi, where people can come and experience development that is community oriented, with community decision-making, and with development appropriate to the region.

Funding is always a problem. We never received any financial support from the Kenyan government. They gave us an office—which they took away as soon as we criticized them. (In a way, it is good they didn't give us money because they would have withdrawn that.) We receive much of our support from abroad, mostly from women all over this world, who send us small checks. And the United Nations Development Fund for Women gave us a big boost, $100,000 in 1981. We also received support from the Danish Voluntary Fund and the Norwegian Agency for International Development. In the U.S. we are supported by the African Development Foundation, which helped us make a film about the Green Belt movement in 1985. Information on the film can be obtained from the Public Affairs Officer of the African Development Foundation, 1400 I Street, N.W., Washington, D.C. 20005.

In the field, we now have about 750 people who teach new groups and help with the compilation of the reports, which we monitor to have an idea of what is happening in the field. At the headquarters we now have about 40 people. When we were kicked out of our office, the headquarters moved back to my house; a full-circle return to where we started.

But it's 10 million trees later—not quite where we started. For myself, now that my two boys and a girl are big—the last boy is still in high school—when we have trained enough women in leadership and fundraising, I would love to go back into an academic institution. I do miss it. My field is biology. But I was into microanatomy and developmental anatomy. I would love to be able to read more about community development and motivation and write about the experience that I have had in the field. And perhaps train people on grass-roots projects. But that will have to wait. I earn maybe a tenth of what I could earn on the international market if I sold my expertise and energy, and I'm sure many people would probably consider me a fool. At home the men don't believe that I don't make a fortune out of the Green Belt movement. But all over the world we women do this sort of thing.

My greatest satisfaction is to look back and see how far we have come. Something so simple but meaning so much, something nobody can take away from the people, something that is changing the face of the landscape.

But my greatest disappointment has been since I returned to Kenya   15
in 1966 after my education in the United States. When I was growing up and going through school, I believed that the sky is the limit. I realized when I went home that the sky is not the limit, that human beings can make the limit for you, stop you from pursuing your full potential. I have had to fight to make a contribution. We lose so much from people because we don't allow them to think freely and do what they can. So they lose their interest; their energy; the opportunity to be creative and positive. And developing countries need all the energy they can get.

I tell people that if they know how to read and write it is an advantage. But that all we really need is a desire to work and common sense. These are usually the last two things people are asked for. They are usually asked to use imposed knowledge they do not relate to, so they become followers rather than leaders.

For example, because I criticized the political leadership, I have been portrayed as subversive, so it's very difficult for me to not feel constrained.

I have the energy; I want to do exactly what they spend hours in the U.N. talking about. But when you really want to *do* it you are not allowed, because the political system is not tolerant or encouraging enough.

But we must never lose hope. When any of us feels she has an idea or an opportunity, she should go ahead and do it. I never knew when I was working in my backyard that what I was playing around with would one day become a whole movement. One person *can* make the difference.

Reading and Responding

1. Draw a line down the center of a page of your reading journal. On one side, write the major successes Wangari Maathai notes, and use the other side to record the difficulties or troubles. Once you've done this, see whether you can determine which factors led to the successes and which ones led to the troubles.
2. Draw a line down the center of a page of your reading journal. On one side, write the major points Maathai makes about men and their attitudes toward the environment. On the other side, write the points she makes about women and their attitudes.
3. Mark the passage in the essay that seems the most powerful, interesting, or important.

Working Together

1. Pool your lists of successes and failures. What can you agree has led to success and what has led to difficulty?
2. Pool your lists of Maathai's statements about men and women, one list on one side of the board, one list on the other side. Discuss the issue of how many of these gender differences are peculiar to African culture. Explain. How many apply to American culture? How many have you experienced yourself? What circumstances account for these differences between African and American culture, if they do exist?
3. Rewrite the list in terms of American culture: cross out any statements that don't apply; shift some from one list to the other; add observations. Or are the lists the same for American culture? Should there be a gender division at all?
4. In light of this discussion, consider Maathai's final statement: "One *person* can make a difference."

Rethinking and Rewriting

1. In light of the discussion in class, write a paper arguing that Maathai's distinctions between the attitudes of men and women *do* apply to the attitudes of Americans about the environment—or that they *don't*. Draw on your own experience. Quote portions of the class discussion.

2. Write an essay supporting the claim that "one person *can* make a difference." Or write an essay arguing against that claim, insisting that one person is too insignificant to affect the course of events. Support your point through research or personal experience.

3. Do a profile of some local figure who has started a grassroots campaign similar to Maathai's. Tell the story of that person and that effort to change things.

4. Imagine that you want to form a group of local people and friends to accomplish some particular task or complete a project. You've called a meeting of anyone interested. Write the speech or talk you would give to that group explaining what you want to do and why it's worthwhile for these people to get involved in it.

"THE CLAN OF ONE-BREASTED WOMEN"

Terry Tempest Williams

> *A resident of the Southwest, Terry Tempest Williams has published seven books, including most recently* An Unspoken Hunger: Stories from the Field *(1994) and* Refuge *(1991), from which the selection here is reprinted. Williams writes from a deep conviction of the natural relationships between people and landscape—a perspective that makes what she discusses here even more painful. Williams lives in Salt Lake City, Utah, where she is Naturalist-in-Residence at the Utah Museum of Natural History.*

As You Read

As you read, mark the passages that affect you most strongly (use a straight line in the margin) and the passages that surprise you (use a wiggly line in the margin).

I belong to a Clan of One-breasted Women. My mother, my grandmothers, and six aunts have all had mastectomies. Seven are dead. The two who survive have just completed rounds of chemotherapy and radiation.

I've had my own problems: two biopsies for breast cancer and a small tumor between my ribs diagnosed as "a border-line malignancy."

This is my family history.

Most statistics tell us breast cancer is genetic, hereditary, with rising percentages attached to fatty diets, childlessness, or becoming pregnant after thirty. What they don't say is living in Utah may be the greatest hazard of all.

We are a Mormon family with roots in Utah since 1847. The word-of-wisdom, a religious doctrine of health, kept the women in my family aligned with good foods: no coffee, no tea, tobacco, or alcohol. For the most part, these women were finished having their babies by the time they were thirty. And only one faced breast cancer prior to 1960. Traditionally, as a group of people, Mormons have a low rate of cancer.

Is our family a cultural anomaly? The truth is we didn't think about it. Those who did, usually the men, simply said, "bad genes." The women's attitude was stoic. Cancer was part of life. On February 16, 1971, the eve before my mother's surgery, I accidently picked up the telephone and overheard her ask my grandmother what she could expect.

"Diane, it is one of the most spiritual experiences you will ever encounter."

I quietly put down the receiver.

Two days later, my father took my three brothers and me to the hospital to visit her. She met us in the lobby in a wheelchair. No bandages were visible. I'll never forget her radiance, the way she held herself in a purple velour robe and how she gathered us around her.

"Children, I am fine. I want you to know I felt the arms of God   *10*
around me."

We believed her. My father cried. Our mother, his wife, was thirty-eight years old.

Two years ago, after my mother's death from cancer, my father and I were having dinner together. He had just returned from St. George where his construction company was putting in natural gas lines for towns in southern Utah. He spoke of his love for the country: the sandstoned land-scape, bare-boned and beautiful. He had just finished hiking the Kolob trail in Zion National Park. We got caught up in reminiscing, recalling with fondness our walk up Angle's Landing on his fiftieth birthday and the years our family had vacationed there. This was a remembered landscape where we had been raised.

Over dessert, I shared a recurring dream of mine. I told my father that for years, as long as I could remember, I saw this flash of light in the night in the desert. That this image had so permeated my being, I could not venture south without seeing it again, on the horizon, illuminating buttes and mesas.

"You did see it," he said.

"Saw what?" I asked, a bit tentative.   *15*

"The bomb. The cloud. We were driving home from Riverside, California. You were sitting on your mother's lap. She was pregnant. In fact, I remember the date, September 7, 1957. We had just gotten out of the Service. We were driving north, past Las Vegas. It was an hour or so before dawn, when this explosion went off. We not only heard it, but felt it. I thought the oil tanker in front of us had blown up. We pulled over and suddenly, rising from the desert floor, we saw it, clearly, this golden-stemmed cloud, the mushroom. The sky seemed to vibrate with an eerie pink glow. Within a few minutes, a light ash was raining on the car."

I stared at my father. This was new information to me.

"I thought you knew that," my father said. "It was a common occur-rence in the fifties."

It was at this moment I realized the deceit I had been living under. Children growing up in the American Southwest, drinking contaminated milk from contaminated cows, even from the contaminated breasts of their mother, my mother—members, years later, of the Clan of One-breasted Women.

It is a well-known story in the Desert West, "The Day We Bombed   *20*
Utah," or perhaps, "The Years We Bombed Utah."[1] Above ground atomic testing in Nevada took place from January 27, 1951, through July 11, 1962. Not only were the winds blowing north, covering "low use segments of the population" with fallout and leaving sheep dead in their tracks, but the

1. Fuller, John G., *The Day We Bombed Utah* (New York: New American Library, 1984).

climate was right.[2] The United States of the 1950s was red, white, and blue. The Korean War was raging. McCarthyism was rampant. Ike was it and the Cold War was hot. If you were against nuclear testing, you were for a Communist regime.

Much has been written about this "American nuclear tragedy." Public health was secondary to national security. The Atomic Energy Commissioner, Thomas Murray, said, "Gentlemen, we must not let anything interfere with this series of tests, nothing."[3]

Again and again, the American public was told by its government, in spite of burns, blisters, and nausea, "It has been found that the tests may be conducted with adequate assurance of safety under conditions prevailing at the bombing reservations."[4] Assuaging public fears was simply a matter of public relations. "Your best action," an Atomic Energy Commission booklet read, "is not to be worried about fallout." A news release typical of the times stated, "We find no basis for concluding that harm to any individual has resulted from radioactive fallout."[5]

On August 30, 1979, during Jimmy Carter's presidency, a suit was filed entitled "Irene Allen vs. the United States of America." Mrs. Allen was the first to be alphabetically listed with twenty-four test cases, representative of nearly 1200 plaintiffs seeking compensation from the United States government for cancers caused from nuclear testing in Nevada.

Irene Allen lived in Hurricane, Utah. She was the mother of five children and had been widowed twice. Her first husband with their two oldest boys had watched the tests from the roof of the local high school. He died of leukemia in 1956. Her second husband died of pancreatic cancer in 1978.

In a town meeting conducted by Utah Senator Orrin Hatch, shortly before the suit was filed, Mrs. Allen said, "I am not blaming the government, I want you to know that, Senator Hatch. But I thought if my testimony could help in any way so this wouldn't happen again to any of the generations coming up after us . . . I am really happy to be here this day to bear testimony of this."[6]

25

God-fearing people. This is just one story in an anthology of thousands.

On May 10, 1984, Judge Bruce S. Jenkins handed down his opinion. Ten of the plaintiffs were awarded damages. It was the first time a federal court had determined that nuclear tests had been the cause of cancers. For

---

2. Discussion on March 14, 1988, with Carole Gallagher, photographer and author, *Nuclear Towns: The Secret War in the American Southwest,* to be published by Doubleday, Spring, 1990.

3. Szasz, Ferenc M., "Downwind From the Bomb," *Nevada Historical Society Quarterly,* Fall, 1987 Vol. XXX, No. 3, p. 185.

4. Fradkin, Philip L., *Fallout* (Tucson: University of Arizona Press, 1989), 98.

5. Ibid., 109.

6. Town meeting held by Senator Orrin Hatch in St. George, Utah, April 17, 1979, transcript, 26–28.

the remaining fourteen test cases, the proof of causation was not sufficient. In spite of the split decision, it was considered a landmark ruling.[7] It was not to remain so for long.

In April, 1987, the 10th Circuit Court of Appeals overturned Judge Jenkins' ruling on the basis that the United States was protected from suit by the legal doctrine of sovereign immunity, the centuries-old idea from England in the days of absolute monarchs.[8]

In January, 1988, the Supreme Court refused to review the Appeals Court decision. To our court system, it does not matter whether the United States Government was irresponsible, whether it lied to its citizens or even that citizens died from the fallout of nuclear testing. What matters is that our government is immune. "The King can do no wrong."

In Mormon culture, authority is respected, obedience is revered, and   30
independent thinking is not. I was taught as a young girl not to "make waves" or "rock the boat."

"Just let it go—" my mother would say. "You know how you feel, that's what counts."

For many years, I did just that—listened, observed, and quietly formed my own opinions within a culture that rarely asked questions because they had all the answers. But one by one, I watched the women in my family die common, heroic deaths. We sat in waiting rooms hoping for good news, always receiving the bad. I cared for them, bathed their scarred bodies and kept their secrets. I watched beautiful women become bald as cytoxan, cisplatin and adriamycin were injected into their veins. I held their foreheads as they vomited green-black bile and I shot them with morphine when the pain became inhuman. In the end, I witnessed their last peaceful breaths, becoming a midwife to the rebirth of their souls. But the price of obedience became too high.

The fear and inability to question authority that ultimately killed rural communities in Utah during atmospheric testing of atomic weapons was the same fear I saw being held in my mother's body. Sheep. Dead sheep. The evidence is buried.

I cannot prove that my mother, Diane Dixon Tempest, or my grandmothers, Lettie Romney Dixon and Kathryn Blackett Tempest, along with my aunts contracted cancer from nuclear fallout in Utah. But I can't prove they didn't.

My father's memory was correct, the September blast we drove   35
through in 1957 was part of Operation Plumbbob, one of the most intensive series of bomb tests to be initiated. The flash of light in the night in the desert I had always thought was a dream developed into a family

---

7. Fradkin, Op. cit., 228.
8. U.S. vs. Allen, 816 Federal Reporter, 2d/1417 (10th Circuit Court 1987), cert. denied, 108 S. CT. 694 (1988).

nightmare. It took fourteen years, from 1957 to 1971, for cancer to show up in my mother—the same time, Howard L. Andrews, an authority on radioactive fallout at the National Institutes of Health, says radiation cancer requires to become evident.[9] The more I learn about what it means to be a "downwinder," the more questions I drown in.

What I do know, however, is that as a Mormon woman of the fifth generation of "Latter-Day-Saints," I must question everything, even if it means losing my faith, even if it means becoming a member of a border tribe among my own people. Tolerating blind obedience in the name of patriotism or religion ultimately takes our lives.

When the Atomic Energy Commission described the country north of the Nevada Test Site as "virtually uninhabited desert terrain," my family members were some of the "virtual uninhabitants."

One night, I dreamed women from all over the world circling a blazing fire in the desert. They spoke of change, of how they hold the moon in their bellies and wax and wane with its phases. They mocked at the presumption of even-tempered beings and made promises that they would never fear the witch inside themselves. The women danced wildly as sparks broke away from the flames and entered the night sky as stars.

And they sang a song given to them by Shoshoni grandmothers:

Ah ne nah, nah
nin nah nah—
Ah ne nah, nah
nin nah nah—
Nyaga mutzi
oh ne nay—
Nyaga mutzi
oh ne nay—[10]

The women danced and drummed and sang for weeks, preparing themselves for what was to come. They would reclaim the desert for the sake of their children, for the sake of the land.   *40*

A few miles downwind from the fire circle, bombs were being tested. Rabbits felt the tremors. Their soft leather pads on paws and feet recognized the shaking sands while the roots of mesquite and sage were smoldering. Rocks were hot from the inside out and dust devils hummed unnaturally. And each time there was another nuclear test,

---

9. Fradkin, Op. cit., 116.
10. This song was sung by the Western Shoshone women as they crossed the line at the Nevada Test Site on March 18, 1988, as part of their "Reclaim the Land" action. The translation they gave was: "Consider the rabbits how gently they walk on the earth. Consider the rabbits how gently they walk on the earth. We remember them. We can walk gently also. We remember them. We can walk gently also."

ravens watched the desert heave. Stretch marks appeared. The land was losing its muscle.

The women couldn't bear it any longer. They were mothers. They had suffered labor pains but always under the promise of birth. The red hot pains beneath the desert promised death only as each bomb became a stillborn. A contract had been broken between human beings and the land. A new contract was being drawn by the women who understood the fate of the earth as their own.

Under the cover of darkness, ten women slipped under the barbed wire fence and entered the contaminated country. They were trespassing. They walked toward the town of Mercury in moonlight, taking their cues from coyote, kit fox, antelope squirrel, and quail. They moved quietly and deliberately through the maze of Joshua trees. When a hint of daylight appeared they rested, drinking tea and sharing their rations of food. The women closed their eyes. The time had come to protest with the heart, that to deny one's genealogy with the earth was to commit treason against one's soul.

At dawn, the women draped themselves in mylar, wrapping long streamers of silver plastic around their arms to blow in the breeze. They wore clear masks that became the faces of humanity. And when they arrived on the edge of Mercury, they carried all the butterflies of a summer day in their wombs. They paused to allow their courage to settle.

The town which forbids pregnant women and children to enter because of radiation risks to their health was asleep. The women moved through the streets as winged messengers, twirling around each other in slow motion, peeking inside homes and watching the easy sleep of men and women. They were astonished by such stillness and periodically would utter a shrill note or low cry just to verify life.

The residents finally awoke to what appeared as strange apparitions. Some simply stared. Others called authorities, and in time, the women were apprehended by wary soldiers dressed in desert fatigues. They were taken to a white, square building on the other edge of Mercury. When asked who they were and why they were there, the women replied, "We are mothers and we have come to reclaim the desert for our children."

The soldiers arrested them. As the ten women were blindfolded and handcuffed, they began singing:

> *You can't forbid us everything*
> *You can't forbid us to think—*
> *You can't forbid our tears to flow*
> *And you can't stop the songs that we sing.*

The women continued to sing louder and louder, until they heard the voices of their sisters moving across the mesa.

> *Ah ne nah, nah*
> *nin nah nah—*

Ah ne nah, nah
nin nah nah—
Nyaga mutzi
oh ne nay—
Nyaga mutzi
oh ne nay—

"Call for re-enforcement," one soldier said.

"We have," interrupted one woman. "We have—and you have no   50
idea of our numbers."

On March 18, 1988, I crossed the line at the Nevada Test Site and
was arrested with nine other Utahns for trespassing on military lands. They
are still conducting nuclear tests in the desert. Ours was an act of civil
disobedience. But as I walked toward the town of Mercury, it was more
than a gesture of peace. It was a gesture on behalf of the Clan of One-
breasted Women.

As one officer cinched the handcuffs around my wrists, another
frisked my body. She found a pen and a pad of paper tucked inside my left
boot.

"And these?" she asked sternly.

"Weapons," I replied.

Our eyes met. I smiled. She pulled the leg of my trousers back over   55
my boot.

"Step forward, please," she said as she took my arm.

We were booked under an afternoon sun and bussed to Tonapah,
Nevada. It was a two-hour ride. This was familiar country to me. The
Joshua trees standing their ground had been named by my ancestors who
believed they looked like prophets pointing west to the promised land.
These were the same trees that bloomed each spring, flowers appearing
like white flames in the Mojave. And I recalled a full moon in May when
my mother and I had walked among them, flushing out mourning doves
and owls.

The bus stopped short of town. We were released. The officials
thought it was a cruel joke to leave us stranded in the desert with no way
to get home. What they didn't realize is that we were home, soul-centered
and strong, women who recognized the sweet smell of sage as fuel for our
spirits.

Reading and Responding

1. When you hear the word *cancer,* what comes to mind? Freewrite about
   this for half a page or so.
2. When you hear the word *radiation,* what comes to mind? Freewrite
   about this for half a page or so.

Working Together

1. In order to get your group discussion rolling, start by individually writing one sentence about the experience of reading this selection; then read your sentences aloud. Once you've heard each person, what conclusions can you begin to draw about how your group was affected by this piece? Make a list of the issues or reactions that stay in your mind after you've finished reading.
2. As a group, discuss what surprised you in this selection. What information was entirely new or startling to you? Make a list of these things.
3. As a group, decide whether or not you agree with the decision of the 10th Circuit Court of Appeals to affirm that the United States government cannot be sued. Assume that you're the Supreme Court and you've agreed to review the appeals court decision. What are the major issues of the case? How would you vote?

Rethinking and Rewriting

1. Write your opinion regarding *Irene Allen vs. the United States of America.* Assume that you're a Supreme Court judge and you're either going to uphold the appeals court decision or you're going to overturn it.
2. Assume that you are Terry Tempest Williams; assume that her family history is your family history, that her medical history is your medical history. Write an open letter to the Supreme Court explaining why you feel so passionately that the Court should agree to reconsider the appeals court decision. Make sure that your letter makes clear all that you feel is at stake here.
3. Look at how this essay ends. Then argue that the protest action Williams took was foolish, that it accomplished nothing. Or argue that her action was significant and important. Either way, explain carefully.
4. Do a modest (five-page) research paper on the causes or suspected causes of breast cancer. What do scientists now think about any environmental causes of breast cancer? If you have some personal experience (yourself or your family members) with some other kind of cancer, investigate that kind of cancer, if you wish.

"THE IDEA OF A GARDEN"

Michael Pollan

In 1983 Michael Pollan and his wife purchased what he describes as "a sliver of a derelict dairy farm on the eastern edge of the Housatonic Valley" in Connecticut. Then executive editor of Harper's *magazine (he is now editor-at-large), Pollan wrote* Second Nature: A Gardener's Education *(1991) as a chronicle of his thought and effort at cultivating that land. The selection here is chapter 10 of that book, a chapter that traces Pollan's sense that "the idea of a garden—as a place, both real and metaphorical, where nature and culture can be wedded in a way that can benefit both—may be as useful to us today as the idea of wilderness has been in the past."*

As You Read

1. As you start reading, look for the major issue that Michael Pollan develops. Mark the passages that define the controversy.
2. Once the controversy itself seems clear, start marking passages that define the two sides. Or start keeping a list of the ways each side is described. When the two sides agree, mark that too.
3. If anything you read here reminds you of earlier readings, make an annotation saying that in the margin.

The biggest news to come out of my town in many years was the tornado, or tornadoes, that careened through here on July 10, 1989, a Monday. Shooting down the Housatonic River Valley from the Berkshires, it veered east over Coltsfoot Mountain and then, after smudging the sky a weird gray green, proceeded to pinball madly from hillside to hillside for about fifteen minutes before wheeling back up into the sky. This was part of the same storm that ripped open the bark of my ash tree. But the damage was much, much worse on the other side of town. Like a gigantic, skidding pencil eraser, the twister neatly erased whole patches of woods and roughly smeared many other ones, where it wiped out just the tops of the trees. Overnight, large parts of town were rendered unrecognizable.

One place where the eraser came down squarely was in the Cathedral Pines, a famous forest of old-growth white pine trees close to the center of town. A kind of local shrine, this forty-two-acre forest was one of the oldest stands of white pine in New England, the trees untouched since about 1800. To see it was to have some idea how the New World forest must have looked to the first settlers, and in 1985 the federal government designated it a "national natural landmark." To enter Cathedral Pines on a hot summer day was like stepping out of the sun into a dim cathedral, the sunlight cooled and sweetened by the trillions of pine needles as it worked its way down to soft, sprung ground that had been unacquainted with blue sky for the better part of two centuries. The storm came through at about five in the evening, and it took only a few minutes of wind before pines more than one hundred fifty feet tall and as wide around as missiles lay jackstrawed on the ground like a fistful of pencils dropped from a great height. The wind was so thunderous that people in houses at the forest's edge did not know trees had fallen until they ventured outside after the storm had passed. The following morning, the sky now clear, was the first in more than a century to bring sunlight crashing down onto this particular patch of earth.

"It is a terrible mess," the first selectman told the newspapers; "a tragedy," said another Cornwall resident, voicing the deep sense of loss shared by many in town. But in the days that followed, the selectman and the rest of us learned that our responses, though understandable, were shortsighted, unscientific, and, worst of all, anthropocentric. "It may be a calamity to us," a state environmental official told a reporter from the *Hartford Courant,* but "to biology it is not a travesty. It is just a natural occurrence." The Nature Conservancy, which owns Cathedral Pines, issued a press release explaining that "Monday's storm was just another link in the continuous chain of events that is responsible for shaping and changing this forest."

It wasn't long before the rub of these two perspectives set off a controversy heated enough to find its way into the pages of *The New York Times.* The Nature Conservancy, in keeping with its mandate to maintain its lands in a "state of nature," indicated that it would leave Cathedral Pines alone, allowing the forest to take its "natural course," whatever that might be. To town officials and neighbors of the forest this was completely unacceptable. The downed trees, besides constituting an eyesore right at the edge of town, also posed a fire hazard. A few summers of drought, and the timber might go up in a blaze that would threaten several nearby homes and possibly even the town itself. Many people in Cornwall wanted Cathedral Pines cleared and replanted, so that at least the next generation might live to see some semblance of the old forest. A few others had the poor taste to point out the waste of more than a million board-feet of valuable timber, stupendous lengths of unblemished, knot-free pine.

The newspapers depicted it as a classic environmental battle, pitting   5
the interests of man against nature, and in a way it was that. On one side were the environmental purists, who felt that *any* intervention by man in the disposition of this forest would be unnatural. "If you're going to clean it up," one purist declared in the local press, "you might as well put up condos." On the other side stood the putative interests of man, variously expressed in the vocabulary of safety (the fire hazard), economics (the wasted lumber), and aesthetics (the "terrible mess").

Everybody enjoys a good local fight, but I have to say I soon found the whole thing depressing. This was indeed a classic environmental battle, in that it seemed to exemplify just about everything that's wrong with the way we approach problems of this kind these days. Both sides began to caricature each other's positions: the selectman's "terrible mess" line earned him ridicule for his anthropocentrism in the letters page of *The New York Times;* he in turn charged a Yale scientist who argued for noninterference with "living in an ivory tower."

But as far apart as the two sides seemed to stand, they actually shared more common ground than they realized. Both started from the premise that man and nature were irreconcilably opposed, and that the victory of one necessarily entailed the loss of the other. Both sides, in other words, accepted the premises of what we might call the "wilderness ethic," which is based on the assumption that the relationship of man and nature resembles a zero-sum game. This idea, widely held and yet largely unexamined, has set the terms of most environmental battles in this country since the very first important one: the fight over the building of the Hetch Hetchy Dam in 1907, which pitted John Muir against Gifford Pinchot, whom Muir used to call a "temple destroyer." Watching my little local debate unfold over the course of the summer, and grow progressively more shrill and sterile, I began to wonder if perhaps the wilderness ethic itself, for all that it has accomplished in this country over the past century, had now become part of the problem. I also began to wonder if it might be possible to formulate a different ethic to guide us in our dealings with nature, at least in some places some of the time, an ethic that would be based not on the idea of wilderness but on the idea of a garden.*

* * *

Foresters who have examined sections of fallen trees in Cathedral Pines think that the oldest trees in the forest date from 1780 or so, which suggests that the site was probably logged by the first generation of settlers. The Cathedral Pines are not, then, "virgin growth." The rings of felled trees also reveal a significant growth spurt in 1840, which probably indicates that loggers removed hardwood trees in that year, leaving the pines to grow without competition. In 1883, the Calhouns, an old Cornwall family whose property borders the forest, bought the land to protect the trees from the threat of logging; in 1967 they deeded it to the Nature Conservancy, stipulating that it be maintained in its natural state. Since then, and up until the tornado made its paths impassable, the forest has been a popular place for hiking and Sunday outings. Over the years, more than a few Cornwall residents have come to the forest to be married.

Cathedral Pines is not in any meaningful sense a wilderness. The natural history of the forest intersects at many points with the social history of Cornwall. It is the product of early logging practices, which clear-cut

---

*In developing some of the ideas for this chapter, I've drawn from a panel discussion on environmental ethics that I moderated for the April 1990 issue of *Harper's* magazine. The participants were James Lovelock, Frederick Turner, Daniel Botkin, Dave Foreman, and Robert Yaro. This chapter also owes a lot to the work of Wendell Berry, René Dubos, William Cronon, William Jordan III, and Alston Chase.

the land once and then cut it again, this time selectively, a hundred years later. Other human factors almost certainly played a part in the forest's history; we can safely assume that any fires in the area were extinguished before they reached Cathedral Pines. (Though we don't ordinarily think of it in these terms, fire suppression is one of the more significant effects that the European has had on the American landscape.) Cathedral Pines, then, is in some part a man-made landscape, and it could reasonably be argued that to exclude man at this point in its history would constitute a break with its past.

But both parties to the dispute chose to disregard the actual history   *10* of Cathedral Pines, and instead to think of the forest as a wilderness in the commonly accepted sense of that term: a pristine place untouched by white men. Since the romantics, we've prized such places as refuges from the messiness of the human estate, vantages from which we might transcend the vagaries of that world and fix on what Thoreau called "higher laws." Certainly an afternoon in Cathedral Pines fostered such feelings, and its very name reflects the pantheism that lies behind them. Long before science coined the term *ecosystem* to describe it, we've had the sense that nature undisturbed displays a miraculous order and balance, something the human world can only dream about. When man leaves it alone, nature will tend toward a healthy and abiding state of equilibrium. Wilderness, the purest expression of this natural law, stands out beyond history.

These are powerful and in many ways wonderful ideas. The notion of wilderness is a kind of taboo in our culture, in many cases acting as a check on our inclination to dominate and spoil nature. It has inspired us to set aside such spectacular places as Yellowstone and Yosemite. But wilderness is also a profoundly alienating idea, for it drives a large wedge between man and nature. Set against the foil of nature's timeless cycles, human history appears linear and unpredictable, buffeted by time and chance as it drives blindly into the future. Natural history, by comparison, obeys fixed and legible laws, ones that make the "laws" of human history seem puny, second-rate things scarcely deserving of the label. We have little idea what the future holds for the town of Cornwall, but surely nature has a plan for Cathedral Pines; leave the forest alone and that plan—which science knows by the name of "forest succession"—will unfold inexorably, in strict accordance with natural law. A new climax forest will emerge as nature works to restore her equilibrium—or at least that's the idea.

The notion that nature has a plan for Cathedral Pines is a comforting one, and certainly it supplies a powerful argument for leaving the forest alone. Naturally I was curious to know what that plan was: what does nature do with an old pine forest blown down by a tornado? I consulted a few field guides and standard works of forest ecology hoping to find out.

According to the classical theory of forest succession, set out in the nineteenth century by, among others, Henry Thoreau, a pine forest that has been abruptly destroyed will usually be succeeded by hardwoods, typically oak. This is because squirrels commonly bury acorns in pine forests and neglect to retrieve many of them. The oaks sprout and, because shade doesn't greatly hinder young oaks, the seedlings frequently manage to survive beneath the dark canopy of a mature pine forest. Pine seedlings, on the other hand, require more sunlight than a mature pine forest admits; they won't sprout in shade. So by the time the pine forest comes down, the oak saplings will have had a head start in the race to dominate the new forest. Before any new pines have had a chance to sprout, the oaks will be well on their way to cornering the sunlight and inheriting the forest.

This is what I read, anyway, and I decided to ask around to confirm that Cathedral Pines was expected to behave as predicted. I spoke to a forest ecologist and an expert on the staff of the Nature Conservancy. They told me that the classical theory of pine-forest succession probably does describe the underlying tendency at work in Cathedral Pines. But it turns out that a lot can go, if not "wrong" exactly, then at least differently. For what if there are no oaks nearby? Squirrels will travel only so far in search of a hiding place for their acorns. Instead of oaks, there may be hickory nuts stashed all over Cathedral Pines. And then there's the composition of species planted by the forest's human neighbors to consider; one of these, possibly some exotic (that is, nonnative), could conceivably race in and take over.

"It all depends," is the refrain I kept hearing as I tried to pin down   15
nature's intentions for Cathedral Pines. Forest succession, it seems, is only a theory, a metaphor of our making, and almost as often as not nature makes a fool of it. The number of factors that will go into the determination of Cathedral Pines' future is almost beyond comprehension. Consider just this small sample of the things that could happen to alter irrevocably its future course:

A lightning storm—or a cigarette butt flicked from a passing car—ignites a fire next summer. Say it's a severe fire, hot enough to damage the fertility of the soil, thereby delaying recovery of the forest for decades. Or say it rains that night, making the fire a mild one, just hot enough to kill the oak saplings and allow the relatively fire-resistant pine seedlings to flourish without competition. A new pine forest after all? Perhaps. But what if the population of deer happens to soar the following year? Their browsing would wipe out the young pines and create an opening for spruce, the taste of which deer happen not to like.

Or say there is no fire. Without one, it could take hundreds of years for the downed pine trees to rot and return their nutrients to the soil. Trees grow poorly in the exhausted soil, but the seeds of brambles, which can lie dormant in the ground for fifty years, sprout and proliferate: we end up with a hundred years of brush. Or perhaps a breeze in, say, the summer of 1997 carries in seedpods from the Norway maple standing in a nearby front yard at the precise moment when conditions for their germination are perfect. Norway maple, you'll recall, is a European species, introduced here early in the nineteenth century and widely planted as a street tree. Should this exotic species happen to prevail, Cathedral Pines becomes one very odd-looking and awkwardly named wilderness area.

But the outcome could be much worse. Let's say the rains next spring are unusually heavy, washing all the topsoil away (the forest stood on a steep hillside). Only exotic weed species can survive now, and one of these happens to be Japanese honeysuckle, a nineteenth-century import of such rampant habit that it can choke out the growth of all trees indefinitely. We end up with no forest at all.

Nobody, in other words, can say what will happen in Cathedral Pines. And the reason is not that forest ecology is a young or imperfect science, but because *nature herself doesn't know what's going to happen here.* Nature has no grand design for this place. An incomprehensibly various and complex set of circumstances—some of human origin, but many not—will determine the future of Cathedral Pines. And whatever that future turns out to be, it would not unfold in precisely the same way twice. Nature may possess certain inherent tendencies, ones that theories such as forest succession can describe, but chance events can divert her course into an almost infinite number of different channels.

It's hard to square this fact with our strong sense that some kind of quasi-divine order inheres in nature's workings. But science lately has been finding that contingency plays nearly as big a role in natural history as it does in human history. Forest ecologists today will acknowledge that succession theories are little more than comforting narratives we impose on a surprisingly unpredictable process; even so-called climax forests are sometimes superseded. (In many places in the northern United States today, mature stands of oak are inexplicably being invaded by maples—skunks at the climax garden party.) Many ecologists will now freely admit that even the concept of an ecosystem is only a metaphor, a human construct imposed upon a much more variable and precarious reality. An ecosystem may be a useful concept, but no ecologist has ever succeeded in isolating one in nature. Nor is the process of evolution as logical or inexorable as we have thought. The current thinking in paleontology holds that the evolution of any given species, our own included, is not the necessary product of any natural laws, but rather the outcome of a concatenation of chance events—of "just history" in the words of Stephen Jay Gould. Add or remove any single happenstance—the asteroid fails to wipe out the dinosaurs; a little chordate worm called *Pikaia* succumbs in the Burgess extinction—and humankind never arrives.

Across several disciplines, in fact, scientists are coming to the conclusion that more "just history" is at work in nature than had previously been thought. Yet our metaphors still picture nature as logical, stable, and ahistorical—more like a watch than, say, an organism or a stock exchange, to name two metaphors that may well be more apt. Chance and contingency, it turns out, are everywhere in nature; she has no fixed goals, no unalterable pathways into the future, no inflexible rules that she herself can't bend or break at will. She is more like us (or we are more like her) than we ever imagined.

20

To learn this, for me at least, changes everything. I take it to be profoundly good news, though I can easily imagine how it might trouble some people. For many of us, nature is a last bastion of certainty; wilderness, as something beyond the reach of history and accident, is one of the last in our fast-dwindling supply of metaphysical absolutes, those comforting transcendental values by which we have traditionally taken our measure and set our sights. To take away predictable, divinely ordered nature is to pull up one of our last remaining anchors. We are liable to float away on the trackless sea of our own subjectivity.

But the discovery that time and chance hold sway even in nature can also be liberating. Because contingency is an invitation to participate in history. Human choice is unnatural only if nature is deterministic; human change is unnatural only if she is changeless in our absence. If the future of Cathedral Pines is up for grabs, if its history will always be the product of myriad chance events, then why shouldn't we also claim our place among all those deciding factors? For aren't we also one of nature's contingencies? And if our cigarette butts and Norway maples and acid rain are going to shape the future of this place, then why not also our hopes and desires?

Nature will condone an almost infinite number of possible futures for Cathedral Pines. Some would be better than others. True, what we would regard as "better" is probably not what the beetles would prefer. But nature herself has no strong preference. That doesn't mean she will countenance *any* outcome; she's already ruled out many possible futures (tropical rain forest, desert, etc.) and, all things being equal, she'd probably lean toward the oak. But all things aren't equal (*her* idea) and she is evidently happy to let the free play of numerous big and little contingencies settle the matter. To exclude from these human desire would be, at least in this place at this time, arbitrary, perverse and, yes, unnatural.

* * *

Establishing that we should have a vote in the disposition of Cathedral Pines is much easier than figuring out how we should cast it. The discovery of contingency in nature would seem to fling open a Pandora's box. For if there's nothing fixed or inevitable about nature's course, what's to stop us from concluding that anything goes? It's a whole lot easier to assume that nature left to her own devices knows what's best for a place, to let ourselves be guided by the wilderness ethic.

And maybe that's what we should do. Just because the wilderness ethic is based on a picture of nature that is probably more mythical than real doesn't necessarily mean we have to discard it. In the same way that the Declaration of Independence begins with the useful fiction that "all men are created equal," we could simply stipulate that Cathedral Pines *is* wilderness, and proceed on that assumption. The test of the wilderness ethic is not how truthful it is, but how useful it is in doing what we want to do—in protecting and improving the environment.

So how good a guide is the wilderness ethic in this particular case? Certainly treating Cathedral Pines as a wilderness will keep us from building condos there. When you don't trust yourself to do the right thing, it helps to have an authority as wise and experienced as nature to decide matters for you. But what if nature decides on Japanese honeysuckle— three hundred years of wall-to-wall brush? We would then have a forest not only that we don't like, but that isn't even a wilderness, since it was man who brought Japanese honeysuckle to Cornwall. At this point in history, after humans have left their stamp on virtually every corner of the Earth, doing nothing is frequently a poor recipe for wilderness. In many cases it leads to a gradually deteriorating environment (as seems to be happening in Yellowstone), or to an environment shaped in large part by the acts and mistakes of previous human inhabitants.

If it's real wilderness we want in Cathedral Pines, and not merely an imagined innocence, we will have to restore it. This is the paradox faced by the Nature Conservancy and most other advocates of wilderness: at this point in history, creating a landscape that bears no marks of human intervention will require a certain amount of human intervention. At a minimum it would entail weeding the exotic species from Cathedral Pines, and that is something the Nature Conservancy's strict adherence to the wilderness ethic will not permit.

But what if the Conservancy *was* willing to intervene just enough to erase any evidence of man's presence? It would soon run up against some difficult questions for which its ethic leaves it ill-prepared. For what is the "real" state of nature in Cathedral Pines? Is it the way the forest looked before the settlers arrived? We could restore that condition by removing all traces of European man. Yet isn't that a rather Eurocentric (if not racist) notion of wilderness? We now know that the Indians were not the ecological eunuchs we once thought. They too left their mark on the land: fires set by Indians determined the composition of the New England forests and probably created that "wilderness" we call the Great Plains. For true untouched wilderness we have to go a lot further back than 1640 or 1492. And if we want to restore the landscape to its pre-Indian condition, then we're going to need a lot of heavy ice-making equipment (not to mention a few woolly mammoths) to make it look right.

But even that would be arbitrary. In fact there is no single moment 30 in time that we can point to and say, *this* is the state of nature in Cathedral Pines. Just since the last ice age alone, that "state of nature" has undergone a thorough revolution every thousand years or so, as tree species forced south by the glaciers migrated back north (a process that is still going on), as the Indians arrived and set their fires, as the large mammals disappeared, as the climate fluctuated—as all the usual historical contingencies came on and off the stage. For several thousand years after the ice age, this part of Connecticut was a treeless tundra; is *that* the true state of nature in Cathedral Pines? The inescapable fact is that, if we want wilderness here, we will have to choose *which* wilderness we want—an idea that is inimical to the wilderness ethic. For wasn't the attraction of wilderness precisely the fact that it relieved us of having to make choices—wasn't nature going to decide, letting us off the hook of history and anthropocentrism?

No such luck, it seems. "Wilderness" is not nearly as straightforward or dependable a guide as we'd like to believe. If we do nothing, we may end up with an impoverished weed patch of our own (indirect) creation, which would hardly count as a victory for wilderness. And if we want to restore Cathedral Pines to some earlier condition, we're forced into making the kinds of inevitably anthropocentric choices and distinctions we turned to wilderness to escape. (Indeed, doing a decent job of wilderness restoration would take all the technology and scientific know-how humans can muster.) Either way, there appears to be no escape from history, not even in nature.

* * *

The reason that the wilderness ethic isn't very helpful in a place like Cathedral Pines is that it's an absolutist ethic: man or nature, it says, pick one. As soon as history or circumstance blurs that line, it gets us into trouble. There are times and places when man or nature is the right and necessary choice; back at Hetch Hetchy in 1907 that may well have been the case. But it seems to me that these days most of the environmental questions we face are more like the ambiguous ones posed by Cathedral Pines, and about these the wilderness ethic has less and less to say that is of much help.

The wilderness ethic doesn't tell us what to do when Yellowstone's ecosystem begins to deteriorate, as a result not of our interference but of our neglect. When a species threatens to overwhelm and ruin a habitat because history happened to kill off the predator that once kept its population in check, the ethic is mute. It is confounded, too, when the only hope for the survival of another species is the manipulation of its natural habitat by man. It has nothing to say in all those places where development is desirable or unavoidable except: Don't do it. When we're forced to choose between a hydroelectric power plant and a nuclear one, it refuses to help. That's because the wilderness ethic can't make distinctions between one kind of intervention in nature and another—between weeding Cathedral Pines and developing a theme park there. "You might as well put up condos" is its classic answer to any plan for human intervention in nature.

"All or nothing," says the wilderness ethic, and in fact we've ended up with a landscape in America that conforms to that injunction remarkably well. Thanks to exactly this kind of either/or thinking, Americans have done an admirable job of drawing lines around certain sacred areas (we did invent the wilderness area) and a terrible job of managing the rest of our land. The reason is not hard to find: the only environmental ethic we have has nothing useful to say about those areas outside the line. Once a landscape is no longer "virgin" it is typically written off as fallen, lost to nature, irredeemable. We hand it over to the jurisdiction of that other sacrosanct American ethic: laissez-faire economics. "You might as well put up condos." And so we do.

Indeed, the wilderness ethic and laissez-faire economics, antithetical   35
as they might at first appear, are really mirror images of one another. Each proposes a quasi-divine force—Nature, the Market—that, left to its own devices, somehow knows what's best for a place. Nature and the market are both self-regulating, guided by an invisible hand. Worshippers of either share a deep, Puritan distrust of man, taking it on faith that human tinkering with the natural or economic order can only pervert it. Neither will acknowledge that their respective divinities can also err: that nature produces the AIDS virus as well as the rose, that the same markets that produce stupendous wealth can also crash. (Actually, worshippers of the market are a bit more realistic than worshippers of nature: they long ago stopped relying on the free market to supply us with such necessities as food and shelter. Though they don't like to talk about it much, they accept the need for society to "garden" the market.)

Essentially, we have divided our country in two, between the kingdom of wilderness, which rules about 8 percent of America's land, and the kingdom of the market, which rules the rest. Perhaps we should be grateful for secure borders. But what do those of us who care about nature do when we're on the market side, which is most of the time? How do we behave? What are our goals? We can't reasonably expect to change the borders, no matter how many power lines and dams Earth First! blows up. No, the wilderness ethic won't be of much help over here. Its politics are bound to be hopelessly romantic (consisting of impractical schemes to redraw the borders) or nihilistic. Faced with hard questions about how to confront global environmental problems such as the greenhouse effect or ozone depletion (problems that respect no borders), adherents of the wilderness ethic are apt to throw up their hands in despair and declare the "end of nature."

The only thing that's really in danger of ending is a romantic, pantheistic idea of nature that we invented in the first place, one whose passing might well turn out to be a blessing in disguise. Useful as it has been in helping us protect the sacred 8 percent, it nevertheless has failed to prevent us from doing a great deal of damage to the remaining 92 percent. This old idea may have taught us how to worship nature, but it didn't tell us how to live with her. It told us more than we needed to know about virginity and rape, and almost nothing about marriage. The metaphor of divine nature can admit only two roles for man: as worshipper (the naturalist's role) or temple destroyer (the developer's). But that drama is all played out now. The temple's been destroyed—if it ever was a temple. Nature *is* dead, if by nature we mean something that stands apart from man and messy history. And now that it is, perhaps we can begin to write some new parts for ourselves, ones that will show us how to start out from here, not from some imagined state of innocence, and let us get down to the work at hand.

* * *

Thoreau and Muir and their descendants went to the wilderness and returned with the makings of America's first environmental ethic. Today it still stands, though somewhat strained and tattered. What if now, instead of to the wilderness, we were to look to the garden for the makings of a new ethic? One that would not necessarily supplant the earlier one, but might give us something useful to say in those cases when it is silent or unhelpful?

It will take better thinkers than me to flesh out what such an ethic might look like. But even my limited experience in the garden has persuaded me that the materials needed to construct it—the fresh metaphors about nature we need—may be found there. For the garden is a place with long experience of questions having to do with man *in* nature. Below are some provisional notes, based on my own experiences and the experiences of other gardeners I've met or read, on the kinds of answers the garden is apt to give.

1. An ethic based on the garden would give local answers. Unlike   40
the wilderness idea, it would propose different solutions in different places and times. This strikes me as both a strength and a weakness. It's a weakness because a garden ethic will never speak as clearly or univocally as the wilderness ethic does. In a country as large and geographically various as this, it is probably inevitable that we will favor abstract landscape ideas— grids, lawns, monocultures, wildernesses—which can be applied across the board, even legislated nationally; such ideas have the power to simplify and unite. Yet isn't this power itself part of the problem? The health of a place generally suffers whenever we impose practices on it that are better suited to another place; a lawn in Virginia makes sense in a way that a lawn in Arizona does not.

So a garden ethic would begin with Alexander Pope's famous advice to landscape designers: "Consult the Genius of the Place in all." It's hard to imagine this slogan ever replacing Earth First!'s "No Compromise in Defense of Mother Earth" on American bumper stickers; nor should it, at least not everywhere. For Pope's dictum suggests that there are places whose "genius" will, if hearkened to, counsel "no compromise." Yet what is right for Yosemite is not necessarily right for Cathedral Pines.

2. The gardener starts out from here. By that I mean, he accepts contingency, his own and nature's. He doesn't spend a lot of time worrying about whether he has a god-given right to change nature. It's enough for him to know that, for some historical or biological reason, humankind finds itself living in places (six of the seven continents) where it must substantially alter the environment in order to survive. If we had remained on African savanna things might be different. And if I lived in zone six I

could probably grow good tomatoes without the use of plastic. The gardener learns to play the hand he's been dealt.

3. A garden ethic would be frankly anthropocentric. As I began to understand when I planted my roses and my maple tree, we know nature only through the screen of our metaphors; to see her plain is probably impossible. (And not necessarily desirable, as George Eliot once suggested: "If we could hear the squirrel's heartbeat, the sound of the grass growing, we should die of that roar." Without the editing of our perceptions, nature might prove unbearable.) Melville was describing all of nature when he described the whiteness of the whale, its "dumb blankness, full of meaning." Even wilderness, in both its satanic and benevolent incarnations, is an historical, man-made idea. Every one of our various metaphors for nature—"wilderness," "ecosystem," "Gaia," "resource," "wasteland"—is already a kind of garden, an indissoluble mixture of our culture and whatever it is that's really out there. "Garden" may sound like a hopelessly anthropocentric concept, but it's probably one we can't get past.

The gardener doesn't waste much time on metaphysics—on figuring out what a "truer" perspective on nature (such as biocentrism or geocentrism) might look like. That's probably because he's noticed that most of the very long or wide perspectives we've recently been asked to adopt (including the one advanced by the Nature Conservancy in Cathedral Pines) are indifferent to our well-being and survival as a species. On this point he agrees with Wendell Berry—that "it is not natural to be disloyal to one's own kind."

4. That said, though, the gardener's conception of his self-interest is broad and enlightened. Anthropocentric as he may be, he recognizes that he is dependent for his health and survival on many other forms of life, so he is careful to take their interests into account in whatever he does. He is in fact a wilderness advocate of a certain kind. It is when he respects and nurtures the wilderness of his soil and his plants that his garden seems to flourish most. Wildness, he has found, resides not only out there, but right here: in his soil, in his plants, even in himself. Overcultivation tends to repress this quality, which experience tells him is necessary to health in all three realms. But wildness is more a quality than a place, and though humans can't manufacture it, they can nourish and husband it. That is precisely what I'm doing when I make compost and return it to the soil; it is what we could be doing in Cathedral Pines (and not necessarily by leaving the place alone). The gardener cultivates wildness, but he does so carefully and respectfully, in full recognition of its mystery.

5. The gardener tends not to be romantic about nature. What could be more natural than the storms and droughts and plagues that ruin his garden? Cruelty, aggression, suffering—these, too, are nature's offspring (and not, as Rousseau tried to convince us, culture's). Nature is probably a poor place to look for values. She was indifferent to humankind's arrival, and she is indifferent to our survival.

It's only in the last century or so that we seem to have forgotten this. Our romance of nature is a comparatively recent idea, the product of the industrial age's novel conceit that nature could be conquered, and probably also of the fact that few of us work with nature directly anymore. But should current weather forecasts prove to be accurate (a rapid, permanent warming trend accompanied by severe storms), our current romance will look like a brief historical anomaly, a momentary lapse of judgment. Nature may once again turn dangerous and capricious and unconquerable. When this happens, we will quickly lose our crush on her.

Compared to the naturalist, the gardener never fell head over heels for nature. He's seen her ruin his plans too many times for that. The gardener has learned, perforce, to live with her ambiguities—that she is neither all good nor all bad, that she gives as well as takes away. Nature's apt to pull the rug out from under us at any time, to make a grim joke of our noblest intention. Perhaps this explains why garden writing tends to be comic, rather than lyrical or elegiac in the way that nature writing usually is: the gardener can never quite forget about the rug underfoot, the possibility of the offstage hook.

6. The gardener feels he has a legitimate quarrel with nature—with her weeds and storms and plagues, her rot and death. What's more, that quarrel has produced much of value, not only in his own time here (this garden, these fruits), but over the whole course of Western history. Civilization itself, as Freud and Frazer and many others have observed, is the product of that quarrel. But at the same time, the gardener appreciates that it would probably not be in his interest, or in nature's, to push his side of this argument too hard. Many points of contention that humankind thought it had won—DDT's victory over insects, say, or medicine's conquest of infectious disease—turned out to be Pyrrhic or illusory triumphs. Better to keep the quarrel going, the good gardener reasons, than to reach for outright victory, which is dangerous in the attempt and probably impossible anyway.

7. The gardener doesn't take it for granted that man's impact on 50 nature will always be negative. Perhaps he's observed how his own garden has made this patch of land a better place, even by nature's own standards. His gardening has greatly increased the diversity and abundance of life in this place. Besides the many exotic species of plants he's introduced, the mammal, rodent, and insect populations have burgeoned, and his soil supports a much richer community of microbes than it did before.

Judged strictly by these standards, nature occasionally makes mistakes. The climax forest could certainly be considered one (a place where the number and variety of living things have declined to a crisis point) and evolution teems with others. At the same time, it should be acknowledged that man occasionally creates new ecosystems much richer than the ones they replaced, and not merely on the scale of a garden: think of the tall-grass prairies of the Midwest, England's hedgerow landscape, the countryside of the Ile de France, the patchwork of fields and forests in this part of New England. Most of us would be happy to call such places "nature," but that does not do them (or us) justice; they are really a kind of garden, a second nature.

The gardener doesn't feel that by virtue of the fact that he changes nature he is somehow outside of it. He looks around and sees that human hopes and desires are by now part and parcel of the landscape. The "environment" is not, and has never been, a neutral, fixed backdrop; it is in fact alive, changing all the time in response to innumerable contingencies, one of these being the presence within it of the gardener. And that presence is neither inherently good nor bad.

8. The gardener firmly believes it is possible to make distinctions between kinds and degrees of human intervention in nature. Isn't the difference between the Ile de France and Love Canal, or a pine forest and a condo development, proof enough that the choice isn't really between "all or nothing"? The gardener doesn't doubt that it is possible to discriminate; it is through experience in the garden that he develops this faculty.

Because of his experience, the gardener is not likely to conclude from the fact that some intervention in nature is unavoidable, therefore "anything goes." This is precisely where his skill and interest lie: in determining what does and does not go in a particular place. How much is too much? What suits this land? How can we get what we want here while nature goes about getting what she wants? He has no doubt that good answers to these questions can be found.

9. The good gardener commonly borrows his methods, if not his goals, from nature herself. For though nature doesn't seem to dictate in advance what we can do in a place—we are free, in the same way evolution is, to try something completely new—in the end she will let us know what does and does not work. She is above all a pragmatist, and so is the successful gardener.

By studying nature's ways and means, the gardener can find answers to the questions, What is apt to work? What avails here? This seems to hold true at many levels of specificity. In one particular patch of my vegetable garden—a low, damp area—I failed with every crop I planted until I stopped to consider what nature grew in a similar area nearby: briars. So I planted raspberries, which are of course a cultivated kind of briar, and they have flourished. A trivial case, but it shows how attentiveness to nature can help us to attune our desires with her ways.

The imitation of nature is of course the principle underlying organic gardening. Organic gardeners have learned to mimic nature's own methods of building fertility in the soil, controlling insect populations and disease, recycling nutrients. But the practices we call "organic" are not themselves "natural," any more than the bird call of a hunter is natural. They are more like man-made analogues of natural processes. But they seem to work. And they at least suggest a way to approach other problems—from a town's decision on what to do with a blown-down pine forest, to society's choice

55

among novel new technologies. In each case, there will be some alternatives that align our needs and desires with nature's ways more closely than others.

It does seem that we do best in nature when we imitate her—when we learn to think like running water, or a carrot, an aphid, a pine forest, or a compost pile. That's probably because nature, after almost four billion years of trial-and-error experience, has wide knowledge of what works in life. Surely we're better off learning how to draw on her experience than trying to repeat it, if only because we don't have that kind of time.

10. If nature is one necessary source of instruction for a garden ethic, culture is the other. Civilization may be part of our problem with respect to nature, but there will be no solution without it. As Wendell Berry has pointed out, it is culture, and certainly not nature, that teaches us to observe and remember, to learn from our mistakes, to share our experiences, and perhaps most important of all, to restrain ourselves. Nature does not teach its creatures to control their appetites except by the harshest of lessons—epidemics, mass death, extinctions. Nothing would be more natural than for humankind to burden the environment to the extent that it was rendered unfit for human life. Nature in that event would not be the loser, nor would it disturb her laws in the least—operating as it has always done, natural selection would unceremoniously do us in. Should this fate be averted, it will only be because our culture—*our* laws and metaphors, our science and technology, our ongoing conversation about nature and man's place in it—pointed us in the direction of a different future. Nature will not do this for us.

The gardener in nature is that most artificial of creatures, a civilized   60
human being: in control of his appetites, solicitous of nature, self-conscious and responsible, mindful of the past and the future, and at ease with the fundamental ambiguity of his predicament—which is that though he lives in nature, he is no longer strictly *of* nature. Further, he knows that neither his success nor his failure in this place is ordained. Nature is apparently indifferent to his fate, and this leaves him free—indeed, obliges him—to make his own way here as best he can.

* * *

What would an ethic based on these ideas—based on the idea of the garden—advise us to do in Cathedral Pines? I don't know enough about the ecology of the place to say with certainty, but I think I have some sense of how we might proceed under its dispensation. We would start out, of course, by consulting "the Genius of the Place." This would tell us, among other things, that Cathedral Pines is not a wilderness, and so probably should not be treated as one. It is a cultural as well as a natural landscape, and to exclude the wishes of the townspeople from our plans for the place would be false. To treat it now as wilderness is to impose an abstract and alien idea on it.

Consulting the genius of the place also means inquiring as to what nature will allow us to do here—what this "locale permits, and what [it] denies," as Virgil wrote in *The Georgics*. We know right off, for instance, that this plot of land can support a magnificent forest of white pines. Nature would not object if we decided to replant the pine forest. Indeed, this would be a perfectly reasonable, environmentally sound thing to do.

If we chose to go this route, we would be undertaking a fairly simple act of what is called "ecological restoration." This relatively new school of environmentalism has its roots in Aldo Leopold's pioneering efforts to re-create a tall-grass prairie on the grounds of the University of Wisconsin Arboretum in the 1930s. Leopold and his followers (who continue to maintain the restored prairie today) believed that it is not always enough to conserve the land—that sometimes it is desirable, and possible, for man to intervene in nature in order to improve it. Specifically, man should intervene to re-create damaged ecosystems: polluted rivers, clear-cut forests, vanished prairies, dead lakes. The restorationists also believe, and in this they remind me of the green thumb, that the best way to learn about nature's ways is by trying to imitate them. (In fact much of what we know about the role of fire in creating and sustaining prairies comes from their efforts.) But the most important contribution of the restorationists has been to set forth a positive, active role for man in nature—in their conception, as equal parts gardener and healer. It seems to me that the idea of ecological restoration is consistent with a garden ethic, and perhaps with the Hippocratic Oath as well.

From the work of the ecological restorationists, we now know that it is possible to skip and manipulate the stages of forest succession. They would probably advise us to burn the fallen timber—an act that, though not strictly speaking "natural," would serve as an effective analogue of the natural process by which a forest is regenerated. The fires we set would reinvigorate the soil (thereby enhancing *that* wilderness) and at the same time clear out the weed species, hardwood saplings, and brush. By doing all this, we will have imitated the conditions under which a white pine forest is born, and the pines might then return on their own. Or else—it makes little difference—we could plant them. At that point, our work would be done, and the pine forest could take care of itself. It would take many decades, but restoring the Cathedral Pines would strain neither our capabilities nor nature's sufferance. And in doing so, we would also be restoring the congenial relationship between man and nature that prevailed in this place before the storm and the subsequent controversy. That would be no small thing.

Nature would not preclude more novel solutions for Cathedral Pines—other kinds of forest-gardens or even parks could probably flourish on this site. But since the town has traditionally regarded Cathedral Pines as a kind of local institution, one steeped in shared memories and historical significance, I would argue that the genius of the place rules out doing anything unprecedented here. The past is our best guide in this particular case, and not only on questions of ecology.

But replanting the pine forest is not the only good option for Cathedral Pines. There is another forest we might want to restore on this site, one that is also in keeping with its history and its meaning to the town.

Before the storm, we used to come to Cathedral Pines and imagine that this was how the New World forest looked to the first settlers. We now know that the precolonial forest probably looked somewhat different—for one thing, it was not exclusively pine. But it's conceivable that we could restore Cathedral Pines to something closely resembling its actual precolonial condition. By analyzing historical accounts, the rings of fallen trees, and fossilized pollen grains buried in the soil, we could reconstruct the variety and composition of species that flourished here in 1739, the year when the colonists first settled near this place and formed the town of Cornwall. We know that nature, having done so once before, would probably permit us to have such a forest here. And, using some of the more advanced techniques of ecological restoration, it is probably within our competence to re-create a precolonial forest on this site.

We would do this not because we'd decided to be faithful to the "state of nature" at Cathedral Pines, but very simply because the precolonial forest happens to mean a great deal to us. It is a touchstone in the history of this town, not to mention this nation. A walk in a restored version of the precolonial forest might recall us to our culture's first, fateful impressions of America, to our thoughts on coming upon what Fitzgerald called the "fresh green breast of the new world." In the contemplation of that scene we might be moved to reconsider what happened next—to us, to the Indians who once hunted here, to nature in this corner of America.

This is pretty much what I would have stood up and said if we'd had a town meeting to decide what to do in Cathedral Pines. Certainly a town meeting would have been a fitting way to decide the matter, nicely in keeping with the genius of *this* place, a small town in New England. I can easily imagine the speeches and the arguments. The people from the Nature Conservancy would have made their plea for leaving the place alone, for "letting nature take her course." Richard Dakin, the first selectman, and John Calhoun, the forest's nearest neighbor, would have warned about the dangers of fire. And then we might have heard some other points of view. I would have tried to make a pitch for restoration, talking about some of the ways we might "garden" the site. I can imagine Ian Ingersoll, a gifted cabinetmaker in town, speaking with feeling about the waste of such rare timbers, and the prospect of sitting down to a Thanksgiving dinner at a table in which you could see rings formed at the time of the American Revolution. Maybe somebody else would have talked about how much she missed her Sunday afternoon walks in the forest, and how very sad the place looked now. A scientist from the Yale School of Forestry might have patiently tried to explain, as indeed one Yale scientist did in the press, why "It's just as pretty to me now as it was then."

This is the same fellow who said, "If you're going to clean it up, you   70
might as well put up condos." I can't imagine anyone actually proposing
that, or any other kind of development in Cathedral Pines. But if someone
did, he would probably get shouted down. Because we have too much
respect for this place; and besides, our sympathies and interests are a lot
more complicated than the economists or environmentalists always seem
to think. Sooner than a developer, we'd be likely to hear from somebody
speaking on behalf of the forest's fauna—the species who have lost out in
the storm (like the owls), but also the ones for whom doing nothing would
be a boon (the beetles). And so the various interests of the animals would
be taken into account, too; indeed, I expect that "nature"—all *those* different (and contradictory) points of view—would be well represented at this
town meeting. Perhaps it is naïve of me to think so, but I'm confident that
in the course of a public, democratic conversation about the disposition of
Cathedral Pines, we would eventually arrive at a solution that would have
at once pleased us and not offended nature.

But unfortunately that's not what happened. The future of Cathedral
Pines was decided in a closed-door meeting at the Nature Conservancy in
September, after a series of negotiations with the selectmen and the owners
of adjacent property. The result was a compromise that seems to have
pleased no one. The fallen trees will remain untouched—except for a fifty-
foot swath clear-cut around the perimeter of the forest, a firebreak intended to appease the owners of a few nearby houses. The sole human
interest taken into account in the decision was the worry about fire.

I drove up there one day in late fall to have a look around, to see
what the truce between the Conservancy and the town had wrought.
What a sad sight it is. Unwittingly, and in spite of the good intentions on
both sides, the Conservancy and the selectmen have conspired to create a
landscape that is a perfect symbol of our perverted relation to nature. The
firebreak looks like nothing so much as a no-man's-land in a war zone, a
forbidding expanse of blistered ground impounding what little remains of
the Cathedral Pines. The landscape we've made here is grotesque. And yet
it is the logical outcome of a confrontation between, on the one side, an
abstract and mistaken concept of nature's interests and, on the other, a
pinched and demeaning notion of our own interests. We should probably
not be surprised that the result of such a confrontation is not a wilderness,
or a garden, but a DMZ.

Working Together

1. Establish the basic facts of the controversy—what is it, how did it originate, what courses of action have been suggested as remedies? Once
   you're clear about these facts, write them in a group paragraph.
2. Write a group paragraph that explains why it's not easy to decide what
   to do with Cathedral Pines.

3. See whether you can collectively summarize what Pollan has to say about the wilderness ethic. Summarize what you understand, and write a list of questions about whatever's confusing.

4. As a group, put Pollan's garden ethic in your own words. Write six sentences about it that you can all agree on.

Rethinking and Rewriting

1. Look at the ten-point discussion of the garden ethic. Of the ten points, choose three as central and argue that if any one of the three were discarded, the garden ethic would fall apart.

2. Pollan mentions several of the writers included elsewhere in this book. Choose one of the selections by one of those writers and show how understanding that selection helps you understand Pollan. Show how this other selection lays the groundwork for Pollan or provides a useful contrast. (Use at least three quotations to help you make your points.)

3. Compare Pollan's recommended actions with the actual decisions and actions made by the Nature Conservancy. Who do you agree with, and why?

4. Apply Pollan's garden ethic to some local issue or controversy regarding land use or land preservation. Model your essay on the last section of Pollan's.

Essay Topics for Chapter 14

1. On the basis of any of the readings in this chapter, write a manifesto that declares your beliefs and that ends by advocating some useful action.

2. Look at any two of the readings in this chapter and compare them according to their strategies for persuasion. How does each work to make its points clearly and effectively? What decisions can you see that these writers have made? End by drawing some conclusions about the kind of writing that makes readers pay attention and reconsider their own thinking.

3. Assume that you have a friend who feels that environmental concerns and environmental solutions are far removed from our lived lives. This friend feels that environmental problems result from big industrial polluters or from the practices other countries pursue. Consequently, this friend doesn't think one person's actions mean very much. Use two of the readings in this chapter to try and convince your friend that the actions of individuals do carry weight and do matter.

4. Using any three of the readings you have done in this chapter (or in this book), explain how you feel about the future of the planet. Are you concerned (why?), optimistic (why?), pessimistic (why?), confused (why?), or some combination of all of these?

5. Identify a group that you belong to—a neighborhood, a sophomore class, a sorority or dorm or fraternity, or the like. What three actions (large or small) could this group take to make some contribution toward solving a local environmental problem? Describe the group and the actions, and explain how those actions could be useful. Then explain why you think you could (or could not) persuade this group to carry out these actions.

6. Explain how one or more of the readings in this chapter has made you rethink something important or led you to change your habits. Explain why the reading(s) had such an impact, and be specific about the new resolve you feel and the new action(s) you're taking.

7. On the basis of one or more of the readings in this chapter, write a letter to the editor—of a local newspaper, a national magazine—urging a particular course of action. Keep your letter concise, but make sure that you explain both the issue you're addressing and the action you want to see readers take.

8. Profile someone you know personally or have read about who has made contributions to improving environmental awareness or environmental conditions. Focus on the person as much as on the contributions. Make this person's interest and this person's actions both come alive.

9. Write a satirical essay that profiles someone you invent—someone who cares not a whit for any environmental issue and acts without any regard for environmental consequences. Follow this person through a typical day.

10. Write an essay that looks frankly at your own understanding of environmental issues and your own actions. In short, take a personal inventory of what you know (what you feel sure about and committed to) and what you don't. Then work from that inventory to a discussion of the changes—if any—that you want to make in your own lifestyle. You could, for example, decide you don't want to make any changes and explain that. Or you could decide that you don't know what to do and explain that. Or you could identify some real changes—large or small—and decide to pursue them.

ACKNOWLEDGMENTS

EDWARD ABBEY, "The Great American Desert," from *The Journey Home* by Edward Abbey. Copyright © 1977 by Edward Abbey. Used by permission of Dutton Signet, a division of Penguin Books USA Inc.

CHRIS ANDERSON, "Forest of Voices," from *Edge Effects* by Chris Anderson. Copyright © 1993 by Chris Anderson. Reprinted by permission of University of Iowa Press.

RON ARNOLD, "Rethinking Environmentalism," from *Ecology Wars: Environmentalism As If People Mattered* by Ron Arnold. Copyright © 1987 by Ron Arnold. Reprinted by permission.

WENDELL BERRY, "Out of Your Car, Off Your Horse," from *The Atlantic Monthly*, February 1991. "Getting Along with Nature" from *Home Economics* by Wendell Berry. Copyright © 1987 by Wendell Berry. Reprinted by permission of North Point Press, a division of Farrar, Straus & Giroux, Inc.

ELIZABETH BISHOP, "The Fish," from *The Complete Poems 1927–1979* by Elizabeth Bishop. Copyright © 1979, 1983 by Alice Helen Methfessel. Reprinted by permission of Farrar, Straus & Giroux, Inc.

MARY CLEARMAN BLEW, "The Sow in the River," from *All But the Waltz* by Mary Clearman Blew. Copyright © 1991 by Mary Clearman Blew. Used by permission of Viking Penguin, a division of Penguin Books USA Inc.

RACHEL CARSON, "Elixirs of Death," from *Silent Spring* by Rachel Carson. Copyright © 1962 by Rachel L. Carson, renewed 1990 by Roger Christie. Reprinted by permission of Houghton Mifflin Co. All rights reserved.

JOAN DIDION, "On Going Home," from *Slouching towards Bethlehem* by Joan Didion. Copyright © 1968 by Joan Didion. Reprinted by permission of Farrar, Straus & Giroux, Inc.

ANNIE DILLARD, "The Silent Neighborhood," excerpted from *An American Childhood* by Annie Dillard. Copyright © 1987 by Annie Dillard. Reprinted by permission of HarperCollins Publishers, Inc. "Life on the Rocks: The Galapagos," "Living Like Weasels," "A Field of Silence," from *Teaching a Stone to Talk* by Annie Dillard. Copyright © 1982 by Annie Dillard. Reprinted by permission of HarperCollins Publishers, Inc.

GRETEL EHRLICH, "The Solace of Open Spaces," from *The Solace of Open Spaces* by Gretel Ehrlich. Copyright © 1985 by Gretel Ehrlich. Used by permission of Viking Penguin, a division of Penguin Books USA Inc.

LOREN EISELEY, "The Bird and the Machine," from *The Immense Journey* by Loren Eiseley. Copyright © 1955 by Loren Eiseley. Reprinted by permission of Random House, Inc.

KEITH ERVIN, "A Life in Our Hands," reprinted by permission of the publisher from *Fragile Majesty: The Battle for North America's Latest Great Forest* by Keith Ervin, The Mountaineers, Seattle. Copyright © 1989.

DAVE FOREMAN, "Earth First!" reprinted by permission from *The Progressive*, 409 East Main Street, Madison, WI 53703.

JANE GOODALL, "The Rains," excerpt from *In the Shadow of Man* by Jane Goodall. Copyright © 1971 by Hugo and Jane van Lawick-Goodall. Revisions copyright © 1988 by Jane Goodall. Reprinted by permission of Houghton Mifflin Co. All rights reserved.

AL GORE, "Ships in the Desert," from *Earth in the Balance* by Al Gore. Copyright © 1992 by Senator Al Gore. Reprinted by permission of Houghton Mifflin Co. All rights reserved.

STEPHEN JAY GOULD, "Nonmoral Nature," reprinted from *Hen's Teeth and Horse's Toes: Further Reflections in Natural History,* by Stephen Jay Gould, with the permission of W. W. Norton & Company, Inc. Copyright © 1983 by Stephen Jay Gould.

MELISSA GREENE is the author of *Praying for Sheetrock,* a nonfiction account of the fall of the "good old boys" and the rise of civil rights in McIntosh County, GA, winner of the Robert F. Kennedy Book Award and the Chicago Tribune Heartland Prize. "No Rms, Jungle Vu" originally appeared in the December 1987 issue of *The Atlantic Monthly.* Used by permission of the author.

DAVID GUTERSON, "Enclosed. Encyclopedic. Endured. One Week at the Mall of America." Copyright © 1973 by David Guterson. Reprinted by permission of Georges Borchardt, Inc. for the author. This essay originally appeared in Harper's Magazine.

CYNTHIA HAMILTON, "Women, Home, and Community: The Struggle in an Urban Environment," from *Reweaving the World,* edited by Irene Diamond and Gloria Feman Orenstein. Copyright © 1990 by Diamond & Orenstein. Reprinted with permission of Sierra Club Books.

MARK O. HATFIELD, "Old Growth and the Media: A Lawmaker's Perspective," by Mark O. Hatfield. Copyright © 1991 Freedom Forum Media Studies Center. Reprinted by permission of the author.

EDWARD HOAGLAND, "Dogs, and the Tug of Life," from *Red Wolves & Black Bears* by Edward Hoagland. Copyright © 1972, 1973, 1974, 1975, 1976 by Edward Hoagland. Reprinted by permission of Random House, Inc.

BARBARA KINGSOLVER, "New Year's Day," excerpt from chapter 12 of *The Bean Trees* by Barbara Kingsolver. Copyright © 1988 by Barbara Kingsolver. Reprinted by permission of HarperCollins Publishers, Inc.

MAXINE KUMIN, "Sleeping with Animals," from *Nurture* by Maxine Kumin. Copyright © 1989 by Maxine Kumin. Used by permission of Viking Penguin, a division of Penguin Books USA Inc.

TED LEESON, "The Farthest Distance between Two Points," reprinted from *The Habit of Rivers* by Ted Leeson, by arrangement with the publisher, Lyons & Burford, 31 West 21 Street, New York, NY 10010. Copyright © 1994 by Ted Leeson.

ALDO LEOPOLD, "Axe-in-hand" and "The Land Ethic," from *The Sand County Almanac, with Other Essays on Conservation from Round River* by Aldo Leopold. Copyright © 1949, 1953, 1966, renewed 1977, 1981 by Oxford University Press, Inc. Reprinted by permission.

BARRY LOPEZ, "Gone Back into the Earth," from *Crossing Open Ground* by Barry Lopez. Copyright © 1988 by Barry Lopez. Reprinted by permission of Sterling Lord Literistic, Inc.

WANGARI MAATHAI, "Foresters without Diplomas," from *Ms* Magazine, March/April 1991.

SAMUEL W. MATTHEWS, "Under the Sun," from *National Geographic Magazine,* October 1990. Copyright © 1990 by National Geographic Magazine. Reprinted by permission.

WILLIAM MCKIBBEN, "The End of Nature," from *The End of Nature* by William McKibben. Copyright © 1989 by William McKibben. Reprinted by permission of Random House, Inc. "Daybreak," from *The Age of Missing Information* by William McKibben. Copyright © 1992 by Bill McKibben. Reprinted by permission of Random House, Inc.

JOHN MCPHEE, "Duty of Care," from *The New Yorker,* June 28, 1993. Reprinted by permission.

W. S. MERWIN, "Unchopping a Tree," from *The Miner's Pale Children* by W. S. Merwin. Copyright © 1969, 1970 by W. S. Merwin. Reprinted by permission.

N. SCOTT MOMADAY, "My Horse and I," from *The Names* by N. Scott Momaday. Copyright © 1987 by N. Scott Momaday. Reprinted by permission of the author. "Sacred and Ancestral Ground," copyright © 1988 by The New York Times Company. Reprinted by permission.

KATHLEEN DEAN MOORE, "Alamo Canyon Creek," an unpublished essay. Copyright © 1994 by Kathleen Dean Moore. Used by permission.

RODERICK NASH, "A Wilderness Condition," from *Wilderness and the American Mind* by Roderick Nash. Reprinted by permission of Yale University Press.

KATHLEEN NORRIS, "The Beautiful Places," from *Dakota* by Kathleen Norris. Copyright © 1993 by Kathleen Norris. Reprinted by permission of Ticknor & Fields/Houghton Mifflin Co. All rights reserved.

JOYCE CAROL OATES, "Against Nature," from *Woman Writers: Occasions and Opportunities* by Joyce Carol Oates. Copyright © 1988 by The Ontario Review. Used by permission of Dutton Signet, a division of Penguin Books USA Inc.

RAY OLDENBURG, "The Problem of Place in America," from *The Great Good Place* by Ray Oldenburg. Copyright © 1989. Used by permission.

SHARON OLDS, "Summer Solstice, New York City," from *The Gold Cell* by Sharon Olds. Copyright © 1987 by Sharon Olds. Reprinted by permission of Alfred A. Knopf Inc.

MARY OLIVER, "Five a.m. in the Pinewoods," from *New and Selected Poems* by Mary Oliver. Copyright © 1992 by Mary Oliver. Reprinted by permission of Beacon Press.

MICHAEL POLLAN, "The Idea of a Garden," from *Second Nature: A Gardener's Education.* Copyright © 1991 by Michael Pollan. Used by permission of Grove/Atlantic, Inc.

DIXY LEE RAY, "Greenhouse Earth," from *Environmental Overkill* by Dixy Lee Ray and Louis R. Guzzo. Copyright © 1993 by Regnery Gateway. All rights reserved. Reprinted by special permission of Regnery Publishing, Inc., Washington, D. C.

ISHMAEL REED, "My Neighborhood," originally titled "My Oakland, There is a There There," Part I. Reprinted with the permission of Atheneum Publishers, an imprint of Macmillan Publishing Company from *Writin' Is Fightin': Thirty-Seven Years of Boxing on Paper* by Ishmael Reed. Copyright © 1988 by Ishmael Reed.

MARC P. REISNER, "A Semidesert with a Desert Heart," from *Cadillac Desert, Revised and Updated* by Marc P. Reisner. Copyright © 1986, 1993 by Marc P. Reisner. Used by permission of Viking Penguin, a division of Penguin Books USA Inc.

PATTIANN ROGERS, "Rolling Naked in the Morning Dew," from *Splitting and Binding,* copyright © 1989 by Pattiann Rogers. Reprinted by permission.

SCOTT RUSSELL SANDERS, "Settling Down," from *Staying Put: Making a Home in a Restless World* by Scott Russell Sanders. Copyright © 1993 by Scott Russell Sanders. Reprinted by permission of Beacon Press.

DAVID SEIDEMAN, "Trouble in Mill City," from *Showdown at Opal Creek.* Copyright © 1993 by David Seideman. Reprinted by permission of Carroll & Graf, Publisher, Inc.

WILLIAM STAFFORD, "Traveling through the Dark," from *Stories That Could Be True* by William Stafford. Reprinted by permission.

LEWIS THOMAS, "The Tucson Zoo," from *The Medusa and the Snail* by Lewis Thomas. Copyright © 1977 by Lewis Thomas. Used by permission of Viking Penguin, a division of Penguin Books USA Inc.

WILLIAM TUCKER, "Is Nature Too Good for Us?" from *Progress and Privilege: America in the Age of Environmentalism,* 1982. Reprinted by permission.

DAVID WAGONER, "Elegy for a Forest Clear-Cut by the Weyerhaeuser Company," from *Sleeping in the Woods* by David Wagoner. Copyright © 1976 by David Wagoner. Reprinted by permission.

ALICE WALKER, "Am I Blue?" from *Living by the Word: Selected Writings 1973–1987.* Copyright © 1986 by Alice Walker, reprinted by permission of Harcourt Brace & Company.

PAUL WATSON, "Shepherds of the Labrador Front," from *Greenpeace Chronicles,* 2nd edition, Vol. 2, Spring/Summer, 1976.

E. B. WHITE, "Sootfall and Fallout," from *The Points of My Compass* by E. B. White. Copyright © 1956 by E. B. White. "Once More to the Lake" from *One Man's Meat* by E. B. White. Copyright © 1941 by E. B. White. Reprinted by permission of HarperCollins Publishers, Inc.

JOY WILLIAMS, "Save the Whales, Screw the Shrimp," reprinted by permission of International Creative Management, Inc. Copyright © 1989 by Joy Williams.

INDEX OF AUTHORS AND TITLES